Special Edition

Using

Using

MICROSOFT®

Site Server

Special Edition Using

Using

MICROSOFT®

Site Server

Barry Wadman, Stephen Peront,
Marc Velez, et al.

Series Editor Peter Hipson

Special Edition Using Microsoft Site Server

Library of Congress Catalog No.: 97-67475

ISBN: 0-7897-1157-5

99 98 97   6 5 4 3 2 1

Interpretation of the printing code: the rightmost double-digit number is the year of the book's printing; the rightmost single-digit number, the number of the book's printing. For example, a printing code of 97-1 shows that the first printing of the book occurred in 1997.

Screen reproductions in this book were created using Collage Plus from Inner Media, Inc., Hollis, NH.

Contents at a Glance

VI | Case Studies

Appendix

Table of Contents

Credits

PRESIDENT
Roland Elgey

SENIOR VICE PRESIDENT/PUBLISHING
Don Fowley

GENERAL MANAGER
Joe Muldoon

MANAGER OF PUBLISHING OPERATIONS
Linda H. Buehler

PUBLISHING MANAGER
Fred Slone

TITLE MANAGER
Al Valvano

EDITORIAL SERVICES DIRECTOR
Carla Hall

MANAGING EDITOR
Caroline D. Roop

ACQUISITIONS MANAGER
Cheryl D. Willoughby

PRODUCT DIRECTOR
Eric Dafforn

PRODUCTION EDITOR
Matthew B. Cox

COPY EDITOR
Kathy Simpson

COORDINATOR OF EDITORIAL SERVICES
Maureen A. McDaniel

WEBMASTER
Thomas H. Bennett

PRODUCT MARKETING MANAGER
Kourtnaye Sturgeon

ASSISTANT PRODUCT MARKETING MANAGER
Gretchen Schlesinger

TECHNICAL EDITOR
Co Truong

SOFTWARE SPECIALIST
Brandon K. Penticuff

ACQUISITIONS COORDINATOR
Carmen Krikorian

SOFTWARE RELATIONS COORDINATOR
Susan D. Gallagher

SOFTWARE COORDINATOR
Andrea Duvall

EDITORIAL ASSISTANT
Travis Bartlett

BOOK DESIGNER
Ruth Harvey

COVER DESIGNER
Sandra Schroeder

Composed in *Century Old Style* and *ITC Franklin Gothic* by Que Corporation.

This is dedicated to my wife, Viviana, and my daughter, Erika.

About the Author

Barry S. Wadman (**bwadman@c-systems.com**) is the CEO of C-Systems (**www.c-systems.com**), Inc. Residing in Concord, Massachusetts, and a graduate of Boston College and Boston University, I specialize in Microsoft electronic commerce solutions. I have been fascinated with electronic commerce for quite a while, and thus, decided to specialize in it. To date, it has been an extremely rewarding experience. I have pioneered sites, such as, Siedler Jewelers (**www.seidlers.com**), and Childshope (**www.childhope. org**) for Boston's Children Hospital. I was part of the small group that first was introduced to Microsoft Merchant Server in August, 1996. We have grown with this product as it has evolved into the new Microsoft Commerce Server, that is part of the Site Server product group. This is the cutting edge of technology. The Internet was beginning to look all the same, and people were turning blue in the face clicking from one pretty thing or piece of information to another. People have not tired of buying, nor selling, and, as a result, this is the new vision for the Internet. I have been working with Microsoft and Back Office for over five years, thus, creating a better environment for the Enterprise.

Acknowledgments

Many people contributed to this book. Although I cannot possibly mention all their names here, I'd like to include certain people and companies who were instrumental in helping me finish this task and complete the book.

The following people worked as contributing authors: Marc Velez, Stephen Peront, Matthew Klein of C-Systems, Greg Croasdill, Christopher Allen, WellsFargo, VeriFone and Cybersource.

We'd also like to thank Hewlett Packard and their representatives, Ardine Williams, Maureen Melon, Ducan Cambel, and Dale McAtee. Of course, I owe a lot to Microsoft and the following people from that organization: Jim Alchen, Brad Silverberg, Russ Stockdake, Gytis Barzdukis, Subbarao Vedula, Vince Orgavan, Jay Jaacks, Scott Harris, Stacey Breyfogle, Keith White, David Ursino, Club Win (the Beta testers for **http://www.seidlers.com**), ClubIE (the main support for Internet Explorer), and the Microsoft Site Builder Network—the pulse for Web developers.

Thanks also go to Barry Press, Tom Masotto from VeriFone, Tim Knowlton, Wellsfargo, HITACHI, Peter Hipson, Childrens Hospital, Programmer's Paradise, Eddie Bower, MSN, Seidlers Jewelers of Boston, and VeriSign.

We'd Like to Hear from You!

As part of our continuing effort to produce books of the highest possible quality, Que would like to hear your comments. To stay competitive, we *really* want you to let us know what you like or dislike most about this book or other Que products.

Please send your comments, ideas, and suggestions for improvement to:

The Expert User Team

E-mail: **euteam@que.mcp.com**

CompuServe: 105527,745

Fax: (317) 581-4663

Our mailing address is:

Expert User Team

Que Corporation

201 West 103rd Street

Indianapolis, IN 46290-1097

You can also visit our Team's home page on the World Wide Web at:

http://www.mcp.com/que/developer_expert

Thank you in advance. Your comments will help us to continue publishing the best books available in today's market.

Thank You,

The Expert User Team

Introduction

Long before our lives were revolutionized by the Internet, we (the indignant customers) were faced with dragging ourselves up out of our comfortable chairs, driving to the store, pulling out some cash, driving home, all just to get a small pizza (with anchovies, right?). Today you simply go from one comfortable chair (the one in front of the TV, of course) to another comfortable chair (this one being in front of your computer) followed by making a few miniscule finger movements (better known as mouse-clicking), then typing in a credit card number, and the pizza (again, with anchovies) is on its way.

Shopping on the Web, electronic commerce (or *e-commerce* as the 'netties' have termed it), has without a doubt transformed the traditional commerce marketplace. Despite e-commerce's underhanded presence in today's marketplace, Bill Gates, Jeff Papows, and many others have been competing, at great lengths, to define what e-commerce is and how to conquer the e-commerce marketplace.

Microsoft broke this e-commerce barrier with the release of Merchant Server 1.0, and has now revolutionized the e-commerce marketplace (on the World Wide Web) with the release of Site Server Enterprise 2.0 (Site Server) and all of its exciting features. ■

Who Should Use This Book

This book is aimed at Webmasters, network, and system administrators, and anyone responsible for installing, configuring, and maintaining a Site Server system. Most of the examples in this book are geared for a large, international enterprise to draw out all of Site Server's features. MIS managers will be interested in using the information in this book to make key decisions about adopting and deploying Site Server.

Finally, this book touches on Web site design and programming with Active Server Pages technology. Although we only touch on using Microsoft Visual InterDev, this book should give you the foundation you need to design, build, and maintain a new online Web site.

How To Use This Book

This book is divided into five sections. Parts I and II give you the foundation necessary to install, configure, and manage a Site Server Web site. Parts III and IV teach you how to extend Site Server's functionality with dynamic databases and Active Server Pages technology. Part V discusses advanced Site Server topics, and the last part, Part VI, presents several case studies to reinforce the lessons learned in this book.

Part I—Getting Started with Microsoft Site Server

Chapter 1, "Introducing Microsoft Site Server 2.0," unveils this new product suite and describes the major functionality of the tools.

Chapter 2, "Web Site Design and Development," prepares you with the knowledge you will need to create a successful site in today's marketplace.

Chapter 3, "Setting Up Your Store," walks you through setting up a Commerce Server 2.0 store by using Microsoft's StoreBuilder Wizard.

Part II—Working with Microsoft Site Server

Chapter 4, "Understanding the Content Replication System," introduces the Content Replication System, giving you the knowledge you need to distribute store information correctly.

Chapter 5, "Implementing the Internet Locator Server," covers the Internet Locator Server (ILS), which shows users how to find each other on a large private intranet and on the Internet.

Chapter 6, "Understanding the Personalization System," tells you about three components that let your customers customize their own page, take polls, and use e-mail.

Chapter 7, "Using the Microsoft Site Analyst," introduces you to the first, of many, important site tools, which helps you analyze information about your store.

Chapter 8, "Using the Microsoft Usage Analyst," unveils the second site tool that helps you analyze information about how much your customers are using your site.

Chapter 9, "Using the Microsoft Posting Acceptor and the Web Publishing Wizard," discusses the Web Publishing Wizard, which enables users to easily upload an entire Web site. This chapter also covers the Posting Acceptor, which allows Web developers to program an interface that will allow your users to send updates to their Web pages via HTTP.

Part III—Understanding Dynamic Databases

Chapter 10, "Understanding SQL Server Databases," introduces you to the concepts behind SQL Server databases, and how they are used within the Commerce Server 2.0 store.

Chapter 11, "Commerce Server Data Components," unveils the usefulness of data components that help you manage data between your store and databases.

Chapter 12, "Getting Data onto Your Pages," helps you display your database information to your customers.

Part IV—Creating Stores with Active Server Pages

Chapter 13, "Introducing Active Server Pages," gives you an understanding of the client/server architecture contained within ASP, which will help you develop successful stores.

Chapter 14, "Introduction to ASP Scripting," provides a discussion of ASP and the scripting within the ASP model.

Chapter 15, "Working with Active Server Web Pages," discusses the important considerations to take when constructing a modular store.

Chapter 16, "Integrating VBScript into ASP," introduces the powerful VBScript tool within ASP applications, helping you understand the benefits of using this tool.

Chapter 17, "Practical ASP Programming," unveils the advanced features of the ASP model.

Chapter 18, "Constructing a Server Component Using ASP," concludes the discussion of ASP by walking you step-by-step through the constructing a server component.

Part V—Advanced Site Server Topics

Chapter 19, "Understanding Microsoft Windows NT Server 4.0," highlights important features of Windows NT Server 4.0 that you will need to know when managing Site Server.

Chapter 20, "Understanding DNS," introduces DNS and how it relates to Windows NT Server 4.0. DNS is used to let customers see your site over the Internet.

Chapter 21, "Working with Internet Information Server," teaches you how to administer IIS so your site can support ASP applications, which is the core model for Commerce Server 2.0 stores.

Chapter 22, "Building the Order Process Pipeline," walks you step-by-step through the creation of the OPP, the most important data-management tool and backbone of every Commerce Server 2.0 store.

Chapter 23, "Constructing Your Own Server Components," teaches you how to create a COM object for Commerce's OPP by using Visual C++ 5.0.

Chapter 24, "Working with the Progistics Shipping Solution," covers how to install and configure the TanData Progistics shipping-and-handling components to work with Commerce Server 2.0.

Chapter 25, "Internet Payment Authentication," describes the key elements of the VeriFone Internet commerce solution with an overview of VeriFone's experience in the development of payment systems, an outline of the company's products for consumers, merchants, and financial institutions, and finally, you see the business process for distributing and setting up VeriFone's Internet payment solution.

Chapter 26, "Enhancing Security with the PIX Firewall," addresses, using hardware, the security issues an Internet site present to your customers.

Chapter 27, "Using the Microsoft Buy Now and Wallet Components," introduces two components which help your store(s) manage money securely and efficiently.

Part VI—Case Studies
Part VI, which includes Chapters 28 through 32, outlines various case studies that show you how to quickly develop and customize your own store by learning about sample stores, such as Eddie Bauer and Siedlers Jewelry. You also learn how to place Web sites on the Web with ease.

Appendix
The appendix, "Commerce 2.0 Components," describes the components Microsoft has provided with Commerce Server 2.0, which you will use within your store(s).

Conventions Used in This Book

Que has over a decade of experience writing and developing the most successful computer books available. With this experience, we learned which special features help readers the most. Look for these special features throughout the book to enhance your learning experience and to help make your reading easier.

- *Italic type* is used to emphasize the author's points or to introduce new terms.
- Screen messages, code listings, and command samples appear in `monospace typeface`.
- Information that the user is asked to type appears in **bold**.

 T I P Tips present short advice on a quick or often-overlooked procedure. These tips include shortcuts that will save you time.

N O T E Notes present interesting or useful information that isn't necessarily essential to the discussion but may help you avoid problems, or offer advice that relates to the particular topic. ▪

CAUTION
Cautions look like this and serve as a warning about potential problems that a procedure may cause, unexpected results, and pitfalls to avoid.

Getting Started with Microsoft Site Server

Introducing Microsoft Site Server 2.0

Identify Site Server's major components

You learn about the components, such as hardware, software, Internet connection, that you need to build your site with Site Server.

See an introduction to electronic commerce and Commerce Server 2.0

You learn about Commerce Server's features that will help you enhance your online store.

Microsoft Site Server 2.0 brings an entire array of features which can be used by businesses to create commerce sites that can be monitored and improved to constantly meet their customer's needs. Site Server's main feature is, of course, Commerce Server 2.0, which enables developers to create and manage robust commerce sites. Commerce Server provides various components, templates, and tools that help businesses reduce the amount of time they spend creating an effective site for selling their products. Commerce Server allows businesses to easily add new content to their sites; to manage the effectiveness of their site by tracking user patterns; and to facilitate the sale of goods and services through their Web site. In addition, Site Server 2.0 offers other features such as User Management, Usage Analyst, Site Analyst, and Content Deployment. Each of these features plays an integral role in your business's presence on the Web. ■

Planning and Building Your Commerce Site

Developing a commerce site requires a great deal of forethought, planning, as well as an understanding of what your customers' needs are and how you want to convey your site to them in such a way that you meet their needs. Here's a bird's-eye view of how you can make a Commerce Server site of your own:

- **Site planning.** The first thing that you need to do is plan your site. Your plan should include figuring out what you want your site to do, how it should look, how the business should run, and what resources are required. As is true of most projects, things may not go precisely according to your plan, but if you don't plan, things may not go at all. We will discuss this further in Chapter 2, "Web Site Design and Development."

- **Putting the hardware and software in place.** The next major tasks are setting up your server site, making sure that all the software you need is installed, and that your site is connected to and communicating with the Internet. We will discuss these concerns in Part II, "Working with Microsoft Site Server."

- **Developing your site.** Get ready, here you will get your hands dirty setting up your site's database, designing the Web pages, and pulling all other pieces together into a site that your customers will want to visit over and over again.

- **Testing.** Before you open your site for business, you will need to test the site thoroughly to discover any problems you (or somebody else) have produced and to fix them. One mentor once told me, "There is too much time spent developing and never enough time debugging. We developers sometimes have egos that destroy our ability." This is so true: If your store is not correctly and completely debugged, your customers will know.

- **Open the site.** Now your effort really starts to pay off. When your site goes live on the Net and those dollars start to flow in, you really understand the power of Site Server.

- **Site maintenance.** In addition to performing the everyday tasks necessary to run your site, you will be involved in a continuous process of maintaining and upgrading your site. Commerce Server site development never really ends.

- **Marketing.** You want to get the word out about your site so everyone will visit your site and your store will prosper greatly. Much like debugging your development, if you do not market your store correctly, you will not have customers.

Commerce Server 2.0

When Microsoft acquired the Sunnyvale, California-based Interse Corporation, Microsoft added an important feature to its Internet/intranet strategy. Interse offers Web site managers (Webmasters) integrated tools to carry out significant parts of their job that used to be cumbersome and time-consuming.

Interse offers management tools that do the following:

- Gather information on how often people visit a Web site.
- Decipher how effectively the Web site served the needs of those people.

- Analyze traffic and other usage data for a Web site. The acquisition of Interse has given a real boost to Microsoft's administration tools. Microsoft was able to build these statistics tools into its own products, for example, Commerce Server 2.0. Commerce Server 2.0 produces viable statistics for evaluation and assists in the targeting of correct audiences, thus improving the scalability of your mall or store(s).

Finally, Microsoft used some products from the MCIS family, Personalization and Replication Servers. These products provide reliable and contiguous updates from staging servers to production.

Now, let's be honest with ourselves, the tools we have discussed thus far are tools that are readily available to everyone from various companies. So, what makes Site Server such a great product? Site Server is unique because it integrates the various tools Microsoft has provided to establish and maintain a retail site, which allows you to focus on what you should be focusing on: the appearance and functionality of your site. Site Server saves you much time and money because it takes care of the programming required to get the various other applications and tools to work together the way you need them to.

Site Server presents a set of software tools that allow you to establish and maintain a site, while Commerce Server 2.0 manages these tools to interact with your mall or store(s) so that you don't have to. The following is a list of the tools that Site Server provides:

- **Site Server**. Site Server is itself a tool that integrates the Web tools provided by Microsoft, much like the controller of a large corporation. Although Site Server is primarily written as the controller for Microsoft products, you can use many other tools to develop and maintain components of your site. Commerce Server then brings all these pieces together. We will discuss more about Commerce Server in Chapters 11, "Commerce Server Data Components," 22, "Building the Order Process Pipeline," and 23, "Constructing Your Own Server Components."

- **An Object Database: Open Database Connectivity (ODBC) database**. Next in importance to Commerce Server is the ODBC database, in which all the data related to your site is managed and through which you will perform the various queries needed to administer your site. Although a good database is important, it is only one key to a successful site. We will take a look at how a SQL database is developed and maintained in Chapters 10, "Understanding SQL Server Databases," 11, "Commerce Server Data Components," and 12, "Getting Data onto Your Pages."

- **Transaction and payment software**. This software provides credit-card verification and communicates with the banking authority. We will discuss more about transactions in Chapter 25, "Internet Payment Authentication." This software ships with Site Server, although it is not a necessary part of Site Server.

- **Internet Information Server (IIS) software**. In Chapter 21, "Working with Internet Information Server," we will thoroughly discuss the advanced features that this server software provides, which will enable your computer(s) to act as Internet servers.

- **Windows NT Server**. Windows NT Server is the operating system that runs the server on which your site is built. Many of the systematic functions of your site are provided by

Windows NT, including security, file, and directory management. In Chapter 19, "Understanding Microsoft Windows NT Server 4.0," we will elaborate on Windows NT's interaction with Site Server.

■ **Security hardware and software.** Site Server was designed with the capability to use many different security schemes, and as such you can choose to protect your site with hardware (such as a Hewlett Packard firewall) or software (which there are many vendors, including Microsoft).

■ **Web-page creation software.** You can use your favorite Web-creation software to design and maintain the appearance and functionality of your site. Chapters 13, "Introducing Active Server Pages," 14, "Introduction to ASP Scripting," and 16, "Integrating VBScript into ASP," discuss Web-page creation as it relates to a Commerce Server 2.0 site, concentrating on the Active Server Pages model.

Among the benefits that Site Server offers is the building blocks on which you can model your site. These building blocks include Web-page templates, Registry settings, database queries, and other major tasks needed for a retail site. You can adapt these building blocks for your own uses, to create quite advanced sites. Microsoft provides most of these building blocks with the Starter Stores that come with Commerce Server 2.0. You can also use the Starter Stores as examples or templates from which you can build your sites.

Site Server Is Like Office, Only Different

If you understand Microsoft Office, you may better understand Site Server. Office itself really is nothing more than the integration of various tools: Word, Excel, PowerPoint, and so on. Office supplies the integration of those tools (primarily through object linking and embedding, or OLE) so that they work together as one. Office really doesn't provide any functionality beyond the tools that work under it, but it does make the tools more powerful and easier to use by integrating them.

Identifying Site Server's Major Players

We will get into the details of what you need later in the book. For now, we will discuss the following sections, which provide an overview of the major components needed.

Hardware

To start, you will need a server (as opposed to desktop) computer with the ability to run Windows NT Server. The size, speed, storage space, and type of machine that you need will depend on the level of activity that you expect your store(s) to bring in, and in general, bigger is better. In addition to these monitors, keyboards, and other peripheral devices, you will need the hardware required for your server to connect to your intranet, as well as the Internet. You will also need a good, reliable backup system (such as a DAT drive). You can purchase additional hardware, such as scanners or digital cameras, if you want to put images of your products on your site. But these will not be necessary for Site Server.

Software

You will use a variety of software to set up, maintain, and run your site. You will, of course, need a copy of Site Server, as well as the following items:

- **An ODBC-compliant database.** The database (such as Microsoft SQL Server 6.5) provides data-storage and manipulation capability for your site.

- **Web-page creation tools.** You can use many tools to create the Web pages through which you present your site to your customers. You probably will use some sort of HTML authoring tools, as well as various utilities to fine-tune your site.

- **Plug-ins for Commerce Server 2.0.** You may want additional plug-ins to expand your site's capabilities, such as Taxware to handle sales-tax computations or Tandata to handle the interface with your shipping partner.

Internet Connection

Your connection to the Internet is the key to making your site usable. You will need to consider several things when connecting your site to the Internet:

- **Bandwidth.** The amount of bandwidth that is available for your site is crucial. If your site bogs down because the 'net-pipe (bandwidth) to your site is too small, you are likely to have very unhappy customers because your site will load more slowly on their machines. Take it from me, there are no customers that will give you more trouble than those who have trouble with your network. (They would rather not be able to launch your site at all rather than having to deal with network problems.)

- **The provider.** Having an Internet Service Provider (ISP) that gives you the kind of service you need is imperative. You should look for a provider that is responsive to your needs. If your site goes down, you want someone to help you get it back up right away. Remember, you want a provider that is flexible and can meet your needs. You will find that a company you can communicate with, particularly in an emergency, will make all the difference in your success.

- **Cost.** The type of Internet access required to maintain a Commerce site may be fairly expensive especially if you go with T1 or T3 line, so be prepared to shop around to various ISPs. The cost of your Internet access should be one factor you consider when choosing your ISP because this will probably be your most expensive bill.

Understanding Electronic Commerce

To really understand electronic commerce, you not only need to comprehend the basics of hardware and software, but also you must understand the people and organizations that are involved.

Almost everyone uses electronic commerce, or e-commerce, in some form or another, and many organizations use e-commerce as part of their everyday operations. The U.S. Government, for example, buys many of its commodity supplies (food, clothing, and so on) via a bulletin-board system. The government organizations that are responsible for supplying food, clothing, and other commodities can dial into a proprietary bulletin board and browse online catalogs of available supplies. Orders can be placed online, payment is made via a payment card (similar to a credit card), and then the supplies are delivered to the requesting agency.

U.S. Government and Commerce

You may wonder why the U.S. Government conducts some of its electronic commerce via a proprietary bulletin board rather than the Internet. The answer is that the Government began to work on its electronic-commerce bulletin boards before the Internet became so widely accessible. When the Internet exploded, many of the bulletin boards were just coming online. Fortunately, the general trend now seems to be for the government to wait for private industry to create and implement Internet-related technology, rather than try to develop its own proprietary systems.

Electronic Commerce and Commerce Server 2.0

Whether developers use Commerce Server to develop a site will depend on the purpose of the site. If your site is dedicated to retail operations, you can expect "retail-typical" customers to use your site. If you use Commerce Server to run an intranet site, you can expect the members of your organization to use it.

There are many valuable features that Commerce Server provides your store(s) or even mall(s) over owning a physical store:

- **Physical versus Virtual.** You can easily tailor your site to its target audience. Suppose the focus of your online store changes, Commerce Server gives you the power to make quick, major changes to your site or even rebuild it. Although you should avoid these changes at all costs with solid planning at the beginning, you cannot always plan everything. A physical store would be marred with inadequate features that would be very expensive and time-consuming to fix, whereas your Commerce Server site can be quickly changed.

- **Cleanliness.** Have you ever gone into a store where the shelves were out of order, the floor wasn't vacuumed, and the front counter was a mess. You don't have any of this maintenance with a Commerce Server site, although this doesn't mean that you don't have any maintenance.

- **Maintenance.** Usually a small physical store could have up to three or four people working throughout the day, re-stocking the shelves, cleaning, and assisting your customers. With a Commerce Server store, this maintenance is cut down drastically. All you will need to do is make sure that there is enough stock for your customers. Thanks to the revolutionary Commerce Server 2.0 you can concentrate on what is important—the appearance of your store—instead of all the maintenance of a physical store.

So, who is going to jump on this Internet retailing bandwagon? Eventually just about every business and most other organizations will have a site of one sort or another within the next five years. The selling points of such sites are fairly obvious, but remember that a site can just as easily be used for other purposes (such as managing the flow of internal resources).

The use of e-commerce is growing at a phenomenal rate because it is a win–win situation. Customers get ultimate convenience (what could be more convenient than around-the-clock access from customers' homes?), as well as better information, more choices, and more privacy. After all, who wants to go down to the crowded mall on Saturday afternoon to shop? Why not do something fun or productive during the day and shop at a more convenient time?

Providers (of goods, services, or information) can get access to new customers no matter where they live. Commerce Server gives retailers expanded global visibility, reduced operating costs, and much better control of inventory. An online presence is not only easy to establish, but also essential for an organization to stay in business in today's marketplace.

Equipment and Software

Most, if not all, major (and many smaller) computer- and technology-related companies are producing tools for the e-commerce marketplace. On the software side, all the names that you know are involved with products that both compete with and complement one another. Microsoft, the biggest player of them all, provides many of the components that are required to operate a site, the most important of which is Commerce Server 2.0. Among these components, Microsoft also provides Windows NT 4.x (soon 5.x) and SQL Server 6.5. It is up to you whether you use Microsoft or another vendor, but remember who has created Site Server (which means they are going to have the edge), but never limit yourself to one company in today's market.

The usual hardware players are also diving in with both specific and general hardware. Specific hardware includes servers from hardware manufacturers such as Hewlett Packard. General hardware (such as monitors, tape drives, and scanners) are provided by a host of companies. The following sections discuss a few of these companies, and their presence in this dynamic e-commerce marketplace.

Banks and Other Financial Institutions

If your site involves purchases (retailing), you will need to have a good relationship with a bank. Because the financial market is such a diverse marketplace today, Microsoft has not included many transaction components with Commerce Server. A Commerce Server site uses transaction software such as Trintecs Payware or vPOS (virtual Point of Sale) to interact directly with your banking partner through their Internet banking gateway. This software will handle your credit-card transactions (approvals, verifications, and charges) when your shoppers purchase items from your store(s). Your banking partner works with you to manage these credit-card transactions, and it is important that you have a good working relationship with your financial institution, because if your business is successful they will most likely be the ones you go to for a loan to expand.

Shipping Partners

If you need to ship products to your customers, you will need a shipping partner. The usual suspects apply (Federal Express, United Parcel Service, and so on), but they are not the only players in the market. Whoever you choose, your shipping partner will need to supply plug-ins for Commerce Server to fully integrate their shipping process into your site. Shipping is very important to your customers, just imagine if your customer purchases an item, pays ahead of time (via the transaction software we just discussed), and doesn't get the merchandise because shipping misplaced it. You can just about guarantee that the customer will not come back to your store.

Independent Software Vendors (ISVs)

Along with the large companies, there are many ISVs which produce shrink-wrapped and downloadable software that supports or runs on Microsoft products, technologies, and platforms. You may want to integrate these plug-ins, for Commerce Server, into your site to increase its functionality. Taxware, for example, can automate the sales-tax aspects of your site. There are many, many ISVs and therefore many, many products they provide. Don't be afraid to shop around: You will be sure to find at least two vendors that provide the same plug-in, and you will want to compare their uses.

From Here...

Designing a site in today's marketplace can be a very daunting process, this means you will have to work harder in the planning stages and have less time to develop and debug. Throughout this book, we will discuss the steps necessary to purchase the correct hardware, design a store, protect your site, and sell your product to many shoppers.

The following highlights what is ahead:

- Chapter 2, "Web Site Design and Development," helps you understand the concerns you will need to consider when designing a Web site.
- Chapter 3, "Setting Up Your Store," takes a detailed look into actually setting up a store, as well as giving you a good foundation in using the Microsoft Sample Stores.
- Chapter 32, "Building a New Site: MSN Store," ends this book, walking you step-by-step through creating your own store.

CHAPTER 2

Web Site Design and Development

Opening a new business involves making many decisions, and one of the largest myths floating around the Web today is that opening a business on the Web is easy. Building a business on the Web involves no magic (besides what Microsoft provides); the risks are the same as in any other business investment that you make today.

Some people think that when you open a business on the Web, you don't have to worry about how customers get to your store, about paying rent for a building, or (the worst lie of all) about continually cleaning up after your store. Anyone who builds a business on the Web with these lies in mind is destined to fail in a matter of time.

When you start a business on the Web, whether you have just one store or a multitude of Web sites, you need to make the same careful decisions that you would make if you opened any other business, and the Web does provide some additional advantages for an entrepreneur. For example, you can have customers from all over the world ordering products from your store(s) without any of them traveling thousands of miles to physically show up at your store.

We can all agree that any good book written about the success of a competitive business emphasizes the fact that a business must have a vision. This fact also applies to a

Building a foundation for fortune

This section shows you how to start your business foundation and how to design this foundation with your vision and future.

Developing the foundation

This section discusses what is involved in the actual development of your site, as well as some of the tools that your business needs to purchase.

Protecting your investment

Starting a business is easy, but keeping the business alive in today's vicious market is a task only for the strong at heart.

Taking the jump

When you have everything ready to go, you want to get into the marketplace. As important as it is to get into the marketplace as quickly as possible, you want to make sure that you do so correctly.

Making a fortune for a lifetime

After you create a successful business on the Web, and just when you think that you have conquered everything, you face one last major task. This section discusses the steps that you take in considering the long-term fortune of your business.

business hosted on the Web. If you are serious about being a successful and competitive business on the Web, the first thing that you need to do is establish a companywide vision.

Although a vision probably is the most important part of your business, it is definitely not the only aspect of success; many other areas of your business need to be taken into consideration. This chapter is not "Five Easy Steps to Success"; how to create a successful business and where to get your information are up to you. Rather, this chapter shows you how to create a successful Web site by using the tools provided by Microsoft. ■

Building a Foundation for Fortune

The first and most important decision is a vision for your company; without it, your company will lack the drive that brings so many businesses to success and fortune. Lack of vision surely ends in disaster.

You are only a couple of pages into this chapter and probably are sick of hearing about this vision thing, but you should take it seriously. Some companies hold off their grand openings just to make sure that they have a clear vision, and these companies almost always are successful.

Any good architect understands what the cornerstone is to a building. If the cornerstone of a building is not set correctly, with the correct material, the building might be constructed completely but is destined to crumble in time.

Vision Is Your Cornerstone

You can think of the vision of your business as having much the same symbolic relationship as that of a cornerstone to a building. If this vision is not set correctly, you may build your business completely around the vision, and everything may appear to go well, but your business will crumble, it is only a matter of time.

Build with Vision

After coming up with a vision for your company, you need to decide what you're going to do with this vision. Having a vision is imperative, but it does not get customers to come, and it certainly does not make customers come back.

You need to build around this vision with everything you do, this type of design and architecture is what will bring customers in. In today's Web marketplace, people are continuously going to and leaving Web sites, knowing this impatience, you can use it to your advantage. Remember that your customers are going to come and go, and plan your site around this, make sure the information is refreshed often, and try to spice the site up. If your site is different and fresh most every time your customers come back, you can be assured that they will come back often.

To return to the cornerstone example, when an architect designs a building, he or she must consider several things, such as whether the building will be constructed near water and whether flooding, or insects will be problems. These considerations, and a million others, help the architect determine what material to use around this cornerstone and how to build it up.

You can apply the same concept to the vision that you create for your business. After you determine what your company should be driving toward, you need to determine what to do with that drive. Planning the architecture for your site can help you plan for quick and often changes, as well as making sure that your business will not be affected severely by anything (much like the architect needs to protect from floods, insects, and such).

Your Vision Opens the Future

The last consideration in your company vision is the future. When you create your vision, keep the future in mind. Many companies confuse "Company Goals" (which should change often) with the "Company Vision" (which should last forever), and adopt a vision that changes often, this instability will show up in your store.

When you create your vision keep the focus on the longstanding position of the company, and try not to focus on what the company should be doing. What the company should be doing will come later, and will be in direct relation to the vision.

Developing the Foundation

You have carefully created a vision that your company can build around and grow with. Now you are ready to actually create the Web site. This step should not be terribly difficult, and with some effort, it can be fun. Following are a few things to remember when you develop your Web site:

- **KISS.** *KISS* stands for Keep It Simple, Stupid. Your visitors will not come back to your site if they can't find what they want to know quickly. A successful Web site is easy to surf, as the Webbies say.

- **Keep initial development costs down.** Any good Web site is continually updated, providing new and exciting displays every day. Which means you will not want to budget all your development costs in the creation of the site. Save some money now and plan to spend it later on site updates.

- **Consider your audience.** Remember your audience when you develop the site. Millions of people on the Web may look at your site (if you are successful), so you need to have information that is not only pertinent to your regular customers, but that also may interest other people. Who knows—maybe those people will become customers.

Developing your Web site requires the right tools, which cost money. Developing a site with the correct tools will save you a lot of stress, and the site will look much better than developing with mediocre tools. Remember that your company is only as good as it is represented to your customer. The following sections describe the tools that can help you develop a successful Web site.

Web-Authoring Tools

Microsoft Visual Studio 97

This suite of Microsoft products is helpful for designing Web applications.

Programming Tools

Microsoft Visual Basic 4.0/5.0

You can develop just about anything for the Web with VB.

Microsoft Visual C++ 4.2/5.0

For advanced programming, you can use VC++. Version 5.0 has some very cool benefits.

Microsoft Visual J++ 1.1

This product helps you develop articulate Web Java applets.

Microsoft Visual Source Save 5.0

This product helps you keep track of your code versions and is especially useful if more than one person is developing your site.

Graphics and Design Tools

Adobe Photoshop 4.0

This program helps you create and design graphics, backgrounds, and just about everything else to spice up your Web site.

Hiring the Right People

If you are not going to develop your Web site, you need to hire someone or some company to develop it. Do not take this task lightly. With the popularity of the Web, many companies focus on site development. Many of these companies do not have the necessary experience to develop a successful site, and choosing the wrong company will be a mistake that you will regret.

Following are some things to remember when you choose a company to develop your Web site:

- Hiring cheap is expensive
- References reflect reliability
- Establish a relationship with your developers. The following sections discuss these topics further:

Hiring Cheap Is Expensive

Many Web-site development companies are available today, but don't be mistaken—the prices are not cheap because of this competition. Many companies try to hook you in with inexpensive prices, but they may not be worth the money.

If you spend a little extra choosing the correct development company, you will save much more later. Don't forget that the better the site development is, the more your customers will want to visit your site.

References Reflect Reliability

Any good development company has references. Don't be afraid to ask what sites the company has developed. Get the addresses of those Web sites, visit the sites, and ask yourself the following questions:

- Did you come away from the site knowing what the company provides?
- Was the site easy to surf and were you able to get where you wanted to go quickly?
- Did the site look good, with graphics and applets that amazed you?

After you look at a site, try to get a reference from the company for which the site was designed. Ask a few questions about the development company. Make sure that your questions are thorough; being thorough now will make a big difference later when you have to deal with the development company.

Establish a Relationship

Most companies in business today are small, sometimes employing only three to five people. Don't be concerned about the number of employees. The mark of a good company is how employees work together and with you, not how many employees the company has.

Take advantage of a small company's size, which gives you an opportunity to get to know the developers as well as everyone else in the company. If you build a relationship now, you will thank yourself later if that company becomes large.

Protecting Your Investment

When you have your store built, you need to make sure that you protect your investment. Too many companies develop Web sites but do not make sure that the sites are prepared for customers who are going to be relentless.

Quality Assurance

Quality assurance (QA) is the process by which a company tests itself to ensure that it can meet the needs of its customers. You can think of QA as being a self-examination; it is a healthy process that every successful company puts itself through.

This section does not discuss all aspects of QA for a company, but two aspects can benefit your company on the Web:

- Web Site

  Content

Ease of Use

Consistency

■ Hardware

Reliability

Upgradability

Remember that QA is not a necessity, but your customers will see the difference whether your site has been designed properly or not, and they will relate it to how your business is run. If your customers do not have faith in your company, they will not stay as customers.

Web Site   When you examine and test your Web site, make sure that the site is full of interesting and helpful content. Be concerned that you have enough information. If your content is placed properly, you never have to worry about having too much information. Remember that customers become frustrated with your company if they cannot get the information that they need from your Web site.

Along with the content on the Web site comes ease of use. You can have all the content in the world on your site, but if your customers cannot get to it, the content is just as useless as if it were not there at all. Make sure that your customers can get to all the information that they need quickly and easily by using some logical format.

The last consideration when testing your Web Site is consistency. If you have content duplicated in many areas, your users become frustrated. Make sure that your site gives users easy access to all the information that they need, but be consistent.

Hardware   One of the most disappointing things that a customer can see is a message like UNABLE TO ACCESS—SERVER BUSY OR NOT RESPONDING. A customer should be able to access your server day or night, rain or shine, whether one other customer is accessing it or a thousand customers are accessing it. The first thing to consider in testing your hardware services is how reliable the hardware is.

If your hardware is not reliable, your customers cannot access your site, which means that they will not be happy. (Funny how everything goes back to these customers being happy, ha?) One of the most common mistakes made today with hardware is to put hardware together with planning for what will happen today, and not what will happen tomorrow, which always leads to slow servers and unhappy customers.

Suppose that a company opens a Web site and expects to have 20,000 customers using its servers for purchasing, so it buys hardware that supports 20,000 people. The problem with this arrangement is that the point of putting a business on the Web is to build the business, not to keep it at the same level. To put this situation in perspective, a company that expects to have 20,000 customers should plan to support 50,000 customers with its hardware.

The second consideration when choosing hardware is upgradability, which goes right along with reliability. Having reliable servers is not enough; you should have reliable servers that can be enhanced when you find that they are getting near their maximum load.

To continue the example earlier in this section, if you expect to have 20,000 customers, you should plan to support 50,000 customers with your hardware, and you should plan to be able to upgrade your hardware in a flash to support 100,000 customers. Anything over the 100,000 will mean adding new hardware.

 When you test your site and hardware, keeping future investments in mind is a good idea. In other words, you should plan your hardware and software in such a way that your company can grow and can come up with new and exciting investments.

Part
I

Ch
2

Taking the Jump: Publishing Your Site on the Web

The time that your company has worked hard for is here; it's time to publish your site on the Web.

With some direction, putting your site up on the Web can be a beneficial and satisfying experience. This section discusses the following topics:

- The grand opening
- The weeks to come
- Investments for the future

The Grand Opening

The Web is not an exception to the rule about first impressions (you know, "First impressions leave the lasting impression"). A recent Web survey asked people what the deciding factor was in their ever going back to a Web site. The results were interesting. Seventy-eight percent of the people surveyed said that they would not go back to a site if did not interest them the first time, even if the site had pertinent information.

This information can be damaging, the people will not come back, if your site does not interest people. Even if your site contains information that, at first site, may not appear to readers as appealing, you still have to make the site appealing if you want people to come back.

The following sections discuss several considerations for the grand opening of your store.

Day The day of your grand opening is important. Try to avoid opening your site on a holiday, but opening right before certain holidays can be beneficial. Having your grand opening right before Christmas probably is the best time; if you open your store before Memorial Day, you probably will not get as much notice.

Like any other decision you can use this decision to benefit your company. But one caution about the day: Don't allow this decision to get in the way of the company's opening. You don't want to wait until Christmas to open your store if you have it ready in March; that type of a delay would be a disaster for your company.

Time As is true of the day, your company can benefit from the time of day when you choose to have your grand opening. Remember that when you open a store on the Web, you are opening it to the world.

Plan to have your grand opening at a time when the core of your customers is on the Web. If you do not already have a customer base, you should plan your grand opening for the customers to whom you are marketing your business.

Special Offers Special offers probably are among the most successful forms of marketing. You should provide some type of special offers to your customers and future customers.

Making some special offers at the time of your grand opening can be beneficial. You should not only have special offers, but also advertise them along with your grand opening. These special offers will serve to tell people about your grand opening and come even though they might not particularly be interested in what you have.

Publicity Publicity goes right along with special offers, because you have to publicize your special offers for anyone to know about them and want to take advantage of your grand opening.

I would suggest that you get in contact with a publicist to help you get your name out into the world. If you are not interested, or cannot afford to hire a publicist full time, I would suggest that you at least hire the publicist for the opening of your store, this initial publicity might be enough to kick your store off to a good start.

Attention You need someone to be at attention 24 hours a day when you have your grand opening. If you do not have someone watching the store and the system crashes, your customers will get the wrong first impression.

The Weeks to Come

The weeks following your grand opening are just as important as the opening itself. After you present yourself to the public through your grand opening, those customers are going to tell other people that you are out there. Being prepared for this wave of interest is important.

One unique aspect of opening a store on the Web is how fast people find information. You will not believe the increase in your publicity when you put your site on the Web.

Investments for the Future

As time goes on, you have to plan for the future. After a while, your site becomes just another site. Is it the type of site that people bookmark? Chances are that if your customers are bookmarking your site, they have a reason to return. This situation is great, but if your site is not updated, the bookmarks go away.

After you get through the grand opening, going right into updating mode is important. Don't be fooled into thinking that you can take a break.

Planning for a Lifetime of Fortune

Now that you have built your fortune, you can begin to plan where you want to go with your company. Building a store is one thing; keeping it successful through the years is different, and very difficult.

Consider a few points that can help you keep your new fortune for a lifetime:

- Maintaining development
- Growing with your vision
- Designing the future

Part
I
Ch
2

Maintaining Development

As discussed earlier in this chapter, you need to update your site continually to keep your customers informed, as well as interested. Maintaining development involves two aspects: adding new content and updating current content. With these two aspects in mind, you should be able to maintain the actual site's development.

You should also update the site's graphics and applets to stay in touch with new technology, which probably is more work than actually keeping the content up to date.

Adding New Content

Regularly putting new content on your site for your customers is critical, because people check for new information every day. One of the best sites in terms of keeping information updated is **http://www.globe.com/globe/**; check it out sometime.

The information at this site is updated hourly, so you never have to worry about going to the site and not finding any new information.

Updating Current Content

Updating current content can be tricky, but if you have a method for referring to duplicated information, you should be able to keep up with this task. Whenever customers go back to a page and search for information, they want the information to be fresh.

Growing with Your Vision

Because you took the time to create a vision (you did, didn't you?), you want to keep it in focus, making sure that your Web site always displays your vision. Don't be afraid to change your site if you feel that the change will help your company.

Remember that if you grow with your vision, your vision grows with you. Along with you growing comes the customers and the rest of the world.

Designing the Future

Because you are going to be updating the information on your Web site, you have a unique opportunity to move ahead of your competitors by providing information and products as soon as they are available (even if they are on the Web, too). Your company could be the next Microsoft in its industry if you follow the steps discussed in this chapter.

So go get 'em! Show the world what you have to offer, and never underestimate yourself. Be far- and high-reaching, and you will do just fine.

From Here...

In this chapter we have discussed the considerations you will need to make when considering your Site Design and Development. From here we are going to implement the design and development of your site, using the concepts we have discussed in this chapter.

The following chapters are just a sample of what is to come ahead:

- Chapter 3, "Setting Up Your Store," will discuss the steps necessary to start your adventure. This is where you will create your first Commerce Server 2.0 store.
- Part II, "Working with Microsoft Site Server," will discuss the various features that Microsoft Site Server provides your store, as well as introduce you to the rich development environment that Microsoft has provided.
- Part IV, "Creating Stores with Active Server Pages," will take a development look at creating your store features and pages using the ASP concepts. These chapters will also serve as an introduction to the rich environment of components Microsoft has provided.

Setting Up Your Store

Now is the time you have been waiting for; you are ready to begin setting up Microsoft Commerce Server 2.0. Before you can install Commerce Server, you need to make sure that you have set up your databases for the starter stores if you want to install these stores. Microsoft has provided four starter stores that you can use as examples to develop your own store. The four stores that have been provided for us are:

> Clock Peddler
>
> Volcano Coffee Shop
>
> Microsoft Press Bookstore
>
> Adventure Works

If you do not want to install the starter stores, you can continue without making any modification. If this server is your production server, you probably do not want to install the starter stores. You want to keep your production server as clean as possible, so installing sample stores would just take up resources and disk space that you want to keep for production stores. We will go over each one of the starter stores in great detail in this chapter.

In most cases, you have one or more machines with Microsoft Commerce Server installed for development only if your business is to develop commerce sites. On your development machines, you should install the starter stores as a reference to aid in developing your production stores.

Setting up your SQL database to use with Commerce Server

Learn how to create database devices and a database so that Commerce Server can customize this database to use with the starter stores.

Create an ODBC System Data Source to communicate with Commerce Server

In order for Commerce Server to be able to communicate with your database, you need to set up an ODBC datasource.

Setting up Commerce Server

You will learn the different options available to you when you install Microsoft Commerce Server

Going over starter stores

You will go through the starter stores in detail and find out how each starter store can benefit you as you create your own store and also how to copy a starter store so that you can create a store using the starter store as a foundation.

Creating a store foundation

You will learn how to create a store foundation and the options you have available to you so that you can create a customized store of your own.

Remember that you must have a separate license for each server on which you have Microsoft Commerce Server. For this reason, if your company is small, you may have one development server that several people use. This arrangement can be practical for development purposes. Keep in mind, however, that if several people experiment on one machine, a good chance exists that people will crash the machine often, depending on what kind of development is going on. Having too many developers on the same machine could seriously slow your development teams. ■

Creating a SQL Database for Your Starter Stores

If you install the starter stores, you need to create a database device and a database in SQL Enterprise Manager.

To create the databases in Microsoft SQL Server, you need to perform the following steps:

1. Go to SQL Server Manager and register the server that you are going to use. To register the server, right click on SQL 6.5 and choose Register Server from the shortcut menu (see Figure 3.1).

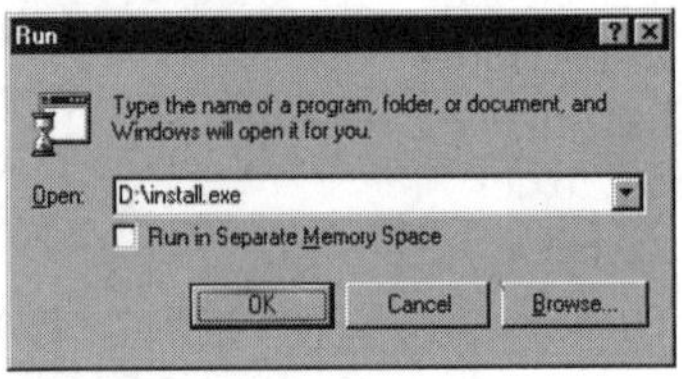

FIG. 3.1
You need to right click on SQL 6.5 to bring up the shortcut menu and register your SQL Server if you have not already done so.

2. In the Register Server dialog box, type the name of the server in Server and in Login Information, select Use Standard Security. For Login ID, use either sa or an account that you have set up that has full access to your database. Click the Register button when you have finished (see Figure 3.2).

3. Click the close button in the Register Server dialog box.

4. Before you can create a database, you need to create two database devices, a data device and a log device. These database devices are created exactly the same way even though they will be used for different purposes. Since you are only using these databases for testing on our starter stores, you do not need to make very large databases. If you create a 20M data device and a 5M log device, this should be more than enough. To create the database devices, expand the tree for the SQL server that you are using by clicking on the + next to your server name.

   Right click on Databases Devices to bring up the shortcut menu. Choose New Device from the shortcut menu (see Figure 3.3).

FIG. 3.2

In this dialog box, you need to choose your server and enter your login name and password.

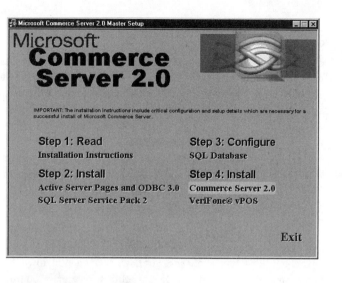

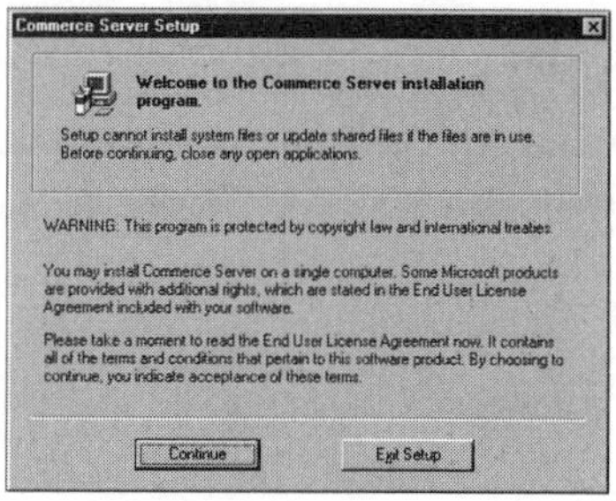

FIG. 3.3

From the expanded Database Device tree, you need to right click Database Devices to bring up the shortcut menu and then choose New Device from the shortcut menu.

In the Name field, the recommended Name is commerceDATA. You can choose to place the database file anywhere you would like. The recommended location is on the same hard drive or partition that you have installed SQL Server on. If you choose the same hard drive, the default directory where all of the other databases reside will be chosen. The last item you need to configure is the database device size. The recommended size for the data device is 20M (see Figure 3.4).

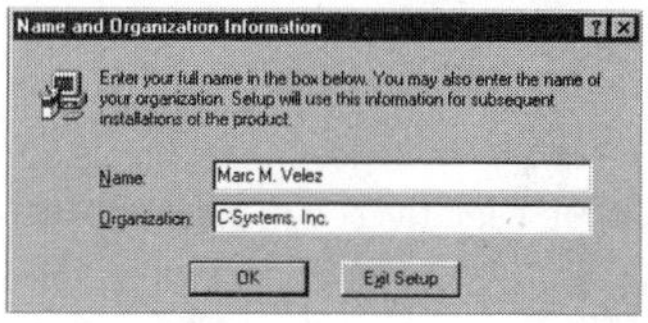

FIG. 3.4

In the New Database Device dialog box, you need to choose a name, location, and size for your database device. When you have filled in this information, click the Create Now button to create the data device.

Part I
Ch 3

To create the log file, follow the same steps as in the previous paragraph. For the Name, choose commerceLOG and for the file size, choose 5M.

5. Now that you have created your database devices, it is time to create the database. To create the database, click the + next to Databases on the tree to expand the list of databases on your server. Right click Databases to bring the shortcut menu and choose New Database to bring up the New Database dialog box (see Figure 3.5).

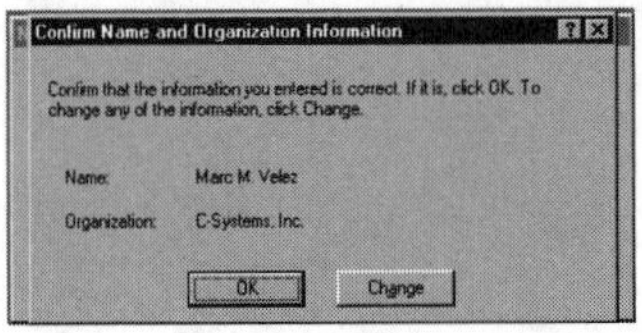

FIG. 3.5

Right click Databases to bring up the shortcut menu and choose New Database.

In the New Database dialog box, you need to choose the Name, Data Device, and the Log Device. For Name, type commerce. For Data Device, pull down the drop-down menu and choose commerceDATA. For Log Device, choose commerceLOG from the drop-down menu. You will see that to the right, the size fields are set to be the total available size of the databases (20M for commerceDATA and 5M for commerceLOG). You will want to leave these values alone since this is the correct size for these databases (see Figure 3.6). When you have filled in all of the information, click Create Now.

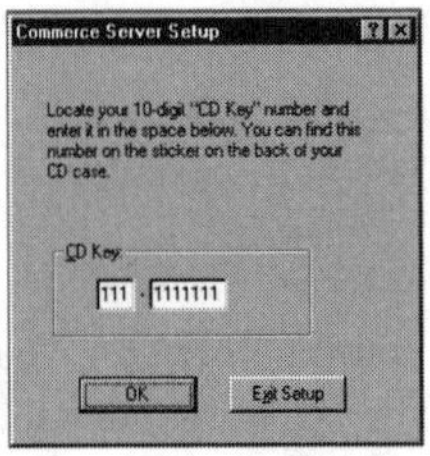

FIG. 3.6

To create the new database, choose commerce for the Name, commerceDATA for the Data Device, and commerceLOG for the Log Device.

Now that you have set up your database to use with your starter stores, you need to set up ODBC system datasources. ODBC system datasources (DSN) allow Microsoft Commerce Server to communicate with your database server, in this case, Microsoft SQL Server. The following steps show how to set up an ODBC DSN for the new database.

CAUTION

When you setup SQL, there are two things that you need to keep in mind. The first thing is that you should never use a blank password for the sa account or any other account on a production machine in your SQL server. The reason for this is that if you use a blank password, you are allowing the means for someone to log into your machine and steal all of your database information, destroy or change your information or even all of the above. If you have strong passwords on your SQL server accounts, you are minimizing the risk of this ever happening.

The second thing that you should consider is creating a separate username and password for each database on your production SQL server. There are several reasons for this:

You may have customers that would like to be able to access their databases directly. You would need to limit access so those customers can only access their own databases.

You have developers that are assigned to a specific project and you do not wish to give them access to other customers' databases.

If a username and password were compromised, you would only be facing problems with one database, not your entire server.

Setting up ODBC for Your Starter Stores

After you set up your databases, you need to set up ODBC on the machine on which you are going to install Microsoft Commerce Server.

1. Go to Control Panel and double click on ODBC. This will bring up the ODBC Data Source Administrator dialog box.

2. Click on the System DSN tab. You will see a list of any system datasources (DSN's) that you have already configured. To add a new DSN, click the Add button to bring up the Create New Data Source dialog box.

3. In the Create New Data Source dialog box, double click on SQL Server in the driver text box. This will bring up the ODBC SQL Server Setup dialog box.

4. In the ODBC SQL Server Setup dialog box, click the option button to bring up additional options. For Data Source Name, type commerce. You can optionally type in a Description if you would like. Server is a drop-down box that will give you a list of any server on your local network. Click the down arrow and choose the SQL Server that you have configured this database on. The only other field that you need to configure is Database Name in the Login section. For Database Name type commerce if this is what you named your database.

5. Click OK when you have finished to bring you back to ODBC Data Source Administrator. Click OK again to bring you back to Windows NT.

6. If you are using a database on a different machine than the machine that you have installed Microsoft Commerce Server on, you must take one more step. You need to use User Manager for Domains to enable the guest account on the server that is running Microsoft SQL Server or, if you are installing on a domain controller, you need to enable the guest account on the domain. When you complete this preliminary work, you are ready to install Microsoft Commerce Server.

Installing Commerce Server

Now that you have setup the databases and ODBC for all of your starter stores, you are ready to begin installing Commerce Server. To begin, select Microsoft Commerce Server from

Master Setup. Master Setup should appear automatically when you insert the Microsoft Site Server Enterprise Edition CD-ROM in your CD-ROM drive. If it does not appear, you simply need to run setup from the root of the CD-ROM.

You see the welcome screen. Read this introduction screen and then click Continue.

Enter your name and the name of your company. Click OK when you finish.

A Confirmation dialog box appears so that you can verify that you have entered your name and company name correctly. Click OK to continue.

The next thing that you need to type is your CD key, which you can find on the back of your CD-ROM case. Make sure that you record your CD key in a safe place, because if you ever lose this key, you cannot reinstall Microsoft Commerce Server without contacting Microsoft for a new CD key.

After you enter your CD key, you see your product identification number. You must use this number if you ever need to call Microsoft for technical support, and you also need this number to register your product. Write the number down and keep it in a safe place. Notice that your CD key is part of this number.

You need to decide which drive and folder to install Commerce Server in. Commerce will take up a great deal of disk space if you have several stores running on the same machine; also, a busy Web server uses a great deal of bandwidth and disk I/O. Therefore, installing this program on a disk drive that is totally separate from your operating system—if possible, on a totally dedicated disk drive—is a good idea. The exception to this rule occurs if you use a large RAID drive to handle your enterprise. A recommended machine that for a production environment is an HP Netserver LH Pro. This machine is a quad Pentium Pro 200 MHz machine that is capable of using up to 2G RAM. The recommended disk drive configuration is as follows. A mirrored 2G partition for the operating system running RAID1 for redundancy. There is also a 2G RAID1 partition for log files. Log files can take up a significant amount of disk I/O and therefore, if possible, you should keep these files on a disk drive that is totally separate from the rest of your system (different physical disk drives and different disk drive controller). Lastly, there is a 60G RAID5 partition for installing all of your programs, databases, and just about everything else. If you want more information about this machine, please visit **http://www.hp.com/netserver**. Figure 3.1 shows a picture of this mentioned machine.

If you want to change the location in which Microsoft Commerce Server is to be installed, choose Change Folder. When you are satisfied, click OK to continue (see Figure 3.7).

In the next screen, you specify whether you want to do a complete installation or a custom installation. If you are installing the program on a development machine, a complete installation probably is the better option, providing things such as the SDK (software development kit), starter stores, and documentation. If you are installing the program on a server that you are going to use only for production, choose a custom installation (see Figure 3.8).

FIG. 3.7
You need to choose the destination folder to install Microsoft Commerce Server.

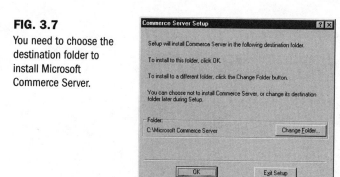

FIG. 3.8
You need to decide how you would like to install Microsoft Commerce Server. It is always recommended that you choose custom installation in order to familiarize yourself with what options you have to choose from.

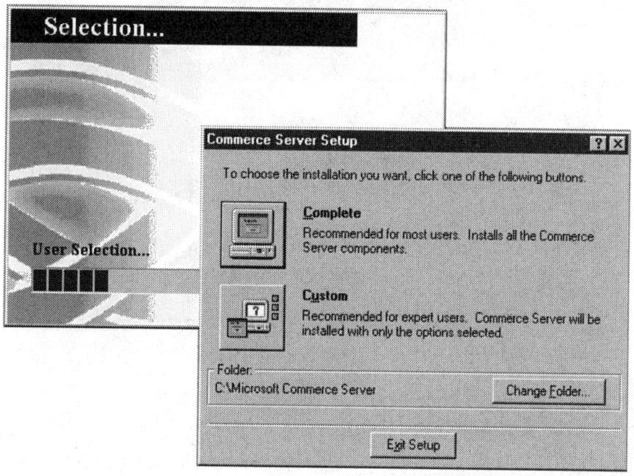

Part
I
Ch
3

For a production store, you want to install all the starter stores and the Commerce SDK. You can also install the documentation, if you want. Most of the documentation is in HTML format, so if you leave it on your production server, people can get to the documentation for Commerce if they are not behind your firewall. If you do not protect these files, of course, any user can see these documents if they know the URL. Although allowing the public to view these documents would not be a security breach, protecting these documents is something that you want to consider. After you select the components that you want to install, click the Continue button (see Figure 3.9).

You need to set up your starter stores. To do so, you need to select the system data sources that you set up earlier in the section "Setting up ODBC for Your Starter Stores." If you are not installing the starter stores, you can skip this section.

The first dialog box that you see is the Adventure Works data-source box. In this dialog box, you see the data sources that you have already set up on your machine. For the starter stores, you can use one database for all four stores. If the only DSN that you have on your machine is the DSN for the starter stores, you see LocalServer and Merchant in the dialog box that appears. Click Merchant and then click Configure to make sure that the DSN is configured properly (see Figure 3.10).

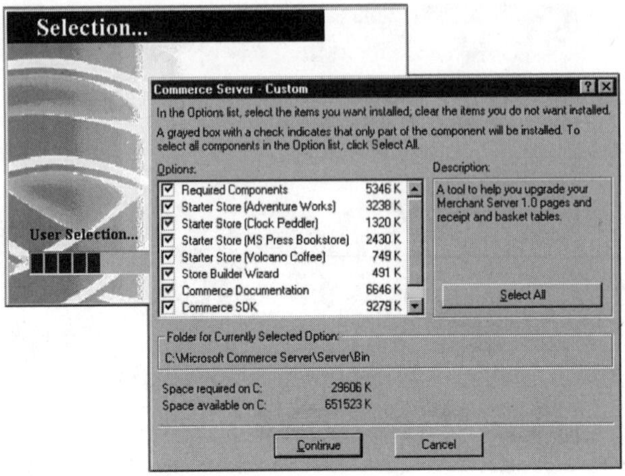

FIG. 3.9
Here, you need to decide which components of Microsoft Commerce Server will be installed.

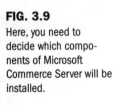

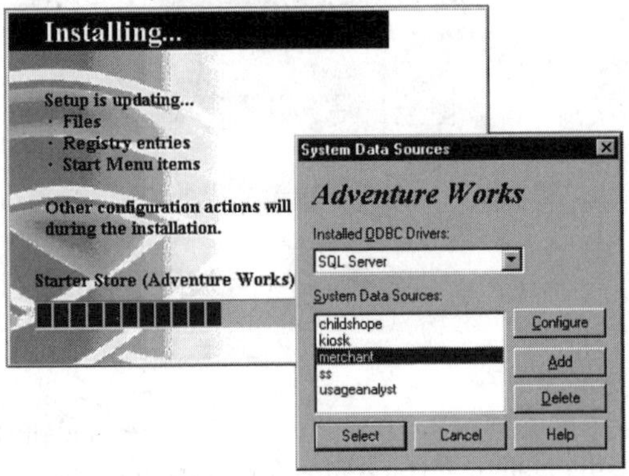

FIG. 3.10
In this dialog box, you need to choose the system data source that you set up previously. This allows your starter stores to be able to interact with a SQL database.

You see the same screen that you saw when you configured the ODBC device in Control Panel earlier in the section "Setting up ODBC for Your Starter Stores." Verify that all your information is correct and then click OK.

The next screen that you see, the SQL Server Login dialog box, is similar to the ODBC setup screen, but this screen has error checking; it also allows you to log into SQL and shows you a list of all available databases. If you do not see the bottom half of the screen (the Options box), click the Options button. Again, verify that all the information is correct, and choose OK.

You are asked to repeat the steps stated in the last paragraph for the remainder of the starter stores that you install. Repeat the steps for as many starter stores as you install.

To continue installing Commerce Server, you must stop any IIS services that are running on your machine: LDAP, WWW, FTP, Gopher, and so on. If you do not stop these services, Commerce Server Setup exits and Commerce Server is not installed properly. To stop these services, simply click OK and they will be stopped for you.

Microsoft Commerce Server installs on your computer and shows you as Commerce Server Setup is copying files.

After Commerce Server finishes copying the files, you get confirmation that the program installed successfully.

Testing Your Installation of Microsoft Commerce Server 2.0

When you finish installing Microsoft Commerce Server, you need to test your installation. You may have been asked to reboot your machine after Microsoft Commerce Server 2.0 finished installing. If you were not asked to reboot, doing so is a good idea anyway. Because you just finished installing several products on your computer, you should reboot so that you can start fresh. Also, by rebooting now, you can make sure that all your services restart without a problem.

When you finish rebooting and logging in, check your event viewer for any errors. If you have any errors, you should take care of them right away before proceeding. If you did not get a message that says that a service did not start, you should expect to see no errors in your event log.

If you are upgrading from Microsoft Merchant Server 1.0, you notice that no Store Service exists for Microsoft Commerce Server 2.0; now Commerce Server is run through the World Wide Web Publishing Service (W3SVC). The Merchant Server Control Panel has also been removed; now most of your configuration is done through the global.asa file. This file is discussed in depth later in the book.

When you finish inspecting your system and are sure that the W3SVC service started, open your Web browser and go to **http://servername/aw/default.asp** to view the Adventure Works store.

> **CAUTION**
>
> If you get an error message, *do not reload the page*. If you get an error the first time that you view a page after starting or restarting the W3SVC, a problem potentially exists in the global.asa file. If you try to reload the page and it reloads, or if you get a different error, the global.asa file has already been read, and it will not be read again until the W3SVC is stopped and restarted or the global.asa file is changed. When trying to debug a problem, the error that you need to look for is the error that you see when the store is reloaded. Again, in order to reload a store, you need to either restart the "World Wide Web Publishing Service" in Control Panel, Services or modify and save the global.asa file for your store.

If you get an error message when you try to load one of the starter stores, you most likely have a problem in the way that the database is set up. The first thing to look at is your ODBC in Control Panel. Go to the System DSN tab and double-click the DSN that you set up. Make sure that you are pointing to the correct machine and that you typed the correct database name. If not, type the correct information.

The next thing to check is whether the MS SQL Server and the SQL Executive services are running on the machine that you have SQL installed on. Last, make sure that you have the guest account enabled so that you can use SQL on the machine.

If your store still does not load properly, go to the directory where the store is installed (usually c:\microsoft commerce server\stores*store name*) and search for dsn_include.asp. Make sure that you have the correct user name in all these files and that the ODBC system DSN names are correct. The username should be in the following format. If you are on a member server or stand-alone server, your MSCSStoreAdmin username should be in the format MACHINENAME\Username. If you have installed Commerce Server on a primary domain controller, your MSCSStoreAdmin username should be in the format DOMAINNAME\Username.

Using Starter Stores

MicrosoftCommerce Server comes with four Starter Stores for you to use. Each store has its own strengths and weaknesses (described in the following sections). The Starter Stores provide a schematic for you to follow and a base upon which you can build your own site. At the simple end of the spectrum, you can use a Starter Store pretty much as it is. You just copy the store, replace the graphics in the asp templates with your own, integrate your bank's credit-card-authorization solution, and open your doors for business. At the other end of the range of possible ways to use the stores is adding your own scripts, modifying the store's database, and totally customizing the store. You can also build your own store from the ground up, but if you do, you probably are not making the best use of your resources.

Following is a brief review of the Starter Stores:

- **Clock Peddler**. Clock Peddler, the first and simplest store, allows you to make an easy transition to the world of e-commerce (see Figure 3.11).

- **Volcano Coffee Shop**. Volcano Coffee Shop, which is a little higher up the scale of complexity from Clock Peddler, was Microsoft's original example on the Internet when they were demonstrating IIS for the first time. This store brings a richer interface to the shopping experience and adds a few more bells and whistles than Clock Peddler has. One feature logs visitors into the store before they shop. This feature is helpful if you want to keep statistics on your users (see Figure 3.12).

- **Microsoft Press Bookstore**. This store is much more sophisticated than the preceding two stores, implementing (among other things) a search engine and image maps. Overall, Microsoft Press Bookstore is a much nicer-looking and much more complicated store than the preceding two. Unlike Volcano Coffee Shop, this store does not require visitors to log in (see Figure 3.13).

FIG. 3.11

Here we have the first page of the Clock Peddler store. As you can see, there is nothing fancy or advanced about this store, it is the simplest of all of the starter stores that are provided with Microsoft Commerce Server.

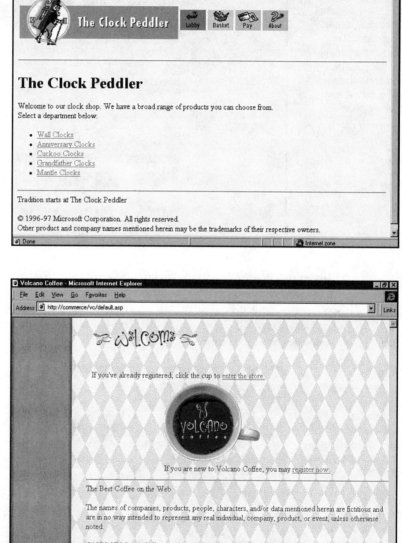

Part

I

Ch

3

FIG. 3.12

The next store is the Volcano Coffee Shop. This was the original store that Microsoft used to demonstrate the first version of IIS. This is a somewhat more complex store than Clock Peddler is. It makes use of tables and it uses some more advanced features in the database for example, giving customers accounts and shopping baskets.

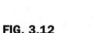

FIG. 3.13

The Microsoft Press Bookstore is one of the two advanced stores provided with Microsoft Commerce Server. As you can see just by looking at the opening page, this page implements some advanced features that we have not looked at yet.

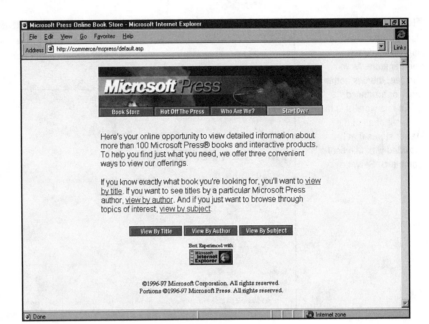

■ **Adventure Works**. Adventure Works is the most sophisticated starter store (see Figure 3.14). The advanced interface offers a full set of tools for administering your site, as well as many merchandising and promotional capabilities. The store also introduces a component called the Microsoft Wallet. This tool allows users to send their names, addresses, and credit-card information.

FIG. 3.14

The Adventure Works store is the most complex store. As you can see just on the first page, there are multiple frames and tables. You also need to log in before you can proceed any further. Once you log in, there are animations, scripts, the Microsoft Wallet and many more advanced features.

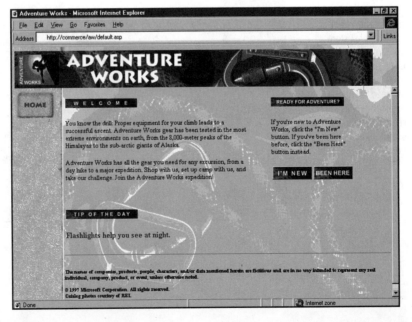

This store is rich with Java and Active X. Adventure Works also uses some fairly complex scripts. Although the capabilities of Adventure Works are quite compelling and sophisticated, be careful before you choose it as your first site. Modifying the store can be tricky, because many connections exist among the components, and some of these connections can be tricky to figure out if you need to change something.

To choose the Starter Store to use, you need to figure out how you want your site to function and how sophisticated you want it to be. The following sections describe the stores in detail, listing the major advantages and disadvantages of each Starter Store to give you some ideas about which one to choose one for your own site.

Clock Peddler

Clock Peddler is the simplest Starter Store and offers the fewest scripts and customization features, but it can be useful if you are trying to set up a basic site. This Starter Store offers basic retail functions such as inventory management and an online catalog of your products. Although simple, this store may be suitable for your site.

When you first enter the store, you see a list of the store's departments. To move to a department, merely click its link.

When you enter a department, you see a list of the clocks that are available in that department. To get more details about an item, including a description and price, you click the item to go to the item's description page. If you want to purchase this item, you add the item to your shopping basket by clicking the Add to Basket button.

When you finish shopping, you move to the checkout area by clicking Purchase. You are asked to input shipping and billing information. If your billing address is the same as your shipping address, click Same As Shipping Address. Click the Total button, and you go to the purchase-verification screen, where you see the subtotal of your order, plus the tax and shipping cost, with the grand total at the bottom. If everything is correct, input your credit-card information and click the Purchase button.

N O T E If this store were real, when your customer clicks the Purchase button, Microsoft Commerce Server would invoke your credit-card-verification software (if you purchased and installed this software). The credit card would be verified, and the purchase amount would be held against the customer's account until you capture the transaction (capturing the transaction actually charges the customer's credit card). The next screen either gives the customer a confirmation number or tells the customer why their credit card has been denied. When you get your confirmation number, save this number, because after you leave, you cannot get this number back easily.

Because Clock Peddler is an example store, when you click Purchase, you go to the confirmation screen, which displays a confirmation number. The purchase is complete. You can either click the Lobby link to continue shopping or leave the store by typing another URL or choosing a bookmark in your web browser.

Part

I

Ch

3

Pros   The main advantage of Clock Peddler is its simplicity. You will appreciate this simplicity, especially if you are creating your first Commerce site. You can start with a simple store and build the store up as your knowledge of Microsoft Commerce Server increases.

Clock Peddler has the basics that you need to create your store: the lobby, departments, products, and tools to process transactions that enable your customers to buy your products. If you want to see an example of a simple store that was created by means of the Clock Peddler store, visit **http://www.childshope.org**.

Cons   On the down side, this store is a generic site that depends solely on its content to get customers to return. If you have a large inventory, Clock Peddler is not the store for you because of the lack of room to grow. The store also does not have much to catch people's attention and keep them interested in staying.

Why Clock Peddler?   Clock Peddler offers simplicity, which is the key to getting online quickly. The lobby is a single entrance to all the store's resources, enabling users to get right to the list of departments and then to the actual merchandise.

You should use Clock Peddler for your first Commerce site unless you have substantial expertise available to help you with one of the more complex stores. When you get your store up and running, you can do many things with it as you learn how to better use Microsoft Commerce Server 2.0 and program asp templates. Also, if you use Clock Peddler to set up a store because you are just learning Commerce Server, you can continue to learn Commerce Server by making the store more complicated. When you are happy with the more complicated and nicer-looking store, you can bring that store into production. Remember that when you put up a site like this store, you most likely will change it often to keep up with new technology and to keep people interested.

Clock Peddler was the model for Childshope (**http://www.childshope.org**), a donation site for Children's Hospital of Boston. When this site was developed, it was decided that a very simple site be used for this store because there are not several items sold. The idea of this store is simply for people to come to the site, see how much good a donation can do for these children and make a donation. There are no products to buy, and it is not a site that users would normally come back to once they make a donation except to donate to again. Because of this, it was decided to make this site as simple as possible. This site was originally a Microsoft Merchant 1.0 site that was converted to Microsoft Commerce Server 2.0. For complete details on the conversion of this site, please refer to the case study of **http://www.childshope.org** in Chapter 29, "Converting an Existing Site: Childs Hope."

When Not to Use Clock Peddler   If you want to track the traffic on your site, such as seeing who is shopping and what shoppers are looking at, Clock Peddler is not the store for you.

If you are looking for the cross-sell and up-sell or other promotion capabilities, Clock Peddler will not meet your needs. Clock Peddler is suitable only for opening a basic site and for learning Commerce Server. If you are looking for some of these advanced features, keep reading about the other starter stores. One of these stores should be able to meet your needs.

If you are looking for a store that grabs people from the moment that they hit your page, this store is not for you. If you are an experienced HTML or ASP programmer, you probably can learn to use Commerce Server by using a more complicated store; Clock Peddler most likely is too simple for you to use even for your first Commerce Server store.

Volcano Coffee Shop

Volcano Coffee Shop offers more features and control for both the merchant and the shopper than Clock Peddler does (see Figure 3.24). The store implements tables, better graphics, a nicer background, and a store manager that has more features. When you enter the store, a table on the left of your screen displays the navigational tools for the shopper to use to browse the store. A search engine enables customers to search for merchandise. This store requires shoppers to register and then to use their passwords to return to the store later. This makes it easier for the merchant to track where users come from, how many users are new users, and how many are repeat users because we are getting detailed information from these users. If your site does not require users to log in, you will not know detailed information about where your users are coming from.

Part
I
Ch
3

Because this store requires you to log in, you are asked to either log in or create a new account each time you go to the store. The first time you visit the store, you need to put in your information. After you input all your information—including your name, address, and password—click Continue to sign in. Your account is created and you go into the store.

Shopper Registration

Requiring your shoppers to register before they log into your store is a controversial issue. On one hand, shopper registration allows you to keep track of your users and how often they log into the store; you can also get statistical data on where users come from and other information. On the other hand, some good arguments exist against requiring users to log in with a user name and password. First, your users could lose their passwords, and you would need to change their passwords for them after they prove their identities to you. Also, because users' user names are their e-mail addresses, reregistering will be difficult for them, because most users have only one e-mail address.

Another argument against requiring people to log in before entering your site is that this requirement discourages people from logging in. Many people are reluctant to give out personal information other than their e-mail addresses. If people are coming to your site simply to browse, they may not want to give you any personal information, especially if they do not know you.

You may be thinking that discouraging users who are not serious about shopping in your store will save you bandwidth, because it will discourage shoppers who are not serious. Consider this: How many times have you gone to the mall with the intention of just browsing and walked out with one or more items? Discouraging people from browsing could cost you sales.

As mentioned earlier in this section, the store uses a table on the left of your web browser for navigation. You can do one of four functions at any time from anywhere in the store: You can go to the store directory, search, view your basket or checkout.

N O T E Another way that this could have been done is to use frames. Programming frames into the
Volcano Coffee store would have been a bit more work, and frames do not work with all
Web browsers. Because the majority of users use either Netscape Navigator or Microsoft Internet
Explorer, using frames would not be too much of a consideration. If you did use frames for a store like
this one, the pages would load a bit quicker for your users, because the navigation frame would load
only one time. Every time a user goes to another part of the store, the frame is almost always the
same.

One special feature of this store is the built-in search engine, which enables users to type key-
words to find items on your site as opposed to having to look for these items.

You can continue shopping, and when you finish browsing the store, you can go to the checkout area to complete your purchase. You are asked to install an ActiveX component called the
Microsoft Wallet, if you do not already have this component installed on your machine. After
you install this component, you should see the Microsoft Wallet. If you are having problems
installing the wallet or just do not want to install it, you can click a link that takes you to a text
form.

N O T E If you noticed, the Microsoft Wallet asked you for all the information that you needed to fill
out when you first registered to shop. What you can do (and you see an example of using
the Microsoft Wallet to register in the Adventure Works section later in this chapter) is have the wallet
load up when you first register. Using the Microsoft Wallet for registration as well as for checkout saves
your customers from having to type all their information if they have the wallet installed on their
machines. If customers decide to install the wallet when they first register, they have to type the
information only when they configure the Microsoft Wallet for the first time; when they check out, the
information will already be there.

Click the Continue button to go to the credit-card-verification screen.

Just like the Clock Peddler store, Volcano Coffee Shop shows the breakdown of charges and
the total charge. If you have already input credit-card information, you can choose that credit
card. If you are making a purchase with the wallet for the first time, you need to input credit-
card information. After you input this information, you are asked for a password. This password is required so that if someone else uses your computer, that person cannot get access to
your credit-card information without your password. When you are satisfied with your purchase, click Purchase Now to complete the sale.

You go to the receipt page. Make sure that your users save their confirmation numbers, because they will not have an easy way of retrieving this number after they leave this page.

This store is reasonably simple. If you want to make a more robust store, such as Adventure
Works, you can make available to users a page in which they can see past purchases. Because
users need a user name and password to log in anyway, this information is reasonably well
protected. Also, you do not show any credit-card information to make sure that your users are
protected.

Pros   Volcano Coffee Shop offers shopper registration so that you can do some advanced traffic analysis of your site. You can do traffic analysis without requiring users to log in, because IIS logs where each hit comes from.

The store also comes with a built-in search engine. This feature enables your shoppers to quickly find the products in which they are interested.

Another advantage of Volcano Coffee Shop is its nice interface with easy-to-use navigation tools provided by the table design of the site. The store is nicer-looking than Clock Peddler and more likely to keep your shoppers interested in further browsing your store.

The Upsale adds a nice touch to this store, allowing the merchant to further reach shoppers through marketing and sales. The Upsale is part of promotions. When users add items to their baskets, they are offered a nicer item. If a user chooses to buy a nicer item, the original item is automatically replaced by the nicer item.

This store also uses the Microsoft Wallet, which makes things much more convenient for your customers, because they can complete their purchases in as few as two or three mouse clicks as opposed to having to type all their information.

Part

I

Ch

3

Cons   The main disadvantage of this store is the fact that it does not offer the sophisticated traffic-analysis, administration, and merchandising tools of Adventure Works. The registration feature can be a slight disadvantage, too, in that some shoppers may resist signing in, so you may lose them as customers.

Why Volcano Coffee Shop?   Volcano Coffee Shop has great potential for a small store, offering advanced features such as a search engine and promotions. The store also uses the Microsoft Wallet, it uses tables for navigation, it has nicer graphics than Clock Peddler does, and it is more likely to grab people's attention.

Volcano Coffee Shop is a wonderful store, extremely versatile and also extremely robust, making it adaptable to almost any merchant environment. The store includes a search feature for ease of navigation and for customers who know exactly what they are looking for. In a store of this size, of course, a customer can find something just as quickly in the products page. If you have a store like this one but have several hundred items, the search feature would be convenient for your customers.

Suppose that you want to set up a greeting-card store. You can easily adapt the Volcano Coffee Shop interface to display the various cards on the site. The search engine enables shoppers to quickly find the cards for which they are looking.

If you want a store that offers some advanced features, or if you are still learning Commerce Server and are starting to get to some advanced features, this store is for you.

When Not to Use Volcano Coffee Shop   Volcano Coffee Shop may not meet your needs if you have several departments or subdepartments. If you need to do many special promotions and a great deal of merchandising, you shouldn't use Volcano Coffee Shop. Another problem with Volcano Coffee is the fact that you cannot navigate to another item without going to the department again. Volcano Coffee Shop gives you the capability to go backward and forward to the places where you have already been, but it offers no other navigational capabilities.

Microsoft Press Bookstore

Microsoft Press Bookstore is a reasonably complicated, tasteful store that catches people's eyes right from the start. This store is a good one to use if you have a large inventory. The store uses such things as image maps (the a–z graphic in the top frame is an image map), frames, a search engine, and the Microsoft Wallet. In addition, the store uses frames to keep the pages organized, offers a more advanced search engine, and is much larger than the previous two starter stores (Volcano Coffee and Clock Peddler).

The first thing that you notice is that you can go right into the store without being asked to register. This feature is attractive for people who come to your store simply to browse; they eventually have to register, but not right away. Users are asked to register or log in the first time that they try to add an item to their shopping baskets. If you ask your customers to register at this point, they are likely to make a purchase unless they change their minds, so this is a good time to ask them for this information.

This store does not implement the Microsoft Wallet until visitors check out. Because customers need to input registration information when they register and when they check out, you should use Microsoft Press Bookstore as a model that you load the wallet when the customer goes to register. This makes things as easy as possible on the customer. Also, if the customer does not want the Microsoft Wallet, he or she always has the option of not downloading it and installing it. They can still use the text forms.

Pros Microsoft Press Bookstore is a sophisticated store but not to the extent that Adventure Works is, because it does not have as many advanced Java applets. The store does have many nice graphics and other features that keep a user's attention, and the way that the products are described and indexed makes this store an excellent solution for a site that has a large inventory.

If you are opening a store that sells computer parts, this store is an excellent choice. You can have an index frame by either manufacturer or by category, and you can have a frame with a description of each part. When people shop for a monitor, video card, or software, they usually look at several items in each category before making a decision.

In some stores, there are no links to go back or to go to other departments so you find yourself constantly clicking the Back button on your web browser to navigate to different departments. If you have a frame with all of the different departments, you are always one click away from being able to navigate to the department that you wish to go to.

By using a frame like the one in Microsoft Press Bookstore, you can avoid having your customers constantly use the Back button on their browsers and provide a much more pleasant shopping experience for your customers.

Cons The biggest disadvantage of this store is the fact it does not have promotions programmed into it, as Adventure Works does. Also, the store does not have many fancy scripts, Java applets, or ActiveX components (you can program these elements into your store as you customize it, however).

Microsoft Press Bookstore is one of the most complicated starter stores, so if you use it as your model, you need to be familiar with Commerce Server to take care of any issues that come up as you program your store. If you are an experienced Commerce Server developer, this store is a good one to use with a production site. You may need to program a promotional interface, if you need one.

Why Microsoft Press Bookstore?　You can use Microsoft Press Bookstore for almost any store. The store has a fair amount of graphics, but not so much that customers have to wait an unreasonably long time to download each page. The store also has a search engine, uses frames, and has a detailed index in one of the frames for easy navigation. This store is a great one to use for just about any type of medium-size to large store.

When not to use Microsoft Press Bookstore　You should not use the Microsoft Press Bookstore if you have the need for a very simple store or if you are trying to create a store that is going to support browsers that do not support frames or advanced features. Some browsers that will not support these advanced features are older AOL browsers, older CompuServe browsers, UNIX text-based browsers, and several others. You should also not use this store if you are trying to familiarize yourself with the basic features of Commerce Server because there are too many things that can go wrong with a store this complicated if this is your first store.

Adventure Works

Adventure Works is the most advanced of the Starter Stores. This store offers many more features than the other stores do, and it does much more to attract customers and keep them interested. This store, which allows customers to dream about climbing mountains or camping in the wilderness, has all the items needed to make any adventure real.

To use this store as a model, you need to do careful planning and have enough time to make sure that you get everything just right. You also need to make sure that you do not go too far. Don't try to get too much on each page. Keep in mind that most of your customers use 14.4- and 28.8-baud modems. Some customers use ISDN or faster connections, but they are the exceptions rather than the rule. If a page takes too long to load, no matter how nice it looks, people lose patience and leave. Adventure Works does a good job of making a page look nice; it has many components (such as Java and ActiveX) on each page without having each page so bloated that it takes a long time to load.

The Adventure Works store is the most complex of the four Starter Stores. This store uses more advanced HTML and ASP features (such as frames, Java, and Active X), but this store is much more than merely a pretty face. You can use numerous features to administer your site, as well as to create special promotions and various kinds of sales (upsales, cross sales, and so on).

This store also uses shopper registration . The store uses the Microsoft Wallet to register shoppers, which makes things much more convenient for shoppers. After signing in, shoppers go directly into the store.

Although you cannot tell by just looking, most pages on the Adventure Works store have three frames. Because the frames are borderless, they are not easy to notice. The top frame is the Geared Up frame, the left frame is the store directories, and the middle frame describes the department that you are in. A script rotates among several items, depending on which department you are in. Links are provided for all items. If you click a link, you go to a page that provides a detailed description of the item and an enlarged picture of it.

Adventure Works has many features that either make you think that it's the greatest thing on earth it or totally confuse you. These features include Java scripts and VB scripts, which are powerful but hard to follow, due to the lack of commenting. On the other hand, if you are developing a Commerce site for one of your customers, the customer probably expects to see something with all of the bells and whistles of the Adventure Works store, so as to attract as many people as possible.

Pros   Adventure Works is a sophisticated store, from its navigational strategy to its use of many advanced technologies. The ActiveX components and the VB and Java scripts make the store fun to visit. Many promotional capabilities are available, including a club that offers special discounts to shoppers who join it. You can find these promotions on the administrative pages. To get to these pages, open your Web browser and go to **http://localserver/aw_mgr/ default.asp**. You see several things that you can do in the store manager.

One big advantage of Adventure Works is its administrative and merchandising tools. These tools can help you run and analyze your site.

Adventure Works also enables you to do promotions via its Promo Manager. These promotions include price promotions and cross-promotions. Although Volcano Coffee Shop allows you to do promotions, the promotions that you can do with Adventure Works are much more advanced. You can have promotions such as buy one, get one at a certain percent off; a discount for members, sales, and other things. With Volcano Coffee Shop, the only promotional tool that is available is Upsell items which simply tries to get a customer to upgrade to a better, more expensive item than the one the customer had originally picked out.

The price promotion is set up to offer a particular type of discount, either to a specific kind of shopper or on a specific product. Initially, the store is set up to offer a promotion to club members and a discount on the purchase of a second pair of boots. As you see in the store manager (**http://_yourserver_/aw_mgr/promo-price_edit.asp?promo_name=Member+Discount**), the member discount gives all members of the club a 10 percent discount. The advantage of such a club to you, the merchant, is that you have more information on club members and may get more sales from them because they get a discount at your site.

If you would like to set up a price promotion for your store, these are the steps that you would take.

1. Go to the Adventure Works Store Manager page at **http://localserver/aw_mgr/ default.asp**.

   If you are using Microsoft Internet Explorer, you probably are not asked to log in. If a dialog box appears, you must log in. Any name and password that is in the administrators group should be sufficient.

2. Log in, if necessary, by entering *DOMAINNAME\Username*.

3. Go to the product(s) or department(s) that you want to discount.

   You need to know the product number (the first column on the left) or the department number (again, the first column on the left). You can also apply the discount to all shoppers or all members. Make sure that you record the department or product number(s) and name(s) that you are going to be discounting to make sure that your changes are accurate.

4. Return to the Store Manager page by clicking the Back button.

5. Click the Promos button to bring you to the Promo Manager screen.

6. Click Price Promotions from the Promo Manager to bring you to the Price Promotions screen.

7. Click Add New Price Promotion to go to the New Price Promotion screen.

8. For Name, enter **My new promotion**.

9. For Description, enter **New price promotion**.

10. For Rank, enter **1** as the rank of the promotion.

11. For Active, select **On** to activate your new promotion.

12. Enter the date on which you want to start the promotion.

    For now, enter the current date.

13. For End Date, enter the date on which you want to end the promotion to end.

    The time period of the promotion must be at least one full day (24 hours).

14. In the Shopper box, choose **All Shoppers**.

15. For Buy, enter **1** in the blank box and choose units, which should be the default choice.

16. Enter the product that you want to put on sale, and enter the product SKU number in the blank field following the `pf_id` and = fields.

17. If you are discounting a department, choose the department ID in the pull-down menu (`dept_id`).

18. In the **Get** section, enter the product ID in the text box all the way to the right if you are discounting a particular product. If you are discounting a department, choose **dept_id** from the first drop-down menu on the left and enter the department ID in the text box all the way to the right.

19. For At, enter the amount of the discount that you want to give.

    This entry can either be a dollar amount or a percentage.

20. Click the Add Price Promotion button.

    Clicking the **Add Price Promotion** button generates the updated Price Promotion List page with the price promotion.

For an example, see Figure 3.15, which shows how to set a 25 percent discount on any second pair of hiking boots.

Part
I

Ch
3

FIG. 3.15

This figure shows what a promotion should look like. Notice the different fields and what you can do with them to customize your own store.

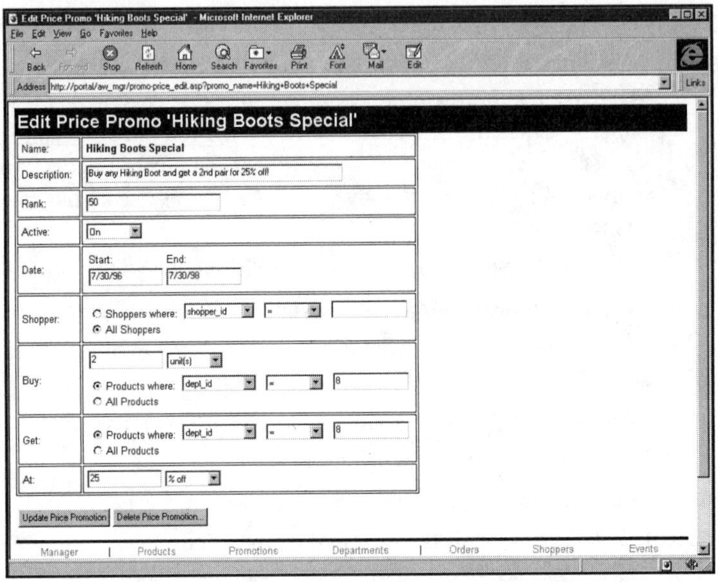

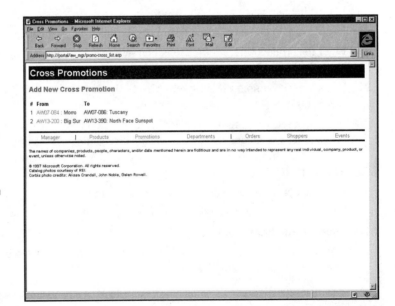

The second promotion is a bit subtler; it is a cross-promotion. After choosing an item, the shopper is prompted to look at another item that may complement the selected item. Thus, the shopper may buy two items instead of one. Cross-promotions are managed in the Cross-Promotion Manager (see Figure 3.16).

FIG. 3.16

This shows the Cross-Promotions manager. Here, you tell Commerce Server that if a customer chooses a specific item, Commerce Server will suggest another item to complement the first item thus encouraging the customer to buy another item in addition to the first.

Cons   The primary disadvantage of this store is its complexity. Because the store is so involved and complicated, it can be difficult to manage and keep organized. For this reason, you need to be careful whenever you make any changes in this store. You should keep a mirror of your production stores on a development machine, for testing purposes; that suggestion goes double for this store. When you make any changes in a section of a store like one, unexpected results may occur in parts of the store that you do not even think to look at. Whenever you make changes, you need to go through the entire store before you implement changes in a production store.

In addition, the databases are more complicated than those of the other stores are. If you implement this type of store, you are almost required to have someone on your staff who is not only an experienced HTML, ASP, VB, Java, and JavaScript programmer but also an experienced SQL programmer and an experienced Windows NT System administrator. This way, if anything goes wrong or customers require changes to be made quickly, someone is always on hand to take care of any issues that come up and to put out any fires.

The other major disadvantage of this store (depending, of course, on how you look at it) is that it requires shoppers to register before they can even browse. This requirement can be a deterrent for users. When they see that they need to give you all their information, many people simply turn away before they even walk in the front door.

Consider instead the way that Microsoft Press Bookstore handles registration. This store does not require users to register until they add items to their shopping baskets. Also, that store uses *cookies* (small files that reside on a user's computer). Cookies uniquely identify users, so when someone visits your page, you know whether that person is a new visitor or a repeat visitor. If you need to track use and repeat visits, having users register when they decide to make a purchase is an excellent alternative. The only thing that you cannot get with cookies is personal information, such as names and e-mail addresses. You can find out where customers come from if you set your tracking to do reverse DNS lookups. With a little work, you can implement this change into the Adventure Works templates.

Why Adventure Works?   Adventure Works is suitable for stores that have a variety of items in different sizes and colors (clothing, sporting goods, office products, and so on). You can also use this store when you want to take advantage of its advanced merchandising and administration features. This store was a model for Seidlers Jewelers (**http://www.seidlers.com**). For a jewelry store, it was decided that Adventure Works was the best store. MS Press was an alternative that was considered but it was decided that the advanced functionality of the Adventure Works store would meet the need of our site more than MS Press so it was decided that the Adventure Works store would be used as the model.

When Not to Use Adventure Works   The prospective merchant should look carefully at Adventure Works before attempting to use it. The store is quite complex, so you need to be sure that you have the expertise to make the changes that you need to make. Using all the fields that are available in Adventure Works, for example, is important. If you try to remove one of the fields, you can be sure that the change will affect another field, and a good chance exists that your store will need some serious overhauling.

Some of the difficulties explained in the previous paragraph were experienced because the Adventure Works store was used as the model for Seidlers Jewelers site (**http://www.seidlers.com**). One piece that was removed resulted in many hours of recoding. This store is only for those who can use its full potential. Thus, you need to examine Adventure Works closely before making a decision.

Creating Your Own Store

After you look at the starter stores, you may have an idea of how you want to proceed with your own store. A new feature in Microsoft Commerce Server 2.0 is the Microsoft Commerce Server Host Administrator. This tool allows you to view and manage all the stores that you have on your system, copy stores, and create a store foundation if you want to create a store from scratch (see Figure 3.17).

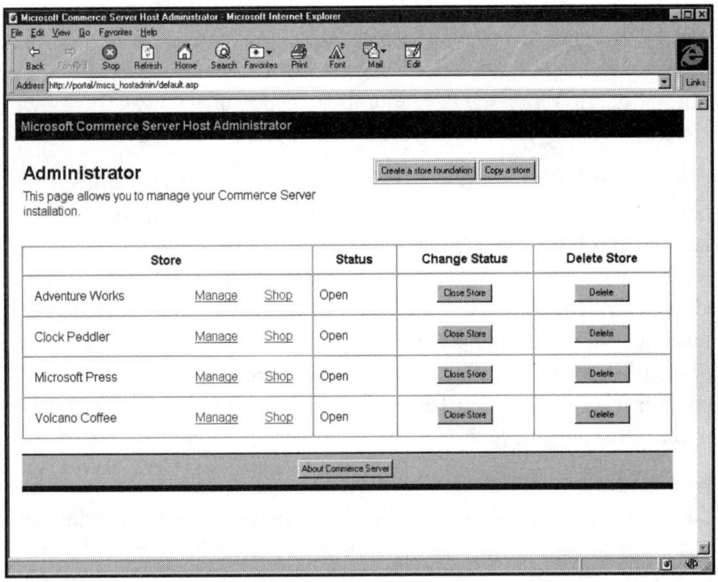

FIG. 3.17

This illustration shows the Microsoft Commerce Host Administrator page. From this page, you can see the status of each of your stores. You can close the store, delete the store, manage the store, and shop in the store by clicking the Shop link. You can also copy any of your stores or create a new blank store foundation.

Copying an Existing Starter Store

The starter stores were provided as a foundation for creating your production stores. According to the license agreement, you are allowed to use any of the code from the templates but you cannot use the pictures or the product descriptions. You also should not take a store and modify it directly because you will no longer be able to use that particular store to develop any further sites. For this reason, Commerce Server allows you to completely copy any store on your site. This next section will go over how to copy a store.

1. To copy a store, you need to go to the following **URL: http://*servername*/ mscs_hostadmin/default.asp**. Click on the Copy a store button to begin. This will bring you into the Starter Store Copy Wizard (see Figure 3.18).

FIG. 3.18

This figure is the introduction page of the Starter Store Copy Wizard. You see an introduction to creating a new store and are prompted to click the next button to proceed.

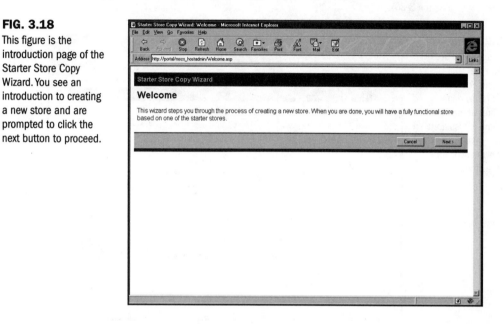

2. When you click Next, you are asked what store you want to copy. Select the store that you want to use and click Next (see Figure 3.19).

FIG. 3.19

You are given a list of all stores that are installed on your Commerce Server that you can copy.

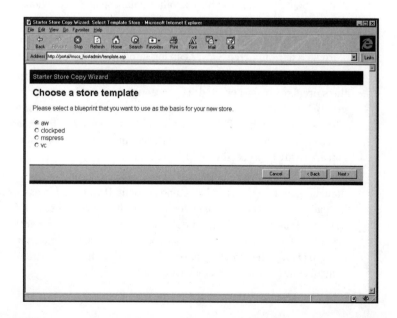

3. Select a short name and a display name for your store. aw is the short name for the Adventure Works store, which is the Display Name. The Display Name is the name that you will refer to the store by. Click Next after you fill in this information (see Figure 3.20).

FIG. 3.20

In this screen, you are asked to enter your store name. You need to enter a display name and a short name. The short name is displayed in the URL and the Display Name is used inside the store.

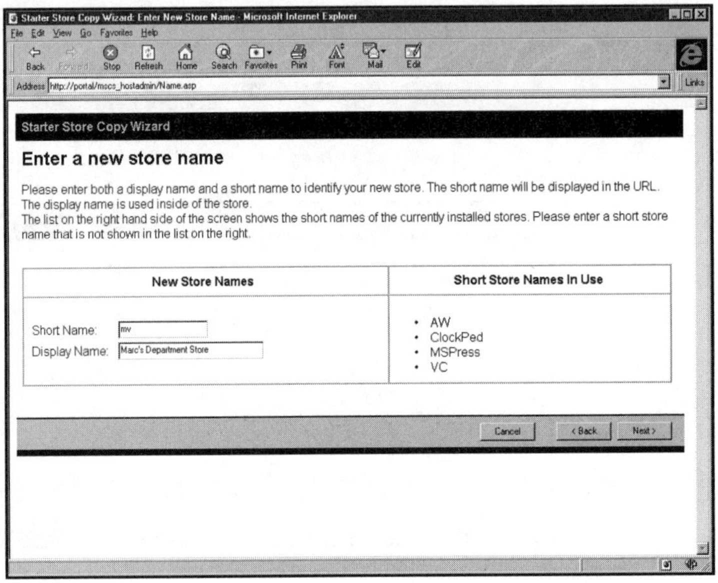

4. You need to choose the type of database driver to use. If you have SQL 6.5 installed, choose SQL Server. If you have another database installed, choose the ODBC driver that you have installed. Click Next to continue.

5. Choose a DSN to use and a database name. You need to type the user name and password so that Commerce Server can log into the database (see Figure 3.21).

6. You need to assign an administrative account—an account that can completely manage the store that you just created. This account does not have to be part of any special group. Being able to choose any account is useful if you are an Internet Service Provider (ISP) and are hosting sites for customers that are allowed to manage their own stores. You can either choose an existing NT account or create a new account. Click Next when you are ready to proceed (see Figure 3.22).

7. You see a list of local computer accounts. Notice that in this screen, you cannot use a domain account, only a local machine account. If you need to use a domain account instead of a local account, you need to go to this store and search for a file called `auth_include.asp`. (This file should be in `<storename>\Manager\include`.) Change the account name to be the account that you want to use to administer the store. You also need to change the directory permissions so that the administrator of the store has full control of the `Manager` directory (see Figure 3.23).

FIG. 3.21

As you remember earlier in this chapter in the section on installing Microsoft Commerce Server, you needed to provide an ODBC DSN name to connect to your SQL Server database. Choosing a Data Source Name is doing the same thing only it is using an HTML interface instead of using a dialog box.

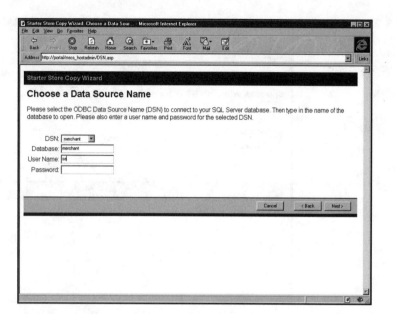

FIG. 3.22

You need to choose if you are going to use an existing account or if you are going to create a new account.

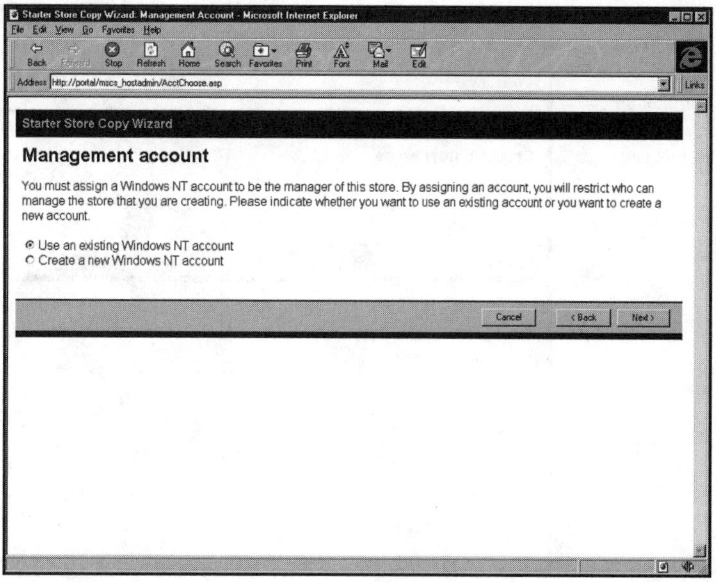

Part

I

Ch

3

8. You have a chance to confirm that you have entered all the information. Click Finish to create your store, click Cancel to forget the whole thing, or click Back to review or correct any information (see Figure 3.24).

FIG. 3.23
This figure shows you a list of available accounts on the server.

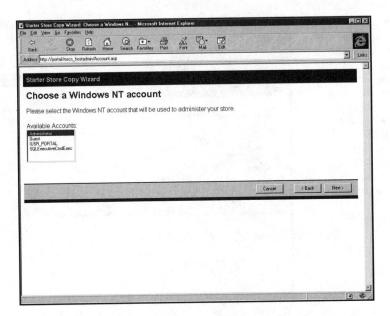

FIG. 3.24
At this point, we have filled in all of the necessary information and are ready to proceed with building the store.

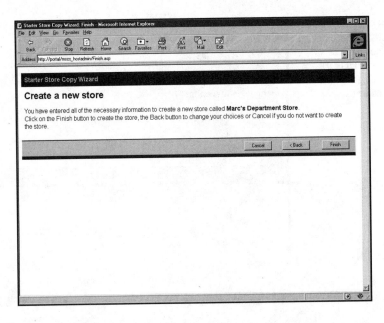

9. If everything went right, in about two minutes, you should see a screen that tells you that you successfully created your store. You can return to the Host Administrator (see Figure 3.25).

FIG. 3.25

This screen gives you confirmation that your store has been created. You are provided with two links; one will take you to the store manager and there is a button that is a link back to the Host Administrator.

Starter Store Copy Wizard: Complete – Microsoft Internet Explorer

File Edit View Go Favorites Help

Back Forward Stop Refresh Home Search Favorites Print Font Mail Edit

Address http://portal/mscs_hostadmin/Complete.asp

Starter Store Copy Wizard

Store Creation Complete

The store **Marc's Department Store** has been created with account **Administrator** assigned to manage it. Click here to go to the store manager.

Return to Host Administrator

Part

I

Ch

3

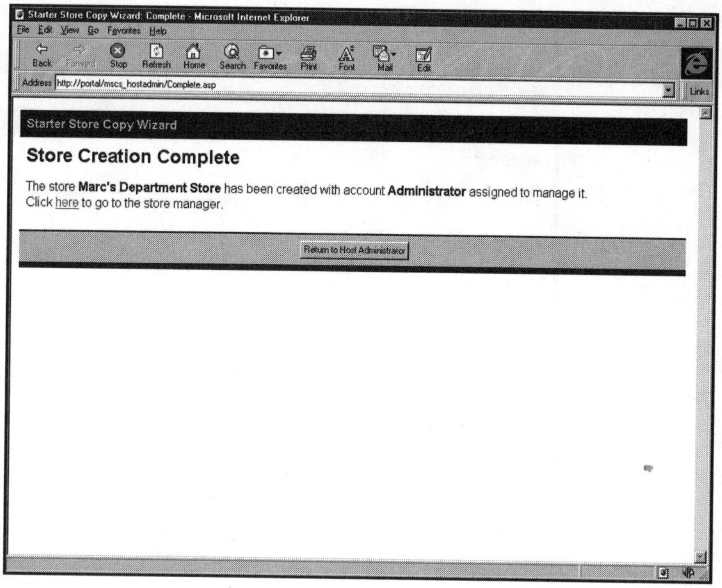

Creating a Store from Scratch

If you decide that you need to create a custom store, you can create a store foundation and then proceed from there. Creating the foundation gives you some templates and store manager pages, and some of the database tables are created for you. You can also choose to have nothing created for you and do everything yourself.

1. To create a foundation, click Create a Store Foundation in the host administrator. You see a brief description. Read this description and click Next to proceed (see Figure 3.26).

2. Select a short name and a display name for your store. Click Next to proceed (see Figure 3.27).

3. Choose the type of ODBC driver to use; then click Next (see Figure 3.28). For this example, we are using Microsoft SQL Server.

4. Select the DSN to use, and type the database name, user name, and password for the database (see Figure 3.29).

5. You need to specify what Windows NT account is to use for a management account. After you specify whether you want to use an existing account or create a new account, click Next (see Figure 3.30).

6. Select an account from the local machine and then choose Next (see Figure 3.31).

7. You can go back and correct some information, cancel the process, or proceed to create the store foundation. Click Finish when you are ready to create your store (see Figure 3.32).

FIG. 3.26

This screen shows the introduction to the Store Foundation Wizard.

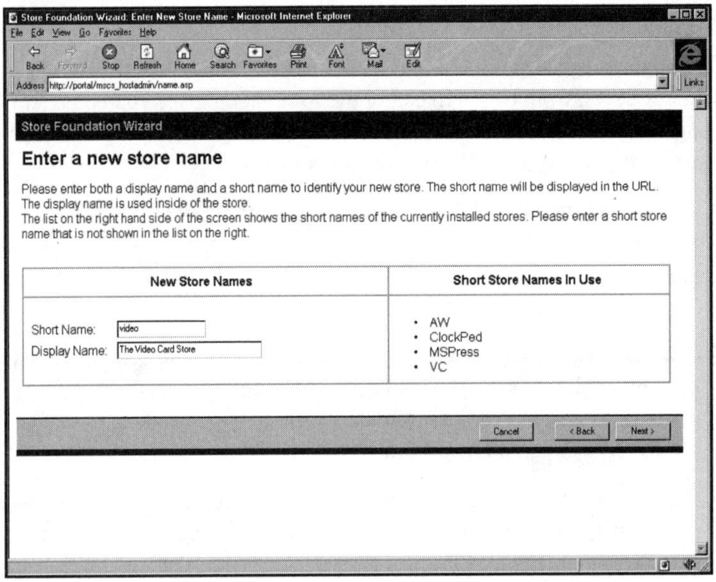

FIG. 3.27

In this figure, you see that you need to enter the Short Name and Display Name for your store.

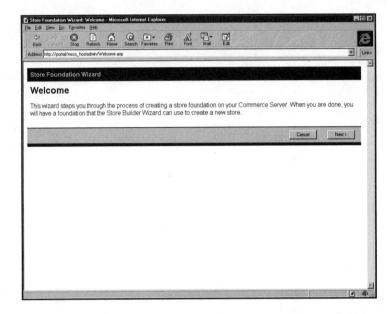

FIG. 3.28

You need to choose which type of ODBC Driver you are going to use.

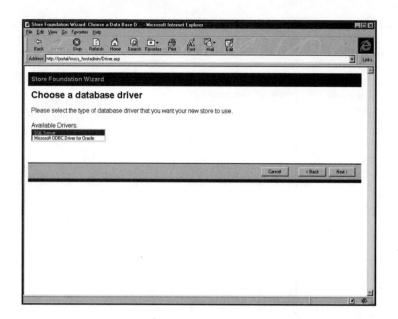

FIG. 3.29

As in the previous section, you need to choose a DSN, Database name, and provide login information to log into the SQL Server.

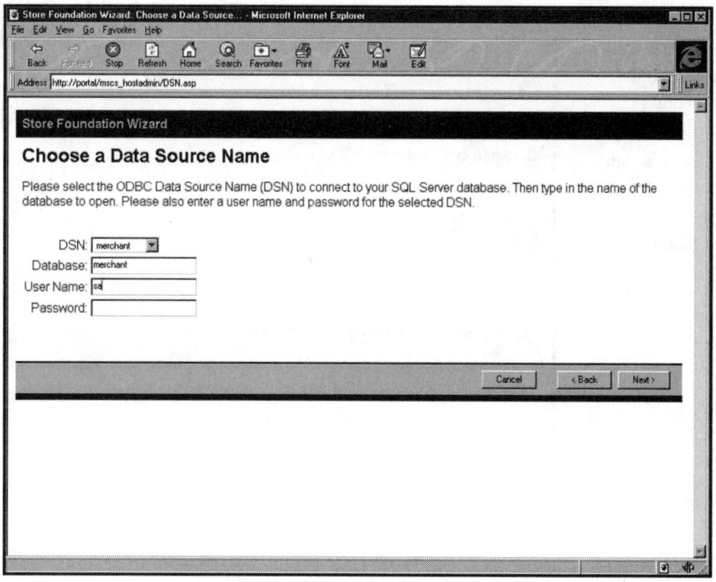

FIG. 3.30

Here, you choose whether you would like to use an existing NT account or create a new account to use for the store manager account.

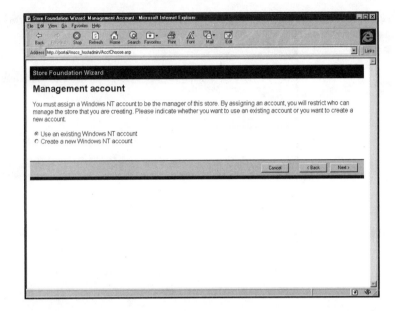

FIG. 3.31

This screen shows you all of the accounts that are setup on your machine. If you were using Commerce Server on a primary domain controller, you would see a list of all the accounts on the domain.

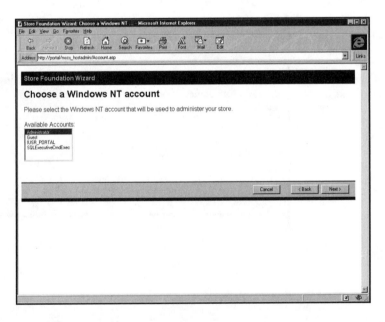

8. After you set up your store foundation, you can create all the templates by hand or use the Store Builder wizard. The Store Builder wizard helps you get your store started so that you can go back and customize it later. Now that your store foundation has been created, you will be brought to a confirmation screen. You have two links available, a link to the store manager page and a link back to the host administrator page (see Figure 3.33).

FIG. 3.32

This screen is the confirmation screen. You can either choose to correct information or go on with creating your store.

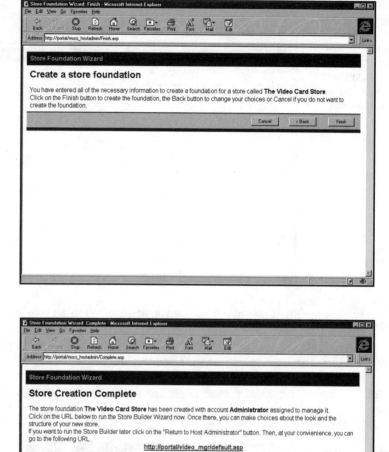

FIG. 3.33

The Store Creation Complete page confirms that your store foundation has been successfully created.

9. To go to the Store Builder wizard, click the link that is provided for you on the Store Creation Complete page. This link takes you to the management page of your new store. The only thing that is in the management page now is a link to the Store Builder wizard. Click this link to proceed (see Figure 3.34).

Part

I

Ch

3

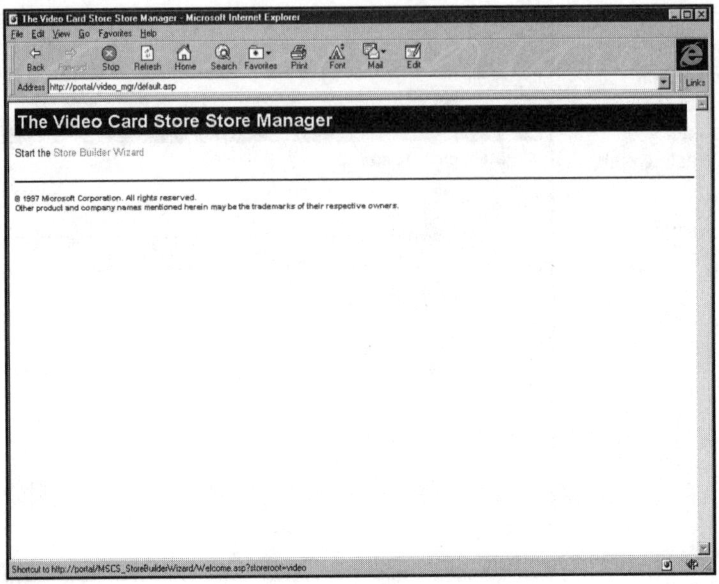

FIG. 3.34

The Video Card Store Manager page. Since the store has not been customized, the only link that is on this page is a link to start the Store Builder Wizard.

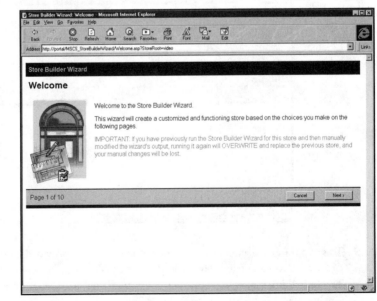

10. You see 10 pages of questions that you must answer to get your store started. Make sure that you answer the questions correctly. After you create your store and begin to customize it, you cannot return to this wizard to make changes. If you try to run the wizard again, it erases your store, and you lose all your changes (see Figure 3.35).

FIG. 3.35

This is the first page of the Store Builder Wizard. You are given an introduction to the Store Builder Wizard and are prompted to click Next to proceed.

11. You need to input a brief description of your store, as well as your store's address, telephone number, and e-mail address. When you finish, click Next (see Figure 3.36).

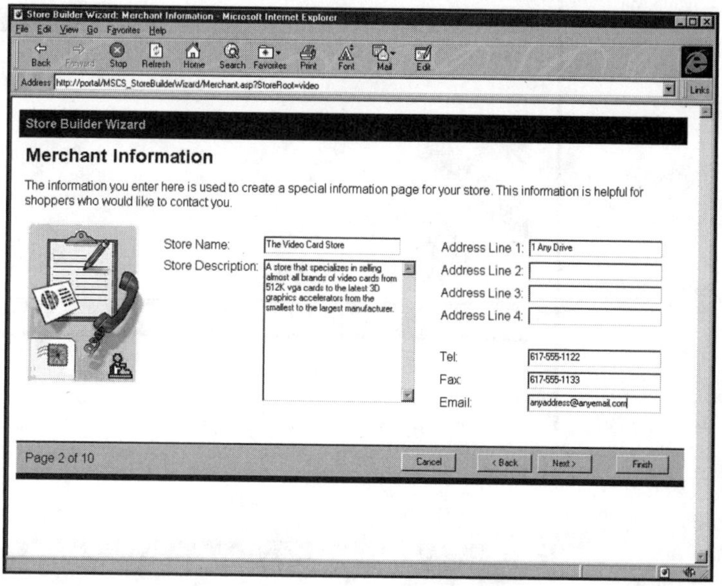

FIG. 3.36
This section gathers information about the merchant such as name, address, e-mail, and a brief description of the store.

N O T E You can click Finish at any time during this process, but doing so is not a good idea until you familiarize yourself with the Store Builder wizard. Right now, you should take the time to learn this wizard, because it can help you tremendously as you build your stores. ▪

12. Choose the location of your store and click Next to continue (see Figure 3.37).

13. Start to customize the look and feel of your store by choosing the navigational bar, font, background color, and button styles. You can also choose to use a logo. If you are not satisfied with the choices that you have, leave the default options selected and change them later. This way, some of the scripting is done for you, and you have placeholders for what you will be using when your store goes to production(see Figure 3.38).

14. The Features page allows you to choose two features, registration and product searching. Choosing to have your customers register before they shop allows your customers to maintain shopping baskets, and customize the store for different shopper characteristics or personalization. You can also limit access to different items or promotions by requiring authentication (see Figure 3.39).

You can also have different levels of membership for your customers. For example, if you give customers discounts based on how much the customers purchase in a given period of time, you will need to have your customers sign in so that the prices your database gives your customers will be accurate. You will also need to use shopper registration if you sell items that are restricted only to certain customers.

FIG. 3.37

Here, you simply need to tell the Store Builder Wizard what locale you are in.

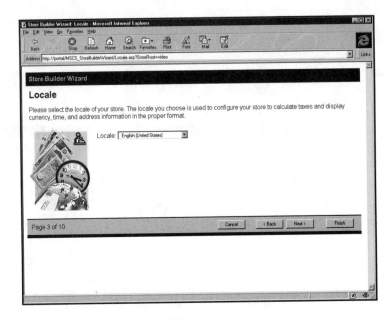

FIG. 3.38

As you can see, there are several choices for your store: which style button, what type of navigation bar, what font you will use, what the background color will be and if you are going to use a logo or not. If you decide to use a logo, the Store Builder Wizard will leave room for you to insert your logo.

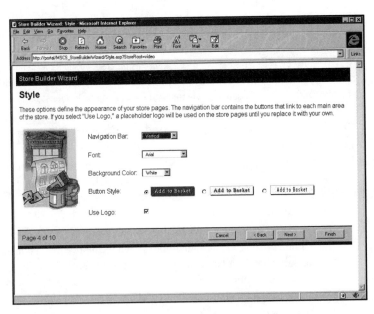

Developing a store in which your customers are given different levels of membership involves some complicated and customized programming on your part, of course. If you want shoppers to be able to browse and register only when they make a purchase, you can do so with a bit of reprogramming.

FIG. 3.39

You need to decide if you are going to require your shoppers to register. You also need to choose to allow product searching.

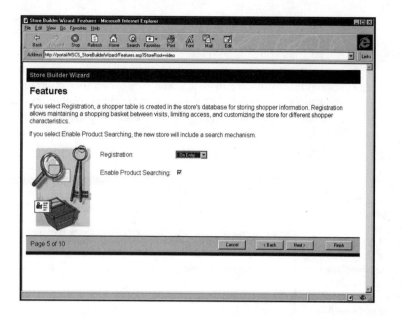

15. You need to decide which product features are applicable to the product that you are selling. Several features are available; if these features are not enough, you can type your own in text box 2, Custom (see Figure 3.40).

FIG. 3.40

In the Product screen, you need to decide which options to include in the text boxes. There are several options that are provided for you and you can also type in custom options if you need additional options.

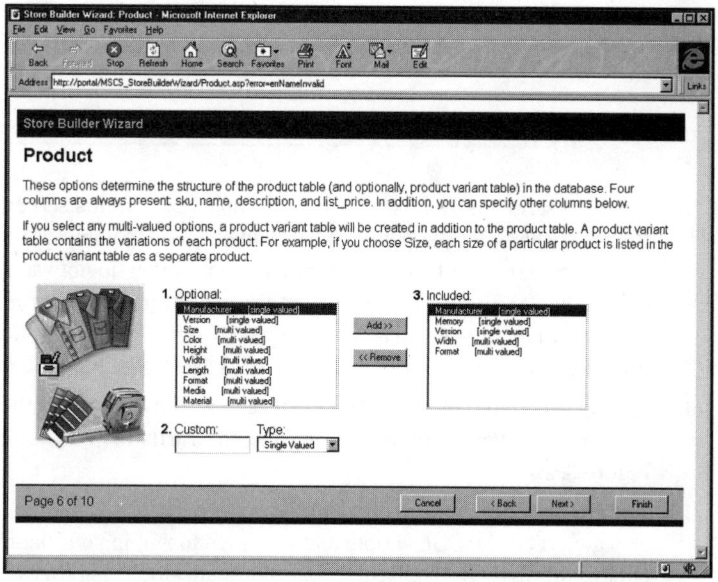

Part

I

Ch

3

16. You need to figure out how much money to charge for shipping and handling. This is a basic way of handling shipping and handling, in that it deals with flat fees. If you will be shipping heavy items, however, a flat shipping fee will not work for your store. You either need to program the additional shipping and handling cost into your store or obtain a program that you can add on to Commerce Server; this program figures out shipping and handling costs based on the size and weight of the item(s) that your shoppers purchase. Even if you are not going to use simple shipping and handling, you can still include additional cost for shipping and handling so that you have a place to add the add-on program when you have a program to use (see Figure 3.41).

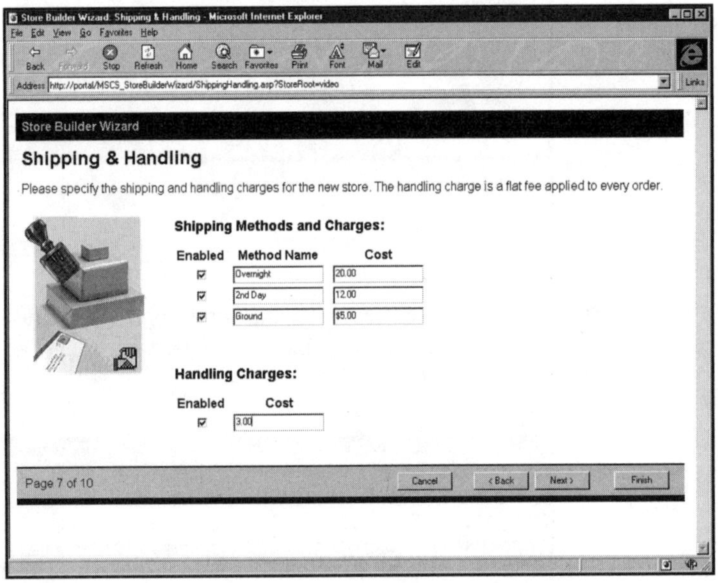

FIG. 3.41

On the Shipping & Handling page, you need to decide how much you are going to charge for shipping and what types of shipping you are going to offer your customers. You will also need to decide if you are going to charge a handling fee and how much.

17. The next screen is Tax. You can enter simple taxes in this screen for up to five states. Before enabling simple taxes, you should check with your accountant to make sure that you are covered. With all the tax laws that exist, you do not want to risk not putting in the correct tax for a state. Also, if you are using a simple tax program that is not going to meet your needs, you can add programs to Commerce Server that do more complicated tax computations. After you add taxes, click Next (see Figure 3.42).

18. Specify what types of credit cards you accept. You know from the agreement that you have with your bank what types of credit cards you can accept on your site (see Figure 3.43).

19. The Output Options page creates all the store templates for you and the global.asa file; it also generates the SQL scripts that you need to run in your database tables. You can also choose to run these database scripts automatically. This process may take a while, so when you click Finish, you can do something else and come back in about 5 to 10

minutes. If you are uncertain about anything that you chose, you can cancel and start again. If you decide to watch, you see everything that is going on in the next page (see Figure 3.44).

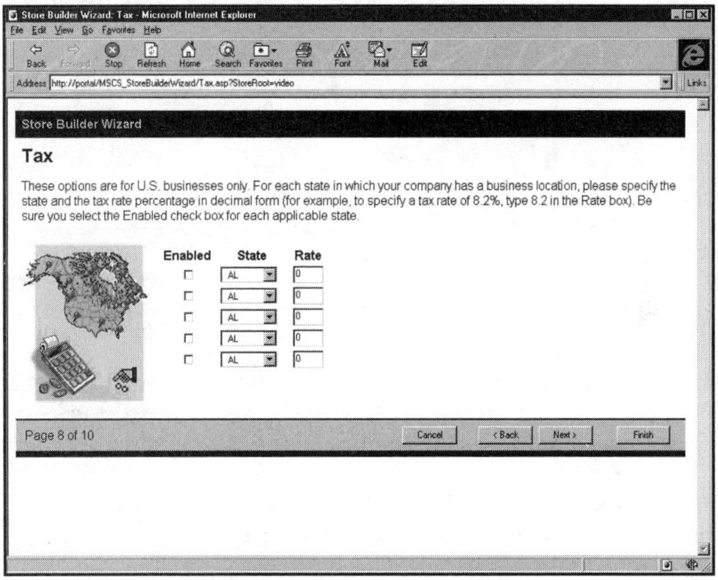

FIG. 3.42

The Tax screen allows you to specify simple tax for up to five states. If you have business offices in more than five states or simple tax is not going to meet your needs, you will need to purchase third-party add-on tax software.

FIG. 3.43

The Payment Methods screen allows you to choose what type of Credit Cards you can use in your Commerce Store.

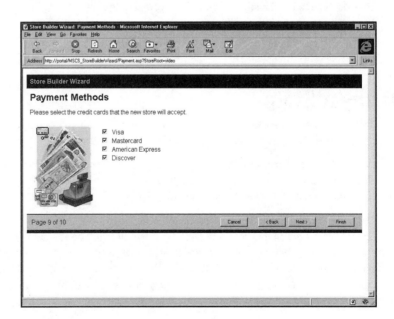

Part

I

Ch

3

FIG. 3.44
The Output Options page determines what the Store Builder Wizard will do when you click the Finish button.

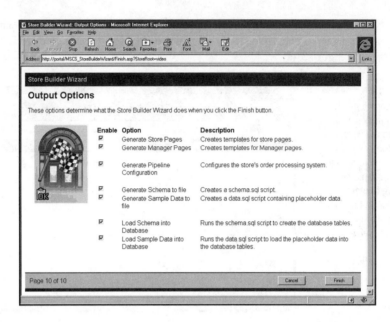

When the Store Builder Wizard finishes, you see a confirmation page with links to your new store. Click go to your store when you are ready.

You have enough to start building a great store, but you have a great deal of work ahead of you. To learn how to build a store of your own, you should refer to Part IV, "Creating Stores with Active Server Pages." The chapters in this section go over in detail the different steps to create a store of your own. Also, to see case studies of some Microsoft Commerce Server sites that have already been developed, refer to Part VI, "Case Studies."

Deleting a Store

If you have a customer that closes their store with you, or if you need to delete a store for any reason, simply choose Delete Store in the Host Administrator.

Delete Marc's Department Store as an example of how to delete a store. As you see from the illustration, Commerce Server requests that you close the store before you delete it. Close the store; then go back and delete it (see Figure 3.45).

As you see in the figure, the store is closed. The close store feature can be a very useful store. If you have a store that is seasonal, you can keep the store on the same machine and simply close it. If customers try to go to a closed store, they get a message saying that the store is closed (and whatever else you choose to include in the message). This feature can also come in handy if a customer has not paid his bill and you want to shut him off to give him a wake-up call but do not want to delete or disrupt any of his files just yet.

FIG. 3.45

As you can see, Commerce Server will allow you to delete the store but you are prompted to close the store before deleting it. This is so no one can browse the store or run any scripts or applications before deleting it; or so that there are no open files when the files are being deleted.

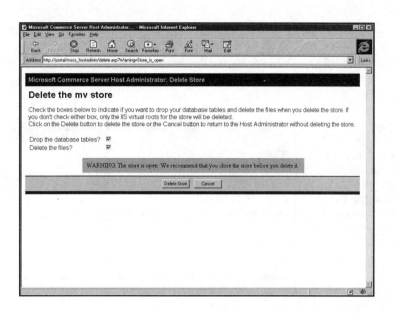

You can reopen a store just as easily as you close it. When you open or close a store, no services need to be restarted, so doing so does not disrupt any of your other stores or other services that are running on this machine (see Figure 3.46).

FIG. 3.46

Now that the store has been closed, it is OK to go ahead and delete the store, all files in the store, and all database tables.

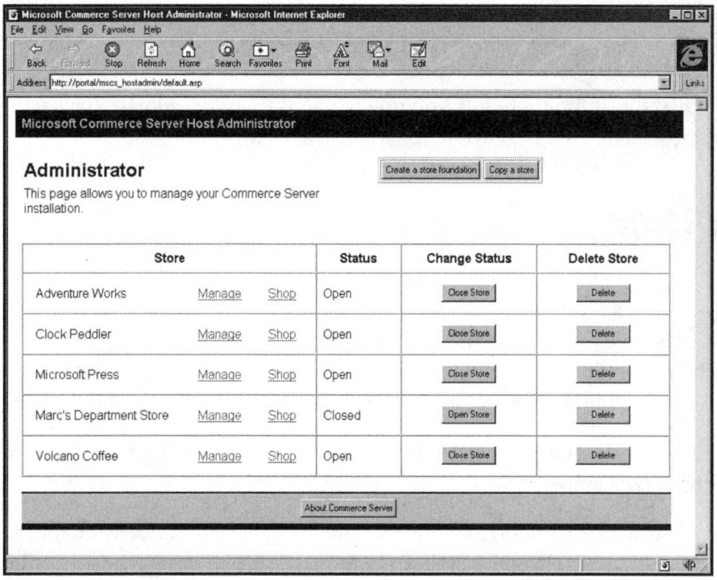

Part

I

Ch

3

Go back and delete that store that you are deleting (Marc's Department Store in this example). As you see in the figure, you have many choices when you delete a store. You can delete only the virtual roots from IIS, leaving the database tables and files intact, or you can delete the files or database tables. When you decide what you want to delete, click Delete Store (see Figure 3.47).

FIG. 3.47

In the Microsoft Commerce Server Host Administrator: Delete Store, you are asked if you want to drop the database tables and delete the files.

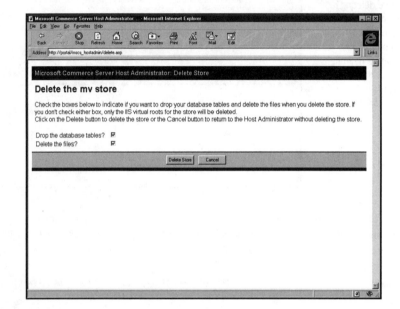

When the store is deleted, you go back to the host administrator page. You know that the store has been deleted because it no longer shows up on this page.

From Here...

This chapter covered how to create a database to use with the starter stores that were provided with Commerce Server, setting up ODBC for your Commerce Server databases and installing Commerce Server. We also learned about the different starter stores and how you can use them to build a production store for yourself or your customers, how to copy the starter stores, or how to build a completely custom store using the Store Builder Wizard.

The following chapters provide further information to help you go on with development of your commerce stores.

- Part III: "Understanding Dynamic Databases." In these chapters, you will learn how to customize Microsoft SQL Server so that you can have more robust stores and custom database tables.

- Part IV: "Creating Stores with Active Server Pages." Since Microsoft Commerce Server uses ASP and not HTML, you will need to learn ASP if you have not done so already. These seven chapters go over how to program with ASP and how to integrate ASP with your commerce site.
- Part VI: "Case Studies." Once you get to this point, you should be pretty familiar with Commerce Server and ASP. You will be able to see by these case studies the problems and issues that come up when developing other stores as well as tips for building your own store.

PART

II

Working with Microsoft Site Server

CHAPTER 4

Understanding the Content Replication System

Content Replication System (CRS) is useful if you have multiple Web servers in your environment. This program allows you to replicate your entire Web site, or any portion of it, at set intervals. You can also update your site when files change. What CRS means to you is that you need to maintain only one Web site and that one Web site can exist on several machines without any intervention from your Web development team or your system administrators. ∎

Comparing Content Replication System and Directory Replication

You may ask why you cannot simply use the Directory Replication that is built into Microsoft Windows NT Server. After all, won't Directory Replication do exactly what you are asking? The answer is no. Directory Replication, although useful for replication in a domain environment, does not do what we are asking. Directory Replication works efficiently only within single- or multiple-domain environments; it does not work well across the Internet, and if you are replicating to a non-Windows NT server, it does not work.

Also, Directory Replication does not by default work through most firewalls. With Content Replication, to grab or pull a Web site, you do not need to configure much more than if you were going to browse the Internet. Pushing through a firewall takes a little more configuration, but Content Replication still does a more efficient job on Web sites than Directory Replication does. The most important advantage of Content Replication over Directory Replication is administration. To administer Directory Replication, you need to be able to log into the Windows NT Server and to use Server Manager. You can completely administer Content Replication via HTTP by using your favorite Web browser.

Content Replication gives companies that need to publish Web content the most reliable, secure, and efficient way to move content across the Web. Content Replication replicates any type of content from one or more remote content servers to multiple-destination content servers; it provides reliable, secure movement of large amounts of data across a network, whether across the Internet or across an Intranet. Content Replication can also move data through a firewall or proxy server and can be used in a variety of applications, including production-server staging, production-server mirroring, and large and/or complex replication scenarios.

A company such as Microsoft, for example, receives several million hits on its Web server every day—too much of a load for one machine to handle, no matter how powerful the machine is. For this reason, the www.microsoft.com site resides on several machines. Another example of a good use for CRS is if you wanted to have your site mirrored all over the country or all over the world. If you have mirror sites, more people can get to your site by using a faster, more reliable link, especially if visitors from other countries frequent your site.

Also, for the sake of dependability, you should have more than one Web server if you are running a busy site. If you have only one server, and if it loses a disk drive or crashes for any other reason and winds up being down for eight hours during a weekday, how many sales are you going to lose? If you house your site on two or more machines, if one machine goes down, the other machine or machines can pick up the slack so that your site is never offline.

Using multiple web servers also makes things much easier on your system administrators. If a minor problem occurs on one of the machines or if you need to make changes to your servers, you can make these changes one machine at a time, and almost no one will notice that a machine went down. Also, your system administrators do not feel pressured to take shortcuts to get the machine back up as quickly as possible; they feel that they have enough time to do the job right the first time.

Installing Content Replication System

1. To install CRS, first make sure that you have the Microsoft Site Server Master CD-ROM in your CD-ROM drive. Click on "Site Creation and Content Publishing", "Content Replication System", and then you can click on "Content Replication System" to go to setup (see Figure 4.1).

FIG. 4.1

Click Content Replication System to begin installation.

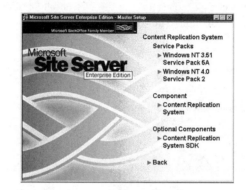

2. The first screen that you see is the welcome screen. Read the information and then click Next.

3. The next screen is the software license agreement. Make sure that you go over this screen carefully so that you are sure of your rights while using this product.

4. Now you prepare to install CRS. The next thing that the CRS setup program (or simply setup) will check is which services are running. If you have any IIS services running, such as the World Wide Web Publishing Service or the FTP Publishing Service, you are prompted to stop these services by setup (see Figure 4.2). If you cannot stop these services, you need to exit setup. Setup can stop the services for you, if you choose to have it do so.

FIG. 4.2

Setup will check for running services and ask you to stop these services.

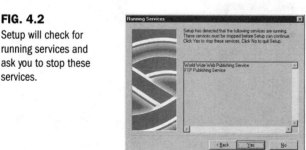

5. Next, you are asked to personalize your product. You are asked for your name and company name. Click Next when you finish.

Part
II

Ch
4

6. You are asked to choose the directory in which to install CRS. The default is C:\CRS; you can change this setting, if you want. To change the directory, click the Browse button. The directory browse dialog box appears. Here, you can type a new drive and/or directory or browse existing directories to find the directory or drive of your choice. If you type a directory that does not exist, setup asks whether you want to create the directory.

7. Next, you are asked to choose a directory for the Web-administration tools and HTML documentation. The recommended directory is wherever your InetPub directory is located. The default is C:\InetPub\CRS.

8. You need to choose the setup type. You can choose Typical, but you have little control over what is installed. For this example, choose a Custom installation (see Figure 4.3).

FIG. 4.3

You need to choose either a Typical or Custom installation.

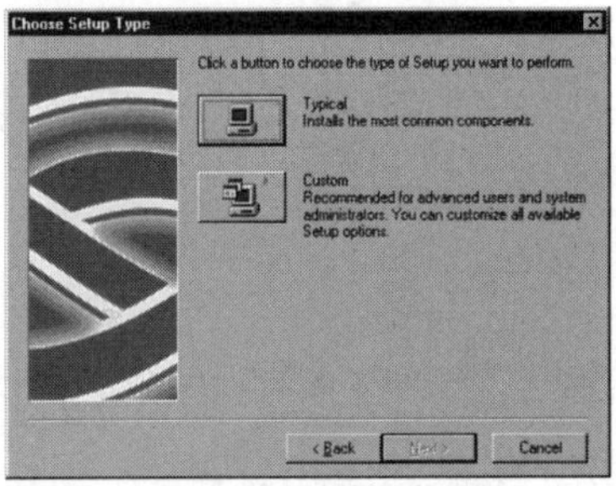

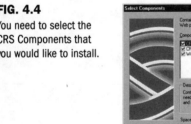

9. When you choose custom, you see the following menu. As you see, all the options are already chosen. You can choose not to install some components. If you want to install only the CRS program itself, and not Web administration or documentation, you can choose to do so. You can also install only the documentation on another computer without installing CRS. When you are satisfied with your selections, choose Next (see Figure 4.4).

FIG. 4.4

You need to select the CRS Components that you would like to install.

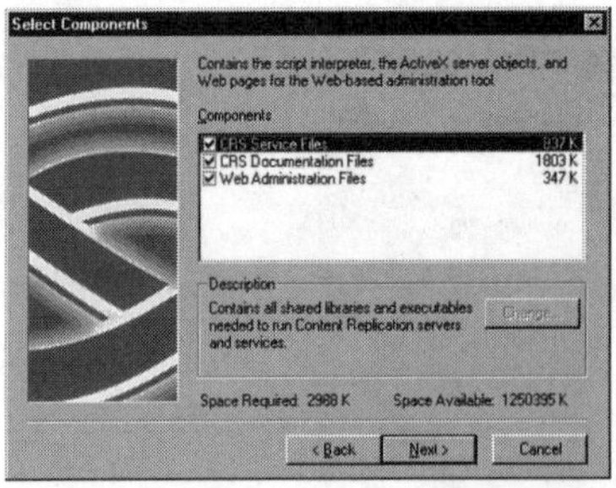

10. The CRS service needs an account to use; it cannot be installed as simply a system account. This account must be an account that is part of administrators group. You can use your own account or the administrator account, but making an account for CRS is strongly recommended. Keeping accounts for users and services separate helps you keep accounts sorted out. Also, if you use your own account and later change your password, the CRS service and any other services that you run under your account no longer run if you forget to change the password in Control Panel, Services. Services that need to run as a specific account and not a system account include Microsoft Exchange Server, Schedule Service, Microsoft SQL Executive, and many others.

11. At this point, you should go to User Manager for Domains, create an account for the CRS service, and make sure that the account is part of the Administrators group. Enter the user name and password. (When you enter the user name, make sure that you enter it in the format DOMAIN\Username.) Then click Next (see Figure 4.5).

FIG. 4.5

You need to assign a username and password to the CRS account.

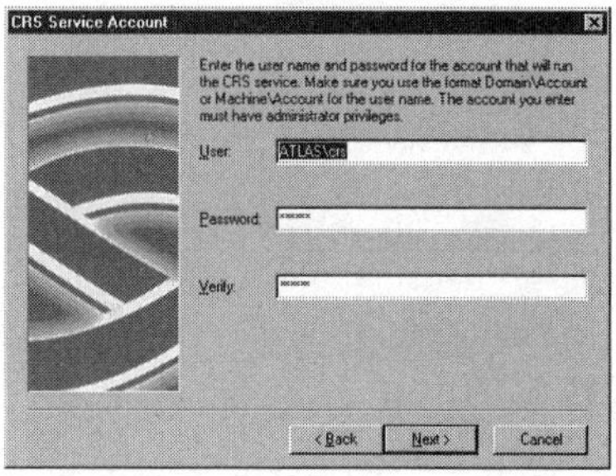

12. If you have not already done so, you need to configure a user name and password for the schedule service. If you have already done so, you can simply fill in the user name and password at the screen you are asked to give a username and password for the schedule service. You can use the CRS account that you just created if you are going to use the schedule service only for CRS. If you are going to use the schedule service for more than just CRS, you may want to give the schedule service its own account.

13. Select a program group for CRS. The default folder is Content Replication System, but you are free to use another folder.

14. Now you see one final confirmation screen, which shows all the settings that you chose to install. If you are satisfied, click Next. CRS begins to copy files to your computer.

15. When CRS Setup finishes copying files, you get confirmation that setup is complete. On the final confirmation screen, you are asked to click Finish. You are also asked if you would like to view the CRS Start Page. If you would like to view this page, highlight this option, otherwise leave it clear. Now click Finish to either view the CRS Start Page or to return to Windows NT.

If you choose to view the CRS start page, you have an opportunity to read the readme file, view all the CRS documentation, go to the CRS Web-administration page, or go to Microsoft's home page or the BackOffice page (see Figure 4.6).

FIG. 4.6
The CRS Start Page.

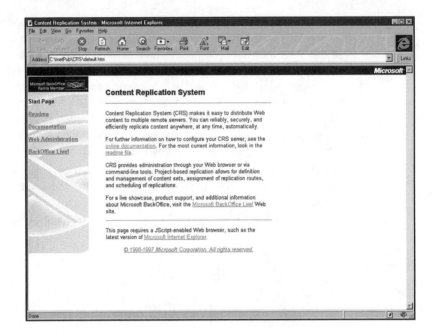

Testing Your Installation

When you complete installation, the first thing that you need to do is make sure that all your services started. Go to Control Panel, Services, and make sure that the following services are running:

World Wide Web Publishing Service

Content Replication Service

Schedule

If these services are not running, start them.

You administer CRS through a WWW interface. If you want, you can administer CRS on the machine on which you installed CRS or on your own workstation. If you administer CRS from the machine that you installed it on, you find a Content Replication group in the Start menu. This group has two options: a CRS Start Page and a CRS Administration page. If you administer CRS remotely, you can simply type the following URL in your web browser: **http:// <servername>/crs.**

This URL takes you to the CRS Start Page, from which you can read the readme file, get information on obtaining product support from Microsoft, read the CRS documentation, go to the Web-administration page, or leave your server and go to BackOffice Live at Microsoft.

Creating a Replicated Site

Using the CRS Web Administration Page

To set up a new site:

Click Web Administration from the Start Page. You see the Web Administration page, which initially contains four items to choose among (see Figure 4.7). These items are:

- **Servers**.   You can choose to administer another server running CRS. To get to another server, you can also simply type its URL.

- **Projects**.   Projects is where you set up the sites that you are going to be replicating. When you click Add Project, another window opens, asking you for the name of your project and the type of replication that you are going to use. You can use push or pull replication. Push replication means that you are going to send all the data from the machine that you are logged into. Pull replication means that you are going to take the information from a remote machine and transfer it to the machine that you are logged into. A good name for you to use for your project name could be the name of the site you are going to replicate. For this example, we will replicate the c-systems.com web site. Type c-systems as the name. Choose pull replication to copy the site from another machine to the machine that you're logged into. Click OK when you finish.

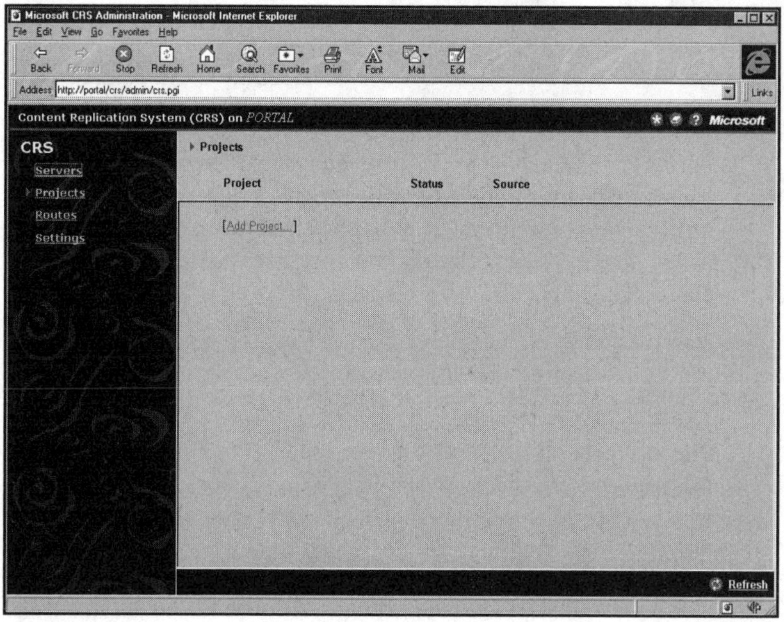

FIG. 4.7
The Microsoft CRS Web Administration Page.

You return to the CRS Web Administration page, which now has another set of menus. The Project menu allows you to configure the replication. On the first page, which is the Source/Target of Pull Project c-systems, you need to input the source URL; the target directory; the user name and password that you are going to use to connect; and the proxy server, if you need to go through one (see Figure 4.8).

FIG. 4.8

CRS Administration Project Menu.

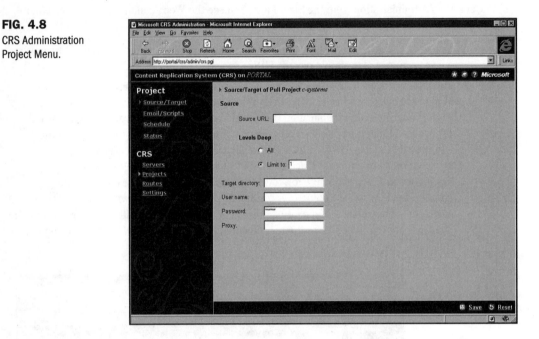

Fill out the required information on the Source/Target of Pull Project c-systems page and make sure that you choose Save in the bottom-right corner of the page (see Figure 4.9). If you do not save your work, you may lose it. When you save your work, you do not receive any notification, so you don't need to worry or keep clicking Save. You will only notice that the Source/Target of Pull Project c-systems page redraws itself.

Now click on Email/Scripts. CRS sends e-mail on certain events to a designated mailbox. You can send mail on all events, or you can leave all the text boxes blank if you do not want to be notified.

The way that CRS is set up in this illustration (see Figure 4.10) is that when replication either fails or succeeds, e-mail will be sent to a distribution e-mail list so that we can keep a record of what has been done. If replication fails, e-mail is sent to another distribution list. This second distribution list sends e-mail to the pager of any system administrator who happens to be on call when replication fails. As soon as replication fails, the administrator can log in and fix whatever went wrong; if a serious problem occurs, the person has to come in and fix it.

You can also run scripts before and/or after your site has been transferred. If you decide to do run a script either before or after replication has been performed, you type in the full path of the scripts here. You also have a space to enter any information that you need to have your administrators see. Again, make sure that you choose Save in the bottom-right corner of the Email/Scripts for Pull Project c-systems page before proceeding.

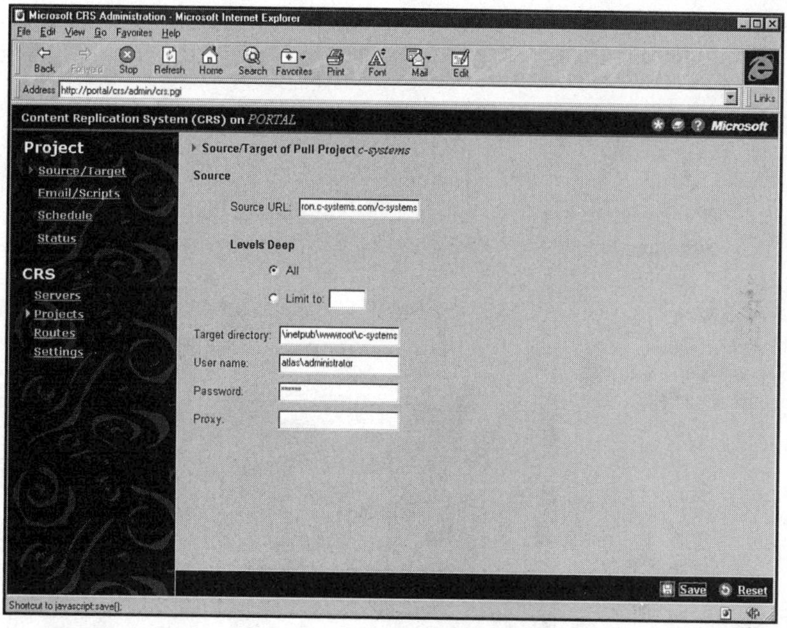

FIG. 4.9
Completed information for Source/Target of Pull Project c-systems page.

FIG. 4.10
Email/Scripts for Pull Project c-systems Web Administration Page.

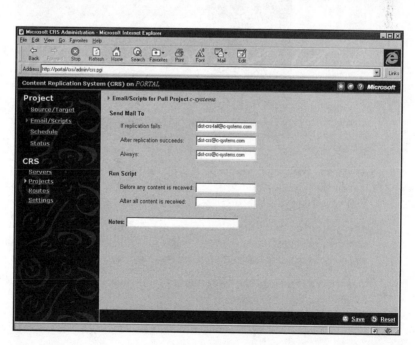

Part

II

Ch

4

After you save your work, you see the schedule Web Administration Page for Pull Project c-systems. You have two options: You can replicate on a schedule, or you can replicate whenever content changes. If you choose to replicate whenever content changes, CRS does a full site replication the first time that it is set up; thereafter, it looks for changes in the site and replicates only those changes. If you decide to do only automatic replication, choose Replicate Automatically and then save your changes.

N O T E   You can replicate on schedule or replicate automatically; you cannot do both. ■

If you want to use a replication schedule, choose Replicate on Schedule and then click Add Schedule to proceed (see Figure 4.11).

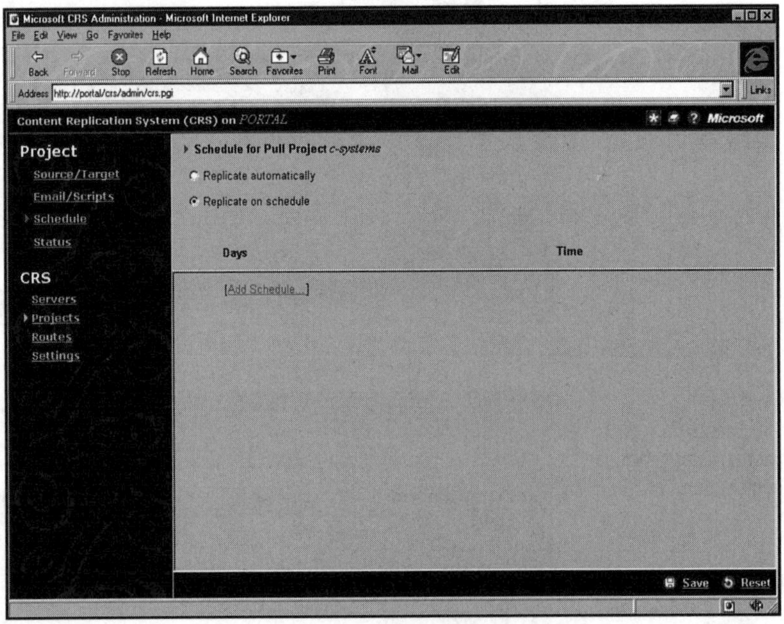

FIG. 4.11

Schedule for Pull
Project c-systems Web
Administration Page.

As you see, replication has been set to occur every day at 2 a.m. You need to use 24-hour format for the time, so if you want replication to occur at 11 p.m., you need to use 23:00. Click OK after you set up your schedule (see Figure 4.12).

After you set up your schedule, you see the schedule on the page. If you are satisfied, you can save your changes. If you want to change your schedule, click the schedule or the pad-of-paper-with-pencil icon. If you want to remove your schedule, click the trash-can icon.

You can click Status to see the status of the site that you are replicating. Status keeps statistics on what you have replicated so far.

■ **Routes**. The next main menu item is Routes. CRS uses routing tables to predefine replication routes. Multiple projects can reference these predefined routes, resulting in a tangible savings in configuration and maintenance time. What using routing tables means is that when you replicate to one server, you can have the same information arrive at another server at the same time. Routing tables work only with push replication. To add a route, choose Add Route, type a name for your route, and click OK (see Figure 4.13).

FIG. 4.12

Add Schedule for Pull Project c-systems web dialog box.

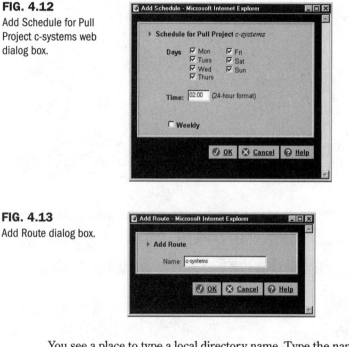

FIG. 4.13

Add Route dialog box.

You see a place to type a local directory name. Type the name of the local directory that stores the site you are replicating, and save your changes.

The next step is adding routing servers. The routing servers are where the information arrives when replication is complete. You can add as many servers as you want. When you finish, be sure to save your work (see Figure 4.14).

■ **Settings**. The last and final screen is the settings screen. In this screen, like the e-mail/scripts screen in the project screen, you can choose who to send e-mail to upon success or failure. You also need to choose a SMTP e-mail relay host. You can also choose a name of which the e-mail was sent from. For this example, send all mail to yourself. If e-mail were being set up for a production system, you would set it up as you did before: having successes go to a CRS distribution list and failures to go a pager distribution list (see Figure 4.15).

FIG. 4.14

Routing Servers for
c-systems Web
Administration Page.

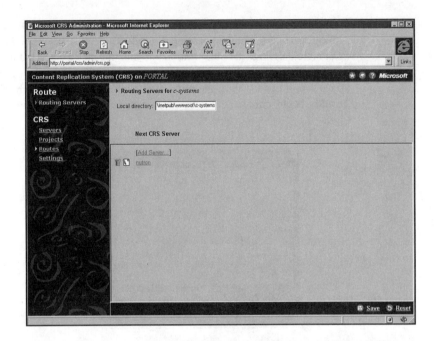

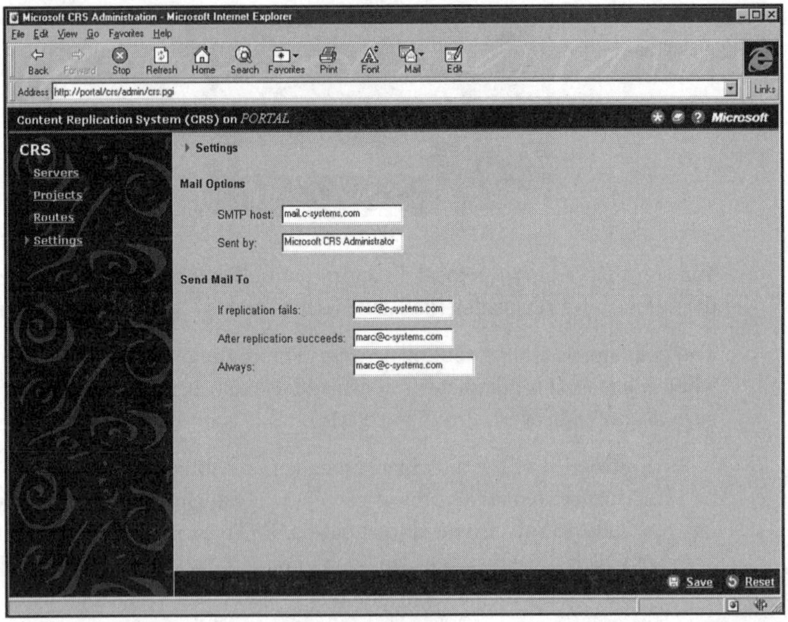

FIG. 4.15

E-Mail Settings Web
Administration Page.

You want to set up test installations of your own so as to become familiar with CRS. You should set up test installations in a lab environment until you become completely familiar with CRS, are satisfied with how you set it up, and are sure that it completely replicates your Web sites and Commerce sites without any problems.

The best way to go about testing is to make your lab as real as possible. If you can, you replicate your production Web site on a test machine by using pull replication. This way, you do not need to make any changes in your production Web server before you are ready. The other advantage of using pull replication is that pull replication should have no more intervention with your production server than someone browsing the whole site with a Web browser.

When you verify that the site is working, set up the server to push-replicate the site on another machine, and verify that this machine is working properly.

After you have run several tests for a few days or weeks, depending on how comfortable you are with CRS and how many configurations you want to do with it, you should be good to go on your production servers. When you do go into production, you should use push replication if at all possible. This way, you can replicate to multiple servers at the same time, and you have more control of what files you are sending. Also, if you have a directory that is not readable—only executable—you cannot replicate any files in that directory. With push replication, you do not have that problem.

A chance exists that you may have to intervene, however. If you are running mirror sites that are not called by the same name, and you have hard links that point to your site, you are going to need to rename these links.

Suppose that you have a coin store called **www.rarecoins.com**. You have your store replicated to other sites, but some of these sites do not use the same name. A site could use **rarecoins.c-systems.com** or something like that. In this case, when you replicate your site, you need to make sure that any hard links pointing to **www.rarecoins.com** are renamed to point to **rarecoins.c-systems.com**. CRS is not capable of renaming your links for you, so you need to do it manually or write a custom program or script that takes this into account for you.

If you are running a Commerce site, you also have to take the database into account. CRS does not replicate the database for you. To replicate the database, you need to use another method. If you have all your machines in one place, you can get away with having one primary database server and a backup database server. This way, you do not need to worry about how you are going to replicate your information; you can set SQL to do a database transfer every night or at whatever interval you want. Just be careful that you are using only one master server at a time and that the other servers are replicating from the master server. You would not want to overwrite a newer database with an older one.

If you are going to use databases that are at different locations, you can have different user information in each database, or you can replicate these databases. (The information about the store remains constant between servers. If you change this information, you need to make sure that all the databases that serve your store have the correct information.) If you decide to

Part

II

Ch

4

replicate all the information, you need to make sure that you allow this information to pass through the firewall.

You do not necessarily need to replicate the database information between sites on a regular basis. Replicating this information between sites is primarily for keeping user information the same. If a user is going to one site, he most likely will keep going to the same site. If you are mirroring with different names, such as **www.rarecoins.com** and **rarecoins.c-systems. com**, your users will almost always keep going to the same site. Very rarely does a user sign into both sites. Therefore, you may not need to replicate the database between the two machines— only the Web content.

The other thing that you need to take into account is the database. CRS does not replicate your SQL databases for you. If you are using SQL databases on different machines but they need to share the same data, you will also need to take this into account. Usually, mirroring databases is not supported or recommended. If you are using a web site over several machines, it is recommended that you use one database server and that you have a backup database server available at all times. You will replicate all of the database information to the backup database server using the standard tools that come with SQL Server so that your database will be as up-to-date as possible.

From Here...

As you can see, Microsoft Content Replication System is something that once you start to use, you will not be able to get along without it. This however is only one of the components that is given to us to use as a resource in Microsoft Site Server. From here, you can go on to installing any component of Microsoft Site Server. Some services that you will find very useful for administering your web site are Chapter 5, "Implementing the Internet Locator Server" and Chapter 6, "Understanding the Personalization System." Another two programs that you will be very interested in are Chapter 7, "Using the Microsoft Site Analyst" and Chapter 8, "Using the Microsoft Usage Analyst."

Implementing the Internet Locator Server

Internet Locator Service (ILS) allows other people on the Internet to find specific users on your system; it also allows you to have real-time meetings and conferences with other users on the Internet or your local intranet. ILS can be used with programs such as Microsoft NetMeeting (which is available at **http://www.microsoft.com/netmeeting**).

Internet Locator Service is designed to permit Internet Service Providers (ISPs) to handle thousands of users per server. Following are some practical uses for ILS.

Setting up ILS

You will learn how to setup Microsoft Internet Locator Server and configure it to meet your own needs.

Testing your installation

You will go through some example ILS pages to see what ILS can do for your intranet or your Internet site.

Putting ILS to the test

The ILS sample site will show you examples of how ILS uses all the different capabilities of ILS.

- To find people who are currently logged onto the Internet without knowing complicated information. Because most ISPs use dynamically generated IP addresses, finding someone is almost impossible if that person does not call while he is logged on to tell you what his IP address is. Also, if the other person gets disconnected, he has to call to give you his new IP address.

- To make Internet telephone calls or conference calls by using software such as Microsoft NetMeeting or Internet Phone.

- To edit documents online with another person using Microsoft NetMeeting as though both of you were logged onto the same network.

MCIS Internet Locator provides a memory-resident database where dynamic user location information is stored. Entries are kept in the database as long as clients refresh them periodically. Users can access the database to determine whether other users are online. Users access this database via their Web browsers. You, as a service provider or system administrator, can use Active Server Pages (ASP) to create a dynamic user directory that users can access. ■

Justifying ILS

You may wonder why you need to use Internet Locator Service if you already have an address book listing all your friends; you should be able to find them easily. This situation is not the case today. Users today may not be so easy to find. People may use different accounts when they travel or may use different accounts at home and at work. Also, most people today use DHCP, so even if you know people's accounts, you may not be able to find them, because their IP addresses change every time they log in. With DHCP, users are assigned a different IP address everytime they log in so it is not easy to find them because their IP address is constantly changing. With Internet Locator Service, the database is updated every time a user logs in or out, so if a person is online, you can find him or her.

The other advantage of using Internet Locator Service is its salability. You can configure ILS so that it can support only a few users and you can also configure it to handle up to 10,000 user connections per server. Most chat servers do not have quite that many people logged on at the same time per server, so as you see, ILS is a program that grows with your needs.

Installing ILS

1. When you are ready to install ILS, click Internet Locator Service from Master Setup. Getting to Master Setup can be accomplished by inserting the Microsoft Site Server CD-ROM in your CD-ROM drive (see Figure 5.1).

2. The Welcome screen appears with information about the product you are about to install. Read this information and click Next to continue.

3. The next screen is the license agreement. Make sure that you read this agreement so that you know what your rights are as you use this product.

4. Next, enter your name and company name. Click Next to continue.

FIG. 5.1

This figure shows the Site Server Master Setup. You need to click Internet Locator Service to begin Setup.

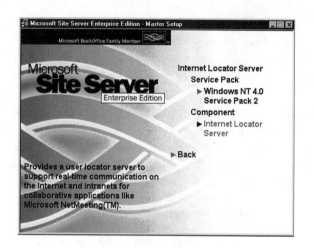

5. Now ILS checks to see if you have any Internet Information Server (IIS) services running such as the World Wide Web Publishing Service or the Gopher Service. If these services are running, a dialog box will appear informing you that these services must be stopped. If you wish to continue, click OK and these services will be stopped for you automatically.

   Unlike other programs, ILS does not give you a choice about where the ILS system files go. The files go to the `%systemroot%\system32\inetserv` directory, which in most cases is `C:\WINNT\System32\InetServ`. You need to choose the virtual root directory that you want the files to reside in, however. The default is `C:\InetPub\ILS`.

6. Now you have the chance to decide which components to install. The recommended installation option is to install all files (see Figure 5.2).

Part
II
Ch
5

FIG. 5.2

This figure shows the recommended installation option, to install all files.

7. When you install ILS, it installs the LDAP (Lightweight Directory Access Protocol) service, which runs as part of IIS. The LDAP service is the Internet address book. You are asked which directory in which to install the LDAP service. The default directory is `InetPub\LDAP`.

If the directory where you choose to install the LDAP service does not exist, setup asks whether it should create the directory for you.

8. The next step is to decide which program folder to install ILS in. The default is Microsoft Internet Locator Service.

9. At this point, you are asked to confirm all your settings—the last chance you get before the program is installed. When you click Next, the program is installed on your computer. Click Next to install the program.

10. When setup finishes copying all the files and modifying the registry, a confirmation box prompts you to click Finish. You also have the option of viewing the Start Page and starting the Administration Tool (see Figure 5.3).

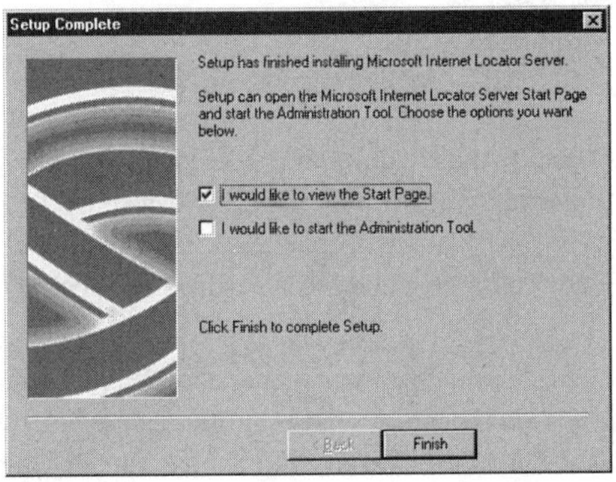

FIG. 5.3
When ILS setup has finished, you are shown a confirmation dialog box. You have two options, you can view the Start Page or you can start the Administration Tool. When you have selected your options, click Finish to complete setup.

Verifying the Installation

1. When you are ready to test your installation, you need to make sure that the services restarted after installation. Go to Control Panel, services, and make sure that the Microsoft LDAP Service and the World Wide Web Publishing Service started. If not, start those services.

2. Next, go to the ILS start page at **http://<server name>/ils**. The start page itself gives you an overview of what ILS can do. You can also read the readme (if you have not done so already), view the online documentation, see what ILS can do with sample templates, verify your installation, and go to BackOffice Live at **http://www.microsoft.com**.

The first thing that you need to do is verify your installation. If something did not go right during installation, you need to correct that problem immediately. Click Installation Verification on the left side of your screen to proceed. The Internet Location Server Installation Verification page appears (see Figure 5.4).

To test the installation, you need to do three things: create an online listing, search for the online listing, and delete the online listing. When you successfully complete all these steps, you can go on to create your own customized templates for your production environment. When you click the Create an Online Listing button, the listing is created automatically; you don't need to fill out any information (see Figure 5.5).

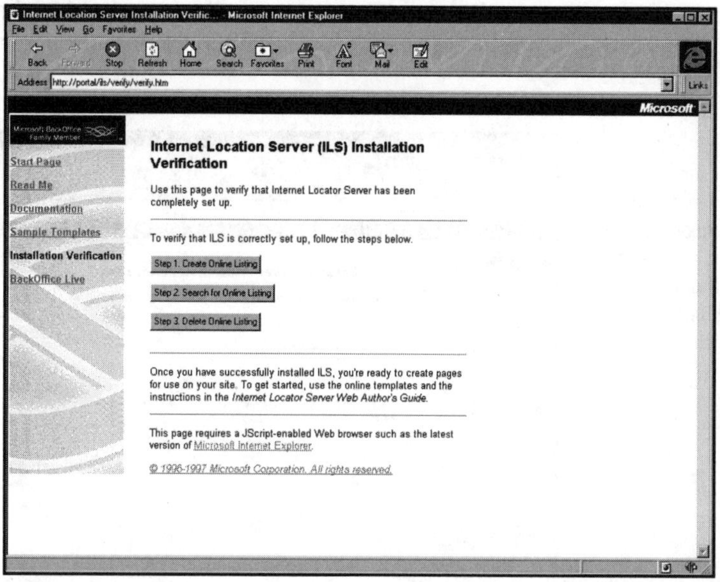

FIG. 5.4

On the Internet Location Server Installation Verification page, you see the steps that you need to take to verify that your installation has been completed successfully.

FIG. 5.5

On this page, you see that your online listing has been successfully created. If you see anything except for this message, there is a problem with the way that you setup or configured Internet Location Server.

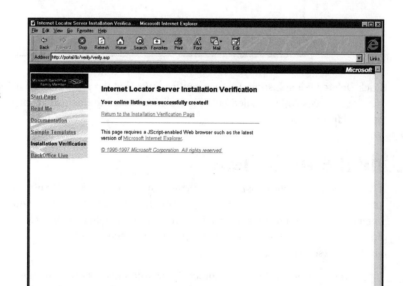

Part
II
Ch
5

When you finish, return to the installation verification page and continue with verification. The next step is to search for an online listing by clicking the **Search for Online Listing** button. You should see the listing for VeraFye@xyz.com return from your search automatically in Figure 5.6. For this example, you do not have to specify a search string, the search string is input automatically for you. Last, go back to the installation verification page and finish testing your installation.

FIG. 5.6

This screen shows the successful search for VeraFye@xyz.com. If you were able to get this far, you are 2/3 of the way to verifying that your install was successful.

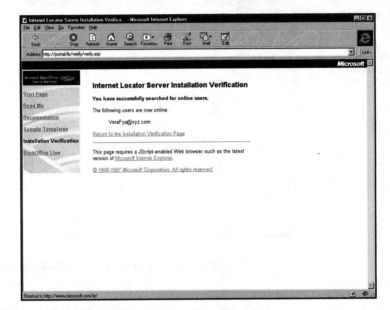

Click Delete Online Listing. You see confirmation that the entry has been deleted and that ILS has been successfully installed (see Figure 5.7). Return to the installation verification page and proceed from there.

Putting ILS to the Test

The next step is to click Sample Templates which is on the left side of your Web browser. You can see in these Sample Templates different examples of what you can do with ILS. The first example is a search page. You can view the names and e-mail addresses of people who are online and search for a specific user or users. The second example is a sample home page for an ILS site (see Figure 5.8).

If you were in a production environment, you would need a program like Microsoft NetMeeting or Intel Internet Phone to perform a search and go online. For the sample templates however, you do not need to have these programs installed. The purpose of the sample templates is to show you the capabilities of ILS even though you do not need these programs.

FIG. 5.7

In this screen, you receive confirmation that the test online listing has been deleted. Now you know for sure that you have successfully installed Internet Locator Server.

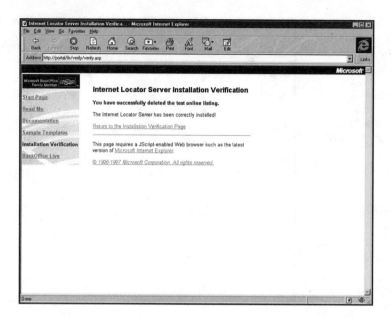

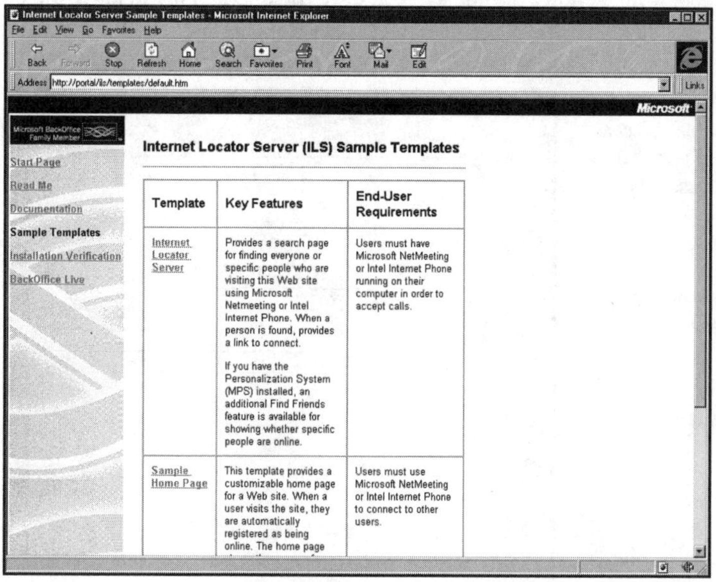

FIG. 5.8

In this screen, you see the two `Sample Templates` provided. You can also see the features and end-user requirements if you were to be using these templates in a production or testing environment. Of course, in a development environment, you would not need these products installed right away although you would need to have them on your computer before you are finished.

When you are ready to proceed click the Internet Locator Server link. You can perform one of three actions. You can set up a friends list, view all users, or search for a specific user (see Figure 5.9).

FIG. 5.9

The Online Search page shows the different actions available with ILS. You will of course have to do some modifications and customization but these pages are a good start.

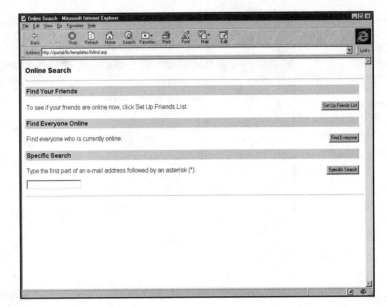

When you set up a friends list, you have the opportunity to enter the e-mail addresses of up to 10 of your friends. When you finish, click Update List (see Figure 5.10).

FIG. 5.10

In this example, you can keep track of up to 10 e-mail addresses. When you return to this page, you will see who is online and there will be links so that you can contact these users.

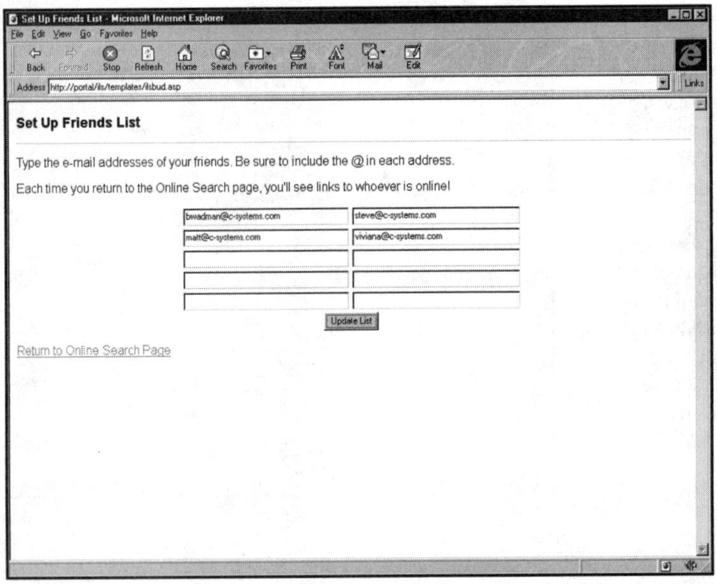

Now whenever you go to the Online Search page, you immediately see whether your friends are online (see Figure 5.11). This is also an example of a personalized Web page. This page does not support saving the search list, but you can do so quite easily with MPS (Microsoft Personalization Server).

FIG. 5.11

As you can see on this page, all of the e-mail addresses that I have entered appear in the Find Your Friends section.

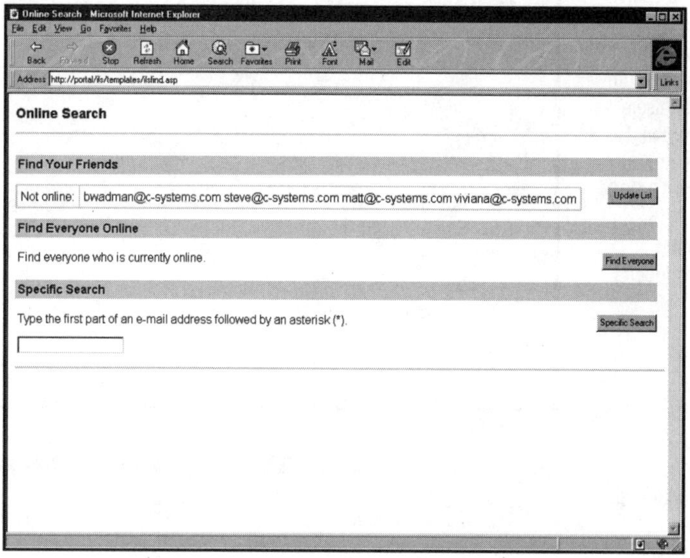

You can click Find Everyone if you want to see all users online. If you have a busy site where hundreds or thousands of people could potentially be online at the same time, you may want to disable this command. If users click Find Everyone Online, viewing this page takes a long time, and if too many people click this, it puts a great deal of unnecessary overhead on your servers. If you just installed ILS, you do not see any users online yet.

The last search that you can perform is a search for an e-mail address. You can search for either a wild card e-mail address or a specific e-mail address. If you wanted to search for someone and you know their e-mail address, you simply type their e-mail address in the Specific Search section on the Online Search (see Figure 5.12) page. If you only know part of their e-mail address, you type the part of the e-mail address you know followed by a * and you will see a list of everyone with the string you typed in their e-mail address.

Now look at the sample home page. To get to the sample home page, you need to click the back button on your browser until you get to the ILS Sample Templates page and click the link to Sample Home Page. When you first go to that page, you are asked to register. When you answer all the questions, click Customize This Page to submit your information (see Figure 5.13).

Part
II

Ch
5

FIG. 5.12

As you can see, when you first install ILS, the `Online Search Results` page shows that there are no users online. If you were in a production environment, this search would return the names of all users online. If you are in a busy environment, you could see up to 10,000 names as this is the maximum number of users that ILS supports.

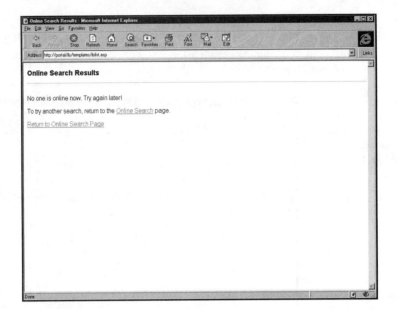

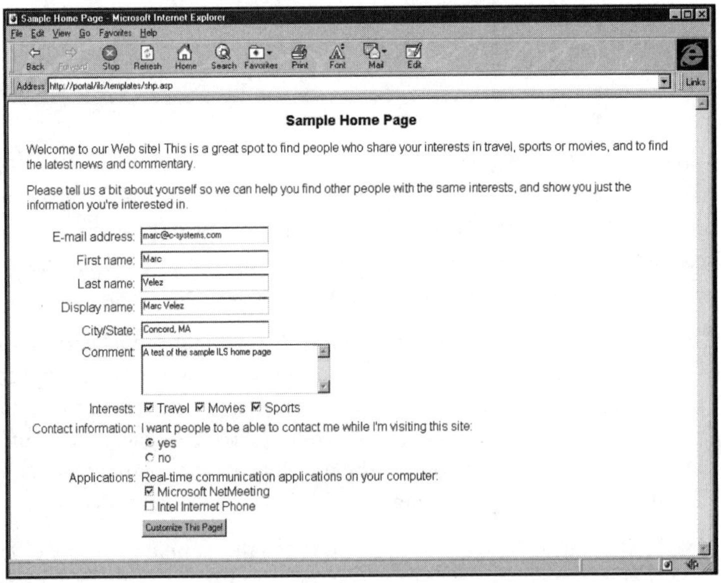

FIG. 5.13

On this registration, you are asked some questions about your name, where you are from and some interests. When you develop your page, you can ask just about any questions that you think your users will be interested in.

From Here...

Internet Locator Server is meant to be a way for users to find each other either on a large private intranet or on the Internet. ILS is scalable in that you can use it for only a few users and you can also use it when dealing with hundreds and even thousands of users. You should browse through the ILS sample site in order to familiarize yourself with what you can do with ILS. When you go through the ILS code, you see notes in templates about what you need to do to customize this site to meet your own needs. You can also go back to the ILS home page and read the online documentation.

The following chapters provide further information in developing your intranet Web site or your Internet Web site or commerce site:

Part II: Working with Microsoft Site Server. This section describes all of the other products that are provided with Microsoft Site Server.

Part IV: Creating Stores with Active Server Pages. All of the sample pages that were discussed in this chapter were created using Active Server Pages. In order to be able to customize your ILS site, you will need to have an understanding of how to use Active Server Pages.

Part

II

Ch

5

CHAPTER 6

Understanding the Personalization System

The next piece of software that this book discusses is Microsoft Personalization System (MPS). This software allows you to personalize your Web site for each user who visits; it also provides a way for users to vote or for you to take polls. With the way that the World Wide Web is growing today, personalized Web sites are the next step in the evolution of the Web.

This chapter discusses the tools that you can use to create such a Web site easily and without having to ask users to sign on each time they log in. After all, making users log in to a Web site sometimes turns them away. ∎

Using Cookies to Create the Personal Touch

You can create a personalized Web site in several ways. The best way is to use cookies. *Cookies* are small text files that are stored on a user's computer. Web browsers use this information for several things.

At first, cookies were used simply to track traffic. Because most Internet users do not get the same IP address when they log in, no way was available to track which visitors were new and which ones were repeat visitors. With cookies, you can track this information.

Now that you have a way to identify users every time they visit a site, why not use that information to take Web browsing to the next level? Three sites that use cookies for more than simply tracking are **http://espnet.sportszone.com**, **http://www.four11.com**, and **http://www.seidlers.com**.

If you ever visit the ESPN site, you notice that it always takes a poll about something. When you visit the page, you see something to vote about. After you vote, you can return to the same page but cannot vote again. Instead, you see the results of the vote being constantly updated. Even if you close your Web browser and go back in, and even if you clear your cache, you always see the voting results and cannot vote again. When you visit that page, the server asks your browser for the cookie for that site. When your browser returns the cookie, the server knows that you have already voted and therefore gives you the voting-results page.

Another page that uses cookies is **http://www.four11.com**. Visitors are encouraged, but not required, to log in; they can register so that they can be found on the Internet. If you are using CU-SeeMe, Microsoft NetMeeting, or Intel's Internet Phone, and you want people to be able to find you easily, you can install the Four11 Connect Client software. Whenever someone is trying to locate you and you are online, you receive notification that you are being called; you can either choose to answer the "phone" or ignore the call. You can also fill out a great deal of other information about yourself.

When you register with this site, you are encouraged to log in every time you visit. To make this process as easy as possible, you are asked whether you want to be logged in from this computer automatically whenever you return. If you answer Yes, the cookie that four11 places on your computer is used to log you in whenever you visit this page.

Another page that uses cookies to log visitors in is **http://www.seidlers.com**. At this site, you are asked to register the first time you visit the site or to log in as a guest. If you choose to register, a cookie is placed on your computer. Whenever you go back to that site, you are logged in automatically; you do not need to put in your name or e-mail address unless you are using another computer.

Personalizing Pages with MPS

Now that you have the technology to automatically log people in, it's time to take it one step further. Because you can show users a somewhat different page when they log in, why not give them a completely personalized page based on certain parameters that you set up for them?

Microsoft Personalization System (MPS) can give your users a completely personalized page. In the past, you could do this only by using custom CGI scripts or writing C programs. This procedure could get expensive, especially for people who did not have C programmers on-site. For this reason, Microsoft came out with MPS. Now Web developers and ASP programmers have the ability to program these custom Web sites without having to hire or contract expensive C programmers.

An example of a completely personalized page is **http://home.microsoft.com**. You have the option of creating your personal Web page from options that Microsoft provides. You can choose which news topics, sporting events, local news, financial news, and other topics of interest you would like to include on your home page. You can also choose a default search engine and use the Microsoft Stock Ticker if you are using Microsoft Internet Explorer 3.01 or later. MPS uses a built-in database to store information about all users. You can keep user information anywhere on your network; it does not have to be on each machine that is running a Web server. This allows you to integrate MPS with a busy site.

In a multiple-server environment, MPS is certified to handle hundreds of connections per second and supports more than 10 million user accounts. Information on each user is stored in a different shared directory and is referenced by number. These reasons are why MPS is so easy to interface with your IIS server. When the user visits the page, IIS reads the cookie from the Web Browser, and the Web server brings up the correct home page for that user.

Some of the key features of MPS are:

- **Rich personalization**. Users can personalize their home pages as much as you allow them to.

- **Simple user identification**. Cookies help you identify users as soon as they hit your Web page; no logging in or any other type of authentication is required.

- **Voting capability**. As discussed earlier in this chapter, you can use MPS to allow users to vote or to take surveys. To provide voting, however, you need to store the results of the vote on an ODBC-compliant database (such as Microsoft SQL Server). Using a database also makes tallying the results much easier.

- **Sendmail capability**. You can use custom scripts to send mail to a user from a customized Web page. You use the sendmail component if you ask users to fill out a survey and you want to e-mail a copy of the survey to users as a receipt. This component requires access to an SMTP mail server on your network.

- **Scalability**. As mentioned earlier in this chapter, MPS can support more than 10 million users. This number probably represents more users than you would expect to visit your Web sites so this program will most likely last you for years to come. MPS also is capable of supporting several hundred hits per second in a multiple Web-server environment.

- **Ease of administration**. All administration is handled through an HTTP interface. No special software is needed, and you do not need to provide special access through your firewall to allow administrators to manage your site.

- **ASP support**. As all new Microsoft products are supporting, MPS supports ASP.

Part

II

Ch

6

■ **Integration with IIS logs**. With MPS, you can enhance the tracking that you have used in the past. You can find out exactly how many users visit your site and what each user is doing. You need to be careful with this information, however, because most users are opposed to having their activities released to the public or any external firms, even for survey or marketing information. This type of tracking, however, helps you see what your target audience is most interested in and can help you plan your site for future growth.

■ **Use of a common security model**. MPS can be integrated with any type of authentication method that IIS supports. These methods are Anonymous Login, Basic Authentication, Windows NT Challenge/Response, and Distributed Password Authentication. Anonymous Login is where users do not need a user name and password to access the Web pages. With MPS, users are logged by cookies on their computer to access specific personalized Web pages. Basic Authentication is where users must type a user name and password to log into the Web site or access specific Web pages. Using Windows NT Security on an NTFS partition does this. You would set permissions on specific directories so that only certain users or groups have access to these directories. This system is insecure, however, because all information is sent over the Internet via clear text. If you are going to be supporting a browser other than Microsoft Internet Explorer, you need to use Basic Authentication because Microsoft Internet Explorer is the only browser at this time that will support Windows NT Challenge/Response. Windows NT Challenge/Response (NTLM) is where the user name and password are sent encrypted over the Internet. Accessing Web pages after using NTLM works exactly the same was as Basic Authentication in that you set your permissions on certain directories using NT security on your NTFS partition. The only difference is that the username and password are encrypted instead of clear-text. The last method is Distributed Password Authentication (DPA). Passwords are again sent encrypted as they are using NTLM. There are several differences between NTLM and DPA however. With DPA, you need to have Microsoft SQL Server and Membership, which is a component of Microsoft Commercial Internet Server. DPA is supported on both Microsoft Internet Explorer and Netscape Navigator. To install DPA support, you would simply install a plugin that is provided by the Webmaster of any site that is using DPA authentication. The other difference between DPA and NTLM is that DPA uses its own user database from SQL Server. NTLM uses the Microsoft Windows NT user database from either the local server or the domain controller to authenticate users.

If you want to learn how to use Membership, you can purchase a book about Microsoft Commercial Internet System.

Installing MPS

This section discusses in detail the steps needed to install and use MPS. MPS is comprised of three components which you use in your ASP applications to administrate the personalization of Web pages, polling and e-mail. You use these components just like you would use any other components within an ASP application. The examples provided with MPS in your

`InetPub\MPS\Samples` directory outline the use of each component, and are basically templates that you can use. If you have trouble understanding how the components work together within an ASP application, please refer to Chapter 27, "Using the Microsoft Buy Now and Wallet Components" which discusses the implementation of the `BuyNow` and `Wallet` controls.

The following steps outline the installation of MPS.

1. To install MPS, you choose Personalization System from Master Setup. Master Setup appears automatically when you insert your Microsoft Site Server CD-ROM in your CD-ROM drive (see Figure 6.1).

FIG. 6.1

This is the Master Setup screen that you run Personalization System setup from.

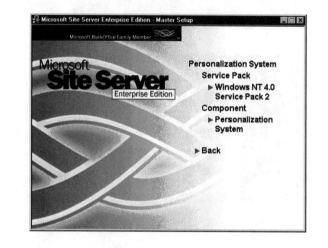

2. You see the welcome screen for MPS. After you read this information, click Next.

3. The software license agreement appears next. Read the entire agreement so that you know your rights and the terms and conditions under which you can use this product.

4. Enter your name and company name. Click Next when you are done.

5. Choose the directory for MPS. To change the directory, click Browse to bring up a drive and directory tree; you can either type the directory name or browse to the drive and directory you want to use. If the directory does not exist, setup can create the directory for you.

6. You are prompted for the virtual root directory. Usually, you put virtual root directories in your `InetPub` directory. These files are used for Web administration, templates, and documentation (see Figure 6.2).

7. If you set up CRS (Content Replication Server) in Chapter 4, "Understanding the Content Replication Server," you were asked to perform either a typical installation or a custom installation. MPS does not give you a choice. This screen allows you to select components to install. The recommended installation is to install all of the MPS components. If you are installing on a computer that is going to run MPS, you should leave all of the options selected. If you are installing for the purpose of remote administration, documentation, or any other reason, you can choose the components that you want to install (see Figure 6.3).

Part
II

Ch
6

FIG. 6.2

In this screen, you need to choose a destination directory for the MPS virtual root. In this directory is the MPS Web administration templates, sample templates, and document components.

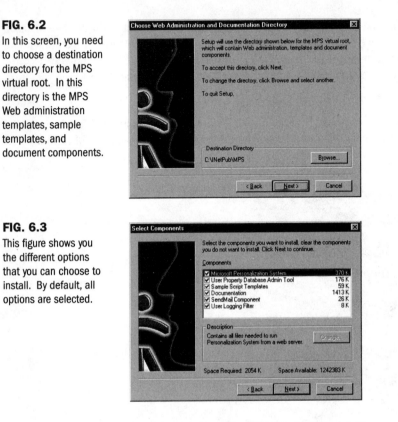

FIG. 6.3

This figure shows you the different options that you can choose to install. By default, all options are selected.

8. MPS allows your users to vote on different issues and allows you to take polls. When a poll or a vote is taken, MPS mails that information to a list or e-mail address that you configure MPS to mail to. To set MPS up to e-mail voting results, you simply need to supply an e-mail or an SMTP server in the next step.

9. If you want to log each transaction, you can enable logging. You can choose to open a new log at a given time or when the log reaches a certain number of lines. You also need to choose a destination directory. Make sure that you set the permissions for this directory so that all users have write permission. If you want to change the directory, click the Browse button, either browse to or type in the new directory and click OK.

10. If you have a busy Web site, chances are that you use multiple machines to host your site. In such a case, you can enable user ID sharing. When users visit a Web site, they are given unique user IDs, usually in the form of cookies. If you have multiple machines, you can allow each machine to use the same database so that when a user visits your site, no matter which machine they hit, they always see the same information. If you enable user ID sharing, you also need to provide the URL of your Web site (**www.site.com**).

11. Choose a program folder for MPS. The default is Microsoft Personalization System. If you want, you can create a new folder or use an existing folder. Click Next when you are done.

12. The last step before installation is confirming all the information that you have typed. Go over this information; if something is not correct, click the Back button and correct the information. This step is also your last chance to cancel installation, because nothing on your system has been changed. When you click Next, MPS is actually installed on your system.

Configuring and Testing MPS

In this section, you configure MPS to run on your network. Click Next to continue with the Property Database Administrator (see Figure 6.4). If you choose to cancel, you can go back to this tool at any time by choosing the User Property Database Admin Tool in your MPS folder.

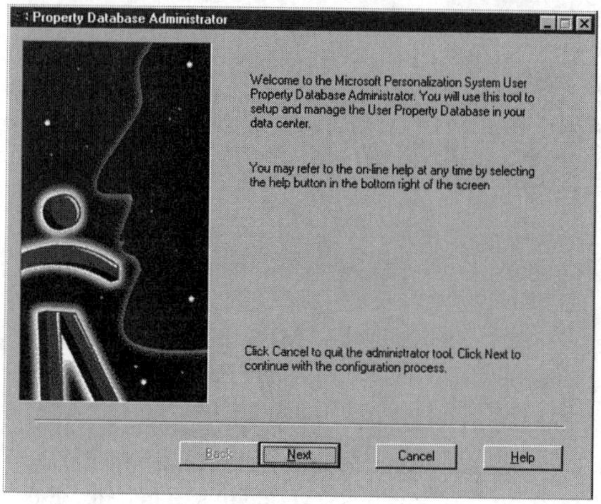

FIG. 6.4
After you finish running setup, the Property Database Administrator is run automatically. You can also go back and run the Property Database Administrator at any time if you need to make any changes.

You are asked whether this machine that you are configuring is the first machine that you are configuring to run the User Property Database.

You need to provide a share name that you have configured for MPS. Type your share name as **\\machinename\sharename** and click Add. You can also have backup servers for fault tolerance. This way, if a machine reboots or crashes, your users are not affected in any way.

The next screen asks you to confirm your list of servers. When you click Next, several directories are created for MPS.

The last screen tells you whether any problems occurred. If not, you get confirmation and can click Exit (see Figure 6.5). If there are any problems, you should first go back to the readme and make sure that your system is running the minimum requirements. For example, you should be running Windows NT 4.0 with at least 32-64M of memory, service pack 2 with all hotfixes (service pack 3 is recommended now that is has been released), and so on. If your system is running the minimum requirements but there is still a problem, you should uninstall MPS from your system and then reboot your machine. When your machine comes back up and you log in, go to control panel, services and stop any service that does not need to be

Part
II

Ch
6

running for the machine to work properly. Also, make sure that you are not running any programs including Exchange Client/Windows Messaging, Outlook, Microsoft Internet Explorer, and so on. Lastly, make sure that you are logged in with Administrator privileges and run setup again. If this still does not work, you should consider calling Microsoft Technical Support and they will help you through the problem.

FIG. 6.5

The confirmation screen tells you that your server configuration is now complete. If there are any error messages on this screen, you will need to resolve these errors before you can run MPS.

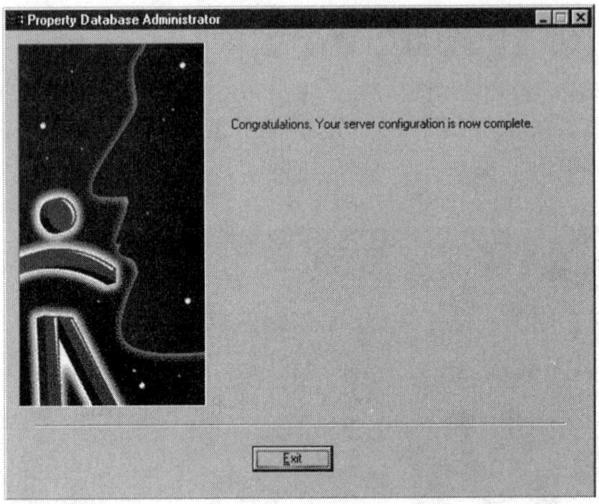

Now setup notifies you that you have set up MPS successfully. You are also prompted to view the MPS Start Page. If you want to view this Start Page, make sure that the World Wide Web Publishing Service has restarted on your machine.

When you are on the MPS start page, you see a short introduction about what MPS is and what it can do for you. The page also provides several links. There are links to the following (see Figure 6.6):

> The readme
>
> how to get product support from Microsoft Product Support Services
>
> MPS online documentation
>
> sample templates
>
> installation verification
>
> vote administration
>
> a link to BackOffice Live at **http://www.microsoft.com**

After you read the readme and are comfortable with your installation, you should verify your installation. Click Installation verification on the left side of your screen. You are asked to vote and are asked for your name and e-mail address.

When you answer the first two questions, you should see the Web page change. When you submit your vote for your name and your favorite color, you immediately see confirmation that your vote was successfully entered. When you enter your e-mail address, you should also receive e-mail immediately after you click the `Send Setup Confirmation Mail` button unless the e-mail server that you are using is delayed for any reason.

FIG. 6.6

When you run the MPS Start Page, by either choosing to go to the Start Page from setup or open your Web browser and go to the URL **http://localhost/ MPS**, you see different options that you can choose from.

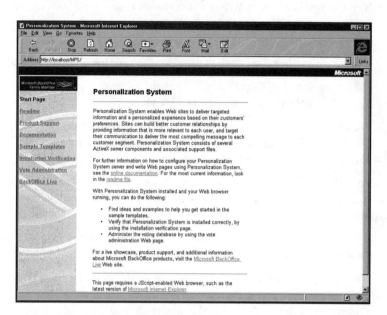

The final step in testing your installation is sending confirmation e-mail. When your e-mail has been sent, you get a message saying that your e-mail has been sent, and you can check your mailbox for final verification (see Figure 6.7). Now you are ready to begin actually using MPS.

FIG. 6.7

The Microsoft Personalization Verification screen is where you test three components of MPS to make sure that your installation is in fact complete. Once you perform the third step, which is Verify SendMail Component Setup, you will see that the text box has changed to a message telling you that e-mail has been sent to your e-mail address.

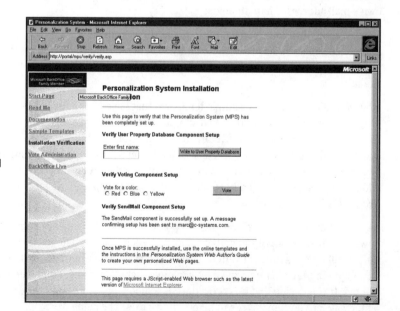

Part

II

Ch

6

Using MPS for the First Time

Now that you have set up MPS, you are ready to learn what MPS can do for you. Click Sample Templates on the left side of your Web-browser window. You see three template components and a sample MPS site.

If you go through each of the templates, you can see the different functions of MPS.

For now, look at the Widget Gadget Company's sample Web site, using all components of MPS. Click All of MPS to get to this sample Web site.

The first thing that you want to do is click Change Your Customization Options. You are asked to enter your first name and vote for the product that you are most interested in. When you finish, click Submit to update your options.

Now when you go back to the home page, you see a customized home page. Your name appears at the top of the page, and the products that you are most interested in appear on the front page of the sample store. You also have the same links that you had before.

If you click Learn About Our Products, you go to the products page. At this site, you see the same page no matter what you set your preferences to.

When you go to the feedback page, you can send a message to the Webmaster. You have the option of giving your e-mail address or remaining anonymous. When the e-mail is sent, you should receive the feedback e-mail immediately, and the sender also gets a receipt soon after.

When you click Submit, you get confirmation that the mail was sent; you also see whom the mail was sent to and also the address that the receipt was sent to. When you are testing MPS, you will be sending and receiving the mail for testing purposes, so most likely you will use your own e-mail address is in both fields.

The last thing that you can do at this sample site is vote for your favorite product. When you go to the vote page, you have the opportunity to vote for one product. The MPS voting component keeps track of whether you have voted; if you have already voted, you are not allowed to vote again.

Now you can take apart the sample templates that have been provided for you and customize each one until it works for your Web site. A good example of a Web site that uses personalization is **http://home.microsoft.com**. You can customize this site so that you can see different sports headlines, news headlines, and so on. If you want additional documentation, you can find online documentation at **http://<your MPS server>/mps**. You can also find additional documentation on how to use and program applications for MPS in the Que book *Special Edition Using Microsoft Commercial Internet System*.

Suppose that each employee on your corporate intranet has a secure login to a Microsoft Windows NT workstation. At the end of every day, each employee needs to account for his or her time by filling out a time card. In the past, each employee would go to `http://timecards`; log in; and put in his or her employee information, including name, employee number, and time worked. If you decide that this procedure is tedious for your employees, you can research a better way for your employees to fill out time cards. Try using MPS.

When employees go to **http://timecards**, they log in for the first time and then go to a personalized home page. Because users are logging in automatically, as soon as they go to this page, all the time-card information is automatically filled out for them except for the days and hours worked. When their time cards are filled out, users can interface with the company database and see their time cards for past days or weeks; they can also see and change personal information.

Once you get the time cards page working perfectly, you decide to create another MPS site. For project reports, your users need to go to **http://projects**; log in; and type the project IDs of what they are working on to find any information about their work or to update the information that they are working on. Again, searching for a specific project takes up time, because users need to search through hundreds of projects in the database or to know the numbers of all the projects that they are working on. Also, some projects are private, so you need to redo the way that users can get access to the projects database.

Again, you can use MPS to create a new and improved projects Web site. You set up MPS on your IIS server or on another machine. Your system administrators or programmers program in certain projects that each user is allowed to see and is given write access to. Whenever a user logs in, he or she automatically sees only projects which they are working on or have access to and cannot search other project databases.

Because this book focuses on Commerce sites, consider how MPS can help a merchant. If you have a large department store, your users may be overwhelmed when they enter to your store. You can advertise a custom Web page for users if they register. Customized Web pages not only encourage users to register with your store, but also keeps them interested in coming back. When you get users to register, you can get a feel for their interests. Ask users what they want to see on their customized home pages, give them a list of all your departments and ask what departments they want to have links from on their custom home pages; and ask them what sales they want to be notified of.

Now your users have custom stores where they can shop. These stores meet all your users' needs; they don't have to go through items they are not interested in. You want users to see parts of the store that they may not think they are interested in, of course, which is why you ask whether you can notify them of sales in other departments. Customized stores is a great way to get cross sales.

From Here...

Microsoft Personalization System is meant to be a way for users to have customized Web pages private intranet or on the Internet. We have looked at some sites that use the components in MPS and one site (**http://home.microsoft.com**) that is using MPS to provide customized home pages to their users. MPS is a server that is meant to be able to provide service to hundreds or even thousands of users. You can have up to ten million users in one MPS site (using multiple servers of course). You should browse through the MPS sample site in order to familiarize yourself with what you can do with MPS. When you go through the MPS sample templates, you see notes in templates about what you need to do to customize this site to meet your own needs. You can also go back to the MPS home page and read the online documentation.

The following sections provide further information in developing your intranet web site or your Internet Web site or commerce site:

Part II: Working with Microsoft Site Server. This section describes all of the other products that are provided with Microsoft Site Server.

Part IV: Creating Stores with Active Server Pages. All of the sample pages that were discussed in this chapter were created using Active Server Pages. In order to be able to customize your MPS site, you will need to have an understanding of how to use Active Server Pages.

Using the Microsoft Site Analyst

With Microsoft Site Analyst, you can completely analyze
your site or any other Internet site. When you enter a
URL, this program goes to that page; clicks every link;
analyzes each page for errors, size, and broken links; and
reports errors to you. Microsoft Site Analyst is also a
powerful tool that tells you whether you have old or outdated pages on your Web site. Over time, most Web sites
become large and sometimes difficult to manage. You may
have outdated links; old pages with incorrect information,
or pages with invalid links because of a programming
error or because a link goes from your site to an Internet
site that changed its URL. Without some automated way of
looking for these problems, you would need to dedicate
staff members to auditing your Web site every so often,
going through the entire site and accounting for every file
and link. This task could take someone hours or even days
if you have a large site.

With Microsoft Site Analyst, you can have all this work
done for you in a matter of minutes to hours, depending
on how large your Web site is. When Site Analyst creates a
report, you know exactly what pages are broken and what
should not be on your Web site. Then you can have the
problem fixed in a matter of hours instead of having to
dedicate several people to do the same work over several
days. ▪

An overview of Microsoft Site Analyst

Understand exactly what Microsoft
Site Analyst can do for you in developing and maintaining your site.

Installing Site Analyst

Learn how to install and configure
Site Server.

Analyze a Web site

You will look at the different reports
that you will see when you go
through and analyze your Web site.

Installing Site Analyst

To install Microsoft Site Analyst, follow these steps:

1. Click Site Analyst from Master Setup. Getting to Master Setup simply done by inserting the Site Server CD-ROM or by running setup on the root of your Site Server CD-ROM. When you run setup, the welcome screen appears. Click Next to continue.

2. The next screen is the license agreement. When you finish reading the license agreement, and if you know, understand, and agree to it, click Yes to continue.

3. Enter your name and company name, and click Next to continue.

4. Choose a directory in which to install Site Analyst. If the default is acceptable, click Next. If you need to change the directory, click Browse to bring up a directory tree of your hard drive and then type a new directory or browse to an existing directory. If you type a directory that does not exist, you are asked whether you want setup to create the directory for you. Click Yes to continue. After you select your directory, click Next to continue.

5. You need to choose a program folder in which to install the shortcuts. The default is Microsoft Site Analyst. If the default is acceptable, click Next. If the default is not acceptable, select an existing folder or type a new folder name in the dialog box. The new folder is created.

6. You are asked to confirm all the information that you just entered. If everything is acceptable, click Next. If you made any mistakes or want to change information, this step is your last chance to do so. Click Back to change any information.

7. If everything is set up correctly, you receive confirmation and can exit setup. You also have the option of viewing the Start Page and running the program. Select the options that you want to use and click Finish.

Configuring Site Analyst

In order for Microsoft Site Analyst to check your Web site, you can either choose a URL or a file, and Site Analyst checks every page and every link from that page that pertains to your site. If a link takes your users to another site, Microsoft Site Analyst simply verifies whether that site is valid and continues checking your site.

To begin, open the File menu and choose New Map from URL or New Map from File to bring up the dialog box. Type the file name and the URL, and choose OK. These screens contain some options (see Figure 7.1):

■ **Explore Entire Site**. When you choose this option, Site Analyst explores the entire site.

■ **Set Routes by URL Hierarchy**. When you choose this option, pages appear as main-route objects in the map according to their relative positions in the site root path. This organizes your map according to the way that your site is structured, not according to the order in which links are discovered on pages.

■ **Generate Site Reports.** When you choose this option, Site Analyst generates site reports automatically. The reports are stored in a location that you specify. When Site Analyst finishes mapping and analyzing your site, the Summary Report appears function in your browser.

FIG. 7.1

The New Map from URL dialog box is where you type in the URL of the site that you would like to analyze. There are also other options that will be discussed in the following paragraphs.

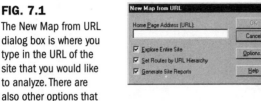

You also see an Options button.

When you click the Options button, you bring up the Mapping From URL Options – New Map dialog box. In the General tab, you can choose the following options (see Figure 7.2):

■ **Ignore the Case of URLs.** This option ignores capital letters in the URL. You need to know whether your Web server is case-sensitive if you decide to use this option. In most cases, Internet Information Server is not case-sensitive. Most UNIX Web servers, however, are case-sensitive.

■ **Ignore Default WebMaps.** This option ignores any default WebMaps on the site that you're mapping. (Some Webmasters create maps of their sites and post those maps. Site Analyst detects such a map and displays it in the map window.)

■ **Verify Offsite Links.** You can also verify the links of other sites. Verifying your offsite links is a good idea if you have an intranet Web server and you are in charge of all the sites. You should also be sure that no links would take you out to the Internet from these sites. If Site Analyst tries to verify the link of a busy site, such as **http:// www.microsoft.com**, verification most likely takes a long time, and you get a big surprise when you view your reports.

■ **Honor Robot Protocol.** If you choose this option, Site Analyst does not look in any directories or sites that are set up to keep out *spiders* (search engines and other automated Web-site robots). If you are going to explore any additional offsite Web sites, Site Analyst also obeys the robot protocols on those sites.

■ **User Agent.** User agent lets you enter the user agent you want Site Analyst to employ when it maps the site. The most common choices are Microsoft (the default), Mozilla 2.0, and Mozilla 3.0.

Part

II

Ch

7

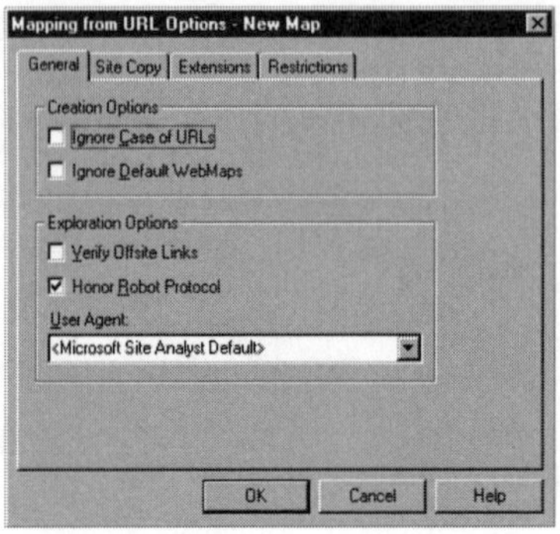

FIG. 7.2

When you click the Options button, you see the Mapping from URL Options – New Map dialog box. There are four different tabs that you can use: General, Site Copy, Extensions and Restrictions.

The next tab in the Mapping from URL Options – New Map dialog box is the Site Copy tab. You have the option of copying the entire Web site that you are analyzing to your local hard drive. If you copy a site that you do not own or administer, you may be violating some copyright laws, so be careful when you use this feature. If you would like to copy the site, you need to check the Copy Site box. When you check this box, you will also see a text box asking you to specify a Local Site Root Directory. If you know the drive and directory, you can simply type it in here. If you are not sure of the directory, you can click the Browse button and you will be given a drive and directory tree. You can browse to the directory of your choice and click OK once you have found the directory that you would like to use. The standard for Web directories is a directory inside of C:\InetPub although you can choose any directory that you would like to use (see Figure 7.3).

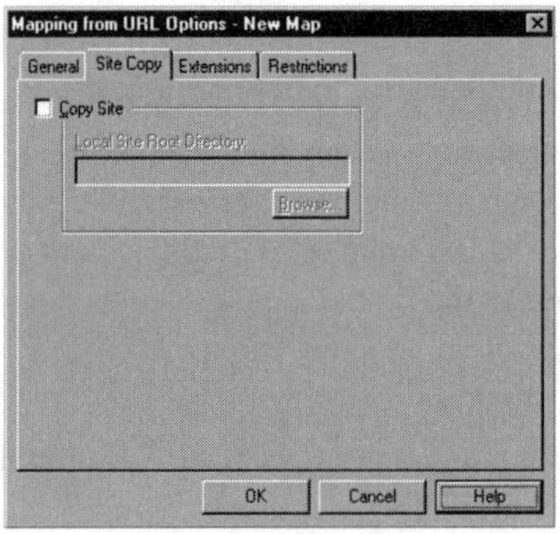

FIG. 7.3

In this figure, you see the Site Copy tab. Site Analyst has the ability to copy an entire site for you. If you would like to take advantage of this feature, click Copy Site and specify the local directory in the text box.

Site Analyst allows you to explore additional domains while you analyze your own site. If you want to analyze additional domains or Web sites, you can do so. You can choose to analyze all other domains from links that Site Analyst encounters, or you can explore a list of predetermined URLs (see Figure 7.4).

FIG. 7.4

The Extensions tab allows you to specify what other Web sites if any you would like to analyze. Be very careful when choosing this option. If you have a link to a very large site, Site Analyst may be running for several hours analyzing a site that you have no interest in at all.

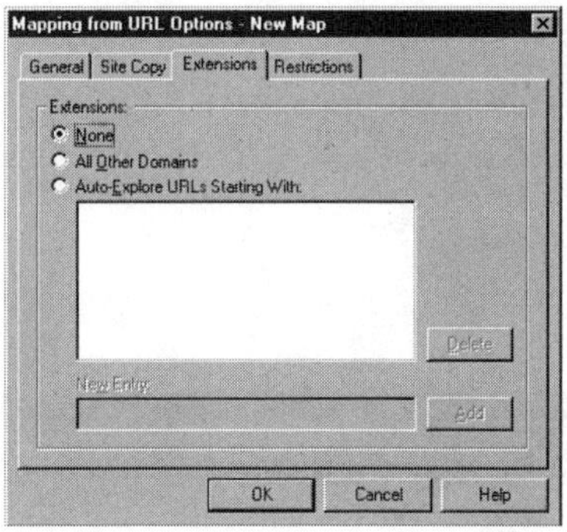

The last tab is Restrictions. If you need to exclude sites from being analyzed, you can do so in this tab (see Figure 7.5). If you are running an intranet with several different sites, you may only be responsible for a small number of those sites. If this is the case, you may wish to make sure that the sites that you are not responsible for are not checked. This will significantly reduce the size of the analysis file as well.

FIG. 7.5

In the Restrictions tab, if you want to make sure that some sites are not checked, you need to click the Restrictions box and under New Entry, type in the URL's or paths that you do not wish to have checked.

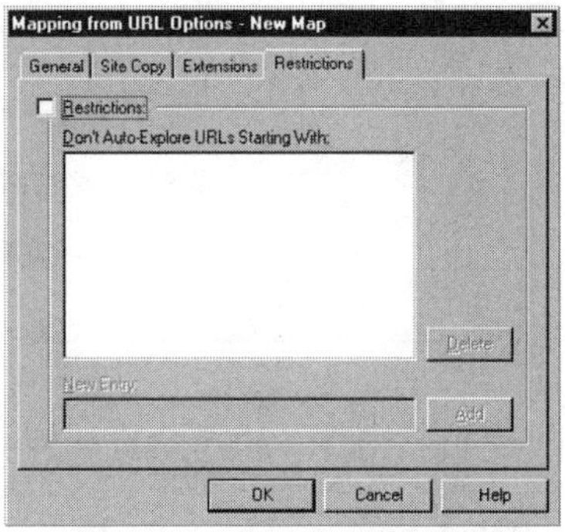

Using Site Analyst for the First Time

After you type your site and set all your options, click OK to begin your analysis. In the Generate Site Reports dialogue box that comes up when you click OK, you are asked what directory you want to use to generate your reports. Choose the directory and the report prefix (the name that all the files start with), and click OK (see Figure 7.6).

Once Site Analyst has finished analyzing your site, your report is generated, and your Web browser opens (see Figure 7.7). There are several links on this page that you can use to completely analyze your site. This page also has several statistics and summary boxes describing what Site Analyst has found on your Web site. A good place to start could be the Error Report page. This page will give you a report of all errors that were found during analysis.

Part

II

Ch

7

FIG. 7.6

In the Generate Site Reports dialog box, you need to type in the Report Directory and the Report Prefix.

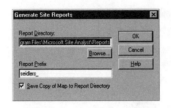

FIG. 7.7

When Site Analyst has finished analyzing your site, it will automatically launch your default Web browser and bring up the summary page.

Now you can begin doing some detailed analysis on your Web site. Although this tool is simple to use, you can get a great deal of information about your Web site as you learn how to use Microsoft Site Analyst. One of the best things about Microsoft Site Analyst is how simple it is to use. You need to simply provide it with a URL and it will generate reports for you based on that URL.

Once these reports are generated, you will have several reports to choose from. To get to these reports, simply click one of the links on the summary Web page. You should be on the summary Web page immediately after Site Server finishes analyzing your Web site. The links that you will see are Site Summary, Pages, Hierarchy, Images, Media, Gateways, Help, Error Report, Internet, Duplicates, Offsite, InLinks, Unexplored, and Index.

■ **Site Summary Report.** In the Site Summary report, you are given a complete summary of your Web site. Object Statistics shows you how many pages, images, links, media applications such as Java applications, etc. are on your Web site. Status Summary shows how many onsite and offsite objects and links are OK, not found, and any other errors that are found. Map Statistics shows how many levels deep your site goes and the average number of links per page. Lastly, Server Summary tells you the URL of the site you have analyzed, which Web server it is running, and which version of HTTP the site is using.

- **Explored Onsite Page Report.** The Pages link takes you to the Explored Onsite Page Report. The first table is a Page Status Summary. You see a summary of how many onsite and offsite pages and links are either OK, showing some type of error, or are unverified. In the next set of tables, you see:

    - The name of each and every page on your site
    - The level of the page
    - The date the page was last modified
    - The size of the page in bytes
    - The load size of the page (the size that the entire page is when the HTML, images, and any other applications on the page are loaded)
    - The number of links on the page
    - The number of offsite links on the page
    - The number of InLinks. An InLink is a pointer to an object in a page instead of pointing to an actual page.
    - The number of broken links

    You will also notice that on this page that most of the statistics are also links to various pages. For example, in the Name column, if you click any of the names, you are taken to that page on the actual site. If you click a number in the Broken Links column, you are taken to another report that tells you exactly what is broken so that you can easily find and fix it.

- **Hierarchy Report.** The Hierarchy Report shows you pages in a tree format. You see the pages by level and all of the pages that fall under that particular level. For example, if you have a products page and a services page on your Web site, you will see first the products page with all pages, links, pictures, mailto's, and so on that fall under the products page. You will also see a similar tree for the services page and all other pages in your site.

- **Images Report.** The Images Report gives you a list of all the images on your Web site. The Image Status Summary shows you a list of onsite and offsite images and links that are either OK or showing some type of error. The next table shows you each image with a link to the image.

    - Name. You see either the location of each image or the name of each image. If you have specified an image name using the ALT tag then you see the image name. If you click any of these images, you will be brought to the actual image.
    - Level. Level shows you how deep in your Web site the image is. You are also given a link to the Hierarchy Report.
    - Last Modified. You see the date that the image was either created or last modified.
    - Size. The size in bytes of the image.

- Type. What kind of image, usually .GIF, .JPG, or .JPEG
- InLinks. The number of times that this image is being accessed.
- INLINE. If there is a * in this box then the image is inline.
- ISMAP. Whether or not the image is also an imagemap.

■ **Media Report.** Media Report shows you the different types of media that you have on your site. Media, in this case, is defined as midi files, wav files, video files, and so on. The Media Status Summary shows you the media and links both onsite and offsite that are either okay, producing some type of error or cannot be verified.

There are also tables for the different types of media (audio, video, other, and so on). In the table, you can see

- Name. The name of the file specified with the ALT tag or the path to the file. If you click the name or the path of the file, you will be taken to this file. If you have the correct application installed on your machine, the program will be executed for you. For example, if you click a wav file and you have Active Movie installed on your computer, the wav file will be played for you.
- Level. This is how far in your Web site this file is.
- Last Modified. The date and time that the file was either created or last modified.
- Size. The size of the media file.
- MIME Type. Each file has to have a different type of MIME Type for the browser to recognize it. The MIME Type column shows what type of file each link is.
- InLinks. How many times this file is referenced on the site.

■ **Gateway Report.** Gateway reports show you links that connect to either an internal or external gateway. Gateways are not like links. A link simply takes you to another site or another page. A gateway in this reference goes to another site and run a query or executes a script. The Gateway Status Summary is the same as for the other reports. You see a table that shows you gateways and links both onsite and offsite that are either OK, with errors or unverified.

There are also tables for

- Name. The name of the gateway or the path to the gateway. If you click this, you will be brought to the gateway.
- Level. How deep in your site this gateway was found.
- Method. The method that is used to pass input to the server, usually GET or POST.
- InLinks. How many times this gateway is called.

■ **Help.** You can get help about any of these reports by clicking this link. You are automatically brought to the help section for the page that you are on. In other words, if you're on the Gateway Report and you do not understand something, if you click Help, you will be brought to help for Gateway Reports.

- **Error Report.** The error report shows all of the errors that are found when the report is run and is sorted by types of errors and then by where the errors are found. In other words, the first error that we see is Pages (404) Not Found. The next error is Images (404) Not Found. On this page, you see the object that is not found followed by all of the pages in your site that reference that object. If you click any of these objects, you will be taken to that page.

- **Internet Service Report.** The Internet service Report gives you an Internet service status summary, as well as detailed information about the different Internet services in your site. Internet services include mailto, news, ftp, Telnet, WAIS, Gopher and so on. In the Internet Services Status Summary table, you see the same table that is in the other reports.

  There are also tables that give detailed reports. These reports are sorted by what type of service is being used. All mailto's are grouped into one category, all ftp links are grouped into another category, and so on. In these tables, you see:

  - Name. If you click the path here, you will be taken to the link or in the case of a mailto, you will be given the opportunity to send mail using your default e-mail program.
  - Level. How deep into your site these services are.
  - Scheme. What service you are using, for example, FTP, Telnet, and so on.
  - InLinks. How many times this particular service is referenced in your site.

- **Duplicates.** Duplicates lets you know how many different objects have been duplicated. A duplicate is defined as an object (picture, media file, and so on) that has the same name and file size. If you do find duplicates, it is better to only use one image or file. Not only will you save disk space on your server, it will be much easier for anyone who is viewing your Web site. If you have a picture that appears several times but is only called from one file, this file only has to be downloaded once by the user. After that, every time this object is called, it is read from the users local hard drive if the user turns caching on in their Web browser.

- **Offsite Links.** Offsite Links give you a report of all links and gateways that take users off your site. This report gives you the name of the site, and if you click the name, you will be taken to the site; the level that this link is and the number of InLinks.

- **InLinks.** The InLinks report gives you a summary of the different links for pages, images, Internet services, media and gateways. If you click any of these reports, you will see details on each link. In other words, if you click the word Pages, you are brought to the InLinks to Pages Report page. Here, you will see a list of all pages and under the page, you will see a list of all pages that reference the original page. The same is true for Images and all other objects on the InLinks report page.

- **Unexplored.** The Unexplored Objects Report lists the objects in the map that Site Analyst did not explore, but did discover. The objects are grouped by object type. Site Analyst didn't explore the objects because either you limited the number of pages and levels to explore when you mapped the site or because the object is offsite. (Offsite objects are not automatically explored.) All objects are reported on this page. URL's of Web pages, Internet services such as ftp, news, etc; mailto's, and so on.

■ **Index.** The last item on your menu is index. If you click Index, you are brought to an alphabetical index of all objects that are on your Web site. You can click any of these items to be brought directly to the object.

From Here...

Microsoft Site Server is a way for Webmasters to easily analyze their Web sites and see very detailed reports of what is happening with their site. Once you master this tool, you will be able to cut down the time that you spend analyzing your Web site trying to make it more efficient.

The following chapters provide further information in developing your intranet Web site or your Internet Web site or commerce site:

■ Part II, "Working with Microsoft Site Server." This section describes all of the other products that are provided with Microsoft Site Server.

■ Part IV, "Creating Stores with Active Server Pages." All of the sample pages that were discussed in this chapter were created using Active Server Pages. In order to be able to customize your ILS site, you will need to have an understanding of how to use Active Server Pages.

Using the Microsoft Usage Analyst

The next component of Microsoft Site Server that will be looked at is Microsoft Usage Analyst. This product takes your IIS logs, reads them into a SQL database, and provides useful statistics for you. You can find out such information as where people are coming from, how many repeat visitors are hitting your Web site, and how many new visitors are hitting your Web site. ■

An overview of Microsoft Usage Analyst

Understand what Microsoft Usage Analyst can do for you in managing your Web site. You can get very useful statistics about who is visiting your site, repeat visitors, new visitors, location of visitors, and a wealth of information.

Preparing to install Microsoft Usage Analyst

Installing Microsoft Usage Analyst is a several-step process. You need to set up a database and possibly ODBC before you can install Usage Analyst for the first time. We will go over in-depth how to set up your databases and ODBC DSN.

Installing Microsoft Usage Analyst

Once you have finished the preliminary work for installation, you are ready to install Usage Analyst.

Analyzing a sample site

You will see how to take the IIS logs from your site, import them into Usage Analyst, choose what report you are going to use and create the report.

Preparing to Install Usage Analyst

You can install Usage Analyst on any machine on your network. You do not have to install the program on your Site Server machine or your Web server, because it imports all the log files into a database. Usage Analyst also uses ODBC, so the database program that you use (SQL Server or Access) does not have to be on your system, either.

To begin installation, click the Usage Analyst that describes your database system, as shown in Figure 8.1. For this chapter, the SQL Server version of Usage Analyst will be used. The reason that SQL Server is recommended is because it can handle much larger databases than Access can, and it is also much faster when dealing with very large databases.

FIG. 8.1

As you can see, you have two choices when you install Usage Analyst, you can either install a version that will run with Access or SQL Server. The recommended install is SQL Server.

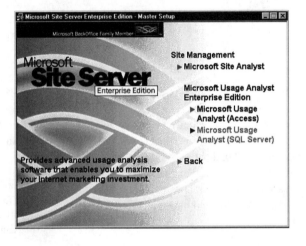

Before you begin installation, you need to take a few steps. You need to set up an SQL database for Usage Analyst to read the IIS log files into.

Setting Up a SQL Database

The first thing that you should do is create a new database. You have the option of using a database device that already exists, but doing so is not a good idea. Microsoft recommends keeping your databases separate for different functions. You should have a separate database for your IIS logs, for each of your Commerce Server production stores, and for any other applications that you are using SQL server for. By using separate databases for each SQL function, if any of your databases become corrupted, this does not affect every application that is on your system; it affects the one database or one application. Also, you do not need to create the database on the same machine that you install Usage Analyst on; you can create the database on any SQL Server on your network.

Creating the Database Device   To create the new database, you need to go into SQL Enterprise Manager, connect to your SQL Server, and perform these steps:

1. When you connect to your SQL Server, go to Database Devices. Right-click Database Devices to bring up the shortcut menu and choose New Device as seen in Figure 8.2. Choosing New Device will bring up the New Database Device dialog box. You want to create a database device and a log device, so you need to create two databases.

FIG. 8.2

In the Microsoft SQL Enterprise Manager, you can create a new Database Device by right-clicking Database Devices and selecting New Device from the shortcut menu.

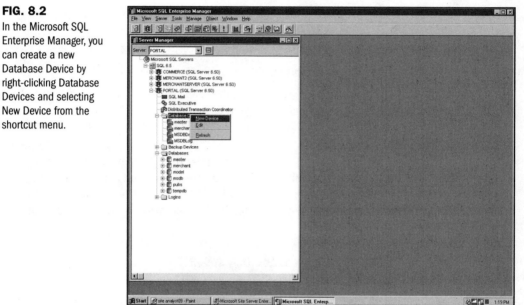

2. The recommended name for the data device is useanalyst_data. The recommended name for the log device is useanalyst_log. The recommended size depends on how much traffic goes through your site each day. The recommended size of the data and log devices are based on the monthly size of your IIS logs. The recommendation is as follows.

Monthly Log File Size	useanalyst_data Device Size	useanalyst_log Device Size
10M	50M	15M
25M	100M	25M
50M	200M	50M
100M	500M	100M
250M	750M	150M

continues

continued

Monthly Log File Size	useanalyst_data Device Size	useanalyst_log Device Size
500M	1,500M	300M
1,000M	3,000M	600M
2,500M	5,000M	1,000M
5,000M	10,000M	2,000M
10,000M	15,000M	3,000M
25,000M	20,000M	4,000M
50,000M	25,000M	5,000M

If you're installing this software on a test machine, make the data device only 20M and the log device 5M. You should not make your database this small in any type of production environment. The size of these databases should be able to hold up to six months' worth of logs.

3. When you decide on the size of your databases, enter this information in the New Database Device dialog box in the Size (MB) text box as seen in Figure 8.3. You also need to enter the location of the database file in the Location text box. After you enter all the information, click Create Now. Creating the database device should be a fairly quick process.

FIG. 8.3
The New Database Device dialog box allows you to create the data device and the log device.

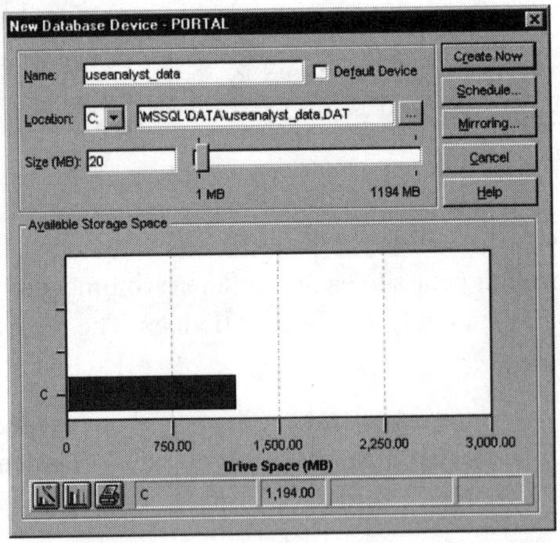

4. If all goes well, you see a dialog box saying that the database device was successfully created (see Figure 8.4).

You need to repeat this process to create your log file.

Creating the Database   Now that you have set up your database devices for your data and log databases, you can create the databases. To do so, right-click Databases and choose New Database from the shortcut menu as seen in Figure 8.5.

FIG. 8.4

You will see this dialog box when you have successfully created your database device for your data and log devices. Click OK when you see this dialog box.

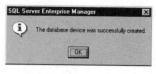

FIG. 8.5

When you are ready to create a new database, right click on Databases and choose New Database from the shortcut menu.

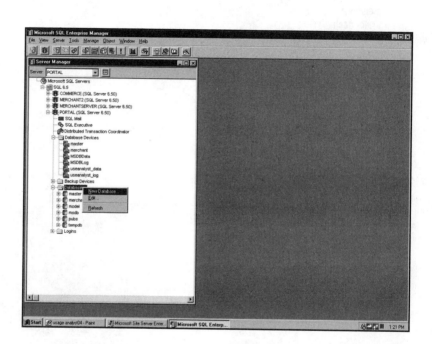

You see a dialog box that allows you to create a new database. You need to name the database. The suggested name is useanalyst. Do not choose Create For Load.

Now you need to select your Data Device and your Log Device from the drop-down lists. For Data Device, choose useanalyst_data; for Log Device, choose useanalyst_log. When you choose your Data Device and your Log Device, the Size (MB) text box will default to the size of the Data Device. In this case, the Data Device is 20M and the Log Device is 5M as seen in Figure 8.6. You can either create the database now or schedule to have the database created at a future date. Keep in mind that depending on the size of your database, creating the database could take several minutes and will take considerable resources on your machine. For this reason, if your machine is a production server, you should schedule the database to be created during off-peak hours.

FIG. 8.6

The New Database dialog box is where the database is created. Here, choose the Data Device and Log Device from the pull-down menus and also type in the size in megabytes that you want for each device.

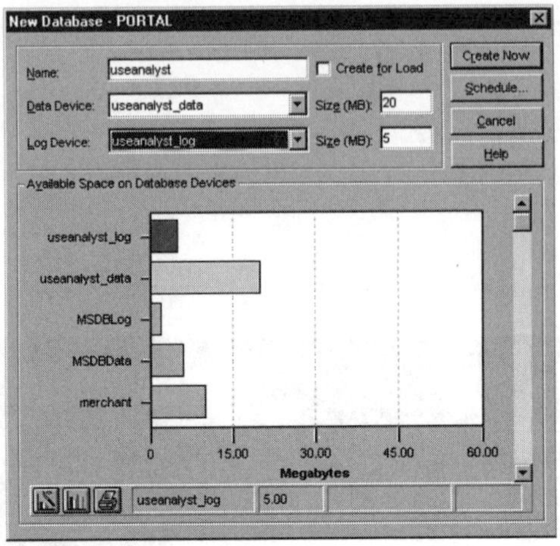

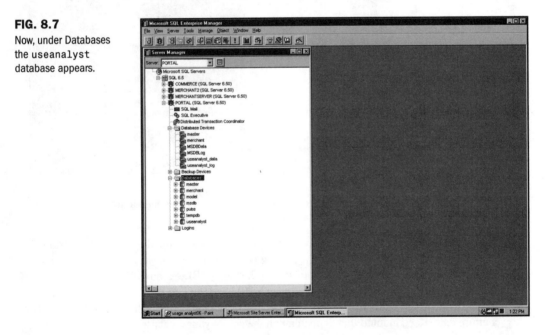

Now you see the database in your database tree as seen in Figure 8.7.

FIG. 8.7

Now, under Databases the useanalyst database appears.

Configuring ODBC to Use a SQL Server Database

If your SQL Server resides on the same machine as you are going to install Usage Analyst on, you are ready to install Usage Analyst (as long as the database has been created). If you are going to use a SQL Server that is on another machine, you must create an ODBC System Data

Source (DSN) so that you can connect to that database. The ODBC DSN is created on the machine on which you are installing Usage Analyst. To create the ODBC DSN, go to Control Panel and double-click ODBC (see Figure 8.8).

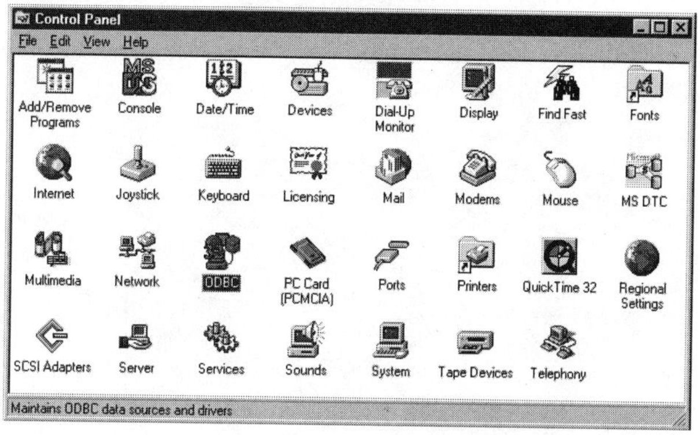

FIG. 8.8

Go to Control Panel and double-click ODBC to bring up the ODBC Data Source Adminis-trator.

1. You need to create a system DSN, so click the System DSN tab (see Figure 8.9).

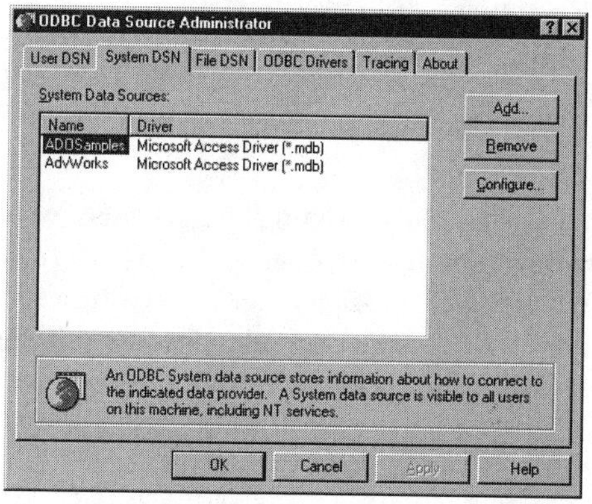

FIG. 8.9

Whenever you add an ODBC object to be used with SQL Server, you will almost always add the object as a System DSN.

2. Click the Add button to add a new DSN. When you click the Add button, the Create New Data Source dialog box appears as seen in Figure 8.10.

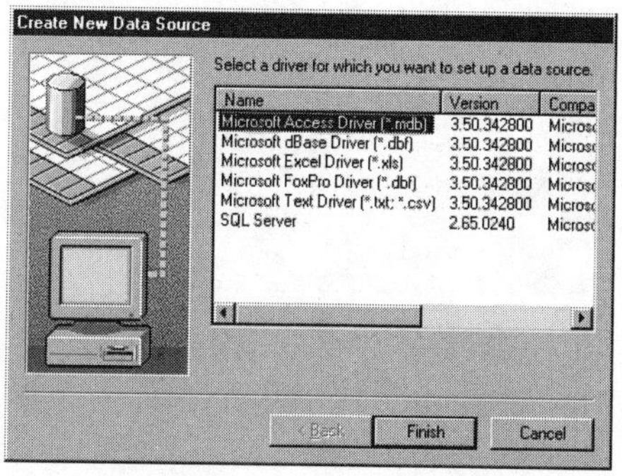

FIG. 8.10

In the Create New Data Source dialog box, you can create a DSN for any type of ODBC driver that you have installed on your machine.

Double-click SQL Server to bring up the ODBC SQL Server Setup dialog box. Enter your Data Source Name and Description (optional), and choose a server from the drop-down list. If your server does not appear, you can type in the name of the server.

Next, you need to choose the database name. To choose the database, you need to click the Options button. Type the database name. Everything else should be left as the default. When you finish, click OK (see Figure 8.11).

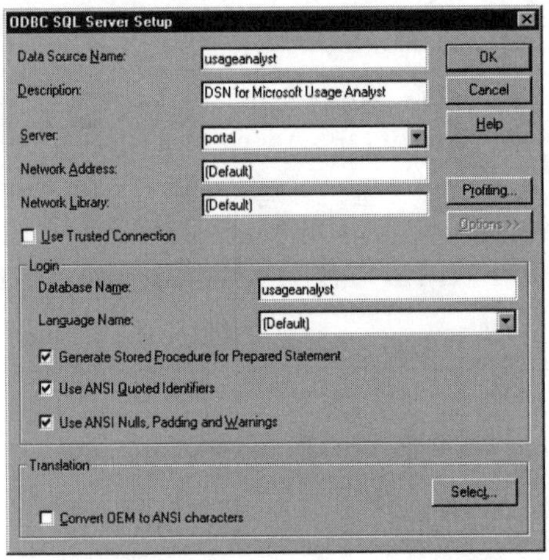

FIG. 8.11

You need to choose all of the options in the ODBC SQL Server Setup dialog box. This figure shows all of the options that are seen when you click the Options button.

No error checking is available when you are setting up the ODBC, so be careful when you set it up that you do not mistype anything. The error checking is performed the first time that you try to use Usage Analyst. When you click OK, you see the new data source when you go back to the System DSN tab of the ODBC Data Source Administrator (see Figure 8.12). When you are satisfied that everything is all right, click OK. You are ready to install Usage Analyst.

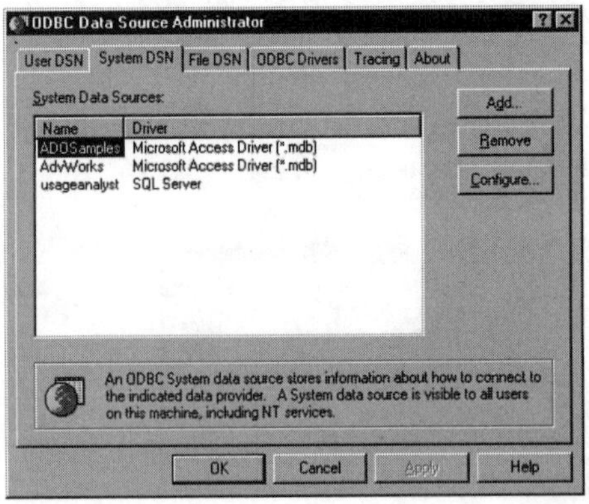

FIG. 8.12

Now that you have added the usage analyst DSN, you will see it in the System DSN tab of the ODBC Data Source Administrator.

Installing Usage Analyst

To install the Usage Analyst, follow these steps:

1. When you go into Setup, you see a notice asking you to close all programs before you install this software. Verify that all programs are closed, and click OK.

2. The next screen is the license agreement. Make sure that you read this document so that you understand the terms and conditions under which you can use and operate this program. You are asked to enter your name and company name. Click OK when you finish.

Installing Components

You need to decide which components you want to install. You have five components from which to choose as seen in Figure 8.13:

■ **Analysis Module**. This module actually analyzes and produces the reports that you see when you use Usage Analyst. Because producing and analyzing these reports takes up a great deal of CPU time, make sure that the computer you install this module on is one that has sufficient CPU speed and memory, and is in close proximity to your database server if SQL is not installed on this machine. Also, just as a reminder, if you have access logs that are several megabytes or larger, Usage Analyst takes a long time to analyze these logs. Make sure that Usage Analyst is not installed on any production servers, if you can possibly help it. If you do not have the resources to keep Usage Analyst off a production machine, try to schedule analysis for off-peak hours, preferably overnight.

■ **Database Module**. You use this module only once, to set up the database on your SQL server. You do not use this module in your normal operation, and if you are moving Usage Analyst to another machine or installing it on a second machine to be used with an existing database, you do not need to install this module.

■ **Help Files**. These files are the online documentation. When you install these files, Usage Analyst Setup installs HTML documentation and also a 14M Microsoft Word document.

■ **Import Module**. This module is what you use to read your IIS logs into SQL. When you import your IIS logs into your SQL database, you can begin to analyze the data. Again, keep in mind that if you have a busy Web site, your logs are going to be large and therefore, take a great deal of CPU time and memory, not only on the analysis machine but also on your SQL Server. Be sure to schedule your time wisely.

■ **Metadata Module**. You use this module to categorize and classify Web-site use data into terminology commonly used in your business, to integrate data from other applications or data sources with the Web-site use data, and to associate ad view and ad click URLs with their common advertisements.

You need to choose the directory in which you want to install Usage Analyst. When you are satisfied with the choices that you have made, click Begin Installation.

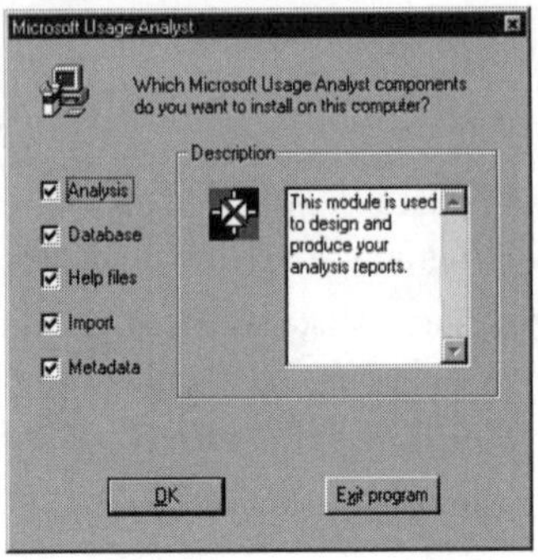

FIG. 8.13

This figure shows the different components that you can install. Also, if you click each component, you will see the component's description in the Description window.

When Usage Analyst is installed on your computer, you see a message telling you that you need to set up your database, if you have not already done so, or if you are installing Usage Analyst for the first time.

If you are installing Usage Analyst for the first time, you should run DBSetup.exe. Choose Run from the Start menu, browse to the directory in which you installed Usage Analyst, choose DBSetup.exe, and click OK to run this program as seen in Figure 8.14. When you install Usage Analyst, you are told that you need to run DBSetup.exe if this is the first time that you have installed Usage Analyst.

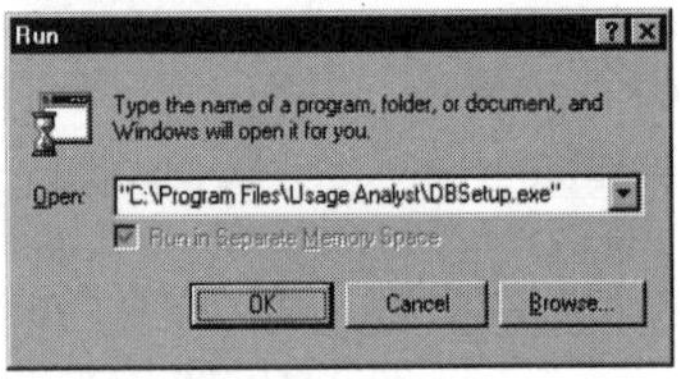

FIG. 8.14

The setup program does not place an icon in the shortcut menus because running this program accidentally will completely clear out an existing database. For this reason, in order to run this program, you must run it manually from the Run dialog box or from a command prompt.

Preparing the Database

The first thing that you are asked is how you want to connect to your SQL Server. You have two choices. You can connect directly to the SQL Server, or you can connect via ODBC (see Figure 8.15). If you are using a SQL Server on your local network and are using TCP/IP or named pipes, you can use a direct connection to the SQL Server. If you are not on the same network, or if you try direct connection and you cannot get it to work, you need to set up a DSN, as explained earlier in this chapter in the section "Configuring ODBC to Use a SQL Server Database."

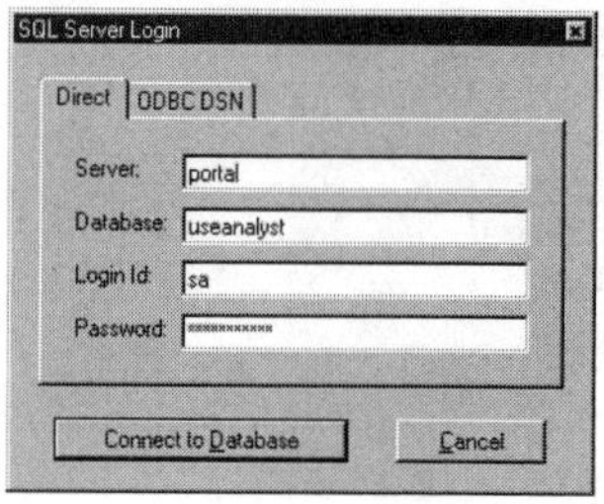

FIG. 8.15

In the SQL Server Login dialog box, you have two choices, Direct or ODBC DSN. If you are using a SQL Server either locally on the same machine that you are using Usage Analyst or on the same LAN, you can use a direct connection. If you are using a SQL Server that is in a different part of the LAN or a direct connection will not work, choose ODBC DSN.

The example in this chapter uses "sa" as the user name. In a production environment, using this name is not a good idea. The recommendation is to have a separate user name and password with full control to each database. By default, the sa account has full control to everything on your SQL Server, just as an administrator has full control of all resources in a Windows NT domain. To keep things secure, you should keep one account per database. If you have users who need to directly connect to the SQL Server, giving each user an account with access to only the information that the user needs is a good idea. This way, users cannot accidentally do anything to interfere with the normal operation of your system.

The next box tells you that default options are set on the useanalyst database. These options are Truncate Log on Checkpoint and Select Into/Bulkcopy (see Figure 8.16). You can find these options and others in SQL Enterprise Manager by double-clicking your database and selecting the Options tab. If you want in-depth information on using and programming SQL Server, you can purchase *Special Edition Using Microsoft SQL Server* (Que).

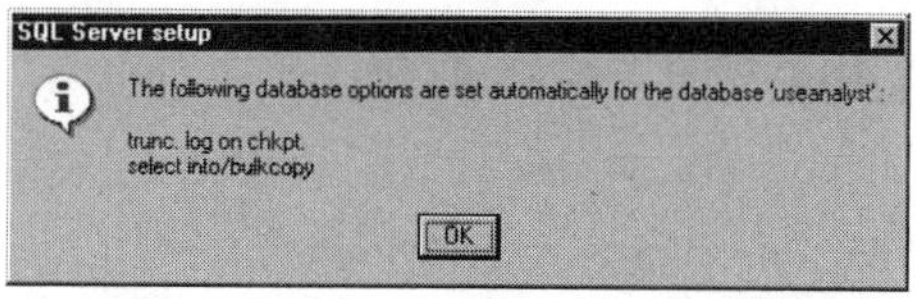

FIG. 8.16

When you have finished running DBSetup.exe, a dialog box appears telling you that certain options are set automatically for the database.

You are ready to initialize the database to use it with Usage Analyst. The recommendation is to leave everything as the default to get the best performance out of Usage Analyst. When you are ready, click Update Destination Database. This process takes 3 to 10 minutes, depending on how fast your computer is (see Figure 8.17).

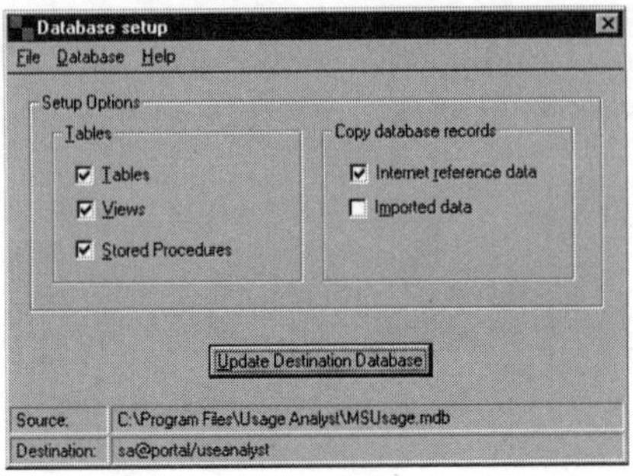

FIG. 8.17

Once you have finished setting up your ODBC or Direct Connection options, DBSetup will ask to initialize the database. DBSetup will create the tables, views, stored procedures, and it can also copy Internet reference data and imported data if you so choose. When you click Update Destination Database and DBSetup finishes running, you will be all set to analyze your first site.

When the database has been set up, you see confirmation box. Click OK, and setup is complete.

Using Usage Analyst

When that you have Usage Analyst installed, you need IIS logs to analyze. If you have a Web site that you want to analyze, you can import the logs to be analyzed. You have a choice of many file formats, so if you have any Web servers that are not running IIS, chances are that you can import these logs and analyze them. Also, if you are logging to a database instead of log files, you can import the information right out of the database.

If you have a busy Web site, however, logging to a database takes extra time and resources. Therefore, you should enable logging to log files and then import these log files into your database. Because you can import your log files into a SQL database anyway, you do not gain much advantage in logging to a database instead of log files.

Running Usage Analyst for the First Time

To run the Usage Analyst, follow these steps:

1. The first thing that you need to do is run the Import Module. From the Start menu, choose Programs, Microsoft Usage Analyst, and Import Module SQL Server. You are asked to connect to the database in the same manner that you did when you set up your database. Fill in all the information and then click Connect to Database (see Figure 8.18).

2. When you open Usage Analyst for the first time, you are told that no Internet site is configured in the database (see Figure 8.19). The Server Manager opens automatically. If the Server Manager does not open automatically, open it by choosing Server Manager from the File menu.

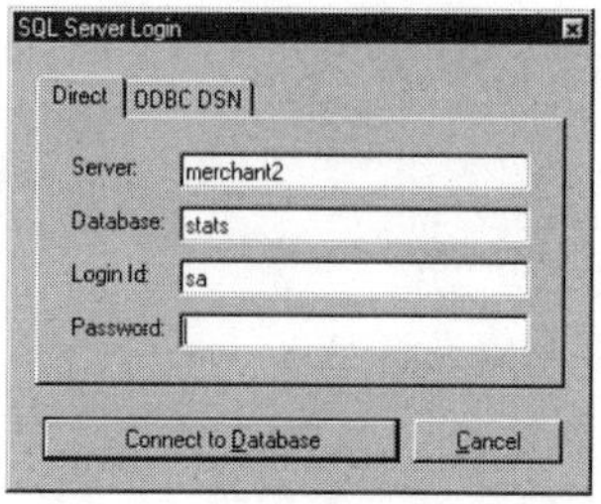

FIG. 8.18

You need to fill out the information to connect to the database in the SQL Server Login dialog box.

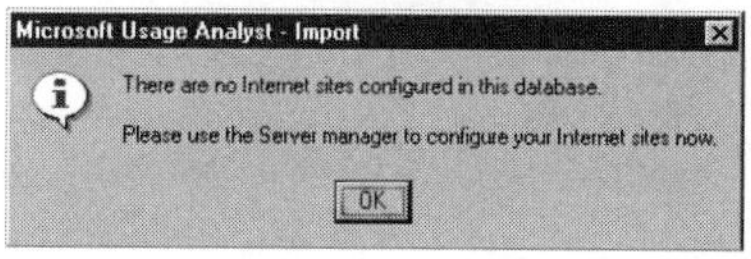

FIG. 8.19

When you open Usage Analyst for the first time, you are told that you need to go to Server Manager to configure your Internet sites.

3. You are asked for the type of log file that you want to import. For this example, use IIS standard log format. Most of the common file formats are listed in the Log Data Source Properties dialog box. Click OK to continue (see Figure 8.20).

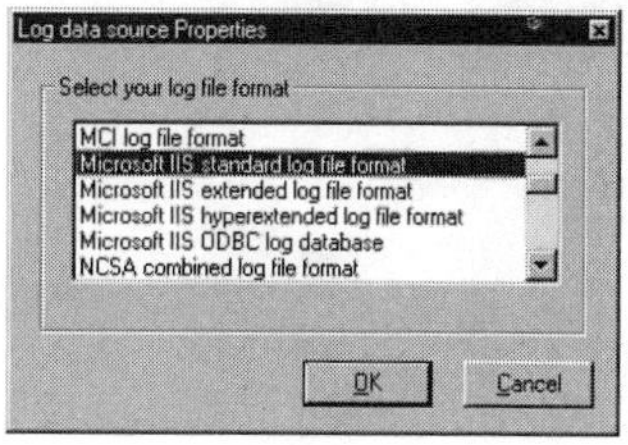

FIG. 8.20

The Log Data Source Properties dialog box allows you to choose the file format of the logs that are going to be analyzed. Usage Analyst supports almost all of the more popular Web server formats.

Configuring Usage Analyst Properties

The next dialog box that appears is Server properties. You need to specify what type of server you are using (WWW, FTP, or Gopher). At this time, Usage Analyst does not support other types of servers, such as the Microsoft NNTP Server that comes with Microsoft Commercial Internet Server (MCIS).

Specify the directory index files. By default, Usage Analyst uses index.html and home.html. IIS uses default.htm as the default file name. If you have multiple-homed servers, you need to input the IP address in the IP Address (Optional) text box. The last things that you need to input are the local time zone and the local domain name (see Figure 8.21). When you finish, click OK; you go to the Site Properties dialog box.

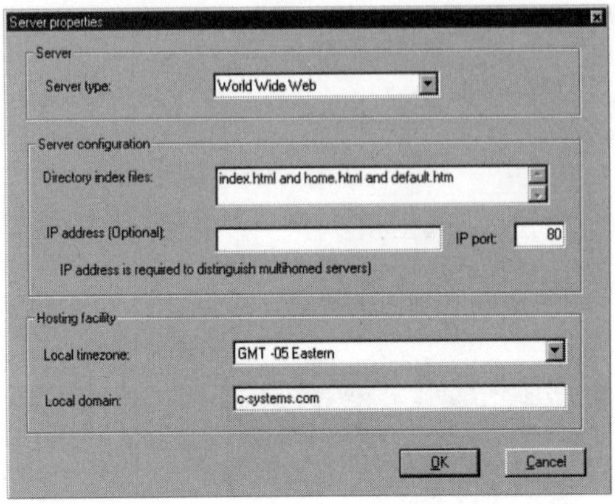

FIG. 8.21

In Server Properties, you need to configure the Server Type, specify the default documents in your Web site, the local time zone and the local domain name.

The Site Properties dialog box allows you to customize how the reports print. In the Basic tab, you need to input the site URL. Optionally, you can input the server file-system path for this site. If you are going to input more than one entry in each of these text boxes, separate the entries with the word *and* (see Figure 8.22). When you finish, click the Excludes tab.

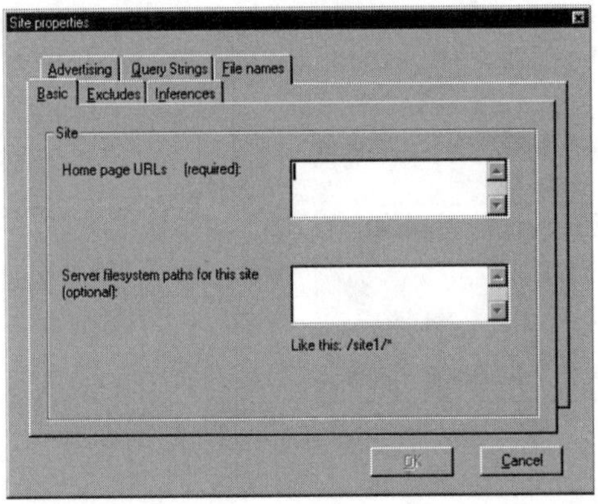

FIG. 8.22

The Basic tab in the Site Properties dialog box.

So that your stats can be as accurate as possible, you have the opportunity to exclude internal hosts and inline images. Again, you can separate the items by using the word *and* (see Figure 8.23).

The next tab is the Inferences tab. This tab has three options. If you are using referrals on your Web page and a referral is missing, you can insert it into your click stream. If someone is visiting your Web page and remains idle, you can configure Usage Analyst so that if the user is idle for a certain amount of time, the visit is ended.

The last thing that you can configure is whether multiple users are allowed to use the same user name. If your Web site authenticates users before allowing them access, decide whether to use this option. Suppose that you require unregistered users to log in by using the account guest. In this case, multiple users use the same user name (see Figure 8.24).

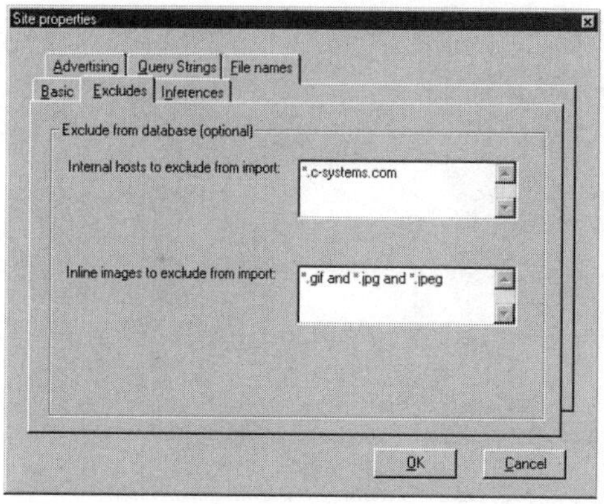

FIG. 8.23

The Excludes tab in the Site Properties dialog box.

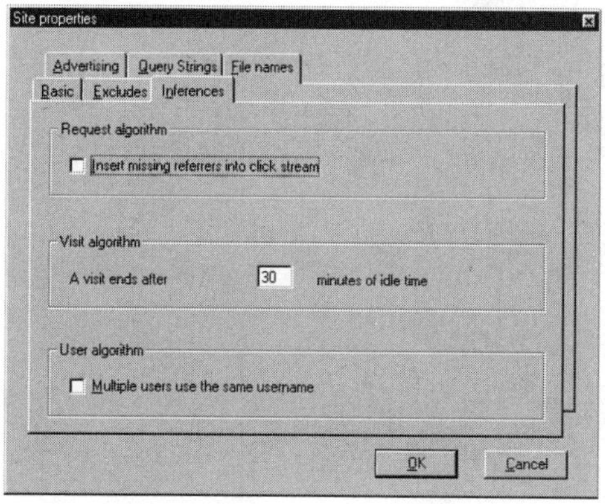

FIG. 8.24

The Inferences tab in the Site Properties dialog box.

The next section is Advertising. In this section, you tell Usage Analyst the paths of all your ads. The first box is Ad View. Suppose that people pay you to advertise their Web sites or product on your Web site. When people visit your Web pages, you have an ad at the top that is either different every time it is visited or rotates through several ads at a given interval. These ads are most likely stored in a separate directory. Usage Analyst can compute which ads are being shown and how often.

If your ads redirect users to another Web site, chances are that some type of script does the redirection, so you track who is going to your advertisers' sites from your Web site. If you enter the path where these scripts are located, Usage Analyst can also give you information about how many customers were redirected to customer sites and to which sites customers were redirected (see Figure 8.25).

The next tab is Query Strings (see Figure 8.26). A file name requested from a Web server has several components. Consider a request for /cgi-bin/getquote?symbols=hp+microsoft&display=table&alpha=beta#top:1000. In this example, /cgi-bin/getquote is the URL, "symbols=interse+hp&display=table&alpha=beta is the query string, #top is a fragment, and :1000 is a parameter.

FIG. 8.25

The Advertising tab.

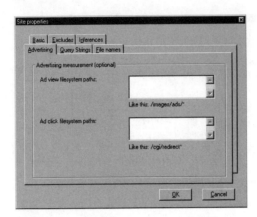

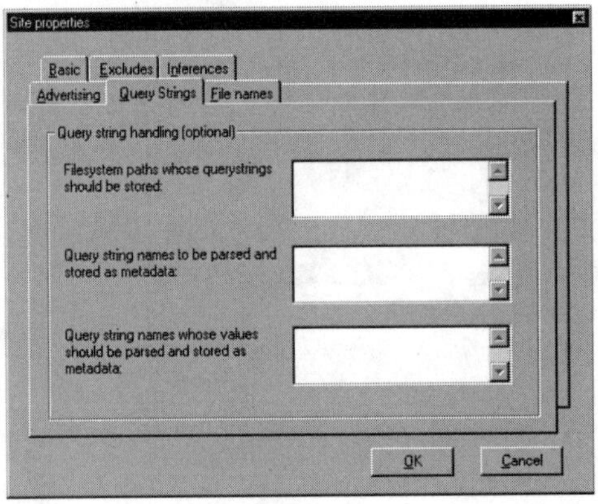

FIG. 8.26

The Query Strings tab.

During import, Usage Analyst removes all fragments and parameters from file names. The program also separates query strings from file names and can store them in the database for the individual requests to your sites, so that you can analyze the requests, visits, and users according to a particular query string. To take advantage of this feature, you must format your query strings in name–value pairs.

You need to specify which query strings to retain by indicating their file path. Typically, you are interested in the information from only a subset of all your file names with associated query strings. If all the CGI scripts that you are interested in parsing are stored in /cgi/ this_is_a_test/, you would type **/cgi/this_is_a_test/*** in the filesystem paths whose query strings should be stored text box. Separate multiple paths with the word *and*. The standard wild-card operators also apply. (Type **/*** to store all query strings, for example.)

Parsing query strings provides an efficient way of incorporating information that you can use in the Metadata module. You can use query-string names to set up metadata dimensions for use in analysis. In the preceding query string, the name display becomes a metadata dimension, and table and graph are its values.

If your query string has a name–value pair that you want to parse and store, specify that name in the query-string names to be parsed and stored as metadata text box. In this example, you type **display**. If you have multiple query-string names, you type **display** and another name.

In the example query string earlier in this chapter, symbols is a multiple-select question. You need to treat this query-string name differently from the string display, because you need to parse the values within the name–value pair to have both hp and Microsoft entered in the database as values for symbols instead of the single value hp Microsoft. For query-string names like these, specify the query-string name whose values should be parsed (in this case, symbols).

The distinction between parsing query-string names and parsing their values is important. In writing a query string, HTTP converts any space to a plus sign (+). The distinction between these two entry boxes in the Import module is essentially how to treat this plus sign. For an HTML fill-in form that accepts a first and last name, the string might include an element "form=John+Smith". If "form" is entered as the query-string name to be parsed, the database shows "John Smith" under "form". (Usage Analyst restores plus signs to spaces.) If "form" is entered as a query-string name whose value should be parsed, the database will show two entries under "form": "John" and "Smith". In general, Usage Analyst expects multiple-value selections to be separated by a plus sign, which is common on most Web sites today.

The last tab in the Site Properties dialog box is the File Names tab (see Figure 8.27). If your Web page is hosted by an ISP and you do not have a domain name, your URL may look like **http://www.c-systems.com/marc/index.html**. Usage Analyst can delete the first-level directory so that you see only the files and directories that pertain to your site. If you want to take advantage of this feature, check Truncate Top Level Directory from Filesystem Paths.

Sometimes, your paths are not exactly the way that you want them to look in the database. Usage Analyst provides a search-and-replace tool for you. To use this tool, you need to do two things. The first thing that you need to do is specify the paths that you want to apply the search and replace to. If you want to change cards to videocards, you put **/cards/*** in the first box. Next, you need to type the search and replace in the second box. To change /cards to / videocards, you type **"s/\/cards/\/videocards"** in the second box.

You can also apply this to multiple expressions by using the word *and* to separate expressions. The backslash (\) is an escape character for this command, which allows the next forward slash (/) to be interpreted as the directory hierarchy divider rather than the regular expression's own separator character. The backslash is required for including any regular expression's special characters within a string for search and replace. Without the backslash, the special characters have their own representation. You can find these expressions by going to file://C:\Program Files\Usage Analyst\Docs\Webdocs\UAN00019.HTM in your Web browser.

FIG. 8.27

The File Names tab.

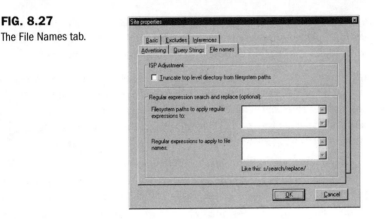

Configuring Usage Analyst Options

When you complete the initial configuration of the Server Manager, you see a window that displays both the Server Manager and the Log File Manager. You also see a tree in Server Manager showing that you have made a successful configuration (see Figure 8.28).

FIG. 8.28

The Log File Manager window.

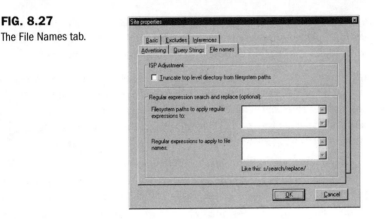

You are ready to move on to the second step of configuration. To continue configuration, choose Options from the Tools menu.

The Import Tab   The first tab in the Import Options dialog box is the Import tab (see Figure 8.29). In the Import tab, you have the following options:

- **Drop Database Indexes**. Analysis requires database indexes, but if the database has indexes, the import is much slower. Therefore, by default, import drops all database indexes and analysis adds them before starting. When you have accumulated a large amount of use data within the database, you want to turn this option off. Adding indexes to the large database takes longer than the incremental time required for import, because each import represents only a small percentage of the data in the database.

■ **Adjust Requests Timestamps To**. If you have sites that are in multiple time zones, and you want to view dates and times in the same time zone, you can turn on this option. All your log files are adjusted to show the same time zone.

■ **Exclude Spiders**. Choosing this option prevents counting hits from search engines, robots, and other agents that you specify in the Spider List tab. This option is also the only way to exclude user agents.

■ **Lookup Unknown HTML File Titles**. When you enable this option, the Import module performs HTML title lookups on new HTML files added to the database during the log-file import. You can perform the same operation manually from the Tools menu.

■ **Resolve IP Addresses**. If you choose this option, the Import module tries to resolve (do an nslookup on) all IP addresses that it encounters in the log file. Resolving all IP addresses could take several hours on a long log file. If you get multiple hits from the same IP address, however, Usage Analyst keeps this information cached, and this helps it go much quicker.

■ **Whois Query for Unknown Domains**. When you choose this option, Usage Analyst does a whois on all domains. To get the domains, however, you need to have Resolve IP Addresses checked. The great thing about Usage Analyst is that it figures out where a domain name is registered and does a whois from that issuing authority. In other words, if Usage Analyst encounters a .com or .net address, it knows to use host rs.internic.net; if you get a .de, it knows the correct host to resolve the domain name. Again, this option takes a long time, most likely even longer than resolving IP addresses. When you resolve IP addresses, you are using your own DNS server, which makes things go somewhat faster. When you do whois queries, you need to use the machine provided by issuing authorities, and if one of these machines is slow or a network backup occurs, things are delayed.

FIG. 8.29
The Import tab.

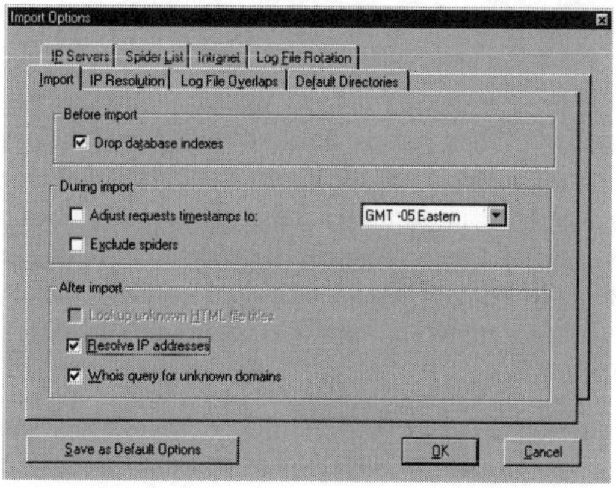

Import Options

| IP Servers | Spider List | Intranet | Log File Rotation |
| Import | IP Resolution | Log File Overlaps | Default Directories |

Before import
☑ Drop database indexes

During import
☐ Adjust requests timestamps to: GMT -05 Eastern ▼
☐ Exclude spiders

After import
☐ Lookup unknown HTML file titles
☑ Resolve IP addresses
☑ Whois query for unknown domains

Save as Default Options   OK   Cancel

N O T E   You need to turn on Resolve IP Addresses and Whois Query for Unknown Domains if you
are going to be doing any detailed reports. Without this information, you cannot get
geographical data for your reports. ▉

The IP Resolution Tab   When you finish setting options in the Import tab, go to the IP Resolution tab (see Figure 8.30). Resolving several thousand IP addresses can take a long time. For
this reason, Usage Analyst can cache this information for you for a given time. When an IP
address has been set, system administrators rarely change the name of the IP address, so if
you cache IP resolutions for 30 days (the default), your information should be accurate.

Sometimes, for whatever reason, system administrators don't assign names to IP addresses. If
users are not behind a firewall, it is more secure not to assign an IP address to keep users
anonymous. For this reason, you can time out a resolution attempt after a given amount of
time. If your name server cannot resolve an IP address after 60 seconds, chances are that it
cannot resolve the address.

The last option is Use a Resolution Batch Size of. You can use this option to resolve a certain
number of IP addresses at the same time. The more addresses that your DNS server is capable
of resolving at the same time, the faster the analysis goes.

FIG. 8.30

The IP Resolution text
box.

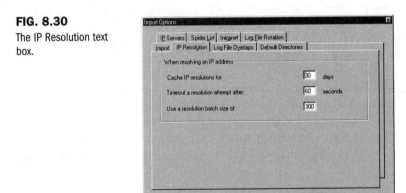

The Log File Overlaps Tab   When you are finished configuring the options in the IP Resolution tab, click the Log File Overlaps tab (see Figure 8.31). Having time periods overlap in your
log files introduces inaccuracies into your database. Several scenarios can produce time overlaps in log-file entries: running logs on separate servers, interrupting and resuming logging on
a single server, accidentally re-importing an individual log file, or concatenating distinct log
files. The Log File Overlaps window allows you to specify how to treat such redundancies. You
can choose several options.

The first thing that you need to decide is the number of minutes for which records must overlap for an overlap to occur. Shorter periods reduce apparent overlap but may affect accuracy of
later analysis for the period in question.

If an overlap is detected, you can do any of four things:

- **Import all records**. The default is to ignore the overlap. This option includes all redundancies in the database.
- **Stop the import**. Stop the import halts the import for the log file(s) in question and continues any other imports that have already started or that are set to go.
- **Stop all imports**. Stop all imports halts the current import of all log files.
- **Discard records and proceed**. Discard records and proceed discards the overlapping records and proceeds.

N O T E   Concatenation of log files makes tracking of overlap extremely difficult and is not recommended. ▪

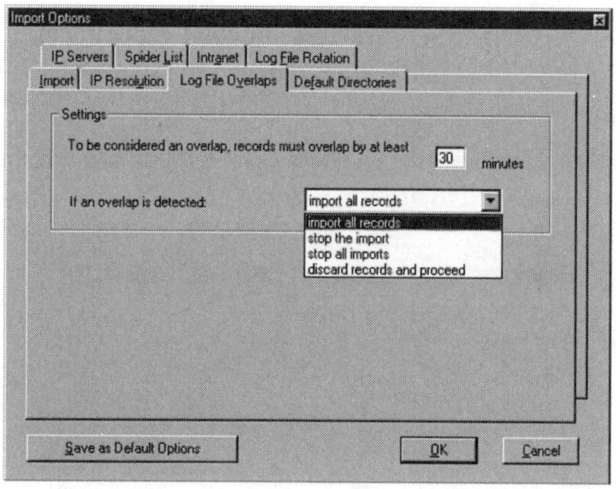

FIG. 8.31

Add a 1- or 2-sentence caption here.

The Default Directories Tab   The next tab is the Default Directories tab. The default directory is the directory that you installed Usage Analyst in. Your log files most likely do not reside there and may not even be on the same machine that you installed Usage Analyst on. You can tell Usage Analyst where you want to look for your log files. The Log files text box sets the default directory when you click Browse when you perform an import. This directory can be either a drive and a path on the local machine or a drive and a path on any machine in your network (see Figure 8.32).

The IP Servers Tab   In the IP Servers tab, you can set the following options (see Figure 8.33):

- **HTTP Proxy**. If you specify a proxy server host name and port, the Import module uses this address for all HTML title lookups.

N O T E   If your proxy requires a user name and password, specify the proxy host name as `username:password@proxyserver`. ▪

FIG. 8.32

The Default Directories tab.

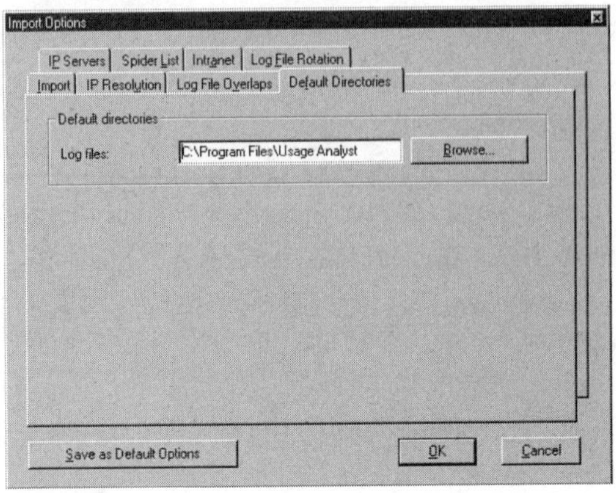

- **SMTP Server**. Usage Analyst needs to send you e-mail on certain events. Because Usage Analyst is not a sendmail server, it needs the name of an SMTP server that it can relay mail through.

- **Local Domain of DNS Server**. Use this option if you are not maintaining your own DNS server or do not want to use the domain name of the DNS server.

FIG. 8.33

The IP Servers tab.

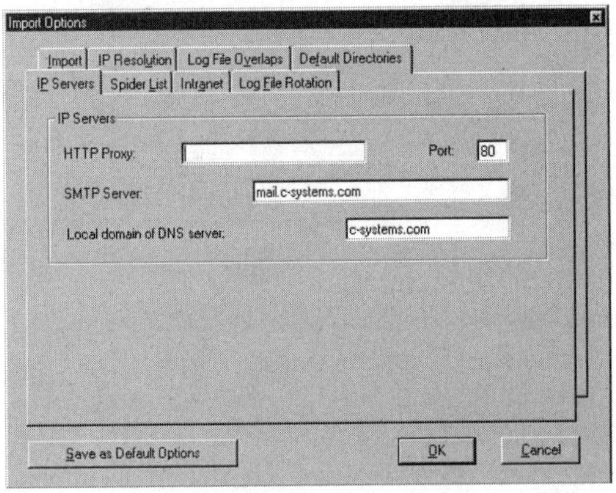

The Spider List Tab   When you finish configuring your IP servers, move to the Spider List tab, where you enter the name of the Spider user agent strings—the names of any search engines or user agents that you do not want to include in your reports. By excluding these agents, you get more accurate reports of actual interactive activity on your site, as opposed to interactive and robot activity on your site.

Most of the popular search engines are listed in this tab. You can add Yahoo and altavista.digital.com, two popular search engines that were not included by default. You can use wild cards in your list, and all fields are separated by the word *and* (see Figure 8.34).

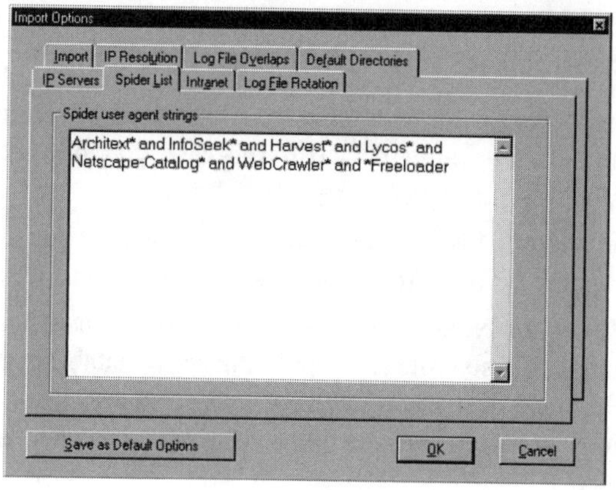

FIG. 8.34
The Spider List tab.

The Intranet Tab   The next-to-last tab is Intranet (see Figure 8.35). If you make the Intranet setting one domain part beyond the organization, you have three-part, two-dotted organization names. Two levels beyond, and Import defines organizations with four-part names in the database.

What this means is that your domain name is something like c-systems.com, which is your Intranet organization. If you have a large Intranet, you may want to give different offices subdomain names. You can have boston.c-systems.com, chicago.c-systems.com, and so on. In such a case, boston is one domain part beyond the Internet organization. If you have a Boston office, all your workstations have names that are a subset of boston.c-systems.com. You may have ws1.boston.c-systems.com, ws2.boston.c-systems.com, and so on. This would be two domain parts beyond the Internet organization.

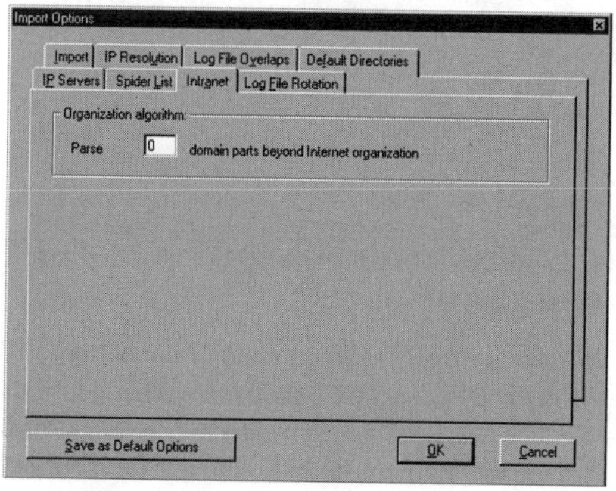

FIG. 8.35
The Intranet tab.

The Log File Rotation Tab   The last tab is Log File Rotation (see Figure 8.36). Because log-file rotation requires an arbitrary cutoff of data produced at your sites, some visits will inevitably be interrupted. For these visits, information is divided between the end of one log file and the beginning of the next. The Import module gives you several options for handling this situation:

- **Commit Open Visits to the Database** (the default). If you commit open visits to the database, these visits are counted twice. In this case, you may get an exaggeration in your statistics, because these visits are counted twice.

- **Discard Open Visits**. This option drops the open visits. If you choose this option, you do not get an accurate report. Your statistics are underreported.

- **Store Open Visits for Next Import**. This option is the most accurate way of handling the log-file rotation. These visits are kept in the active database, and you get the results of these visits the next time you rotate your logs. This option takes more time than the other two options, however, because these visits must be called up from the cache at each new import.

- **Clear Open Visits Cache**. You cannot see this option in Figure 8.36, because it is a button hiding behind the At the End of an Import menu. This option clears all the open visits so that you can start fresh for your next import.

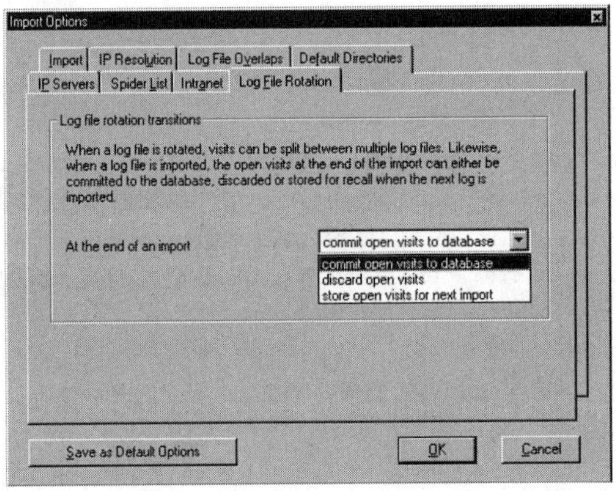

FIG. 8.36

The Log File Rotation tab.

Importing Your First Log

You should be all set to import your first log. To import your first log, open the Log File Manager, and follow these steps:

1. Choose Log File Manager from the File menu. At the bottom of the screen, you see a window for New import (see Figure 8.37). You need to choose the log location and browse for the file. For Log Location, you can choose ODBC or file. For this example, use a file, which is the recommended method to use for a busy Web site. Click Browse and go to your IIS logs directory. Choose the log that you want to import. When you are ready to begin, click the red arrow button at the top of the screen.

If you have a large log file to import, now is a good time to go get a cup of coffee or take a break. The example log file is only 175K so it will be imported pretty quickly. When the import has finished, there will be a confirmation box that tells how long the import took and an Import Statistics box that gives useful information.

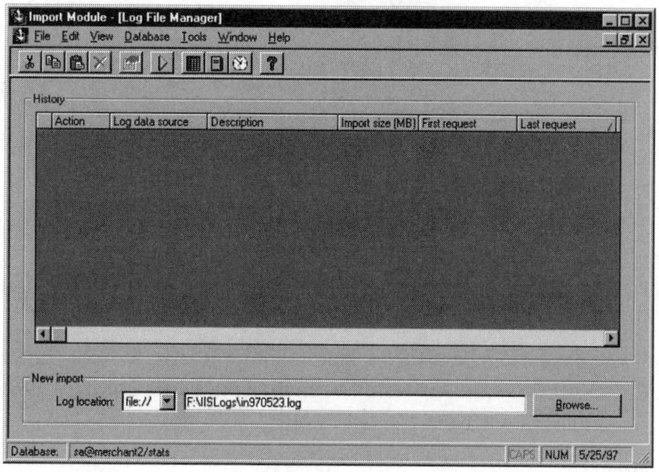

Part
II

Ch
8

FIG. 8.37

The Import Module –
(Log File Manager).

2. After you import the log file into the database, you can exit the Import module and open the Analysis module (see Figure 8.38). Again, you are asked to connect to the database. When you connect to the database, you are asked what type of report you want to use. You can use one of several reports that are provided for you, or you can use a report that you program yourself.

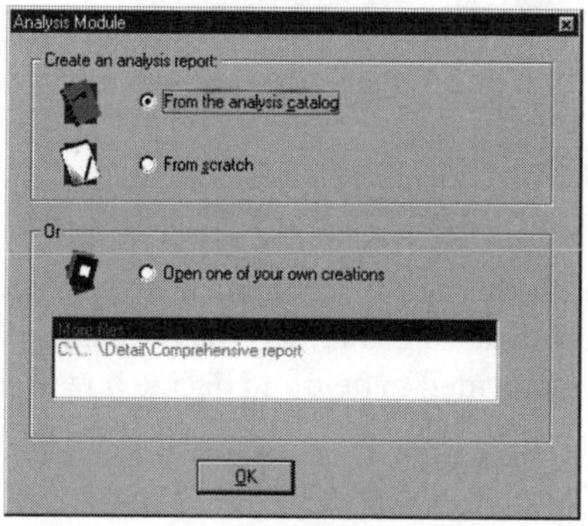

FIG. 8.38

In the Analysis Module dialog box, you can choose to either create an analysis report from the analysis catalog or from scratch. You can also choose to open up an analysis report that you have created.

3. This example discusses only at the comprehensive report, which gives you as much information as you could ever want. When you become more familiar with this program, you can look at the other reports to see whether a report with less information meets your needs better than the comprehensive report does. You can find the comprehensive report under Detail Reports as seen in Figure 8.39. Choose the type of report to use and then click Next.

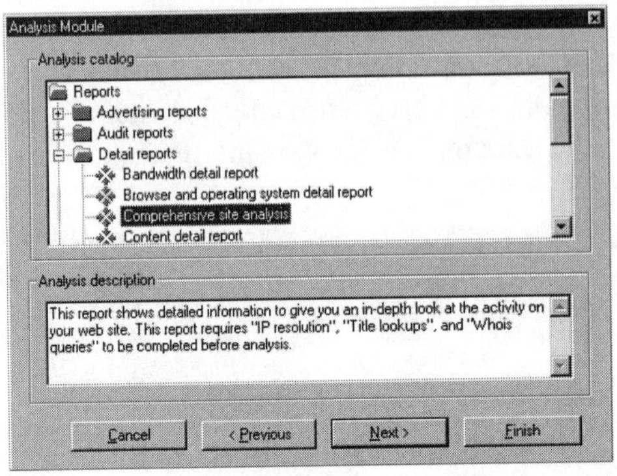

FIG. 8.39

In the Analysis Module dialog box in the Analysis Catalog window, you see a list of different types of reports that you can use for your analysis.

N O T E For the example in this chapter, you will only use the Comprehensive site analysis report. You will find just about any information that you can think of if you use this report.

4. If you have a database that spans several weeks or month, you can choose to analyze the entire database or a specific range of days (see Figure 8.40). After you make your selection, choose Next.

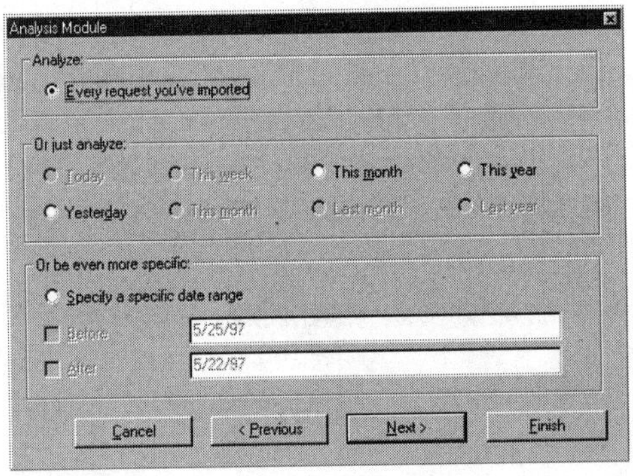

FIG. 8.40

In this dialog box, you can choose what days you are going to analyze from the log file(s) that you have just imported.

5. The next screen allows you to filter any information from your analysis. You can include or exclude any portion of the data from analysis. You have many options to choose among. Three examples are provided to help you decide how you want to use this option (see Figure 8.41):

- In the Filter Name Reference list box, you can choose what type of information that you are going to filter.

- The Examples window gives three examples of how to filter.

- Once you have decided what information, if any, you are going to filter, you need to type it in the Filter text box.

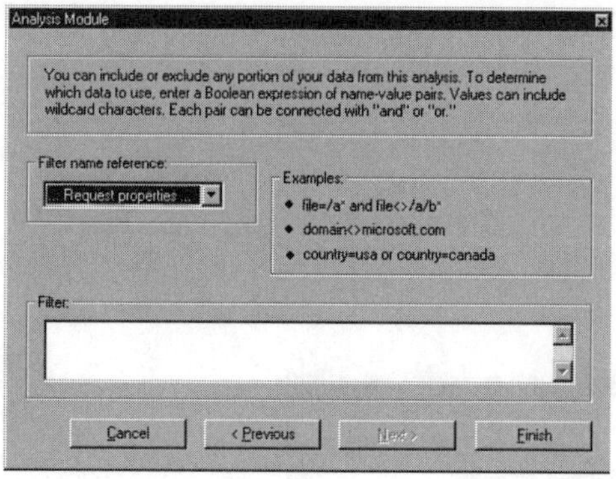

FIG. 8.41

In this dialog box, you can include or exclude any information from the analysis.

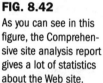

When you click Finish, Usage Analyst builds a comprehensive report that will look something like Figure 8.42. The next step is to save the report. Choose Save from the File menu and name your report. After the report has been saved, you can analyze it. When you are ready to create the analysis report, click the red arrow.

FIG. 8.42

As you can see in this figure, the Comprehensive site analysis report gives a lot of statistics about the Web site.

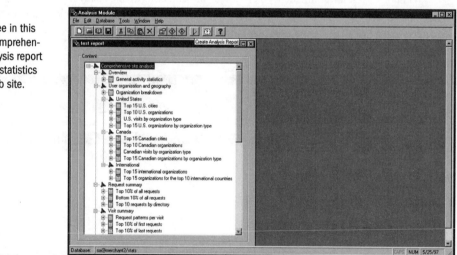

When you start the analysis report, you are asked to name the report and the file format that you want to use (see Figure 8.43). The easiest report to use is an HTML report, but you can also save it as an Excel or Word document. After you name the document and decide the format, click OK, and Usage Analyst starts performing the analysis.

You see a status report while Usage Analyst analyzes the data. Figure 8.44 shows the Analysis statistics dialog box. This process may take some time.

FIG. 8.43

The Report Document dialog box allows you to choose the file name of the completed report and the format in which you would like the output.

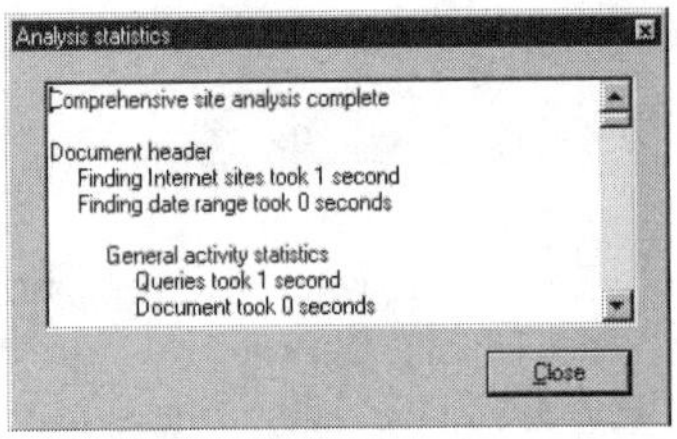

FIG. 8.44

The Analysis Statistics dialog box shows how long each step of the analysis took.

When Usage Analyst finishes, you receive confirmation. Usage Analyst also opens your Web browser and shows you the report (see Figure 8.45). The report is very long and detailed. Since this report is so long, there are links at the top of the report that will take you to the different analysis reports on this report page.

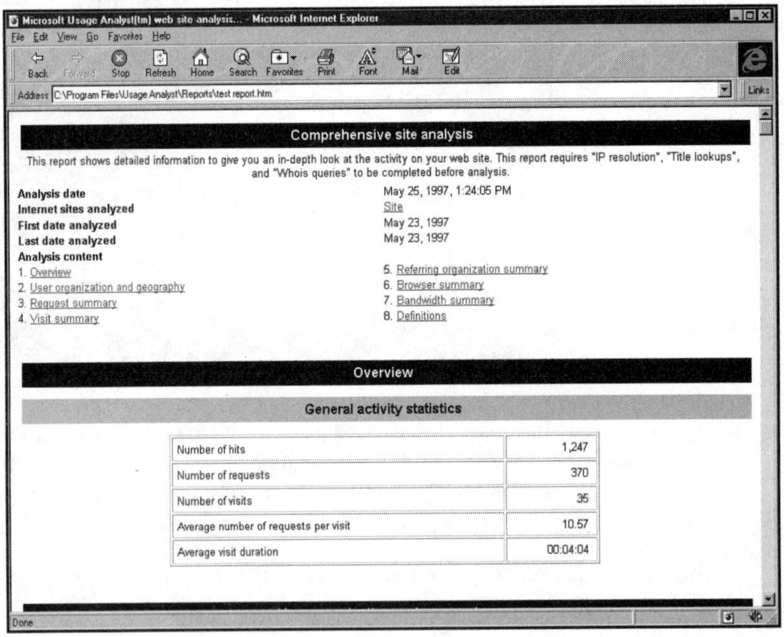

FIG. 8.45

As soon as Usage Analyst has finished analyzing the Web site, it will open the default browser.

You see several pages of reports. At this point, you have enough information to begin using Usage Analyst to look at your production data and to start customizing your own reports. As you go on, this tool will be one that you will never want to live without.

Microsoft Usage Analyst is a way for Webmasters to be able to perform very detailed tracking on their Web sites. A raw log file has the basis for some very detailed reports but this process can be very time-consuming. When you first see the log files, you see several IP addresses, paths, and a bunch of other numbers separated by commas. A program such as Usage Analyst will take the log files and analyze all of the IP addresses. When you see the report, you will not see an IP address, you will instead see a host name, a domain name, a city and state for the domain name so that you will know exactly where geographically people are coming from, and other pertinent information. ●

CHAPTER 9

Using the Microsoft Posting Acceptor and the Web Publishing Wizard

The tools that are provided are Microsoft Web Publishing Wizard and Microsoft Posting Acceptor. Both products are provided with Microsoft Site Server as a convenience. These tools were still in beta when Microsoft released Microsoft Site Server to manufacturing, so you need to check periodically to find out when these tools are going to be officially released. You can get the latest versions of these products from **http://www.microsoft.com/ windows/software/webpost**.

To install these products, you simply choose install from master setup or download the files and double-click them. When you double-click the files and agree to the license agreement, Microsoft Web Publishing Wizard and Microsoft Posting Acceptor are automatically installed for you. You have no options to choose, and both products are installed in your Windows directory, so you do not need to choose the default directory.

An overview of Web Publishing Wizard and Microsoft Posting Acceptor

Understand what Microsoft Web Publishing Wizard and Microsoft Posting Acceptor can do for you and how these tools can help you. With Publishing Wizard, users can very easily upload the entire web site. With Posting Acceptor, your web developers can program an interface that will allow your users to send updates to their web pages via HTTP.

Installing Web Publishing Wizard and Posting Acceptor

Installing these programs is very easy; there is basically nothing that you need to configure. You simply click the setup programs and everything else is automatic.

Going over how to use Web Publishing Wizard and Posting Acceptor

We will go over how to use these programs. With Posting Acceptor, there is some programming that you must do in order for Posting Acceptor to work. The final chapter on the installation section goes over the two web publishing tools that Microsoft has provided for us as a part of Microsoft Site Server. The tools provided are Microsoft Web Publishing Wizard and Microsoft Posting Acceptor.

N O T E   If you are used to publishing your web pages using Microsoft FrontPage, you will not be able to use this tool when developing a Microsoft Commerce Server Site. Microsoft FrontPage will not work properly with ASP and the calls that Commerce Server uses. ■

CAUTION

When you install Web Publishing Wizard, if you get an error message saying that setup cannot register the DLL, you may have an older version installed. You need to uninstall the older version and reboot. If you still get this error, you need to uninstall Web Publishing Wizard 1.5 (go to Add/Remove programs in Control Panel). After you uninstall, you need to go to regedit and search for webpost. Delete anything that has a reference to these DLLs. Now you should be able to reinstall without a problem.

When you have these products installed, you need to reboot your machine (actually, you need to reboot only for Posting Acceptor). After you reboot, you should be all set to start using Publishing Wizard and Posting Acceptor. ■

Using Web Publishing Wizard

With Microsoft Web Publishing Wizard, you can upload your Web content quickly and easily. When Publishing Wizard installs, it creates a program group called Web Publishing Wizard. When you choose the program, you are asked a few simple questions. You are asked for the directory information of the files that you want to upload. Web Publishing Wizard uploads the directory, all files, and all subdirectories unless you choose not to include subdirectories.

Next, you choose the method that you want to upload. You can choose Automatic, Front Page Extended Web, HTTP Post, FTP, or Content Replication System. The next thing that you choose is the URL of your Web pages. You type the URL that you would use to view these pages with a Web browser even if you are using FTP.

If you are using automatic configuration, when you type your address, the files start to upload for you automatically. If you choose the server type manually, you are told if the server is not configured to accept the way that you are posting. If you choose anything except FTP, Web Publishing Wizard automatically finishes and uploads the files for you. If you choose FTP, you see a screen asking for your user name and directory name before you proceed. When you are ready, click Finish. If you need to log in, you see a dialog box asking you to enter your user name and password.

Using Posting Acceptor

With Microsoft Posting Acceptor, you can upload files to a Web server that is compliant with HTTP Post (RFC 1867). To use Microsoft Posting Acceptor, you need to configure it by using ASP pages. Posting Acceptor is not a simple program that you can install and expect to work out of the box; an ASP developer must do a great deal of customization.

Several modules come with Posting Acceptor. The mapping module is a self-registering server that creates the appropriate entry in the Posting Acceptor's mapping-modules registry during registration. You have the option to accept the default mapping module or create other modules to suit your needs.

A mapping module must be an in-process server that supports the IMapper interface, defined as follows:

```
const IID IID_IMapper = \
{0x66BE7351,0x83A0,0x11D0,{0xA3,0x17,0x00,0xC0,0x4F,0xD7,0xCF,0xC5}};
```

This interface supports one additional method besides the standard ones.

```
HRESULT STDMETHODCALLTYPE GetLocation(
/* in */ LPCTSTR szUrl, // Destination URL ("TargetURL"variable)
/* in */ LPCTSTR szUsername, // User uploading files
/* out */ LPSTR szDestination, // Physical disk location buffer
/* in */ DWORD dwDestinationLength); // Length of the buffer
```

For the acceptor, the length of the buffer is always MAX_PATH.

You can enable or disable a mapping module by setting its value in the registry to 1 (enable) or 0 (disable).

Using Content Replication System with Posting Acceptor

A mapping module for Content Replication System (CRS) is installed automatically when you install Posting Acceptor. If you have CRS installed on your system, you can use it to replicate content posted to your server or to other servers.

To use Posting Acceptor with CRS, set up an automatic project with a MapURL pointing to the content directory of your project. With the TargetURL being a superset of the MapURL, posted content is saved in the content directory via the CRS mapping module.

If the TargetURL is **http://www.yourserver.com/content/html**, the MapURL is **http://www.yourserver.com/content**.

Using CRS with Posting Acceptor   This section provides a detailed example of how to use CRS with Posting Acceptor. In the example, the Internet Service Provider (ISP) wants users to post files to an intermediate machine instead of posting directly to the live WWW servers. The ISP has a posted file dropped into a directory that is running an Automatic Mode CRS project. User posts are then replicated to the end WWW servers.

The intermediate system is called **tempserver.c-systems.com**, and the WWW server is called **www.c-systems.com**. All systems are running Windows NT Server 4.0 and IIS 3.0.

On **www.c-systems.com**, the ISP has configured the IIS virtual directory **/webusers maps to: d:\inetpub\webusers**.

On **tempserver.c-systems.com**, the content directory for dropping of files is e:\uploads.

User accounts on **tempserver.c-systems.com** must be in the CRS Users group.

CRS Setup   On **tempserver.c-systems.com**, create the following project:

```
crs addproj stage e:\uploads www.c-systems.com /automatic /fastmode /mapurl
http://www.c-systems.com
```

On **www.c-systems.com**, create the following project entry:

```
crs addproj stage d:\inetpub\wwwroot\webusers
```

On **tempserver.c-systems.com**, start the CRS project.

```
crs startrep stage
```

Posting Acceptor Setup and Configuration

This example assumes that the posting acceptor sample has been installed on the system.

On **www.c-systems.com**, add the following line to the default page of root:

```
<META name="postinfo" content http://tempserver.c-systems.com/scripts/
postinfo.asp>
```

On **tempserver.c-systems.com**, create a postinfo.asp file with this content:

```
<% Response.Buffer = True %>
Version=1.5
[WebPost.PostWPP]
PostingURL="http://<%= Request.ServerVariables("SERVER_NAME") %>/scripts/
➥cpshost.dll?PUBLISH"
BaseURL="http://<%= Request.ServerVariables("SERVER_NAME") %>/webusers/<%=
Request.ServerVariables("LOGON_USER") %>"
<Picture>Note
```

tempserver.c-systems.com turns off anonymous access so that the postinfo.asp file can determine LOGON_USER.

To keep the system from being overwhelmed by excessive amounts of content posts, for example, the results from a denial of service attack, Posting Acceptor has implemented limitations on two posting values. The limitations are placed on the total number of outstanding posts and on the maximum post duration, both of which are adjustable in the registry.

- MaximumOpenTransactions. This value controls maximum outstanding posts (default is 200 posts).
- OpenTransactionsTimeout. This value controls maximum outstanding post duration (default is 600 seconds, or 5 minutes).

To configure for outstanding posts, in a registry editor, open the registry key, HKLM\Software\ Microsoft\WebPost\Acceptors\CPSHost. Adjust the value limitations to suit your needs.

If you want to perform additional configuring after a post is received, Posting Acceptor can call a secondary (or post-processing) URL with all the form data except that of the posted files uploaded from the client. In place of the content is a list of locations and sizes of the files posted to the server. You can edit the PostInfo file if you want to specify a post-processing URL.

To specify a post-processing URL for WebPost API clients, modify the PostInfo file for WebPost.

To specify a post-processing URL for Netscape Navigator and other HTTP clients, modify the HTTP sample page (uploadN.asp) that contains the file upload from information.

You can make it easy for your users to upload their Web content. Getting your server configured to accept Web posts may look like a great deal of work but in the end, the work is well worth it. By allowing your users to post via HTTP, you will make things easier on them. The advantages are:

- You do not need to run an FTP server on your Web server. Every service that you run takes up precious CPU time, and running an FTP server only for posting is no longer necessary. Also, if users are logging onto an FTP server, they need to send their information through the Internet via clear text. If the information goes through an intranet, sending user information via clear text is not a problem, but if people are going through the Internet, someone using a packet sniffer can find out this information. If you send user names and passwords via HTTP by using Windows NT Challenge/Response, the user names and passwords are encrypted.

- If users are on the same network, they are authenticated with their current user names and passwords; therefore, they do not have to reenter this information when they post their information.

- Allowing updates via HTTP requires the system administrator to allow HTTP traffic through the firewall only if the Web server is on the other side of a corporate firewall.

From Here...

When you use Web Publishing Wizard, your users can send their Web content without even having to know what protocol they are using, because Web Publishing Wizard automatically tries to find this information and uses it to post the Web page. Also, Web Publishing Wizard reliably transfers your entire Web directory. If you are using FTP, unless you have a good FTP client, you need to transfer one file at a time, and some FTP clients do not handle directories well.

Understanding Dynamic Databases

CHAPTER 10

Understanding SQL Server Databases

Early WWW catalog sites were just a collection of HTML files that held the catalog's product hierarchy and a file for every product or family of products in the catalog. If you wanted to remove, add, or update a product, you had to manually edit those files, hacking your way through, trying to remember all the files that needed to be changed—a boring, error-prone task. Then one day someone decided to hook a Web site to a database and use a CGI to create the catalog pages, and there was no looking back. ∎

Understanding the Commerce Server database environment

Understand how robust database systems can make modern commerce sites more manageable.

Installing Microsoft SQL Server as a database system

Learn the steps to install the SQL Server product in your server.

Administrating the database

Learn about issues regarding creating data devices and databases for storing your application's data.

Planning databases for your applications

Understand some of the important issues in planning the requirements for a database system.

Optimizing relational database performance

Learn how to modify system parameters to optimize performance based on your system's requirements.

Understanding the Database Environment

Web sites have come a long way. User expectations for reliability and speed now demand true production-level software. A professional Web site can not get away with flat-file databases and homegrown query systems. High-traffic merchant sites, such as 1-800-FLOWERS (www.1800flowers.com), require systems with robust back-end databases, fully developed query tools, and dynamic content generators. With these tools in place, running a commerce site on the Internet becomes more a matter of managing inventory than of managing HTML pages. Microsoft Commerce Server provides these tools and more.

Commerce Server uses its database as more than a simple storage area for product information. Commerce Server also uses its database as a "blackboard" to store the user's current shopping information and shopping basket. Because this data is centralized, Commerce Server's processing can be spread over many Web servers, all coordinating their information via a single database. As the load on your first Web server increases, additional servers can be added and can be connected to the same database. All of this configuration is transparent to the user as he or she is interacting with the data in your database, not with any one Web server.

Figure 10.1 shows two examples of Commerce Server setups. The top example shows a single server running both Commerce Server and the database server. In this case, all the processing for the store is done on one machine. The user connects directly to the server running Commerce (or indirectly, if a firewall is in place).

The example on the bottom of Figure 10.1 shows a Web server farm running Commerce Server. The farm is constructed by placing a load-balancing or round-robin router in front. The user makes requests to this piece of hardware, which then forwards the request to a Web server running Commerce Server. Each of the Commerce Server machines uses a network connection to connect to the database server. This way, if a Commerce Server machine needs to be added or removed, the reconfiguration can be done without affecting the operation of the site.

The Database Connection

Commerce Server establishes its database connections using the Open Database Connectivity (ODBC) software package and drivers. ODBC is a standard and open method for connecting applications to a relational database system. Therefore, you can use any database system that has ODBC drivers for NT. You could store your data in a SQL Server database on the same machine as your Web site, for example, or you could connect to a DB2 database on a legacy IS system somewhere else on your network. In general, your store can be designed to access data no matter where it lives on your network.

To use ODBC to access the data in your database, you need to make sure that the proper drivers are installed for your database system on each computer system that needs to access the data. Microsoft Windows NT 4.0 comes with drivers for Microsoft SQL Server, dBASE (IV and 5), and Oracle v7. For other systems, contact your database vendor to get the correct ODBC drivers.

FIG. 10.1
Single and multiple
server configurations.

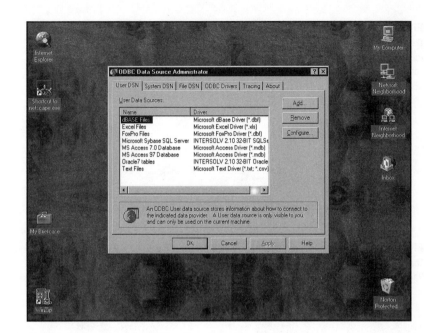

You need to repeat the following steps on every NT server or workstation that uses ODBC to connect to the database:

1. When the proper database drivers are installed, run the ODBC configuration utility from NT's control panel.

2. When the main appears, as shown in Figure 10.2, click the System Datasource Name (DSN) tab.

3. The DSN tab will bring up the dialog shown in Figure 10.3. Click the Add button to create a new System DSN entry for the database.

4. In the next screen, select the correct ODBC driver for the database. (See Figure 10.4.)

5. The next screen is unique for each ODBC driver; the one pictured in Figure 10.5 is for Microsoft SQL Server.

6. Enter a name for your DSN. By default, SQL Server's ODBC driver makes the DSN the same as the database name. To use another name, click the Options button and explicitly name a database to connect to.

7. Enter a description for the DSN. This step is optional but may help guide users when they see a list of DSNs at some later point.

8. Select the database server of the database. The drop-down list contains all available SQL Servers in your domain.

9. If your database administrator has informed you of any other special requirements for your database, click the Options button to specify advanced options for the ODBC connection.

Part
III

Ch
10

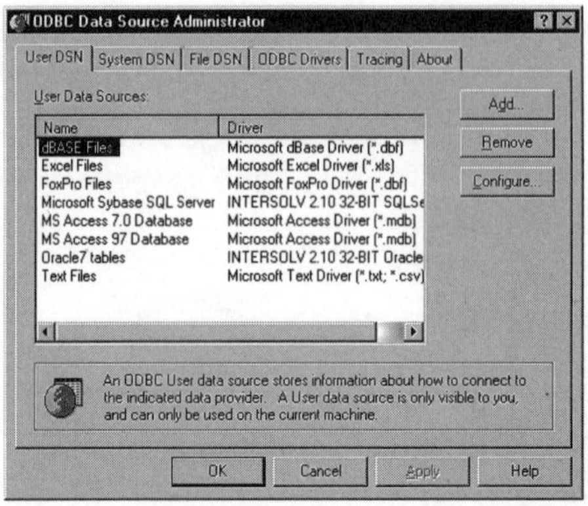

FIG. 10.2

The ODBC Control Panel's main dialog screen.

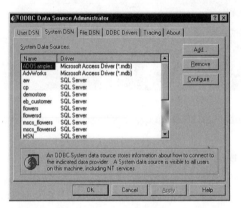

FIG. 10.3

The ODBC Control Panel's DSN screen.

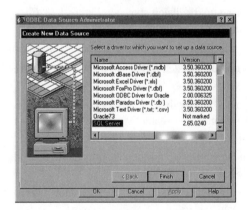

FIG. 10.4

The Create New Data Source screen.

10. Click the OK button when you finish.

When you complete these steps, a DSN representing this ODBC connection for your database is available. Repeat this task for all machines that need access to the database.

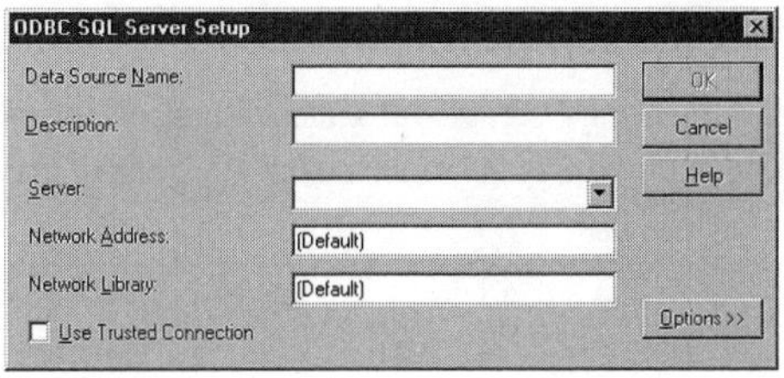

FIG. 10.5

SQL Server ODBC
Setup screen.

Data Language

ODBC drivers and ODBC-compliant databases use the ANSI Structured Query Language (SQL) for moving data to and from the database. SQL is the standard data-manipulation language used by all relational database systems. Books by the score have been written about SQL, which is a topic unto itself and beyond the scope of this book.

A simple SQL query looks like this:

```
SELECT lastname FROM authors WHERE firstname = "greg"
```

This query gets the values from the lastname field for all records in the database table authors where the firstname field matches the string "greg." As you can see by this example, simple SQL queries are easy and powerful. When you get used to writing SQL, you can write complex queries that connect data from multiple tables, order data by specific fields, and even (with SQL Server) perform string manipulations on-the-fly as part of the query.

Database Requirements

Although Commerce Server works with any ODBC-compliant database system, by far the most popular with Commerce Server sites is Microsoft's SQL Server. If you choose to use another DBMS, be sure that it can handle the transaction load that your commerce site generates. Desktop database systems such as Microsoft Access and Microsoft FoxPro work for test systems but are not sufficient for any real traffic on your Web site.

The examples in this chapter use Microsoft's SQL Server version 10.5 and its ODBC drivers. Because most of the examples are written with the standard ODBC interface and standard SQL, you should be able to apply them regardless of which database system you choose to use.

Tip from the Trenches

Unless you are trained in the care and feeding of relational database systems, if you will be acting as your own database designer and administrator, you want to get some good books or training on your database system. Databases are not kind; they are finicky beasts at best. A little knowledge ahead of time will definitely save you some sorrow in the long run.

You should know something about how relational databases work and the SQL language that's used to access the data. Small changes in either of these can affect the performance many fold. You also need to develop backup plans, recovery plans, and loading and reporting tools. Planning is the key to database success.

continues

Part

III

Ch

10

continued

Remember that after you go live, changing the database without experiencing hours, if not days, of downtime is difficult. And unless you have a good backup strategy, recovering from a database failure may be impossible.

Installing SQL Server

This portion of the chapter briefly covers how to install and configure Microsoft SQL Server version 10.5 and how to create a database for Commerce Server. If you are going to be using another database system, the specifics of the examples may not be useful, but the required tables, fields, and database schema (database definition) are the same.

Microsoft SQL Server can be purchased as a stand-alone unit or as part of the Microsoft BackOffice suite. For more information on Microsoft SQL Server, please contact an authorized reseller. The following sections summarize the requirements for SQL Server installation, starting with the requirements for Commerce Server, followed by the requirements for SQL Server itself.

N O T E SQL Server must be installed on the same NT server or another in the NT domain before Commerce Server is installed. Commerce Server wants to create and load databases for the starter stores as part of its installation, if SQL Server is not available, the Commerce Server installation fails. ▩

Commerce Server's Requirements for SQL Server

Version   Microsoft SQL Server version 10.5 with Service Pack 3 installed.

License   Commerce Server requires an unlimited user license for SQL Server.

SQL Server Hardware and Software Requirements

SQL Server requires a mid- to high-level NT server configuration to work well with Commerce Server. The following sections detail the minimum requirements to set up a basic SQL Server system. Later, the chapter gives you some hints about additional hardware that really makes SQL Server fly.

OS

- ▩ Windows NT 4.0 (NT Server, patch level 2 recommended)

CPU

- ▩ Intel 486 or better (Pentium Pro recommended)
- ▩ Alpha AXP
- ▩ MIPS
- ▩ Power PC

Memory

- 16M minimum (32M or more recommended)

Disk Space

- SQL Server Base System: 56M
- Master DB: 25M
- SQL Server Books Online: 15M
- Commerce Server Starter Stores: 30M

Other Requirements

- CD-ROM drive for installation

NOTE Microsoft recommends that you do not install SQL Server on a primary or backup domain controller (PDC or BDC). These machines usually are pretty busy maintaining security information and managing login information for an NT domain; therefore, they are not suitable as database servers. ■

Installing Basics

In a basic Commerce Server environment, you have two options where you can install SQL Server: You can install it with Commerce Server and IIS on your Web server, or you can install it on a separate machine in the same NT domain.

In the following installation example, SQL server will be installed on an Intel x86 system running NT Server 4.0. The system has 32M of RAM and 4G of disk space on 2 disks.

1. Before installing SQL Server, you will need to create an account for the SQL Server Executive. You can optionally use the local system account, but then SQL Server cannot interact with other servers on the network. If you will be using SQL Server's replication utilities to manage your data within an NT domain, you need to make this account a domain-level account.

2. To create an account for the SQL Server Executive, run the User Manager for Domains tool from the Start / Programs / Administration Tools menu of NT.

3. Choose New User from the User menu.

4. When the New User dialog appears, see Figure 10.6, enter at least a user name and password for the account. Make sure that the User Cannot Change Password and Password Never Expires boxes are checked. You need to be sure that the password for the account does not change or expire; if it does, SQL Server will not start until it is reconfigured to match the account information.

5. You will need to make this account part of the Domain Administrator's group. To do this, click the Groups button on the New User dialog. When the Account Group Membership dialog appears, as in Figure 10.7, select the Domain Admins group from the Not a member of list of groups and press the Add button. Now make this group the primary group for the account by selecting it in the Member of list and pressing the Set button.

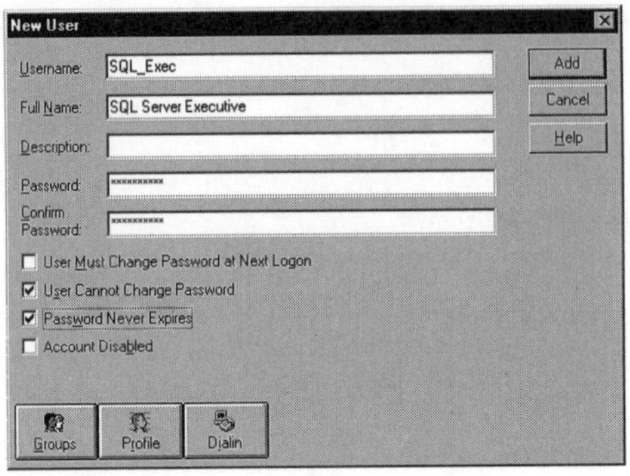

FIG. 10.6

The User Manager's Add New User dialog is used to add new accounts to an NT system or domain.

6. Click the OK button to leave the Group Memberships screen.

7. When you get back to the User Manager's Add New User dialog, click the Add button to add the new account. After the account is added, press the Close button to return to the User Manager screen.

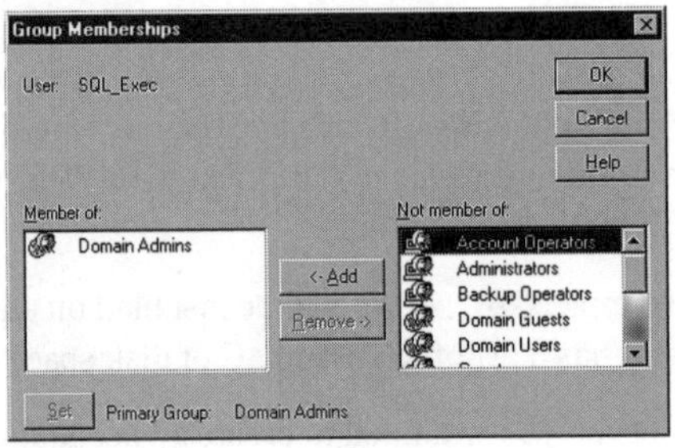

FIG. 10.7

The New User Account Group Membership is used to set the privileges for an account.

8. The SQL Server Executive account needs some additional privileges to perform SQL Server network tasks. To set up these privileges, select the account that you just created and then choose User Rights from the Policies menu.

9. Click the Advanced User Rights button to show all the available privileges. One at a time, add the following rights to the new account:

   - Increase quotas
   - Log on as a service
   - Act as part of the operating system
   - Replace a process-level token

10. Click OK to add each right. When you are done, exit the User Manager.

Now that the SQL Server executive account has been prepared, you can begin the installation of SQL Server 6.5. The following steps will guide you though an example installation session.

1. Insert the SQL Server 6.5 CD-ROM into your system's drive and open the \i386 directory.

2. Run setup.exe to start the installation program.

3. When the Welcome screen appears, as in figure 10.8, click the Continue button to begin the installation process.

FIG. 10.8

SQL Installation Welcome screen.

4. Register your installation by entering your name, company, and product ID code in the spaces provided (see Figure 10.9). Click the Continue button to move on.

FIG. 10.9

SQL Server's installation registration screen.

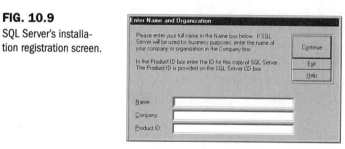

5. The installer will now display the information you have supplied, verify that you have entered the correct registration information (see Figure 10.10). If so, click the Continue button to move on. If you need to change any of the registration data, click the Change button to go back to the registration screen.

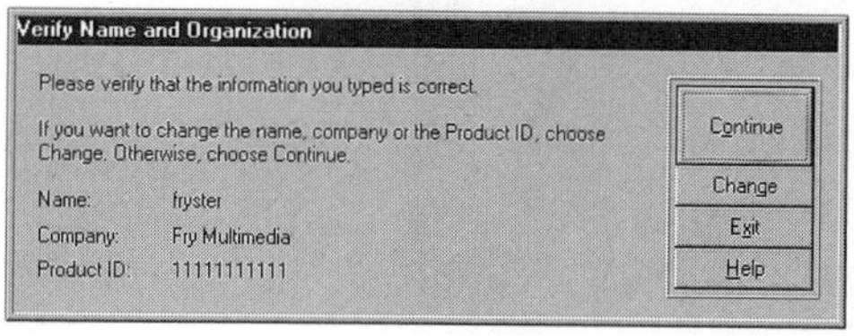

FIG. 10.10

SQL Server's installation registration verification screen is used to verify the that the information you entered is correct.

6. The next screen, shown in Figure 10.11, presents SQL Server's installation options. If you are installing for the first time, choose Install SQL Server and Utilities to install SQL Server. If you are upgrading from an earlier version, choose Upgrade SQL Server.

T I P   For remote administration of SQL Server, you can install just the administration utilities on another NT machine. Do this by running the installer and choosing Install Utilities Only at this point in the installation.

7. After you choose your option, click the Continue button to move to the next screen.

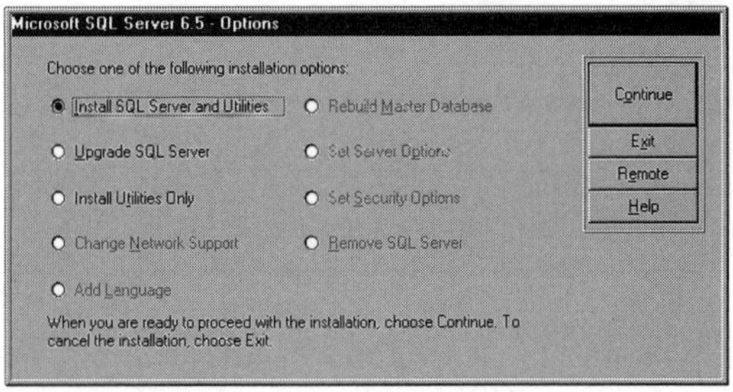

FIG. 10.11

Installation Options screen is used to configure the SQL Server installer's actions.

8. The next screen is the SQL Server Licensing Mode screen. This screen allows you to choose the licensing mode for SQL Server. The two modes are per Server and per Seat. For a Commerce Server installation, you want to use the per Server option. To use this option, you need an unlimited user license.

9. After you choose your option, click the Continue button to move to the next screen.

10. In the next screen, enter the license mode information for the version of SQL Server you have purchased.

11. After you enter the license information, click the OK button to move to the next screen.

12. The next screen, shown in Figure 10.12, prompts you to specify where to install SQL Server. The default directory is C:\MSSQL. After you select the installation area, click the Continue button to move to the next screen.

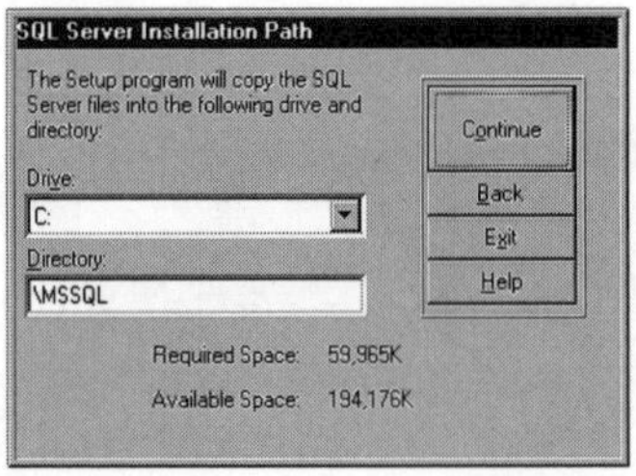

FIG. 10.12

The installer's installation path screen prompts you where to install the SQL Server software.

13. The next screen, seen in Figure 10.13, prompts you where to create the SQL Server's master database device and how large to make it. The default location is C:\MSSQL\DATA\MASTER.DAT and the default size is 25M.

14. The master database device contains two databases: the master database (master) and the temp database (tempdb). The master database contains configuration information about your SQL Server system. Keeping this database safe is important, because if it gets deleted or corrupted, SQL Server will not run. SQL Server uses the temp database as temporary storage while processing queries. This database can have a great deal of I/O during normal database operation.

     Because Commerce Server requires the Temp database to be larger than its installed 2M size, you should change the master database device's size to at least 30M.

15. After you set the proper values, click the Continue button to move to the next screen.

FIG. 10.13

The SQL Server installation program's master data device setup screen is used to specify the size and location of the master device.

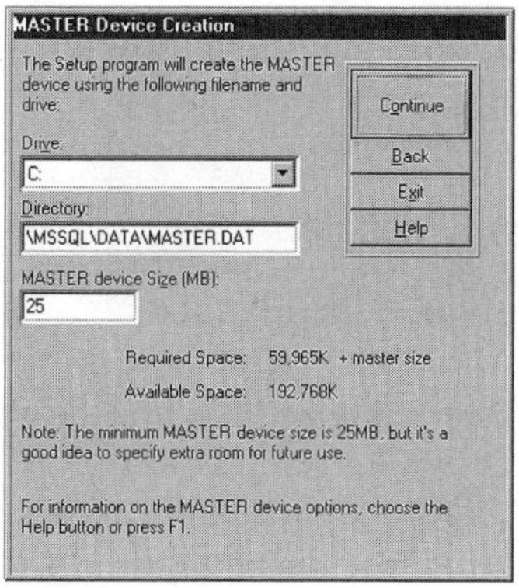

Part III

Ch 10

16. The next screen, shown in Figure 10.14, gives you the opportunity to install SQL Server's Books Online. You have three choices: Install these documents on the Hard Disk, Install to Run from the CD, and Do not Install.

TIP These books are an indispensable resource for programming and administrating SQL Server. A full text search is built into the environment, so you can look for any information in any or all of the SQL Server documentation with a simple click. You should find the space to install this feature.

17. After you choose your option, click the Continue button to move to the next screen.

18. Now you're in the final stretch of the installation. The next screen, shown in Figure 10.15, is used to set some of SQL Server's more miscellaneous settings. If you are working with foreign character sets or want to serve information to other servers, you need to specify that information on this screen.

19. Commerce Server requires that SQL Server start before it can start itself. Therefore, if you want your Commerce system to start automatically when NT reboots, you need to make sure that SQL Server autostarts, too. To make sure that SQL Server starts at system boot, make sure that the Auto Start SQL Server at Boot Time check box is checked.

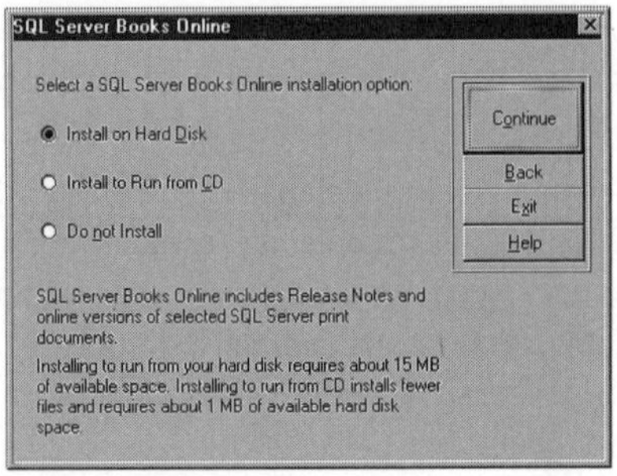

FIG. 10.14

Install SQL Server Books
Online screen.

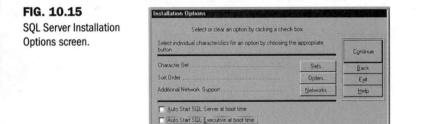

20. After you choose your options, click the Continue button to move to the next screen.

FIG. 10.15

SQL Server Installation
Options screen.

21. In the final installation screen, shown in Figure 10.16, you are prompted for the administrator user name and password for SQL Server. This account needs to have administration privileges on the server which you are installing. Otherwise, SQL Server may not have the capability to create or use all the resources it needs for normal operation (named pipes, network connections, and so on).

FIG. 10.16

Executive Account
Information screen.

22. After you enter this information, click the Continue button to complete the SQL Server installation.

SQL Server is now installed on your system, but you're not through yet. For Commerce Server to run properly, you need to install the latest of Microsoft's service packs for SQL Server, but don't worry—that process won't take as long.

Installing SQL Server Patches

Before installing Commerce Server, you need to apply the service pack 3 patch kit to SQL Server 6.5. This service pack 3 (or later) is required for using SQL Server with Commerce Server.

Installing the service pack is very straightforward, so it will not be covered here. The quickest way to obtain the latest service pack for SQL Server is to download it from Microsoft's WWW site (www.micrsoft.com). The kit will be downloaded as a self-extracting executable file. For best results, create a new directory named SP3 (or whatever the service pack is numbered), move the executable there and then run it. This way you will have a directory that contains just the service pack.

To install the service pack, just run the setup.exe file found in the directory where you unpacked the kit. The service pack software will then locate your SQL server installation and proceed with the update.

Changing SQL Server Default Settings

SQL Server's default configuration settings work well for general cases. Usually, few settings need to be changed. You want to change two settings right away, however.

First, the SQL Server administrator user account, sa, is created with a blank password. The first task you want to perform is change the password. The sa account can do anything from looking at any of the data to deleting databases. These are not actions that you want just anybody doing.

Second, you want to increase SQL Server's memory setting. This setting tells SQL Server how much of your server's memory to allocate for its use. SQL Server uses this memory for its executable, resources, data cache, and procedure cache. The more memory you can give SQL Server, the faster it will run.

The default memory-allocation setting is based on the amount of installed memory on the server; the setting is 8M for less than 32M of memory and 16M for more than 32M. These numbers are all right for servers with up to 32M of memory, but 32M is too little for a production Commerce Server system. As RAM is fairly cheap now, you should have 64M or more installed on a SQL Server for your Commerce Server database.

When all that memory is installed, you can follow these guidelines for setting SQL Server's memory setting:

- For servers with 32M to 64M of memory, allocate 50 percent of the memory to SQL Server.
- For servers with more than 64M of memory, allocate 70 percent of the memory to SQL Server.

These guidelines are rough; the amount of memory to allocate really depends on your application and the other programs that are sharing the SQL Server machine.

Configuring SQL Server to Work with Commerce Server

When SQL Server is installed, you have to make some modifications in its standard setup so that it works with Commerce Server. If at any time, you want to find more details about the settings you are changing, you can look them up in the SQL Server Books Online that you installed with SQL Server. If you don't have these handy online reference materials, you can install them from the SQL Server installation disks. These books are extremely helpful and are well worth the investment of disk space required to install them.

For SQL Server to support Commerce Server, you need to make the following changes in the default setup:

- Set SQL Server to autostart at boot time.
- Increase the number of user connections that SQL Server supports.
- Increase the amount of memory that SQL Server allocates.
- Change the administrator's (sa) password (not required, but should be).
- Increase the size of the temp database.

These changes all made using SQL Server's administration tool, Enterprise Manager, which was installed with SQL Server. You can also install these tools on another NT Server or NT Workstation on your network. The Enterprise Manager can be started by selecting its icon from the startup menu, where it will be found in the SQL Server 6.5 group.

The first setting you need to change or verify has to do with getting SQL Server to start when NT boots up. This is done by setting the Auto Start at Boot Time flag in the server's configuration settings. You also were able to set this when SQL Server was installed. If this setting was not turned on there, or if you were not the installer, you should follow the these steps to change or verify that the setting is correct.

1. Start SQL Server's Enterprise Manager from NT's start menu. The icon will be found in the SQL Server 6.5 group that was created when SQL Server was installed. When Enterprise Manager is running, you will see a screen that looks something like Figure 10.17.

FIG. 10.17

SQL Server 6.5
Enterprise Manager's
main screen.

2. If the server that you want to configure is not displayed in Enterprise Manager's server list, you need to register the server by right-clicking the SQL 6.5 icon and choosing Register Server from the shortcut menu. This menu will look like the one in Figure 10.18.

FIG. 10.18

SQL Server Enterprise Manager's server management pop-up menu.

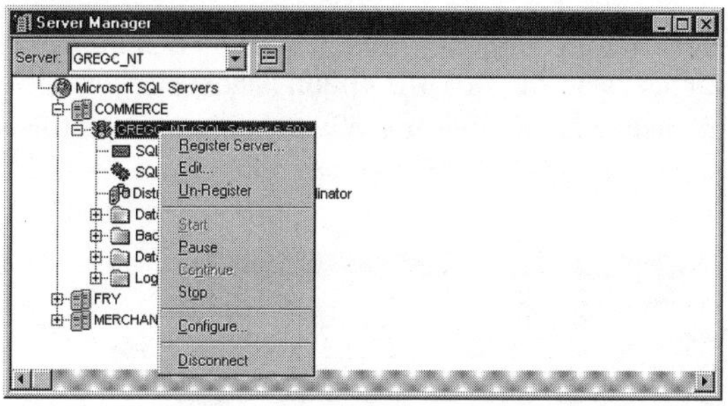

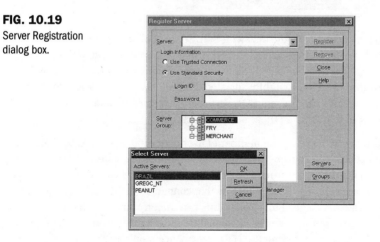

3. When the server registration screen appears, seen in Figure 10.19, enter the server name and a valid SQL Server user name and password for that server. For a list of available servers, click the Servers button.

4. The user specified when registering the server needs to have administration privileges on the server you are registering. If you are using SQL Server's security, the account information is for a SQL Server user name and password defined in SQL Server. If you are using NT Security, the account information is for a user name defined in the NT system. If you are using integrated security, either type of users will work. A typical user account to use when registering a server is sa, the system administrator's account.

FIG. 10.19

Server Registration dialog box.

5. When you have filled out the server registration information, click the Register button to return to the main Enterprise Manager window.

Part
III

Ch
10

6. If the SQL Server database server is not already running (the stoplight's icon shows a red light), you need to start it by right-clicking the server's icon and choosing Start from the shortcut menu. When the light turns green, the server has started.

7. Right-click the server that you want to configure and choose Configure from the shortcut menu. A tabbed dialog box screen appears, with the Server Options tab selected, as seen in Figure 10.20.

8. If the Auto Start Server at Boot Time option is not set, then click on the box to the left of the text so that a checkmark appears. When you have done this, press the OK button to return to the main Enterprise Manager screen.

FIG. 10.20

The Server Options tab of the Server Configuration screen.

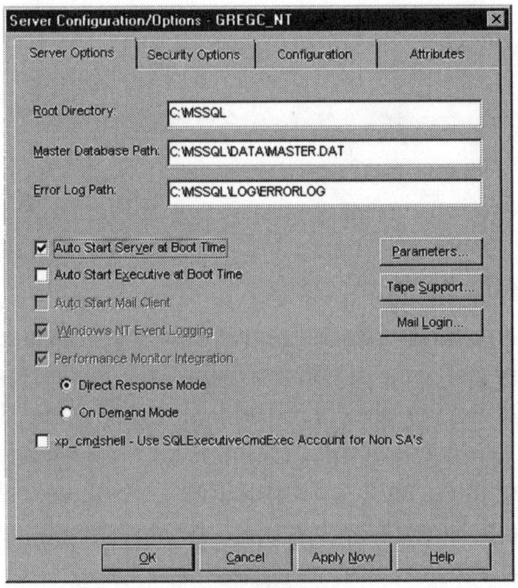

The next settings you may need to change deal with SQL Server's allocation of resources. When SQL Server starts up, it reserves and allocates certain resources. Most of the settings that are created when SQL Server is installed will work just fine for Commerce Server, however there are two that may need to be slightly adjusted. You will need to be careful here, changing some of these settings can prevent SQL Server from restarting, and if SQL Server can't start, then it is very hard to change these settings back.

The first setting to change is to increase the number of user connections allowed by SQL Server. SQL Server preallocates resources for a predefined number of connections to its databases. Every connection that is opened from a program into the SQL server system consumes one of these slots. If you are running other programs that connect to the database along with the Commerce Server system, you need to increase this parameter. You know that you need to change this setting if you start getting failures to connect to the database. You can monitor the number of active user connections by using the NT performance monitor tool and selecting the user connection parameter in the SQL Server section.

CAUTION

Each user connection uses 37K of the RAM that SQL Server has allocated, so don't just crank the user connections up to 1,000, or SQL server may run out of memory and fail to restart.

Another resource to modify is the default memory allocation. This is the amount of memory that SQL Server allocates on start up. The default is 8M for a 16M server and 16M if you have more than 32M of memory.

The default settings don't really give SQL Server enough memory for a Commerce Server application. However, if SQL Server is running on a memory-thin server, 16M or less, don't adjust the memory setting. If you have 32M or more of memory installed, use the following guidelines:

- 32M to 64M of memory, allocate approximately 50 percent of the memory to SQL Server.
- greater than 64M of memory, allocate approximately 70 percent of the physical memory to SQL Server.

If you are running many other processes or programs on your server or see excessive swap-file activity, lower the amount of memory allocated this setting. You may have to change the setting a few times to work out the best balance for your server.

1. To change these settings, you need to run SQL Enterprise Manager.
2. Right-click the server that you want to configure and choose Configure from the shortcut menu. A tabbed dialog box appears, with the Server Options tab selected.
3. Select the Configuration tab (see Figure 10.21). Use the scroll arrows to move down the list of server configuration parameters until you get to the Memory row. Change the number in the Current column to the desired amount.

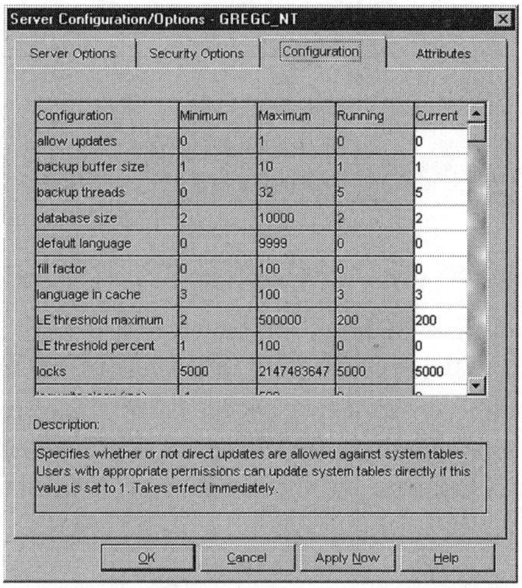

Part III

Ch 10

FIG. 10.21

The Server Configuration tab.

4. This setting is a memory amount in 2K units. To allocate 24M of memory, you need to change this setting to (about) 12200.

5. Use the scroll arrows to move down the list of server configuration parameters until you get to the User Connections row. Change the number in the Current column to the desired amount.

6. You need to stop and restart SQL Server for this setting to take effect.

7. To stop SQL Server, right-click the server's icon and choose Stop from the shortcut menu. When the icon's signal light turns red, the server has stopped. When the server has stopped, you can restart it by right-clicking the server's icon and choosing Start from the shortcut menu.

So that you can begin using SQL Server right away, SQL Server's installer creates the system administrator's account with a blank password. To ensure the security of your system, you need to change this password.

1. To change the SQL Server system administrator's, you need to run SQL Enterprise Manager.

2. Select and connect to the SQL Server for which you want to change the settings. Choose Logins from the Manage menu. The screen shown in Figure 10.22 appears. Use the Login Name combo box to select the sa account. Enter a new password in the Password box and click the Modify button to change the settings.

FIG. 10.22

The Manage Logins screen.

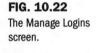

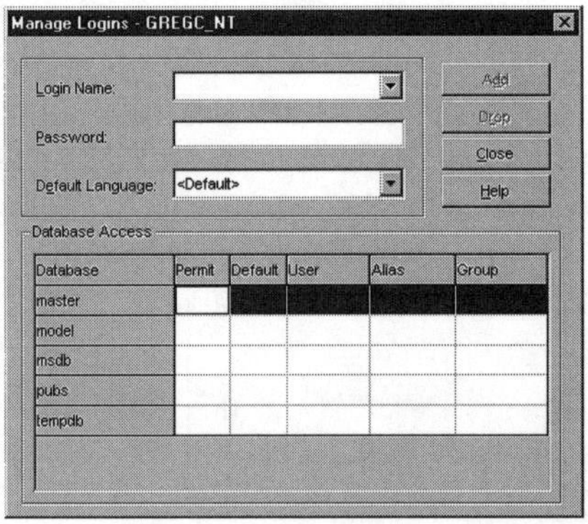

3. Click the Close button to exit this dialog box.

The last bit of configuration magic to do here is to increase the size of SQL Server's temp database. This database is used by SQL Server to store intermediate data while running queries. SQL Server's installation process creates a very conservatively sized temp database of only two megabytes. This is too small for Commerce Server's needs during its installation process. You need to increase the size of this database by at least 4M to accommodate Commerce Server.

The following steps will show how to allocate more space for the temp database. These same steps can be used to increase the size of any SQL Server database.

1. To change the size of temp database, you need to run SQL Enterprise Manager.

2. Make sure that the server is registered and running. Click the plus sign (+) next to the server you need to make changes on to open the server's contents.

3. To increase the size of the temp database, you will first need to create a new database device to extend the temp database into. To do this, right-click on Database Devices and choose New Device from the shortcut menu, shown in Figure 10.23.

FIG. 10.23
SQL Server Enterprise Manager's Database Device management pop-up menu.

4. Using the New Database Device screen that appears, see Figure 10.24, create a new database device of at least 4 megabytes. Do this by entering 4 in the Size (MB) box. Name the new device tempdb. This will create a tempdb.dat file in your file system that will be used for the new data device. When you have made these changes click the Create Now button to create the data device.

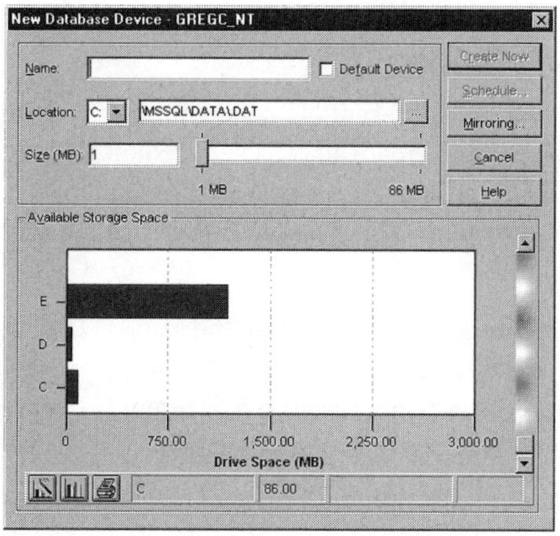

FIG. 10.24
The SQL Server Enterprise Manager's New Database Device screen is used to create a new data device.

5. When the New Database Device screen closes you will be back at the SQL Server Enterprise Manager main screen. Now that the data device is created, you can extend

the tempdb database into it. To do this, in the server manager window locate the server's contents for the server you are working with. Click on the plus sign (+) next to Databases label. Locate tempdb in the list of databases and then double-click on its name to edit the database configuration.

6. When the Edit Database screen appears, click the Expand button.

7. In the Expand Database screen that appears, as seen in Figure 10.25, click the Data Device list box and select tempdb, the device that was created in Step 4. Enter the number of megabytes that you wish to allocate for tempdb in the Size (MB) box. If you created a 4 megabyte data device, then enter 4 to expand the database by 4 megabytes. Click the Expand Now button to expand tempdb into the new data device.

FIG. 10.25

The Expand Database dialog box.

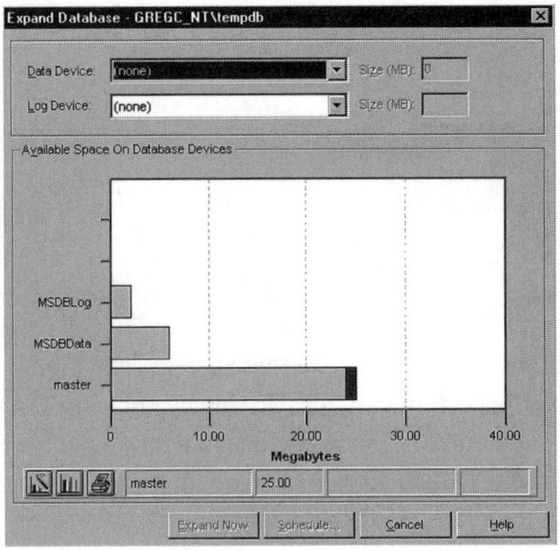

Additional Configuration Tasks

If you want to run SQL Server on a different NT server from the one that IIS and Commerce Server are installed on, you need to create an NT user account on the SQL Server machine to allow access to it. When IIS is installed, it creates a user account called IUSR_*machinename* to use as an anonymous access account. This account is then used to access resources on the NT server.

If SQL Server, IIS, and Commerce Server reside on the same NT server, no account-access problem occurs. IIS can use the IUSR_*machinename* account to create named pipes to access the data in SQL Server. If SQL Server is on a different NT server, however, the IUSR_*machinename* account has no access on that machine, unless you add it.

You can add these privileges to the IUSR_*machinename* account in one of several ways:

■ If both of the NT servers reside in the same NT domain, you can change the IIS anonymous access account to be a domain account. This way, using one account, Commerce Server and IIS have access privileges on both machines.

- Make a user account with the same name, IUSR_*machinename*, and password on the NT server on which SQL Server is installed. This allows IIS to connect by using the user name with which it has been configured with which for both servers.

- Make the NT server on which SQL Server is installed a member of the same domain as the IIS server and follow the first suggestion.

Starting SQL Server

This section covers the basic techniques for creating databases for SQL Server.

If you are used to Microsoft Access or other desktop database systems, you are accustomed to a model in which the database and its storage file are synonymous. SQL Server, however, uses a different setup. The files that are visible on the system are known as *devices*. SQL Server uses devices to store databases, transaction logs, and backups.

Databases are objects that are stored in data devices. When you create a database, you must allocate space from a device to store it in. When the database runs out of space, more space can be allocated from the same device or from another one under that server's control.

Using SQL Server Data Devices

The first step in creating a database for SQL Server is creating a physical data file to store the database in. SQL Server calls these data files devices.

Devices come in two types. *Data devices* are used to hold databases and transaction log files, and *dump devices* are used to hold database backups. The next few sections discuss data devices and the databases that use them.

Database devices are the .DAT files that SQL Server creates in the NT file system. Although these files are just files in the file system, it would not be wise to move or delete these files without first dropping (deleting) any databases that reside within them. SQL Server maintains its own database—master—which tells it where the data devices are and what databases exist within each device. Any tampering with the master database or with the database device files may cause SQL Server to invalidate the data device, making all the data stored within inaccessible.

TIP Device files are fairly safe from tampering when SQL Server is running. SQL Server keeps the files locked so that users and other programs cannot corrupt or delete them. When SQL Server is not running, however, these files are vulnerable to tampering, accidental or otherwise. Make sure that your databases and files are being backed up on a regular basis.

SQL Server allows database administrators to set up complex relationships between databases and data devices. You need not keep a one-database-to-one-data-device relationship. A data device can contain one, more than one, or even just part of a database that spans several data devices.

Although you can have multiple databases in a single data device or a database that is spread across several data devices, neither method is suggested for planning of production SQL Server systems. The main drawback to these configurations is that they are not easy to deal with when you need to recover from a database failure. For most production applications, it is wise to maintain a one-to-one relationship between database and device.

The exception to this one-to-one relationship of the database to data device is when your database becomes too large to fit on one physical hard drive. In this case, however, you should think of upgrading your system's drives rather than using one of these nonstandard database configuration.

Creating a Data Device

When you need to create a new data device in the SQL Server database system, its usually in preparation for creating a new database. The following section will show the steps required to create a new data device for SQL Server.

1. Start SQL Server's Enterprise Manager.

2. Connect to the SQL Server on which you will create the data device and open it by clicking the plus sign (+) next to its name.

3. Right-click the Database Devices (see Figure 10.26) item and choose New Device from the pop-up menu.

FIG. 10.26
Pop-up menu for database devices.

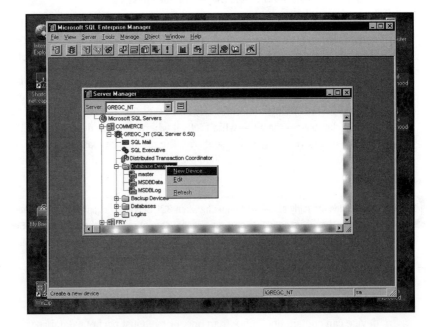

4. When the New Database Device screen appears, as seen in Figure 10.27, you will be prompted to specify the name, location, and size of your database device. The graph at the bottom of the screen shows how much space is available on each of your local drives.

5. Enter a name for your device. As you type, you will see your entry reflected in the Location line, followed by .DAT. By default, SQL Server will make a file for the data device with the same name as your device.

FIG. 10.27

The New Device screen in SQL Server's Enterprise Manager allows you to specify and create a new data device.

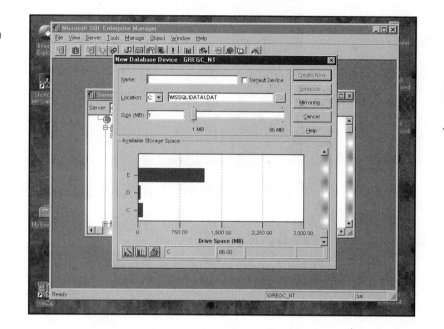

6. Specify the location for the data device by setting the drive letter and directory in the Location line. If you do not know the directory that you want to create the device in, click the ellipsis (...) button. A dialog box appears, as in Figure 10.28, allowing you to browse the file system to select the proper location for your device file.

7. Set the size of the database device by entering a value (in megabytes) in the Size.

8. When you have all the information entered, click the Create Now button to create the database immediately, or click the Schedule button to have SQL Server schedule creation of the device later. You may want to use this option if your SQL Server is in production and you need to process database changes at an off time.

After you finish these tasks, the newly created data device appears in the list of available devices. If the device does not appear in the list, right-click the Database Devices item and choose Refresh from the shortcut menu.

Part
III

Ch
10

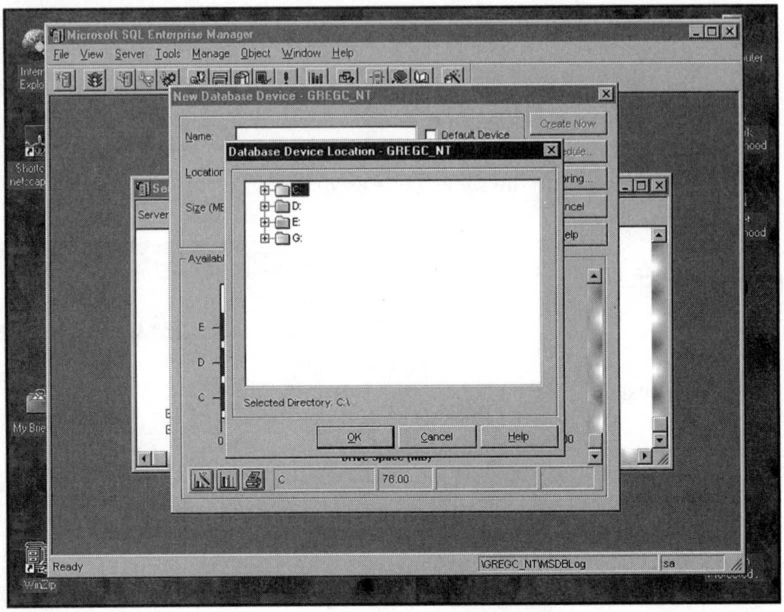

FIG. 10.28

The file system dialog box on the New Device screen allows you to locate where you want to create the data devices.

Extending a Data Device

After you have created a data device, even if you have assigned a database to it, its size can be increased. This is called "Extending" the data device in SQL Server terms. The only limit to the size that data device file can be extended to is the remaining space on the hard drive it was created on.

To extend a data device follow these steps:

1. Start SQL Server's Enterprise Manager.

2. Connect to the SQL Server on which you will create the data device and open it by clicking the plus sign (+) next to its name.

3. Expand the list of database devices by clicking the plus sign (+) next to the Database Devices folder on the screen.

4. Double-click on the database device you need to expand.

5. When the Edit Database Device screen appears, you can change the size in the Size (MB) box. There is a note next to the box that will indicate what the maximum size of the device can be, based on the available disk space.

6. Click the Expand Now button to change the size of the data device.

Using SQL Server Databases

In many other database-management systems (DBMS), databases are a logical collection of data within the whole system. In SQL Server, however, databases are partitioned collections of data tables, procedures, indexes, and supporting information. Therefore, you have to create a database object before you populate it with tables, views, and stored procedures.

Placing data in separate database objects does not prevent you from combining data from several databases. You can still access the data in another database on the same server by writing a query that specifies the entire path to a table, *database.owner.tablename,* within the database. Notice that if both databases have the same owner, dbo, for example, the owner can be omitted, *database..tablename.*

A database has two portions: the data section and the transaction log. The data section holds the database structure, data and procedures. The transaction log is a special data area that records all the changes that are made in the database. Every action that changes data, structure, or permissions in the database also gets written to the transaction log. This way, if the database ever gets corrupted, you can use the transaction log to rebuild it from a known state.

The data section and transaction log can be created in the same data device or in separate devices; for most production situations, you want to create them in separate devices.

Part III

Ch 10

Creating a Database

The following section will show the steps required to create a new database for SQL Server.

1. Start SQL Server's Enterprise Manager.

2. Connect to the SQL Server on which you will create the data device.

3. Right-click the Databases item and choose New Database from the shortcut menu shown in Figure 10.29.

FIG. 10.29
The Database menu.

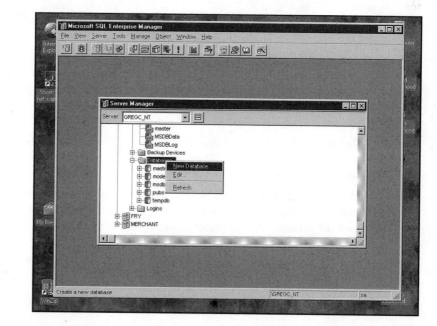

4. When the New Database screen appears, as in Figure 10.30, you are prompted to specify the name, location, and size of the database you are creating. The graph at the bottom of the screen shows how much space is available in each of the available data devices.

5. Enter a name for your database. This name is used to reference the database within SQL Server. The name of the database is also used when setting up DSN string for database connections using ODBC.

FIG. 10.30

Selecting the database device.

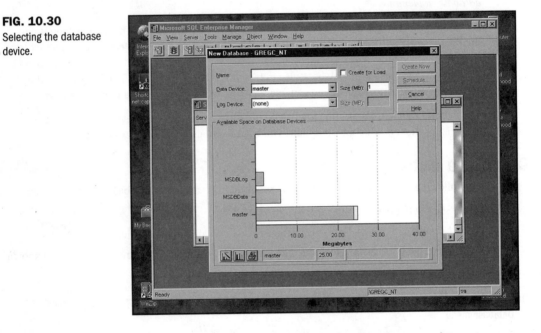

6. Select a data device to create the database in from the Data Device drop-down list, as shown in Figure 10.31. If you have not created a data device for this database, choose <new> to create a data device. If you select <new> here, then you will be prompted to create a new data base device. Instructions for creating a database device were shown in Creating a Data Device.

7. In the Size (MB) field on the screen, specify the size in megabytes to allocate from the data device to the database. The Size (MB) field defaults to the maximum available space in the data device.

8. From the Log Device drop-down list, choose one of the data devices to create the database transaction log in. If you want to keep the transaction log in the same device and the database, choose <none>. If you want to create a new data device to keep your transaction log in, choose <new> to create a data device. If you select <new> here, then you will be prompted to create a new data base device. Instructions for creating a database device were shown in Creating a Data Device.

FIG. 10.31

Selecting the
Transaction Log device.

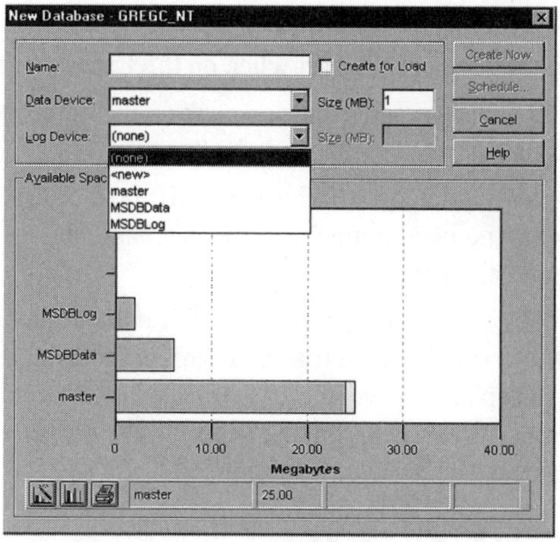

9. In the Size (MB) field, specify the size in megabytes (M) to allocate from the selected data device to use for the transaction log. The Size (MB) field defaults to the maximum available space in the data device.

10. When you have all the information entered, click the Create Now button to create the database immediately, or click the Schedule button to have SQL Server schedule creation of the database later. Databases take about one minute to create for every 100M you allocate. (Depending on processor speed and load, your mileage may vary.) You may want to use the schedule option if your SQL Server is in production. Creating a new database will take CPU, I/O and memory resources from the server, if the server is in production, you may want to process database changes at an off time.

Extending a Database

After you have created a database and start using it with your application, you may find that your initial size estimates were a little low. If this happens you can increase the size of the database very easily. First you will need to extend the data device that the database is being stored in. Then you can allocate that extended space to the database. In fact, you can take these steps while the database is in operation, without the application or the users being effected.

To extend a database follow these steps:

1. Start SQL Server's Enterprise Manager.

2. Follow the steps described in the section Extending a Data Device to increase the size of the device the database is stored in.

3. Expand the list of databases by clicking the plus sign (+) next to the Databases folder on the screen.

4. Double-click the database you need to expand.

5. When the Edit Database screen appears, click on the Expand button.

6. When the Expand Database screen appears, click on the database devices drop-down list and select the database device you expanded in Step 3.

7. Enter the new size for the database in the Size (MB) box. There is a note next to the box that will indicate what the maximum size of the database can be, based on the available space in the selected data device.

8. Click the Expand Now button to expand the database immediately, or click the Schedule button to have SQL Server schedule the expansion of the database later. Databases take about one minute to expand for every 100M you allocate. Extending a database will take CPU, I/O and memory resources from the server, if the server is in production. You may want to process database changes at an offtime.

Some SQL Server Tuning Information

Database tuning is definitely a mysterious art. It takes many years of experience to really become effective at the process and be able to do "fine-tuning" of the database system. However, there are some simple things that even the newest database administrator can do to make SQL Server get to the 90 percent efficiency mark.

The main things to look out for are memory usage and disk I/O. Both of these are fairly simple to tune on a basic scale. In addition, using the Performance Monitor tool that comes with NT 4.0, you can tack these two resources in real time and see how they effect server performance.

Memory   Memory is the most crucial resource for SQL Server. The more memory that you can give SQL Server, the better its performance is. This is because SQL Server attempts to cache often-used data and stored procedures in memory rather than re-read them from the hard disk. Caching data gives a huge boost in the area of read performance because a read from the memory cache is much faster than a read from the hard disk.

One way to see whether you have allocated enough memory to SQL Server is to monitor the SQL Server's cache-hit ratio using NT's performance monitor. To get an accurate reading, monitor the cache-hit ratio while your application is running with a real or simulated load. As a general goal, try to get the cache-ratio to remain at or above 90 percent. This means that SQL Server is going to the cache rather than the disk 90 percent of the time.

Remember that you have to leave some memory for NT and the other processes that are running on your server, so don't set SQL Server's memory setting too high. When the NT server starts to page excessively, back down from your SQL Server memory allocation. Paging occurs when NT is moving something from real memory to the page file (virtual memory) to make room for application code or data. When NT starts to page, overall system performance degrades rapidly. You can monitor NT's paging activity by looking at the page fault rate with the Performance Monitor.

FIG. 10.32
The NT Performance
Monitor.

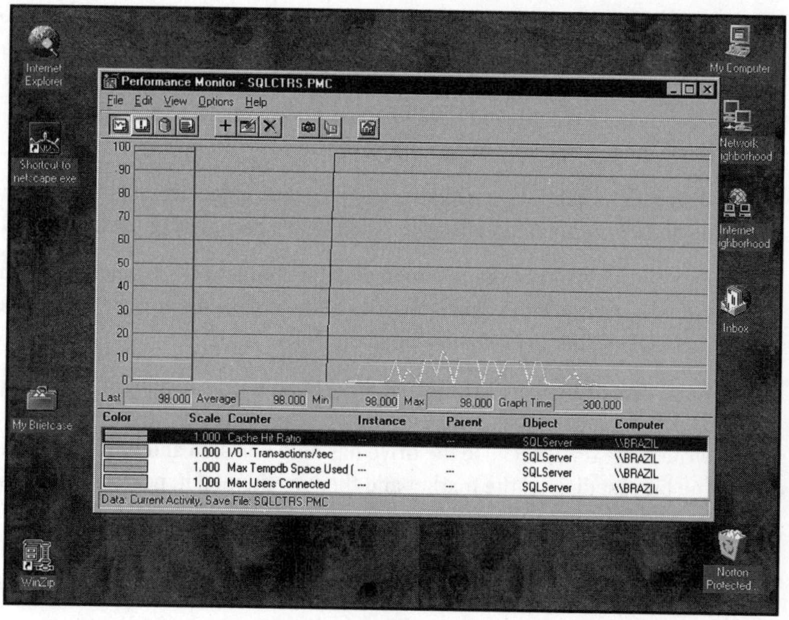

As mentioned previously, when SQL Server is installed, the default memory allocation setting is based on the amount of physical RAM installed in the server; the setting is 8M for less than 32M of memory and 16M for more than 32M. These numbers are all right for servers up to 32 MB of memory, but 32M is too little for a production Commerce Server system. As RAM is fairly cheap now, you should have 64M or more installed on an SQL Server for your Commerce Server database.

When all that memory is installed, you can follow these guidelines for setting SQL Server's memory setting:

- For servers with 32M to 64M of memory, allocate 50 percent of the memory to SQL Server.

- For servers with more than 64M of memory, allocate 70 percent of the memory to SQL Server.

The memory setting reflects the amount of memory that SQL Server allocates as a working set and locks while it is in operation. It is best if this amount never exceeds the amount of physical RAM that the server has installed. SQL Server can use virtual memory for this setting, but it performs very poorly. For best results, memory must be real RAM.

To adjust SQL Server's memory setting, follow the steps shown in the section Configuring SQL Server to Work with Commerce Server. For memory changes to take effect, you must stop and restart SQL Server. This is because SQL Server allocates and locks this memory when it starts, and the memory allocation cannot be adjusted while SQL Server is in operation.

Part
III

Ch
10

In fact, because SQL Server allocates and locks its memory, this reduces the amount of memory that NT has available for other programs. You may see other memory-hungry processes report out-of-memory errors when SQL Server is running. If you see these errors, you have three choices—you have to add more memory, reduce the allocation for SQL Server, or move those processes to another server.

Disk I/O Disk I/O is a hidden performance killer. The fact that you have a problem is not obvious, except that you hear the disk heads hammering back and forth all the time.

You can avoid any of the common disk I/O bottlenecks by planning your data layout. To do so, you need to know the characteristics of the databases you are using, the transaction log files that SQL Server keeps, and a bit about NT.

First, disk drives can do only one thing at a time: read a bit or write a bit. If you put all of NT, SQL Server, databases, and Commerce Server on one drive, each has to wait its turn to read or write some data, because the drive has only one arm and one spindle. Therefore, if you bought the biggest disk on the market and then partitioned it, performance is worse than if you had bought four little drives.

When a record is read from a SQL Server database, if the data is not in the memory cache, a page of database is read from the disk. Some database queries may have to read many pages from the database to even begin returning data.

When a record is written to a SQL Server database, a record is first written to the transaction log; then the data is written to the database. Both these operations must occur for the database to be written to.

As part of NT's normal operation, the disk that holds the operating system and virtual memory page file is accessed at random times, but in many cases, the operating system has to wait for the disk I/O to complete before moving on. If any other disk operations get in the way of completing this I/O, overall system performance suffers.

In most cases, you are wise to lay out the information on your drives in the manner shown in Table 10.1.

Table 10.1 Suggested Drive Setup

Drive	File System	Files	I/O Type
1	FAT	NT and paging file	Mostly reading and writing page file
2	NTFS	Data devices	Reading and occasionally writing database files
3	NTFS	Log devices and database backups	Writing transaction logs
4	NTFS	Commerce Server WWW files	Reading Web files and images

This way, the different types of I/O are isolated from one another. You can combine some of these on the same disk—the Web files and the page file, for example. Database I/O activity is severely impaired by placing databases on the same disk as the transaction log, however, because SQL Server uses these files to simultaneously write and record database activities.

Planning Your Database

Database designing and planning are really an art form. There is no way to cover it sufficiently here in a few pages. The following sections cover some basic aspects, but for best results, you need to get a good book (or a good consultant/employee) to help you.

To plan your database, you need to start by creating some rough estimates for data related to your store:

- How many products will you have?
- How many shoppers a day do you expect?
- How long will you keep baskets alive?
- Will you be logging traffic information?
- How long will you keep the log information online?

Part
III

Ch
10

After these questions have been answered, you can use the planned table and field information to calculate the space required. To do so, add all the field sizes, in bytes, for a single record of a table, and multiply by the total number of records required for the table. In the case of the product table, the number of records in the table is equivalent to the number of products you want to keep in the database. For the logging tables (traffic log and receipt), you will need to calculate the total number of records by multiplying the number of records you get per day by the number of days you want to keep the records online. Note that in the traffic log table, one record is logged for each page that a user requests (much like the Web server's log file); therefore, this table can grow rapidly.

TIP The traffic log table for 1-800-FLOWERS grew at a rate much faster than expected in the weeks after the site went live. In fact, due to a major holiday during that period, the table grew to 2.5 million records in the first month. During that time, the site ran out of database space and had to expand the database to three times the calculated size. So beware—your estimates may be a little shy of reality. Make sure that ample resources are available and that you watch database growth during the first month or so of operation. You can then use this live data to feed back into your estimates and adjust your hardware and maintenance needs accordingly.

Once you have calculated the total size requirements for your data, you might want to multiply the result by 1.5 to 2 to make sure that the unexpected success of your store, doesn't cause you problems. Hard disk costs are currently running at an all-time low, so overestimating your storage requirements is not nearly as costly a mistake as underestimating. The down time for upgrading your store's hardware might well be much more than the cost paid for a larger drive to begin with.

From Here...

This chapter covered many of the basic issues surrounding database management, mainte-nance and planning. With this foundation, and armed with tools such as Microsoft Access or Visual Interdev, you should be able to build databases and tables that will be the backbone of your Commerce Server Application.

Now that you have been thoroughly swamped with information about the care and feeding of relational database systems, the next few chapters move on to the Commerce Server side of the database connection. These chapters will cover the following topics:

- A Commerce Server data components reference.
- How to use the data components effectively in your application.
- Reading data from the database and getting it onto the page.

Commerce Server Data Components

This chapter discusses the data-related components that come with Commerce Server. For each component, the chapter covers the methods or actions and the syntax, and also shows some examples of how the component is used. ∎

Learning about Commerce Server's data components

Understand the important aspects of each of Commerce server many data components.

Understand how the components are created and used

Each component is discussed and its use with Commerce Server is explained.

Examining the methods and parameters used for each component

The methods and parameters for each component will be displayed. You will see what types of data each method needs and a short example of the correct calling syntax.

Commerce Database-Related Components

Commerce Server comes with a set of components that allow a developer to interact with a store's data. These components are much simpler to use that those that come with ASP and provide a simple gateway from the store to the database.

The data-related components fall basically into two categories; those that use SQL and data cursors, familiar relational database interactions; and those that use direct dictionary access via data keys. The SQL-based components are typically used for accessing general information about the store and its products. The dictionary-based components are typically used only for the Commerce Server specific objects such as the order data.

Using the *Content* Component

The Content component is used to manage data sources and queries used in your application. By using this component's methods, you can create and maintain the objects and definitions that are used throughout the Commerce Server application's environment to access the database.

The Content component's methods allow you to define two types of information: queries and data sources. The queries are stored with the Content component. Each query is associated with a name string that is used to access and execute it in the context of the application. Datasource components are defined by means of the Content component and also are associated with a name string. This string is used in the store to access the Datasource component. The Datasource component is discussed later in this chapter.

> **TIP** Content and related components typically are used where you need to use SQL to interact with your database. Product queries and stored content queries are typical of these types of interactions. For working with data related to the shopping basket or receipts (anything with the MarshaledOrder field), you should use the DBStorage component.

Creating the *Content* Component   The Content component is a top-level component that must be created by means of the CreateObject method of the IIS 3.0 Server component. To create a Content component, the component identifier value to pass into the CreateObject method is "Commerce.Content".

Example:

```
Set storeContent = Server.CreateObject("Commerce.Content")
```

Method List

Method Name	Description
AddDatasource	Creates a Datasource component based on a DSN.
AddQuery	Creates a query for use by the Content data sources.
Datasource	Returns the Datasource component associated with a variable.

***AddDatasource* Method**   The `AddDatasource` method defines a `Datasource` component for this `Content` component by using a defined file or system data-source name (DSN). You must use the ODBC utility in the Windows NT Control Panel to define DSNs before you use the resulting `Datasource` component to access data.

Syntax

```
Content.AddDatasource(Alias, ConnectionString, [RowsetSize, MaximumRows])
```

Parameters

`Alias`

A string that identifies a `Datasource`; used with the `Content.Datasource` method to access the `Datasource` component.

`ConnectionString`

An ODBC connection string that contains all the required connection information. Typically, this string takes the form:

```
"DSN=clockped;UID=cp_user;PWD=onetwothree;DATABASE=clockped"
```

`RowsetSize (optional - default = 1)`

A number, greater than 0, that specifies the number of rows to return at one time from a query. The default (1) maximizes the efficiency of server-side cursors by allowing the server to fetch only one row at a time from the database.

`MaximumRows (optional - default = 0)`

The upper limit of the number of rows to return from the database. The default (0) returns all the rows that a query generates.

Applies To   Any defined `Content` component.

Example

```
<%
REM First create the main content component
Set storeContent = Server.CreateObject("Commerce.Content")

REM Now define the Datasource components based on the
REM databases we use

Call storeContent.AddDatasource("products",
➥"DSN=cp;UID=cpusr;PWD=one;DATABASE=cp")
Call storeContent.AddDatasource("tracking",
"DSN=cp_track;UID=cpusr;PWD=one;DATABASE=cp_track")
%>
```

***AddQuery* Method**   The `AddQuery` method adds a query to the `Content` component. When defined, the method can be used by all the `Datasource` components also defined in the `Content` component.

Part

III

Ch

11

Queries can contain placeholders for parameters. These placeholders take the form :n, in which n is a number starting at 1 and increasing for every new parameter in the query.

Syntax

```
Content.AddQuery(Alias, QueryString Timeout, CommandType, MaximumRows,
CursorType, CursorSize, RetrievalMethod)
```

Parameters

Alias

A string that identifies this Query in a Datasource; used with the Datasource.Execute method.

QueryString

A SQL query string. Typically, this string takes the form "SELECT * FROM PRODUCT".

Timeout

An optional value that specifies the number of seconds to wait for a query to complete. If this value is set to 0 or omitted, it defaults to the value set for the database driver.

CommandType

An integer constant that specifies the kind of query that QueryString represents. Specifying the precise type (as opposed to adCommandUnknown) results in faster execution time. The default value is 8 (adCmdUnknown). The following table lists the possible constant values.

Constant	Value	Description
adCmdText	1	Evaluates SQLText as a textual definition of a command.
adCmdTable	2	Evaluates SQLText as a table name.
adCmdStoredProc	4	Evaluates SQLText as a stored procedure.
adCmdUnknown	8	Specifies the type of command for the SQLText is not known. adCmdUnknown is the default.

MaximumRows

Limits the number of rows returned by the query. If this value is set to 0 or omitted, it defaults to the value set for the database driver. You can use this parameter to prevent runaway queries that could return a great many rows. Specifying a value greater than 0 for queries that always return a small number of rows, however, can substantially reduce the speed of query execution.

CursorType

An optional integer constant that references the ADO cursor type. CursorType is used most often in conjunction with the CursorSize parameter. The default value is 0 (adOpenForwardReadOnly). This parameter can contain one of the values listed in the following table.

Constant	Value	Description
adOpenForwardReadOnly	0	Forward-only cursor, identical to a static cursor except that you can only scroll forward through records. Using this setting improves performance in situations when you need to make a single pass through a recordset. This is the default value.
adOpenKeyset	1	Keyset cursor, like a dynamic cursor, except that you can't see records that other users add, although records that other users delete are inaccessible from your recordset. Data changes by other users are still visible.
adOpenDynamic	2	Dynamic cursor. Additions, changes, and deletions by other users are visible, and all types of movement through the recordset are allowed, except for bookmarks if the provider doesn't support them.
adOpenStatic	3	Static cursor, a static copy of a set of records that you can use to find data or generate reports. Additions, changes, or deletions by other users are not visible.

CursorSize

Specifies the number of rows to gather at one time from the database. Specifying a default of 1 optimizes the server-side cursor by ensuring that the server never has to retrieve more than a single row in server memory at a time. The default value is 1.

RetrievalMethod

An optional parameter that specifies the method to use to retrieve data from the query result set. The default value is 2 (Unknown). You can use the values listed in the following table for this parameter.

Value	Description
0	Block retrieval. This value indicates that the result set contains no long text or binary data or that the database fully supports block retrieval of long data.
1	Row retrieval. This value indicates that the database supports the retrieval of long data, but only on a row-by-row basis.
2	Unknown. When you use this value, you effectively ask the system to determine for itself which method to call by searching for fields that contain binary data. This is the default value.

Part
III

Ch
11

N O T E If you are using an Oracle database, the block-retrieval method is unavailable; you must use the row-retrieval option. ▦

Applies To Any defined Content component.

See Also

Datasource.Execute

Example

```
<%
REM First create the main content component and a datasource
Set storeContent = Server.CreateObject("Commerce.Content")
Call storeContent.AddDatasource("products",
➥"DSN=cp;UID=cpusr;PWD=one;DATABASE=cp")

REM Now define some queries
Call storeContent.AddQuery("allprod_byprice", "SELECT * FROM product ORDER ➥BY
price")
Call storeContent.AddQuery("findprod", "SELECT * FROM product WHERE sku = ➥:1")
%>
```

Datasource Method The Datasource method is used to create a datasource object variable that contains a connection to a specific database. The methods single parameter, Alias, is a string identifier that will indicate which of the DSNs stored in the Content component to use. The Alias string must match the string used to create the datasource DSN in the AddDatasource method.

Syntax

Content.Datasource(Alias)

Parameters

Alias

A string used to identify a uniquely defined Datasource. This string is set in the AddDatasource method.

Example

```
<%
REM First create the main content component and a datasource
Set storeContent = Server.CreateObject("Commerce.Content")
Call storeContent.AddDatasource("products",
➥"DSN=cp;UID=cpusr;PWD=one;DATABASE=cp")

REM Now define some queries
Call storeContent.AddQuery("allprod_byprice", "SELECT * FROM product ORDER ➥BY
price")

REM Now execute the query
Set productDS = storeContent("products")
Set prodCursor = productDS.Execute("allprod_byprice")
%>
```

Applies To   Any defined Content component.

See Also

AddDatasource, Datasource

Using the *Datasource* Component

The Datasource component is defined by the Content component and is used to execute queries against a database. The results of the query, if any, are stored in a SimpleList of Dictionary components. For more information on Dictionary components, please refer to the component's description in this chapter. The query that the Datasource component executes can be a stored query defined in its parent Content component or one defined in the Execute method.

The Datasource object is typically used for retrieving read-only data from the database. This data becomes the content for a page and is used to populating ASP-coded templates. A good example of this is a page where a set of product selections are displayed to the user in the form of a catalog page.

Creating the *Datasource* Component   The Datasource component is created by the AddDatasource method of the Content component. You need to define the Datasource in the Content component based on an existing ODBC file or system data-source name (DSN). You also need to supply a string variable or alias to refer to the Datasource component within the application.

Method List

Method Name	Description
Execute	Executes the indicated query. If results exist, they are returned in a SimpleList of Dictionary components.
CreateADOConnection	Creates an Active Data Objects (ADO) connection to the database.
ExecuteADO	Executes a SQL query using an ADO connection. Results are returned in an ADO Recordset.

Query Parameters   Queries used in the Execute method can contain parameter placeholders or markers that are filled in at execution time. These markers take the form :n, in which n indicates the location of the associated parameter value in the parameter list. If the number of parameters required by the SQL query are not supplied in the Execute method, an error is generated.

It is important to note that parameters passed into a query are variants, a VBScript datatype that is used for generic storage. To ensure proper storage or datatype matching, you will need to cast the data into the proper type. In SQL Server queries, this is done using the CONVERT function and in Oracle, use the conversion macros (TO_NUMBER, TO_DATE, and so on).

Reading Query Results   The Execute method returns any results in a SimpleList of Dictionary components. The fields that are returned by the query define the Dictionary component's contents. Therefore, you do not need to predefine the Dictionary's structure, it is created automatically using the fields returned by the query. By using the VBScript control statements For Each or For loop, you can move through the SimpleList component and read the data from the Dictionary component. The number of Dictionary component items in the SimpleList is specified in the SimpleList.Count property. For more information, see the section on the SimpleList component.

Execute Method   The Execute method runs the specified query and returns any results in a SimpleList of Dictionary components. The method has two formats. The first format uses a query defined in the Datasource component's parent Content component by the AddQuery method. The second format uses a query defined in the method call.

Syntax

```
Datasource.Execute(QueryName, [Parameters])
Datasource.Execute(QueryString, [Parameters])
```

Parameters

QueryName

The variable string name that used to define a SQL query in the Datasource component's parent Content component by means of the AddQuery method.

QueryString

A SQL query string. Typically, this string takes the form "SELECT * FROM PRODUCT".

Parameters (Optional)

One or more parameters to pass into the query that is being executed. You must have at least as many parameters as you do parameter markers in the query.

Example

```
<%
REM First create the main content component and a datasource
Set storeContent = Server.CreateObject("Commerce.Content")
Call storeContent.AddDatasource("products",
➥"DSN=cp;UID=cpusr;PWD=one;DATABASE=cp")

REM Now define some queries
Call storeContent.AddQuery("allprod_byprice", "SELECT * FROM product ORDER ➥BY
price")

REM Now execute the query
Set productDS = storeContent("products")
Set prodCursor = productDS.Execute("allprod_byprice")
%>
<TABLE BORDER=1>
<TR><TH>SKU</TH><TH>Product Name</TH></TR>
<%
REM Read the results
```

```
for I = 0 to prodCursor.Count
%>
<TR><TD><% prodCursor(I).sku %></TD>
<TD><% prodCursor(I).name %></TD></TR>
<%
next I
%>
</TABLE>
```

Applies To

Datasource

See Also

Content.AddQuery

CreateADOConnection Method   The CreateADOConnection method creates an Active Data Object (ADO) connection to the database. This is a read-only connection that can be used with the ExecuteADO component to return query results in the form of an ADO recordset, which may be more familiar for some Visual Basic programmers.

Syntax

Datasource.CreateADOConnection()

Parameters   The call to CreateADOConnection does not take any parameters.

Example

```
<%
REM First create the main content component and a datasource
Set storeContent = Server.CreateObject("Commerce.Content")
Call storeContent.AddDatasource("products",
➥"DSN=cp;UID=cpusr;PWD=one;DATABASE=cp")

REM Now execute the query using ADO
Set productDS = storeContent("products")

productADO = productDS.CreateADOConnection()

myRecordSet = productDS.ExecuteADO(productADO, ", "SELECT * FROM product ➥ORDER
BY price")
%>
```

Applies To

Datasource

See Also

Datasource.ExecuteADO

ExecuteADO Method   The ExecuteADO method runs the specified query and returns any results in an ADO recordset object. This method requires that an ADO connection had been created using the CreateADOConnection method.

The method has two formats. The first format uses a query defined in the `Datasource` component's parent `Content` component by the `AddQuery` method. The second format uses a query defined in the method call.

Syntax

```
Datasource.ExecuteADO(Connection, QueryName, [Parameters])
Datasource.ExecuteADO(Connection, QueryString, [Parameters])
```

Parameters

`Connection`

The `connection` parameter is an open ADO connection created with the `CreateADOConnection` method.

`QueryName`

The variable string name that used to define a SQL query in the `Datasource` component's parent `Content` component by means of the `AddQuery` method.

`QueryString`

A SQL query string. Typically, this string takes the form `"SELECT * FROM PRODUCT"`.

`Parameters (Optional)`

One or more parameters to pass into the query that is being executed. You must have at least as many parameters as you do parameter markers in the query.

Example

```
<%
REM First create the main content component and a datasource
Set storeContent = Server.CreateObject("Commerce.Content")
Call storeContent.AddDatasource("products",
➥"DSN=cp;UID=cpusr;PWD=one;DATABASE=cp")

REM Now execute the query using ADO
Set productDS = storeContent("products")

productADO = productDS.CreateADOConnection()

myRecordSet = productDS.ExecuteADO(productADO, ", "SELECT * FROM product ➥ORDER
BY price")
%>
```

Applies To

`Datasource`

See Also

`Datasource.CreateADOConnection`

Using the *DBStorage* Component

The DBStorage component interacts with a Commerce Server database on a record level rather than at a query level as the DBStorage component does. This component is directly connected to a table in the database and acts as a local cache for the table. Using key and value pairs to find matching records, an application can directly manipulate the data.

Typically, DBStorage objects are used to store application level data about a shopping session. Some examples of a application data are the order form, shopper information, and receipt data. Global components such as these are created in the global.asa file and accessed throughout the application.

When a DBStorage component is initialized using the InitStorage method, it is configured to return data in one of two forms; an OrderForm component or a Dictionary component. Once initialized, the all interaction with the DBStorage component must use references to the proper storage component type. If the wrong type is used, either an error will occur or the action will produce unexpected results.

Creating the *DBStorage* Component   The DBStorage component is a top-level component that must be created by with the CreateObject method of the IIS 3.0 Server component. Once a DBStorage component is created, it must be initialized using the InitStorage method before any other DBStorage methods are called. The InitStorage method associates the new DBStorage component with a data source and a table and sets up field mapping information.

Example:

```
Set myOrderFormStorage = Server.CreateObject("Commerce.DBStorage")
Call myOrderFormStorage.InitStorage(myDatasource, "dbTable", "shopper_id",
"Commerce.OrderForm", "marshalled_order", "data_changed")
```

Method List

Method Name	Description
CommitData	Writes data from the DBStorage component to the database.
DeleteData	Deletes a record from a DBStorage component.
DeleteDataKey	Deletes all records from DBStorage component based on. key/value pairs.
GetData	Gets a record from a DBStorage component.
InsertData	Adds a record to DBStorage component.
InitStorage	Initializes a DBStorage component.
LookupData	Gets a record from a DBStorage component.
LookupMultipleData	Gets several records from a DBStorage component.

Part III
Ch
11

Property List

Property Name	Description
Mapping	Maps a database field to an established entry in the DBStorage component.

CommitData Method   The CommitData method saves the data stored in the DBStorage component to the database. The data is written to the table and fields defined in the InitStorage method.

Syntax

DBStorage.CommitData(Null, DataComponent)

Parameters

Null

The first parameter is not used in the v1.0 release of Commerce Server. To avoid unreliable behavior, put the value Null as the first parameter.

DataComponent

An OrderForm or Dictionary component previously loaded with data from this DBStorage component.

Example

```
<% REM -- Add an item to the order
Set myOrder = myOrderFormStorage.GetData(Null, shopperID)
set myItem = myOrder.AddItem(CStr(Request("sku")), Request("quantity"),
request("price"))

REM -- Commit changes to DB
call myOrderFormStorage.CommitData(Null, myOrder)
%>
```

Applies To

DBStorage

See Also

InitStorage

DeleteData Method   The DeleteData method is used to delete the data that matches the item stored in a Dictionary or OrderForm component from the DBStorage component.

Syntax

DBStorage.DeleteData(Null, DataComponent)

Parameters

Null

The first parameter is not used in the v1.0 release of Commerce Server. To avoid unreliable behavior, put the value Null as the first parameter.

DataComponent

An OrderForm or Dictionary component previously loaded with data from this DBStorage component.

Example

```
<% REM -- Clear the shopping cart
   REM -- Get the current order and delete it

Set myOrder = myOrderFormStorage.GetData(Null, shopperID)
call myOrderFormStorage.DeleteData(Null, myOrder)
%>
```

Applies To

DBStorage

See Also

InitStorage, InsertData

DeleteDataKey Method   The DeleteDataKey method removes some or all of the data stored in the DBStorage component. Selection of which rows to delete is based on the supplied key values.

Proper use of the key field is determined by how the DBStorage component was initialized. If there is only a single key field, such as a unique ID field, then a simple value can be specified. If there are multiple keys, then a Dictionary component can be created to hold all of the key field values.

Syntax

DBStorage.DeleteDataKey(Null, Key, Value)

Parameters

Null

The first parameter is not used in the v1.0 release of Commerce Server. To avoid unreliable behavior, put the value Null as the first parameter.

Key

Data used to identify the data to be deleted.

Value

The value of the key. Used to identify the records to be deleted.

Applies To

DBStorage

See Also

`InitStorage, DeleteData`

***GetData* Method**   The `GetData` method retrieves some of all of the data stored in the DBStorage component. Selection of which rows to return is based on the supplied key values.

Proper use of the key field is determined by how the `DBStorage` component was initialized. If there is only a single key field, such as a unique ID field, then a simple value can be specified. If there are multiple keys, then a `Dictionary` component can be created to hold all of the key field values.

The `GetData` method returns the selected data in either an `OrderForm` component or a `Dictionary` component. The type of component returned is determined by how the `DBStorage` component was initialized.

Syntax

`DBStorage.GetData(Null, Key, Value)`

Parameters

`Null`

The first parameter is not used in the v1.0 release of Commerce Server. To avoid unreliable behavior, put the value `Null` as the first parameter.

`Key`

Data used to find the data to be returned.

`Value`

The value of the key. Used to identify the records to be returned.

Applies To

`DBStorage`

See Also

`InitStorage, LookupData`

***InitStorage* Method**   The `InitStorage` method initializes a `DBStorage` component. This method must be called after the `DBStorage` component is created and before any other method is called on the component.

`InitStorage` performs two important tasks when initializing the `DBStorage` component. The method first associates the component with some data by defining a `Datasource` and table. As part of this definition key fields and required data fields are defined.

The other task that `InitStorage` does is to specify what type of component will be used to hold the data returned by this `DBStorage` component. There are two choices here, a component or `Dictionary` or `OrderForm` component. The `Dictionary` component is a generic `DBStorage` object that will hold whatever data is retrieved from the database for the component. The

OrderForm component, on the other hand, is has a specific format that is required for the Order Processing Pipeline. This style of component is typically used to hold a shopper's order.

InitStorage allows for the definition of a special field on the table that will store a "marshaled" object. Commerce Server will store data from variables in this object when there is no field on the database that matches the variable's name.

Syntax

```
DBStorage.InitStorage(Datasource, Table, Key, DataComponent [,MarshalColumn]
[,DateColumn])
```

Parameters

Datasource

A Datasource component.

Table

A table on the database supplied in the Datasource parameter.

Key

The name of a column that has a unique identifier for each row in the table supplied in the Table parameter.

DataComponent

The style of storage that the DBStorage component will use. All data passed into or returned from the DBStorage component will use the same style of data component for storage. The possible values are Commerce.OrderForm and Commerce.Dictionary.

MarshalColumn (Optional)

A field on the table that will be used to store "Marshaled" data. This field must be defined to have an image datatype.

DateColumn (Optional)

A field on the table that will be used to store an update timestamp for the record. This field must be defined as a datetime or small_datetime datatype.

Example

```
Set myOrderFormStorage = Server.CreateObject("Commerce.DBStorage")
Call myOrderFormStorage.InitStorage(myDatasource, "dbTable", "shopper_id",
"Commerce.OrderForm", "marshalled_order", "data_changed")
```

Applies To

DBStorage

See Also

OrderForm Component, Dictionary Component, Datasource Component, Content
➥Component

Part
III

Ch
11

***InsertData* Method**   The InsertData method adds data records to the DBStorage component.

Syntax

DBStorage.InsertData(Null, DataComponent)

Parameters

Null

The first parameter is not used in the v1.0 release of Commerce Server. To avoid unreliable behavior, put the value Null as the first parameter.

DataComponent

An OrderForm or Dictionary component previously loaded with data from this DBStorage component.

Applies To

DBStorage

See Also

OrderForm Component, Dictionary Component

***LookupData* Method**   The LookupData method a single row stored in the DBStorage component. Selection of the row to return is based on the supplied key values.

Proper use of the key field is determined by how the DBStorage component was initialized. If there is only a single key field, such as a unique ID field, then a simple value can be specified. If there are multiple keys, then a Dictionary component can be created to hold all of the key field values.

The LookupData method returns the selected data in either an OrderForm component or a Dictionary component. The type of component returned is determined by how the DBStorage component was initialized.

Syntax

DBStorage.LookupData(Null, Key, Value)

Parameters

Null

The first parameter is not used in the v1.0 release of Commerce Server. To avoid unreliable behavior, put the value Null as the first parameter.

Key

Data used to find the data to be returned.

Value

The value of the key. Used to identify the record to be returned.

Applies To

DBStorage

See Also

InitStorage, GetData

LookupMultipleData Method The LookupMultipleData method retrieves some of all of the data stored in the DBStorage component. Selection of which rows to return is based on the supplied key values.

Proper use of the key field is determined by how the DBStorage component was initialized. If there is only a single key field, such as a unique ID field, then a simple value can be specified. If there are multiple keys, then a Dictionary component can be created to hold all of the key field values.

The LookupMultipleData method returns the selected data as a SimpleList of Dictionary components.

Syntax

DBStorage.LookupMultipleData(Null, Key, Value)

Parameters

Null

The first parameter is not used in the v1.0 release of Commerce Server. To avoid unreliable behavior, put the value Null as the first parameter.

Key

Data used to find the data to be returned.

Value

The value of the key. Used to identify the records to be returned.

Applies To

DBStorage

See Also

InitStorage, LookupData, GetData

Mapping Property The Mapping property is used to map Dictionary or OrderForm fields to fields on the table the DBStorage component is connected to.

Syntax

DBStorage.Mapping.Value("DictionaryField") = "tablefield"

Parameters

DictionaryField

Part
III

Ch
11

The name of the field in the `Dictionary` or `OrderForm` data component to map to the assigned table data field.

Applies To

DBStorage

See Also

InitStorage

Commerce General Data Components

The following components deal with the general issues of managing and storing data in the Commerce Server application. These utility components do not read or write data directly to the database.

Using the *SimpleList* Component

The `SimpleList` component provides a list or open-ended array object for storing lists of similar data items. The result of SELECT query execution is returned as a `SimpleList` of `Dictionary` components.

Entries in a `SimpleList` list have a variant datatype. This means that any data can be stored in the list regardless of its base data type. A `SimpleList` just acts as an indexed container for items, it's up to the application what is stored inside of it.

The `SimpleList` component supports a `Count` property, which can be used as the upper bounds of a VBScript `FOR` statement to iterate though the list. Similarly, the VBScript `FOR EACH` statement can be used to iterate through the list.

The index for a `SimpleList` component is 0 based, this means that the first item in the list is has an index of 0. If an index is used that is beyond the end or beginning of the `SimpleList` component's index bounds, an error is generated.

Creating the *SimpleList* Component   The `SimpleList` component is a top-level component that must be created by with the `CreateObject` method of the IIS 3.0 `Server` component. Once a `SimpleList` component is created, the component's `Add` and `Delete` methods can be used to manipulate the data stored in the list.

Example:

```
Set myListOfThings = Server.CreateObject("Commerce.SimpleList")
Call myListOfThings.Add("now")
Call myListOfThings.Add("is")
Call myListOfThings.Add("the")
Call myListOfThings.Add("time")

REM Write "the" to the output page
response.write(myListOfThings(2))
```

Method List

Method Name	Description
Add	Adds a new data item to the end of the list.
Delete	Deletes an item from the list.

Property List

Property Name	Description
Count	The number of items currently in the list (read-only)

Add Method   The Add method inserts a new item at the end of the list.

Syntax

```
SimpleList.Add(DataItem)
```

Parameters

DataItem

The data item to be added to the list.

Example

```
Call myListOfThings.Add("now is the time")
```

Applies To

SimpleList

See Also

Delete

Delete Method   The Delete method removes an item from the list. The item that is deleted is the one at the index supplied. The indexes for the remaining items in the list are adjusted to fill in the hole left by the deleted item.

Syntax

```
SimpleList.Delete(Index)
```

Parameters

Index

The index of data item to be deleted from the list.

Example

```
Call myListOfThings.Delete(2)
```

Applies To

SimpleList

Part
III

Ch
11

See Also

Add

Count Property   The Count property is a read-only value that can be used to determine the number of items currently in a SimpleList component.

Syntax

```
total = SimpleList.Count
```

Applies To

SimpleList

See Also

Add, Delete

Using the *Dictionary* Component

The Dictionary component is used to store name/value pairs. The internal data structure of a Dictionary component is defined at runtime, an application can add new name/value pairs to the dictionary as needed.

When a Dictionary component is stored in a SimpleList, the dot (.) operator between the SimpleList name and the Dictionary component's field name.

The Dictionary component has no methods, but does support two properties, Count and Value. Value is the default property and does not need to be specified.

Creating the *Dictionary* Component   The Dictionary component is a top-level component that must be created by with the CreateObject method of the IIS 3.0 Server component. Once a Dictionary component is created, name/value pairs can be used to store data in the component.

Example

```
Set myDictionary = Server.CreateObject("Commerce.Dictionary")
myDictionary.time = "12:01"
myDictionary.date = "05/24"
myDictionary.name = "greg"

REM write "greg" to the output page
Response.Write (myDictionary.name)
```

Property List

Property Name	Description
Value	The value of a name field stored in the dictionary.
Count	The number of name/value pairs currently in the dictionary (read-only).

***Count* Property**   The `Value` property is used to access the value for a named field currently in a `Dictionary` component. This is the default property for a `Dictionary` component and may be omitted.

Syntax

```
data = Dictionary.Field.Value
data = Dictionary.Field
```

Applies To

```
Dictionary
```

***Count* Property**   The `Count` property is a read-only value that can be used to determine the number of name/value pairs currently in a `Dictionary` component.

Syntax

```
total = Dictionary.Count
```

Applies To

```
Dictionary
```

Using the *OrderForm* Component

The `OrderForm` component provides a convenient mechanism for storing information about a shopper's order. The `OrderForm` component combines the `SimpleList` component with the `Dictionary` component to form a specialized storage system.

The `OrderForm` component contains information about the order. There is a dictionary of name/value pairs that contain the order control information. These values are described in Table 11.1. The first element of the `OrderForm` component, `Items`, is a `SimpleList` of `Dictionary` components that describe every item the shopper has placed into the shopping cart. The contents of this list is described in Table 11.2.

Some of the element name begin with an underscore character "_". This indicates that these elements are not saved in the `OrderForm` component's storage table. These are only saved when an order is completed and the Commerce Server application is configured to save receipts.

Table 11.1   Contents of the *OrderForm* Component

***OrderForm* Element**	**Description**
`Items`	A `SimpleList` of `Dictionary` components, one for each item in the order. See Table 11.2 for a detailed view of each entry.
`shopper_id`	The shopper ID that this order belongs to.
`date_changed`	The date of the last update for the order.
`order_id`	A unique identifier for this order.

continues

Table 11.1 Continued

OrderForm Element	Description
[order form data]	One name/value pair for every input field on the order form.
_Basket_Errors	A SimpleList of strings describing errors related to products in the basket.
_Purchace_Errors	A SimpleList of strings describing errors related to the Order Processing Pipeline.
_total_total	Total of the purchase for this order. Generated by running the Order Process Pipeline.
_oadjust_subtotal	The total price of the adjustments made to this order. Generated by running the Order Process Pipeline.
_shipping_total	The total shipping cost for the order, if any. Generated by running the Order Process Pipeline with a configured shipping phase.
_tax_total	The total sales tax cost for the order, if any. Generated by running the Order Process Pipeline with a configured tax phase.
_handling_total	The total handling cost for the order, if any. Generated by running the Order Process Pipeline with a configured handling phase.
??_tax_included	The total shipping cost for the order, if any. Generated by running the Order Process Pipeline.
_payment_auth_code	The credit card payment authorization code for the order, if any. Generated by running the Order Process Pipeline with a configured credit card verification phase.

Table 11.2 Contents of the Items *Dictionary* Component

OrderForm Item Element	Description
SKU	The value of the SKU parameter passed in the OrderForm AddItem method.
Quantity	The value of the quantity parameter passed in the OrderForm AddItem method.
name	The value of the name field returned by the product query. This query is defined in the QueryProdInfo phase of the Order Process Pipeline.
list_price	The value of the list_price field returned by the product query. This query is defined in the QueryProdInfo phase of the Order Process Pipeline.

OrderForm Item Element	Description
placed_price	The value of the price parameter passed in the OrderForm AddItem method.
[product data]	The values of all the fields returned by the product query. This query is defined in the QueryProdInfo phase of the Order Process Pipeline.
_n_unadjusted	Generated by running the Order Process Pipeline.
_oadjust_adjustedprice	Generated by running the Order Process Pipeline.
_iadjust_regularprice	Generated by running the Order Process Pipeline.
_iadjust_currentprice	Generated by running the Order Process Pipeline.
_oadjust_discount	Generated by running the Order Process Pipeline.
_tax_total	The sales tax cost for this item, if any. Generated by running the Order Process Pipeline with a configured tax phase.
_tax_included	Generated by running the Order Process Pipeline.

Creating the *OrderForm* Component   The OrderForm component is a top-level component that must be created by with the CreateObject method of the IIS 3.0 Server component.

Example:

```
Set myOrderFormStorage = Server.CreateObject("Commerce.DBStorage")
Call myOrderFormStorage.InitStorage(myDatasource, "dbTable", "shopper_id",
"Commerce.OrderForm", "marshalled_order", "data_changed")
```

Method List

Method Name	Description
AddItem	Adds a new product to the items list.
ClearItems	Removes all the products from the items list.
ClearOrderForm	Removes all the data stored in the OrderForm component.

***AddItem* Method**   The AddItem method inserts a new item at the end of the list.

Syntax

```
OrderForm.AddItem(SKU, Quantity, Price)
```

Parameters

SKU

The SKU or other single unique identification code for the product being placed in the basket. This value will be used in the QueryProdInfo stage of the Order Processing Pipeline as the parameter to the product query.

Quantity

A number indicating the number of items of this type to add to the basket.

Price

The placed price for this item. This value can be used to override the price of the product stored in the database.

Example

```
Call myOrderForm.AddItem("123-44", 1, 1999)
```

Applies To

OrderForm

See Also

ClearItems

ClearItems Method   The ClearItems method removes all of the elements from the Items list, effectively emptying the contents of the shopper's shopping cart.

Syntax

```
OrderForm.ClearItems()
```

Example

```
Call myOrderForm.ClearItems()
```

Applies To

OrderForm

See Also

AddItem, ClearOrderForm

ClearOrderForm Method   The ClearOrderForm method removes all of data from the OrderForm component.

Syntax

```
OrderForm.ClearOrderForm()
```

Example

```
Call myOrderForm.ClearOrderForm()
```

Applies To

OrderForm

See Also

ClearItems

CHAPTER 12

Getting Data onto Your Pages

To use Commerce Server effectively, you need to know a little about the SQL language. Structured Query Language (SQL) is a database query and programming language originally developed by IBM. Today, many of the leading vendors of relational databases use the standard SQL definition of the American National Standards Institute (ANSI). ■

Understanding the SQL language

A brief overview of the Structured Query Language (SQL), including descriptions of the most often used query types.

Defining the data connections for Commerce Server

Learn where and how to define the connections between your Commerce Server application and its database.

Retrieving data by using queries and datastore components

Learn how Commerce Server applications use components to interact with its database.

Reading the returned data and creating pages

Using an example catalog system, learn how to move content from the database to the page.

Reviewing Structured Query Language

The SQL language can be broken into three categories of database-related activities. In the SQL language definition, each of the following categories is also referred to as a language:

- Data Definition Language (DDL): Used to create, modify, and delete databases and database objects such as tables and indexes
- Data Manipulation Language (DML): Used to store, manipulate, and retrieve data from a database
- Data Control Language (DCL): Used to create, modify, and delete database users and data-access controls

Microsoft SQL Server's implementation of SQL follows the ANSI standard closely and enhances it with many extensions and functions. This extended language, known as *Transact-SQL*, can be called by queries and stored procedures. SQL Server also supports many built-in functions for manipulating numeric, string, and data values. For more information about Transact-SQL and SQL Server's built-in functions, see the SQL Server manuals or the SQL Server books online.

The SQL language is a large subject and beyond the scope of this book. If you are not already trained and will be doing database-related development for a Commerce Server site, you need to get some background and training on the subject.

Some good tools can take some of the mystery out of developing SQL queries and databases, however. Both Microsoft Access and Microsoft Visual Interdev allow developers to build queries and databases graphically. Both of these tools allow a developer to connect to an existing database through ODBC drivers. How well the tools work depends on how well the ODBC drivers are written. In some cases, you have full control of the remote database; in others, you are severely limited in terms of what you can do. If you are using SQL Server, you should be able to do most of your development work with these tools.

Using the graphical query builder built into Access or Visual Interdev is a straightforward process. After you establish a connection to the database, you can begin to build SQL queries. To do so, follow these simple steps:

1. Create a new "Local Database Query" in Visual Interdev or click the "New" button on the queries tab in Access.
2. Drag the tables you need in your query from the dataview or tables screen to the newly created query window.
3. Where you need to join two tables, click the joining field in one table and drag it over to the target field on the table you want to join it to.
4. Drag the fields you wish to show in your output and drop them onto the output grid.
5. Specify any sorting or selection criteria.
6. Run the query.

When the query performs to your requirements, you can cut and paste the SQL code into your source.

In addition to building queries, these tools allow direct access to the data stored in the database. A developer can interactively add and modify the data stored in the database's tables. This ability to alter the data interactively can come in quite handy during the development and testing phases of a store.

Identifying Types of SQL Queries

For a Commerce Server project, the most common elements of the SQL language that are used are known as Data Manipulation Language (DML). You will need to know about the four basic types of DML queries:

- SELECT: Used to read data from the database.
- INSERT: Used to write data to the database.
- UPDATE: Used to update data in the database.
- DELETE: Used to delete data from the database.

Following is an example of a SELECT query:

```
SELECT
  product.*
FROM
  product,
  productXCategory
WHERE
  product.id = productXCategory.prodid AND
  productXCategory.catid = 1
ORDER BY
  product.sku
```

This SELECT query combines data from two tables, product and productXCategory. The query specifies that the two tables are joined using the common entries in their productID fields. This results in a virtual table containing one record for every combination of the matching productIDs.

Next the virtual table is scanned looking for records where the value of the catid field is 1. These records are kept in the virtual table and all of the others are dropped.

Finally this query sorts all of the remaining records by using the SKU field and the resulting set is returned.

> **N O T E** You will need to be careful when joining tables. If the tables are very large, or there are many matches between the two fields, then the query can take a very long time to execute and consume a lot of resources.
>
> Make sure that the fields you choose to join contain fairly unique values or that you supply other selection values in the where clause of the query.

Part
III

Ch
12

continues

continued

If you still find that the query takes a long time to run, then you may wish to add indexes to the tables on the fields you are joining. ▪

Following is an example of an INSERT query:

```
INSERT INTO
 product
 (name, sku, list_price)
VALUES
 ("left handed spanner", "PROD-0901", 998)
```

This INSERT query appends one row to the product table, setting the name to "left handed spanner", the sku to "PROD-0901", and the list_price to 998. Any other fields in the table for this row are set to NULL, the empty value.

Following is an example of an UPDATE query:

```
UPDATE
 product
SET
 name = "cheap-o hockey puck",
 list_price = 499
WHERE
 sku = "PROD-0321"
```

This UPDATE query changes all products for which the sku value is "PROD-0321". The name field is set to "cheap-o hockey puck", and the list_price is changed to 499.

Following is an example of a DELETE query:

```
DELETE
FROM
 product
WHERE
 sku = "PROD-0110";
```

This DELETE query deletes from the product table all rows in which the sku field has the value "PROD-0110".

Defining Commerce Server Data Connections

Commerce Server is intended to be tightly integrated with one or more databases. In creating Commerce Server sites it is important to understand how applications interact with data.

When designing a Commerce Server application, you will need to define the interactions that the application will have with the databases and what databases those will be. When these definitions are understood, then these relationships can be coded in the application.

Almost always, these definitions are put into the application's global.asa file. This file contains all of the global variable and component definitions for the application. You will want this file to do the following things:

- Define the data sources
- Define the queries that will drive the data interactions
- Define the application local storage components

The next few sections introduce these concepts and show how the components are defined in the global.asa file.

Defining Commerce Server Data Sources

Connections to the database from Commerce Server are managed through an ODBC data-source specification standard called a data-source name (DSN). A DSN specifies a set of information about connecting to a database, including the database name, a user ID, and a password. For Commerce Server to work properly, you need to supply a complete set of information in the DSN so that the connection can be established without operator intervention.

Following is an example DSN string:

```
"DSN=AnExample;UID=greg;PWD=secret;DATABASE=db1"
```

This string defines a DSN named AnExample. When an application uses this string to connect to a database server, an attempt will be made to open a database named db1. This connection to the server will use the username greg and the password secret.

You can specify a DSN for Commerce Server in two ways. The first (and recommended) method is to create a full DSN definition by using the ODBC32 control panel. When defined, the DSN can be referenced by name in the AddDatasource method of the store's Content object. The data-source definitions for the Content components are specified in the global.asa file for your store.

N O T E The reason that an ODBC-defined connection is preferred is that this definition is reusable in other applications, say Access or Visual Interdev. If you make use of this common definition and if for some reason the security information or database location needs to be changed, then you will only have to change the definitions in one place. If each application had its own DSN definition, then you would need to modify each to reflect any database change. ■

Following is an example of adding a data source based on an externally defined DSN:

```
call content.AddDatasource("myDB","DSN=AnExample")
```

This example associates the data source myDB with the DSN AnExample, which is defined by ODBC32 in the system DSNs. You can also specify the user ID, password, and database, if you want to override (or simply document) the settings in the ODBC system's DSN definition.

An advantage of using this method is that a problem occurs in connecting to the datasource, you can access system DSNs by using other ODBC client tools, such as Access and Excel.

If you do not use ODBC to specify a full DSN, you can define one when the AddDatasource method is called. To do so, specify the entire DSN string as shown above in the DSN parameter.

Following is an example of adding a data source based on a locally defined DSN:

```
call content.AddDatasource("myDB",
➥"DSN=AnExample;UID=greg;PWD=secret;DATABASE=db1")
```

Defining Commerce Server Queries

In Commerce Server, database queries are associated with a `Content` component and can be defined in advance in the `global.asa` file.

The following code sample adds a query called `product` to the `myContent` `Content` component:

```
Call myContent.AddQuery("product",
➥ "SELECT Product.*
➥  FROM Product
➥  WHERE ProductID = :1",
➥ 0,adCmdText,0,adOpenForwardOnly,0)
```

You can use the query later by supplying the name of the query into the `Execute` method for a `Datasource` component.

The following code sample shows how to run a query using the `Execute` method:

```
set items = myDataSource.Execute("product",
➥ CInt(Request("sku")))
```

You can also define queries at runtime by passing the query string into a `Datasource` component's `Execute` method.

The following code sample shows how to run a query that has not been predefined using the `Execute` method:

```
set items = myDataSource.Execute("SELECT Product.*
➥  FROM Product
➥  WHERE ProductID = :1",
➥ CInt(Request("sku")))
```

N O T E   Defining the queries in the code this way is not very efficient in the long run. If you define
all the queries in the `global.asa` file, then you can reuse those definitions throughout the
application. Also, when maintenance time comes, it is much better to know that all of the query
definitions are in one place. If you have to change the query for efficiency, or because one of the tables
has changed, then you will only need to look in one place to make the changes. ■

Defining Storage Components

There are two types of local data storage components in Commerce Server.

- The `Dictionary` Component: Used for general local storage of data.
- The `OrderForm` Component: Used to store the order data. An `OrderForm` component is the only type storage component that can be passed into the order pipeline.

For the most part, Dictionary components are created and used on an as needed basis. These components are typically used to store the data returned from a SQL query on execution. In many cases, in fact, when more than one row is returned by a query, a SimpleList of Dictionary components is created.

To define a global Dictionary component named myDictionary the following lines of code would be added to the global.asa file.

```
Set myDictionary = Server.CreateObject("Commerce.DBStorage")
Call myDictionary.InitStorage(myDataSource,
➥    "product", "product_id", "Commerce.Dictionary")
```

In the first line of this code a DBStorage component is created named myDictionary. The second line then initializes myDictionary as a Dictionary component and connects to the product table of the database by using product_id as the key field.

When data is read from the product table using the myDictionary component, all the fields of the table will be stored in the component. Each field can be accessed by name, using the format myDictionary.name.

An OrderForm component is very similar to the Dictionary component, however, it is used to store a very specific kind of data—orders. Orders contain the shopping basket data and the data that has been entered by the user during the store checkout phase of the application. There is typically only one OrderForm component defined in an application, and it is used as the input data to the order pipeline process.

To define a global OrderForm component named myOrderFormStorage the following lines of code would be added to the global.asa file.

```
Set myOrderFormStorage =
➥    Server.CreateObject("Commerce.DBStorage")
Call myOrderFormStorage.InitStorage(myDataSource,
➥    "my_basket", "shopper_id", "Commerce.OrderForm",
➥    "marshaled_order", "date_changed")
```

In the first line of this code, a DBStorage component is created named myOrderFormStorage. The second line then initializes myOrderFormStorage as an OrderForm component and connects to the my_basket table of the database using shopper_id as the key field.

When data is read from the my_basket table using the myOrderFormStorage component, all the fields of the table will be stored in the component. Each field can be accessed by name, using the format myOrderFormStorage.name.

Getting Product Information on the Page

The following sections provide some real-world examples of using Commerce Server to dynamically create a catalog system. In these sections, you build a small application that shows product categories, displays the products in each category, and allows you to place products in the shopping basket.

Defining the Sample Database Schema

The database used in the examples is a little different from the ones in the starter stores, just to provide some variety. This (very) simple database has four tables that contain all of the information used to run the store.

- ■ Product: This table contains the information used to describe the products used in the store.

  Product
  ProductID
  Name
  Description
  List_Price
  Active

- ■ Category: This table contains information describing the various categories of products in the store. Categories are used in this store to indicate groups of related products.

  Category
  CategoryID
  Name
  Active

- ■ ProductXCategory: This is used to show what products are in what categories. This table allows you to have a many-to-many data relationship between the categories and the products. A many-to-many relationship means that you can have a product that is in multiple categories, as well as having multiple products in one category.

  ProductXCategory
  ProductID
  CategoryID

- ■ Basket: This table is used to store the shopping basket information for store shoppers.

  Basket
  ShopperID
  DateChanged
  MarshaledOrder

An interesting convention used in this store, but not the starter stores, is the Active flag. This flag allows you to disable products and categories temporarily without removing them from the database. This allows the person managing the store to turn off the access to a product when it is temporarily unavailable for some reason.

Defining the *global.asa* file

The first thing that you need to do is define all the data-related components and queries in the global.asa file for your application. When defined, these objects can be referenced from your Active Server Pages (ASP) scripts to create dynamic content for the store.

Listing 12.1 is from the `global.asa` file for the test store. The sections that follow will explain some key sections of the `global.asa` file in greater detail.

Listing 12.1 Code for the Test Store

```
<SCRIPT LANGUAGE=VBScript RUNAT=Server>

Sub Application_OnStart

REM -- ADO command types
    adCmdText     = 1
    adCmdTable    = 2
    adCmdStoredProc = 4
    adCmdUnknown  = 8

REM -- ADO cursor types
    adOpenForwardOnly = 0
    adOpenKeyset  = 1
    adOpenDynamic = 2
    adOpenStatic  = 3

REM -- Define the content component "myContent"
Set myContent = Server.CreateObject("Commerce.Content")

REM -- Define the datasource component "myDS" in
REM -- myContent and specify a complete DSN
Call myContent.AddDatasource("myDS",
➥ "DSN=myDSN;UID=user;PWD=secret;DATABASE=myDB", 1, 0)

REM -- Declare a component "myDataSource" as an instance
REM -- of the datasource myDS
Set myDataSource = myContent.Datasource("myDS")

REM -- Define queries used in the store
Call myContent.AddQuery("product",
➥ "SELECT Product.*
➥  FROM Product
➥  WHERE ProductID = :1",
➥ 0,adCmdText,0,adOpenForwardOnly,0)

Call myContent.AddQuery("categories",
➥ "SELECT *
➥  FROM category
➥  WHERE (active = 1)
➥  ORDER BY SortOrder",
➥ 0,adCmdText,0,adOpenForwardOnly,0)

Call myContent.AddQuery("products-by-cat",
➥ "SELECT Product.*, Category.*
➥  FROM Product
➥  INNER JOIN ProductXCategory ON
➥  Product.ProductID = ProductXCategory.ProductID
➥  INNER JOIN Category ON
➥  ProductXCategory.CategoryID = Category.CategoryID
```

continues

Part

III

Ch

12

Listing 12.1 Continued

```
➥   WHERE (Product.Active = 1) AND
➥   (Category.Active = 1)",
➥ 0,adCmdText,0,adOpenForwardOnly,0)

Call myContent.AddQuery("products-in-cat",
➥ "SELECT Product.*
➥ FROM Product
➥ INNER JOIN ProductXCategory ON
➥   Product.ProductID = ProductXCategory.ProductID
➥ INNER JOIN Category ON
➥   ProductXCategory.CategoryID = Category.CategoryID
➥ WHERE (Category.CategoryID = :1) AND
➥   (Product.Active = 1) AND
➥   (Category.Active = 1)",
➥ 0,adCmdText,0,adOpenForwardOnly,0)

REM -- Create a Shopper Manager
Set myShopperManager =
➥   Server.CreateObject("Commerce.StandardSManager")
Call myShopperManager.InitManager("myStore", "cookie")

REM -- Create a storage object for the
REM -- order forms (shopper's basket)
Set myOrderFormStorage =
➥     Server.CreateObject("Commerce.DBStorage")
Call myOrderFormStorage.InitStorage(myDataSource,
➥ "my_basket", "shopper_id", "Commerce.OrderForm",
➥ "marshaled_order", "date_changed")
```

Connecting to the Database

The first part of the global.asa file that we will examine is where the database connections are defined. To define a connection, first a Content component is created. Then, in the context of that content component, a database connection is defined by using the AddDatasource method and supplying a DSN string.

Once these two steps have been performed, then a Datasource component can be assigned from the Content component. Here are the lines of code from the global.asa file that create the Content object myContent, which is used throughout the store. This code also defines a data source called myDS in myContent that will connect to the store's database. Finally, the code creates the Datasource object myDataSource, which references the DSN.

```
Set myContent = Server.CreateObject("Commerce.Content")
Call myContent.AddDatasource("myDS", "DSN=MSN;UID=sa;PWD=;DATABASE=MSN", 1, 0)
Set myDataSource = myContent.Datasource("myDS")
```

Defining Queries

The next interesting part of the store's global.asa file, is where the queries are defined that are used in the store. The queries get added to the Content component using the AddQuery method. The SQL statements in the following example code have been broken in a syntax-readable way. In a real `global.asa` file, the entire `AddQuery` call must be on one (long) line.

N O T E You will notice that all the example query definitions contain optional parameters. These parameters specify additional query attributes to the database engine.

The settings shown in the following string provide the optimal performance for small, read-only queries:

```
--""--0,adCmdText,0,adOpenForwardOnly,0
```

The following code adds a query named product to the content object. The product query can be executed anywhere in the application to retrieve a product from the database. This query requires that one parameter be passed in. When the query is executed, the parameter will be placed into the placeholder :1. This parameter is used to specify the ProductID of the product to fetch from the database.

```
Call myContent.AddQuery("product",
➡ "SELECT Product.*
➡  FROM Product
➡  WHERE ProductID = :1",
➡ 0,adCmdText,0,adOpenForwardOnly,0)
```

The next sample, shows adding a query to the content object that will be used in the application to get the list of active categories from the database.

```
Call myContent.AddQuery("categories",
➡ "SELECT *
➡  FROM category
➡  WHERE (active = 1)
➡  ORDER BY SortOrder",
➡ 0,adCmdText,0,adOpenForwardOnly,0)
```
```
""""
```

This next query does the work of getting the data about the active products in a category. The query takes a single parameter, the CategoryID to get the products. The query also specifies that both the product and the category must have their active flags set to 1, meaning that they are active and can be displayed.

```
Call myContent.AddQuery("products-in-cat",
➡ "SELECT Product.*
➡  FROM Product
➡  INNER JOIN ProductXCategory ON
➡   Product.ProductID = ProductXCategory.ProductID
➡  INNER JOIN Category ON
➡   ProductXCategory.CategoryID = Category.CategoryID
➡  WHERE (Category.CategoryID = :1) AND
➡  (Product.Active = 1) AND
➡  (Category.Active = 1)",
➡ 0,adCmdText,0,adOpenForwardOnly,0)
```

Displaying Categories

Once the data connections and the queries that are needed for the store have been defined in the `global.asa` file, Active Server Pages (ASP) can be developed that use those queries to display navigation and content pages. The following ASP code examples will show how to make use of the defined queries to build a simple catalog system.

The first page of the catalog system is the categories page, cat.asp, shown in Figure 12.1. This page displays a list of the product categories defined in the database. Each category name is a link that when clicked, brings up a list of products in that category. Since all of this page's content is being created on-the-fly from the database, the store's administrator can change the category listing by adding or deleting categories from the database. Any changes will automatically appear when the page is next generated.

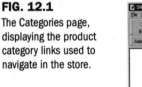

FIG. 12.1
The Categories page,
displaying the product
category links used to
navigate in the store.

Listing 12.2 is from the categories page, cat.asp, of the catalog system. This script does all the work of reading the categories from the database and placing navigation links for each one on the page.

Listing 12.2 Code for the Categories Page

```
<%@ LANGUAGE = VBScript %>
<!--#INCLUDE FILE="include\shop.asp" -->
<% REM -- body %>
<%
set categories = myDataSource.Execute("categories")
%>
<HTML>
<HEAD>
 <TITLE>SHOPPING CATEGORIES</TITLE>
</HEAD>

<BODY>
<P ALIGN="center">
Please select a category to shop
</P>
<BR>
<TABLE CELLSPACING=20 WIDTH=100% ALIGN=CENTER>
<% for each category in categories %>
 <TR>
  <TD ALIGN=CENTER>
```

```
  <FONT SIZE=6">
  <A HREF="catprod.asp?catid=<% = category.categoryid%>">
  <% = category.categoryname %></A>
 </TD>
 </TR>
<% next %>
</TABLE>
<HR>
Products from the shop
</BODY>
</HTML>
```

This script first runs the `categories` query defined in the `global.asa` file. This is done by calling the `execute` method for the `myDataSource` component. The resulting simple list is assigned to the categories variable that will be used later in the script.

```
<%
set categories = myDataSource.Execute("categories")
%>
```

The next interesting section of code creates an HTML table and using the data returned by the query adds one row to the table for every entry in the list. Each table row will display one of the active product categories defined in the database. Each name will serve as the link to a page that will display the products in that category.

To do this, the `for each` looping mechanism is used. This loop will move sequentially through the list from the first to the last entry. For each entry in the list, the `for each` loop assigns the data of the current entry to a variable named `category`. The script can then read the data from this variable and use it in the active content on the page.

```
<TABLE CELLSPACING=20 WIDTH=100% ALIGN=CENTER>
<% for each category in categories %>
 <TR>
  <TD ALIGN=CENTER>
   <FONT SIZE=6">
    <A HREF="catprod.asp?catid=<% = category.categoryid%>">
    <% = category.categoryname %></A>
  </TD>
 </TR>
<% next %>
</TABLE>
```

For each element in the list, the script creates a link to the category's product display page and passes a variable named `catid`. The value for `catid` is set to the current list element's CategoryID. The script then gets the category's name from the current list element and puts it on the page. Finally the script closes the HTML link and moves to the next element in the list.

When all of the elements in the list have been processed, the HTML table is closed and processing is finished. The rest of the page contains standard HTML page tags.

The next page of the catalog system is the Category-Products page, `catprod.asp`, shown in Figure 12.2. This page displays the list of the products in a selected category. Each product name is a link that when clicked, brings up the product order page for the selected product.

Part
III
Ch
12

The product names displayed here are the active products that are listed in the
ProductXCategory table for this CategoryID. The store administrator can change what products are in each category at any time. Any changes to category or product definitions will
automatically appear when the page is next generated.

FIG. 12.2

The Category-Products
page, displaying the
products in a selected
category.

Listing 12.3 is from the Category-Products page, catprod.asp, of the catalog system. This
script has one external parameter, catid, that gets passed in as part of the page's URL. The
value of catid has been set to a known CategoryID in the database by the categories page.
This CategoryID is used as a parameter to the query products-by-cat to get the products that
are defined to be in this category. The results of that query are then read and the list of products displayed on the page.

Listing 12.3 Code for the Category-Products Page

```
<%@ LANGUAGE = VBScript %>
<!--#INCLUDE FILE="include\shop.asp" -->
<% REM -- body %>
<%
 set items = myDataSource.Execute("products-in-cat", CInt(Request("catid")))
%>

<BODY>
<P ALIGN="center">
<FONT FACE="Arial,Helvetica,Sans Serif" SIZE=6>
Here are the products you selected.
</FONT>
</P><BR>

<TABLE>
<% for each item in items %>
 <TR>
  <TD>
   <A HREF="product.asp?sku=<% = item.productID %>">
   <FONT COLOR="00FF00" FACE="Arial,Helvetica,Sans Serif"SIZE=3>
```

```
    <% = item.productname %>
    </FONT>
    <TABLE ALIGN="right" BORDER="1">
     <TR>
      <TD BGCOLOR="FFFFFF" WIDTH=50>
       <A HREF="product.asp?sku=<% = item.productID%>">
        <% = MSCSDataFunctions.Money(item.list_price) %></A>
      </TD>
     </TR>
    </TABLE>
   </TD>
  </TR>
 <% next %>
 </TABLE>
 <HR>
 Products from the shop
 </BODY>
 </HTML>
```

The first thing this script does is execute the products-by-category query defined in the
global.asa file. This is almost the same as the code in category page, except this query requires a parameter specifying the category to display products from. Since the CategoryID is
passed into the page as part of the URL, the Request function is used to get the value and pass
it into the query. The resulting simple list is assigned to the items list variable that will be used
later in the script.

```
set items = myDataSource.Execute("products-in-cat", CInt(Request("catid")))
```

The next interesting section of code creates an HTML table and using the data returned by the
query adds one row to the table for every entry in the list. Each table row will display one of
the active products from the selected category. Each name will serve as the link to a page that
will display the product information.

Part
III

Ch
12

To do this, the for each looping mechanism is again used. For each entry in the list, the for
each loop assigns the current item's data to a variable named item. The script can then read
the data from this variable and use it in the active content on the page.

```
<TABLE>
<% for each item in items %>
 <TR>
  <TD>
   <A HREF="product.asp?sku=<% = item.productID %>">
   <FONT COLOR="00FF00" FACE="Arial,Helvetica,Sans Serif"SIZE=3>
   <% = item.productname %>
   </FONT>
   <TABLE ALIGN="right" BORDER="1">
    <TR>
     <TD BGCOLOR="FFFFFF" WIDTH=50>
      <A HREF="product.asp?sku=<% = item.productID%>">
         <%= MSCSDataFunctions.Money(item.list_price) %></A>
    </TD>
   </TR>
  </TABLE>
```

```
    </TD>
    </TR>
<% next %>
</TABLE>
```

For each element in the list, the script first opens a link to the product description page, `product.asp`, and passes a variable named SKU. The value for SKU is set to the current list element's `ProductID`. The script then gets the product's name from the current list element and puts it on the page and closes the link. Then the script puts the product's price on the page and links that to the product's display page too.

When all of the elements in the list have been processed, the HTML table is closed and processing is finished. The rest of the page contains standard HTML page tags.

The last page of the catalog system is the Product page, `product.asp`, shown in Figure 12.3. This page displays detailed information about the selected product. In addition to the product information there is an Add To Basket button that allows shoppers to add this product to their shopping basket.

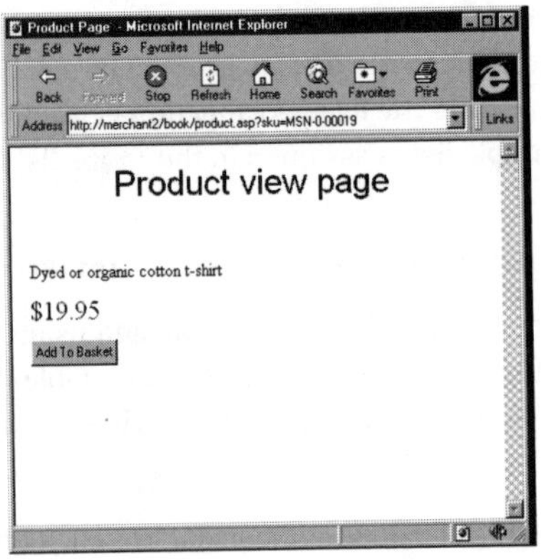

FIG. 12.3

The Product page displays detailed product information.

The following code is from the Product page, `product.asp`, of the catalog system. This script has one external parameter, SKU, that gets passed in as part of the URL. The value of SKU is set in the Category-Products page and is a `ProductID`. This value is used as a parameter to the stored query product. The results of that query are then read and the detail product information is displayed on the page.

```
<%@ LANGUAGE = VBScript %>
<!--#INCLUDE FILE="include/shop.asp" -->
<HTML>
<HEAD>
    <TITLE>Product Page</TITLE>
</HEAD>

<% REM -- body %>
<%
set product = myDataSource.Execute("product",
➥CInt(Request("sku")))(0)
```

```
%>

<BODY>

<P ALIGN="center">
<FONT FACE="Arial,Helvetica,Sans Serif" SIZE=6>
Product view page
</FONT>
</P><BR>

<FORM METHOD="post" ACTION="xt_orderform_additem.asp">
 <INPUT TYPE="HIDDEN" NAME="sku" VALUE="<% = Request("sku") %>">
 <TABLE CELLPADDING="5">
  <TR>
   <TD VALIGN="TOP" WIDTH="400"><FONT SIZE=+2>
    <% = product.productname %></FONT>
   </TD>
  </TR>
  <TR>
   <TD VALIGN="TOP" WIDTH="400">
    <% = product.description %>
   </TD>
  </TR>
  <TR>
   <TD><FONT SIZE="+2">
    <% = MSCSDataFunctions.Money(product.price) %></FONT>
   </TD>
  </TR>
  <TR>
   <TD>
    <INPUT TYPE="SUBMIT" NAME="Add" VALUE="Add To Basket">
   </TD>
  </TR>
 </TABLE>
</FORM>
```

The first thing this script does is to execute the product query defined in the global.asa file. As in the Category-Product page, this query requires a parameter. In this case it needs the ProductID that is to be displayed. Since the ProductID is passed into the page as part of the URL, the Request function is used to get the value and pass it into the query. Since this page is designed to display one product, this code skips getting a simple list, and assigns the result of the query directly to a component. To do this, a (0) is added after the Execute method to make the assignment directly access the first, and only, element from the list.

```
set product = myDataSource.Execute("product",
➥CInt(Request("sku")))(0)
```

The next interesting section of code creates an HTML Form that will allow the user to add this product to the shopping basket. To do this, the form's action is set to xt_orderform_additem.asp function and the value stored in the variable SKU is passed on to it using an HTML input hidden tag.

```
<FORM METHOD="post" ACTION="xt_orderform_additem.asp">
 <INPUT TYPE="HIDDEN" NAME="sku" VALUE="<% = Request("sku") %>">
```

To display the product information to the user, the page is formatted with an HTML table. The product's name, description, and price are all read from the Dictionary component and written to the page. The product's price is reformatted using the Money data function so that it appears in the standard monetary units for this store locality (country).

```
<TABLE CELLPADDING="5">
  <TR>
   <TD VALIGN="TOP" WIDTH="400"><FONT SIZE=+2>
    <% = product.productname %></FONT>
   </TD>
  </TR>
  <TR>
   <TD VALIGN="TOP" WIDTH="400">
    <% = product.description %>
   </TD>
  </TR>
  <TR>
   <TD><FONT SIZE="+2">
    <% = MSCSDataFunctions.Money(product.price) %></FONT>
   </TD>
  </TR>
  <TR>
```

The final step for this page is adding the HTML submit button that will allow this user to add the item to their shopping cart.

```
<TD>
    <INPUT TYPE="SUBMIT" NAME="Add" VALUE="Add To Basket">
   </TD>
  </TR>
 </TABLE>
</FORM>
```

From Here...

In this chapter, various examples were used to show how to get the data from a relational database to the Commerce Server application pages. From establishing database connections and queries in the global.asa file, to writing the product information to a template page.

In upcoming chapters, you will integrate this knowledge with:

- ■ The use of Active Server Pages (ASP) technology.
- ■ Using VBScript programming to interact with and react to the data retrieved from the database.
- ■ Using advanced features of ASP to get the most out of your data.

Creating Stores with Active Server Pages

Introducing Active Server Pages

A decade ago, everyone was excited about a new technology architecture that was going to revolutionize the way that business is conducted in corporate America. This technology would provide a new paradigm for information processing, facilitating collaboration and information sharing across a vast number of systems and organizations. What was this new technology? Client/server computing.

Now the chorus sings again about the latest revolutionary technology: the World Wide Web. You learned in eighth-grade Social Studies that history is bound to repeat itself and those who do not learn from the mistakes of the past are doomed to repeat them. Now we are poised on the edge of the next technological precipice. Numerous systems-development failures have occurred with client/server architecture, but many successes have occurred as well. By understanding the strengths of the client/server architecture, you can implement it in your Active Server Pages (ASP) development.

This chapter discusses what ASP is and why understanding it is imperative for developing Commerce Server 2.0 stores. Because understanding how the client/server model works is an important part of understanding ASP, the chapter first discusses the client/server aspect and then moves to ASP. ■

Understanding client/server architecture

This provides a brief overview of the architecture and how it has evolved over the years.

Examining client/server on the Web

The client/server revolution of the early eighties was a boon to developers for a number of reasons. Looking at its implementation in the past enables you to leverage the inherent strengths of client/server in your ASP development.

Understanding static versus dynamic content creation

Scripting enables for a simple yet powerful method of adding dynamic content to your Web site.

Leveraging scripting in a distributed environment

The choices you make as you decide where to place functionality, on the client and on the server, will expand your application options.

Reviewing Client/Server Technology

Do you remember the first time that you used a PC database? For many of you, that database was dBASE. dBASE and programs like it (Paradox, FoxPro, and Access) provide a quick and easy way to create two-tier client/server applications. In the traditional two-tier client/server environment, much of the processing is performed on the client workstation, using the memory space and processing power of the client to provide much of the functionality of the system. Field edits, local lookups, and access to peripheral devices (scanners, printers, and so on) are provided and managed by the client system.

In this two-tier architecture, the client has to be aware of where the data resides and what the physical data looks like. The data may reside on one or more database servers, on a midrange machine, or on a mainframe. The formatting and displaying of the information is provided by the client application as well. The server(s) routinely only provide access to the data. The ease and flexibility of using these two-tier products to create new applications continue to drive many small-scale business applications.

The three-tier architecture (later called *multitier*) grew out of this early experience with distributed applications. As the two-tier applications percolated from individual and departmental units to the enterprise, people discovered that these application do not scale easily—and in our ever-changing business environment, scalability and maintainability of a system are primary concerns. Another factor that contributes to the move from two-tier to multitier systems is the wide variety of clients within a larger organization. Most of us do not have the luxury of having all our workstations running the same version of an operating system, much less the same OS. This inconsistency drives a logical division of the application components, the database components, and the business rules that govern the processes that the application supports.

In multitier architecture, each of the major pieces of functionality is isolated, as shown in Figure 13.1. The presentation layer is independent of the business logic, which in turn is separated from the data-access layer. This model requires much more analysis and design on the front end, but the dividends in reduced maintenance and greater flexibility pay off time and again.

Multitier Enterprisewide Applications

Imagine a small company. The company may produce a product or sell a service, or both. The company has a few hundred employees in one building and needs a new application to tie its accounting and manufacturing data together. This application is created by a young go-getter in the accounting department who creates an elegant system in Microsoft Access 1.0. The system easily supports the 20 accounting users, all of whom have identical hardware and software.

A few years, the company grows by purchasing a competitor in another part of the country, effectively doubling its size. The need for information sharing is greater than ever. The Access application is given to the new acquisitions accounting department, but alas, all the people in that department work on Macintosh computers.

The company faces several challenges and opportunities at this juncture. The company can purchase new hardware and software for all computer users in the organization, or it can invest in creating a new application to serve both user groups.

FIG. 13.1
Multitier architecture
supports enterprisewide
applications.

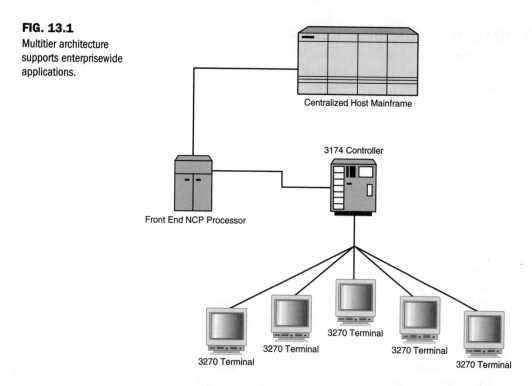

Centralized Host Mainframe

3174 Controller

Front End NCP Processor

3270 Terminal

3270 Terminal

3270 Terminal

3270 Terminal

3270 Terminal

For the purpose of demonstration, assume that the company chooses the second option. Several questions come to mind:

- What model allows the company to provide the information infrastructure that is needed to run the business?

- How can the business ensure that the application won't need to be rewritten after the next acquisition?

- How can the business provide external clients access to parts of the system?

A few years ago, you may have suggested using a client/server cross-platform development toolkit or a 4GL/database combination, which supports multiple operating systems. Today, the answer most likely is an intranet application. A multitier intranet solution provides all the benefits of a cross-platform toolkit without precluding a 4GL/Database solution. If created in a thoughtful and analysis-driven atmosphere, the multitier intranet option provides the optimal solution. Designed correctly, the intranet application provides the flexibility of the client/server model without rigid conformance to one vendor's toolkit or supported platform.

In the company's new model, the client application is the browser that supports data entry, local field edits, and graphical display of the data. The entry to the database information is the intranet Web server. The Web server interacts with several back-end data sources and business-logic models through the use of prebuilt data access objects (DAO). These objects are created and managed through server-side scripting on the Web server. You can implement this scenario with ASP technology, using the information, tools, and techniques discussed in this chapter.

Part
IV

Ch

13

Client/Server with Inter/Intranet(s)

The same multitier architectures that businesses have been effectively using on their LANs and WANs can now be taken advantage of on the Internet and intranet. The client (browser) and the server, when designed correctly, can provide the best of the traditional client/server architecture with the control and management of more-centralized systems.

Developing a multitier client/server system involves three basic steps:

1. Selecting the network component
2. Designing the application architecture
3. Creating the user interface

This section examines each of these steps. By the end of the following discussion, you will understand how to effectively use the client/server model in your Internet/intranet development.

The most important step, of course, is the first. Before undertaking any new development effort, you need to have a thorough understanding of the information that your users require. With this knowledge, you can develop a firm, well-documented feature set. From these pieces of information, you can complete the functional specification for the new application.

N O T E With the advent of RAD (Rapid Application Development) tools, writing code first and asking questions later is tempting. Although this method can be successful in small applications, it can lead to major problems in a more-substantial systems-development effort. Remember that your users can have a system with two of the following three attributes: fast, good, and cheap. The fast/cheap combination has never been a good career choice. ▪

Identifying the Client/Server Components

You have the idea, the specifications, and the will to continue. (Right?) Now you can use the client/server model to complete your detail design and start development. But first, examine each of the steps (bet you're glad that this process doesn't have 12 steps) and how the client and server component roles are defined.

The Network Component

In traditional client/server development, the choice of the communication protocol is the basis for the system. Choosing among the vast number of protocols and selecting appropriate standards is the first step. Specifying connectivity options and internal component specs (routers, bridges, and so on) is a vital decision in creating a system.

In the Internet world, these choices are academic. You use the existing TCP/IP network layer and the HTTP protocol for network transport and communication.

The Application Architecture

Now you get to the heart of your application-design decisions. Sadly, you have no quick and easy answers when you begin to choose the data stores that your application interacts with.

Remembering that the choices you make now will affect the system over its entire useful life is important. Making the correct choices of databases, access methods, and languages guarantees the success or failure of your final product.

A helpful way to think about your application is to break it down into functions that you want to perform. Most client/server applications are built around a transaction processing model. This model allows you to break the functions into discrete transactions and handle them from beginning to end.

In the Internet world, thinking of a Web page as being a single transaction set is helpful. The unit of work that is done by any one page—either a request for information or the authentication of actions on data that is sent—can be considered to be a separate transaction. Using this model, you can easily map these document-based transactions against your data stores. The Active Server Pages environment, through server-side scripting and DAOs, enables you to leverage this model and to create multitier client/server Internet applications.

If your application will use legacy data from a database contained on a back-end or host-based computer, you need to have a facility for accessing that data. The ASP environment provides a set of component objects that enable connectivity to several DBMS systems.

Through the use of scripting on the server, you can also create instances of other OLE objects that can interact with midrange or mainframe systems to add, retrieve, and update information.

Front-End Design

As you have already learned, one of the great benefits of the client/server architecture is its fundamental guidelines to provide a multiplatform client application. With the advent of the World Wide Web and the Web browser, you can provide active content to users from a variety of platforms. Although great movement toward standardization of HTML is occurring, many vendor-specific features appear in browsers today.

This situation means that you have a couple of important choices to make, similar to the choices that you have to make when you create traditional multiplatform client applications. When you develop with traditional cross-platform toolkits, you have several options:

■ **Code to the lowest common denominator.** This option involves selecting and implementing the features that are available on all the client systems that you want to support. This method is a good way to support everyone, but you have to leave out those features within each system that make the system unique. You may want to implement a container control for your OS/2 application, for example, but no similar control is available for the Mac. As a consequence, this multi-platform attempt falls out of the common-denominator controls list.

- **Create a separate application for each client.** This option ensures that each client application makes full use of the features of the particular operating system. The big drawback, of course, is that you have multiple sets of client code to support. This singular approach may be achievable for the first version, but having to manage the numerous code bases you will accrue and carry through system changes to each code base can be a huge effort.

- **Make the majority of the client code shared.** The last option is a good choice in most scenarios, because the majority of the code is shared between applications. You can then use conditional compilation statements to include code that is specific for any client system. This multi-platform approach is even easier when you use a browser as the client. Within an HTML document, if a browser does not support a particular tag block, it ignores it.

Summarizing Client/Server Architecture

As stated laboriously in the preceding sections, the client/server architecture has been a buzzword for years now. Many definitions of this architecture exist, ranging from an Access application with a shared database to an all-encompassing transaction processing system across multiple platforms and databases.

Throughout all the permutations and combinations, the following major themes remain consistent:

- **Requester/provider relationship.** The client and the server have well-defined roles, the client requesting a service and the server fulfilling the service request.

- **Message-based communication.** The communication between the client and server (or among the client, middleware, and server) is a well-defined set of rules (messages) that govern all communications, a set of transactions that the client sends to be processed.

- **Platform independence.** Due to the clearly defined roles and message-based communication, the server or service provider is responsible for fulfilling the request and returning the requested information (or completion code) to the client. The incoming transaction can be from a Windows client, an OS/2 machine, or a Web browser.

- **Dynamic routing.** The client can send a transaction to a service provider and have the request fulfilled without having to be aware of the server that ultimately fulfills the request. The data or transaction may be satisfied by a database server, a midrange data update, or a mainframe transaction.

Generating Web Pages

When I first started surfing the Web, one of my first finds was a wonderful, informative site offering the latest and greatest in sporting equipment. The site had a well-organized page with interesting sports trivia, updated scores during major sporting events, and a broad selection of equipment and services.

Over the next few months, I visited the site from time to time to see what was new and interesting in the world of sporting goods. What struck me was the fact that the content did not seem to change over time. The advertisements were the same; the information provided about the products was the same; and much of the time, the "updated" information was stale. Last summer, while looking for new wheels for rollerblades, I was surprised to find that the site's Christmas special was still running.

People surf the Web for several reasons: to find information, to view and purchase products, and to be informed. Nothing is worse than going to a fondly remembered site and being confronted with stale advertising or outdated information. The key to having a successful site is providing up-to-date, dynamic content.

Most of the information provided by current sites on the Internet consists of links between static informational pages. A cool animated GIF adds to the aesthetic appeal of a page, but the informational content and the way that it is presented are the measures by which the site is ultimately judged.

To provide the most useful and entertaining content possible, you must be able to provide almost personal interaction with your users. You need to provide both pre- and post-processing of information requests, as well as to manage interactions across your links. You must provide current (real-time) content and must be able to exploit the capabilities that the user's browser exposes. One of the many components available in the ASP environment is an object through which you can determine the capabilities of the user's browser. This component is just one of the many features that you can use to provide a unique, enjoyable experience for your users.

A great, yet basic and simple, example of something that shows you how a page is changing with each hit is the hit counter. This capability, although easy to implement, in itself shows the user that the page is continually changing. Also, you can easily have the date and time show up as a minor part of your pages. All these little things (in addition, of course, to providing current information) help your Web site to seem new and up-to-date each time a user visits it.

Adding Scripting to Active Server Pages

A variety of tools enable you to create Internet applications. The best of the new breed of tools, called *scripting languages*, enable you to add value to your Web pages by providing client-based functionality. You can perform field edits and calculations, write to the client window, and employ a host of other functions without having to make another trip to the server for additional information.

What is so exiting about the newest scripting technology is the fact that it is implemented not only on the client, but now also on the server. With ASP, you can leverage your knowledge of scripting on the server. In addition to the basic control and flow that many scripting languages provide, you can access objects from within your scripts to provide additional functionality and power. These objects provide you the capability to communicate with those multiple tiers of information in the client/server model.

To make a quick process check, you now know about the client/server multitier architecture and how to use it effectively on the Internet and in an intranet. You have a good understanding of the type of content that you must provide, and you know about scripting, which can tie all the pieces together and make them work. The next step is deciding what functionality should go where.

Obviously, a great chunk of the processing ultimately resides on the server. All database access and access to other internal data sources is provided by the server. Interpage linking and responses to user requests also are handled on the server. The decision about what functionality to place in the browser client is the same as you discovered when reading about the challenge of supporting multiple operating systems in the traditional client/server environment. There are many opinions from many scholors as to the best approach to conquer the feat of multiple OS applications, the following is a list of approaches commonly used to provide this multiple OS Client/Server architecture.

- **The lowest-common-denominator approach**. This approach provides the greatest guarantee that your active content can be viewed in its entirety on any browser.
- **The OS-specific (browser-specific) functionality approach**. By determining the capabilities of the browser as the information is requested, you can tailor the returned document to exploit the browser's capabilities.
- **A combination of the two approaches**. Most sites that you visit today have a link to a text-only version of the document. This capability is important, not only to ensure that all users can get the information, but also to enable those users who have less-capable equipment to have a full and rich experience from your active content.

The scripting language that you use on the client depends wholly on the capabilities of the browsers that request your pages. Java Script is supported in the Netscape Navigator family of browsers. VBScript and Java Script are supported in the Microsoft Internet Explorer browser. Given the remarkable changes in browser software over the past year, you can expect the two major scripting dialects to be supported across all major browsers in the near future.

When used within the confines of Internet Explorer, VBScript and Java Script are functionally equivalent. Both languages provide a rich, Basic-like scripting language that is interpreted by the browser at runtime to provide client-side intelligence and an enhanced user experience.

VBScript is a subset of the popular Visual Basic language. For the legions of Visual Basic developers, VBScript is a natural progression and useful tool for creating interactive Web pages. With the release of Active Server Pages, scripting has been taken to another level. Now you can use the same versatile scripting to add value to the server-side of the process as well as to the client side.

From Here...

Figuring out how to best employ scripting in an Internet environment can be a daunting task. You have learned how you can benefit from the experience of thousands of developers who have used multitier architecture to create enterprisewide applications. You can create Internet applications with the same transaction-based, flexible, and client-neutral functionality that has been driving businesses for the past decade.

In the next chapter, "Introduction to ASP Scripting," you take a leap forward and see how you can apply this information to the ASP architecture.

- Chapter 14, "Introduction to ASP Scripting," will further discuss the client/server model discussed in this chapter and how the model relates to ASP scripting.
- Chapter 15, "Working with Active Server Web Pages," will show you how to use ActiveX, OLE, and OOP methods within the ASP realm.
- Chapter 16, "Integrating VBScript into ASP," will cover the basic concepts on how to integrate VBScript and ASP to use the ActiveX and OLE controls.
- Chapter 18, "Constructing a Server Component Using ASP," will discuss the components that ship with Commerce Server 2.0, these are the components you will implement in your ASP applications.

Part
IV

Ch
13

Introduction to ASP Scripting

Up to now, this book has covered the information that you need to create your first Active Server Page and your first ASP application with Microsoft Commerce Server 2.0, and you have seen the essence of Internet/intranet design. Chapter 14, "Introducing Active Server Pages," discusses the basics of information architectures and gives you a feel for the historic roots of ASP development, as well as a good understanding of the client/server model.

This chapter introduces the players in the new game: the ASP development game. This chapter also serves as a wrap-up of the material covered thus far. The aim here is coherence, giving you a firm conceptual foundation from which to build a solid understanding of the underlying technology of ASP and how it relates to Commerce Server 2.0. ■

Learn what an Active Platform is

You see the abstract features of Microsoft's Active Platform, and you learn about the Active Desktop and the Active Server: two symmetric programming models that will revolutionize the development of client/server programming for the Internet and for intranets of all sizes.

Get acquainted with the plumbing of ASP

Learn the implementation details of ASP and what makes them work.

The inside of ASP

You've seen how ASP's abstract parts relate and what its infrastructure looks like; now see what the inside of an `.asp` file looks like.

Defining Active Platform

In November 1996, Microsoft formally introduced the Active Platform at the Site Builders Conference and the Professional Developers Conference. At those events, the audience saw a graphic similar to the one shown in Figure 14.1, which outlined the major parts of Microsoft's vision of the future of Internet development. The two pillars of client-side and server-side scripting have a common tool set and are both based on consistent standards and protocols. ASP's Client/Server implementation is a complete model and is presented in detail in the rest of this chapter.

FIG. 14.1

The Active Platform incorporates similar functions for the client and the server, exploiting their individual strengths.

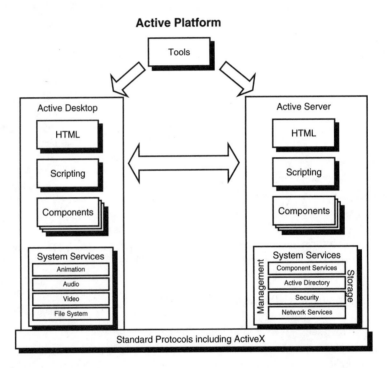

The Active Platform Vision

The Active Platform is Microsoft's vision of the next generation of distributed computing, exploiting the best of the centralized programming models, as well as the best of decentralized programming. The Microsoft vision has profound implications for the Internet (not merely for industrial-strength Client/Server programming) and for the way that systems are developed and deployed. Microsoft's model creates applications that are logically centralized and physically decentralized. A *logically centralized* system can be administered from anywhere. Such a system is conceptually simple and, when properly tooled, easy to manage. *Physically decentralized* systems can be more efficient, fault-tolerant, powerful, and scalable, as long as the high speed connection to centralize their uses is available.

Two Profound Paradigm Shifts

Microsoft's vision has two more key features. First, until the advent of the Active Server, programmers spent too much time worrying about infrastructure (programming Database Management System connections, for example) and not enough time in their core competence (that is, doing something useful with the records fetched from the Database Management System (DBMS)). By bringing the system services closer to the program and abstracting these services into server components, ASP promises productivity gains absolutely unrivaled in the history of computing.

The other feature of Microsoft's vision for ASP is in one of the company's key design goals for ActiveX Data Objects: *universal access,* not *universal storage.* This preference for knowing where everything is instead of collecting everything in one place is the natural extension of the overall mission of ASP: keeping things logically centralized and physically decentralized.

What strikes me most about this vision is the fact that both sides of the diagram are almost identical, evidently different only to the extent of system services. You may protest "I thought you said this was Client/Server programming," but don't allow looks to deceive you. Under this apparent similarity are important differences.

Scripting

As you will clearly see, client-side scripting and server-side scripting have different missions in life. Client-side scripts most often add improved user interface (when HTML forms are used) and data validation. Server-side scripts are practically unlimited, but they are used primarily to capture business rules and access to data (the second and third tiers in three-tier Client/Server programming).

For example, suppose you want to limit the number of items a shopper can select from your store (maybe you are short on stock, and you want the product to get around). A common programming practice would be to evaluate the number of items selected against some MAX value, and if the shopper has selected too many, let them know.

You could write this evaluation into the HTML document, which would result in the evaluation being done on the shopper's machine. This results in an excess of work to be done, because the MAX value is contained on the server, which means the browser would have to query the server for this value.

The advantage of using ASP (notice the Server in ASP) is that you can use ASP to do these evaluations before the HTML (generated) document is passed to the users machine, this saves much time when you introduce many of these queries. Later in this book we will discuss other ways to make these evaluations using some features provided by Commerce Server 2.0.

The important thing to stress is that server-side can, if properly implemented, create client-side scripts that will save your shopper's much time. One of the most important issues in Internet development is choosing between programming to the broadest audience and programming for the richest online experience. Server-side scripting is important for two reasons:

■ Server-side scripts can sense the capabilities of requesting client programs.

■ These scripts can be as powerful as you, the designer, want, regardless of how thin the client is.

In today's Internet, a major difference among Web clients is whether they recognize ActiveX controls or not. Again, the Active Server Page doesn't care one way or the other. If ASP senses the capability to interpret ActiveX controls, it presents those controls; otherwise, it includes static images (or text, if necessary).

Of far greater importance than these mundane issues is the fact that ASP promotes a new level of processing power into Web servers. Remembering that Web servers were never designed to be application servers is critical; they were designed to deliver HTML. The application model remains today's Web server's primary mission, even on the Active Platform, but with ASP, this design constraint ceases to be a constraint at all.

The scripts that are contained in ASP, especially those that are driven by Active Server components (discussed in the following section), bring virtually all the power of traditional client/ server programming to the Web server. Indeed, to the extent that Active Server components are used, ASP can do things that even the most sophisticated client/server programs can't, as you will see in the next section.

Components

The single most important feature of ASP is definitely the supporting of components within an ASP page. Their importance to ASP is understandable when you step back and see how pervasively Microsoft has embraced components in virtually everything it creates. Microsoft engineers have "componentized" everything from the Internet Explorer to Windows NT 5.0. Components give programmers many advantages, including lower development time and cost; added flexibility; easier maintenance; and, most important, easy scalability.

For the ASP development community, on the server side, server components are either intrinsic to the Active Server or user-defined. On the client side, ActiveX controls provide functionality similar to that of server components.

N O T E Because the word *component* is a generic term meaning any kind of part, this book uses the expression *server component* to refer to that special feature of ASP. ■

Active Server Components

Active Server components do two basic things: directly expose operating-system services to your ASP and encapsulate business rules in a way that is extremely easy to program. Perhaps even more important in the long run, Active Server components are easy to create. With programming tools and environments optimized to work with the Active Platform, writing sophisticated server components no longer is the province of advanced programmers.

A truism in programming says that the best programmers are users. Active Server components prove that statement to be not only true but important as well. In the summer of 1996, it was estimated that the number of lines of Visual Basic code finally exceeded the number of lines of code written in COBOL, the perennial champ. Perhaps the biggest reason why Visual Basic is so prolific is that users, not professional programmers, wrote these "extra" lines of code. Active Server component development brings the same ease of programming to the Internet that Visual Basic brought to creating Windows programs.

To get a feel for what server components are and what they do, examine a few of those that ship with the Active Server:

- Browser Capabilities—The Browser Capabilities component is the component that permits an Active Server Page to determine what kind of browser or Web client program is making a request. The component makes this determination by looking to the User Agent HTTP header and looking up the identified browser in the browscap.ini file. All the listed features of the browser are exposed as properties of the Browser Capabilities component.

- TextStream—The Browser Capabilities component is a clever piece of code, but it doesn't have anything to do with the operating system. One component that does get closer to the OS is the TextStream component. This component relies on the FileSystem object, which, as its name suggests, accesses low-level file I/O. With this component, opening or creating text files in the directory system is a simple, direct process. Navigating the files' contents is an equally straightforward process.

- Database Access—One Active Server component may keep you up nights. The Database Access component exploits an operating-system service of earthshaking importance: objects in the directory system.

Actually, the earth won't shake until Windows NT 5.0 ships; at that time, ActiveX Data Objects (ADO) will be incorporated into the Windows NT Directory Services. That is, you will be able to manage the directory system like a database. Files will become database objects with properties that are exposed to ADO.

You can already see what these properties will look like when you right-click the file and choose the Properties menu option for any file on your Windows Desktop. By the way, these directory services aren't restricted to the Windows Explorer and the local file system; they reach out to every file system on the Internet!

A key design goal of ADO is to provide universal access to information, and I do mean *universal*. To ADO, whether the data is a record in an ODBC database or a message stored in Exchange Server doesn't matter. Whether the data is stored on your own hard drive or on one in the Smithsonian doesn't matter, either; ADO finds it and presents it to your application (possession no longer is nine-tenths of the law). Again, this universalism is the logical conclusion of the Web. The Web doesn't allow you to take possession of HTML; it just allows you to see HTML. ADO doesn't allow you to possess the data, either; it just makes the data available to your application.

Part
IV

Ch

14

N O T E   When you make a connection to a data store with ADO, you can specify how long to wait
for a connection to be made. If the connection isn't made in time, the attempt is abandoned, and the data provider returns a trappable error to ADO. Not all data providers will support this
feature. ▨

Now imagine programming when most of the work done by your applications is done with the
aid of other people's server components. Whether you use a server component to access an
interactive feature in your Web site or you access network functionality in Windows NT 5.0,
you can do far more programming of the real task at hand rather than wasting time doing
things that every other programmer in the world is doing at the same time you are.

Even if the objects exposed by Active Server components don't qualify as true objects in the
minds of the purists, the kind of objectcentric programming that will become commonplace in
ASP development will have an impact great enough that most of us will forget about polymorphism and inheritance.

ActiveX Controls

ActiveX controls are used like server components, only on the client side. That is, you instantiate an ActiveX control in a client-side script with the OBJECT tag; then you manipulate this
control through its exposed properties and methods. Most ActiveX controls enhance the user
interface of your Web applications, but some can simply return a value directly to your application. You can write an ActiveX control that makes a complex calculation from given inputs, for
example. The control receives the inputs through its properties, and the resulting calculation is
returned to the calling application through a separate property.

On the other hand, Active Server components never have a user interface; they are designed to
render services to your server application for the purpose of producing standard HTML output. In other words, ASPs are never used directly by people. ASPs produce the HTML that
users see, and that HTML may include ActiveX controls. Sensing browser capabilities, manipulating text files, providing HTML source code with a randomly selected image, and filling the
controls in an HTML form with data from a database are all examples of the usefulness of
server components.

One of the most important aspects of the relationship between the Active Desktop and the
Active Server is the fact that server components can be made from existing ActiveX controls.
In fact, Microsoft encourages this approach, for three reasons.

■ You don't need to reinvent the wheel.

■ Incorporating ActiveX controls into server components is too easy for you to not exploit
this advantage.

■ Especially important in the context of Java and ActiveX controls, this approach gives you
direct access to the Windows graphical user interface.

Indeed, more and more of Windows will be available to the ASP developer through this
medium, so get used to taking advantage of it now. Dividends await the astute.

You may be tempted to suggest that Microsoft also wants you to use ActiveX controls for self-serving reasons, but this allegation carries less weight now that the Open Group is responsible for the standard.

NOTE The Open Group, created in 1996 to act as the holding company for The Open Software Foundation (OSF) and X/Open Company Ltd., provides a worldwide forum for collaborative development and other open-systems activities. ■

System Services

Writing a book about emerging technology is never easy. Writing this book was particularly challenging because even the operating system was making profound changes under our feet. When the first readers open the pages of this book, Microsoft may have already shipped the next generation of its Windows NT operating system—Windows NT 5.0. At the same time, Microsoft will be developing and shipping servers that are meant to be integral parts of Windows NT, most of which cost nothing to add on.

These servers are awesome achievements in data processing. Products such as the Microsoft Transaction Server (MTS), the Message Queuing Server (MQS), and the Index Server are vital parts of the extended Active Platform. A detailed discussion of these products would require a separate book for each one.

The point is that as powerful and revolutionary as the Active Platform is, it does not fully empower you as a user, programmer, or developer until you implement them into related technologies, such as those just mentioned.

When you become a proficient developer of Active Server components developing sophisticated, two-tier Client/Server apps, using DCOM (Distributed Component Object Model) to deploy your components and ASPs, you will not want to administer this large project without the managerial genius of Microsoft Transaction Server.

If you expect difficulties and delays in the actual day-to-day use of your application, and if you don't want the entire system to come down while you sort out the inevitable traffic jams on the Internet, you will be forced to implement the Message Queuing Server.

Understanding the Active Server Programming Model

Now that the abstract features of the Active Platform have been discussed, you will now learn about the Active Server programming model. How do you actually implement ASP?

As you can see in Figure 14.2 the processing environment of ASP is much richer than your run-of-the-mill Web site. Actually, the full richness of this environment is impossible to depict; the programming environment of the Active Server is both rich and accessible to all programming-skill levels.

Part
IV

Ch
14

FIG. 14.2

The programming environment of the Active Server is both rich and accessible to all programming skill levels.

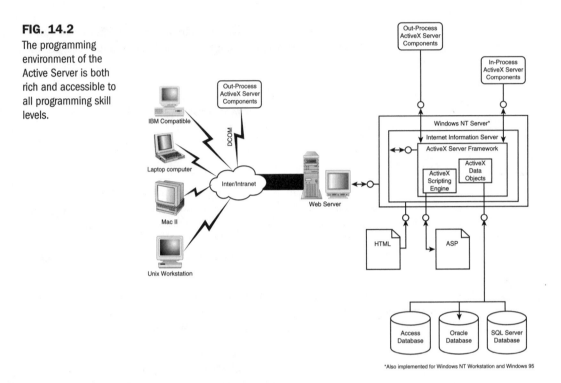

*Also implemented for Windows NT Workstation and Windows 95

ASP serves all clients, versions, and platforms because ASP produces nothing but HTML. The constraint is not in ASP but in HTML. If you want ASP to produce HTML that's rich in ActiveX controls, ASP complies without complaint, but any clients that are not ActiveX-enabled do not work the way you expect them to. With ASP, you can produce HTML code that's consistent with the capabilities of the client, from the most basic feature set to the most advanced.

This discrepancy is best displayed by business and science that most severely test the practical feasibility of the Web, because computation drives most of the need for their data processing.

Because computation is encapsulated in components, and because ASP is a componentized development and deployment environment, ASP shines brightly, attracting the best programming talent in the world. Instead of having to write large, complex applications, these programmers can write compact, computationally intense programs. That situation is a fundamental paradigm shift of the first order.

This paradigm brings up the next-most-noticeable feature of the out-process server, DCOM.

Distributed Component Computing

As you may know, the entire vocabulary of OLE was supplanted recently by Component Object Model (COM). With the advent of Windows NT 4.0, COM evolved into the Distributed Component Object Model (DCOM). This specification was designed to permit developers to store their Active Server components (or to access someone else's) anywhere on any network. Understanding that part of your ASP application can be out on the Internet is imperative; the application doesn't have to be on your own Web server.

Currently, only out-process servers can be deployed with DCOM. The implication in the Microsoft literature is that one day, in-process DLL servers will run in another server's address space on a remote machine.

An Overview of Server Types

If you look in your Windows directory, you see two predominant file types: `.exe` and `.dll`. The `.exe` file can be activated directly by the user; the `.dll` (which stands for Dynamic Link Library) file, on the other hand, can be used only by another program. As such the `.exe` file runs in its own address space and the `.dll` file runs in the address space of another `.exe` file. The `ASP.DLL` (the ASP program) file, for example, runs in the address space of `INETINFO.EXE` (the Internet Information Server program).

Any program that runs in its own address space is called an *out-process server*, and any program running inside an out-process server is called an *in-process server*.

At this point, you may be asking, "So what? Isn't the Internet just one big computer system where you can call any file on any server and have the results delivered to the client that addressed you with the request? What does DCOM give you that's unique?"

Fair enough, but let us warn you at the outset that the answer you read here will make much more sense when you understand how to create your own Active Server components.

The simplest way to answer the question is to say that DCOM permits the ASP developer to create instances of objects from components that are not on the same machine, and to do so in the context of a single program: a single HTTP transaction.

To better understand this complex Client/Server model, again think about what would have to happen in a large, complex ASP application if you want to use the Internet instead of DCOM. To use the Internet to access other servers and their resources, you need a separate HTTP transaction. You can't nest HTTP transactions, because they're all self-contained units. When you call a server with an URL, you initiate an HTTP transaction with a request, and your client waits for the HTTP response. If your ASP application already has been called and is in the process of delivering the requested resource, it can't stop what it's doing, initiate another HTTP request, and then incorporate the response into the response that it then makes itself. Do you see the quandary?

With DCOM, these problems are solved. You use the out-process Active Server component that you are accessing with DCOM *exactly as though it were on your own computer.* You instantiate the component just like in-process DLL servers, and you manipulate it with its exposed methods and properties exactly as you do its lightweight cousin, the in-process server. Think of DCOM as being an "Internet inside the Internet." Microsoft sure has you running around in circles using this absolutely brilliant Client/Server model.

From Desktop Apps to Client/Server Apps

ASP has everything a programmer (or power user) needs to turn his or her old desktop applications into full-blown, three-tier client/server applications almost overnight.

In "Active Server Components" earlier in this chapter, you saw that a great deal of Visual Basic code is out there. Porting the business rules contained in that code to VBScript is a slam dunk. Using Visual Basic 5.0 Control Creation Edition to turn those programs into real DLLs is simple now; accessing data through ActiveX Data Objects is an integral part of ASP; and using DCOM to distribute these ActiveX Data Objects around the world, if necessary, finishes the transformation.

And more is in store. Porting legacy applications is one thing, but writing new code from scratch (still using your tried-and-true friend, Visual Basic) you now can create *asynchronous servers*. These servers take your requests, return a success code, and then do time-consuming processing, updating the client program's user interface later, when everything's done. This Client/Server model allows the user to see progress with the user interface while the important information is generated.

Suppose that you are a financial adviser, and you have a client who makes a request of one of these asynchronous servers. Your client wants to know his current position in the market but doesn't want to sell his stock unless his portfolio is in real need of rebalancing. He launches Internet Explorer and calls a portfolio server hosted by you, the financial adviser. Your server knows what assets your client holds, as well as where the last asset-allocation model is stored. The server retrieves the model and reruns it.

Your asynchronous server then makes a request of the virtual operations center (which collects the transaction and pricing data for all your clients, as well as those of several other financial advisers across the country) and updates your client's portfolio with the most-current data.

N O T E Hiding in the preceding story is a subtle but important advantage of ASP apps. These apps can hide the details about how you interact with the structure of a database system, yet they give your client all the access to that data that he needs. The watchword is *control*. No one has to know anything about your system—only what methods and properties are exposed by its mediating objects. ▪

While the transaction data is being collected, your asynchronous server makes another request of yet another asynchronous server that handles mutual-fund analysis. Your server asks for the top 10 mutual funds whose asset classes match those required by the asset-allocation model that it passes along for reference.

While it waits for the list of funds, your asynchronous server gets updated with the results of the latest transactions, and it sees that the market has been good to your client. Then your portfolio server rebalances your client's portfolio, which is lopsided in stocks, and makes another request of the mutual-fund server for any new asset class that it selected as a result of optimizing the portfolio.

Your asynchronous server places all this data, and its recommendations for sells and buys, in an e-mail message and sends the message to you, with an Urgent flag attached. You see the urgent message appear on-screen while you read your personal edition of one of the main investment e-zines (also driven by an ASP application). You review the results of processing and, in the interest of prudence, make the necessary changes that the overaggressive portfolio server suggested.

When the dust settles, your client gets an e-mail message, notifying him that all processing has been completed and is ready for his review and approval. He sends an HTTP request to another Active Server Page, which displays the new information, and your client approves it for implementation.

Every piece of the preceding programming scenario can be written today by a sufficiently skilled ASP developer.

Seeing Where ASP and HTTP Fit Together

Three entities are involved in an HTTP transaction: the Web client, the Web server, and the human being.

The Web client and Web server communicate by using HTTP headers. *Headers* are collections of data that the client and server exchange to ensure that regardless of the contents of the body of the HTTP transaction, the entire transaction remains coherent and complete.

The data displayed to the human being is transmitted from the Web server to the Web client, and the Web client transfers the text and the interpreted HTML source code to the screen or printer, so that the human can read it.

ASP permits the developer to affect all facets of the HTTP transaction. The ASP objects known as *Request* and *Response* interact with the HTTP body and headers, respectively. This feature gives the ASP developer almost unlimited flexibility in management of interaction on the Web.

Using these two objects allows the developer to authenticate secure HTTP transactions and control the contents of the STATUS header, blocking access to requested content when such access would violate established security policy. You can implement even complex authentication schemes by using new headers that are defined just for your ASP application.

The Active Server is implemented as an ISAPI (Internet Server Application Programming Interface) filter running under Microsoft Internet Information Server (IIS). Whenever a Web client makes an HTTP request of a Web server, the Active Server ISAPI filter gets a chance to intercept the request. If the request is for an .asp file, the Active Server takes over from IIS, parses the entire file from top to bottom, processes the server script(s), and returns an HTML output file to IIS. IIS then returns this data stream to the requesting Web client.

Part

IV

Ch

14

> **N O T E** Be careful when you enter an URL for your .asp files. Depending on the browser you use if you don't use the protocol prefix HTTP://, the browser interprets the request as a call to display a file. This command bypasses IIS, so the filter never gets its chance. As a result, under

continues

continued

Windows NT, the contents of the file are displayed, instead of the results of the .asp source code. Under Windows 95, if a file has been associated with the .asp extension, an excellent ASP editor, such as HomeSite, then that program launches and opens your .asp file outside the Web client window. ▨

Because an .asp file needs to execute IIS, remember to use the protocol prefix "HTTP://" in the URL.

The Active Server is running in the same address space as IIS, and IIS is running as a service under Windows NT, so both IIS and the Active Server inherit all the security features of the Windows NT operating system. Security comes through four access mechanisms: the IP address, the user account, the virtual directory, and the NT File System (NTFS).

User-account access is granted by means of either of two authentication methods: basic authentication or NT Challenge/Response authentication. Virtual directories enable IIS to control access to specific directories (and all subdirectories) that are identified by a single name (alias). Access Control Lists (ACLs), a product of the NTFS, permit you to specify access permission for individual users or groups, which allow you to control access to sites when using NTFS under NT 4.x with IIS 3.x.

N O T E Use the Microsoft Internet Service Manager to specify IP address restrictions (from the Advanced tab) and to configure virtual directories (from the Directories tab). Specify ACLs in Windows NT Explorer through the Security tab of the Properties dialog box of the directory or file to which you want to restrict access. ▨

Because the Active Server is linked to IIS through the ISAPI filter mechanism, and because IIS runs as a service under NT, all your .asp files have direct access to these programming assets. Because these services are available to your ASP applications they are highly scalable and their performance doesn't degrade as demands on them increase.

Because everything is running as a service under NT, other services may be available to your ASP programs. Of these services, you are most likely to use the other two perennial Internet severs: FTP and Gopher. Other important servers are the Microsoft Index Server, a Personalization Server, and a Proxy server. Microsoft Exchange Server now has a Web interface as well, and the directory services provided by NT also are ready to be pressed into action.

Finding ActiveX in ASP

You've seen that HTTP is what gets an Active Server Page running, but what makes it tick? In a word, ActiveX. But what kind of ActiveX?

If you did any advanced HTML programming before coming to ASP, you already may be familiar with ActiveX controls. ActiveX controls are slimmed-down OLE Automation servers. That is, Microsoft reduced the number of object interfaces required by OLE objects so that they would work more efficiently in the bandwidth-challenged world of today's Internet. ActiveX controls, therefore, work wherever OLE Automation servers worked in the past.

ActiveX controls usually have a user interface and some way to interact with it at runtime. Other ActiveX controls have no user interface, such as computation engines or text-formatting functions.

You can extend the Active Server by using Active Server components. Understanding that ASPs are objectcentric programs is important. Most of the work done in an .asp file is done by some kind of object.

N O T E The term *objectcentric* is used to distinguish the informal kind of object that is common in computer programming, from the formal objects in full-blown object-oriented programming (OOP) languages such as C++, Java, Smalltalk, and Delphi to the informal object in semi-OOP languages like VB. Most of the features of real objects are available in objectcentric languages, but some of the most problematic—such as inheritance—are missing. ▪

The most important feature of all objects is that they are self-contained programs that encapsulate data and source code. In ASP development, objects expose collections, methods, and properties by which work is requested and results are accessed.

The Active Server is a collection of objects, but it also can interface with any other programs written to the ActiveX specification. In the same way that ActiveX controls are OLE Automation servers on a diet, Active Server components are ActiveX controls with a reduced set of interfaces.

Specifically, the only interfaces that an Active Server component needs to support are IUnknown, IClassFactory, and IDispatch. The other feature that is recommended (though not required) for a program to be an Active Server component is a type library.

N O T E The ActiveX scripting engine with which the Active Server Engine interfaces is the same one with which the Web client interfaces. If you develop a scripting engine of your own, all you need to do is incorporate the ActiveX scripting interface into your own scripting engine, and your work will work on both the client and the server. ▪

Because Active Server components run on a controlled server and not on a user's desktop, they have full access to the server's file system and network resources. This easy access to server resources makes them a natural alternative to client-side scripting technologies such as Java and the twin client-side scripting engines: VBScript and JavaScript.

An Active Server component can be instantiated in the global.asa file and stored as a Session property. This component can be accessed simultaneously by all sessions (assuming that it uses one of the multithreading models supported by the Active Server). Here, then, are the reasons why in-process Active Server components are so superior to the traditional CGI implementation of Web interactivity:

- ▪ The server doesn't do any context-switching.
- ▪ The Active Server component runs in the address space of the server.

Part
IV

Ch
14

■ With Application scope, only one instance of the object exposed by the Active Server component is necessary to enable its use across all sessions of your ASP application.

ASP and HTML, What Is What

You've seen how Web clients access IIS (IIS is running as a service of Windows NT) and how IIS communicates with the Active Server (which is running in the address space of IIS).

The last step of this IIS process is to display the results of all the users, although this is generally done with ASP generated HTML, we will discuss the following:

■ **Basic HTML output.** Although an .asp file contains text, HTML source code, and scripts, the only thing that it produces is HTML. The Active Server is merely an HTML factory; it writes HTML code for you. You might actually write this code along with scripting logic that determines what, if anything, is returned to the client. Alternatively, the end results might come from an .asp file that generates HTML entirely on its own from source code stored in a database record.

N O T E When you call an ASP program that contains only .asp source code, which generates no HTML, your Web client complains because no data appears in the response body. Sometimes, the program doesn't even run. ■

If the program does run, the error message that invariably appears includes an apparent non sequitur: The operation completed successfully. This message means that the Active Server ran to completion, but the client wasn't happy with the result.

If you need to create what is basically an ASP utility (a function that does not deserve to be made into a full-fledged Active Server component), find a way to return some HTML, even if it's merely a <BR>. Even better is a redirect to another .asp file.

■ **Data-driven HTML.** Most HTML on the Internet always has been, and still is, static. Forms provide a basic level of interactivity, and ActiveX controls can give static HTML pages a dynamic appearance and enhance interactivity, but all this appearance is dependant on the client software supporting the ActiveX specification.

Using ASP immediately does two things for you: It enables the highest form of interactivity on the Web (namely, secure commercial transactions), and it encourages the greatest amount of dynamic content.

Whether that content changes because the Ad Rotator randomly selected another banner ad or because the structure of the HTML page was generated to suit the ActiveX control-enabled client program, your ASP application did everything automatically.

■ **Special cases.** With sufficient experience, you may find that nothing is beyond your reach when ASP extends your grasp. This new power doesn't come without exacting a cost, however. To really improve your reach with ASP, you have to meet at least the following two challenges:

- .asp files can populate client-side scripting objects with data that is accessed through ADO.
- The files can be used to generate data inside the Microsoft Layout Control's .alx file.

To whet your appetite, we close this section with a brief introduction to the programming problems posed by the particular challenges of these two special cases.

Dynamic Client-Side Scripts

The first challenge presents itself when the server is called to create a dynamic client-side script. The most frequent occurrence of creating dynamic client-size scripts almost certainly is filling out online forms.

Suppose that you have an HTML FORM that contains SELECT tags and TEXT fields. Further suppose that the specific variables displayed in these controls are stored in your database. The OnLoad event of your scripted page normally populates the SELECT tag. With ASP, the server-side script first fetches the SELECT options from the database; then it writes the client-side script that runs when the OnLoad event fires. The result is a dynamic SELECT tag.

HTML Layout Controls

When you get past the more common dynamic HTML challenge, you are likely to confront the second challenge: using the ActiveX Layout Control in your .asp file. The trick is to give the file created in the ActiveX Control Pad an .asp extension, instead of the standard .alx value. Other requirements involve protecting the .asp delimiters embedded in the .alx/ .asp file, but details dictate a prerequisite knowledge of .asp syntax.

The ActiveX Control Pad and the *.alx* File

Standard HTML is a structural language, not a page-layout language like PostScript. HTML is interested only in specifying the components of a document, not in their relative positions on the page. Microsoft introduced what it calls a 2-D control: the Microsoft HTML Layout Control. This control permits the HTML author to specify precise locations for controls. With this control, you can also specify the layering of objects and their transparency. The results can look spectacular.

These specifications—and any scripts that manipulate the controls contained within the Microsoft HTML Layout Control—are stored in a separate file that uses the .alx extension.

Creating an instance of the Microsoft HTML Layout Control is facilitated by the Microsoft ActiveX Control Pad program. This small application is designed to identify and configure ActiveX controls and to create the ALX file.

At any rate, being able to use the sophistication of .alx files *and* .asp files in the same file perhaps is the most impressive example of how ubiquitous .asp source code will be in your Web applications. Are you beginning to see how the advent of the Active Server Page is going to empower Web developers like nothing else in the history of the Internet?

The Structure of ASP

No structure exists, per se, in an .asp file that isn't already in the structure of the HTML, Visual Basic, or JavaScript code. In this respect, .asp files are not really programs. Indeed, a single .asp file can implement any combination of supported scripting engines, using languages as diverse as Perl, Rexx, Visual Basic, and JavaScript. ASP is an ecumenical programming environment.

HTML and ASP, What Is What

An acceptable practice (though not necessarily recommended) is to rename your HTML files with the .asp extension and turn them all into ASP which is really all that's required to make an ASP application.

If you only want to control more of the HTTP headers in your HTML files, you may see minimal .asp source code in those renamed HTML files. But if you want to turbocharge those sluggish old HTML files, or if you want to stop maintaining two versions of your Web site (one for the interactive-impaired), read on.

HTML Mixed with *.asp* Source Code

When you choose to add .asp source code to your HTML files, you have to make several more choices. If you are silent, the Active Server engine makes a few of these choices on your behalf. The choices fall into two categories: whether to use scripting and, if so, what kind(s) of scripting.

For the purposes of this discussion, .asp source code consists of either native ASP commands or scripting commands. *Native commands* are those that access Active Server Engine objects and components. *Scripting commands* rely on a particular syntax as well which means that you have to tell the Active Server Engine which language to use to interpret the commands. If you are silent, the engine uses VBScript by default.

This choice is not trivial when you are using ASP to write client-side scripts. As soon as you opt for this feature in your Web site, you're back to square one. Are you writing to a captive audience such as an intranet, in which all the client programs are the same brand and version? Even if all the browsers are the same brand and version, do they all support VBScript, or do you have to rely on the more ubiquitous JavaScript?

N O T E   As noted in the introduction to this section, you don't have to choose one scripting engine; choose the ones that suit your needs. If you have a nifty Perl program that you want to use, use it. If you will do most of your server-side scripting in VBScript because you are most fluent in that language, use it. And if you need a generic, client-side scripting engine, use JavaScript while you're at it. ■

After you make the preliminary choices, you must begin to contend with the challenge of separating the HTML source code from its ASP counterpart.

You have two basic choices: Use code delimiters <%...%> or the HTML <SCRIPT>...</SCRIPT> delimiters. When you mix scripting engines, you must use the <SCRIPT>...</SCRIPT> tags, because you have to identify the scripting engine to the Active Server. You identify the language with the LANGUAGE parameter. The comment delimiter is different for each scripting engine as well, and comments are an integral part of the <SCRIPT>...</SCRIPT> tag.

> **N O T E** Comments are necessary in client-side scripts because browsers that cannot interpret scripts need to ignore everything within the <SCRIPT>...</SCRIPT> tag. If you use a comment in the server-side version of a script, however, nothing happens. In other words, do not use comment lines when you define server-side scripts. ▪

.asp Source Code

As mentioned earlier in this chapter, you can write an .asp file with only .asp source code, but if you intend to have a client program call the file, and the output doesn't have a stitch of HTML, your client is going to balk.

An important advantage of using scripting delimiters is that the .asp source code never is visible to the reader of the HTML that is sent by the Active Server Page, because the source code is processed entirely at the server. This invisible-source-code trick holds whether you use the <%...%> or the <SCRIPT>...</SCRIPT> option. To the extent that you have client-side scripts in the HTML output, however, you are directly exposing your programming expertise to anyone who looks at the HTML source code.

Scripting Functions and Subroutines

For server-side scripting functions and subroutines to work, they must be delimited by the <SCRIPT>...</SCRIPT> tags, and the RUNAT parameter must be set to Server so that the client scripting engine doesn't get its hands on it. You cannot use the <%...%> delimiters to define a function, because you cannot give names to .asp code blocks. Even if you could, you have no inherent way to get a code block to return a value: the required function of a function.

To use .asp files to generate client-side scripts, you need to mix the <SCRIPT>...</SCRIPT> tags with the .asp source code delimiters: <%...%>. That is, client-side scripts consist of <SCRIPT>...</SCRIPT> blocks. When those scripts need content generated by the server (namely, filling form controls with database contents, as mentioned earlier in this chapter), you must tell the Active Server Engine which code is to be executed at the server and which is to be streamed to the client and executed there.

This sounds complicated doesn't it? It's not, really; most of the secret is in the fact noted a couple of paragraphs ago: The Active Server Engine doesn't run a script unless the RUNAT parameter equals Server. Obviously, then, all other occurrences of scripts run at the client, and the <SCRIPT>...</SCRIPT> commands are just plain old HTML, dutifully sent back to the client in the response body of the HTTP transaction.

No hard and fast rule about where to put your functions and subroutines exists, but a common practice is to put them in the <HEAD> section of your HTML file. Sometimes, you can install short functions directly with the HTML command.

Server-Side Includes

Server-Side Includes are powerful tools for programmer productivity. In a sense, SSIs are the most basic kind of reusable code; their primary purpose is to insert text-file contents into .asp files. Server-Side Includes can contain other Server-Side Includes, so you can stuff an incredible amount of text into an .asp file with a single command.

Because Server-Side Includes are included in your .asp files before any of the files' ASP commands are executed, SSIs can't do anything fancy, such as looking up database records, but they can call other SSIs.

Server-Side Includes (SSIs) insert text into the place in your file where the you specify, much like the C++ pre-processor directive #include but different in that they are included at run-time not by a pre-processor. In other words, SSIs replace themselves at runtime. This distinction can be important when the resulting text has a particular role to play and that role has a particular place in the file to play it. At other times, this distinction is not so important.

One of the most common uses for the SSI is when you need to refer to constants in your .asp source code. The adovbs.inc file contains all the VBScript constants used by ActiveX Data Objects.

A final point about Server-Side Includes is that they really don't add any marginal overhead. In a UNIX shop, however, .html files usually are not opened before they are sent on to the client program. But to process a SSI, the server must open the .html file and the SSI file. Then the server must insert the text in the SSI into the .html file at the proper location. Finally, the server must close the .html file and send it on to the Web client.

Under the Active Server, the .asp file has to be opened anyway, so the extra effort of inserting the text is negligible. Anyway, this entire file I/O is processing in the address space of Windows NT, so even in the worst case, the overhead of processing .asp files in this way is nothing compared to the power that you get in the bargain.

From Here...

This chapter introduced the results of what can be described only as the most spectacular course correction ever attempted by an American corporation.

In less than a year, Microsoft redeployed all its resources to incorporate and exploit the revolution in data processing that is the Internet. If the definition of an asset is "anything that enables you to do something you couldn't do before," the Internet is one of the most amazing assets ever to appear on this planet; look at what its mere presence did for Microsoft. But if the Internet is a consummate example of an asset, the technologies that Microsoft has built and delivered can be described only as a mutual fund of technology. This mutual fund goes by the name of the Active Platform.

Perhaps the most remarkable Internet-development asset in this mutual fund is the Active Server Page. Designed to be used by anyone who can deliver content to the Internet (and that's practically anyone who can type), the ASP is typified by a single file that can be packed with an incredible amount of processing power. You can mix a virtually unlimited number of scripting languages in a single .asp file, using each language for the kind of work for which it's optimized. In that single file, you have immediate access to all the processing power of the Active Server Engine's internal objects and components.

And if those objects and components don't do what you need them to do, you can build your own Active Server component. When registered, your component is accessed and will behave exactly like those components that ship with the server. You can build those components in any language that conforms to the COM specification, from C++ to Java to Visual Basic 5.0. Also, you can store those components anywhere on the planet and use them as though they were on your desktop. With ASP, you have no separate files to compile (or even store). Everything can be contained in a single file extension, if you want.

Nothing comes close to the breadth and depth of processing horsepower that you have at your fingertips when you master the Active Server framework.

So what do you say? Should we get started?

The following chapters will provide more information related to implementing this Client/Server model using Commerce Server 2.0.

- Chapter 15, "Working with Active Server Web Pages," will show you how to use ActiveX, OLE, and OOP methods within the ASP realm.
- Chapter 16, "Integrating VBScript into ASP," will cover the basic concepts on how to integrate VBScript and ASP to use the ActiveX and OLE controls.
- Appendix A, "Commerce 2.0 Components," will discuss the components that ship with Commerce Server 2.0, these are the components you will implement in your ASP applications.

Part
IV

Ch
14

CHAPTER 15

Working with Active Server Web Pages

The people, places, and things with which you come in contact each and every day are the objects of your life. You have a transportation object (your car), a companion object (your spouse, child, or pet), and other objects that you interact with throughout the day. This example is a suggesting that you are living a mechanical life, but rather that you can express the relationships between yourself and those things around you by thinking about the attributes that define those objects. This set of specific, meaningful attributes allows you to differentiate between the kitchen chair and the sofa. Both objects provide you a place to sit, but each objects has its own specific function within your life.

Abstracting the essence of real-world objects, events, and processes and then creating a road map or blueprint of that occurrence is the rationale behind object-oriented development. This chapter examines objects, their attributes, and their relationships with other objects. By understanding the pieces of the underlying technologies (OLE and ActiveX) and how each technology fits into the Active Server Pages environment, you become a more proficient and educated developer. ■

Learning about objects

Understand important keys to extensibility within Active Server Pages by examining objects and components.

Understanding the benefits of components

Find out how component technology solves many problems that traditional developers face.

Examining the Component Object Model and OLE

Creating objects within ASP is simply creating OLE or ActiveX components. Understanding OLE and how it works, allows you to leverage its features in your ASP development.

Using distributed computing

From transactions to distributed objects, we will discuss the future of distributed processing.

Understanding Object-Oriented Development

The terms *object* and *component* are used somewhat interchangeably within this chapter. When you see *component*, you can think *object*, but with one main difference—The component is always packaged separately from the application, as a dynamic link library or as a COM or ActiveX object. This distinct seperation of memory usage provides several benefits that are examined in this chapter.

In the aftermath of World War II, the United States was the world's provider of choice for goods and services. Shortly after that time, a man named Dr. W. Edward Demming spoke about a new concept in manufacturing: total quality management (TQM). At the time, not many U.S. companies were interested in TQM—they already were the world's first and best suppliers. So Demming took his message to the Japanese, who quickly took his teachings to heart. Now, some 50 years later, that country is beating most others in quality production at nearly every turn.

In the past ten years, the idea of total quality management was revived in the offices of corporate America. What corporations once spurned, they began to embrace. Out of this new focus on quality, methods and techniques were developed to examine problem processes within an organization and ferret out the causes.

The next steps involved process redesign and, in many cases, process automation. The developer was given a process map that showed the new process to be automated and, more specifically, the way that the data flowed through the process. Many developers then used this road map to develop the new application. The problem with the result was that it was a data-centric—not process-centric—design.

For the developer, this road map was a godsend, giving him or her a step-by-step, data-driven guide to developing the system. Many systems continue to be developed in this manner today. Several issues arise, however, from this traditional, structured application-development methodology.

Working from a data-driven process map, the developer tends to focus on creating functions that allow the to data flow as it does in the map. This process is a great way to implement the application, based on the process flows. In reality, however, most processes that are reengineered are changed again (*tweaked*) just before or shortly after implementation. So a step that was in the beginning of the process might be moved to the middle, and a few weeks later, it might be moved to the end and then back to the beginning. Adapting the procedural, data-based application to these changes is a major effort, and in most cases, the application cannot adapt to the requested modifications.

The need to change an application rapidly in a changing environment faces every developer. As a solution to this issue, many development shops have moved to object-oriented design and development. Traditional application development involves using a structured methodology, looking at top-down functional decomposition of the processes involved and their associated systems. When you use data-flow diagrams and structure charts, the processes are identified, as is the data that moves through the processes.

Object-oriented development strives to decrease the complexity of a problem by breaking the problem into discrete parts, which then manifest as objects. The objects in this problem domain are then discovered and abstracted to a level at which the inherent complexity within the real-world object is removed.

You are left with some number of objects that have a state (data members) and that provide services (methods) for other objects within the domain. The nice thing about encapsulating functionality within objects is that they are self-sustaining units. If a process step is changed within a flow, you do not need to change the object itself—just its place within the program.

As new requirements are added, you can easily add new functionality to the object. Even better, when a new application is required, you can use existing objects in the new development, either directly through combination or through inheritance, all of which you learn about in this chapter. Even though no support exists for object-oriented development with VBScript, you can apply many of the hard lessons you will learn about the value of code reuse and encapsulation (data hiding) in your ASP development as you develop your skills.

Understanding Classes and Objects

To you, the Active Server Pages developer, an *object* or *component* is a prebuilt piece of functionality that you can immediately integrate into your scripts. Components such as database connectivity, interaction with a host environment, and other functions that you cannot perform through scripting alone. By understanding the principles that drive the component implementation, you are better able to leverage components' use in your development.

At its most basic level, an object is an instantiation of a class. A *class* is a blueprint for the creation of an object and the services that reside within it. The class describes the state of the object by using data members (private) and provides services (member functions or methods) that are available to owners of the object (those that are public members) and to the object itself for internal use (nonpublic members: protected or private). The class also can be related to other classes through inheritance or composition.

Which came first, the object or the class? Who has the time or energy to try and figure out the answer? The question certainly falls into the chicken-or-egg category don't you think?

Using Abstractions

When you begin trying to identify objects within your problem domain, you are struck by the complexity of the world in which you live. *Abstraction* is a useful way of reducing your environment's complexity to manageable pieces. When you use abstraction, you pick out the most important elements or properties of an object that allow you to view the object from a higher place—a reduced complexity.

If you look at a piece of paper under a microscope at high magnification, you see millions of fibers intertwining in no discernible pattern. As you lessen the magnification, the fibers begin to run together. Eventually, you reach 0x magnification (looking at the page on a table, perhaps), and the fibers within the paper are abstracted to such a level that they become insignificant.

To understand the use of a paper you could abstract it's uses associating actions with categories (such as using the paper in a printer or to write on). The more an object is abstracted, the smaller the number of intricate details are involved. You can abstract something too much, of course, to the point at which you lose the essence of the object. As a developer, you determine the level of abstraction that enables you to integrate the object into your code.

As you abstract objects, you identify those attributes that are essential to understanding the object. When you identify the attributes, you can move into the services or member functions that manipulate the object attributes that you abstracted.

Protecting Your Object's Data: Encapsulation

As your applications begin to interact with the objects in your Active Server Pages scripts, you set properties and call methods of those objects. All your interactions with those objects take place when you access them through a well-defined set of functions, or a *public interface*. When you execute a method of an object, you don't need to know how the object performs its duties; you just need the object to get the job done.

The idea of having a public interface and private implementation is one of the key OO (object-oriented) concepts. You may have heard this concept referred to as *data hiding*; another name for this technique is *encapsulation*. In essence, all the implementation details, all the internal variables that are created and used, and all the internal support functions are encapsulated within the object. The only view into the object that you, as a user of the object, have is the public interface.

Encapsulation provides several benefits. First, you don't need to know how the requested service is implemented; you only need to know that the object performs the requested service. The second benefit is that the underlying implementation of the services that the object provides can change without the public interface's changing. The client (calling procedure) often is totally unaware that the implementation of the function has changed, because it never has access to that part of the object.

Many people refer to this type of system as being a *black-box interface,* which is a fair analogy. Imagine that you are creating a transaction program to interface with a legacy database system. You define a set of transactions that the black box (or object) accept; then it returns the result set to your client application.

A few months later, however, the protocol changes to TCP/IP. Your client application is never aware of the protocol that the black box is implementing, and the change does not affect the client app at all, because the public interface (the transaction set) does not change. The benefits of encapsulation are that the public interface remains constant and that the implementation can be changed without affecting the object's users.

Understanding Inheritance

The only thing that you need to know to understand *inheritance* is how to use *kind of* in a sentence, as in "A bicycle is a *kind of* vehicle." The idea behind inheritance is that you create a class of a base type (say, vehicle) and then derive a new class from the base class (bicycle). The neat thing about inheritance is that all the functionality residing in the base class is available to the derived class.

Those functions that are unique to the derived class are then implemented within the new class, called the *subclass*. Then you have the opportunity to derive a new class (say, Huffy) from the bicycle class. The Huffy class has all the methods from each of the classes that it is derived from. This derivation is called single inheritance, because a subclass is derived from only one base class.

In the preceding example, the vehicle base class has functions that include starting, stopping, and turning. All the vehicles derived from the base class (bicycle, car, motorcycle, and boat) have the methods of the base class, but their implementations are different. To turn right in the car class, the steering wheel is turned; in the Bicycle class, the handlebars are moved. I think you get the idea.

In another case, you can derive an object from more than one base class. This derivation is called *multiple inheritance*. Suppose that you are creating an object to provide a visual interface for the abstraction of a document scanner. You can derive a ScanView class from a ViewWindow class and a ScannerControl class.

Using Polymorphism

You may be asking, "So what? Why do I need the base class when many of the functions in the subclasses are implemented differently anyway?" The answer is illuminating. *Polymorphism* allows you to use a variable of a base-class type to reference any of the classes derived from that base type. This morphing implies that you can have a procedure that accepts as a parameter an object variable that is declared as a vehicle.

Then you can call the procedure by passing any of the subclasses of vehicle that have been derived: boat, car, and so on. The great thing is that when you say objectVar.TurnRight() within the procedure, the *appropriate method within the subclass* is invoked. As you can see, polymorphism is unbelievably powerful.

Your application can control any type of vehicle, turning left or right, starting, or stopping, regardless of the class of vehicle that it is controlling. Just as important, each time you create a new abstraction of a vehicle, you don't need to start from scratch; all the basic functions already have been defined for you. The methods that need additional implementation code are all that you have to add. Notice in the following code that the procedure takes as a parameter a pointer to a vehicle:

```
Bicycle bike;
Drive(&bike);

void Drive(Vehicle * veh) {
   veh->TurnRight();      // will invoke the method TurnRight in
                          // the Bicycle class, not the vehicle class
}
```

When the method TurnRight is called from within the Drive procedure, the correct method, within the subclass, is called.

Here's another example. You are working for the zoo and are in the midst of creating an audio application that reproduces the sounds of all the zoo's animals. You create a base class called Animal that has an associated member function, Speak.

Next, you derive each of your subclasses: goat, bird, and so on. Back in the application proper, the user selects an animal sound to hear. An instance of that animal subclass is created and passed as an Animal. Then, when the Speak method is called, the appropriate animal sound is played.

Comparing Static and Dynamic Binding

To enable implementation of polymorphism with your classes and objects, the object variable veh within the Drive function, listed in the "Using Polymorphism" section, must be associated with the actual Bicycle object at runtime. In effect, the object is sent the "turn right" message and figures out how to implement it. This capability to assign the object type during the program's execution is called *dynamic binding* and is the method through which polymorphism is executed.

Static binding, on the other hand, is what happens when all object references are resolved at compile time. During static binding, the object associated with any object variable within the application is set by the object declaration. As you can see, dynamic binding is imminently more powerful and is required within an OO environment.

Working with Composition

In the section "Understanding Inheritance" earlier in this chapter, inheritance is expressed as a "kind of" relationship. Classes created through composition are expressed through a "part of" relationship. A car is a type of vehicle, for example, but a vehicle is not a part of a car. When you use composition to create a class, you find those classes that are a part of the class that you are building. An engine is a part of a car. Wheels are a part of a car. A windshield is a part of a car. You can create a car class composed of engine, wheel, windshield, and any other parts that are appropriate to the car class.

The car class is derived from vehicle, but those other "parts" of the car class—the engine object, the wheel object, and so on—become private member variables of the car class. The following example shows a class definition for the hypothetical Auto class:

```
Class Auto: public Vehicle { // inheritance from Vehicle class
Public:
  Auto();
[td]Auto();

      Private:                      // composition of objects within the class
Engine engine;      // engine object as private member variable
Wheels wheels;      // wheels object as private member variable
};
```

The Bottom Line Object Reuse

By now you are probably asking yourself, "Why all the fuss about object-oriented development?" The most important feature that OO provides is the capability to create new applications from existing code without introducing new bugs. This is not to say that you will have no bugs within your implementation—just you should have no bugs *within* these production-hardened objects that you are going to use.

This capability to reuse proven, production-ready code is one of the main forces driving the OO movement into corporate development. As the business environment continues to become more complex, developers need to be able to quickly represent that complexity within the systems that they build.

In addition, the rapid changes in the current business environment demand systems that developers can modify easily, without having to recompile an entire application each time a change is made. If you develop your system with component objects, when the objects are enhanced, the client does not need to be changed.

Using Object Orientation and Components in ASP Development

The object-oriented methods of inheritance, composition, and polymorphism are not implemented in VBScript within the ASP environment. Nevertheless, you can take the overriding principle of OO development to heart as you develop ASP applications.

That principle is reuse of existing, production-ready code. You can create libraries of functions that you can include within your Active Server Pages applications. You also can imbed the functionality of ASP component objects and other third-party components within the functions that reside in your library.

Several prebuilt components that ship with Active Server Pages. If you had to reproduce the functionality of each of the components, either by using native scripting or by creating your own components in Visual Basic or Visual C++, you would expend a considerable amount of time and money. The wonderful thing about components is that they give you innumerable choices for implementing solutions to a particular problem.

We know some developers have a particularly disturbing disorder. This disorder has been known by many names over the years, but we tend to refer to it as *NBH* (*not built here*) Syndrome. Anything that these developers do not create within their development shop is no good, nohow. Although it is true that these developers have created some exciting applications over the years, they could have cut development time by at least half had they integrated other development groups' code into their own.

The same is true of components. "Sure, I'll build it myself. How long could it take?" is easy to say, and many developers have fallen into this trap. One good example of a build/buy component decision that often comes to mind is the ubiquitous calendar control. (A calendar control is a user interface component that allows you to select a date from a calendar by clicking a calendar graphic.)

Hundreds of applications require this type of functionality. Although the project is not an overwhelming one to design and build, why should you bother? Numerous calendar components are available out there in the market; they have been tested and proved in production. Why waste time implementing an object that is available in the market? You have business process expertise. You understand the specific business logic that rules the process.

Put your development time to best use by implementing the business processes. Don't waste time reinventing the wheel. In the build-versus-buy decision, remember that a development project's success is determined by how well an application meets a business need, not by who built a particular component of an application.

We'll hop off the soapbox now. We were getting a little light-headed up there anyway.

Understanding the Component Object Model

The history of the Component Object Model (COM) follows somewhat the history of Windows and the applications that were created for use on the system. In the early days of the Windows environment, the need for users to be able to share data across applications was paramount. The capability to copy and paste data between applications via the Clipboard was the first step.

In the late '80s, Microsoft implemented the *dynamic data exchange* (DDE) protocol to provide this Clipboard functionality in a more dynamic implementation. The only problem was that this new dynamic implementation was quirky, slow, and somewhat unreliable.

By 1991, DDE was effectively replaced by a new technology called *object linking and embedding,* or OLE 1.0. The new OLE enabled applications to share data or to link objects, with the linked data remaining in the format of the application that created it. When you embedded or linked objects, they would show up within the client application. When the linked data needed to be edited, the user would double-click the object, and the application that created the base data would start.

As nice as OLE 1.0 was, it still was a far cry from the easy application integration promised by Microsoft. From this point, Microsoft came to the conclusion that the only way to provide truly seamless object integration was to create little pieces of functionality that could be plugged from one application into another to provide specific services. From this idea was born the idea of *component objects*—objects that could provide services to other client applications. The Component Object Model (COM) specification came out of this desire to create a standard for component objects.

COM, as implemented with OLE 2.0 in 1993, became more than just a specification for component objects. COM supports a vast range of services that allow components to interact at many levels within the application environment. The same service that provides local processing can be invoked on a remote machine to provide similar services, all of which are transparent to the user.

Component Design Goals

As Microsoft moved from DDE to OLE 1.0 and finally to the component model specification, several design goals guided the company in the development of COM and OLE. This set of functionality was derived partly from the history of creating monolithic, complex applications, but more so from the ongoing maintenance and inevitable changes that an evolving environment demands on any system.

To create a truly generic interface architecture, the model was created with the following goals in mind:

- **Generic access path**. For any components that reside on a system, a method must be in place to provide the capability to find any available service through a unique identifier.

- **Transparent access**. In a distributed computing environment, the client must not be required to know specifically where a service resides. The access to the component and the services that it provides must be transparent to the user, whether the component is running locally on the same system in the same process, in a different process on the same machine, or on a system across the country.

- **Implementation independence**. The component services must be designed with a well-defined binary public interface that allows the use of a component by any compliant client, without regard to the actual implementation details or language that created the component.

- **Adaptability to change**. As implementations change or as new functionality is added, the component must continue to support existing public interfaces. The current Component versioning schemes allow the component to be modified without a resultant change in the client application.

- **Advanced versioning capabilities**. The component object must be capable of telling the client program what compatible versions are available to the client within the component, so that new versions of the component do not break older client applications.

- **Interoperability among service providers**. The components themselves must provide standard binary interfaces that allow them to operate across vendors and operating systems. Without a standard across service providers, interoperability is impossible.

- **Conformity with Object Oriented development**. The component model must support key Object Oriented principles such as inheritance, composition, and polymorphism. The key objective is to provide enhanced object reuse to enable creation of dynamic, component-based applications—no more complex, monolithic designs.

All the design goals in the preceding list boil down to providing developers the tools to create dynamic, flexible applications that are swiftly created and easy to maintain. As business processes continue to become more complex and require increasing levels of adaptability, the old monolithic development architecture is breaking under the weight of the changes. In traditional development, when one part of an implementation within a system changes, the entire application must be recompiled to ensure that all references to functions are correct. The need to provide dynamic changes without compiling new versions of applications is another central goal of the component model.

To support larger applications and distributed data, client applications must be able to access appropriate services, wherever they reside, to fulfill user requests. Once again, whether a service resides on another machine, across the hall, or across the continent, the client must not be aware of the difference.

As corporations move toward improving quality, every process is being looked at and, where appropriate, redesigned. The requirement for new applications continues to outpace information systems' capability to keep up. By creating new applications from proven, existing components, developers can build new applications more quickly and more reliably. As improvements are made in base components and rolled into production, each new application can benefit from the new refinements immediately, and existing applications

COM the Component Solution

COM is an object-based model, a specification and implementation that defines the interface between objects within a system. An object that conforms to the COM specification is considered to be a *COM object*. COM is a service that connects a client application to an object and its associated services. When the connection is established, COM drops out of the picture. COM provides a standard method of finding and *instantiating* (creating) objects and of providing the communication between the client and the component.

Under COM, the method of bringing client and object together is independent of any programming language that created the app or object, as well as from the app itself. This independence provides a *binary interoperability standard* versus a language-based standard. COM helps ensure that applications and objects that are created by different providers, often writing in different languages, can interoperate. As long as the objects support the standard COM interfaces and methods for data exchange, the implementation details within the component itself are irrelevant to the client.

COM Interfaces

Client applications interact with components through a common collection of function calls named *interfaces*. An interface is a public agreement between a service provider and a service requester about how to communicate. The interface defines only the calling syntax and the expected return values for the member function. No definition or even hint is provided about how the service provider actually implements the services. The interfaces that are available within an object are made known to COM through the IUnknown object, which then makes them available to other applications.

Here are some key points to help you understand what a COM interface is and is not:

- *The interface is not a class.* A class defines the public and private functions and data within the object, as well as the implementation of those functions. The interface is a description of the public view of the class but has no implementation details.

■ *The interface does not change.* Each time an interface is defined for an object, it creates a new public interface for the object. No inherent versioning occurs. As each new service is added, an additional interface is added as well, with its own unique identifier. In this way, all previous interfaces always are available to a client program.

■ *The interface does not define the object.* An object is defined by its class. The interface is a means, at a binary level, of allowing a client and the component to communicate via COM's introduction services.

■ *The client sees only the interface.* When a client instantiates a COM object, it is returned a pointer to that object, through which it can invoke its services. The private data of the object, along with its implementation, is hidden from the client application.

All COM objects must implement a generic interface known as IUnknown. IUnknown is the base interface of a COM object; the client uses this interface to, among other things, control the lifetime of the object that is being instantiated. It is the first interface pointer returned to the client. To find out what additional interfaces are supported by the object, call the QueryInterface method of IUnknown, using the initial IUnknown pointer. QueryInterface is called with a requested interface and returns a pointer to the new interface if it is implemented within the object.

QueryInterface must be implemented in all COM objects to support adding additional functionality to objects without breaking existing applications that expect the original object—in effect not requiring the client application to be recompiled. Through the QueryInterface, objects can simultaneously support multiple interfaces.

In Figure 15.1, you see an example of how the interfaces supported by an object can grow over time, as well as how new interfaces don't break existing applications. In the top pane, you see that the first version of the client is connected to the component's interface A. Later, a second version of the client also uses interface A. In the second pane, when the component is modified to add a new interface, the new client takes advantage of the newer functionality. Notice that the original client still is fully functional and using the original interface of the object. Powerful stuff, huh?

A New Versioning Scheme

Using a naming convention to ensure that all functions have unique names within an application is a perfectly viable solution to the name-collision problem. The compiler catches any name collisions within modules at runtime. In the object universe, where the object can live on a local computer or a remote host, the number of opportunities for getting the wrong object increase exponentially. To make sure that the correct object always is instantiated, COM uses globally unique identifiers (GUID).

Globally unique identifiers provide a method to ensure that each object residing on a system has a unique ID that identifies it. GUIDs are 128-bit integers generated by an algorithm that guarantees that they are unique at any given place and time in the world. The parameters to the function that determine the GUID are the machine's Internet address and the date and time when the function is called.

FIG. 15.1
An object's interfaces never change; the developer just adds new ones.

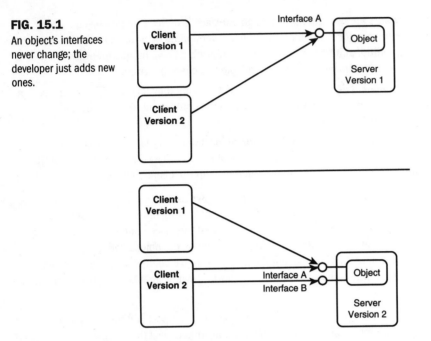

Creating a COM Server

A COM Server is a piece of code that allows the COM service locator to find and call upon it to enable the classes residing within the server to be instantiated. The servers can be implemented as a dynamic-link library (DLL) or as executables (.EXE).

The server must implement a *class factory* (IClassFactory) interface for each interface supported. The class factory is responsible for creating the object for the client. The general graphical syntax for expressing interfaces within servers portrays an interface for an object as a socket or plug-in jack (a circle, sometimes shaded). The known interfaces are defined on the right or left side of the object, with the IUnknown interface coming out of the top of the server. Given this representation, Figure 15.2 shows the structure of a COM Server.

FIG. 15.2
A graphical illustration of the structure of a COM Server.

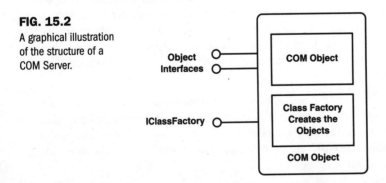

In-Process and Out-of-Process Servers

A server is implemented in relation to the context of the client that uses it. A server executes *in-process,* meaning within the address space of the client, or *out-of-process,* meaning in another process on the same or a different machine. These server types break into three conceptual types:

- **In-process (in-proc) server**: a server loaded into the address space of the client on the same machine. In the Windows environment, the in-proc server is implemented as dynamic-link libraries. In other environments, the implementation is different.

- **Local server**: an out-of-process server that executes its own process on the same machine as the client. The local server is implemented as an .EXE.

- **Remote server**: a server (out-of-process, of course) that executes on a machine other than the client. A remote server can be implemented as a DLL or an .EXE.

During this discussion of the COM Servers, think of the server in terms of the objects that the server creates instead of as being the server itself. As far as the client knows, all the objects are accessed through the function pointer to the object, whether in-process or out-of-process, on the same machine or a different one. This transparent access mechanism is illustrated in Figure 15.3.

FIG. 15.3
The client and server have location transparency within the COM model.

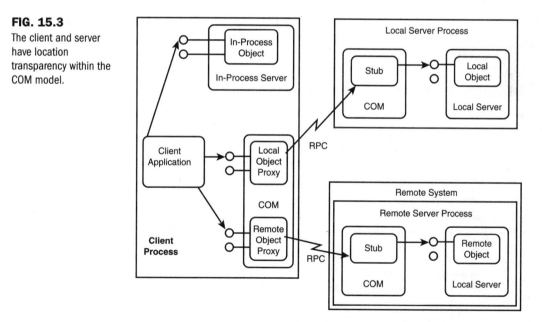

Because all function pointers are, by default, in the same process, all the COM objects accessed by the client are accessed in-process. If the object is in-process, the client connects directly to the object. If the client is on another machine, the client calling the object is a stub object created by COM; this object in turn picks up a *remote procedure call* (RPC) from the "proxy" process on the client machine. The net result is that through COM, the client and the server believe that they are dealing with in-process calls.

COM's Implementation of Inheritance

COM itself does not support the traditional method of inheritance, and for this reason, many object purists consider it to be of little value. Within the framework of object-oriented development, the inheritance mechanisms available under COM are *aggregation* and *containment/ delegation.*

In containment/delegation, two objects participate to fulfill a service request. One object (the outer object) becomes a client of the second object (the inner object). In effect, the request passes the service call or reissues the method, from itself to the inner object to be fulfilled. The client of the outer object is not aware of this handoff, so encapsulation requirements are fulfilled in containment/delegation.

The outer object, being a client of the inner object, accesses its services only through the COM interface, just like a normal client. The outer object delegates the fulfillment of the service to the inner object. So although inheritance is not explicitly supported in COM, the capability to call the methods of the contained object provides similar functionality to calling the method of a base class from a subclassed object.

In aggregation, the interfaces of the inner object are again exposed to the client application via IUnknown, but in this case, the client interacts directly with the inner object through an interface pointer to the inner object returned.

The Lifetime of COM Objects

All COM objects must support two basic operations. The first operation—exposing and navigating between the interfaces provided by an object—is covered in "COM Interfaces" earlier in this chapter, in the discussion of IUnknown and the QueryInterface member function. The second operation is a method to control an object's lifetime.

Speaking of an object's lifetime when that object is an in-process server is very different from discussing an object's lifetime in a heterogeneous, distributed environment. Because COM objects support multiple instances, a way must exist to ensure that all clients have completed their use of an object before it is destroyed. Object destruction is handled by using *reference counting* within the COM object.

During Active Server Pages development, you create objects and then release them when they are no longer needed. In C++ development, any memory that you dynamically allocate must be freed. If the memory associated with an object is not freed when all the object's users are done using it, you have what is called a *memory leak.*

This is obviously not a problem if you are leaking 1k/day, but suppose you are in a transaction environment in which you might perform thousands of transactions per hour, those leaks will add up fast!

The same care that you take to free any objects that you create in ASP is also handled for objects within the COM environment. Each COM object must implement the two IUnknown functions, AddRef and Release. These two functions are used to fulfill the reference-counting specification, as the mechanism to manage the object's life. Each time an object is instantiated, the reference count is incremented. The count is decremented as clients implicitly call the release function. When the reference count eventually returns to zero, the Release function destroys the object.

A Few Words About OLE

Over the years, many developers were confused as OLE 1.0 came on the scene, followed by COM and then by OLE 2.0, which was totally different from OLE 1.0. Also, much confusion has occurred about whether COM and OLE are the same thing. Can one exist without the other?

OLE is a group of services and specifications that sit on top of the basic COM architecture and COM services. OLE 2.0 is the first implementation of this extended COM specification.

As an Active Server Pages developer, you are interested primarily in the custom services supported through the OLE specification. These services include OLE documents, OLE controls, OLE automation, and drag-and-drop.

OLE acts as a facilitator for the integration of component objects into applications and into a system itself. OLE, through COM, provides an open, widely supported specification to enable developers to create component software. In the real world, the distinction between COM and OLE has become cloudy. Just remember that OLE is drawing on all the basic object services that COM provides to standardize the next level within component development.

Understanding Distributed Computing

The movement away from monolithic computer architectures began with the first client/server revolution. For several reasons, information-technology managers were enamored with the multitier architecture that client/server proposed, as discussed in Chapter 14, "Introducing Active Server Pages."

First, a logical division of work was made among the client, the business logic, and the database back end. The client would be responsible for data input and front-end validation, as well as for the graphical user interface and display. The business-logic tier would handle the process-specific validation and calculation, and also send and receive the appropriate data to and from the database server.

Breaking the application into these logical pieces provided several benefits for the business. First, as each tier was created, it could be tested independently, which made debugging much easier. Also, as the pieces were put together, the appropriate hardware could be selected for each tier. The capability to scale the application by splitting processing across multiple machines also was a boon to rapidly growing enterprises.

As new applications were developed, the existing middle and back-end services often could be reused, again enhancing the speed at which new systems could be implemented. Developers faced several challenges in developing and managing these systems. The mechanisms for the tiers to interact (protocol, transaction format, and so on) often were proprietary and specific for a certain type of operating system. Moving pieces of functionality between the tiers, when doing so made sense, was difficult—and often not worth the time and effort.

Suppose that a key piece of data validation that is called hundreds of times per client session is bringing the application to its knees, due to the network traffic getting to the remote tier. Ideally, you just pick up this validation functionality and place it closer to the clients—or even on the clients themselves. Sadly, in the current environment, this solution requires you to recompile all the client code, as well as to change the interface for the validation routines.

In an effort to leverage the multitier architecture that makes client/server computing so attractive, as well as to deal with the problems that occur during its use, Microsoft created the DCOM specification.

Distributed Objects DCOM

To address the concerns and problems associated with traditional program development on the desktop, the COM specification was created. As discussed in "Understanding the Component Object Model" earlier in this chapter, COM provides the architecture and mechanisms for creating binary-compatible components that can be shared between applications.

The goal of distributed computing in a component-based environment is to ensure that the components working on a local machine look the same to the client as they do on a remote machine. Distributed COM (DCOM) is built on the foundations of COM, and just as OLE provides a new level of services for the desktop on top of COM, DCOM extends COM's component architecture across the enterprise.

One of DCOM's primary goals is to provide to the enterprise the same reduction in complexity that COM and OLE provide in desktop development. For developers, this simplicity means not having to learn a new set of interfaces, because COM and DCOM use the same component model. The open, cross-platform support of COM and DCOM provides the mechanism to allow objects to reside anywhere within the enterprise, transparently accessible from the desktop or other component servers.

The location of the component that provides the service must be transparent to the local machine. Consider the case of a client accessing a remote database. You can provide a service on the local machine that connects to the remote database and then execute queries against that database.

In this scenario, the client must be aware of several things:

- First, the client needs to know where the physical data resides.
- Second, the client needs a connection to the database. In most cases, this connection is permanent for the duration of the query session. Permanent connections may not be a

big concern when only one or two users are accessing the database concurrently, but when the application scales, hundreds or even thousands of connections can be a huge overhead burden on the database server.

■ Finally, the client must speak the language of the connection that provides the link between client and database. The majority of a user's time on the client is spent performing local tasks, formatting the data, creating queries, or building charts. Usually, the user uses the database connection for a short time, yet the server is carrying the overhead of that connection.

Take the example a step further and examine a typical corporate application. A company that processes mortgages uses applications with extensive calculations to perform risk analyses on potential customers. In a distributed application built on component technology, the calculation engine is a component on a server. The component pulls a variety of information from legacy databases and then performs the calculations.

As the business environment changes and new federal laws are introduced, the calculations need to be modified. Due to its basis in COM, the DCOM calculation component is the only object that needs to be modified, leaving the data-entry and processing applications as they are. In working with the database, the DCOM object may maintain five or six concurrent connections to the database, or it may in turn connect to another DCOM object that handles all database interaction. In either case, as requests come in, the database service spins off a thread to handle the request on one of the available connections. In this way, hundreds of users can be supported with only a few concurrent connections to the database.

DCOM Architecture

DCOM is created as an extension to the Component Object Model. As stated earlier in this chapter, COM provides a specification and mechanism to allow clients and objects to connect to other objects. When COM objects run outside the process of the client, COM provides the interprocess communication methods between the objects in a transparent fashion. When the interprocess communication takes place across a network, DCOM steps in to replace the interprocess communication with a network protocol.

DCOM Benefits

You gain several benefits from using DCOM. These benefits are inherited directly from COM and fall out when the two new technologies are integrated. The following sections outline a few of the most impressive benefits.

Component Reuse   Under COM, the client and the server believe that they are running in the same process. A COM object that was originally created to perform services on a client desktop can easily be moved to perform the same functions on a server. DCOM provides the transparent access between the objects running on different machines. This multitier model allows the objects to live in relation to one another in the most appropriate place, and as that place changes over time, the objects can be moved to other locations quickly.

Language Neutrality   DCOM has effectively inherited all the benefits of the binary compatibility specification of COM. As new COM objects are created in a variety of languages, you can scale them immediately for distributed performance under DCOM.

Scalability   When the same system can support one or hundreds of users, it is said to be scalable. *Scalability* refers to the ability to scale (increase or decrease) the number of users on the system without affecting the application's performance.

Suppose that you just created a new COM component-based application that includes a user interface, business-rules logic, a transaction manager, and a database-services component. This application is amazing for several reasons, the first of which is that you currently are unemployed.

Second, all the COM components are running on the same machine. Next week, you decide to start your own business in the garage, and your application is up and running. Business picks up, and you hire four people to use the new system to keep up with demand. To allow all the new workers to use the same database, you move the (now shared) database-access component to another server (which happens to be where the database lives). You don't have to change the client application at all (location independence). A few months later, business takes off further, and you find that all your business logic, which is quite complex, takes forever to process on your client machines.

You go out, purchase a nice SMP box, and move the logic component to that box. Again, you don't need to recompile any code. You just change the DCOM configuration on the clients, and voilá—you are back in business.

This scenario could be followed by the meteoric rise and phenomenal growth of your company (and the continued scaling of your application). You get the idea. The point to remember is that you can take a component-based application that resides on one box and split it across multiple machines.

From Here...

You spent this chapter learning about object models, COM, and distributed computing. You now can use this information as you begin to develop applications in the Active Server Pages environment. Here's what you can look forward to in the chapters on the ASP objects and their uses:

- Chapter 16, "Integrating VBScript into ASP," will cover the basic concepts on how to integrate VBScript and ASP to use the ActiveX and OLE controls discussed in Chapter 16.
- Chapter 17, "Practical ASP Programming," will show you how to implement practical objects within you ASP application, as well as discuss the *Application* and *Session* objects.
- Appendix A, "Commerce 2.0 Components," will discuss the components that ship with Commerce Server 2.0, these are the components you will implement in your ASP applications.

Integrating VBScript into ASP

To take full advantage of Active Server Pages (ASP) features, you must first learn to integrate other languages into the HTML programming of ASP. The most commonly used scripting language today is Microsoft Visual Basic Scripting Edition (VBScript). In this chapter, you learn how to integrate the VBScript scripting technology into HTML programming by using ASP. You should quickly discover the advantages of being able to integrate other scripting languages into this environment. ■

Connecting Microsoft and BASIC

This section briefly examines the history of the BASIC language and Microsoft's role in its development.

Understanding the Visual Basic family tree

This section discusses the Visual Basic family of tools.

Examining scripting and HTML

This section shows you how scripting looks within an HTML file and how the two (scripting and HTML) integrate to create dynamic content.

Understanding client versus server scripting

Scripts can be executed at the client, on the server, or at both ends of the connection.

Looking at other scripting languages

VBScript is the default scripting language of Active Server but is not the only option for ASP script development. In this section, languages are discussed and how you can change what language you are using.

Connecting Microsoft and BASIC

The history of the BASIC language is a good place to start in putting the development of VBScript and Active Server Pages into perspective. Beginners All Purpose Symbolic Instruction Code, commonly known as BASIC, was developed in 1964 at Dartmouth College by Kenney and Kurtz. BASIC was designed to provide students an easy-to-understand procedural language that would be a stepping stone to more powerful languages such as FORTRAN.

In the intervening 30-plus years, a great deal has happened to this introductory computer language. The language has grown and become more feature-rich over the years, due mainly to its vast acceptance in the marketplace. The story of the evolution of the BASIC language into the default language of Active Server Pages scripting began in 1975, when a young man named Bill Gates was attending Harvard University.

Attracted by an article about the forthcoming M.I.T.S. Altair computer, Paul Allen and Bill Gates developed a version of BASIC that would run on the Altair and that eventually was licensed to M.I.T.S. for its Altair computer. When version 2.0 was released later that same year, it was available in two versions: 4K and 8K. Imagine the entire development system implemented in 4096 bytes! Today, you would be hard-pressed to find a Microsoft Word template that is that small.

BASIC was the first product ever sold by Microsoft. Two years later, after porting its version of BASIC to other platforms (CP/M, for example), the exclusive license with M.I.T.S. for Microsoft BASIC ended. In 1979, Microsoft released MS-BASIC, a 16-bit product for the 8086.

Bill Gates won the opportunity to provide the operating system for the new IBM personal computer after IBM's courtship of Digital Research Inc. to license its CP/M operating system failed. Microsoft licensed the SCP-DOS operating system and modified it to run on the IBM-PC. Version 1.0 of the MS-DOS operating system, bundled with MS-BASIC, was the engine that drove the beginning of the personal computer revolution.

Over the years, Microsoft saw how attractive BASIC was and created a compiler for the language in the form of QuickBasic. QuickBasic reigned supreme until version 4.5, when it was replaced by PDS BASIC (Professional Development System).

Few people had any idea in the spring of 1991 that their lives were going to change dramatically. Visual Basic was announced at the Windows World '91 conference on May 20, 1991. The Visual Basic environment was to provide graphical application development and an integrated debugger and to create compiled executable Windows programs, all using the BASIC language. Many Windows developers still remember the first time that they used Visual Basic version 1.0. After thrashing their way though learning the C language and building Windows applications with Microsoft C and the SDK, developers couldn't believe the power inherent in this innocuous little visual development package.

Visual Basic for Windows was followed by Visual Basic for DOS. When the DOS version came out, many programmers still had DOS machines. The DOS version of VB addressed the RAD methodology on the DOS platform. Even though the product never made it past version 1.0, it was useful for creating graphical applications for the DOS environment.

By the time Visual Basic version 4.0 was released in 1995, countless programmers were hooked on the Visual Basic development environment. Visual Basic's easy learning curve, intuitive interface, and bundled components, combined with its incredible extensibility and tightly integrated environment, make it the logical choice for millions of developers each day.

Understanding the Visual Basic Family Tree

As you learned in the preceding section, getting from the M.I.T.S to Visual Basic for Windows took some time. Over the past few years, the Visual Basic family has been fruitful (and has multiplied). In the next several sections, you examine the various incarnations of the Visual Basic language as it is available today and develop a greater appreciation for the differences and similarities in the VB family. (Figure 16.1 shows the family portrait.) For all you Visual Basic programmers out there (VB and VBA), the following sections examine what VBScript leaves in and, more important, what it leaves out.

FIG. 16.1
Each member of the VB family has an important role to play.

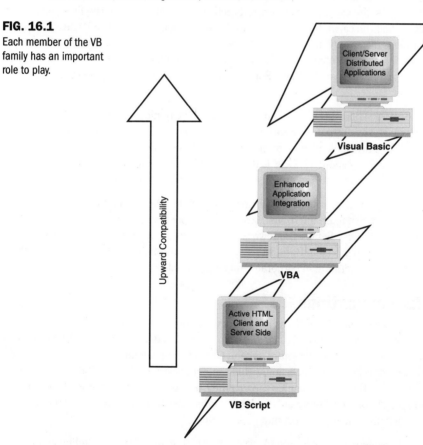

Visual Basic

The Visual Basic programming tool is a professional development environment suitable for developing multiple-tier, enterprise-level client/server applications. The product's inherent extensibility in the form of supporting OLE and ActiveX controls and its capability to integrate Win32 API calls, as well as third-party DLLs, provide a rich environment for creating applications.

Visual Basic is used by millions of programmers all over the world, mainly for development of personal and corporate applications. Over the past few years, commercial applications developed in VB have been showing up in the marketplace.

The current version of VB (5.0) is available in three packages: Standard, Professional, and Enterprise. The Standard package is ideal for the computer hobbyist or student, providing all the base functionality without including (in the price or the package) several custom controls that are appropriate for larger-scale development. The Professional Editon provides additional custom controls, the capability to interact directly with databases (not requiring data-bound controls), and the capability to create remote automation servers. The Professional and Enterprise Editions differ only in their capability to provide remote data objects. The Professional Edition is suitable for many needs in corporate application development. The Enterprise Edition also integrates Microsoft's Visual SourceSafe, a source-code-management and team-development tool.

In December of 1996, Microsoft made Visual Basic Control Creation Edition available for down-loading from its Web site (**http://www.microsoft.com**). VB CCE was a new version of Visual Basic that provided a first look at some of the features that were integrated into Visual Basic 5.0. The remarkable thing about VB CCE is the fact that it can create ActiveX controls, which you can integrate into your Web applications on the client and server sides.

As the Visual Basic product continues to mature, it will remain the tool of choice for millions of developers, who will use it to create robust, scalable, multiple-tier applications. With the introduction of Microsoft's Active Server framework and its middleware-transaction-processing product, code-named Viper, Visual Basic will come to the forefront as the tool for creating the client side of the next generation of corporate and commercial applications.

Visual Basic for Applications

Visual Basic for Applications (or VBA, as it is commonly known) is a powerful subset of the Visual Basic environment. At the end of 1996, Microsoft released VBA version 5.0. The company has integrated VBA across the entire suite of Office 97 applications and has made it available to third-party developers for inclusion within their applications. At the 1996 fall Comdex computer show, more than 40 companies showed their products with an integrated VBA programming engine. As of the printing of November's *ComputerWorld*, an additional 60 third parties had signed up to integrate VBA into their products.

VBA is a shared development environment within the hosting application, including an integrated code editor and support for debugging. With its support for OLE automation, VBA is often used as an integrating tool to create custom applications from within Word, Excel, or Access. VBA developers can use any application that exposes its objects as OLE or ActiveX controls. Many of the familiar tools from the Visual Basic IDE made it into VBA 5.0. Features such as the code window, project explorer, properties window, and object browser make the VBA environment similar to its bigger sibling.

In Office 97 products, as well as other products that host VBA 5.0, users have access to Microsoft Forms which help when creating a development environment with the same forms metaphor as Visual Basic. Because VBA 5.0 applications use the same forms environment, any form object created in one application can be used by any other application. This tight integration and code reusability makes VBA the language of choice for embedded programming engines.

One wonderful aspect of VBA is the fact that you can learn the language within one application or environment and immediately transfer that knowledge to other products. In addition, you can easily scale up to the complete Visual Basic environment or move down to create powerful Internet/intranet applications with VBScript and Active Server Pages. For anyone who wants to learn to develop with VB within an application environment, VBA is an excellent choice.

Visual Basic Scripting Edition

The Scripting Edition of Visual Basic is a smaller subset of the Visual Basic for Applications language. This Edition is intended for use in Internet/intranet application development and currently is supported in Microsoft Internet Explorer version 3.0 and later. The scripting edition brings much of the power and flexibility of the Visual Basic language to the Internet and intranets.

On the client side, the product gives developers the opportunity to interact with ActiveX controls to create active and interesting content. On the server side, the scripting language is used and integrated within HTML to provide a new level of functionality and ease of use in Web-site development.

For VB or VBA programmers, the transition to Active Server Pages development by using VBScript from a traditional client/server environment will be less a challenge of learning the idiosyncrasies of a sister language than a challenge of changing to the new Net development paradigm. Programming in any language consists of expressions, statements, and procedures. The trick is to figure out how the language integrates with the environment in which it is to be implemented. In the case of VB or VBA, the environment is the Windows operating system.

VBScript, on the other hand, is implemented on the client by using ActiveX controls, as well as on the server in ASP, integrating a variety of components to create dynamic pages. You deal with not only the scripting language, but also with its integration into HTML code. At first, having your code in pieces throughout the HTML page takes some getting used to. But just as mastering the VB IDE was a struggle, you will master VBScript and Active Server Pages development.

If you are coming to Active Server Pages development from a strictly HTML background, you also have a learning curve to climb. If you have been developing Perl or REXX scripts, the language features of VBScript are not very foreign to you. Also, you have become used to adding additional tags as the HTML standard has emerged. You can treat VBScript and the associated implementation as being just some additional tags to integrate.

Be sure, however, to use the new components that ship with Active Server Pages. This powerful set of ASP components includes such features as session management, application management, and database connectivity. You could easily use VBScript for some minor chores and revert to the old CGI way of doing things for database access and other local processing tasks. Learning to use the VBScript language and its associated ASP components is worth the effort.

Identifying VBScript's Feature Set and Limitations

You probably are really looking forward to a huge table filled with every difference between the VB language syntax and VBScript. What you find in the next few pages is a list of some of the most important or widely used functions that your typical Visual Basic developer might immediately miss. The coverage is not exhaustive. If you must have the complete list, line by line, of the differences between VBA and VBScript, refer to the VBScript documentation that ships with Active Server Pages.

Array Handling

Arrays are useful in hundreds of situations, and when you have an array of objects, that number jumps again. Many times, changing the base of an array variable for a specific implementation is useful. If you were to create an array representing the days in February, for example, starting the array at 1 and going to 28 would make sense but this is not possible in VBScript; all arrays must have a lower bound of 0. The same is true of multidimensional arrays: All lower bounds begin at 0. Starting arrays with 0 doesn't affect the performance at all; you just need to remember that to get to element *n*, you always subtract 1. In VBScript, your February array index would go from 0 to 27.

Collections and Classes

Two of the most cherished features in the most recent release of Visual Basic are collections and classes. The addition of classes to the Visual Basic language enables you to get that much closer to fully supported object-oriented development. You cannot create a user-defined collection within VBScript.

You also cannot create a class. If you do want to add functionality within a class, create the class in Visual Basic, create an OLE component, and then create an instance of the class from within an Active Server Pages script by using the `CreateObject` syntax.

The Active Server Pages environment includes several collections, which you treat just as you would in Visual Basic: walking the collection, setting items, and so on.

Conversion

Several conversion functions are supported in VBScript. The most glaring omission is the Format command, which is the one command that surely will be missed the most. This command is in the list for inclusion in the next release of VBScript.

Data Types

No intrinsic data types are available in VBScript. The only data type available is Variant, which makes complete sense, considering that VBScript is an OLE-implemented language. All passing of values between OLE objects is performed through Variant variables.

Dynamic Data Exchange

Dynamic Data Exchange (DDE), the venerable method of interprocess communication, is the forerunner of OLE. Given the built-in support of OLE objects, DDE is not supported in any form in VBScript. This feature, if included, could potentially violate the integrity of the client machine. Imagine a script that runs during startup, looks for Windows Explorer via DDE, finds it, and then sends messages telling it to format your hard drive!

Dynamic Link Library Support

One feature of Visual Basic that makes the product so extensible is the capability to declare and call functions within Dynamic Link Libraries (DLL). This feature provides you the method to call any of the Win32 API functions and a host of other functions that are available in third-party DLLs. Although many of the functions of DLLs are now available as OCX/ActiveX controls, there are probably many controls that you created over the years which you still wish to use.

You have a few options. First, port the DLL to an ActiveX object. Next, if you don't have the source or do not want to change the DLL, you can wrap the DLLs functions within a VB class and then create an OLE Server for use in your ASP scripts.

Debugging Support

One of the nicest features of VB is its integrated development environment (IDE). You could debug your application line by line, changing variable values on-the-fly. No IDE is available for VBScript and Active Server Pages development (yet), and VB does not support the Debug.Print, End, and Stop commands.

Again, you can easily build a simple component to provide the Debug.Print functionality. On the client side, in December of 1996, Microsoft released Microsoft Script Debugger for Internet Explorer, which enables interactive debugging of scripts that execute within Microsoft's Internet Explorer client. This product is available for free downloading at **http://www.microsoft.com/workshop/prog/scriptie**.

Error Handling

Error handling is available when you develop ASP applications. The familiar `On Error Resume Next` command is still available, although branching on errors is not. You also have access to the `Err` object to retrieve error numbers and descriptions. When an error occurs in your `.asp` scripts, error messages are sent back to the client as HTML, and depending on the severity of those messages, they can also be written to the IIS log and the NT Server log.

File Input/Output

All the language features that enable access to local files (File I/O) on the system in which an application is running have been removed from VBScript to enhance the security of the language on the Internet and in intranets. This file I/O protection prevents an errant VBScript program executing on a browser from damaging data on the client machine.

User-Defined Types

The last feature of VB that is not included in VBScript is the capability to create user-defined types. No better construct is available for dealing with database and transaction-oriented data than the user-defined type, which will be sorely missed.

The Last Word

Several features are not yet (or never will be) available in VBScript. As the language is deployed and continues to mature, the features that are requested most often and that do not violate the security constraints will be added to the language. VBScript must be a smaller subset of VBA security and size for two main reasons:

- The VBScript code will execute on the client and the server systems. If the VBScript code had access to the native file system on the computer on which it is running, it could potentially wreak havoc with the data contained within. Imagine pulling up a new page and having your hard drive mysteriously formatted or having key files destroyed. Just as you safeguard your computer with virus-protection programs, Microsoft has safeguarded your browser by limiting the functionality of the VBScript language.

- VBScript must be a subset because of the "weight" of the language. The language is designed for use over the Internet and in intranets. If you end up shipping the OLE scripting engine over the Net to fulfill a request, you want to ensure that the language is relatively small, so as to minimize transfer time.

Regardless of the real or perceived shortcomings of the VBScript language, nothing is better or more powerful for creating and implementing dynamic content over the Net than using VBScript within Active Server Pages.

Security is not as big an issue when code executes on the server as opposed to executing on the client. Assume, for the moment, that any component you build will not damage the machine. That said, you can easily add any missing functionality in the VBScript language by creating an OLE component. Because VBScript can create an instance of any OLE or ActiveX component, you can easily provide the native VB functionality to your server-side VBScript Active Server Pages.

Examining Scripting and HTML

A *script* is composed of a series of commands that are executed by the host environment, meaning that scripts are executed on the client or on the server. Active Server Pages contains scripts that execute within the client browser as well as the server. Within a script, you can perform a variety of activities, such as the following:

- Create a variable and assign a value to it
- Perform operations on variables
- Group commands into callable blocks of code called *procedures*
- Dynamically create client-side scripts from the server

The scripts within an ASP page are passed to a scripting engine within the client or server environment. A *scripting engine* is a Component Object Model (COM) object that is called to process the script. Within the scripting engine, the script is parsed, checked for syntax, and then interpreted. The resulting actions, deciphered by the interpreter, are then performed within the host environment. Because the scripting engine in the Active Server Pages environment is a COM object, you can add additional scripting engines to support multiple scripting languages. Support for VBScript and Java Script is bundled with Active Server Pages.

Script Delimiters

Within an HTML file, you use delimiters around tags to tell the client that you are requesting an HTML tag, not just text to be displayed. You also need delimiters to tell the host environment that scripting occurs within the page. The scripting delimiters that you wrap around scripting are <% and %>. Text within the script delimiters is processed within the host environment before the page is executed. Following are a few examples of how a script with delimiters looks within an ASP page:

```
<HTML>

<HEAD>
<TITLE>Scripting in HTML</TITLE>
</HEAD>

<BODY>
<P>We will now create a variable, assign a value to it and then <BR>
display the value of the variable within our page</P>

<% strName ="steve" %>

<P>We have created a script variable called strName and have<BR>
assigned a value to it. The value is <%=strName%> </P>
</BODY>

</HTML>
```

Notice that you can intersperse scripting commands almost anywhere in an `.asp` file. The script expression is evaluated, and the resulting value is inserted into the HTML file that is sent to the client. Within the first set of scripting delimiters, you create a variable `strName` and assign the value `steve` to it, using the equal sign to perform the assignment. When you want to display the value of the variable on the client, you again use the equal sign to place the value in the HTML file `=strName`.

Scripting Statements

Creating variables or putting single values in-line in an `.asp` file is referred to as a *single expression*. Single expressions are bits and pieces of code that resolve to a value. *Statements*, on the other hand, are complete logical units that perform one type of action. Following is an example of an `If` statement:

```
<%
IF (Time > #8:00:00AM# and Time < #5:00:00PM#) THEN
strMessage= "Get Back to Work!"
ELSE
strMessage = "You should be at home, resting."
END IF
%>

<P> Sir or Madam, <%=strMessage%> </P>
```

Imagine the poor unsuspecting office worker who happens to pull up this page from the corporate intranet. If the time is between 8 a.m. and 5:00 p.m., the employee gets a "Dilbert"-style management command. At any other time, the employee is reminded that he or she has much better places to be than work. Many of us are not fortunate enough to have a standard 8-to-5 job, but presenting the employees with appropriate pictures of what they should be doing remains a good example of a scripting statement within HTML code.

Scripting Blocks

Just as you enclose tables and forms in beginning and ending tags, you encode script blocks in beginning and ending tags. The `<SCRIPT>` and `</SCRIPT>` tags notify the host environment to expect a block of scripting code within the tags. By using these tags, you can create procedures that can be called from anywhere within the page. (A procedure is several scripting commands that are grouped to perform a specific function.) If you try to define a procedure within script delimiters alone, you generate syntax errors.

To combine scripting languages and procedures, and examine at some scripting code in action. You are going to create two simple procedures—one in VBScript and one in JavaScript—to be invoked within the same page. For now, don't worry too much about the scripting syntax; just try to get a feel for how the scripting is integrated into the ASP page. First, create the VBScript procedure, as follows:

```
<SCRIPT LANGUAGE=VBScript RUNAT=Server>
```

```
Sub vbwrite
response.write("Hello from VBScript")
End Sub

</SCRIPT>
```

The following JavaScript procedure is invoked next:

```
<SCRIPT LANGUAGE=JavaScript RUNAT=Server>
Sub jwrite
response.write("Hello from JavaScript")
End Sub
</SCRIPT>
```

Putting everything together with a little HTML results in the following:

```
<HTML>
<HEAD>
<TITLE>Mixing Scripts</TITLE>
</HEAD>
<BODY>
<P>First we have output from VBScript</P>
<% Call vbwrite %>

<P>Now from JScript</P>
<% Call jwrite %>
</BODY>
</HTML>
```

The VBScript and JavaScript scripting languages are functionally equivalent and use much of the same syntax. If you start using other scripting languages, such as Perl and REXX, you find that these languages are quite different in syntax from VBScript and JavaScript but retain the same programming constructs. But if you are a crack Perl or REXX developer and want to make the transition to Active Server Pages development without learning a new language, you are in luck. Because the scripting engine is a COM object, which is called to process a file under ASP, you can integrate a Perl or REXX script processor into Active Server Pages.

N O T E Notice that the preceding example uses an additional attribute of the <SCRIPT> tag:, RUNAT. This attribute, which determines where the script is executed, is a nice transition into the following sections, which discuss the primary scripting language and client-side and server-side scripting. ■

Procedures are an ideal way to create logical units of functionality that can be called from within your Active Server Pages script. To reach the next level of functionality and to provide a medium for code reuse, ASP provides the capability to include code from another source file in an ASP script. This capability, called *server-side includes*, is a syntax used for inserting the contents of one file into another.

This include capability is a familiar one to C and C++ developers, who have been including header files since the day they began application development. Still, this simple feature adds an additional level of functionality to Active Server Pages. If you have a great procedure in a file called `grtproc.htm` and want to add the procedure to a new file, you would use the server-side include syntax as follows:

```
<!--#INCLUDE FILE="grtproc.htm"-->
```

Now you could call the great procedure in `grtproc.htm` in your new `.asp` file.

Changing the Primary Scripting Language

Embedding scripting within your ASP pages, using only the scripting delimiters, is referred to as *primary scripting*. The code in primary scripting is executed against the default scripting engine for the page. In Active Server Pages development, the default scripting engine is VBScript. You can select a different scripting language for a page or block of script within a page by setting the `<SCRIPT>` tag as follows:

```
<SCRIPT LANGUAGE=JavaScript>
```

This code line notifies the host that the script within the page uses JavaScript syntax.

You can also mix multiple scripting languages within a page by changing the scripting language tags within the page itself, as follows:

```
<SCRIPT LANGUAGE=JavaScript>
...Java Script Code Here
</SCRIPT>

<SCRIPT LANGAUGE=VBScript>
...VBScript Code Here
</SCRIPT>
```

Comparing Client-Side and Server-Side Scripting

We have taken much time, in earlier chapters such as Chapter 13, "Introducing Active Server Pages," and Chapter 14, "Introduction to ASP Scripting," to emphasize the client/server architecture and the architecture's importance in developing a Commerce Server 2.0 store. Here, again, we stress the importance of the client/server architecture, but with a new twist. Here we discuss the client/server architecture when using VBScript.

Client-Side Scripting

Client-side scripting refers to the scripts that are interpreted and executed in the client browser. When you are scripting for the client, you have access to the object model that is available within the browser. You also create scripts to interact with user-interface objects on the client.

Several tools are available for creating client-side pages and their associated scripting. The ActiveX Control Pad is a good example of such a tool. This Microsoft-developed, freely available product enables you to design Web pages, adding ActiveX controls and standard HTML fields at design time. The program then generates the HTML code to create the page. When the page is created, you can edit the file and add scripting to provide such client-side features as field validation, custom responses to user actions, and a host of other capabilities inherent in the client's browser. The ActiveX Control Pad is available at **http://www.microsoft.com**.

As mentioned earlier in this chapter, the opportunity for field validation of data at the client is an important feature of client-side scripting. You can have the page validate the data *before* it is sent to the server. This ensures that you do not immediately receive a message from the server, requesting that you provide complete or correct information. In addition to providing validation errors more quickly to the user, which reduces network traffic. In the following example, you create a simple page containing a field that you validate:

```
<HTML>
<HEAD>
<TITLE>Scripting in HTML</TITLE>
</HEAD>

<BODY>
Enter a Value <INPUT TYPE=INPUT NAME=TxtField SIZE=20>
<INPUT TYPE=BUTTON VALUE="Submit" NAME="BtnSubmit">
```

You have created an input field named `TxtField` and a button for submitting the page. Next, you create an event that executes when the `BtnSubmit` button is clicked, as follows:

```
<SCRIPT LANGUAGE=VBScript>
<!--
Option Explicit
Dim bValid

Sub BtnSubmit_OnClick
bValid = True
Call CheckField(TxtField.Value, "Please enter a value in the field.")

IF (bValid) THEN
MsgBox "Thank you for filling in the field"
END IF

End Sub
```

> **CAUTION**
>
> Although the default language of Active Server Pages is VBScript, in the Internet Explorer (IE), it is not. If you do not explicitly state `LANGUAGE=VBScript`, the default language in IE, JScript generates errors within your pages.

The first line is the SCRIPT tag, which tells Internet Explorer that you are preparing to provide scripting instructions in the VBScript language. The next notable section is the procedure created to respond to the click of the `BtnSubmit` button. The syntax `OnClick` makes perfect sense and should be familiar to you if you have any experience with developing in VB, where the procedure would be named `BtnSubmit_Click`. This procedure executes when the button is clicked. The script then checks the field (see the following code) to see whether it contains a value. If so, the field information is sent to the server. If not, the user sees a message to input an appropriate field value.

```
Sub CheckField(ByVal strFieldValue, ByVal strMessage)
If strFieldValue = "" Then
MsgBox strMessage, 0
bValid = False
End If
End Sub
-->
</SCRIPT>
</BODY>
</HTML>
```

This last bit of code is the procedure that implements the field validation. Notice that you are only checking for any text entered in the field. You could have written a more involved procedure that could check for a range of values or convert the values to all uppercase or lowercase. For now, don't worry too much about the syntax of VBScript (the rest of this section is devoted to that topic). You should just begin to get a feel for how client scripting is integrated into the HTML code.

When you create a page with scripting and define procedures within script tags, the default RUNAT (where the script executes) is the client. Any scripting that you include within the scripting tags without specifying the RUNAT attribute executes on the client.

Server-Side Scripting

This section is the meat and potatoes of the scripting discussion. *Server-side scripting* occurs when the scripts within the page are executed at the server, before the page is ever sent to the client browser, as shown in Figure 16.2.

FIG. 16.2

Active Server Pages scripts execute on the server before passing the page to the client.

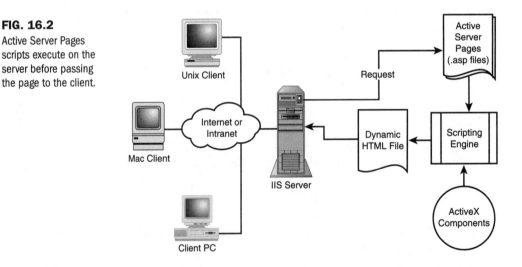

This distinction is incredibly important; it means that the server is responsible for generating the HTML that is ultimately sent to the client. You do not have to worry about the client's connecting to a database, reading from a file, querying an online service, or performing any of the thousands of other actions that take place on the server to fulfill the client request.

Active Server Pages provides server-side scripting for the Internet Information Server Web server. In addition to enabling custom scripting to be developed, you can integrate almost any ActiveX component (one that doesn't require a user interface, of course) into your server scripts. Server-side scripting and components open the door wide and enable a level of functionality that is difficult—if not impossible—to achieve with traditional methods of server-side processing.

Server-side scripting blocks are executed at the server when the ASP interpreter finds the scripting tag with the RUNAT attribute set to SERVER:

```
<LANGUAGE=VBScript RUNAT=SERVER>
```

When an Active Server Pages page is requested, the server calls ASP. The .asp file is read through from top to bottom. Any scripting that needs to execute on the server is performed; then the dynamically created HTML page is sent back to the client.

Notice that the code in the CheckField subroutine (in the preceding section) creates a message box to respond to user input. If you mistakenly add the RUNAT=SERVER to the client code, the message box is never displayed on the client, because the server has no interface in which to display a message box. What you could do at the server is generate custom messages based on the time of day or data in a database and then pop those messages into the client browser when the validation takes place, which is done by dynamically generating client-side scripts from the server.

Modifying Client Scripts from the Server

When you create Active Server Pages applications, you normally are interested in creating dynamic content for your clients to view. You can create dynamic content by interacting with ActiveX components and databases, and even with legacy systems, to provide dynamic, up-to-date information.

One of the most exciting aspects of the capability to create dynamic HTML content is the capability to create client-side scripting on-the-fly. In essence, you dynamically create scripting based on server information and embed it in the HTML page that you return to the client. Then these dynamically created scripts execute on the client's browser.

The more you think about this capability, the more situations you think of in which to use this powerful new functionality. You can create custom on_load events that are invoked when the page is loaded onto the client. You can also dynamically create scripts that respond to user events on the client.

Currently, many pages on the Web are full of VBScript and JavaScript. The problem with these pages is that after they are created and posted to the Net, you cannot do anything to change them without editing the source file. Now, by using Active Server Pages, you can prepare scripting variables on the server side to be used by the client.

Suppose that you want to create a VBScript array for use on the client with real-time information stored in a legacy system. Without server-side scripting, querying information from a legacy system would be problematic at best. Using server-side scripting, you can query the legacy system by using a database-access component and then populate the array before returning the page to the client. In another scenario, you could have custom client-side validation scripts generated by the server, based on external values stored in a database.

When an Active Server Pages script is run, ASP processes any commands within a comment block with the scripting tags <% and %>, regardless of where the tags are within the script. In the following code, the server-side script executes within ASP, even though the script resides in a scripting block that has no RUNAT=SERVER parameter:

```
<SCRIPT LANGUAGE=VBScript>
<!--
<% server side scripting commands %>
-->
</SCRIPT>
```

In the following example, the server script creates three VBScript subroutines that subsequently execute on the client machine:

```
<HTML>
<HEAD>
<TITLE>Client Side Scripting From The Server</TITLE>
</HEAD>

<BODY>
<%
tmeServerTime = Now
For i = 1 to 3
%>

<SCRIPT LANGUAGE=VBScript>
<!--
Sub Server_Time_<%=i%>()
MsgBox "The time at the server is <%=tmeServerTime%>" _
& " on pass <%=i%>"
End Sub

Server_Time_<%=i%>()
-->
</SCRIPT>

<%="Server side loop " & i & "<BR>"%>
<%
Next
%>
</BODY>
</HTML>
```

When you execute this code in your browser and look at the source, you see three VBScript procedures, named `Server_Time_1`, `Server_Time_2`, and `Server_Time_3`. Each of these procedures was generated dynamically from the execution of the ASP script on the server.

Although this example is simplistic, it should give you a sense of the power of this ASP capability. (Thanks to Dave Kaplin at Microsoft for explaining this powerful feature in a thread from the Denali list server.)

You probably want to ask "Where do I put what?"—meaning "How do I decide what scripts should execute on the client and which on the server?" The answer is that most of the client procedures usually deal with data validation. All the other procedures—accessing data, communicating with host systems, and so on—take place within the server-side scripts. No hard-and-fast rule exists, though. Experience is the best teacher in this case.

Part
IV

Ch
16

> **CAUTION**
>
> Remember that not all browsers support VBScript or even support scripting at all. If you want to provide client-side scripting, be sure to interrogate the `Browser Capability` object to see which scripting language is supported. Then you can return the appropriate client-side scripts.

Looking at Other Scripting Languages

The default language of Active Server Pages is VBScript. ASP also supports JavaScript out of the box. The OLE object model for scripting engines, which Active Server Pages supports, enables you to easily integrate other scripting languages and their associated engines into ASP.

The capability to host a variety of languages within the Active Server Pages environment is an incredibly powerful feature. If you are a developer with years of experience generating Perl scripts, you do not need to forgo all that valuable knowledge; you can become productive in ASP development immediately. As you begin to learn VBScript or JScript, you can incorporate additional features, such as dynamic client-side scripting.

REXX is one of the most widely used scripting/macro languages in existence today and is available for platforms ranging from OS/2 to the AS/400 to the mainframe. Some versions of REXX are even implemented today as visual languages. VisPro/REXX is one such example of a visual REXX environment. This OS/2 application provides an easy-to-use, incredibly powerful visual development metaphor, leveraging the REXX language. For more information about VisPro/REXX, point your browser to **http://www.vispro.com**.

For the countless REXX developers who are working today, the ability to plug a REXX scripting engine into Active Server Pages again opens the gates wide, allowing the greatest number of people to maximize their Internet/intranet development.

Selecting a Scripting Language for a Page

For languages that follow the Object.Method syntax and use parentheses to enclose the proce-dure parameters, add the selected language by using the LANGUAGE tag. The syntax of the LANGUAGE tag is

```
<% @ LANGUAGE = ScriptingLanguage %>
```

Be sure to add this tag as the first line in your .asp file. If you want to change the default script-ing language of all .asp pages, you need to change the value of the DefaultScriptLanguage entry in the NT Registry to the new script type.

For languages that do not conform to the Object.Method syntax, you must add a Registry key with the corresponding language name and value to the ASP\LanguageEngines Registry entry.

From Here...

In this chapter we have discussed the advantages that VBScript brings to your ASP applica-tions. You have probably already concluded, as you should, that the addition of VBScript within ASP is a very powerful tool that you will need to learn to embrace.

From here we will further discuss the advantages that VBScript brings to your Commerce Server 2.0 store(s) and mall(s), through the following chapters:

■ Chapter 17, "Practical ASP Programming," puts together the ASP features we have discussed up until now. This chapter helps you understand the "practical" way to implement the features that ASP provides to your application.

■ Chapter 18, "Constructing a Server Component Using ASP," discusses the implementa-tion of Server Components within ASP. This chapter helps you put together advanced ASP applications, as well as build a bridge, which will help you cross-over from an ASP developer to a Commerce Server site developer.

■ Chapter 23, "Constructing Your Own Server Components," gives you the powerful tool of creating your own components for your ASP applications. In this chapter you learn to create your own component by using Visual C++ 5.0.

■ Part VI, "Case Studies," takes you on an in-depth study of Commerce Server 2.0 stores. Along the way, you encounter many ASP and VBScript examples that will give you an example of how to implement the features of VBScript within ASP.

CHAPTER 17

Practical ASP Programming

Many aspects of Active Server Pages (ASP) programming allow the developer to really focus on what he or she should: the project. Many Web developers get caught up trying to get the Web site to communicate properly when they should be programming the functionality. This chapter discusses the features of ASP programming that allow the developer to accomplish his or her job quickly.

With a solid understanding of these topics, you can confidently create ASP applications by using the basic ASP features. ■

Tracking user sessions

In most Web applications, tracking users and their activities from page to page requires a large portion of the overall programming effort.

Setting up an application

Active Server Pages uses directory structures and the global.asa file for managing applications.

Understanding *Application* and *Session* objects

This section will give you an overview of the Application and Session objects' scoping, events, and properties.

Understanding the *Application* object's events and properties

The Application object provides a mechanism to track sessions and to store variables and objects for application-wide use.

Understanding the *Session* object's practical applications

Use the Session object to manage a user's flow from page to page, track user input, and cache information.

Managing States and Events with *Application* and *Session* Objects

Managing users as they navigate an application represents a common and easily handled challenge in the traditional client/server application-development world. In the Web world, by contrast, Internet application developers find managing this challenge—or, in essence, maintaining a user's state—to be one of the greatest challenges in building a comprehensive Internet-based application. Because HTTP transactions between a browser and a Web server are independent, with no persistence or connection state being maintained, even tracking a user as she moves from one page request to another can be a difficult task.

For managing a user from the first page request, Active Server Pages incorporated a model based on *cookies* to generate a unique ID for users' browsers. At the first page request, the session OnStart event fires. This event sets the scope of several properties for the life of this unique browser's session. At the same time, the event defines a Timeout property to manage the session length. The Timeout property measures inactivity from the cookied browser (the cookie for the browser containing the Timeout property). This chapter explores in detail the capability to track users, but goes way beyond that capability in exploring the valuable functionality extended to programmers through the Session and Application objects.

N O T E   *Cookies* are a feature of HTML 2.0 that enable an HTML author to write a variable or named piece of information to the client browser. If the browser supports HTML 2.0 or later, this information is saved as a file by the client browser program on the user's hard drive, and the browser automatically sends that information with any browser request to that domain. The cookie has a duration property as well. ■

ASP Manages User Sessions

In the typical Visual Basic client/server development environment, the Visual Basic program operates as the client, capturing any user input and responding to events such as mouse movement. These user inputs, ranging from mouse movement to the pressing of a keyboard key, give the programmer absolute control in managing the user's choices and experience. The Web world of development has some important distinctions that frame the entire development model.

Because Active Server Pages operates completely at the server, from executing VBScript to storing variables, the normal Visual Basic model does not apply. The VBScript source code and the objects that it invokes and references come into play only when a user connects to the server by processing a form page or selecting a URL. In short, Active Server Pages is invoked only when a user moves from one page to another. At this point, when a browser requests a page, the HTTP request or transaction sends only the simple HTTP transaction, including the requested page, form or URL fields, and some general browser-related information (such as cookies).

N O T E For a more detailed description, please refer to information about the HTTP transaction standard, which you can find by searching for "HTTP transaction standard" on the Web. ∎

The simple HTTP record layout passed between Web server and Web browser creates a challenge for managing an application. One of the key challenges becomes tracking users as they move between pages. Tracking users includes maintaining, in an easily accessible way, some unique tracking ID, as well as any information that must be displayed or manipulated (such as a shopping basket of selected products in an order-processing system). Several standard workarounds have emerged for dealing with this challenge, and Active Server Pages builds on the best of these approaches.

Tracking User Sessions: The Web Challenge

A key challenge in Web programming is tracking each user from one page to the next and making information from previous pages available on subsequent pages. This challenge can be met by using several basic approaches. But without Active Server Pages, the problem requires complex functions for generating unique IDs and difficult workarounds for keeping track of information—in other words, maintaining variables scoping during a user's working session.

Part
IV

Ch
17

The challenge of tracking a user's session requires generating a unique ID and then ensuring that on every subsequent page, that ID and any added user information continue to be available. Two basic techniques before Active Server Pages for accomplishing this task include:

- Using the cookie feature of browsers
- Creating hidden fields/URL variables on a page

If you use the second technique, you must ensure that the hidden field or URL variable gets passed to all subsequent pages and is created as a new hidden field or URL variable on those pages, which is done to always keep the variable alive as a hidden form field or URL variable.

An enhanced approach to moving hidden fields around involves maintaining a variable's scope by using a database or text file on the server to store this information based on the unique ID. Constantly retrieving unique ID's every time a new page gets requested followed by passing the unique ID to sequentially called pages as hidden fields and URL variables requires careful planning, because all possible page selections and flow must be carefully considered to ensure that unique IDs are not lost.

Generating Unique IDs for Tracking Users

Creating a unique ID and saving it as a variable requires more effort than you might expect. After generating and saving a unique ID, you must carefully manage the ID to make it available to all subsequent pages during the user's session. There are many approaches to generating unique IDs which generally result from some combination of date and time, user input, and IP addresses or, by using a database to generate a unique ID such as a counter field in Microsoft Access. Unfortunately, all these approaches require careful planning.

Take the approach, for example, of setting up a Microsoft Access table with a counter field and using the counter fields as the unique IDs for users entering the Web page. The first step is inserting a new record when the user first hits the page. Because the insertion of a new record does not return the counter field, however, a query must be done to retrieve that ID field.

You can't just request the last ordinal record, because within a second or so of the insert command, a second user may have requested the same page and inserted a subsequent record. As a result, you must actually take some value, such as date/time, and insert that value as well so that you can retrieve the counter value. Even with this approach, you run the risk of having two transactions with same date/time values, down to the second. To further complicate matters, you must have the date/time field available as a form field in the HTML document to pass it as a parameter.

Managing UIDs and Scoping with Cookie/Form/URL

Regardless of how you generate your unique ID, the immediate challenge that follows becomes keeping that ID alive or always in scope from one page to the next. Without the Active Server Pages Session object, one approach involves ensuring that every HTML page passes the ID as either a URL variable or a Form field, depending on whether the page request results from a hyperlink or Form's processing. This takes the form illustrated in Listing 17.1.

N O T E The empty string tests in Listing 17.1 determine whether the variable exists, because Active Server script returns an empty string when you attempt to reference an HTML field that does not exist. ■

Listing 17.1   HIDDEN_VARIABLES.ASP: Scoping Hidden Variables from Page to Page

```
<%
' Check if parameters are from a form or URL
' -----------------------------------------------
IF NOT request.form("router") = "" THEN
' Parameters are Form Based
' -----------------------
IF NOT request.form("userid") = "" THEN
userid = request.form("userid")
ELSE
userid = 0 'New User
END IF
' Scope Router Variable for page processing
'--------------------
router = request.form("router")
ELSEIF NOT Request.QueryString("router") = ""
' Parameters are URL Based/Hyperlink
' ------------------------------
IF NOT request.QueryString("userid") = "" THEN
```

```
userid = request.QueryString("userid")
ELSE
userid = 0 'New Users
END IF
' Scope Router Variable for page processing
' ...............................
router = request.QueryString("router")
ELSE
' Variables not correctly passed, an error has occurred
' set error routing flag
' .................................
router = 0 'Error Routing for Lost Variables
' close IF, all variables set at this point
' .....................
END IF
%>
```

Cookies drive another approach to managing user IDs from page to page. In a cookies-based model, no hidden information must be moved from page to page, because the cookie provides a variable that the server writes to the browser and that the browser stores locally by domain name. As a result, whenever the browser requests a page from a site within the domain name, such as **http://www.melnick.com**, the browser passes the cookie variable along with the rest of the request to the Web server.

Listing 17.2 shows how a cookie evaluation simplifies the process of scoping user IDs and routing variables compared with managing the process from page to page. A point much more important than the complexity of the code comes from the fact that users may not necessarily move in a linear process through your Web pages. Users may bookmark and jump directly to a page, type an alternative URL directly in a browser, or click the Refresh button or the Back button. All these maneuvers create uncertainty or more errors in the Listing 17.1 approach to managing users. Unlike the approach in which hidden variables are kept alive, with cookies, the variables are passed regardless of which page the user starts from. Your code loses its dependence on any order of page processing.

CAUTION

Cookies have received a great deal of attention in recent months, and browsers (including Microsoft's Internet Explorer 3.0) currently enable features to limit and potentially disable the use of cookies.

In both Netscape 3.0 and IE 3.0, the user can set a flag that forces the browser to prompt the user every time a site attempts to write a cookie. This prompt gives the user the option of rejecting the cookie. In addition, third-party programs are available to effectively disable cookies as well. In practice, cookies have become so prevalent that setting the prompt becomes quite annoying and, as a result, probably is not actively used by any but the most vigilant and fearful users.

Listing 17.2 COOKIES_VARIABLES.ASP: Cookies and User IDs

```
<%
' Check if cookie variables are available
' ----------------------------------------
IF request.cookie("router") = "" THEN
' Cookie Not Yet Set
' ......................
userid = 0 'New Account
router = 0 'New Account
' Route to new account area and set cookie
' ......................
ELSE
userid = request.cookie("userid")
router = request.cookie("router")
' Close IF all variables set at this point
' ......................
END IF
%>
```

Without the use of cookies, or when cookies use tracks only the user ID and not other supporting information, the process of passing the variables from page to page requires the use of both
hidden fields and URL links that add variables to them. As illustrated in Listing 17.3 both Form
and URL variables must be used, so the user can't move to another page without passing the
variables that you assigned.

Listing 17.3 FORMURL_FIELDS.ASP: Scoping Variables Through HTML

```
<html>
  <body>
   <FORM ACTION="next.asp" METHOD="post">
     <!------------------------------------->
     <!--- hidden fields are added to URL link --->
     <!--- so the link passes values       --->
     <!------------------------------------->
     <a href="profile_top.asp?userid=<%=userid%>&
➥router=<%=router%>">
Next Page
                 </a>
   <a href="profile_display.asp?userid=<%=userid%>&
➥router=<%=router%>">
Next Page
     </a>
     <!------------------------------------->
     <!--- hidden fields are stored for passing--->
     <!--- in form submit action       --->
     <!------------------------------------->
   <INPUT NAME="router" VALUE="<%=router%>" TYPE=HIDDEN>
   <INPUT NAME="userid" VALUE="<%=userid%>" TYPE=HIDDEN>
     <CENTER>
      <INPUT TYPE=SUBMIT VALUE="Continue" NAME="btn">
     </CENTER>
   </FORM>
```

```
    </body>
    </html>
```

The methods discussed previously provide a framework for how most of the CGI-based programs currently operate with respect to variables, scoping, and user tracking. These techniques are based on a combination of HTML fields, cookies, and unique ID generation. All these techniques become more stable and more insulated from the developer in the Active Server Pages Session and Application objects.

Modeling with Active Server Pages

Active Server Pages provides an object model, which insulates the developer from all the challenges related to tracking users and generating unique IDs. The Session and Application objects not only provide support in generating unique IDs and maintaining the scope of variables, but also implement the beginning of an event-driven model for developers. Active Server Pages defines an application as an execute-permission-enabled directory served by Internet Information Server. As a subset of the application, a session results when a browser requests a page from an application directory. The session involves one unique browser, so as other browsers request pages from the same application directory, they invoke additional sessions.

The first user to request a page from a directory that makes up an application invokes both an Application and a Session object. As subsequent users request pages, they invoke additional Session objects. The invoking of an Application object kicks off the Application OnStart event, which executes scripts stored in the global.asa file. In addition, you can append variables and objects to the Application object as new properties. When a developer's .asp file adds a new Application property, the Web server's memory space is used to store the variable for use by future .asp files invoked.

As a browser requests a page or file from the application directory, the Web server checks to see whether that browser is involved in an active session. If not, the Web server returns the requested page to the browser and also writes a session ID value as a cookie to the browser. By writing this cookie, the Web server provides a unique ID for tracking this user session or browser during the scope of the session.

The Web server maintains this ID and also monitors the Timeout property set for this session. If the timeout expires, the Web server abandons all information associated with this session. In addition, at the same time that the Web server writes the cookie, it processes the OnStart event, executing any scripts stored in the global.asa file for the Session OnStart event. Similar to Application objects, Session objects can have additional properties appended, enabling the storing of variables and objects for use by .asp files processed during that browser's session.

Setting Up the Application

Developing an application primarily involves establishing a directory that is served by Internet Information Server and has execute permissions. This directory location contains the source code for the application. The source code includes individual files that follow the naming convention .asp. Web browsers request these files similarly to the way that they request files ending in .htm or .html. In addition to general ASP pages, each application can have a single file named global.asa, which stores scripts for the OnStart and OnEnd events for applications and sessions.

> **CAUTION**
>
> Though not explicitly stated in this section, to use Active Server Pages, the directory containing the described files must reside on a Windows NT Server with Internet Information Server set up for your directory.

Defining Application's IIS Directory

Building an Active Server application requires planned use of the hierarchical and logical directory trees created when configuring Internet Information Server. In general, a single-served directory forms the application. All source files, including files ending in .asa and .asp, reside in a single-served directory. For more complex applications, a series of directories may be appropriate.

In Table 17.1, the Root directory contains all pages associated with nonregistered users. This area may use Session objects to do extensive tracking on the pages that users visit to try to build profiles of nonregistered visitors. In the Root/Members directory, on the other hand, the purpose of the Session object may be much more focused on the maintenance of logon status and member permissions. Finally, the Root/Secure/ directory would maintain Session information on administrative privileges available and perhaps support the maintenance of a comprehensive audit trail.

Table 17.1   Sample Directory Structure

Directory	Description
/Root/	All visiting or non-logged-on users request pages
/Root/Members/	Logon page and all subsequent pages that require a logged-in user
/Root/Secure/	Administrative area for site administrators to manage member accounts and system settings

The key point to remember is the scope of the Application and Session objects. Within each of the directories, the Application objects and Session objects are completely different, with different roles, different scopes, and no relationship between the objects in separate directories.

Understanding *global.asa* and the *Application* object

The global.asa file provides the Application and Session objects the script, if any, to be invoked on the OnStart and OnEnd events for Application and Session objects. Scripts for the OnStart and OnEnd events exist within the script tags with the RunAt property set to Server. These script tags can contain functions that can add properties to the Session and Application objects for use by subsequent .asp files within the scoped session or application.

Following is an example of how a global.asa file may be used. In the Application object, The OnStart event adds properties to the Application object to initialize a series of variables for maintaining information on how many members and visitors have come to the site since the application started. By contrast, the Session object deals with a specific user starting a new session.

The OnStart event for the Session object increments applicationwide information and initializes user-specific information. In addition, the Session object's OnStart event alters the default Timeout setting and sets the timeout to 30 minutes, which means that after 30 minutes of no page requests, the session is abandoned. Finally, when the Timeout expires and the Session object's OnEnd event is invoked, this event decrements applicationwide tracking information.

Part
IV

Ch
17

Managing Source Code or *.asp* and *.asa* files

Source code must be contained in an .asp or .asa file. This requirement stems from the method that the Internet Information Server uses to process Active Server Pages. When the Web server receives a request for a file, the Internet Information Server first checks the registered ISAPI filters. Active Server Pages rely on an ISAPI filter to catch .asp files before returning anything to the Web browser.

These files are then processed by the ISAPI (Internet Server API) filter, which strips out all "<%%>" tags, compiles VB Script, invokes any components called, and makes Application and Session objects available during the processing of all Active Server scripts. All these actions happen before the Web server returns the results to the Web browser.

N O T E   You can view ISAPI filters by opening the Registry and looking under the IIS-related setting in the current control set. Review Chapter 21, "Working with Internet Information Server" for more information on the Registry. ▨

T I P   .asp and .asa files are just standard text files, which enables you to use any editor to manage your source code. Microsoft's Source Safe, originally designed for managing source code associated with C++ or VB project files, is an effective tool for tracking version and checkout status on a multiple-developer project, and Internet Studio could provide script-development support as an .asp file-development tool.

Any type of file can exist in an Active Server Application directory, including HTM/HTML, graphic images, video, sound and .asp/.asa files. The important distinction is that only .asp/.asa files invoke the filter that makes Session and Application objects available during script processing.

The Internet Information Server also contains features such as Server-Side Includes (SSIs), which you may use to further enhance your application-management capabilities. This capability enables you to insert .asp or other files into a requested .asp file before the Web server invokes the ISAPI filter. The SSIs are processed before script execution. SSIs features extend your capability to store files in different directories and still maintain a single Application directory for purposes of Application and Session object scoping.

> **CAUTION**
>
> Be careful in using Server-Side Includes during development. The IIS keeps track of the last modification date/time of files, but the IIS caches frequently used files in memory. In other words, a direct page request causes the Web server to check whether a cached file has been modified since its last execution. If the file has been modified, the Web server re-compiles the file. Unfortunately, SSIs do not follow this checking process and as a result do not get re-compiled. In these cases, the Web server must be restarted to flush cached .asp files.

Using *Application* and *Session* Object

In leveraging Application and Session objects for the development of your application, carefully consider what information and objects should be stored at the application and session level. A good example of the value of Session objects is storing a user's logon status for security. With a misunderstanding of the Session object's scoping, you could create a major security hole. The primary Application and Session object methods, properties, and events include:

Abandon Method	Session
Timeout Property	Session
SessionID Property	Session
OnStart Event	Session/Application
OnEnd Event	Session/Application

Scope of *Application* and *Session* Objects

The most exciting feature of the Application and Session objects involves the capabilities to scope the objects beyond a single page and, more important, to scope the Session object to a single user. Specifically, users invoke the Application object when they request a page from an application directory for the first time since the Web server last started.

This Application object lives on from that moment until all sessions time out or the Web server restarts. In contrast to invoking the Application object, users invoke the Session object when they request a page from a browser that is not currently involved in an active session. The Session object, unlike the Application object, times out based on a 20-minute default or a custom Timeout property that you can set at runtime.

> **CAUTION**
>
> Avoid the temptation to store everything at the session level. While at first, the convenience of the Session object can lead to caching everything about the user, remember that all this information must be maintained in the memory space of the Internet Information Server.

When a user invokes a Session object, all the Session's properties and methods become available at runtime every time the same user requests an .asp file. A user's session at the Web site now can be managed through the Session object. As long as error trapping addresses the situation in which a user times out, you have complete control of a user's session and the ability to add properties to the Session object.

These properties can include anything from strings and status flags to database RecordSet objects. The Session object and its scope now create the first stable method for developers to manage a user's experience at a Web site, as a user moves from page to page or even from your site to another site and back to your site.

N O T E The Internet Information Server (IIS) manages the Session object by writing a cookie, or long integer, to the client browser. If IIS restarts, the Session abandons, or if the browser prevents cookies, the Session object attempts to reinitialize on every page request. ■

You must understand the scope of the Session object in the context of the Web. The Internet Information Server creates the Session object by writing a long-integer cookie to the client browser and maintaining the long-integer key and related properties, such as the Timeout property and last hit date/time, in the Web server's memory.

Beginning of an Event Model

The event model available in the Session and Application objects represents the beginning of bringing event-driven programming to the Web but stops short of providing what you may be hoping for. Because the Active Server Pages process at the Web server and not the client, your source code cannot respond to the range of events that the client handles, such as mouse movements and keyboard presses. Instead, your code is invoked when the user processes a form or clicks a hyperlink. These events generate a request to the Web server, which invokes your source code.

The Application and Session objects provide two events each: the OnStart event and the OnEnd event. The client invokes these events when the following methods are called:

- ■ Application_OnStart: invoked the first time users request an .asp file from an application directory since the IIS last started or the application timed out.
- ■ Application_OnEnd: invoked when all sessions time out.
- ■ Session_OnStart: invoked by users when their browser requests an ASP page from the application directory either for the first time or after a previous session with the client browser has been abandoned.

■ `Session_OnEnd`: invoked when a user's session `Timeout` property value exceeds the number of minutes allowed since the last page request or when your code invokes the `Abandon` method.

When a user invokes an `Application` or `Session` event, you can execute functions on the Web server. All source code invoked by `Session` and `Application` events must be stored in the `global.asa` file within an application's directory. The format of this text file follows the model in Listing 17.4.

Listing 17.4   GLOBAL.ASA: Sample *Application/Session* Event Code

```
<SCRIPT LANGUAGE=VBScript RUNAT=Server>
SUB Application_OnStart
END SUB
</SCRIPT>
<SCRIPT LANGUAGE=VBScript RUNAT=Server>
SUB Application_OnEnd
END SUB
</SCRIPT>
<SCRIPT LANGUAGE=VBScript RUNAT=Server>
SUB Session_OnStart
END SUB
</SCRIPT>
<SCRIPT LANGUAGE=VBScript RUNAT=Server>
SUB Session_OnEnd
END SUB
</SCRIPT>
```

The scope of variables used in the `global.asa` scripts does not extend to the page actually requested before the event. To store a variable for use in the current requested page or subsequent pages, you must save the information to an `Application` or `Session object` property. The properties of these objects provide the only means for allowing scripts in an `.asp` file to use the information available in the scripts run during these events. As a result, these scripts become useful primarily for saving information directly to a database or file, or for saving information to `Application` or `Session object` properties for use during the scope of the application or session.

Taking some time to understand how to leverage these events provides big benefits in helping your program manage a range of issues, from enhancing the user's Web experience to tracking site statistics. Don't make the mistake of overlooking the value of these events.

 TIP
Session and Application events provide a key mechanism to manage user-status control mechanisms, such as logon security.

Understanding Methods: Locking, Stopping, and Abandoning

Like events, the currently available methods seem to be quite limited compared with the event-driven development environments that you may currently use in non-Web based programs. However, these methods present a powerful beginning for the Web programmer. The only methods currently available to Session and Application objects include the Application Lock and Unlock methods and the Session Abandon method.

The Application Lock and Unlock methods allow you to change values to the properties shared across the application without fear of creating conflict with multiple users potentially changing the same property values concurrently. This locking control may seem to be intuitive to database developers who work in multiple-user environments that share this risk.

The Abandon method plays a valuable role for managing a session. Although during development and testing, the method can be useful for flushing a working session and beginning again, it also has a role in the final application. If a user requires the capability to log on and then perhaps log on again as a different user, the Abandon method could be used to allow the previously stored logon information to be cleanly dumped for a new logon.

These methods provide important functionality in using the Application and Session objects, but for real functionality, you must look to the properties provided and use the capability to add properties to the Application and Session objects.

Part
IV
Ch
17

Built-in Properties or Your Own

At first glance, the list of currently available properties appears to be quite unimpressive. The real secret lies behind the built-in properties, in the capability to add properties dynamically. Still, the two built-in Session properties play an important role in all application development and should not be overlooked. The available properties include Session SessionID and Session Timeout.

The capability to add properties on-the-fly provides the developer an approach to maintaining persistence or state. By having a server-based Session object manage variables, a user's activities and input can be used during their entire session or visit to your Web application. The capability to build your own variables is demonstrated later in this chapter.

The *Application* Object: How Much It Can Do

The Application events and methods provide the infrastructure necessary to maintain applicationwide information that can be leveraged for managing all users within an application. Uses range from tracking the number of currently active users to dynamically altering content provided to a particular user, based on the activity of other users at large. These features lay the foundation for building interactive communities and more. The following sections discuss the use of these events and methods.

Using the *Application OnStart* Event   The Application OnStart event can be likened to the initial load event of an application. This load event is not the load event of a single client, but the load event of the multiple-user Web-based application. As a result, one use is to initialize a series of variables that you need to access frequently in your application. The example in Listing 17.5 opens a database and assigns a recordset of system error messages to the Application object. As a result of loading this object, now *any page* processed can reference the recordset during execution and can use the recordset to loop through and display a particular error, based on a given situation.

Listing 17.5   SAMP_EVENTS.ASP: Sample *Application OnStart* Event

```
<SCRIPT LANGUAGE=VBScript RUNAT=Server>
SUB Application_OnStart
REM Open ADO Connection to Database
Set Conn = Server.CreateObject("ADODB.Connection")
Conn.Open("DSNName")
RS = Conn.Execute("SELECT * FROM TblSysMessages;")

REM Set Recordset to Application object and Close ADO
IF rs.recordcount <> 0 THEN
application.lock
Set application.ObjErrMsg = RS
application.unlock
ELSE
Rem Error Condition
END IF
rs.close
conn.close
END SUB
</SCRIPT>
```

N O T E   The loading of the database recordset involves the Server object and the ADO database Connection object, which is discussed in more detail later in Part III of the book. ▦

Using the *Application OnEnd* Event   The Application OnEnd event can be likened to the close of active forms or an application, but it provides more than that, because it manages the environment for not just a single-user system but for the multiple-user Web-based environment. As a result, one use is to flush all temporary user accounts that may have been created during the course of the day.

This type of activity previously was available only by using time stamps and scheduled batch programs, running as services in the background. Now, when all users time out, a database cleanup (or any other type of cleanup) can take place. The following example runs a SQL statement to purge all partially completed orders taken by a Web-based order-processing system:

```
<SCRIPT LANGUAGE=VBScript RUNAT=Server>
SUB Application_OnEnd
REM Open ADO Connection to Database
Set Conn = Server.CreateObject("ADODB.Connection")
```

```
Conn.Open("DSNName")
RS = Conn.Execute("Delete * FROM Orders where
    complete_status=0;")
conn.close
END SUB
</SCRIPT>
```

Application Locking Methods

Similar to database record and page locking, `Application` locking simply ensures that no other user has simultaneously attempted to update the `Application` object's property. This locking feature applies only to the application, and not the `Session` object, and should be followed to avoid creating any conflict or lost data. The following section of code shows you a specific use of the `Session` `OnStart` event:

```
<SCRIPT LANGUAGE=VBScript RUNAT=Server>
SUB Session_OnStart
application.lock
application("counter") = application("counter") + 1
application.unlock
END SUB
</SCRIPT>
```

Scoping *Application*-Wide Variables

Adding properties to the `Application` `object` provides one of the key values of the `Application`-object model. `Application` properties added this way are similar to global constants and variables in Visual Basic.

Practical uses of the `Application` properties include the capability to cache frequently used information to conserve resources. Current Web development environments require either database/file lookups or the passing of information from one page to the next in hidden fields. The first approach requires extensive resources as an application's load grows. The latter approach becomes difficult as users click the Refresh and Back button or bounce from page to page through direct typing of URLs.

With the `Application` `object`, information can be saved to an `Application` `object` property as the result of a single lookup. From then on, any user can access that information. When a Web-based store opens its doors as a result of the first user request (`Application` `OnStart` event), a store's greeting (including number of visitors, date/time, or current sale items) can be saved to an `Application` property, as illustrated in the following code sample:

```
Application.lock
Application("dateinfo") = date
Application("timeinfo") = time
Application("visitors") = Application("visitors") + 1
Application.Unlock
```

As a result, all subsequent pages can display that information as part of a standard greeting, as shown in the following code:

```
<HTML>
<BODY>
Welcome to our store, open for business since <%=Application("timeinfo")%> on
↩<%=Application("dateinfo")%> with <%Application("visitors")%> so far.
</BODY>
</HTML>
```

More important than cached activity information, resources can be conserved by limiting the number of times components must be brought in and out of memory on the server. If you run a database-intensive site, you may start your application by placing statements in every page to load DLLs into memory.

The example below not only loads the Connection component's DLL, if it is not currently loaded, but also closes the object, allowing it be taken out of memory. For a frequently accessed site, loading the DLL when the application loads and leaving it in memory for frequent use may make more sense.

```
Set Conn = Server.CreateObject("ADODB.Connection")
Conn.Open("DSNName")
RS = Conn.Execute(SQL)
conn.close
```

The example below is an example of leaving the DLL in memory through the application.

```
Set Conn = Server.CreateObject("ADODB.Connection")
Conn.Open("DSNName")
Application("conn") = Conn
```

When you load the Conn object into the Application Conn property, it can now be referenced by all pages for use.

```
set db = Application("Conn")
set rs = db.execute(sql)
```

N O T E   The preceding examples provide only a starting point for the range of uses that the Application object can play in the ASP application model that you develop. Take the time to think through the activity and caching issues that relate to your application before implementing a model for your use of the Application object. ■

Managing Users with the *Session Object*

The Session object, more than the Application object, drives your Web-based environment. Look closely at how the deceptively small number of methods and events can streamline your method for managing a user's experience, as well as your system-level tracking and control of that user. The Session object, like the Application object, enables new properties to be defined on-the-fly. More important, the Session object's properties, like those of the Application object, can be referenced on any page, anywhere, and at any time during that active session.

Session Events, Properties, and Methods

SessionID is, without a doubt, the prebuilt property to watch. This property provides the persistence in a user session that you should be looking for, but the OnStart event, OnEnd event, and Abandon method also play a valuable role in managing your application. The following sections document basic application of the prebuilt events and methods.

Session OnStart Event

The Session OnStart event can be likened to the initial load event of a form or application. The event provides a mechanism to identify the first activity of new users and allows the initialization of whatever user information your application requires for managing the user session.

At the OnStart event, you cab reference Application-object properties to track the new user in the context of your multiple-user environment, but you also want to bring into existence any user-specific information that you need for managing that user's session. The event kicks off the script set up in the global.asa for the Session OnStart event in the following form:

```
<SCRIPT LANGUAGE=VBScript RUNAT=Server>
SUB Session_OnStart
Rem Load User Specific Information
Session("NewUserStatus") = 0
Rem Load Application level info
Application.lock
Application("usercount") = Application("usercount") + 1
Application.unlock
END SUB
</SCRIPT>
```

N O T E Although this chapter discusses the use of the global.asa file in detail, don't lose sight of the fact that you don't need to create any functions in the global.asa or even a global.asa at all.

Session OnEnd Event

The Session OnEnd event can be likened to the close of active forms or an application. This event does not require user action, however. In fact, the OnEnd event most often is triggered by user inaction or timeouts. This event often provides a mechanism for cleanup or closing of open resources. The system loses all session information after this event, so any session information that you want to save, you must save during this event.

This event can be invoked by the user if he hits a page that executes the Abandon method. The Abandon method and the Timeout property provide the two mechanisms for terminating a session.

CAUTION

A crash or stopping of the Web server also terminates events, because the Web server's memory space is where all session and application information resides.

Following is an example of cleanup that can be done at the end or termination of a session:

```
<SCRIPT LANGUAGE=VBScript RUNAT=Server>
SUB Application_OnEnd
REM Clean up user activity information
Set Conn = Server.CreateObject("ADODB.Connection")
Conn.Open("DSNName")
SQL = "Delete * FROM UserActivity where
➥sessionID
       = " & session.sessionid & ";"
RS = Conn.Execute(SQL)
conn.close
END SUB
</SCRIPT>
```

SessionID Property

The Active Server creates the SessionID when a user first requests a page from an Active Server application. The SessionID gets written as a cookie with a long-integer value to the browser and provides the core mechanism the server uses to track session information stored in memory.

You should not use the SessionID as a unique ID to track users across multiple sessions, because the value's uniqueness is guaranteed only for the current application. This value gives your application the time it needs to generate an ID that can be used across multiple sessions, and it provides a unique ID for all sessions that are currently running. You can reference the SessionID on any page in this form:

```
session.sessionID
```

This value provides a key mechanism for managing users as they move from page to page, and it relieves you of the responsibility of trying to uniquely track individual users during a multiple-page request session.

Session Timeout Property

The server stores the Session Timeout property as a long integer that represents minutes and that defaults to 20. The server takes full responsibility for tracking this 20-minute period. Timeout is tracked from the last date/time when a page request is received by the browser. The Timeout property can be altered at runtime; you can set it in the Session OnStart event or any subsequent page.

In determining how to manage this property, you should consider the rate of hits by a single user during a session. For sites that have long intervals between page requests—such as pages that require research, long review, or large amounts of input—you may want to increase the Timeout. More rapid sessions may require a shorter Timeout. Changing this property takes this form:

```
session.timeout = 30
```

> **CAUTION**
>
> When the `Timeout` occurs, all session information is lost, and the next page request is treated as a new session.

Session Abandon **Method**

The `Session Abandon` method provides a vehicle for you to force a session to terminate. Uses include the situation in which your user community takes the time to log off or in which you implement a discrete site-exit page that invokes the `Abandon` method.

The method takes this form:

```
Session.abandon
```

> During development, a page with the `Abandon` method provides a useful mechanism for restarting sessions. A lingering session often makes testing difficult.

Managing a User Session

The `Session object` provides a rich environment for managing user sessions. The following sections show a few examples of how you can put this object to work for developing efficient applications. As described in the first part of this chapter, the challenge of managing a user session has historically required difficult, code-consuming techniques for generating unique IDs and then for keeping session-related information alive from page to page.

Generating a Unique ID To Manage Users

As illustrated in Listing 17.6, the `SessionID` property is used to generate a session ID to keep track of a user's session. During this process, if you need to track users over a longer life than just one session, you still need to create an ID that guarantees uniqueness for your application. This process generally involves a database for storing this user and his or her related information.

When you design a database to store user information, you can rely on the wealth of features in databases to generate a guaranteed unique ID. A simple example of generating a unique user ID involves leveraging the counter field of a Microsoft Access database. The code example in Listing 17.6 uses the current date and the `SessionID` to insert a record and then queries the table to retrieve the counter value when the record has been created. As the final step, the example sets the new counter value to a new session property for reference on subsequent pages.

> **N O T E** Certain variable status designations, such as the `logonstatus` variable, have been subjectively assigned values for tracking that in no way reflect any preset or required approach to the tracking process. ■

Listing 17.6   SESSIONTRACKING.TXT: Managing the Tracking of Users with Session Variables

```
<%
Set Conn = Session("conn")
Select Case session("logonstatus")
Case 1 ' Already Past finished this insert step
msg = "<Center><h2><blink>Please Record your new
Member ID:
➥" & session("memberid") & "
</blink></h2></center>
➥<h3>Your Ideal Mate
Profile has already been saved,
➥please complete the process and
➥relogon in edit
mode to alter you profile </h3>"
Case 2 ' Proper Status for Insert of new account
set rsInsert = Server.CreateObject("ADODB.Recordset")
Conn.BeginTrans
rsInsert.Open "Members", Conn, 3, 3
' ----------------------------------------
'Insert Record Using AddNew Method of ADO
' ----------------------------------------
rsInsert.AddNew
rsInsert("SignOnID")    = session.sessionid
rsInsert("AdmCreateDate") = Date()
rsInsert.Update
Conn.CommitTrans
rsInsert.Close
' ----------------------------------------
'Look up generated record by referencing SessionID/Current Date
  ' ----------------------------------------
  sql = "SELECT Members.SignOnID, Members.memberid, Members.AdmCreateDate FROM
➥Members WHERE (((Members.SignOnID)=" & session.sessionid & ") AND
➥((Members.AdmCreateDate)=Date())));"
  Set RS = Conn.Execute(sql)
  msg = "<h2><Center> Please Record your new Member ID:
➥" & rs("memberid") & " </center></h2>"
  ' ----------------------------------------
  ' Set Session object with memberid value
  ' ----------------------------------------
  memval = rs("memberid")
  session("memberid") = memval
  session("logonstatus") = 3
  rs.close
End Select
%>
```

N O T E   You could add time and User IP addresses to the record inserted into the database for greater certainty of uniqueness. ▪

Caching User Information, the *Session* Object

When the user has a unique ID, the next use of the Session object focuses on the capability to cache user information that you previously would have stored in a database or text file for constant lookup and editing. The process of querying a file or database every time users hit a page just to make basic information about their sessions or accounts available reflects the status quo for current Internet applications.

The lookup of a shopping basket for a user shopping in a Web-based store or the lookup of account information for personalizing a user page, is a good example of implementing the unique ID. Although some developers attempt to move that information from one form page processed to the next, this problem creates serious challenges for application design.

A good example of a Session-object property is storing a system message for display on subsequent pages, as well as trapping basic name and last-time-online-type information. Like the properties of the Application object, the properties of the Session object can range in complexity from integers and string values to RecordSet objects. The following example provides for storing personal information and redirection following a successful logon:

Listing 17.7

```
<%
'----------------------------------------------------------
' Lookup User Info
'----------------------------------------------------------
sql = "SELECT members.admonlinedate, Members.MemberID, members.pass,
Members.FName,
➥Members.LName, Members.AdmExpDate,
Members.AdmStatus FROM Members "
➥sql = sql & "WHERE (((Members.MemberID)=" & request.form("memberid")
& "));"
set db = session("conn")
set rs = db.execute(sql)
'----------------------------------------------------------
' Logon Fail
'----------------------------------------------------------
IF rs.eof THEN 'No Record Found Bad ID
rs.close
session("msg") = "<h3><center>No Member ID equaling <em>" &
➥request.form("memberid") & "</em>
exists</center></h3>"
response.redirect "fail.asp"
ELSE
'----------------------------------------------------------
' Success Logon Approved, Load Session and Status
'----------------------------------------------------------
session("logonstatus") = 1
session("memberid") = rs("memberid")
session("AdmOnlineDate") = rs("AdmOnlineDate")
session("fname") = rs("fname") 'First Name
```

continues

Listing 17.7   Continued

```
' Update User Database Record with Last Logon Date
sql = "UPDATE Members SET"
sql = sql & " Members.AdmOnlineDate = #" & Date() & "#"
sql = sql & " WHERE Members.MemberID=" &
request.form("memberid") & ";"
set rs2 = db.execute(sql)
rs.close
response.redirect "start.asp"
END IF
%>
```

As illustrated in the preceding code sample, the statement setting the logonstatus property equal to a value creates the logonstatus property as a new Session property. No special statements to dimension the property are required, and when this information gets loaded into the Session object, it can be referenced on any page requested by the browser that is sending the matching SessionID. The process of referencing the properties requires only a single statement in this form:

```
session("propertyname")
```

Using *Session* Objects for Security, Status, and Caching

For managing an application, the Session properties can play the role of tracking user status and security information. Because Session properties exist at the server without any information being passed to the browser except for the SessionID, session properties provide an effective method of managing logon and other statuses.

You can include an .asp file with no purpose other than the validation of a user's logonstatus by using the Server-Side Includes feature of IIS. This approach to user authentication provides an effective method of trapping any user who attempts to request a page that he or she doesn't have authority to view. This method relies on the Session properties alone and not on any NT-based security controls, as illustrated in the following excerpt of code:

```
<%
SELECT Case session("logonstatus")
Case 0 'New Session No Status
session("msg") = "<h3><center> Your are currently not
logged in or
➥your logon has
timed out </center></h3> Please
logon to continue your session,
➥sorry for any
inconvenience</h4>"
Response.Redirect "logon.asp"
Case 1 'Authenticated User Properly Logged On
Case 2 'New Member in Sign Up Process first page
Case 3 'New Member in Sign Up Process Record Created
END SELECT
%>
```

The process of actually validating a user after she enters a user account and password further illustrates how to manage a site's security and user's status through the Session object. The example in Listing 17.8 builds on the preceding code, which simply adds Session properties after a successful logon, and in this case evaluates all possible results of a user's attempt to log on. The following example relies heavily on the Response object's redirect feature to route the user, based on the results of the logon validation.

Listing 17.8 LOGONVALIDATE.TXT: Validating and Redirecting Users Requesting .asp Files

```
<Script Language=VBScript runat=server>
FUNCTION redirect()
Session("msg") = session("msg") & " Please enter a valid Member ID
➥and Password, if you have forgotten
your ID try our Search based on
➥First Name, Last Name and your password"
Response.Redirect "logon.asp"
END FUNCTION
</script>
<%
'---------------------------------
'---------------------------------
'Level 1 Basic Validation Testing
'---------------------------------
'---------------------------------
'Test for Already Logged In
'---------------------------------
IF session("logonstatus") = 1 THEN 'Already Validated
session("msg") = "<h3><center>You are already logged
in</center></h3>"
Response.Redirect "start.asp"

'Test for Entry of Member ID prior to Running Search
'---------------------------------
ELSEIF request.form("memberid")="" THEN ' NO Member ID Entered
session("msg") = "<h3><center>No Proper Member ID
Entered</center></h3>"
Redirect 'Call Function to Exit Back to Logon Screen
'Run Search
'---------------------------------
ELSE 'Run Database Lookup
sql = "SELECT members.admonlinedate, Members.MemberID,
members.pass,
➥Members.FName, Members.LName,
Members.AdmExpDate, Members.AdmStatus FROM
Members "
sql = sql & "WHERE (((Members.MemberID)=" &
request.form("memberid") & "));"
set db = session("conn")
set rs = db.execute(sql)
END IF
'---------------------------
```

continues

Listing 17.8   Continued

```
'.............................
'Level 2 Validation Testing
'.............................
'.............................
'Member ID Entered Now Run Search for Record
'.............................................
IF rs.eof THEN 'No Record Found Bad ID
rs.close
session("msg") = "<h3><center>No Member ID equaling <em>" &
➥request.form("memberid") & "</em>
exists</center></h3>"
Redirect 'Call Function to Exit Back to Logon Screen
'Customer Record Found Now Check Password
'.............................................
ELSEIF not request.form("password") = rs("pass") THEN
rs.close
session("msg") = "<h3><center>Member ID OK
➥but Bad Password Entered</center></h3>"
Redirect 'Call Function to Exit Back to Logon Screen
'Password OK now Check Expiration and Status
'.............................................
ELSEIF not rs("admstatus") = 1 and rs("admexpdate") > date THEN
rs.close
session("msg") = "<h3><center>Not Active or Expired
Account</center></h3>"
Redirect 'Call Function to Exit Back to Logon Screen
'.............................
'.............................
' Level 3. Success Logon Approved, Load Session and Status
'.............................
'.............................
ELSE
session("logonstatus") = 1
session("memberid") = rs("memberid")
session("AdmOnlineDate") = rs("AdmOnlineDate")
session("fname") = rs("fname")
' Update users last online date
sql = "UPDATE Members SET"
sql = sql & " Members.AdmOnlineDate = #" & Date() & "#"
sql = sql & " WHERE Members.MemberID=" &
request.form("memberid") & ";"
set rs2 = db.execute(sql)
END IF
rs.close
response.redirect "start.asp"
%>
```

The example in Listing 17.8 uses a script tag to create a callable function for redirecting the user in the event that she fails the logon process at any step. The user is forwarded to the start page with logged-on status only in the event that she passes all checks, including password, account number, currently active status, and valid expiration date.

From Here...

You should now have a good understanding of how to create and manage customers by using the ASP scripting language. You should also be able to create fairly sophisticated sites by using the server/client programming techniques discussed in this chapter. Now you are ready to move on to the advanced features of ASP programming discussed in the next chapter.

We will further discuss the management of customers within the Commerce Server 2.0 store, in the chapters to follow. You will also learn to differentiate what administration Commerce Server 2.0 provides for you as well as what administration you will need to provide your store using ASP.

- The appendix in this book discusses some components that are installed with Commerce Server 2.0 which will help you in the adminstration of user and store information.

- Chapter 18, "Constructing a Server Component Using ASP," teaches you how to create your own components which you will be able to administrate user and store information that Commerce Server 2.0 does not already adminstrate for you.

- Chapter 22, "Building the Order Process Pipeline," introduces you to what is probably the most powerful tool that Commerce Server 2.0 provides your store. This chapter helps you understand how the OPP is the heart of all user and store administration in a Commerce Server 2.0 store/mall.

Constructing a Server Component Using ASP

Many times, you want to use server-side functions that just cannot be accomplished through the use of a scripting language, either alone or in combination with the components that ship with Active Server Pages. When you hit this particular wall, you have a few options. First, you can check the market and try to find prebuilt components that satisfy your requirements. Second, you can contract with a third party to build a component for you. Last, given the time and inclination, you can build your own component.

When you create your own server components, you have the benefit of using a component built by someone who really understands your business. As you encapsulate line-of-business functions within your components, you can use them on your server and in your client applications or even give them to your clients for use on their systems (for a nominal fee, of course).

This chapter focuses on creating server components with the Visual Basic programming language. If you are familiar with VB, this chapter is a snap! If you are coming to VB a little later in the game, this chapter provides you the skills to begin creating components right away. ■

Justifying Visual Basic as a Component Creator

For several reasons, Visual Basic is an ideal tool for creating many of the server components that you use. VB has grabbed the hearts and minds of millions of developers out here in the real world. As you already have learned, VBScript is a subset of Visual Basic. Everything that you've learned about VBScript is immediately applicable to development in the VB environment, which has several useful features that are not available in its younger sibling.

Hundreds of custom controls, such as ActiveX components, currently are available for use with Visual Basic. More controls seem to be available each day. The rub is that most of these components require an interface for use in development. VB provides a perfect way to wrap the functionality of these third-party components for use in your Active Server Pages development. In addition to the custom controls available in Visual Basic, you have access to the Win32 API. You can access any number of functions on the server that are impossible to get to by using scripting alone. You also can use almost any DLL (dynamic-link library) to add additional functionality to the components that you create.

Millions of developers have used Visual Basic for years because of its ease of use and flexibility, as well as the speed with which it allows them to develop applications. If you were to hire a new Active Server Pages developer, he or she would be likely to have VB skills. If not, those skills are just a class or two away.

Another advantage of developing your server components in VB is that so many resources are available to help you. CompuServe, America Online, and Prodigy offer forums. The Microsoft Web site provides a wealth of information about VB (a knowledge base and newsgroups), as well as links to other valuable sites. Hundreds of quality sites are dedicated to Visual Basic.

Another benefit of developing your components in Visual Basic is that so many excellent sources of information are available to help you in your own neighborhood. Hundreds of texts at your local bookstore provide even more information about creating objects in VB than you'll find in this one chapter.

N O T E   When this book was written (the Summer of 97), Commerce Server 2.0 presented threading problems during creation of custom Visual Basic 5.0 components for the order-processing pipeline, discussed in Chapter 22, "Building the Order Process Pipeline." For compatibility, this chapter uses Visual Basic 4.0 in examples. ■

Finding a Touch of Class

Component creation is the process of building objects that you instantiate in your Active Server Pages scripts. To create objects in Visual Basic, you need to define a blueprint to expose the functions within your object to other applications—in this case, ASP. You use classes to provide this blueprint, or definition and interface, for your objects.

Creating class modules in Visual Basic is the method by which you can develop reusable components. Public procedures within classes are the method by which you can expose functionality from within your class to other objects within your application and to other applications within the system. By creating your functionality within the class framework, you can harness the incredible power and ease of use of Visual Basic for your component needs.

Introducing Classes

As you begin to develop components, consider some of the following details of class development.

A *class* is the description, or blueprint, of the object that is created when the class is instantiated. You can follow some basic guidelines from general object-oriented development to ensure that your class is a good component candidate.

The idea of *data-hiding*, or encapsulation, is a fundamental principle of object-oriented development. Encapsulation is the process by which a class is designed to provide access to the data variables within your class only through the member functions of the class. Effectively, you hide the class data from the client program. Encapsulation ensures that the client application does not unwittingly corrupt the Private object data. Encapsulation also allows you to change the Private members of your class "under the covers," without changing the Public interface.

Think of your component in terms of properties and methods. The *properties* are a set of definitions that control attributes of your component. *Methods* are the actions that the component takes on your behalf. Look to the components that ship with Active Server Pages and Visual Basic to see how the properties and methods work together to provide the components' functionality.

Always strive to limit the functionality of a component to a basic set. Don't try to put the entire business in a single component. Try to view component creation as being an exercise in creating building blocks. If the blocks are too big, you lose flexibility in the design. If the blocks are too small, building the structure takes forever.

Part
IV

Ch

18

Creating and Destroying Class Objects

When the client application instantiates your object (class), you have an opportunity to perform one-time initialization actions for your class. You do this initialization of data in the Class_Initialize event of the class object. The Class_Initialize event is a handy place to initialize Private data members and perform any initial error checking, as well as any other functions that need to occur before any class methods (functions) are invoked.

You also have an opportunity to perform actions immediately before the object is destroyed. This processing is performed in the Class_Terminate event of the class. You can destroy any memory that was allocated during the life of the class or perform any other required cleanup.

Instantiating an Object

After you define and code the class, you can create an instance of the class in Visual Basic by initializing an object variable to that class type, as follows:

```
Dim TestClass as New ClassName
```

You also can instantiate a class object by using the `CreateObject` method within your script, as follows:

```
Dim TestClass
Set TestClass = Server.CreateObject("Component.ClassName")
```

The variable `TestClass` now has a reference to the newly created object. Now you can invoke any of the methods of the newly created object by using the method name with the newly created object reference, as follows:

```
Avalue = TestClass.MethodName(Parm1, Parm2... ParmN)
```

When you finish with the object, set the object variable to `Nothing` to ensure that all memory associated with the object is released, as follows:

```
Set TestClass = Nothing
```

Understanding Class Methods

The *methods* of a class are the set of `Public` functions and subroutines that reside within the class. Methods are just a convenient way to talk about the procedures that are available to the user of a component. These methods are like the methods available to any of the otjër "objects" within Visual Basic: the form methods, the button methods, and all the other intrinsic objects in VB that expose their functionality (methods) to you as a developer.

Any subroutine or function that you create in your class module is visible to the client program if it is declared as `Public`, as follows:

```
Public Function CalculatePayment(LoanAmount, Term, InterestRate)
```

When you use the `Public` identifier before the function declaration, the `CalculatePayment` function is *visible* to any client that instantiates the class or to any variable that is assigned a reference to it. `Private` functions within a class are used to provide functions and services that the `Public` functions can use to fulfill client requests.

Using Property Procedures

In Visual Basic development, as well as HTML development, user-interface objects have properties that you set to determine the appearance and actions of these elements. To access the background color of a text box in the VB environment, you access its `BackColor` property, as follows:

```
text1.BackColor = &H00FFFF00&
```

The use of properties is a simple and intuitive way to access the attributes of an object. You can provide the same functionality to access the properties of your components. Property procedures use the familiar VB and ASP syntax , using the `<object>.<method>` notation with any component that you create. Using property procedures also allows you to immediately validate the value of the property being set. If invalid data is passed in or a value out of range is provided, the component can respond immediately, instead of waiting for some point downstream in your code to notify the calling program of the error.

After you determine what properties you want to provide for your class, you set aside `Private` variables to hold these properties. You then need to provide the framework for accessing and updating these class properties.

The *Let* Procedure   The `Let` procedure enables your class users to set the value of a class property under the class's control. Following is a `Let-property` procedure:

```
Public Property Let HostName(aHost)
  IF Not Len(aHost) THEN
   Err.Raise vbObjectError + CTRANSACT_ERR_HOSTLEN,
"CTransact.Host", _
           "Set Host Name: Host Length Invalid"
  ELSE
   m_sHost = aHost
  END IF
End Property
```

You certainly could declare the `Private` class variable `m_sHost` (declared as a string) as a `Public` variable and then allow the user to set the host name directly. If you had publicly declared the variable, you wouldn't have the opportunity to ensure that the host name is valid. Within the `Let` procedure in the preceding code, in addition to testing for a zero-length string, you could also try to ping the host to ensure that the address is valid or to perform additional validations on the passed-in value. When you use the `Let` procedure, you can provide the calling application immediate feedback about the status of the component property being set.

In addition to allowing for data validation when the property is set, you can update other associated variables within your class. If another property—say, the port to connect to—is based on the host that is entered, you can set the port property when the host name is set.

You cannot set the port property if you just declared the `m_sHost` variable as `Public`. Using the `Let` procedure can ensure that you don't get any component breaker values in the `Private` variables of your class. If, for example, a user were to put a `NULL` value in a variable, the `NULL` value could easily generate a runtime error in another method that references that variable. The rule continues to be "better safe than sorry."

The *Get* Property   The majority of your coding sets property values of the objects created within the script. You probably could go the better part of a day without ever requesting the value of an object's property, but at times, you need to check a property and determine its value. A good example is the `.text` property of an entry field.

To provide the "getting" of a property within your class, you create a `Property Get` procedure. Using the preceding example, you provide the `HostName` property procedure to your calling application with the following procedure:

```
Public Property Get HostName() As Variant
  HostName = m_sHost
End Property
```

Using Public Procedures in Your Classes

The Let and Get procedures are wonderful for creating properties within your class. Eventually, though, you need your class to perform some function to become useful. To expose functionality to an external application from within your class, you declare a function or subroutine Public. Declaring a function as Public enables the application that created an instance of your class to access the procedure.

Any procedure that is not directly used by the client application should be declared Private. Declaring Private functions ensures that the client does not inadvertently call a function or subroutine that it should not call. Private functions are used to perform internal activities for the component.

As you see in "Creating Your Server Component," later in this chapter, the Public interface usually is the smallest part of the class code. The component interface is intentionally kept small and simple. If the implementation of the method changes (the Private functions), you do not need to change the external (Public) function declaration.

Handling Errors Within Your Classes

You can handle errors within your classes in two ways. The first way requires you to provide all methods as functions and to return a completion code for all Public procedures. This method requires a well-defined set of return codes and requires the client program to check for errors in line after each call to the component returns.

A better way to handle error conditions within your class is to use the VB error-handling framework. If an error occurs within a class module, you use the Raise method of the Err object to pass notification of the error to the calling program. The error percolates through the procedure levels to a place where an error handler has been registered within the calling program.

You notify the client application of an error by calling the Raise method of the Err object. The syntax for raising an error is:

```
Err.Raise(Number, Source, Description, HelpFile, HelpContext)
```

The only required parameter is Number. When you are creating server components, you usually should include the Source and the Description parameters as well. Suppose that you are trying to open a local file in a method in your new class. The file cannot be opened because the program cannot find the file on the disk. A runtime error that the component invoked in your code looks something like this:

```
Err.Raise vbObjectError + 55, "CFileMgr.ReadFile ", _
"Cannot find file specified"
```

The constant vbObjectError is a base number to which to add your component-specific error number. The vbObjectError is the constant that is used when raising runtime errors within an OLE server.

Exposing Your Class with OLE Servers

Up to now, this chapter has discussed the class module and how it provides the blueprint for your Active Server Pages when your component is invoked. Class structure is well and good, but components live by more than class alone. You need to wrap the class in a suitable way so that you actually can create an instance of it. To do so, you create the class within an OLE server.

You can create two types of OLE servers with Visual Basic. OLE servers can run either out-of-process or in-process. The distinction is evident in the server names. An *out-of-process* server executes in a separate process from the client application that creates an instance of the server (component). An *in-process* server is packaged as a dynamic-link library and, when instantiated, shares the process space with the application.

An in-process server has inherent strengths that ensure that it is the type that you build when creating your server components. First, because the server is running in the same process space as the calling application, the component is faster, because data does not have to be passed across process boundaries. Second, because the server is packaged as a DLL, if it is already loaded in memory when a new instance is created, the new object has virtually no load time.

Keep in mind several restrictions when creating in-process servers as components in Visual Basic:

- **The servers are available only as 32-bit code.** You must create the components by using Visual Basic Professional or Enterprise Edition, version 4.0 or later. No 16-bit code support is provided.
- **One `Public` class member is required.** Because the visible functionality of your object is defined by the `Public` classes within your DLL, at least one class must be `Public`.
- **No user interface is allowed.** Any user interface that you embed in your class is not visible to the browser requesting information from an Active Server Pages script and potentially could lock the server process that is requesting the service.
- **No static or global variables are allowed.** If you package multiple classes in your component, avoid the use of globals or statics in any shared modules. Globals and statics only complicate your coding and can lead to incorrect or corrupted memory across multiple instances of any given object.

Creating Your Server Component

You're ready to begin creating your Active Server Pages component. You may be working in a heterogeneous environment, interacting with PCs, minis, mainframes, and even UNIX boxes. The component that you are going to build provides access to several transactions living on a multiple host systems.

Suppose that for years, your hypothetical company has been processing TCP/IP requests from external vendors to authorize credit-card transactions. You have a well-defined transaction header structure that is used to send a transaction through the system. You want to provide the same authorization transactions from your Web servers.

Several commercial packages (even Microsoft's own Internet Control Pack) provide generic TCP/IP communications. The problem with most of these packages is that they are set up to provide an event when a transaction (or any data, for that matter) is received from a previous request. By design, these packages are *asynchronous,* meaning that the receipt of the response from the transaction occurs sometime later.

The program or thread execution does not *block* waiting on a response from the server, which is ideal for interactive client/server applications in which you are doing other things while waiting for a response (or multiple responses). Due to the stateless nature of connections on the Internet, no facility is available to continue to process the script and then respond to this "transaction complete" event later.

You are going to build is a TCP/IP transaction class that allows you to call a method that sends a transaction to your host system and waits for a response before returning from the procedure call. All formatting of the transaction takes place within the class, as well as all the communications details.

The only things that the script must provide are a host name and port to connect to, an account to validate, and an amount to authorize. You can probably think of situations in which you would want to leverage TCP/IP transactions from your servers. You can easily modify this component to accept different header and transaction types. Out of the box, the component should give you a good sense of the steps involved in building your own server components.

The first thing that you need to do is ensure that you have a copy of the 32-bit version of Visual Basic, either the Professional or Enterprise Edition. Then open a new project to begin creation of your transaction component.

Optimizing the Server

When you start a new project in Visual Basic, several custom controls and object references get added to your project for free, or seem to be free at the time; in fact, they are not free at all. If you open the file AUTO32LD.vbp (in the directory where the VB32.exe lives on your system) in Notepad, you see the default objects that are loaded each time you request a new project. To permanently change these defaults, you can edit this file to remove the object references.

Any component or reference that you do not use, but do retain in your project when it is built, tags along for the ride, even though it never is invoked. Unreferenced components add overhead to your application and swells the number of disks required to distribute your new component.

To reduce this overhead, remove all the custom controls that you can from your newly created default project.

1. Choose Custom Controls from the Tools menu or press Ctrl+T.

2. Choose References from the Tools menu.

When Form1 is selected, choose Remove File from the File menu (this removes the form from the project).

The first step brings up a dialog box with all the controls available for your use (see Figure 18.1), as well as those that currently are active in your project. The active controls have their check boxes checked. Remove all the currently selected objects by removing the checks in all checked boxes. Then click the OK button to save your changes.

FIG. 18.1

Lighten up the application by removing unused controls.

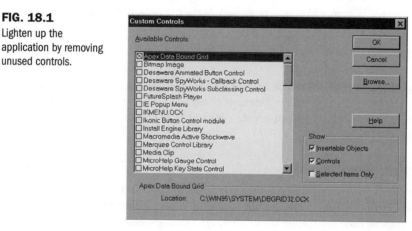

The second step brings up a dialog box with all the references that are available for your use, in addition to those that are currently in use for the project. If you are not going to be performing any database functions with the Jet database engine, remove the reference to the DAO library. Removing these controls will cut your distribution down by more than a megabyte. If you do not need any other references, remove them as well by unchecking the checked boxes.

Your server component has no user-interface attributes, so remove the default form that loaded in your new project. To remove Form1, select the form in the project window. If the project window is not visible, press Ctrl+R to display it.

Although all functionality that you expose to your client application (in this case, an Active Server Pages script) is through the Public methods of a class, component-level initialization can still take place when the component is created. Component-level initialization takes place in the Sub Main procedure of the component.

To add the Sub Main procedure to your new project, you need to add a code module. To do so, follow these steps:

1. Choose Module from the Insert menu.
2. Press F4 to pull up the module properties.
3. Change the name Module1 to CTransact_Main.
4. Move back to the newly named CTransact_Main code window.

5. Type **Sub Main**.

6. Press Enter.

These steps add a new module to the project. The module defaults to Module1 in the project window. You are creating a component that provides transaction processing for your server, and this component is called CTransact, so you call the module with Sub Main in it CTransact_Main.

You now have created an empty Sub Main procedure in the CTransact_Main module much like the following:

```
Sub Main()
End Sub
```

Because you perform no component-level initialization in your transaction component, you can leave the Sub Main procedure empty. Even though no explicit initialization takes place, you must have a Sub Main procedure defined in your component, or you receive an error when you try to instantiate the component.

The Project Dialog Box

Now is a good time to save your project. Before you do so, though, set up the project so that the compiler creates an OLE in-process server instead of a normal Windows executable program. The settings for code generation are located in the Options dialog box. To get to those settings, follow these steps:

1. Choose Options from the Tools menu to display the Options dialog box.

2. Select the Project tab.

N O T E   The menu options for Visual Basic 4.0 specified in the steps in this chapter have changed in version 5.0.

As shown in Figure 18.2, you notice several user-definable options for the project. The first thing that you need to do is specify the Project Name. The Project Name is the name that you use when specifying an object to create within your Active Server Pages script.

Select the Project tab from the Options dialog box, then do the following:

1. Enter the name **CTransact** in the Project Name field.

   The StartMode setting specifies whether you build a normal Windows executable file or an OLE server. You want to build an OLE server.

2. Select the OLE Server option button.

   The last field that you edit in the project is the Application Description edit box. This edit box is the text that you see when you browse the objects and components that are currently available on a system. You want to provide a concise description of your component.

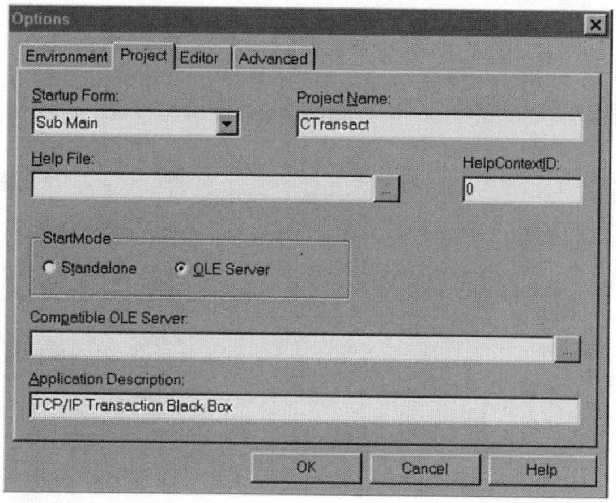

FIG. 18.2

The Project tab defines your component naming.

3. Type **TCP/IP Transaction Black Box** in the Application Description field.

4. Jump over to the Advanced tab and select the Use OLE DLL Restrictions check box.

   Selecting the OLE DLL Restrictions check box ensures that as you debug your application, the same restrictions placed on an in-process OLE server apply to your component during debugging.

5. Click the OK button to save the project changes that you just made.

6. Choose Save Project from the File menu.

   You are prompted to save the CTransact_Main.bas module in the default directory. Accept the default directory or create a new directory from the Save As dialog box, and then save the module. When you are prompted for the project name to save, replace the Project1 name with CTransact.

Congratulations! You have just completed the first task in creating your component.

Creating Your Transaction Class

Now the real work begins. Up to now, you have been dealing with the administration of creating a server component, setting up the project, selecting project options, and creating a main procedure. Now you begin to develop the class data and methods that perform the transactions that you have been working toward.

The first step is creating the class module. The class information lives in its own class code module—a file with a .CLS extension. To create the class module, choose Class Module from the Insert menu.

Now you've added a new class module to your project. If the class module is not currently selected, select the module in the project window by double-clicking the name Class1 or by selecting Class1 and then clicking the View Code button in the project window. Remember that if your project window is not visible, you can display it by pressing Ctrl+R.

Part
IV

Ch
18

In the next few steps, you rename your class, set it to `Public`, and select the instancing options.

1. With the class code window active, press the F4 key to display the class properties window, which looks like the one shown in Figure 18.3.

FIG. 18.3

Editing class properties
is just like changing any
VB object's properties.

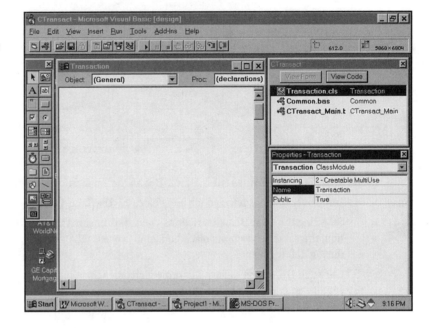

2. Change the name Class1 to `Transaction`.
3. Set the `Public` property to True.
4. Set the `Instancing` property to Creatable MultiUse.

The first of the preceding steps—changing the name—is important, because the name of the class is referenced when you create an instance of your component. Just as you take care in naming your class methods, you need to make a good choice for the class name.

The `Public` property determines the visibility of the class outside your OLE server. If you were to leave the class private, no one could access any of the transaction functions that you build into the class.

The last property of your class that you set was the `Instancing` property. This property determines how the OLE server is managed when it is instantiated by a client application. You selected the `Creatable Multi-Use` property, which enables the object, if already created, to be supplied by the existing object. If no object currently exists, one is created.

Contrast `Creatable Multi-Use` with the `Creatable Single Use` option, in which each `CreateObject` request causes a separate copy of the OLE server to start. The `Creatable Multi-Use` option uses memory more efficiently than the `Creatable Single Use` option and is the primary choice for externally created components like the one that you are building.

The Winsock Methods

To perform TCP/IP transactions, you use the Windows Sockets library calls in this section. One nice feature of Visual Basic allows you to declare just about any dynamic-link library and use it in the VB environment. To use these Winsock functions within your component, you need to declare them to Visual Basic, which is done with the `declare` statements shown in Listing 18.1, in the general code of the `Transaction` class.

Listing 18.1 TRANSACTION.CLS—Declaring the Winsock Functions to Visual Basic

```
'Winsock calls in VB format, for 32 bit, WSOCK32.DLL
Private Declare Function bind Lib "wsock32.dll" (ByVal s As Long, _
                addr As sockaddr_type, _
                ByVal namelen As Long) As Long
Private Declare Function inet_addr Lib "wsock32.dll" (ByVal s _
                As String) As Long
Private Declare Function gethostbyname Lib "wsock32.dll" _
                (ByVal hostname As String) As Long
```

You use several other Win32 API functions in your class. You can find all the declarations for these functions in the `TRANSACTION.CLS` module, in the `declarations` section.

Several helper procedures within the class handle the dirty work of the TCP/IP communications. Generally, the flow of the transactions follows this path:

1. Connect to the host.
2. Send the transaction to the host.
3. Receive a response.
4. Check the return code of the response.
5. Pass the response back to the calling application.

Each of the preceding steps has a `Private` procedure that handles one part of the communications chore. Listing 18.2 shows the code for the `fn_Connect` function, which connects to the host system. All the helper procedures perform one activity and return a Boolean value if the activity is completed successfully.

Listing 18.2 TRANSACTION.CLS—The *Connect* Function

```
Private Function fn_Connect(iSocket As Long, lAddress As Long, iPort As Integer)
➥As Boolean
  Dim sockaddr As sockaddr_type
  Dim rc As Integer

  sockaddr.sin_family = AF_INET
  sockaddr.sin_port = htons(iPort)
```

continues

Listing 18.2   Continued

```
    sockaddr.sin_addr = lAddress
    sockaddr.sin_zero = " "

    rc = connect(iSocket, sockaddr, Len(sockaddr))
    If rc = SOCKET_ERROR Then
     Err.Raise vbObjectError + CTRANSACT_ERR_CONNECT,
          "Transaction.fn_InitSockets", fn_GetLastSockError()
     Exit Function
    End If

    fn_Connect = True
End Function
```

If the connection fails, an error is raised, passing back the error code as well as text that describes the reason for the connection failure. The `fn_GetLastSockError` function returns the error text for the most recent socket error, using a call to the Windows Sockets extension function `WSAGetLastError()`. For additional information about the Winsock 1.1 specification, check out the Microsoft Web site at **http://www.microsoft.com**.

Private Class Variables

The first thing that you need to do after setting up the declarations for Winsock and Win32 API functions is create your `Private` class variables, as shown in Listing 18.3. These variables are dimensioned as `Private`, so that your client does not have access to them and cannot accidentally change one of their values at an inopportune time.

Listing 18.3   TRANSACTION.CLS—Declaring Class Variables *Private*

```
'Module Level Variable Declarations
Private msHost As String        ' Holds the host name
Private mlHost As Long          ' 32 bit host address
Private miPort As Integer        ' Host port to connect to
Private miConnectTimeout As Integer  ' connect timeout
Private miReceiveTimeout As Integer  ' receive timeout
Private msBuffer As String        ' buffer to hold transmitted data
Private mbInProcess As Boolean    ' in process flag
```

Having all these `Private` variables to use in your class is great, but you also need to get some pertinent information from the component user so that you can send your transaction on to the correct host. The section "Using Property Procedures" earlier in this chapter discusses property procedures that enable your users to set properties within your component. Two properties that must be set for you to perform your transaction are the `Host` and `Port` properties. These properties provide you with the name of the host to send the transaction to, as well as the port to which the host is listening. The property procedure for the `Host` property is shown in Listing 18.4.

Listing 18.4 TRANSACTION.CLS—Property Procedures and Data Hiding

```
Public Property Let Host(aHost As String)
  If Len(aHost) = 0 Then
   Err.Raise CTRANSACT_ERR_HOSTLEN, "Transaction.Host", _
"Set Host Name: Host Length Invalid"
   Exit Property
  End If
  mlHost = fn_GetHostByName(aHost)
  If mlHost = 0 Then
   Err.Raise CTRANSACT_ERR_HOSTBYNAME, _
"Transaction.Host", fn_GetLastSockError()
   Exit Property
  End If

  msHost = aHost
End Property
```

Notice in Listing 18.4 that you are handling errors by raising runtime errors that your component user catches in his or her code. If the Host length sent in by the application is 0, you raise an error. Also, if the host name cannot be resolved to a physical address (the fn_GetHostByName function provides the name-resolution services), an error is raised.

If you were setting properties just by giving your component user access to a Public variable sHost, you would have to check for a valid host name each time you performed a transaction. By handling this check through the use of a property procedure, you can raise the error, if needed, immediately when the property is set.

Part

IV

Ch

18

The Public Transact Method

The CTransact class has only one Public procedure. This procedure initiates the transaction and returns a completion code to the calling program. The function must be declared as Public so that it is visible from outside the component.

The first part of the method (or procedure) is the declaration. Parameters are passed to the method, and a return code of type Long is sent back when the transaction is complete, as shown in the here:

```
Public Function Transact(transaction As Integer, Version As Integer, _
    inBuffer As String) As Long
```

Several authorization transactions can be processed by the back-end service. Also, to support new versions of transactions as time goes on, a version is passed in as a parameter. This use of parameter passing is a handy way to enhance transactions without having to change any of the clients that are currently using a previous version. The buffer that is passed in is the authorization string formatted by the Active Server Pages script.

The first part of the code, shown in Listing 18.5, ensures that a valid Host property has been set, as well as a value for the Port property.

Listing 18.5   TRANSACTION.CLS—Verifying that Required Class Properties Have Been Set

```
If miPort = 0 Then
   Err.Raise CTRANSACT_ERR_PORTNOTSET, "CTransact.Transact", _
        "Port must be set prior to invoking Transaction method"
   Exit Function
   End If
   If mlHost = 0 Then
   Err.Raise CTRANSACT_ERR_HOSTNOTSET, "CTransact.Transact", _
        "Port must be set prior to invoking Transaction method"
   Exit Function
   End If
End If
```

You check for a valid host when the property is set, but you must also ensure that the property has been set before you begin the transaction. You could have added another Private variable as a flag (say, blnHostSet), but checking the value of the miPort and mlHost variables is just as easy and also saves a bit of memory (the less module-level variables you use, the better).

The interaction with the host system is performed through a standard header that is defined by the type TRAN_HDR. All the transactions are performed by means of this header, and the return code from the transaction is put in the ReturnCode member of the TRAN_HDR type. Ideally, you send the structure in the transaction. In the C or C++ programming languages, you would just cast the structure variable as a char * or a void * and be done with it. In Visual Basic, you need to send the transaction as a string. To do so, you create a little C DLL to perform the conversion from a string to a type and back again.

The next part of the code fills in the TRAN_HDR type, converts it to a structure, and prepares to send the transaction over the wire (see Listing 18.6).

Listing 18.6   TRANSACTION.CLS—Using the VBUTIL *CopyStructToString* Function to Simplify the String Conversion

```
hdr.PacketNumber = Format$(transaction, "00000000")
hdr.Version = Format$(Version, "0000")
hdr.ReturnCode = "9999"
hdr.OperatorNumber = ""
hdr.RecordLength = Len(hdr) + Len(inBuffer)

msg = Space$(Len(hdr))
rc = CopyStructToString(hdr, msg, Len(hdr))
```

Notice that you must preallocate the msg (which hosts the string representation of the TRAN_HDR type) string by filling it with spaces equal to the size of the header into which you are going to copy it. If you forget to preallocate the msg string, you receive an error.

Now comes the heart of the communications functions. All the TCP/IP functions have been created for you as Private procedures in the class, and the procedure for calling them within the Transact method is shown in Listing 18.7. As each function is called, the function returns codes that are checked after the call is made to ensure that you are still communicating with the host system.

Listing 18.7 TRANSACTION.CLS—TCP/IP Functions in the *Transact* Method

```
socket = fn_OpenSocket()
  If socket = 0 Then
    Err.Raise CTRANSACT_ERR_OPENSOCKET, "CTransact.Transact",
➥fn_GetLastSockError()
    Exit Function
  End If

  If fn_Connect(socket, mlHost, miPort) Then
   If fn_SendData(socket, msg & inBuffer) Then
     msBuffer = fn_ReceiveData(socket, 60)
     If Len(msBuffer) Then
      rc = fn_CloseSocket(socket)
      rc = CopyStructToString(hdr, msBuffer, Len(hdr))
      retCode = hdr.ReturnCode
      ' remove rich header from data buffer
      msBuffer = Mid$(msBuffer, Len(hdr) + 1)
     Else
      Exit Function
    End If
   Else
     rc = fn_CloseSocket(socket)
     Err.Raise CTRANSACT_ERR_SEND, "CTransact.Transact", fn_GetLastSockError()
   End If
  Else
   rc = fn_CloseSocket(socket)
  End If
```

A couple of return code type variables are used in the Transact method. The first variable, retCode, holds the value of the returned code from the host transaction. The retCode variable is a four-character string variable. The second, rc, is an integer that holds the transaction-specific return code that is sent back to the calling program. When you receive the return code (retCode) from the host, you interrogate it, as shown in Listing 18.8, to return the appropriate value to the calling application.

Listing 18.8 TRANSACTION.CLS—Formatting the Return Code for Your Calling Application

```
'Based upon the return code from the transaction, pass a value
  'to the calling app
  Select Case Left$(retCode, 2)
   Case "00"
     rc = TRANSACT_RC_SUCCESS
   Case "IL"
     rc = TRANSACT_RC_INVALID_ACCOUNT
```

Part

IV

Ch

18

continues

Listing 18.7   Continued

```
  Case "IR"
    rc = TRANSACT_RC_INVALID_TRAN
  Case Else
    rc = TRANSACT_RC_SERVER_ERROR
End Select

Transact = rc
```

Compiling the Component

The last step in building your transaction component is generating the DLL. In "The Project Dialog Box" earlier in this chapter, you set the project options to generate an OLE server. Now you just need to instruct the compiler to generate an OLE DLL. Follow these steps:

1. Choose Save Project from the File menu.
2. Choose Make OLE DLL File from the File menu.

That's it! You have built your first Active Server component. You can use this component with Visual Basic, Access, Excel, or any other application that supports OLE components. The new component was registered automatically for you on the system where it was initially created.

Using Your New Server Component

Now that you have built the component, you need to create the form and Active Server Pages script to invoke that component. If you are going to use the component on a machine other than the one that you created it on, you need to register the component on that machine.

Registering Your New Object

When you create the OLE DLL file in the Visual Basic environment, the component is registered automatically on the machine where it is compiled. If you want to move the DLL and associated support files to another machine, you need to register the new control after you place it on the system. You can distribute your new control in a couple of ways. If you are going to distribute your component, you can create an installation program by using the VB Setup Wizard or another third-party installation package. The control is registered during the installation process.

You also can just move the files to the new machine and register the control by using the REGSVR32.EXE program that ships with Visual Basic. You can find the registration application on the Visual Basic CD-ROM in the \TOOLS\PSS directory. Here's how to register the control by using the REGSVR32 program:

1. Move the component DLL and any supporting files (VB40032.DLL, for example) to the new machine.

2. Copy the REGSVR32.EXE file to a directory that is in the path on the target system (\WINDOWS\SYSTEM, for example).

3. Switch to the directory where you copied the DLL file.

4. Type **REGSVR32 COMPONENT.DLL.**

   When the component has been registered, you see a "successfully registered" dialog box.

5. Click OK to dismiss the dialog box.

Testing the Component

The easiest way to initially test your new component is to start another instance of Visual Basic, create a simple form, and create an instance of the component. Then you can set the properties and call the Transact method, which allows you to fine-tune the component before you try to integrate it into your Active Server Pages scripts.

To test the component, start another instance of Visual Basic. Add a command button to the Form1 that's displayed at startup. Double-click the newly created command button to bring up the code window. Then type the code shown in Listing 18.9 in the code window to test your new component.

Part

IV

Ch

18

Listing 18.9   form1.frm—Test Script for the New Component

```
Private Sub Command1_Click()
  Dim tran As New Transaction
  On Error GoTo COMMAND_ERR

  tran.Host = "localhost"
  tran.Port = 7511
  rc = tran.Transact(1000, 0, "TEST TRAN")
  MsgBox rc
Exit_Sub:
  Exit Sub

COMMAND_ERR:
  MsgBox "Error: " & Err.Number & " " & Err.Description
  Resume Exit_Sub
End Sub
```

The only action left to take before testing your component is adding a reference to it to your new project. Follow these steps:

1. Choose References from the Tools menu.

2. Scroll down the list and check TCP/IP Transaction Black Box.

While testing, it's helpful to force errors to ensure that error handling within the component is functioning correctly. You can comment on the line tran.Host = "localhost", for example, which generates an error because, as you may remember from the HostName property procedure code in "The Let Procedure" earlier in this chapter, you must set the host before calling the Transact function.

The error is raised in the component and caught in the calling application by this directive:

```
On Error GoTo COMMAND_ERR
```

In your Active Server Pages development, you are not displaying message boxes on your server, but at minimum, you surely want to log any communication errors for further study and return an appropriate response to your client.

Testing the Component on Net

To test the component on your server, you need to build a simple form that calls an Active Server script and passes the appropriate parameters to it (account number and authorization amount). Then you can create your transaction object, call the Transact method, and return the results to your client.

From Here...

In this chapter we have taken a very large step towards advanced site development. We discussed the advantages that server components can provide you, and we also created what might have been your first server component.

We will now discuss how you can use this new information to create advanced Commerce Server 2.0 stores which will meet the needs of your customers. The following are some of the chapters that you can look forward to later in this book:

- Chapter 22, "Building the Order Process Pipeline," will discuss how you can implement these server components into the Commerce Server OPP.

- Chapter 23, "Constructing Your Own Server Components," will discuss constructing server components using Visual C++. This chapter will further the discussion of commerce server components by demonstrating their ability to integrate directly with the OPP's internal information.

Advanced Site Server Topics

CHAPTER 19

Understanding Microsoft Windows NT Server 4.0

Microsoft Windows NT Server is Microsoft's most powerful and resilient operating system. This operating system was specifically designed for servers to operate in either large or busy environments, although it is fully scaleable and will also work in a much smaller environment. In this chapter, all references to Windows NT will refer to Windows NT Server unless otherwise specified.

Windows NT offers many advanced features and is scalable in different types of environments, including small, busy environments and large, busy environments. You can run Windows NT Server in large corporations that have several thousand computers in a network. You can also run it in an environment that has only a few computers but uses all those computers as Internet servers and will get hit hard.

Microsoft also offers a workstation version of this package called Windows NT Workstation. This version of the operating system is made for single-user workstations and is designed to coexist with Windows NT Server (shown in Figure 19.1). Microsoft Windows NT Server is also the required operating system for using Microsoft Commerce Server. ■

Minimum requirements to run Windows NT Server and Commerce Server

You see the hardware necessary to run both of these servers.

Windows NT Service Packs

You learn about Service Packs, which are the means by which product updates are distributed.

File system options for Windows NT

Before you choose a file system for Windows NT, you learn about the differences between two different file systems: FAT (File Allocation Table) and NTFS (New Technology File System).

Various functions of Windows NT Server

You learn about what Windows NT Server does. In particular, you see the functions of a Primary Domain Controller, Backup Domain Controller, and Stand-alone Server.

Networking Windows NT

You configure network services and protocols for Windows NT Server.

Administering Windows NT Server

After your Windows NT Server is set up, you learn about ways to ensure continued high performance of your system.

FIG. 19.1
Windows NT Server is the operating system on which Commerce Server runs.

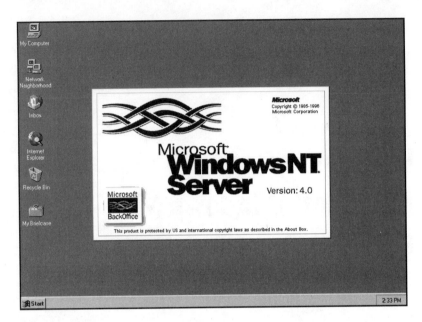

This chapter gives you an overview of Windows NT, focusing primarily on what you need to know to run Microsoft Commerce Server, so it won't tell you *everything* that you need to know about NT. If you aren't familiar with NT, you should get some good books or other reference material on it before you try to do much with Commerce Server. A good book on Windows NT Server is *Special Edition Using Windows NT Server 4, Second Edition* (0-7897-1388-8).

N O T E Throughout this book, Windows NT Server 4.0 is used. Although the previous version of Microsoft Merchant Server runs under Windows NT 3.51, the new version of Microsoft Commerce Server does not run under anything earlier than Windows NT 4.0 with Service Pack 2 and IIS 3.0 installed.

The Hardware

According to Microsoft, the minimum hardware required to run Windows NT Server is

- 486 processor running at 66 MHz or faster
- 32M of RAM
- 500M of hard disk storage
- VGA-compatible video card
- TCP/IP compatible network card

The minimum hardware requirements to run Commerce Server are

- *Pentium processor running at 166 MHz or faster.* You are probably best off with a Pentium Pro 200 or faster.

- *128M of RAM.* Microsoft recommends 64M, but if you are going to be running Commerce Server and a database on the same machine, you will do much better with the added memory.

- *2.5G of hard disk storage.* You are going to want a large database, especially if you plan to have a busy store.

- *VGA-compatible video card or better.* The HP NetServers that we use come with 512K or 1M video cards built onto the motherboard. Since you will administer your Commerce Server system remotely, this should not be a factor in your machine choice.

- *TCP/IP network card that takes up the full bandwidth of your slot.* (PCI should work on all Pentium boards.) If you are going to run a database on a separate machine, you want to have a second network interface card to ensure that your network is not overburdened with database traffic.

  Consider having two networks: one for your regular traffic and the other for internal traffic among machines. You can use this network to run backups and to communicate among machines on your local network. You get much-improved performance for a busy machine. If you are running two computers—one for commerce and one for a database—you can simply connect your machines via crossover cable. This way, you guarantee that the only traffic coming over this network card is traffic between these two machines. Having two network cards per computer also keeps your main network clean.

- *Fastest Internet connection that you can get and afford.* You also need to monitor your bandwidth closely. When you get to the point at which you are using about 60 percent of your total available bandwidth and your business is increasing, you want to order more bandwidth. If you have a fractional T-1 or T-3, raising your bandwidth is most likely a simple matter; you probably need only flip a switch on your CSU/DSU. If you have to order another T-1 or upgrade from a T-1 to a T-3, however, this process is time-consuming; it can take up to eight weeks from start to finish.

- *Backup system.* You need a reliable backup system of some kind—preferably a tape-based drive or if you have several gigabytes of data, an optical backup system. We are using an HP 40E DLT tape drive to backup our network. This is an external DLT tape drive that allows up to 40G (compressed) per tape. If you are doing incremental backups to your machines, 40G should be able to last you for several days.

When you decide on a Windows NT Server system to purchase, you need to check the "Hardware Compatibility List" to make sure that all your hardware is compatible with Windows NT. You can find the "Hardware Compatibility List" (HCL) by going to **http:// www.microsoft.com/ntserver/info/hwcompatibility.htm**. There is a hard copy of the HCL that comes with Windows NT Server but with all of the new products coming out, this hard copy list is usually outdated by the time it is printed. For this reason, I strongly recommend checking the HCL on the online site.

One of the most important things to keep in mind is that you want to buy an approved system—not a bunch of approved parts with which to build a system. A system that you build yourself is not likely to be reliable, and reliability is the name of the game for a Commerce Server. Microsoft and other distributors have spent a great deal of time and effort to make sure that certain systems work solidly with Windows NT Server.

Part
V

Ch
19

I needed a development machine a while back, so I decided to save some money and build one myself. I bought all the parts in the HCL and put a machine together. However, I had nothing but problems with it. I replaced almost every part of the machine until it was working correctly with Windows NT Server. I had to get a new motherboard. After I got the motherboard, I needed to upgrade the BIOS to fix some conflicts. It still did not work, so I continued to investigate. The video card was conflicting with the SCSI BIOS, so I bought another video card.

The new video card was also conflicting with the SCSI BIOS, so I decided to replace the SCSI card. I had Adaptec send me a SCSI card with the latest BIOS (1.25 at the time when this book was written), which solved many problems. The video card still was not working, however, so I got my money back for the video card and bought a Matrox Millennium at the recommendation of my friend. After I got the latest drivers for the card and updated the BIOS, my computer finally worked. All this took a year. If I had simply spent a few extra dollars, just think of all the work that I could have gotten done in that amount of time.

Using HP NetServers to Run Microsoft Site Server

For our Commerce Server sites, we use and recommend Hewlett Packard NetServers. We currently operate two of these machines. One machine is an LH Pro dual Pentium Pro 200 with 224M of RAM and 16G of hard disk space in a RAID 5 array. The other machine is an LX Pro quad Pentium Pro with 512M of RAM, 2G of mirrored disk space for the operating system, 2G of disk space for log files, and 60G of disk space in a RAID 5 array for running applications. These systems were specifically designed to run Windows NT Server and are guaranteed to work well with Windows NT Server for years to come. If you want more information on any of these HP NetServers, see **http://www.hp.com/netserver**.

If you are going to buy a system that has not been proven to run Windows NT Server or is not an approved NT Server system, you should get a *written* guarantee from your vendor that the machine will run Windows NT Server. This guarantee will help you if your site crashes or if you run into a situation like mine.

You would be better off to stick with systems that are approved, however. Your Commerce site is likely to be important to you, so why take unnecessary risks?

TIP Before you install Windows NT, read the Readme file. You already know to do that, of course, but an absolutely amazing number of people do not read these important documents. In the Readme, you will find important information that may not have been available at the time when NT was packaged. Make sure that you look to see what's there; you will save yourself a great deal of time and effort.

Windows NT Service Packs

Microsoft offers what it calls Service Packs and hotfixes when it finds either enough bugs or a critical bug in its products. At the time when this book was written, Service Pack 3 for Windows NT was available as well as several Post Service Pack 3 hotfixes.

To install Commerce Server, you need at least Service Pack 2; however, Service Pack 3 is recommended. To find the latest Service Pack for Microsoft Windows NT Server, go to **http://www.microsoft.com/NTServerSupport/Content/ServicePacks/Default.htm** and choose `Where can I get the latest Service Pack?`. On this page, you are given a list of several different places where you can download the latest Service Pack. Also, as of Service Pack 3, you are given an opportunity to download the strong 128-bit encryption version of Service Pack 3. Downloading this version is highly recommended if you are in the United States or Canada. With this version, if you are going to be using HTTPS on your Web server, you will be able to use the strongest encryption available, providing your customers with the most secure way of transferring their credit card information or any other information that they need to provide. If you want to find out what has been fixed in the latest service pack, click `Do I need the latest Service Pack?` and then click `List of Bugs Fixed in Windows NT 4.0`.

When you download the Service Pack, put the file in an empty directory and run it. The Service Pack will do a verification on itself and then it will extract the files into your temp directory (whatever you set your temp directory to in your environment, usually C:\TEMP). When all of the files have been extracted, UPDATE.EXE will automatically be run to install the Service Pack. To install the Service Pack, follow the instructions. It is recommended that you allow Windows NT to create an `uninstall` directory for you, just in case something goes wrong.

If you are in the United States or Canada, you most likely have the 128-bit version of Microsoft Windows NT Server. If you have this version, and if you downloaded the 40-bit Service Pack from **ftp.microsoft.com**, you get a warning telling you that the Service Pack is about to replace your 128-bit security files with 40-bit files because of U.S.-Government export regulations on security. You most likely want to choose Skip. If you overwrite this file, you can no longer use high-grade security. If you overwrite this file then when you apply for your encryption certificate to use HTTPS, or if you already have an encryption certificate, you cannot use it with strong encryption.

If you would like to have Service Pack 3 mailed to you instead of downloading the large file, you can go to **http://www.microsoft.com/NTServerSupport/Content/ServicePacks/Cdsp.htm**. This page provides instructions for ordering a Service Pack CD. When you call, make clear to the operator that you need the 128-bit nonexportable version of the Service Pack if you are in the U.S. or Canada and you meet the requirements for owning this version of the Service Pack. If you do not make it clear to the operator, you will get the same version that you can download from Microsoft's FTP Server.

Part
V

Ch
19

Choosing a File System for Windows NT

Here are some very important considerations when you choose which file system you are going to install on Windows NT. One of the first things that you need to decide is which file system to use on your hard disk. You have two choices: New Technology File System (NTFS) or File Allocation Table (FAT). Several differences exist between the two types of file systems. NTFS is an advanced file system that was developed specifically for Windows NT. With NTFS, you can implement several features that you cannot implement with FAT under MS-DOS or

Windows 95. A new type of file system, called FAT32, also is available. FAT32 is a better version of FAT, and it supports disks larger than 2G. Unfortunately, the only type of operating system that can read this file system is Windows 95 Service Release 2. If you are going to be dual-booting Windows 95 and Windows NT, make sure that you use regular FAT or FAT16.

Security

NTFS allows you to assign read, write, and change permissions to files. Then only authorized users can read, write, or change files or directories according to the permissions that you put into place. With FAT under Windows NT, or even Windows 95 or MS-DOS, you cannot implement any type of security. Everyone can read, write, or delete any files on your system, so you have no privacy or security for your server—definitely not a good idea for a Commerce Server. Also, with NTFS, you can give accounts to registered users and allow them access to certain areas of your Web site.

Efficiency

With NTFS, your files are handled in such a way that the storage space required for those files is used most efficiently. NTFS is also a much faster file system than FAT, which means that when you access large files or several people access files on your server simultaneously, you see a significant increase in speed compared with FAT.

With a FAT file system, your files can easily become fragmented. If you have partitions larger than 250M, the space is used inefficiently, and you do not get the most usable space out of your hard disk. Also, under Windows NT, you can have only up to 4G partitions with FAT. With NTFS, you can have partitions up to 16 exabytes, which is equal to 16 million terabytes of data—probably enough to hold you for a little while, at least.

Auditing Capability

In an NTFS partition, you can have file auditing. File auditing enables you to monitor file activity on your site. You may want to audit files if you have a public area where you need to write or change permissions for users, or if you find that some user is making unauthorized changes or deletions.

You enable auditing in User Manager for Domains. The general procedure for auditing files consists of two main tasks. First, turn on file auditing in User Manager. Second, select which events you want to audit in either File Manager or Windows NT Explorer, as well as the users/groups that you want to audit. Then you find out which users are making changes in these files.

Here's a step-by-step guide to setting up file auditing:

1. Go to User Manager for Domains. You can find this program by going to the Start menu and choosing programs. In Administrative Tools, you will see User Manager for Domains.

2. Choose the Audit command from the Policy menu.

   You see the Audit Policy dialog box (see Figure 19.2).

FIG. 19.2

The Audit Policy dialog box enables you to choose the file events that you want to audit.

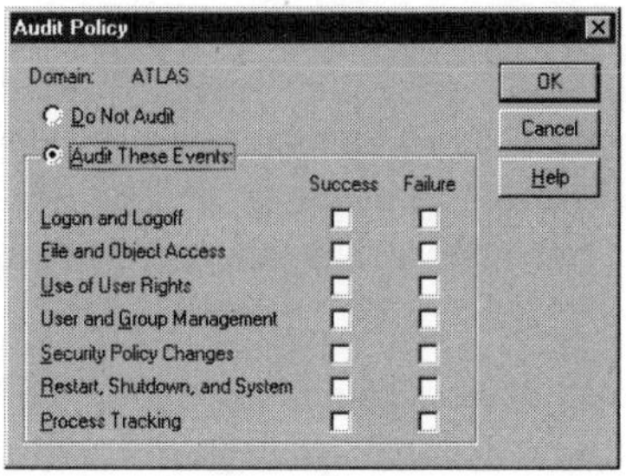

3. Choose the events to audit.

You do not have to choose any events in User Manager if you do not want to, but you do need to enable auditing in User Manager for Domains for any security auditing to work. If you want to enable auditing on your file system so that you can track people who are deleting files, you can do so through the auditing function. Remember that your file system must be NTFS; FAT does not support any type of auditing.

Now that you have set up auditing in User Manager for Domains, you can exit this program and open up Windows NT Explorer to continue. You must at this point decide which files or directories you wish to audit.

1. When you decide what directories or drives to audit, go to Windows NT Explorer. You can find Windows NT Explorer by going to the Start menu and choosing Programs. You will see Windows NT Explorer as part of these program files.

2. Right-click the drive or directory that you want to audit to bring up a shortcut menu.

3. Choose Properties from the shortcut menu. You should see the directory name properties dialog box.

4. Click the Security tab.

5. Choose Auditing. You will see the directory auditing dialog box.

6. Click Add to bring up the users and groups list.

7. Add the users and groups that you want to audit. Click OK when you have added all the users and groups that you wish to audit.

8. Choose the events that you want to audit, and decide whether you want to replace auditing on existing files or subdirectories.

9. Click OK.

The system writes this information to your hard disk. If you choose to replace information on the entire disk, this procedure can take several minutes, because you are making changes in the entire file system.

Fault Tolerance

With Windows NT and NTFS, you can set up a software fault-tolerance solution. The advantage of setting up a RAID system by using software is that it can be much less expensive than buying a hardware RAID solution. Windows NT supports RAID 0, 1, and 5; it also supports disk mirroring. You can enable and manage all these solutions with Disk Administrator. Be aware, however, that if you use Windows NT RAID, you cannot mirror the operating system. With a hardware RAID solution, you can mirror the operating system, because Windows NT is not aware that you are using any type of redundancy. The different types of RAID that Windows NT supports are

■ RAID Level 0 stripes data across all disks without redundancy or parity. This level is best suited for maximized transfer rates and transfer sizes. Spare drives are not useful on this level.

■ RAID Level 1 mirrors data across multiple disks. Data is duplicated on another set of drives. If one drive fails, then the data is still available on the other mirror. This level has the highest cost per megabyte and is best suited for smaller capacity applications. Typically, only one drive is mirrored at a time. Spare drives are not useful on this level.

■ RAID Level 5 stripes data and parity information at the block level across all the drives in the array. Parity is written onto the next available drive rather than a dedicated parity drive. Reads and writes may be performed concurrently. Level 5 also calculates parity during the write cycles, but uses an Exclusive-OR (X-OR) algorithm. This algorithm is best suited for smaller data transfers. Spare drives take over in the event of a drive failure.

■ With fault tolerance, if one of your physical hard disks crashes, you do not lose any data, because enough data is on the remaining hard disks for all your data to be reconstructed without any data loss. If you are using a hardware RAID solution, you may even be able to replace and rebuild a failed hard disk without even having to turn off your machine and reboot. This type of disk drive is called hot-swapable. Using a hardware RAID solution with hot-swapable disks makes things much more convenient for your users, because no interruption in service occurs.

Learning the Various Roles of Windows NT Server

The next thing that you need to decide is the role of your Windows NT Server. The three roles that a Windows NT Server can perform are

■ *Primary Domain Controller (PDC)*—A Primary Domain Controller performs domain authentication and holds the master copy of all user databases, user profiles, logon scripts, and so on. A PDC can also perform any function that a server can perform. Your PDC can be a Microsoft Exchange Server, Microsoft SQL Server, Print Server, DNS Server, IIS Server, Microsoft Commerce Server, and so on.

Domain authentication occurs when a user logs on to a system. When a user logs on through Windows 95, Windows 3.1, or Windows NT, the user name and password are sent to the PDC or the Backup Domain Controller (BDC). The PDC or BDC checks the user name and password against the information in the user's database. If those items are correct, the system logs the user on. At that time, an access control list is generated, providing information about what services, files, and so on the user has access to, as well as what the user cannot access. The user's privileges are also established at that time.

■ *Backup Domain Controller (BDC)*—A BDC can perform any of the functions that a PDC can perform, including all aspects of authentication. What a BDC does not do is hold the master copy of the information. The BDC needs to go to the PDC to receive updates of any user information, scripts, and so on.

■ *Stand-alone Server (Server)*—A Windows NT Server that is configured as a stand-alone server can perform all the preceding tasks *except* domain authentication. A stand-alone server can be useful if you have a large domain and need to keep domain authentication separate from your servers, or if you need several servers on your network in addition to your PDC and BDC.

This chapter does not discuss the workgroup role, because the most efficient way to set up your Windows NT network is in a domain.

The Roles of Primary and Backup Domain Controllers

You obviously need a PDC to begin establishing your domain. You should also use at least one BDC. A BDC is important for a couple of reasons. One reason is that the BDC has all the authentication information, so it can take part of the load off the PDC. A more important reason is that if your PDC goes down for any reason or needs to be rebooted, your BDC must be capable of performing most of the PDC's functions so that your network does not go down while your PDC is unavailable.

Be aware, however, that you cannot make any changes in the user database or any files that are replicated from the PDC to the BDC's or any other servers, because the master copy resides on the PDC. If you make any changes in these files while the PDC is down, you lose these changes when the PDC comes back up and overwrites them. If you need to take your PDC down for any length of time, you want to temporarily promote one of your BDCs to a PDC and demote your PDC to a BDC. (To promote a BDC to a PDC, you need to go to Server Manager, select the BDC that you want to make a PDC, and choose Promote to Primary Domain Controller from the Computer menu.)

Depending on the size of your network, you may want to have your Windows NT Commerce Server running on either your BDC or PDC. If these machines are busy doing other tasks, you may want to use a stand-alone server as your Commerce Server.

An IIS Bug and the Fix for It

If you choose your BDC to house your Internet Information Server (IIS) with Windows NT 4.0, you may experience a bug. (At the time when this book was written, Microsoft was aware of this bug and planned to rectify it in a future release.) The bug occurs because the BDC has no local user-account database until it synchronizes with the PDC. The problem that you may run into is that IIS needs a dedicated guest account called IUSR_*<machine name>* to allow access to your machine. When your BDC attempts to set up this account, if it has not yet synchronized with your PDC, the account is lost when your BDC synchronizes with your PDC.

You can rectify this problem in three ways.

An Easy Way   Defer installment of IIS until your BDC is all set up and has been synchronized with your PDC.

A Bit More Work   If you chose to install IIS with your initial installation of Windows NT 4.0, you can add the account with User Manager for Domains. Follow these steps:

1. Go to User Manager for Domains as explained in a previous section and make an account called IUSR_<machine name> (see Figure 19.3). From the User menu, choose New User. Fill in all of the information. For the description, you can use something like, **Internet Guest Account**. You can, of course, make the password anything you would like.

FIG. 19.3

Creating the IUSR_<machine name> account.

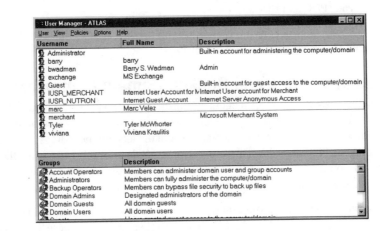

2. Select User Cannot Change Password and Password Never Expires (see Figure 19.4).

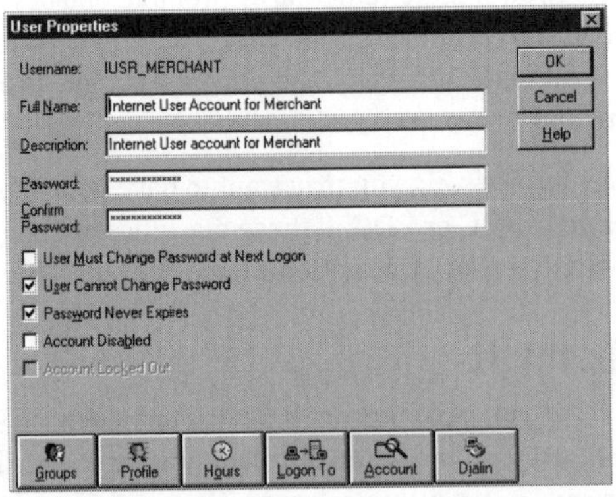

FIG. 19.4

Setting user properties in the User Properties dialog box.

Make sure that this account is part of the Domain Users group and the Guest group so that access to your machine is restricted. You can choose any password that you want. To add the user to these groups, select the Groups button to bring up the Group

Memberships dialog box. From the list of groups on the right, double-click the Domain Users and Guest groups to make this user a member of these two groups.

3. Go to Internet Service Manager and all the services that you will be using, such as WWW, FTP, and Gopher (see Figure 19.5). To get to Internet Service Manager, go to the Start menu, Programs. Choose Microsoft Internet Server and then choose Internet Service Manager.

FIG. 19.5

Setting IIS.

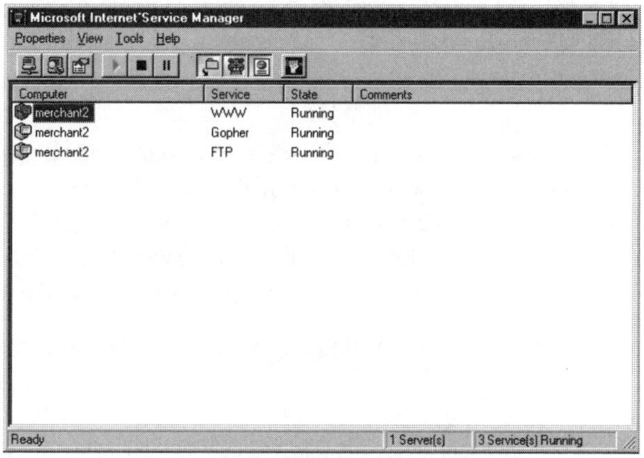

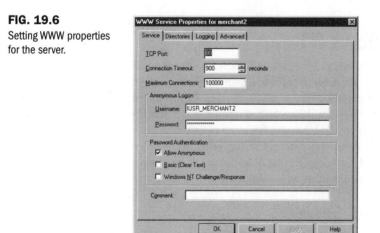

4. To go to properties (see Figure 19.6), double-click the desired service. When you bring up the Properties dialog box, you will be able to configure all of the service properties for the desired service such as anonymous login username, directories, logging, and advanced features such as allowing and denying certain IP addresses.

FIG. 19.6

Setting WWW properties for the server.

Part
V

Ch
19

5. Under the Service tab in the Properties dialog box in the Anonymous Logon section, enter the user name that you selected in User Manager for Domains, and use the same password. Without this information, anyone who tries to go to your Web server will need to have a user name and password on your system before they could view any pages.

6. In the Password Authentication group, choose the type of authentication that you need.

 T I P   You should use Allow Anonymous if you are going to have a Web server that is accessible to everyone. If you need to password-protect certain areas, you can choose to allow plain-text authentication or Windows NT Challenge/Response.

If you allow plain-text authentication, when someone sends a user name and password over the Internet, that information is in plain text unless you are using SSL (Secure Sockets Layers). If you use SSL, this information is encrypted. If you choose Windows NT Challenge/Response, the information is encrypted by Microsoft Windows NT encryption. Microsoft Internet Explorer supports this type of encryption.

Another Easy Way   You can also reinstall IIS, which adds the user account and the correct permissions.

N O T E   When you purchase your server software, you may find that especially with SQL Server, you may exceed the number of allowed connections that you are licensed to use. Microsoft offers an unlimited server license so that you never run into this problem. If you plan to have a busy Web site, purchasing unlimited licenses is something that you may want to consider so that your customers are never denied access to your pages merely because you do not have enough licenses. ▧

Networking Windows NT

The next thing to decide when you set up Windows NT Server is which network services and protocols to install. If you are setting up IIS or Commerce Server on your NT Server, you need the TCP/IP protocol, which is the only protocol that Commerce Server and IIS support. TCP/IP is one of the most robust and widely accepted protocols; it is also the only protocol that you can use on the Internet. If you find that all your machines need to be on the Internet, and you don't have any databases or servers that require any other protocols, you should consider using TCP/IP as your only protocol. Having as few networking protocols helps keep your network as clean and easy to manage as possible.

An Overview of the DNS Server

A new service that is available with NT Server 4.0 is DNS (Domain Name Service) Manager. Microsoft supplies a fully interactive GUI (graphical user interface) DNS Server with NT Server 4.0 so that you can manage DNS on your domain name and Class C addresses. When you decide which machines to put a DNS Server on, you need to keep several things in mind.

■ First, if you are going to register a domain name with the InterNIC or obtain Class C addresses from the InterNIC or your Internet Service Provider (ISP), you need at least two DNS Servers to hold name service.

■ If you have a Web server or Web servers with light to moderate traffic, and you are doing any type of logging, having at least a local DNS Server on each of your Web servers is a good idea. This way, your Web server(s) can resolve DNS names on their own, thereby preventing delays if another DNS Server is unavailable or busy.

If you have a busy Web server, you do not want to put a DNS Server on your Web server, because this increases the load on that server. Instead, you may want to have one or two machines dedicated to doing DNS and have your Web servers simply point to that machine. That way, your Web servers can dedicate all available system resources to Microsoft Commerce Server.

An Overview of the NETBios Protocol

The NETBios interface is required for Windows NT networking. NETBios enables you to browse the network by using your machine's names. If you call your machine nutron, for example, your machine's NETBios name is nutron. When you are in Windows and you click Network Neighborhood, you see a list of machines, domains, and workgroups; you get this information through the NETBios service.

An Overview of the IPX/SPX Protocol

The IPX/SPX protocol is used primarily for communication with Novell servers. If you have any Novell machines on your network, you need to install IPX/SPX on at least your Windows NT Server if you want your Windows clients to communicate with your Novell server. If you want all your clients to communicate with your Novell server directly, you need to install IPX/SPX on all your client machines, as well as your servers. Some databases are capable of using only IPX/SPX; if you are running any of these databases, you also need to install IPX/SPX on all machines that need access to these databases.

An Overview of DHCP

The DHCP (Dynamic Host Configuration Protocol) service enables you to configure TCP/IP on all your client machines automatically. This capability is convenient because you do not have to worry about configuring each of your client machines individually; the configuration is done for you automatically. You should not set up any of your Web servers or DNS Servers as DHCP clients, because every time you log on, your computer gets a different IP address. If you were using DHCP on your Web servers or DNS Servers, users from the Internet would not be able to find your servers and this would of course defeat the purpose of having these servers.

To set up a DHCP Server, you need to first install the DHCP Server service. Follow these steps:

Part

V

Ch

19

1. Go to Control Panel and double-click the Network icon to bring up the Network dialog box.

2. Click the Services tab.

3. Click Add to bring up the Select Network Service dialog box.

4. Choose Microsoft DHCP Server.

5. Click OK.

   You are asked for your Windows NT Server CD-ROM or the local or network path where your Windows NT Server files reside.

6. Insert the required CD-ROM or type the correct path.

7. Reboot your machine at the prompt.

8. After your machine reboots, make sure that the Microsoft DHCP Server has started.

   To verify that the Microsoft DHCP Server service has started, go to the Start menu, choose Settings and Control Panel. Double-click Services and scroll down to Microsoft DHCP Server. Verify that DHCP Server is set to Automatic and that DHCP Server has started. If the DHCP Server has not started, you will need to check your Event Viewer to find the cause of the problem. If you did not get any errors installing DHCP Server, there should not be any problems starting DHCP Server.

9. Go to the Start menu, choose Programs, and go to Administrative Tools.

   You should notice a new item: DHCP Manager.

10. Choose this program to configure your machine as a DHCP Server.

   With DHCP Manager, you can configure any DHCP Server on your network; your machine should be added to the server list automatically. You should see local machine (see Figure 19.7).

FIG. 19.7
The DHCP Manager.

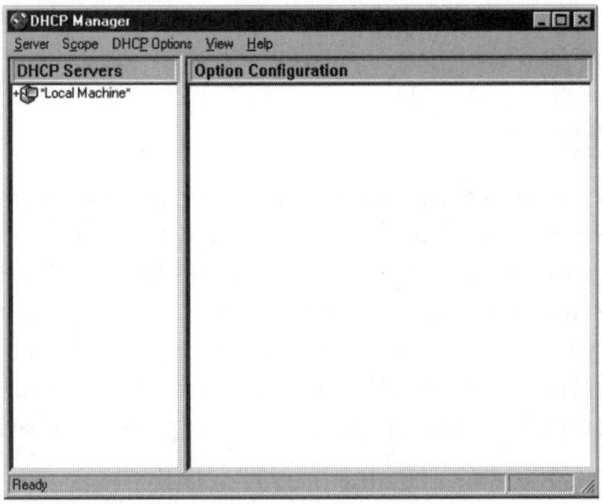

11. Choose Create from the Scope menu. The Create Scope dialog box appears.

12. In the IP Address Pool box, enter the beginning and ending IP addresses that you want your DHCP clients to use.

13. Add Netmask to the Subnet Mask box.

You also have the choice of excluding addresses that the DHCP Server uses.

14. Decide how long you want clients to keep an address.

The default is three days. You can choose Unlimited, or limit the time to a specific number of minutes, hours, or days (see Figure 19.8). When you have filled in all of the necessary fields, click OK to close the dialog box. When you click OK, you will receive another dialog box telling you that the new scope has been created but not activated. Click Yes to activate the new scope or No to wait. If you decide to activate the scope at a later time, you can go to the Scope menu and choose activate.

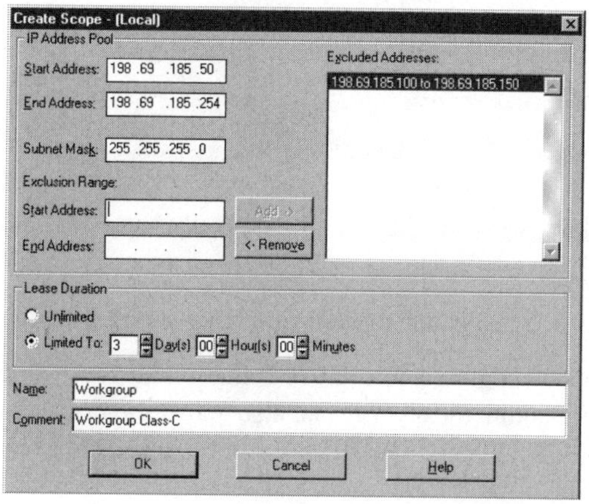

FIG. 19.8

Setting the scope of user access to the local network.

You also have the option of adding the DNS Servers and the gateway (router) address so that all machines do not have to be configured separately. To add a gateway address to a scope, follow these steps:

1. Click the DHCP Server scope.

2. Choose the Scope option from the DHCP Options menu (see Figure 19.9).

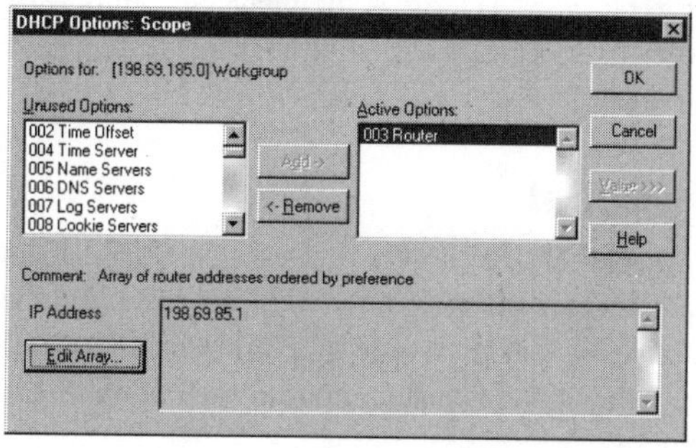

FIG. 19.9

The DHCP Options: Scope dialog box.

Part

V

Ch

19

3. Find the Router option in the Unused Options box and add it to the Active Options box.

4. Click Value. This expands the box so that you can type in the value of what you are adding.

5. Click the Edit Array button to bring up the IP Address Array Editor (see Figure 19.10).

FIG. 19.10

The IP Address Array Editor.

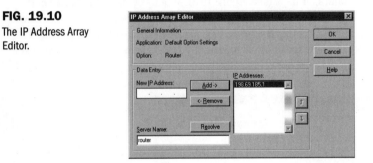

6. Enter the IP address of your router and, optionally, the DNS name of your router.

7. Click OK.

Now the IP addresses of your DNS Servers have been added to your DHCP scope.

Now you do not have to configure a gateway or router on all your workstations, because configuration is done there automatically. You can also follow the preceding steps to add DNS Server IP addresses, WINS Server IP addresses, and several other options.

Integrating Windows NT and Macintosh

Windows NT Server can also act as a file and print server for any Macintosh client. To set this up, you need to install Services for Macintosh. When you have Services for Macintosh set up, you need to set up volumes for your Macs to be capable of seeing shared directories. Unlike Windows clients such as Windows 3.1, 95, and NT, Macs are not automatically capable of seeing shared files and directories. You need to go into File Manager under the macfile menu and set up Mac-accessible volumes. When you set up these volumes, all the Macs on your network can see these files and directories—as long as they have accounts with proper permissions on your Windows NT Server or you have set up the guest account for login access and the guest account has access to the files.

Using the NetBEUI Protocol

The last networking protocol that this chapter covers is NetBEUI. This protocol is a proprietary networking protocol that can be used only on Microsoft Windows or MS-DOS networks. This protocol is not routable, so it is good only for communications between local networks. This protocol has little overhead and is fast compared with TCP/IP and IPX/SPX when you are dealing with small networks.

Securing NT

When you have Windows NT installed and all your network services configured, you want to secure your system, because it most likely has direct access to the Internet. If you have a popular Web site, people may try to hack into it. You should be prepared for any attack and make your system as secure as possible.

The best place to start is in User Manager for Domains. You need to set up account policies. Some of the things that you can set to secure your system are the following (see Figure 19.11):

- Lockout after X number of failed logon attempts—To prevent a user from trying to guess someone else's password, you can choose to have the account locked out after a certain number of failed logons. You can have the account locked out indefinitely or only for a certain number of minutes. If you have the account locked out indefinitely, the user needs to find an administrator to unlock the account for her. Most people use this option only when security requires a user to change his password immediately when the account is locked out.

FIG. 19.11

The Account Policy dialog box.

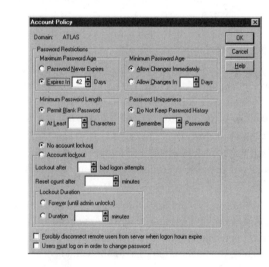

Part
V

Ch

19

- Minimum requirements for passwords—You can set the minimum number of characters that users can have in their passwords; the longer a password is, the more difficult it is to guess. You can also choose how often users are required to change their password, to prevent anyone from having a password for an unreasonably long period. If a user keeps his password for a long time, a greater chance exists that someone will obtain the password.

Windows NT has the capability to remember a certain number of passwords and can prevent users from reusing passwords within a given period. For password security to be most effective, you may also want to set a minimum password life to keep users from changing a password and then immediately changing it back.

TIP Good passwords are any combination of two words, a combination of letters and numbers, a word in which you remember where you replace letters with numbers, and so on. If you have a word that you want to use, you can replace the letter I in the word with !, E with 3, O (letter) with 0 (digit), and so on. This system makes guessing passwords difficult.

■ Remote administration—If you need to set up remote administration, you want to set up trust relationships. By setting up trust relationships, you eliminate the need for users to send passwords over the Internet. Thus, if someone is using a packet sniffer to see what you are doing, that person cannot get a password to your domain.

If you are going to administer a Microsoft Exchange Server, you need to set up a trust. If you do not set up a trust, you cannot administer Exchange remotely. Even if you can log on to the machine as an administrator, Exchange does not allow you to administer it. (Hopefully Microsoft will fix this bug in a service pack for Exchange 5.0.)

If you are concerned about security and the potential for another user to see what you are transferring, the most secure way to administer a Windows NT Network remotely is to dial directly into your Windows NT Server and force RAS to encrypt all transferred data. That way, if someone is trying to watch what you are doing, all he sees are the encrypted packets going through the line, which are useless.

■ File and directory permissions—The next thing to do is set up file and directory permissions to protect any individual files as well as specified directories. If you have any files that need to be secured, keep these files off your Web server or any other servers that are directly connected to the Internet and that are not protected by a firewall.

■ Security logging—Another thing that you can do with User Manager for Domains is set up security logging. You can choose the type and level of logging to see any failed logon attempts and to lock out any user whom you think may be attempting to enter your system improperly.

■ TCP/IP security—Windows NT provides another way to secure your system. In Control Panel, Networking is an option for security in the Advanced IP Addressing dialog box. By using this feature, you can allow or disallow access to TCP ports, UDP ports, or IP services. Unfortunately, the only options are to allow full access to all of the ports or to deny all access to a specific port or ports; it does not keep an access list of authorized addresses (see Figure 19.12). If you want to keep an access list, you need to do so in your router or in your firewall.

Fortunately, IIS does provide this feature. If you have a Web site for which you need to restrict access to certain IP addresses, you can do so with IIS. To enable this feature, you need to open Internet Service Manager.

To open Internet Service Manager, go to the Start menu Programs and select Microsoft Internet Server. Open Internet Service Manager.

Double-click the service you would like to configure to bring up the Properties dialog box.

FIG. 19.12

The TCP/IP Security
dialog box.

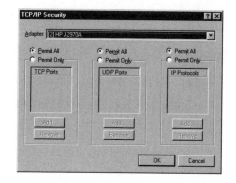

Click the Advanced tab. From here, you can decide how you would like to configure your access list. You have two choices. The first choice is Grant All Except Those Listed Below. This option allows all IP addresses to access your IIS server except for any IP addresses or block of IP addresses that you deny. The second option is to Deny All Except for Those Listed Below. This option denies all IP addresses except those IP addresses or blocks of IP addresses that you specifically allow in.

Administering Windows NT Server

When your system is set up and secured, you need to perform certain routine tasks to ensure optimal performance of your system. Microsoft provides several tools that help you administer your system.

Windows NT Backup

With Windows NT Backup, you can back up selected files or all files on your computer or any computer on the network. You can also back up the Registry on the local Windows NT computer. Backing up is important, because if a hard disk crashes for any reason or a user accidentally deletes a file, you need a way to recover quickly so that you can minimize any downtime. You may think of backing up your servers as being a long, tedious process and if you are using a fault-tolerance system such as RAID, you may ask why you need to bother.

You should back up the systems on your network for several reasons, the most important of which is security. If your servers are broken into and important information is deleted, you may be set back several weeks or months, or you may never be able to recover. If you have a store, and if someone breaks into your system and deletes all the orders, you may never be able to recover those orders unless you have a reliable backup system. If you are able to recover the orders, you will most likely only be able to recover these orders because angry customers are calling and e-mailing, asking you where their orders are. If your system was backed up recently, you minimize the risk of losing any data.

Part

V

Ch

19

If some sort of natural (or manmade) disaster strikes, you need a good backup system to be able to recover. To have a reliable backup system, you need to have more than one backup of your data. Many organizations make at least two backups of valuable information. One backup is readily available on-site, and another backup is stored off-site, possibly in a safe deposit box or in a remote office. This way, backups are available under almost any circumstances.

You, of course, need to back up your system so that in case of a hardware failure or a system crash that causes you to have to rebuild your entire system, you will have the necessary information. You can certainly reinstall all your software from the original media, but reconfiguring everything on your system could take days. If you have a complete backup of your system, you can rebuild your system in a matter of hours.

You also need good backups to protect yourself and your users from human error. You certainly will have cases in which someone deletes a file that he was not supposed to delete. This file could be an important data file. If you have a recent backup of this file, you can recover this file quickly and minimize any data loss as well as effort required to re-create that data.

Event Viewer

The Event Log or Event Viewer is one of the most useful tools for debugging problems. With the Event Log and Event Viewer, you can see any messages that any system drivers, applications, or services generate.

If you try to start Microsoft Commerce Server but it does not start, you can go to the Event Viewer and find out exactly why Commerce Server did not start. Also, Event Viewer has a security log. For security logging to work, you need to allow Security Logging in User Manager for Domains. When security logging is enabled, you can see any security issues that you chose to log.

Using Event Viewer is a fairly straightforward process. To get to Event Viewer, go to the Start menu, Programs, Administrative Tools, and choose Event Viewer. When you go into Event Viewer for the first time, you go into the system log. The system log gives you information about anything that is going on with the system (such as drivers that have loaded).

The security log gives you information about any security auditing that you have enabled. (Enabling auditing is explained in "Choosing a File System for Windows NT" in this chapter.) When you have auditing enabled, you can look at things such as who is deleting files from specific directories, who is trying to read or delete files to which they do not have access, and who is rebooting your machines and when. This capability is useful for catching a user who is abusing his privileges and for finding out whether someone is trying to break into your machine.

The last log is the application log, which gives you information on anything that you decided to log on your applications and messages that are automatically generated by your applications. You can choose, for example, to enable auditing in Microsoft Exchange Server, and every time you receive a mail message, the application log logs where the message is coming from and who is sending it. This log also gives you any error messages on your applications.

One last thing that you can do with the event log is filter events. This way, if you have a large event log and you are trying to go through a specific event, you can do so easily.

Remote Administration

With remote administration, you can work on your system remotely. This capability is useful if a system administrator needs to get into your system during off hours or in case of an emergency. You do remote administration by setting up trusts between NT Server domains. The requirements for being able to establish a trust relationship is that you must be running Windows NT Server as part of a domain. When you set up Windows NT, you can choose to set up Windows NT to run in a workgroup environment or a domain environment. In order to be part of a trust relationship, you must be part of a domain environment.

Another thing that you can do in a Windows NT environment is give people specific permissions to each machine. If you need to allow someone into a specific machine as administrator but do not want to give that person access to the entire domain, you give him an account on the machine to which you are giving him access. To access the machine, the user first needs to map a drive, which is the only way that he can log on to the machine. When the user maps a drive and logs in with his user name and password, he has full access to the machine. He can use Server Manager to stop and start services; he can use User Manager to create and modify accounts; he can use Performance Monitor to monitor performance on specific services or the entire machine; he can do just about anything except reboot the machine and install software.

In NT 4.0, remote administration is much easier than in previous releases. In previous releases, you needed to know the machine name and set up an `lmhosts` file. Now you only need to know the DNS name of the machine or the machine's IP address. When you map a drive, make sure that when you log on, you specify the machine name and your user name in the login. If you are going to map a drive on `machine1.c-systems.com` by using a DOS prompt, the command is

```
net use <drive letter> \\machine1.c-systems.com\c$ /user:machine1\marc
```

c$ is the administrative share for the C drive. At this point, you are prompted for a password or see an error message. When you type the correct password, you log on to the machine.

> **N O T E** If your user name and password are the same on the machine on which you are logged on and the machine to which you are logging on, Windows NT notices that fact and does not prompt you for a password again. ■

Another thing that you can set up between Windows NT Servers (if you are using Windows NT Server 4.0) is PPTP (Point to Point Tunneling Protocol). PPTP is a dedicated link between two Windows NT Servers. The significant feature in PPTP is the fact that it encrypts the data sent between NT Servers. This encryption helps ensure security for transferring files over the Internet or administering your server.

You can also dial into a Windows NT Network domain by using RAS. To use RAS, you need to grant dial-in permission to users whom you want to allow to dial in.

Part
V

Ch
19

Go to Administrative Tools and open Remote Access Administrator. Make sure that the service is running; then choose Permissions from the Users menu. Select the users to which you want to allow dial-in access. When you do this, your users can dial in to your RAS Server and access your network.

When your users log on, they do not necessarily have full access to all computers on the network, as though they are physically located on the network. The main difference is that Windows NT checks security information against the machine to which the users are logged into, not the fact that they have just connected to your network through RAS. Users need to share the drive to log on to the machine before they can access any files or resources on the machines. Instead of logging on with the machine name, users must log on with the domain name.

To log on to machine1 in the merchant domain, users need to use the following command:

```
net use <drive letter> \\machine1\home /user:merchant\marc
```

Users are prompted for a password and can then use files and resources on the machine.

Disk Administrator

Disk Administrator enables you to partition and format your hard disks. You choose which type of format to use, such as FAT or NTFS. To get to Disk Administrator, go to the Start menu, Programs, Administrative Tools, and choose Disk Administrator.

You can also set up fault tolerance from Disk Administrator. The types of fault tolerance that you can set up are RAID 0, RAID 1, and RAID 5. You want to use some type of fault-tolerance system on your Windows NT Server, whether it be hardware (which comes with the Hewlett Packard NetServer LH PRO) or a software RAID solution provided under Windows NT Server by means of Disk Administrator. As explained in the "Fault Tolerance" section in this chapter, if you can afford a hardware RAID solution, this method is a more reliable and resilient way of protecting your data; it is also much faster.

Check Disk

Check Disk is a tool that you can use to scan your disk for bad sectors, cross-linked files, or other file disk errors. Check Disk can also repair any errors that it finds automatically, if you choose to have it do so. You cannot run Check Disk immediately, because Check Disk needs full control of your system. To run Check Disk, from a DOS prompt, type chkdsk **<drive letter> </F>** (to fix errors on the disk); **</V>** (to display the full path of every file name on the disk); **</R>** (to locate bad sectors and recover readable information); **</L:size>** (NTFS only to change the log file size to the specified number of K or /L to display the current size). You can also run Check Disk in Windows NT Explorer and run it. You are prompted to either cancel Check Disk or run it the next time you reboot your machine.

To run Check Disk from Windows NT Explorer or Disk Administrator, click the drive that you want to check and display the Properties for that drive by right-clicking. Choose error checking. Click Automatically Fix File System Errors and Scan for and Attempt Recovery of Bad Sectors, if you want (highly recommended, because you are not in an interactive window when you reboot your machine and Check Disk is running).

defrag

With defrag, you can defragment your hard drive. defrag moves all the sectors of a file into contiguous space so that access to these files is faster. No defrag utility is installed with Windows NT Server; you need to install one yourself.

Server Manager

Server Manager enables you to administer your local Windows NT Server, as well as any Windows NT Server or Workstation that is on your network or in any trusted domain. With Server Manager, you can see which users are connected to your computer; look at which directories are shared and which of those directories are in use; see which resources (including directories and printers) are in use; manage replication; choose who will be notified of any administrative alerts; share or stop sharing directories; change permissions of shared directories; stop, start, or disable services; and add Windows NT Workstations or Servers to your domain.

To get to Server Manager, go to Administrative Tools and choose Server Manager. When you are in Server Manager, you should see all the computers in your domain (see Figure 19.13). Click the computer that you want to manage (see Figure 19.14). As you see in Figure 19.14, you have several options in the Computer menu.

FIG. 19.13

Looking for all the machines in the domain.

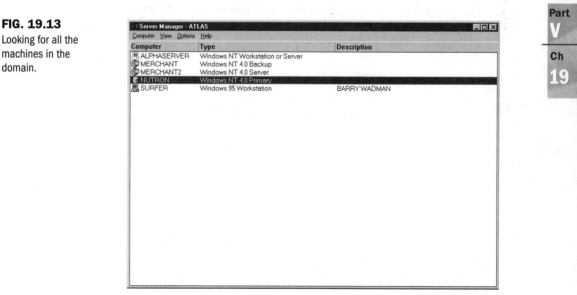

FIG. 19.14

Three options available under the Computer menu.

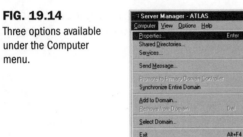

The first option is Properties (see Figure 19.15).

FIG. 19.15

The Properties dialog box.

With this function, you can see users who are connected to the computer, see directories that are shared (including hidden shares), see the files that are in use, manage replication, and see administrative alerts.

Figure 19.16 shows an example. In this case, MERCHANT and MERCHANT2 are connected to NUTRON. MERCHANT2 is using an IPC$, which is a named pipe, and C$, which is a hidden administrative share of the C drive on NUTRON.

FIG. 19.16

Seeing the users on NUTRON.

Shares shows all the directories on the machine that are shared, including hidden directories. As you see in Figure 19.17, you can see who is connected to a share, how long that user has been connected, and whether he is using the share. You can also disconnect the user or all users who are connected to the share.

FIG. 19.17

Determining the shares on a machine.

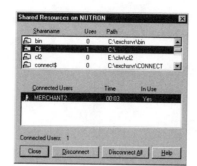

The next button in the Properties dialog box is the In Use button, which enables you to see any resources that are opened or in use on your machine. For an example, see Figure 19.18. In this example, the directory Microsoft Internet is in use and the file support.txt is open. If you see a resource that should not be open or if you need to close all resources, you can do so from the Open Resources dialog box.

FIG. 19.18

The Open Resources dialog box.

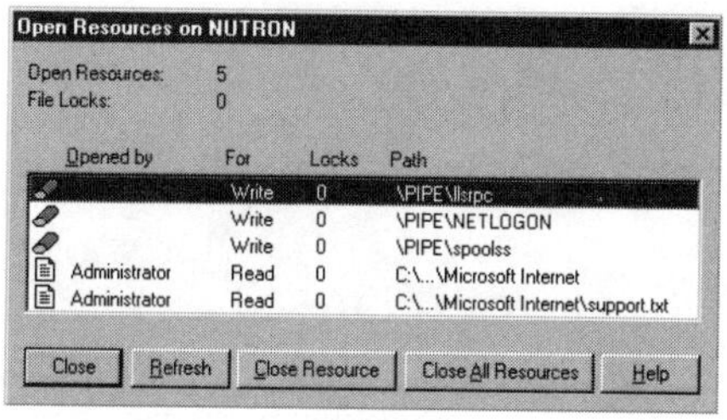

Replication allows you to manage the replication service (see Figure 19.19). With replication, you can copy files from any Windows NT Server to any other Windows NT Workstation or Server.

FIG. 19.19

The Directory Replication dialog box.

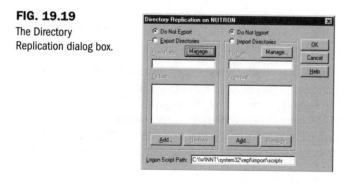

The last button is the Alerts button. When you click the Alerts button, it brings up the Alerts dialog box. In this dialog box, you can specify who any administrative alerts should go to (see Figure 19.20). You simply type the name in **New Computer or Username** and then click the

Add button. Then the user sees any alerts as long as the alerter service and the messenger service are running on the machine that the user is logged on to.

FIG. 19.20

The Alerts dialog box.

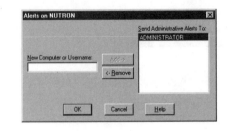

Also in the Computer menu is the Shared Directories command. When you choose Shared Directories, this brings up the Shared Directories dialog box. With this feature, you can manage any shared directories in any of your Windows NT Servers or Workstations. You can share any directory or stop sharing any directory, including hidden directories (see Figure 19.21).

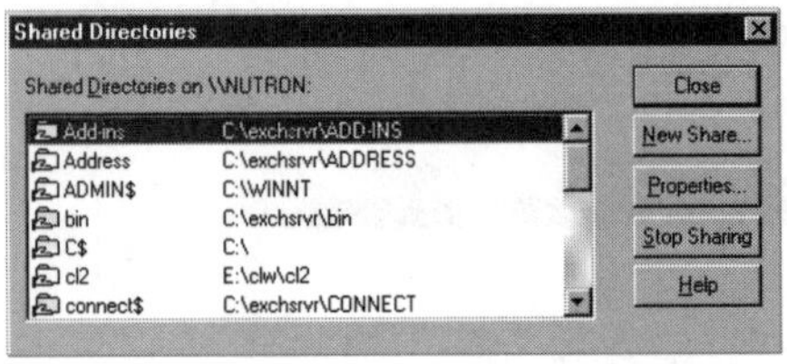

FIG. 19.21

The Shared Directories dialog box.

The Services item in the Computer menu enables you to manage any services on your Windows NT machines. Choosing Services from the Computer menu is the same as choosing Services from Control Panel. With Server Manager, however, you can go into Services for any Windows NT Server or Workstation on your network and stop, start, disable, or change any services that you need to.

Send Message allows you to send a message to any users who are connected to your machine. This feature is useful for sending important messages that you need to get to all users. When you use this feature, your message appears on-screen immediately.

Promote to Primary Domain Controller allows you to promote a Windows NT Server that is acting as a BDC to be a PDC. Being able to change the status of your domain controllers is useful if you need to take your PDC offline for any period. Although a BDC performs all the functions that a PDC does, a BDC does not store any changes to user profiles, user database information, or any other information that resides on the PDC. When your PDC comes back online, all that information is overwritten with the old information that was on the PDC before you took it offline.

Synchronize Entire Domain forces all your BDCs to go to the PDC and get any information that has changed, including all user information.

With Add to Domain, you can add Windows NT Servers and Workstations to your domain. If you are moving a Windows NT Server or Workstation from another domain to your domain, you need to add them with Server Manager so that they can participate in domain security and access resources on the network. Unlike Windows 95 and Windows 3.1, in which you need only a login name and password, your Windows NT Workstation or Server also must be added to the domain by means of Server Manager. If you are setting up a Windows NT Workstation or Server client from scratch, when you choose to add the computer to the domain, Windows NT asks you for the user name and password of an administrator. If you supply the correct information, the Windows NT Workstation or Server is added to the Windows NT Domain without you having to go into Server Manager.

Remove from Domain enables you to remove any Windows NT Server or Workstation from your domain. You may need to remove a machine from your domain if you are renaming the machine, moving it to another domain, or removing it from the domain.

Select Domain enables you to manage Windows NT computers in another domain in which you have administrator privileges.

Registry Editor

With Registry Editor, you can edit your local Registry, edit the Registry of any Windows NT Workstation or Server on your network or a trusted network, and import and export Registry keys and hives. Two versions of the Registry Editor come with Windows NT 4.0: `regedit` and `regedt32`. If you look at these two versions of the Registry Editors, you notice several differences. `regedt32` looks like the old Windows NT 3.51 Registry Editor and also resembles the Windows 3.1x Registry Editor. `regedit` looks like the new Windows 95 Registry Editor. At certain times, you prefer to use one version instead of the other. Unlike other programs, Microsoft decided not to include shortcuts for either of the Registry Editors when they designed all of the different versions of Windows (NT, 3.1x, and 95). They did this because this is a very powerful and dangerous tool. If a user decided to try out the Registry Editor and deleted or changed something, the user could put his computer in a very unstable state, so much so that it may not be able to be booted anymore. For this reason, you need to run the Registry Editor by either going to a DOS prompt and typing **regedit** or **regedt32**, or you can choose Run from the start menu and type **regedit** or **regedt32**.

regedit   You can use this version of the Registry Editor only to edit the Registry on your own machine or a Windows 95 machine; you cannot use it to edit the Registry of another Windows NT machine. `regedit` is easier to use than `regedt32`; it resembles the Windows Explorer and has a newer interface. `regedit` also has advanced searching capabilities that you cannot get in `regedt32`. With `regedit`, you can search all the Registry hives with one search command. You can also search for a specific key value, as well as for the key itself. In addition, you can export Registry text script files with this version of `regedit`, which you cannot do with `regedt32`.

regedt32   This version also has its disadvantages and advantages. `regedt32` is not as advanced for searching as `regedit` is. You also cannot export Registry trees as text file scripts; you can export them as text files, but you cannot reimport these scripts or import them to another Registry. What you can do is edit the Registry of remote computers. This feature is important, because when your network is set up, you most likely want to work from only one computer that you have set up for the way that you like to work and then administer all other computers from that computer.

Also, if you do any advanced Registry editing, you can edit certain values with `regedt32` that you cannot edit with `regedit`. One example is a binary value, or `REG_BINARY`. You may not edit this type of value, but if the need ever arises, you need to use `regedt32`.

`regedt32` has a bug. At times, you need to save information in the Registry of one computer and import it to another computer. To do so, you need to use `regedt32` and go to the tree that you want to export. If you want to move a Merchant 1.0 store onto another machine to convert it to 2.0, for example, you need to move the Registry over as well. To use Seidlers Jewelers as an example, go to `regedt32` and under `HKEY_LOCAL_MACHINE`, go to `\SOFTWARE\Microsoft\MerchantServer\Stores\sj`.

Next, choose Save Key from the Registry menu. The Registry on `MERCHANT2` is being edited on the computer called `NUTRON`. When you save the Registry key, save the key on the C drive of your local machine and call it `sj.reg`. Now go into Windows NT Explorer and look for the file `sj.reg` on `NUTRON`. As you notice, the file is not there. Go to your C drive on `MERCHANT2`. Notice that the file `sj.reg` is in your C drive. Saving a file as explained above is the only way to save a Registry key. If you try to map a drive to the C drive on `MERCHANT2` and save the key there, you get an error.

If you want to restore a key, you have to use a similar method. If you want to restore the `sj.reg` on a machine called `SERVER1` and are logged on to the machine locally, you need to map the C drive of `SERVER1` and place the `sj.reg file` there. You also need to place the `sj.reg` file on your local hard drive.

To restore the file, choose Restore from the Registry menu. Before you try to restore the Registry, make sure that you are in the key that you want to restore. In other words, if you are going to restore the Seidlers store, you need to be in `\SOFTWARE\Microsoft\MerchantServer\Stores` before you choose Restore. When you restore the file, you choose the file from your local hard drive; `regedt32`, however, reads the file from the machine that the Registry is on. This situation makes little sense and took me about a month of trial and error to figure out, but if you follow these instructions, editing the Registry on remote computers should work for you without a problem.

Repair Disk Utility

With the `rdisk` utility, you can create or update your emergency repair disk. With the emergency repair disk, you can recover from any problem that arises from a corrupted Registry, corrupted drivers, and several other problems that can prevent your Windows NT machine from booting up. To run `rdisk`, type **rdisk** at a DOS prompt or run the utility from the `run` command.

Performance Monitor

With Performance Monitor, you can keep track of where your resources are being used on your local computer or any other Windows NT computer in your network or a trusted network. Performance Monitor is useful if you notice that a particular machine is slowing down and you need to track down the problem. You can monitor more than 200 events: memory, CPU, hard drive, virtual memory, network connections, network throughput, services that you are running in Windows NT Server, and so on. Performance Monitor can be found by going to the Start menu, choosing Programs, Administrative Tools, Performance Monitor.

Windows NT Diagnostics

This tool enables you to view the hardware configuration on your machine and to see which drivers and services are running. By clicking the Services tab, you can see which services or devices are running or stopped. If you double-click a service or device, you see detailed information on that service or device.

The Resources tab enables you to see the hardware configuration of your machine. You can see the IRQs, the I/O ports, the DMAs, the memory addresses that your hardware devices are taking up, and the device drivers that are installed on your machine.

The Environment tab enables you to view your local and system environment variables.

In the Network tab, the General button enables you to see your access level. Which workgroup or domains you are logged on to, which version of network software you are using, how many users are logged on, the user names that are logged on, the logon servers that users are using, and which domain users are logging on to. The Transport button enables you to see which network drivers are installed on your machine. The Settings button enables you to see the settings of your network protocols and transports. You can see things such as whether you are logging election packets, whether you are using raw data to transfer, and whether you are using encryption. The Statistics button enables you to see things such as how much data has been received and transmitted, how many errors occurred, how many packets have been timed out, what the average response time is, and how many jobs are queued.

The Version tab shows you which version and build of Windows NT you are running, your serial number, and to whom NT Server is registered to.

The System tab shows you the date of your BIOS, how many CPUs are installed, and the types of CPUs (Alpha, Intel, MIPS, PPC, and so on).

The Display tab shows you what type of display adapter you are using, the date on the video BIOS, the current settings of your adapter, the chip type, the DAC type, the manufacturer of the video card, and how much memory is on your video card.

The Drives tab shows you all the drives that are connected to your machine, either physically or through a network. You can view by type or by drive letter.

The Memory tab gives you statistics about the physical memory and virtual memory on your machine.

Network Client Administrator

With this tool, you can install Windows NT clients over the network, so that you do not have to use a CD-ROM or floppy disks. You can install Windows NT Server, Windows NT Workstation, Windows 3.1, Windows 95, or any other client software that supports network installations. You must have a separate client license for each client that you install, of course. To get to the Network Client Administrator, go to the Start menu, and choose Programs, Administrative Tools, Network Client Administrator.

System Policy Editor

The System Policy Editor enables you to configure security policies on your machine. To get to the System Policy Editor, choose Administrative Tools from the Start menu and then choose Programs, System Policy Editor. To view or change policies on your local machine, choose Open Registry from the File menu. You see Local Computer and Local User (see Figure 19.22). Double-click Local Computer, and you see a list of things for which you can set policies. You see a similar list if you choose Local User. When you finish, save your changes.

FIG. 19.22
System Policy Editor.

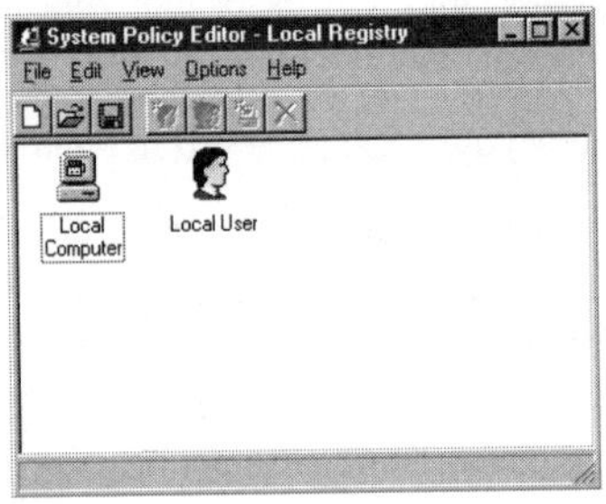

Administrative Wizards

With this tool, you can perform several administrative tasks. There are several wizards that can help simplify administration for someone who is fairly new to Windows NT (see Figure 19.23). You can add accounts, modify groups, accounts, set permissions on files or folders that are in an NTFS partition, add a printer (local or network), add or remove Windows NT programs or utilities, uninstall programs that you have previously installed (only 32-bit programs support uninstall), install a new modem, run Network Client Administrator, or run License Manager.

In this chapter, we have learned about the decisions that you need to make when you are going to be purchasing a machine to run Windows NT Server on, what considerations that you need to make before installing Windows NT Server, whether the machine should be a PDC, BDC, or a stand-alone server. We learned about the different types of file systems that can be used, FAT and NTFS, and the advantages and disadvantages of each. We also learned about administering your Windows NT Server and about remote administration, how to get around some bugs when trying to edit the Registry of a machine remotely and lastly the different types of network protocols Windows NT supports.

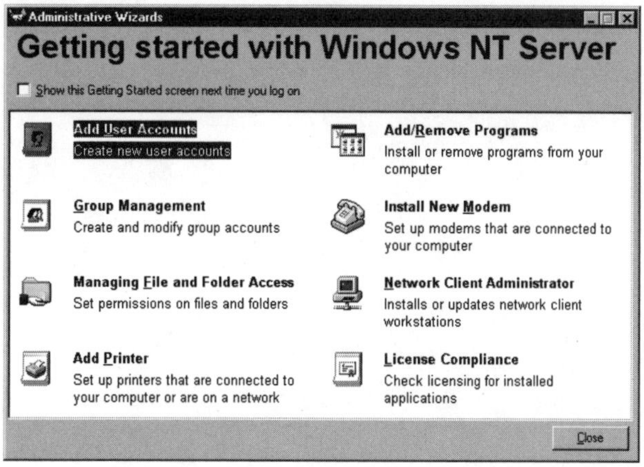

FIG. 19.23
The Administrative
Wizards.

From Here...

You should be able to configure your Windows NT Server and have it ready to install Microsoft Site Server, Microsoft SQL Server, and any other software that you need to install. At this point, you can go on to either Part III, "Understanding Dynamic Databases," or Part I, "Getting Started with Microsoft Site Server."

Part
V

Ch
19

CHAPTER 20

Understanding DNS

DNS (Domain Name Service) is used to map IP addresses to host names. Without DNS, you would have to memorize the IP address of every server on the Internet that you want to visit. This requirement would make going to your favorite Web site tedious, because you would have to use numbers up to 12 digits rather than URLs that contain words, which are much easier to deal with. DNS is a useful tool for navigating on the Internet, and it has evolved greatly over the years. ■

How to incorporate your viewing preferences into Excel's display settings

Windows 95 supports most five disk compression schemes, Double-Space, DriveSpace, Stacker, SuperStor, and AddStor.

How to hide unwanted information in worksheets

Look here to find out how best to use customized worksheets.

Reviewing the History of the DNS

In the original state of the DNS, system administrators needed to keep large files with the DNS names of every machine on the Internet that they wanted to access. With the Internet growing at the tremendous rate that it has over the past several years, these files started to get very large. If System Administrators needed to keep a file with all of the domain names and host names of each and every computer on the Internet, this file would be several gigabytes. Also, since there are so many changes to DNS records every day, this several gigabyte file would need to be updated on a daily basis. Everyone would need computers with large hard drives dedicated to simply doing DNS, when in a small operation you would not necessarily need that much equipment for DNS. You would need DNS in big or small company. Also, if someone made a change to a host or other record, there would be no telling how long it would take for those changes to propagate to the rest of the Internet if the System Administrator did not update this file on a regular basis.

Because of the increased difficulty in maintaining such files, the entire system for doing DNS needed to be changed. Now, all system administrators are responsible for keeping records of their own domain names and IP addresses. System administrators keep these records on a minimum of two machines so that if one machine goes down, the information is always available.

Whenever a user on the Internet tries to reach any of these machines, a DNS lookup is performed, and eventually, that machine is queried for the information. For a simple lookup to be performed, several things need to happen.

The first thing that happens is that the local DNS server is queried and asked whether it knows this host; if so, the information is returned immediately by the local DNS server. If the local DNS server does not know about this host, it must find the information and return it to the user in a reasonable period of time (usually, fewer than 2 seconds). The server does this by asking other DNS servers on the Internet if they know about this host. The servers that it will ask are called root servers. Every DNS server has a list of root servers. A *root server* is a strategically placed machine that knows something about every (or almost every) domain name that is currently registered. For almost every domain name, this type of server has the IP address of the name servers that are responsible for that domain name or IP address. When the local DNS server goes to the root server and asks whether it knows about that domain name, the root server most likely returns the IP address of an authoritative name server. The local DNS server then goes to that name server and asks it for the information. At this point, that name server should be capable of returning the requested information.

If you try to visit **http://www.seidlers.com**, for example, you query your local name server. Chances are that your local name server does not have this information, so your local name server goes to the root server. (An example of a root server is rs.internic.net.) The root server tells your local DNS server to check either commerce.c-systems.com or merchant2. c-systems.com for the information. Your local server then goes to either of these machines and asks for the information. These machines at this point return the IP address 205.181.30.50.

ON THE WEB

If you want a complete list of root servers, you can find it at **ftp://rs.internic.net/domain/named.root**. This file is kept in every DNS server and is updated periodically, so you should check it every three to six months for changes in root servers.

Several types of DNS servers exist. Up until Microsoft Windows NT Server 4.0, the most popular DNS server was BIND, which is always available at `ftp://ftp.isc.org/isc/bind/src/4.9.5`. A UNIX version is available, as well as a Windows NT version. This version of DNS is stable, but unfortunately, it requires maintenance of DNS through simple text files. No error checking occurs while you work, so if you make a mistake, you do not know until you try to start your DNS server and it does not start for you.

Also, if you make certain errors with BIND 4.9.x, the DNS server starts without a problem but does not load your zone. If you have several domain names on a server and you make a mistake with `seidlers.com`, for example, your DNS server starts and all your domain names are loaded *except* `seidlers.com`. Unfortunately, you do not notice this unless you happen to check your logs as you start your DNS server, or unless someone else tries to access `seidlers.com` and cannot because the zone is not available. For example, if you were to have a record that looked like:

```
seidlers.com.      IN      MX      mail.c-systems.com.
```

Notice that there is no number before mail.c-systems.com. This error would cause the zone for seidlers.com not to load but all other domain names and IP addresses in your DNS server would continue to load without a problem.

With Microsoft Windows NT 4.0, Microsoft included a new service called Microsoft DNS Server. This new DNS server is a GUI-based DNS server that allows a person who does not know a great deal about DNS to run a DNS server. The service also allows an experienced system administrator to run a DNS server by using text files that he is used to or to use the graphical interface so that he can minimize any chance of making a mistake.

Installing Microsoft DNS Server

Before installing the Microsoft DNS Server, you need to make sure that you have TCP/IP installed. When you installed Microsoft Windows NT Server, TCP/IP should have been installed by default. The first thing that you need to do is install the Microsoft DNS Server. To install Microsoft DNS Server, follow these steps:

1. Open Control Panel and double-click Network. You will see the network dialog box. Here you can change several things. You can change your network adapter card, networking protocols, networking services, your computer name, and the domain or workgroup name that you computer is part of.

2. Click the Services tab.

3. Choose Add.

4. Choose Microsoft DNS Server.

5. Click OK.

    You are prompted to insert your Windows NT Server CD-ROM or to specify the local or network path where your Windows NT installation files are located. After the files are copied, you see the service installed (see Figure 20.1).

FIG. 20.1

Microsoft DNS Server is installed.

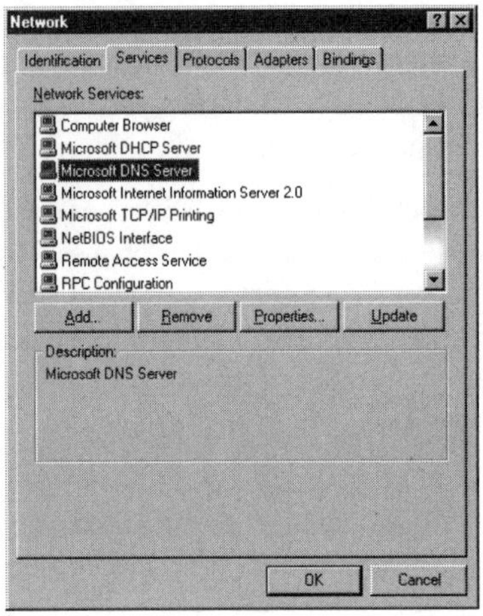

6. Click OK to close the Network dialog box.

At this point, you are going to be prompted to reboot your computer. If you are converting from Bind 4.9.x or another DNS server, you will not want the Microsoft DNS Server service to start when your computer is rebooted. To prevent the Microsoft DNS Server Service from starting, you need to answer "no" when you are asked to reboot your computer. Control Panel should still be open. Click the Services icon and scroll down to "Microsoft DNS Server" and choose the startup button on the right. Change the startup type from "Automatic" to "Manual" and click "OK." Now you can close services and at this time, you can reboot your computer.

When you have rebooted your computer, you will need to re-install any service packs and hotfixes that you have ever installed. At this time, Microsoft is recommending that all Windows NT users install Service Pack 3 and all of the hotfixes. Please see the Windows NT Chapter for information on the service packs and hotfixes and where to find these files. There is a very important hotfix that deals specifically with the Microsoft DNS Service. This file can be found at ftp://ftp.microsoft.com/bussys/winnt/winnt-public/fixes/usa/nt40/hotfixes-postSP3/dns-fix/. Although this file is found in the postSP3 directory, this file is not dependant on installing SP3, you can install this file regardless of what service packs you have installed on your system. This service pack is very important because it fixes several bugs that have been found since the first release of the Microsoft DNS Server.

If you are converting from a UNIX or another DNS server, refer to the following sections. If you are setting up a new DNS server, you can skip the next section and go to "Installing a New DNS Server."

Converting from UNIX

After your computer reboots, you may need to set up a few things. If you are migrating an existing DNS server to your Windows NT server, you need to copy your files from your DNS server to your Windows NT machine and have Microsoft DNS Server point to these new files.

If you are coming from a UNIX environment, you're used to having an `/etc/named.boot` file with all the information on any zones, domain names, Class Cs, and so on for which you are doing DNS. In Windows NT, you can use the `named.boot` file to start the migration process, but after the first time you start the Microsoft DNS Server, all the information is written to the Registry, and you no longer use a `named.boot` file. If you should, however, decide that you would like to continue using a named.boot file, you can override this feature by editing the registry directly. Be very careful if you should decide to edit the registry directly because if you change the wrong key, you can cause your system to have unexpected results or possibly to no longer be able to boot into Microsoft Windows NT Server. The registry key is HKEY_LOCAL_MACHINE\SYSTEM\CurrentControlSet\Services\DNS. Change "start" from 2 to 3. This will force Microsoft DNS Server to use data files instead of the registry. Once you are ready to boot from the registry, you can change this key back to "2" and stop and start the Microsoft DNS Server service, and your boot file will be imported to the Registry. In Microsoft DNS Server, however, all the files are kept in your `%SYSTEMROOT%\system32\dns` directory. The first thing that you need to do is make some changes in your named.boot file. Because all files must be in the `%SYSTEMROOT%\system32\dns` directory, the following command is not supported, so you need to comment this line out:

```
directory
```

If you have the following line

```
cache . named.root
```

or something similar, it is automatically saved when the boot file gets converted to the Registry. Any forwarders that you have also get saved into the Registry.

Next, you have to fix the directories for each domain name and Class C that are in your boot file. If you are using relative directories, you won't have to change them. That is, if your boot file looks like this,

```
primary childshope.org     childshope/hosts
```

it is recognized, and you simply have to create the `c-systems` directory and add the `hosts` file to this directory. Please notice that you need to change all your forward slashes (/) to backslashes (\).

Part

V

Ch

20

If your entry looks like this,

```
secondary childshope.org 205.181.30.20 childshope/hosts
```

you need to add the c-systems directory. The hosts file is added automatically when the DNS service starts and the zone transfer occurs.

When your named.boot file is all set up and formatted to be used with Windows NT Server, you need to make all your directories, if you have any, and copy all your domain, Class-C, and other related files to their respective directories. Once this has been done, there is one final step that you must take. Microsoft DNS Server will not recognize a file called "named.boot." You need to rename your "named.boot" file to simply "boot."

Now you should be ready to start the Microsoft DNS service. Follow these steps:

1. Open Control Panel and choose Services. You will see the services box appear.

2. Scroll down to Microsoft DNS Server and start the service.

   If everything is correct, the service starts without a problem. If a problem exists, the service does not start, and you need to run the Event Viewer to see where the problem is. Look in the system log for any entries that have DNS as the source. If you have a great deal of information in your system log, you can filter your events so that you see only DNS events. To do so, choose Filter Events from the View menu (see Figure 20.2).

FIG. 20.2

Filtering events.

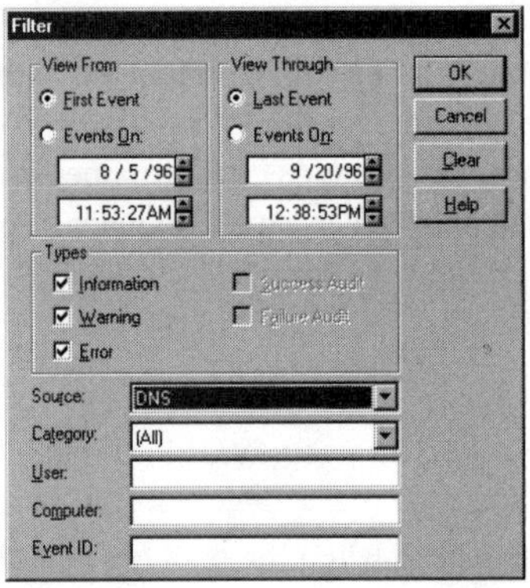

From the Filter Events dialog box, choose DNS from the Source drop-down menu. Now you will only see events pertaining to the DNS Server, and you can find out where the error is and fix it. ("Adding Zones to Your DNS Server," later in this chapter discusses some error messages that you may get.)

N O T E You need to be aware of one important thing. In UNIX, if you have a broken record in a zone, that zone is not loaded. In Microsoft DNS Server, however, if you have a zone that contains an illegal record, the service fails to start until you fix the zone. Microsoft includes this excellent feature in this version of the Microsoft DNS Server. In other versions of BIND (Berkeley Internet Name Daemon), if a zone is incorrect, you do not see it unless you are specifically looking at your log files or if someone is unable to reach you. In the Microsoft DNS Server, you know immediately if something is wrong and can fix the problem before it causes any damage.

When the Microsoft DNS Server starts and all the information from the boot file is read into the Registry, you no longer use the boot file. Instead, you use the graphical DNS Manager (see Figure 20.3). The first thing that you need to do is add your machine to the list of servers that you can manage.

FIG. 20.3

The Domain Name Service Manager.

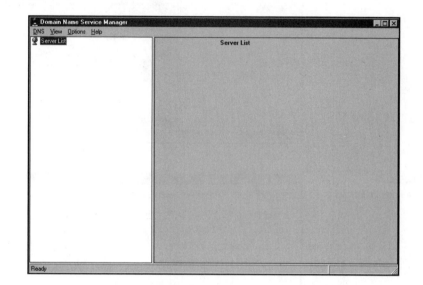

3. From the DNS menu, choose New Server. You will be prompted to enter the name or IP address of the DNS server that you wish to manage.

4. Enter the name or IP address of your DNS server in the dialog box and click "OK."

When you connect to the server, it appears in your server list with all the zones for which the server is doing DNS. The server also gives you a list of statistics for the DNS Server. If you double-click the server, it gives you the cache and a list of zones that are on that server (see Figure 20.4).

5. Now you will see a tree with your server name and one item called cache. Verify that your cache files are correct by double-clicking cache, or click cache and then press F5 to refresh.

Your screen should look similar to Figure 20.5.

This figure shows a list of all the root servers that your DNS server looks to if it is not doing DNS for the zone. The cache also keeps information for sites that you have recently visited so that a lookup does not have to be done every time you visit a site.

When you complete all these steps, you have successfully converted your DNS server from a UNIX server to a Windows NT server.

Part
V

Ch
20

FIG. 20.4
Server statistics generated by the Domain Name Service Manager.

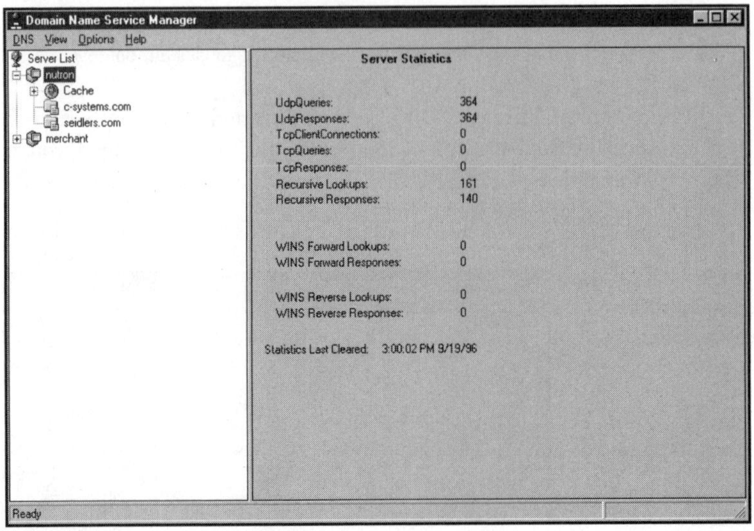

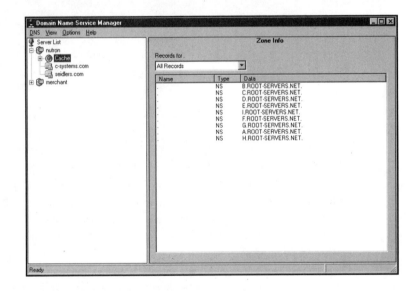

FIG. 20.5
Zone information.

Installing a New DNS Server

If you are going to be setting up a new DNS server, follow these steps after your computer has been rebooted:

1. Open Control Panel and choose Services. The services dialog box will open up.

2. Scroll down to the Microsoft DNS Server service and verify that the service has been started. It should have been started automatically when your computer was rebooted.

Because you do not yet have any zones, the service should have started for you without a problem. Now that the service has been started, you can begin to configue your DNS server.

3. Open up the DNS Manager. You can find DNS Manager by going to the start menu, choosing Programs, Administrative Tools, and choosing DNS Manager.

   You should see DNS Manager without any servers (refer to Figure 20.3). At this time, you can add your machine as a server.

4. From the DNS menu, choose New Server. You will see a dialog box asking you for the name or IP address of the DNS Server that you would like to administer.

5. Add the name or IP address of your machine in the dialog box.

TIP If you are administering a remote DNS server, you also have the option of entering the full DNS name of the machine. If I am at home and want to administer the DNS server for c-systems.com, I enter **nutron.c-systems.com** for my DNS server instead of simply **nutron**.

Now your machine should appear in the list, and the only thing that you should see is cache (see Figure 20.6).

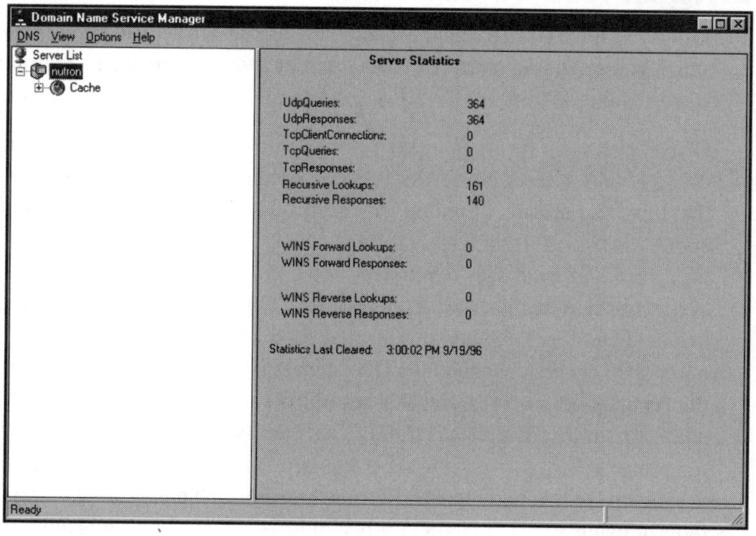

FIG. 20.6
Installing a new DNS.

6. Double-click cache.

   You should see a list of root servers. If you see something similar to Figure 20.7, your DNS server has been successfully installed as a cache-only DNS server.

Part
V

Ch
20

FIG. 20.7
Root-servers listing.

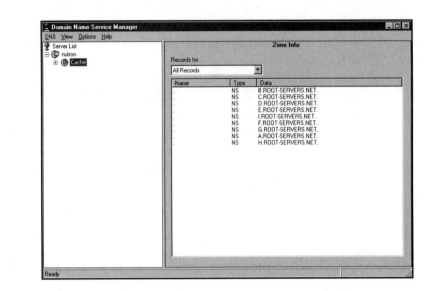

Adding Zones to Your DNS Server

When you have DNS Manager installed, you may want to add a domain name or a Class C for which you are doing name service. You may also want to cache a domain name or Class C that you are doing secondary DNS for or a domain name that several of your users visit often.

DNS Servers can be classified as primary and secondary DNS Servers for zones that they hold information for. If a DNS server is considered the primary DNS server for a zone, this means that this DNS server is holding the master database for this zone. Anytime information is given about this zone, this information must come from this machine. This does not mean that everytime someone tries to resolve your domain name or IP addresses that it will always look to the machine that is classified as primary. What it means is that all machines which are classified as secondary DNS servers for that particular zone will read the information from the primary DNS server. A secondary DNS server is a server that has the same exact information as the primary DNS server, and this server can also answer any requests for a particular domain name. The only difference is that the secondary DNS server will retrieve the information from the primary DNS server whenever the information on the primary DNS server has changed. Setting up DNS in Microsoft DNS manager is much easier than doing it with previous DNS tools or using BIND in UNIX. With Windows NT, everything is done through a graphical DNS manager, which does not allow you to make any mistakes that prevent your zone from loading. Some of the most common mistakes in doing DNS on UNIX machines are:

- Forgetting to put a number in an MX record, as follows:

```
IN        MX      childshope.org.
```

The correct way is:

```
IN        MX      1 childshope.org.
```

- Forgetting to put a period at the end of a record. Although this mistake does not prevent the zone from loading, it causes major problems in name resolution.

- Mixing up different types of records, as in this example:

```
IN        A     1 childshope.org. or
IN        MX    205.181.30.20
```

If you actually want to modify the DNS files directly, you can do so by going to %SYSTEMROOT%\system32\dns and modifying the files directly, just as you would for any other version of DNS or BIND. For these files to be read in correctly, you then need to stop the DNS server and restart it. Then the new files are read in. If any mistakes occur in the files, however, the DNS server no longer starts, and the event viewer gives you specific messages about what is wrong. It is strongly recommended that you don't modify any DNS files directly unless you are an experienced DNS administrator, as you can create many more problems than you bargain for. If you do make a mistake, you waste more time trying to correct these problems than you would if you had taken the extra time to use the GUI DNS Manager in the first place.

To actually set up the zone, you need to go into DNS Manager. Follow these steps:

1. Double-click Server List, if your server does not appear.

2. Double-click the server where you want to add the new zone so that the DNS tree is expanded and you can get a listing of all zones that are on this DNS server.

3. Either right-click the server to bring up a shortcut menu or click the DNS menu and then choose New Zone (see Figure 20.8).

FIG. 20.8
Choosing New Zone.

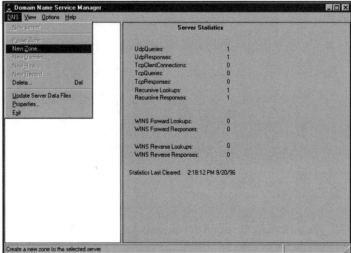

Setting Up a Secondary DNS Zone

When you set up a secondary DNS zone, you go into the DNS Wizard. Now is a good time to use a wizard. When you open the Wizard, it asks you several questions about how you want to create the zone. The easiest zone to create is a secondary one. After you create a secondary zone, nothing else needs to be configured, because the secondary zone is getting all its information from the primary domain server and storing it in your server.

In the following example, you set the DNS server to cache the information for `childshope.org`.

When you choose New Zone, you see the dialog box shown in Figure 20.9.

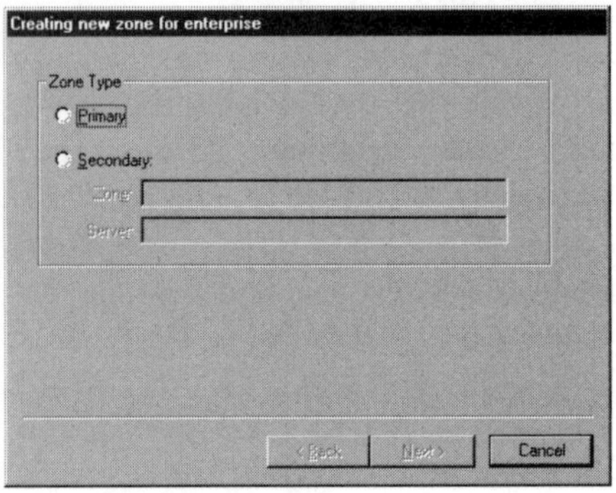

FIG. 20.9

Creating a new zone.

1. The zone type we are using is a secondary zone. From the dialog box, choose Secondary and type the name of the zone that you want to cache in the zone box and the name or IP address of the existing DNS server in the "Server" box (see Figure 20.10).

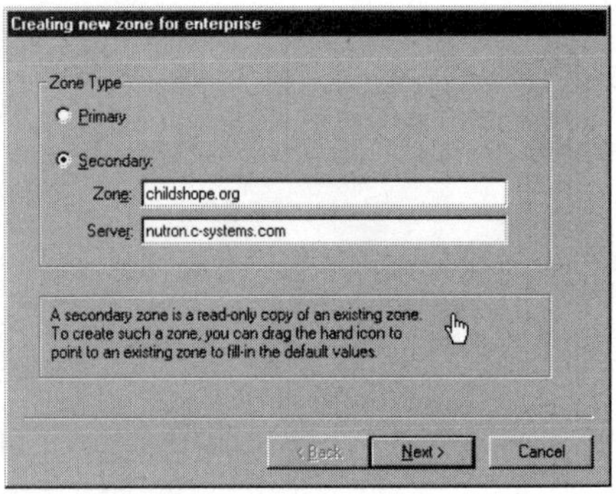

FIG. 20.10

Creating a new secondary zone for `c-systems.com`.

2. Click Next.

   You are asked to confirm the zone name and to choose a file to name the zone. You are given a default file name. If you want, you can change the file's name and even place it in a separate directory.

3. If you want to keep the default information, choose Next.

   If you would like to change the file name or the directory name, you can do so here. If the only change that you are making is to the file name, simply type in the new file name in the "zone file" section of the dialog box. If you wish to use a directory, you can type in the directory name and file name in the following format: directoryname\filename. If you type c-systems\hosts, for example, the file is put in %SYSTEMROOT%\system32\dns\ c-systems\hosts (see Figure 20.11).

FIG. 20.11

Zone and file name information.

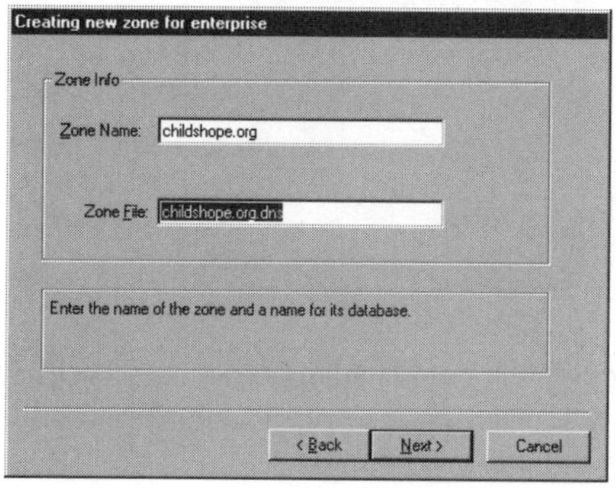

Now you need to have the IP address of the primary name server. If you don't know the address, you can open an MS-DOS window and use the nslookup utility. (This utility is explained in further detail in the nslookup section at the end of this chapter.)

4. From a DOS prompt, type **nslookup nutron.c-systems.com** (see Figure 20.12).

As you can see, the IP address is 205.181.30.20.

FIG. 20.12

Using nslookup to resolve an IP address.

5. Type the IP address in the IP Master(s) box.

6. Click the Add button.

If you want to cache from more than one DNS server, you can also add additional servers in this dialog box. After you enter the IP addresses of the name server(s) you will be using, click Next again.

Now that you have all the necessary information, you are prompted one last time to confirm that everything is correct and to set up the zone.

7. Click Finish.

The new zone is created (see Figure 20.13).

Part

V

Ch

20

FIG. 20.13
Click the Finish button
to create the new zone.

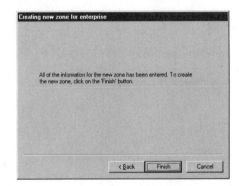

You should see your new zone now. Double-click it or press F5 to confirm that everything is set up properly. If everything is correct, you see all the information for the new zone, as shown in Figure 20.14.

FIG. 20.14
The new zone.

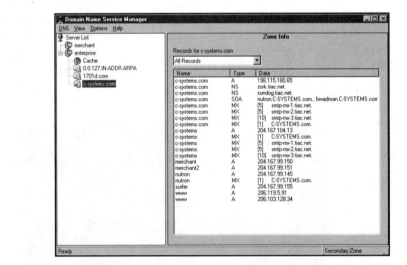

Now your zone is successfully set up. Because this zone is a secondary zone, your DNS server looks for updates on a regular basis; you shouldn't have to do anything else to this zone.

Setting Up a New Zone

Setting up a new zone is the most complicated thing that you can do with the DNS server. Before you set up a new zone, you have several things to decide and a great deal of planning to do. The first thing that you need to do is to set up a domain name.

Before you can set up a domain name, however, you must register it with the InterNIC (United States and Canada only). And before you request the domain name from InterNIC, you must decide which two or more machines are going to do name service for your domain name. This decision is important, because when you choose a DNS server, the name and IP address of that server is registered with the root servers. You can no longer simply change the name of your machine by changing the DNS of the machine; you must file changes with InterNIC and wait for your changes to propagate to the root servers. The process can take as little as three business days or as long as four weeks.

Applying for a Domain Name   After you choose your two or more DNS servers, you are ready to apply to InterNIC for the domain name. You can apply for the domain name in two ways. The easiest way is to use the online WWW registration form. To get to this form, go to **http://www.rs.internic.net**; click the Registration Services link; and fill out the WWW-based Registration Template.

If you don't have access to a graphical Web browser, if you simply prefer to fill out the form yourself and send it in, or if you have a large number of domain names that you need to register and want to read the form into a template, you can get the plain-text form from `ftp://rs.internic.net/templates/`; the form is called domain-template.txt. Because the forms are continually changing, checking this site often for new templates is a good idea. At the time this book was written, InterNIC was using form 3.0.

Filling out the form is a fairly straightforward process, but first you need to know a few things about the process.

Here is the form as you see it when you download it from the InterNIC:

```
[ URL ftp://rs.internic.net/templates/domain-template.txt ]          [ 8/96 ]

******** Please DO NOT REMOVE Version Number ************

Domain Version Number: 3.0

***** Please see attached detailed instructions ***********

NOTE REGARDING ITEM 2 - SEE RFC1591 FOR DETAILS
     .COM is for commercial, for-profit organizations.
     .NET is for network infrastructure machines and organizations.
     .EDU is for 4-year, degree granting colleges/universities (schools, librar-
➡ies, museums register under country domains)
     .GOV is for United States federal government agencies.
         (state and local governments register under country domains)
     .ORG is for miscellaneous, usually non-profit, organizations. (orgs/
➡individuals that do not clearly fit in any of the above)
```

Use the authorization section to indicate whether you want to register a new domain name, modify an existing domain name, or delete a domain name.

```
Authorization
0a. (N)ew (M)odify (D)elete....:
```

Auth Scheme is for modifying or deleting a domain name only. If you are modifying or deleting a domain name, you need to choose one of the three following authorization schemes:

Part

V

Ch

20

- MAIL-FROM—This scheme probably is the most common authorization scheme. When you use this scheme, the headers of your mail are checked to make sure that the changes are coming from an authorized contact. You can get information about an authorized contact by using a whois client. If you have access to a UNIX account, you can type **whois <domain name>**. You see an administrative contact and a technical contact. You can also get whois information by going to **http://www.rs.internic.net** and choosing the whois function. Every time a change is requested, the administrative and technical contacts receive e-mail asking them to confirm these changes. When these changes are confirmed by one of these contacts, the changes are made.

- CRYPT-PW—With this authorization scheme, you need to supply a password to make any changes in your domain name.

- PGP—With this method, you are given a PGP (Pretty Good Privacy) key. You fill out your form and encrypt it with the key that you are given. The InterNIC has the key to decode the message, and if the message decodes, your changes are made. If the message does not decode, it is unreadable, and your message is ignored.

```
0b. Auth Scheme...............:
```

Auth Info is only if you are using CRYPT-PW. You need to send your plain-text password in this field to make your changes. This will validate your identity.

```
0c. Auth Info.................:
```

The Purpose/Description field serves two purposes. If you are registering a new domain name, this field is required. You need to supply a one- or two-line description of your organization. Your description is not shown in any information that is made available to the public, such as a whois. InterNIC uses this field to make sure you are authorized to have the type of domain name that you are applying for.

```
1. Purpose/Description........:
```

InterNIC does not give domain names for personal use. The different types of domain names are as follows.

- .com. If you are applying for a .com domain name, you must be a business.

- .net. If you are applying for a .net domain name, you have to be a network infrastructure, such as an Internet Service Provider (ISP) or Internet backbone (MCI, BBN Planet, Digex, UUNET, and so on).

- .edu. The .edu domain name is for an educational institution, such as a college or university.

- .gov. The .gov domain name is for a branch of the federal government—the Department of the Treasury or the Department of Defense, for example.

- .mil. The .mil domain name is for a branch of the armed forces, such as the Coast Guard, Army, Navy, Marines, or Air Force.

- .org. The last type of domain name is .org, which is for not-for-profit organizations, such as charities, churches, and schools that do not qualify for an .edu domain name.

Enter the complete name of the domain (such as `c-systems.com`). Make sure that you include the suffix (`.com`, `.net`, and so on), and do not use any host names within the domain name. `www.c-systems.com`, for example, is not a valid domain name. `c-systems.com` is the domain name, and `www.c-systems.com` is a host name within the domain name.

```
2. Complete Domain Name.......:
```

"Organization Using Domain Name" asks for the organization information for the organization who is going to be using the domain name.

```
Organization Using Domain Name
3a. Organization Name..........:
3b. Street Address.............:
3c. City.......................:
3d. State......................:
3e. Postal Code................:
3f. Country Code...............:
```

These three sections (administrative, technical, and billing contact) are for contact information for your organization. The administrative contact is the person who is responsible for the domain—usually, the person who actually owns the domain name. The technical contact is the person who is responsible for administrating the domain name. If you register your domain name through an ISP, the ISP usually is the technical contact. The billing contact is the lucky person who gets the bill!

Although most of the information is self-explanatory, you need to be aware of a couple of items. The first item is the "NIC Handle." If you are registering a new domain name, you leave "NIC Handle" blank; InterNIC assigns a new NIC handle to you when your domain name is registered. If you already have a domain name, you also have a NIC handle. You can get this information by doing a `whois` on your own domain name. NIC handles are two to three letters followed by two to three numbers. MV486, for example, my NIC handle.

You need to decide which type of contact you should have. You can have either an individual contact or a role contact. You should ideally have at least one role contact, usually for the technical contact. That way, if something needs to be done to your domain name or if someone leaves the company, a fallback will always be used regarding the domain. A recommended e-mail address that people commonly use as their technical contact is `hostmaster@yourdomainname.com`.

```
Administrative Contact
4a. NIC Handle (if known)......:
4b. (I)ndividual (R)ole........:
4c. Name.......................:
4d. Organization Name..........:
4e. Street Address.............:
4f. City.......................:
4g. State......................:
4h. Postal Code................:
4i. Country Code...............:
4j. Phone Number...............:
4k. Fax Number.................:
4l. E-Mailbox..................:
```

```
Technical Contact
5a. NIC Handle (if known)......:
5b. (I)ndividual (R)ole........:
5c. Name.......................:
5d. Organization Name..........:
5e. Street Address.............:
5f. City.......................:
5g. State......................:
5h. Postal Code................:
5i. Country Code...............:
5j. Phone Number...............:
5k. Fax Number.................:
5l. E-Mailbox..................:

Billing Contact
6a. NIC Handle (if known)......:
6b. (I)ndividual (R)ole........:
6c. Name.......................:
6d. Organization Name..........:
6e. Street Address.............:
6f. City.......................:
6g. State......................:
6h. Postal Code................:
6i. Country Code...............:
6j. Phone Number...............:
6k. Fax Number.................:
6l. E-Mailbox..................:
```

Name Server is for information about your nameservers. You need one primary DNS server and at least one secondary server. If you want to have more than one secondary server, you simply need to copy the "Secondary Name Server(s)" information for as many secondary name servers as you would like to use.

```
Primary Name Server
7a. Primary Server Hostname....:
7b. Primary Server Netaddress..:

Secondary Name Server(s)
8a. Secondary Server Hostname..:
8b. Secondary Server Netaddress:
```

Invoice Delivery specifies how you want your bill to be delivered. You can either have a bill e-mailed to you every year or you can get a hard-copy bill mailed through the postal service each year.

```
Invoice Delivery
9. (E)mail (P)ostal...........:
```

```
An initial charge of $100.00 USD will be made to register the Domain name. This
charge covers any updates required during the first two (2) years. The Billing
Contact listed in Section 6 will be invoiced within ten (10) days of Domain name
registration. For detailed information on billing, see:
```

```
ftp://rs.internic.net/billing/billing-procedures.txt
http://rs.internic.net/guardian/
```

The party requesting registration of this name certifies that, to her/his knowledge, the use of this name does not violate trademark or other statutes.

Registering a Domain name does not confer any legal rights to that name and any
disputes between parties over the rights to use a particular name are to be
settled between the contending parties using normal legal methods. See RFC 1591
available at:

```
ftp://rs.internic.net/policy/rfc1591.txt
```

By applying for the Domain name and through the use or continued use of the
Domain name, the applicant agrees to be bound by the terms of NSI's then current
Domain name policy (the 'Policy Statement') which is available at:

```
ftp://rs.internic.net/policy/internic.domain.policy
```

(If this application is made through an agent, such as an Internet Service
Provider, that agent accepts the responsibility to notify the applicant of the
conditions on the registration of the Domain name and to provide the applicant a
copy of the current version of the Policy Statement, if so requested by the
applicant.) The applicant acknowledges and agrees that NSI may change the terms
and conditions of the Policy Statement from time to time as provided in the
Policy Statement.

The applicant agrees that if the use of the Domain name is challenged by any
third party, or if any dispute arises under this Registration Agreement, as
amended, the applicant will abide by the procedures specified in the Policy
Statement.

This Registration Agreement shall be governed in all respects by and construed in
accordance with the laws of the United States of America and of the State of
California, without respect to its conflict of law rules. This Registration
Agreement is the complete and exclusive agreement of the
applicant and NSI ("parties") regarding Domain names. It supersedes, and its
terms govern, all prior proposals, agreements, or other communications between
the parties. This Registration Agreement may only be amended as provided in the
Policy Statement.

Setting Up the Name Service   After you apply for your domain name, you need to set up a
name service for it. You need to decide on host names, IP addresses, Mail eXchanger records,
and so on. You do not have to decide everything at this time, however. If you register several
domain names for customers or for any other reason, you can generate a standard DNS file and
copy it for all your new domains until you decide how to set up all the individual data items.
This section explains how to set up a new domain from scratch by using the graphical user
interface in DNS Manager.

1. To set up a new domain from scratch, open DNS Manager and click the DNS server
   where you want to add a new zone.

2. Right-click the DNS server name to bring up a shortcut menu or click the DNS menu
   and choose New Zone to bring up the new zone dialog box (see Figure 20.15).

FIG. 20.15

Choose New Zone to set up a new zone under your domain.

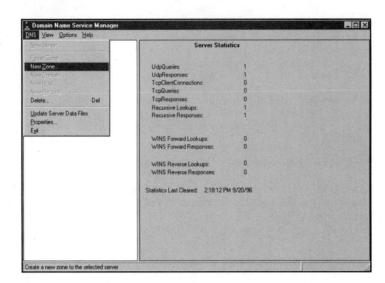

3. When the new zone dialog box comes up, choose Primary in the zone type section.

4. Click Next.

5. Enter the name of the zone and the name of the zone file in the zone info box. Click next to proceed (see Figure 20.16).

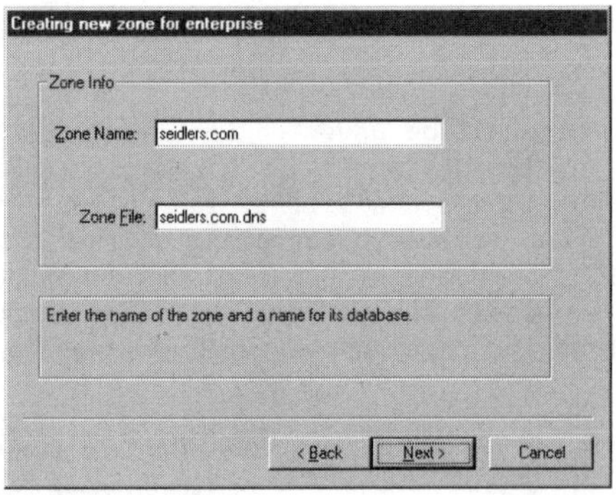

FIG. 20.16

Creating a new zone.

6. Click Finish.

   The new zone is established.

Adding Records to the New Zone   Next, you need to add records to your domain name (see Figure 20.17). You can add several types of records. This section covers the records that are the most important and the most commonly used.

Watch for Periods   One thing to which you need to pay close attention is the location of periods. Sometimes, you see a record such as enterprise.1701d.com. (notice the period at the end of the record). At other times, you see a record that does not have a period at the end—for example, `enterprise` (no period). You need to be careful where you do and do not put periods. If a period appears at the end of a line or a record, the line or record is read as is. If no period appears at the end of a line or a record, the domain name is appended to the end of the record. For example,

```
seidlers        IN       A        205.181.30.50
```

is expanded to read

```
seidlers.seidlers.com.       IN       A       205.181.30.50
```

because no period appears after `seidlers`.

If you have

```
seidlers.seidlers.com.       IN       A       205.181.30.50
```

it is used as is. If you have

```
seidlers.seidlers.com       IN       A       205.181.30.50
```

a problem exists. seidlers.seidlers.com is translated to

```
seidlers.seidlers.com.seidlers.com.       IN       A       205.181.30.50
```

which is not correct. For this reason, be careful how you do and do not use periods.

FIG. 20.17
Adding records to the new zone.

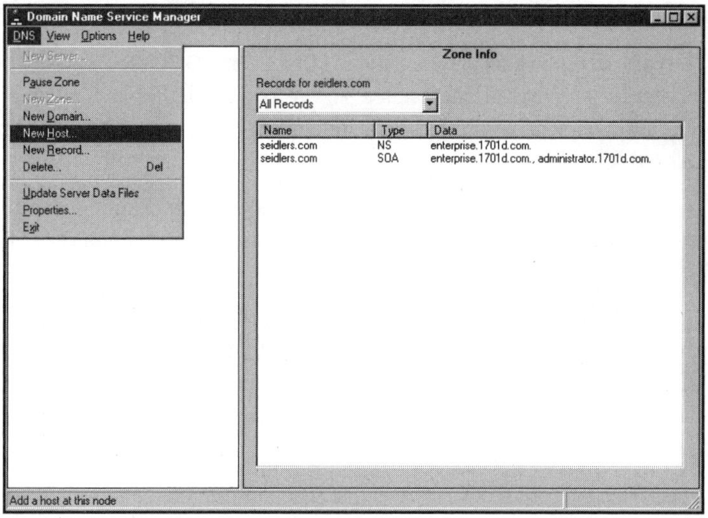

N O T E You can use the `nslookup` utility to check how your records actually look. `nslookup` is covered at the end of this chapter in the nslookup section. ▪

SOA Record   An SOA (Source of Authority) record looks something like this:

```
@                     IN     SOA      nutron.c-systems.com.      postmaster.c-
systems.com.   this all needs to be on one line (this line and the one before it)
  (
```

```
22              ; serial number
3600            ; refresh
300             ; retry
3600000         ; expire
3600          ) ; minimum TTL
```

To help you understand SOA records, look at each item in this example.

In the first line, `nutron.c-systems.com.` is the primary name server.

Also in the first line, `postmaster.c-systems.com.` is the e-mail address of the person who is responsible for the domain name. Notice that the line is `postmaster.c-systems.com.` and not `postmaster@c-systems.com`. The at symbol (@) is a reserved character in a DNS record, and although it may work, it is not recommended for the sake of compatibility.

The serial number in this case is `22`. The serial number is important; it tells the secondary name servers when an update occurs. Every time this number increases, the secondary name servers know that something has changed and that they need to update their information.

Be careful with your serial number. If your serial number is lower than any of your secondary name servers, your zone expires on that server. Then your secondary name server can no longer respond to queries about this domain name and people can no longer find you. As long as your serial number is the same on all your servers, and as long as all your secondary name servers can transfer information from your primary name server, your domain name does not expire.

The refresh time is `3600`, which means that every 3,600 seconds, all your secondary name servers look to your primary name server to see whether any information has changed. If so, your secondary name servers do a zone transfer from your primary name server to get the updated information.

The retry time is `300`. If your secondary name servers cannot get the information from your primary name server, they try to get the updated information every 300 seconds until they retrieve the information successfully.

The expire time is `3600000`. If your secondary name servers are unable to get information from your primary name server within a time frame of 3,600,000 seconds, they expire the zone. When a zone expires, a secondary name server is asked for information about this domain name. The servers say that it does not have this information; therefore, your site can longer be found.

A zone can expire for several reasons. Some of the most common reasons are the following:

- You lowered your serial number in your primary name server. If your serial number gets lowered in your primary name server, your secondary name servers assume that incorrect or out-of-date information appears somewhere. If your serial number is not increased, the information expires.

- Bad information appears in your DNS record. If any bad or malformed records appear in your DNS record, your zone does not transfer. If you do not correct this information within your expire time, your zone expires.

- Your primary DNS server is offline or not actually running a name server.
- You changed the IP address of your primary name server and did not change the address from which the secondary name server was getting its information.

NS Record   The NS (Name Server) record tells anyone who is looking up any records in your domain name where the authoritative name servers are. You always have at least two NS records for your domain name—one for each of the domain name servers, which you chose when you registered the domain name. You can have additional name servers to balance out the load without having to register them with InterNIC. One of the most common uses for NS records is to delegate a subdomain name.

A *subdomain name* is a host name within a domain name. nutron.c-systems.com, for example, is a subdomain name of c-systems.com. If you have an internetwork in which you want to delegate a subdomain name to a remote location, you can do so with an NS record. You delegate the zone to the new name server, and every time someone looks to a record within this subdomain name, your DNS server points that person to the new name server. You may have NS records that look like this:

```
childshope.org.           IN      NS      merchant.c-systems.com.
                          IN      NS      merchant2.c-systems.com.
boston.childshope.org.            IN      NS boston.childshope.org.
                                  IN      NS ns.childshope.org.
                                  IN      A 205.181.30.20
```

If you are using boston.seidlers.com as an NS record, you also have to assign boston.seidlers.com an A record; because you are pointing to it for a DNS server, you need an IP address to point to.

A Record   An A record associates one or several IP addresses with a host name, as in the following example:

```
www.seidlers.com.        IN        A        205.181.30.50
```

If you have a Web server that you need to balance through several machines, you should assign it several IP addresses. Some Web servers support redirecting, but to support redirecting, you are depending on one Web server to be up and running all the time. If you use DNS to balance the load among several machines and a machine goes down, you have at least one more machine to handle your incoming Web requests, and you do not have any loss of service. To assign several IP addresses to a single hostname, your records look like this:

```
www.clubwin.com.         IN        A        205.181.30.50
                         IN        A        205.181.30.60
```

Now whenever someone goes to www.clubwin.com, your DNS server alternates between the machines to which the name request goes. This arrangement is called *round-robin DNS*.

CNAME Record   A *Canonical NAME (CNAME) record* is a convenient record, if you have in several domains a record that is going to point to the same IP address. This type of record is also useful if you have a record that you need to point a name to and you know the record's IP address may change on a regular basis. This type of record is commonly used when several domain names all need to point to the same Web server. You also can use it when you have several different Web servers and typing the IP addresses of all the Web servers for each domain name is inconvenient. In addition, you use a CNAME record if you ever need to add or delete an IP address, which can be difficult to keep track of.

A CNAME takes only one line and points the same way that the master record is pointing. The following example shows how a CNAME line looks:

```
www.sbn3.com.        IN       CNAME         www.microsoft.com.
```

With other types of records, you can have as many different records per host name as you need. But with a CNAME, you cannot have any other type of record. You cannot add an A record or an MX record after you create a CNAME. Also, you cannot have a CNAME for the actual domain name. Because seidlers.com is the domain name, you cannot have any CNAME records for that host name. In other words, the following example would be illegal:

```
seidlers.com.        IN       CNAME         microsoft.com.
```

If your zone looks like the above example, your zone will fail to load and your secondaries will expire your information.

One more thing to remember about CNAMEs is they take an extra lookup. In the first CNAME example, a server not only has to look at the DNS server for microsoft.com to get the information, but also has to find the DNS server for c-systems.com and get the necessary information to find that host.

MX Record   The last type of record for a domain name that this chapter discusses is MX. An MX record is a Mail eXchange record; you use it to define where mail is to be sent. An MX record looks like the following example:

```
seidlers.com.        IN       MX        1 mail.c-systems.com.
                     IN       MX        5 mail2.c-systems.com.
```

This record is read in such a way that all mail going to seidlers.com tries to go to mail.c-systems.com first. If mail.c-systems.com is down, mail goes to mail2.c-systems.com and is spooled until mail.c-systems.com is up and capable of receiving mail again.

Use priorities to set where mail goes. You set priorities by using numbers before the host names. The smaller a number, the higher the priority. Priorities can go from 0 (highest) to 65,535 (lowest). The mail resides on the machine that has the highest priority or the lowest number. If you have a large number of users or if you want redundant mail servers, you want to set up load balancing between mail servers. All of your mail servers will of course have the exact same information on them. By using DNS, you can give more than one mail server the same priority. Giving more than one mail server the same priority distributes mail evenly to all the mail servers for your domain name. In the event that one of the mail servers is down, your DNS server immediately tries to send the mail to another mail server so that your mail is delivered instantly. An MX record looks something like the following example:

```
seidlers.com.        IN       MX        5 mail.c-systems.com.
                     IN       MX        5 mail2.c-systems.com.
                     IN       MX        5 mail3.c-systems.com.
```

You can have several more types of records when you create a domain name, but most of them do not make any difference on your DNS server; most of them are simply used for information purposes.

A Sample DNS Database File

Now that you have seen the records that you are most likely to use, you're ready to see how those records look in an actual host file. Normally, if you use Microsoft DNS Server, you do not have direct interface with the host file. If you are doing any type of troubleshooting, however, you need to know how to read this record to make sure that all the information is valid so that you don't take the chance of breaking your DNS server.

Following is a sample host file:

```
@           IN     SOA     seidlers.com.        postmaster.seidlers.com.        (
            25              ;serial number
            3600             ;refresh
            300              ;retry
            3600000         ;expire
            3600)            ;minimum TTL

            IN     NS       merchant.c-systems.com
            IN     NS       merchant2.c-systems.com.

seidlers.com.    IN     A        205.181.30.50
            IN     MX       1 mail.c-systems.com.
            IN     MX       5 mail2.c-systems.com.
www         IN     CNAME    seidlers.com.
```

This example shows how different types of records can be used together in a host file.

Adding Records to a Domain

Now that you are familiar with all the different types of records and how they interact, you can add records to the new domain that you set up earlier.

To begin, add all the applicable NS records to your domain name by following these steps:

1. Choose New Record from the DNS menu or right-click your domain name to bring down a shortcut menu. The "New Resource Record" dialog box will appear.

2. Choose NS Record from the Record Type box.

3. Type the host name of your name server.

4. Click OK.

   Your record is added.

Repeat this process until you have added all your desired name servers.

The next thing to do is add your host names. To do so, follow these steps:

1. Choose New Host from the DNS menu (see Figure 20.18). The "New Host" box will appear.

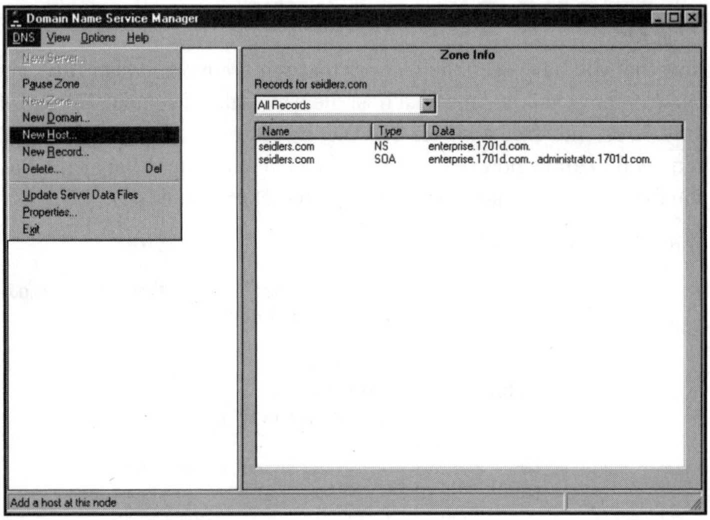

FIG. 20.18

Adding a new host name.

You see a box asking you for the host name and the host IP address. You cannot use this dialog box to assign an IP address to your domain name; you use the New Record command to do that.

2. Enter the host name in the "host name" box and the IP address in the "IP Address" box.

3. Click Done (see Figure 20.19).

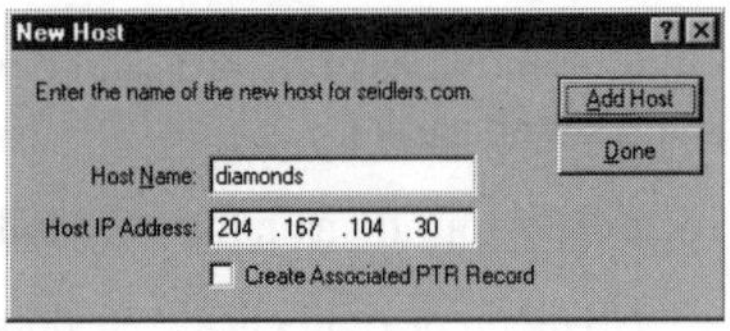

FIG. 20.19

The New Host dialog box.

You see the names that you have added and the IP addresses next to them (see Figure 20.20).

You should now add your MX records so that you can receive mail sent to one or several of your host names. Follow these steps:

1. Right-click the domain name and choose New Record from the shortcut menu to bring up the "New Resource Record" dialog box.

2. Choose MX Record from the "Record Type" box.

You see the New Resource Record dialog box (see Figure 20.21).

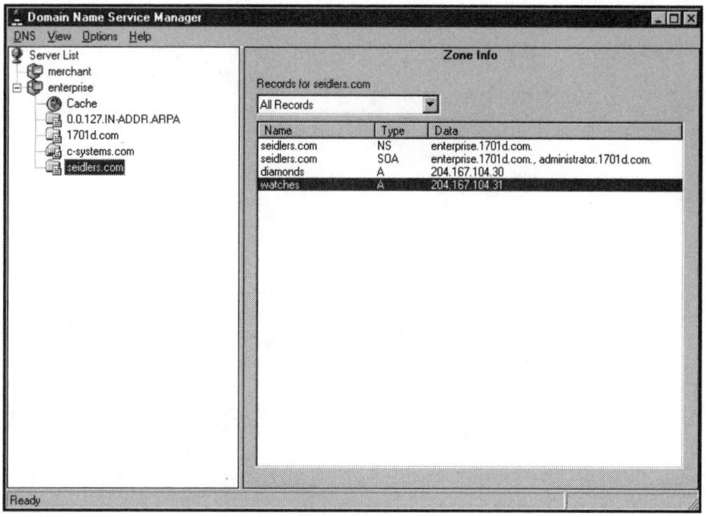

FIG. 20.20

The host names and IP addresses that you added.

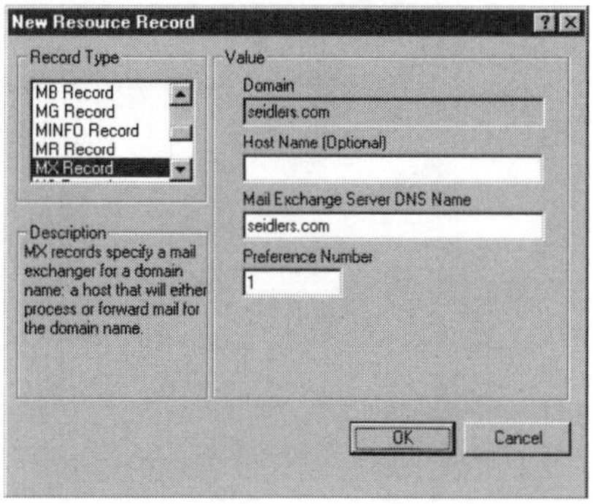

FIG. 20.21

The New Resource Record dialog box.

3. Type in the host name if you would like your mail to go to a specific host other than the actual domain name.

   If you do not type in a host name, the record is added to the actual domain name. In this example, the MX record is added for seidlers.com, because no host name exists.

4. Because you want all mail to reside on that server, give it a priority of 1. Type "1" in the Preference Number box.

5. Click OK when you have finished adding your new MX record.

In this next example, all mail going to watches.seidlers.com is set to reside on watches.seidlers.com (see Figure 20.22).

In Figure 20.23, you see all the records that you added: the A records for diamonds and watches, the MX records for diamonds and watches, and the CNAME record to have www.seidlers.com point to www.c-systems.com.

Part

V

Ch

20

FIG. 20.22

Setting the mail server.

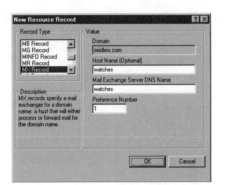

FIG. 20.23

All records for seidlers.com.

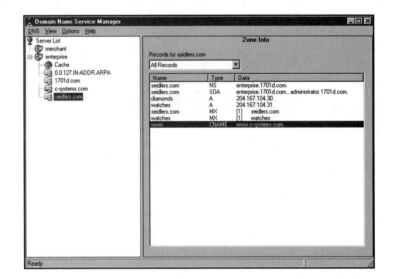

Understanding Zone Properties for a Domain

Now that you have the records that you want set up, go into seidlers.com and look at the properties for the zone (see Figure 20.24). The first thing that you see when you go into Properties is the General window, which shows you the zone file name and the zone type. If the DNS server that you are using is the primary DNS server for a zone, then the primary box will be checked in "Zone Type." If the DNS server that you are using is the secondary DNS server for the zone, secondary will be selected and there will be one or more IP addresses typed in under "IP Masters." The IP addresses that appear in "IP Masters" are the IP address(es) for other computers that have information for that zone, usually one of which is the primary DNS server.

Next is the SOA Record tab, which shows all the SOA information. You can also change this information (see Figure 20.25).

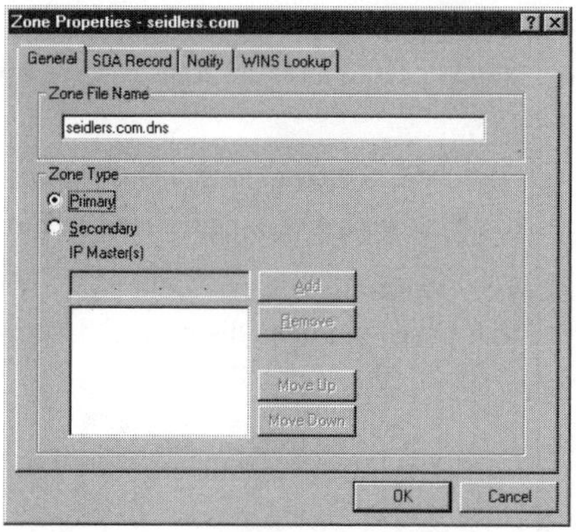

FIG. 20.24
Properties for
`seidlers.com`.

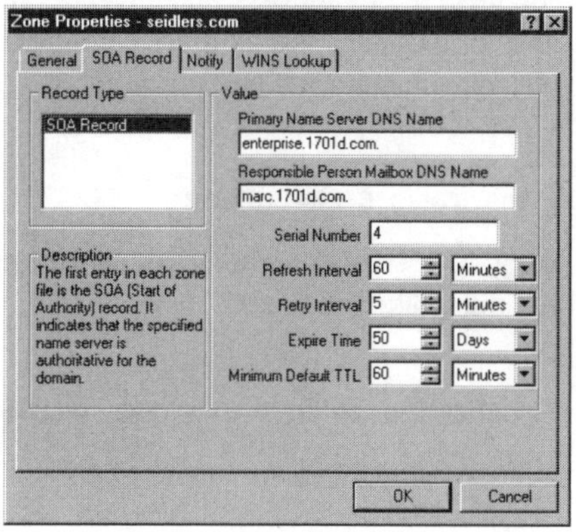

FIG. 20.25
The SOA Record tab for
`seidlers.com`.

The next tab is the Notify List tab. If the information in the tab refers to a primary name server, you have the option of having the server notify all the secondary name servers in your list if any information changes. This option forces the secondary name servers to update their information immediately, instead of waiting for the amount of time that you allotted in the refresh information that you set. If you are using WINS on your network, you can specify a WINS server by using the WINS lookup area.

Setting Up Name Service for Your Class C

If you have a Class C of addresses, you need to set up name service for them. Setting up resolution for a Class C is similar to setting up a domain name but different in several ways. A Class C is a block of 254 IP addresses that would be assigned to you by either an authority like Internic or your Internet Service Provider. Now if you are going to be receiving only a single class-C, this would be assigned to you by your ISP.

When you set up resolution for a Class C, you are setting up something called *reverse lookup*. When you set up a host name, you perform a two-step process. The first step is setting up a host name to resolve to an IP address. You can have as many host names resolve to the same IP address as needed. The next step is having an IP address resolve to a host name, which is the topic of this section.

The first thing that you need to know is the Class C or block of Class Cs for which you are going to set up a name service. You can also set up a name service for a Class A or a Class B.

You use three types of records when you set up reverse lookup for a Class C. These records are SOA, NS, and a type of record that hasn't yet been discussed: the PTR (IP address to name pointer) record.

The SOA and NS records are exactly the same as they are for a domain name. The PTR record is in the following format:

```
9    IN    PTR    enterprise.1701D.com.
```

In this case, 9 is the last set of digits of the IP address, and enterprise.1701D.com. is the actual host name. Setting up DNS for a Class C is a bit more complicated. You cannot just simply name the Class C. A Class C looks like this in a DNS server:

```
104.167.204.IN-ADDR.ARPA
```

```
104.167.204.IN-ADDR.ARPAis the Class C 204.167.104.
```

To find out the Class C of an entry, reverse the numbers. To turn a Class C into an entry that you can put in a DNS server, you must take the Class C, reverse all of the fields, and add IN-ADDR.ARPA to the end of it.

Another example is the Class C 199.8.170. To do reverse-resolve DNS for this Class C, you need to add the following new zone:

```
170.8.199.IN-ADDR.ARPA
```

To add this zone, perform the following steps.

1. Open DNS Manager.
2. Create a new zone by right-clicking your DNS server entry and choosing "New Zone" from the shortcut menu.
3. The "Creat New Zone" dialog box will appear. Choose Primary from "Zone Type."
4. Click Next.
5. In the "Zone Info" box, enter **170.8.199.IN-ADDR.ARPA** as your zone name.

   The default file name will be **170.8.199.IN-ADDR.ARPA.dns**. I have always preferred using the actual name of the class-C for the file name plus a .rev as the file extension. I recommend changing the file name to 199.8.170.rev.
6. Change the file name to **199.8.170.rev**.
7. Click Finish.

   You see your new zone (see Figure 20.26).

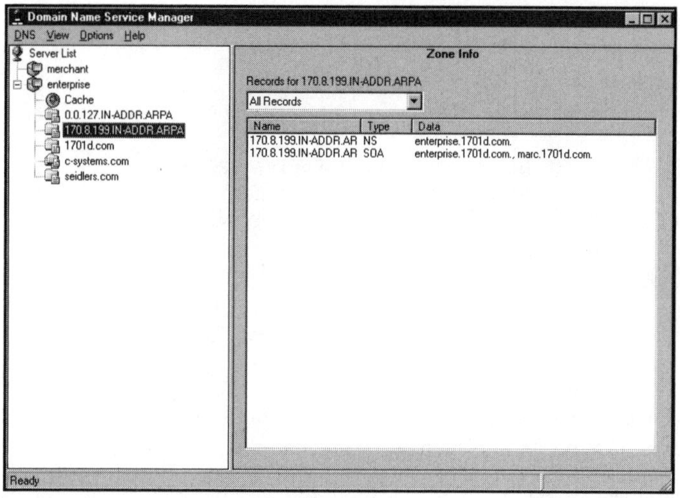

FIG. 20.26

The new zone.

The next thing that you need to do is add all the name servers that will be carrying DNS for this Class C. If you received this Class C from an ISP, be sure to put their name servers in your NS records as well as your own, because all the root servers will be looking to your ISP first for the information.

When all your name servers are added, you can add the PTR records. Go to your zone, right click and choose New Record from the shortcut menu. In the New Resource Record dialog box, you notice fewer choices than you had for a domain name (see Figure 20.27).

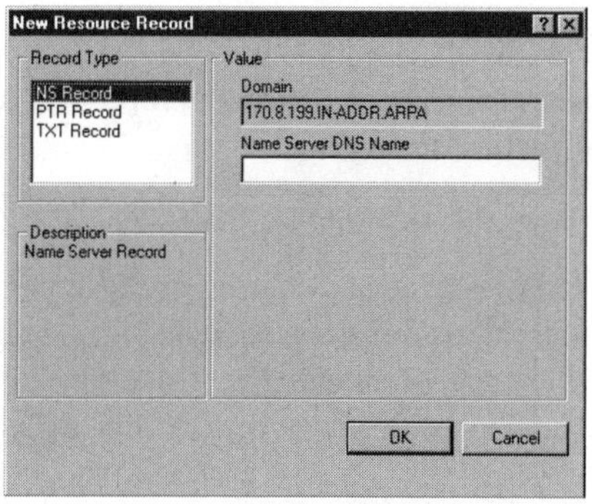

FIG. 20.27

New Record Resource dialog box for PTR records.

Add your host names by using the New Resource Record as described in the previous section until they are all added. Enter the IP address and the host name; then click OK. When your hosts are added, you are ready to go.

Following is a sample host reverse-resolve file:

```
@              IN    SOA    enterprise.1701d.com.          marc.1701d.com.
(
```

Part

V

Ch

20

```
          2              ;serial number
          3600             ;refresh
          600            ;retry
          86400            ;expire
          3600           );minimum TTL

          IN     NS      enterprise.1701d.com.
          IN     NS      ns.1701d.com.

;
;   Zone records
;

1             IN     PTR     router.1701d.com.
2             IN     PTR     ns.1701d.com.
```

As you can see, this file is not complicated, but remember one thing: Use your periods where they need to be, or you will have problems.

If you have `router.1701d.com` without the period, for example, it turns into the following:

`router.1701d.com.170.8.199.IN-ADDR.ARPA.`

As you can see, putting your periods where they belong is very important.

You will notice that all the way to the right in the above example, the 1 at the beginning of this record does not have a period after it. This is because without the period, it turns into `1.170.8.199.IN-ADDR.ARPA`, which is the actual IP address of `router.1701d.com`.

Changing a Zone from Secondary to Primary

Changing a secondary zone to a primary zone is a fairly straightforward process.

Right-click the zone that you want to change and choose "properties" from the shortcut menu. This will bring up the "Zone Properties" dialog box.

In the "zone type" box, change from secondary to primary, and click OK.

Refresh the zone by right-clicking your zone and choosing refresh from the shortcut menu. You should not see anything different in your zone info box on the right side of the DNS manager. In order to verify that your changes were effective, make sure that you restart your DNS server. It is much better to find out any problems now while you are working on it rather than later.

To stop and start the Microsoft DNS Server service, go to a command prompt and type **net stop dns**. Alternatively, stop the Microsoft DNS Server service in Control Panel Services; then restart it by typing **net start dns** or restarting it in the services box.

If your DNS service does not restart, you need to go to the Registry and make sure that everything changed over properly from secondary to primary. Open Regedit and go to `HKEY_LOCAL_MACHINE\SYSTEM\CurrentControlSet\Services\DNS\Zones\<zonename>`.

You should see the following keys:

- DatabaseFile—This key is the file name that you are using for your zone file.

- MasterServers—This key is the IP addresses of your master servers (you see it only for a secondary zone). Do not modify this field directly, because the IP addresses are converted to hexadecimal.

- Type—Type is interpreted as follows: 0 is for the cache, 1 is for a primary DNS server, and 2 is for a secondary DNS server. There was a bug in the Microsoft DNS Server that if you changed from primary to secondary or vice-versa, this registry key would not change. Microsoft has recently released a fix for this problem and several other problems that have been found with the Microsoft DNS Server. You can find this fix by going to **ftp://ftp.microsoft.com/bussys/winnt/winnt-public/fixes/usa/nt40/hotfixes-postSP3/dns-fix/**. Although this is a hotfix for Service Pack 3, you do not need to have Service Pack 3 installed to use this updated version of the Microsoft DNS Server, this will work with any service pack. If you ever did decide to install a service pack on your machine (Service Pack 3 or earlier) you would need to re-install this hotfix or your DNS server would be overwritten. When Service Pack 4 comes out, since it is a later service pack, this hotfix will of course be included.

- UseDatabase—This field should always be 0.

Using *nslookup*

This utility is useful for debugging problems with your DNS server. To use the utility, you simply type **nslookup** and press Enter. You are prompted with the default server and a > prompt.

You need to be familiar with several commands. The first command that you need to use is the server command. With this command, you can choose any DNS server to look at. When you are in an nslookup window, if you are not at the server that you need to look at, type **server <servername>** (see Figure 20.28).

FIG. 20.28

Running nslookup.

Part

V

Ch

20

When you are at the server, you can check several things. The first thing that you want to check is whether your zone is functioning properly. To see whether `enterprise.1701d.com` is an authoritative name server for `1701d.com`, type the following:

```
nslookup
server enterprise.1701d.com
1701d.com
```

Since `nslookup` did not return a nonauthoritative answer, the zone is functioning properly. If you are not an authoritative name server, you get something that looks like Figure 20.29.

FIG. 20.29

This nameserver is not an authoritative name server.

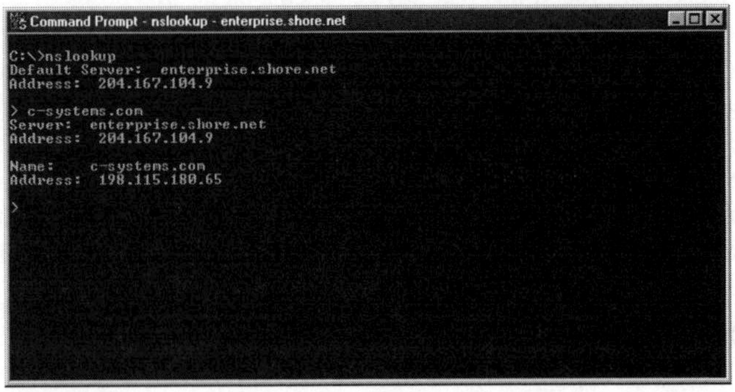

You can also look up all records for a domain name, `A` records, `MX` records, `SOA` records, `PTR` records, and `NS` records. You can use `set type=any`, which gives you any combination of these records.

To look up A records, type the following:

```
nslookup
set type=A
c-systems.com
```

To get all the Mail eXchanger records for `c-systems.com`, type the following:

```
nslookup
set type=mx
c-systems.com
```

To get all the authority information about `c-systems.com` (including responsible DNS server, responsible e-mail address, serial number, refresh time, retry time, expire time, and TTL time), type the following:

```
nslookup
set type=soa
c-systems.com
```

To get all this information about a domain name, use the `ls -d` function. You can use this function only on an authoritative name server. To use the function, type the following:

```
nslookup
server 1701d.com
ls -d 1701d.com
```

This enables you to see everything about the 1701d.com domain (see Figure 20.30).

FIG. 20.30

Everything that you need to know about the domain 1701d.com.

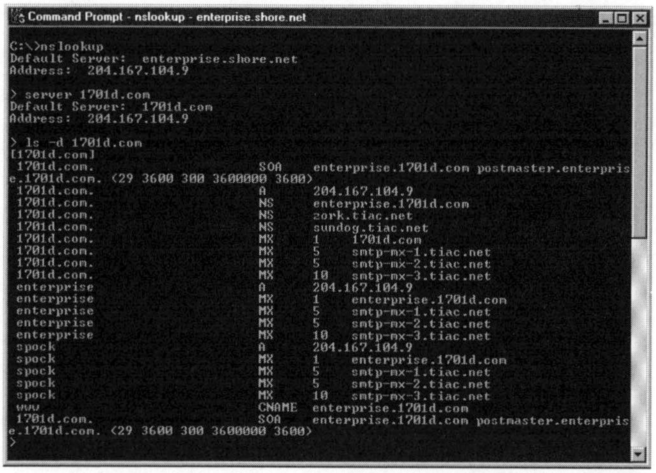

In this chapter, we have learned about different domain name servers that are avaliable on UNIX and Microsoft Windows NT Server platforms and we have also learned how to use the Microsoft Windows NT DNS Server in order to host domain names on our Windows NT Servers. When you are hosting a DNS server, there are many mistakes that can be made that will either cause a zone not to load at all or cause records to load with the wrong information. When you use the Microsoft DNS Server, these mistakes will be avoided because there is a graphical DNS manager that does very extensive error checking before any records are entered into the DNS server. We have also learned how to register a domain name with Internic by filling out the domain template form or by going to the Internic web page and filling out the form. The last thing that we have learned is how to use a DNS tool called nslookup. ●

Part

V

Ch

20

CHAPTER 21

Working with Internet Information Server

Internet Information Server (IIS) was developed exclusively for Windows NT. Developing IIS exclusively for Windows NT makes IIS the most efficient way to unleash the power of Windows NT and not rely on ported code, which always brings on legacy code that is not optimized for Windows NT.

IIS is the World Wide Web server that allows the world to connect to your home page (**www.yourcompany.com**). At the moment, IIS is the only server that Commerce Server works with. IIS also allows you to host an FTP site, but beware—FTP grabs all the bandwidth that you can give it, thus taking bandwidth from your Commerce site.

IIS and Commerce work with each other to produce the end result and that is e-commerce. IIS is the transport that brings the Internet to Commerce Server. ■

An overview of Microsoft Internet Information Server 3.0

Understand what Internet Information Server (IIS) 3.0 can do for your Internet and intranet Web sites and why it is the recommended choice for Microsoft Windows NT Server.

Installing Internet Information Server

With IIS 2.0, installing was a very simple process because it was installed with Microsoft Windows NT Server. You need to download and install IIS 3 from **http://www.microsoft.com/iis**. This whole process is described in detail.

An overview of the different features of IIS

IIS is not only a Web server, it also is a Gopher server and an FTP server. This chapter touches on those two features of IIS and the benefits of both services.

Requesting an SSL Key

One of the most important things in an E-Commerce site is security. You want to get a key that is as strong as you can possibly get so that your customers can be assured that their credit-card and personal information is not compromised in any way.

Installing IIS

Installing IIS is now a minimum two-step process since the release of IIS 3. First, you need to make sure that you have IIS 2 installed. If you do not have IIS 2 installed, you cannot install IIS 3. IIS 2 should have been installed for you automatically when you installed Windows NT Server, so this section will not cover installing IIS 2, there will only be a very brief overview of installing IIS 2. The best way to install IIS 2 is go to Control Panel's Network tool, and on the Services page, click the Add button. When the Select Network Service dialog box appears, scroll down to Microsoft Internet Information Server. Insert the Windows NT Server CD-ROM when prompted. Once the files are copied, you are prompted to reboot your machine.

To install IIS 3, you first must get the update from Microsoft. If you are on a high-speed line, the best way to get IIS 3 is directly from Microsoft's IIS home page at **http://www.microsoft. com/iis/default.asp**. Click the Download IIS 3.0 button and follow the instructions to register and download the product. Remember that when it comes time to download, you should choose the site that is closest to you so that your download will be as fast as possible. You will be given several to download. You need to read about each component and decide which add-ons you would like to download. The most important pieces for you to download are Microsoft Active Server Pages and Microsoft Index Server. Active Server Pages (ASP) is the actual update that will bring you to IIS 3. Index Server is a tool that you will find very useful. It allows you to enable searching on your Web site with very little extra programming.

N O T E   If you downloaded and installed IIS3 (asp.exe) before late March or April 1997, chances are that you have an old, outdated version of IIS3. Microsoft posted several updates to IIS3 between the date it first came out and March 1997 but never posted any type of updates on its home page or IIS page. It was just by chance that some people knew about these updates and decided to download the new version. Also, since this was not documented by Microsoft, there is not a list of changes or fixes available that can be posted. To find out if you are running the latest version, you can go to your *systemroot* directory (usually C:\WINNT), go to the *system32\inetserv \asp\cmpnts* directory, and look at the date of some of the files in there. If the files are dated 3/14/ 97 or later, you are using the latest version of IIS 3. If the files are older, you need to download the newest version of asp.exe and reinstall.

If you need to install IIS 2, upgrade to IIS 3, or update your existing version to the latest version of IIS 3, you are also going to need to reinstall service pack 3 and *all* of the hotfixes that you have installed to date. The reason for this is that when you install any version of IIS, it will overwrite certain IIS files and system DLLs that have been updated by the service packs and hotfixes. If you do not re-install the services packs and hotfixes, your system may have unpredictable results. If you try to re-install any hotfixes and your system is telling you that you are using the latest hotfix even though you know that you are not, you need to run regedit or regedt32 and delete this Registry key: HKEY_LOCAL_MACHINE\ SOFTWARE\Microsoft\Windows NT\CurrentVersion\HOTFIX. When you completely delete this Registry key, you can reinstall all your hotfixes. ▪

Installing IIS 3 after you finish downloading it is very simple; you just click asp.exe and follow the steps. Make sure that you install all the options. IIS 3 also includes a new version of ODBC, version 3.0, that you need to run Commerce Server. Once you have finished installing or upgrading to IIS 3, you need to reapply all your service packs and hotfixes as explained in the preceding note. After you reinstall all these files, you are all set to begin using Active Server Pages.

A client could use FTP to update pages if the client is changing art or making corrections in some code. You must set permissions and an account for that person in User Manager, as discussed in Chapter 19, "Understanding Microsoft Windows NT Server 4.0." Be a bit cautious when giving users accounts to modify Web sites or allowing unskilled personnel access to these accounts. As an administrator, you will be responsible to repair any damage caused to the clients account. Sure, it will just be a restore from tape, but restoring data from backup takes time—time that customers cannot shop nor access the site.

This is a very simple layout. Some tools ease you through the configuration of IIS. In configuring a virtual server (WWW), your first step is to open the server. Figure 21.1 shows the Internet Service Manager.

FIG. 21.1

You see all the installed IIS services on your machine in the Internet Service Manager. If you have the Internet Locator Service installed, you see the LDAP protocol; if you have the Microsoft Commercial Internet Server News Server installed, you see the NNTP Service, and so on.

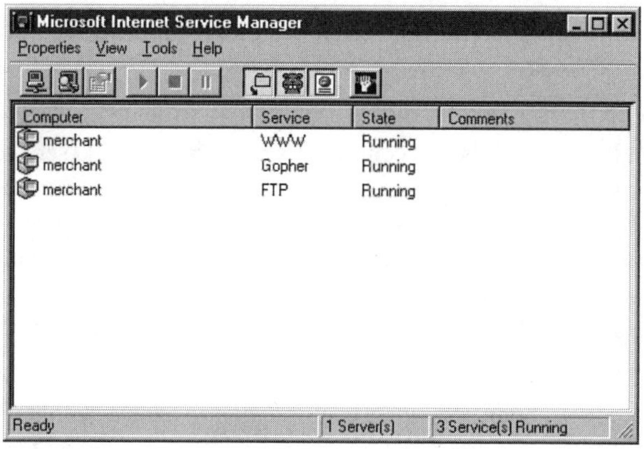

A virtual server is simply a device that resolves **www.yourcompany.com** to a specific IP address. You can run many virtual accounts on that same server; thus, one server does the work for many sites, eliminating the need for more servers.

Figure 21.2 shows the Service, Directories, Logging, and Advanced tabs.

Part

V

Ch

21

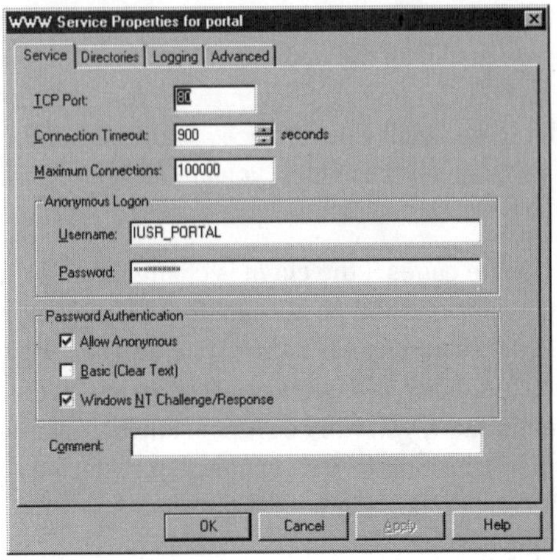

FIG. 21.2

Double-clicking WWW in the Microsoft Internet Service Manager brings up the WWW Service Properties dialog box for the machine you are editing. In the dialog box, you see the Service, Directories, Logging, and Advanced tabs.

Service Page

The first thing that you see is the Service page, on which you can set the TCP/IP port for the Web server, the connection timeout, the maximum number of connections, the authentication information, and types of authentication.

The standard TCP/IP port for a Web service is port 80, which is the default. The connection timeout is set to 900 seconds. If a computer is connected for 900 seconds without any activity, the computer is automatically disconnected. You may want to lower this timeout value if you have a busy site and don't want open idle connections to your server. The maximum connections are set to 100,000, which means that up to 100,000 users can connect to your site simultaneously. If you have a graphic-intensive page or use your Web site to transfer files and do not have enough bandwidth to support this many simultaneous connections, you may want to lower this number.

Next is Anonymous Logon. When IIS is installed, it assigns a default user name and password in the Username and Password text boxes and creates the account for you. It is recommended that you use the IUSR_*machinename* account for all your IIS services.

N O T E   When you install Commerce Server, you may need to add the IUSR_*machinename* account to the Administrators group on either your machine or your domain. For this reason, you should change the password on this account as often as you change your administrator account password. ▓

CAUTION

Try to avoid giving the IUSR account administrator privileges at all costs. Commerce Server uses NTFS permissions for security. When Commerce Server installs on your machine, the Manager pages are protected

---

against unauthorized use by setting the permissions on these pages so that only users in the administrators group can have access. If you put the IUSR account in the administrators group, you are allowing all users access to your store manager pages. This means that any user can get into your store, modify your database, change prices on any items, see all your customer files, and so on. As you can see, when you give an account access to the administrators group, you can cause all kinds of problems that you may not even realize until it is too late. Just as a good UNIX administrator limits set-uid root programs to those programs that absolutely need them, you should exercise the same caution whenever allowing users access to the administrators group.

The last section that you see is Password Authentication. In the Password Authentication section, you are given three options. By default, Allow Anonymous and Windows NT Challenge/Response are checked. Basic (Clear Text) is left blank because it is not recommended that users send user names and passwords through the Internet using clear text.

- *Allow Anonymous*. If you select Allow Anonymous, users can get to your Web site and read any files that your IIS service account (IUSR_*machinename*) has access to read.
- *Basic (Clear Text)*. If you have private areas on your Web site, you will need to select Basic (Clear Text) or Windows NT Challenge/Response. If you do not have Allow Anonymous selected or you have files on your server that your IIS service account does not have read access to, users will need to authenticate by using a user name and password that is either in the local account or part of a trusted domain. If you are using a Web browser other than Microsoft Internet Explorer 3.0 or above, you will need to have users send user names and passwords in clear text because these browsers can't encrypt user names and passwords in a format that IIS can read. There is a way to encrypt user names and passwords even if you are using Basic (Clear Text) authentication. If you bring your users into an HTTPS (HHTP Secure) area and have them sign on after they are in this secure area, their user name and password will be encrypted when it is sent.
- *Windows NT Challenge/Response*, also known as NTLM. The only difference between Basic (Clear Text) and NTLM is that NTLM encrypts the user name and password automatically as soon as it is sent, whether or not IIS is running from a secure HTTPS server. NTLM will work only with Microsoft Internet Explorer 3.0 or greater; it will not work with Netscape or any other browsers.

Directories Page

On the Directories Page is a summary window of all the IIS directories and aliases that you are using. The page contains three buttons: Add, Remove, and Edit Properties.

If you check the Enable Default Document box, whenever someone goes to your site, if they do not specify a file name, the file name in the Default Document text box will appear. The default document for IIS is default.htm. Other Web servers use index.htm or index.html. If you are

Part

V

Ch

21

transferring from another Web server that uses something besides default.htm as the default document, you can change it in the Default Document text box. Also, an undocumented feature is that you can have multiple default documents if you simply separate your default documents with commas.

> **N O T E** If you use multiple default documents and are using FrontPage Extensions, there could possibly be problems with the way that FrontPage uploads pages to your Web site. If your default document is set to "default.htm, index.html," FrontPage may name the default document in every directory to default.htm, index.html. If this happens, you will need to go through your Web site and rename all those files. ▪

The Add and Edit Properties dialog boxes show a few types of directories that are described in the following sections. The only difference between the Add and Edit Properties dialog boxes is that when you click Edit Properties, you are editing an existing directory; when you click Add, you are adding a new directory.

When you go to the Edit Properties dialog box, the first thing that you see is Directory. This is the full hard drive and path to the files that you are allowing access to.

> **N O T E** Internet Service Manager will allow you to edit IIS services not only for the machine that you are logged into locally, but for any machine on your network or even other machines on the Internet that you have control of. If you are editing a machine remotely, you will *NOT* be able to browse directories; you will need to type the path if you are adding a directory or editing a directory. ▪

Next, you see options for either Home or Virtual directories. Home Directory is the place where a user goes if he types **www.*yourdomainname*.com** without any parameters. You can also specify virtual directories. A *virtual directory* is a directory that is outside the directory tree of your home directory. If you have your home directory set to be c:\inetpub\wwwroot and need to put a large document on another drive, you can set http://www.*yourdomain*.com/public to go to d:\public\www or whatever you choose.

You use the Virtual Server field if you are going to have more than one home directory. In Windows NT Server, you can specify an unlimited number of IP addresses per network card. You can have one home directory per IP address. A practical application for using the Virtual Server option is hosting Web pages for several domain names. You can assign a different IP address for each of your customers' domain names so that each customer can have **http://www.*yourcustomersdomainname*.com** go to each of their individual home pages.

Directory Browsing Allowed is if you want to allow your users to see a list of files in a directory. You should not allow users to get a list of files in a directory unless you know whom you are allowing access to. Allowing this type of access can be a potential security breach, allowing users to read and download any files that you may have in this directory tree. You also may have private files and directories that users would not know about if directory browsing were not allowed.

Home   A home directory is the default directory that a user gets when he or she goes to http://www.*yourdomainname*.com. Users can get to any subdirectory within that home directory, provided that you give the guest account the proper permissions by using File Manager if you are using an NTFS file system.

Virtual Directories   A virtual directory is a subdirectory outside the home directory that you can give users access to. You can have www.*yourdomainname*.com/users go to an entirely different directory from your default home page. Being able to specify directories outside the default directory is useful when you need to split your users over several drives for the sake of disk space or performance. Using virtual directories is also necessary if you need to have a directory in which execute permission is required. Giving execute permission in every directory is not a good idea, because you don't want people to be running programs anywhere on your Web server—only in specified areas. You need to restrict permissions on certain directories to maintain system security and also to control what your users have and do not have access to.

Virtual Server   The most common use of a virtual server is for hosting Web pages that have several domain names (www.*domainname*.com) going to the same machine. To host Web pages for different domain names and give each user a separate home directory, you need to specify a different IP address for every domain name. If you are using DNS for your virtual Web customers, you can refer to Chapter 20, "Understanding DNS," for assistance in setting up DNS for your site.

N O T E   If you find that you have too many customers on one machine and this is slowing the machine down, before you invest in another machine, there is another step that you can take. Windows NT Server will support multiple network cards. If you split up the IP addresses that you are using between multiple network cards, you may find that your machine is going fast enough so that you do not, at this time, need to start adding new machines. ▧

Make sure that you have a sufficient number of IP addresses for the amount of virtual servers that you think that you need. To obtain class C IP addresses (254 usable IP addresses), see your ISP. InterNIC no longer issues individual class C addresses; it issues them in blocks of 64 class C addresses or more, and then only to ISPs or companies that have very large intranets like Microsoft or HP.

Logging Page

The third page is Logging. Logging is a useful feature of any Web server. If you enable logging, you can track where your users are coming from. It helps you compile geographical data on your users and your potential customers. Logging also helps you sniff out any potential hacking attempts.

Another useful feature tracks how much bandwidth your users are using. If your customers are generating more than a certain amount of traffic each month, you may want to charge them for the excess traffic.

IIS supports logging in one of two ways. The first way is to log to a comma-delimited text file. This way is recommended because it is much faster. If you have a busy Web site, Microsoft recommends logging to a file so that you will not slow down your site. Once you have these log files, you will be able to import these log files into a log file analysis utility such as Microsoft Usage Analyst. Microsoft Usage Analyst will import these log files into a database such as Microsoft SQL Server. See Chapter 8, "Using the Microsoft Usage Analyst," for detailed instructions.

When you log to a file, you are given two options of how to log, either Standard Format and NCSA (National Center for Supercomputing Applications) format. The default is Standard Format. The next option is whether to automatically open a new log file. You can choose Daily, Weekly, Monthly, or whenever the log file reaches a certain size. The default is to rotate the log daily. The last option is the log file directory. The default is C:\WINNT\System32\LogFiles. If you are using a different drive for file logging or would like your log files in a different directory, you can change the default directory. Figure 21.3 shows the logging dialog box.

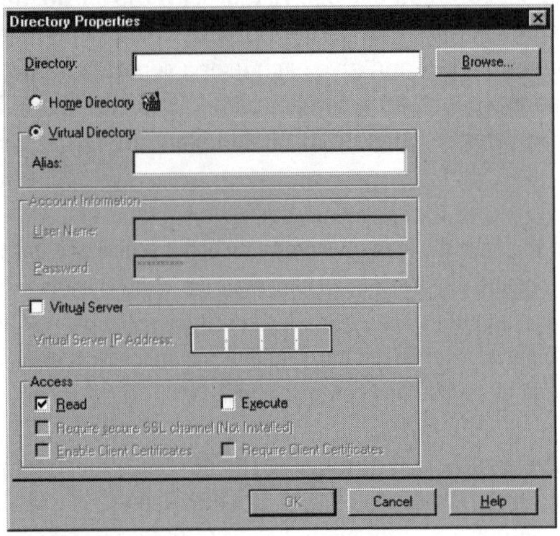

FIG. 21.3
You can either log to a file or to a SQL/ODBC database.

The second option for logging is to log to an ODBC-compliant database such as Microsoft SQL Server. This is not recommended, however, because logging to a database takes up more processor time and memory than logging to a text file, thus slowing down the response time of your Web server.

Advanced Page

The last page is Advanced, which has two useful features. The first is the Grant/Deny Access section. If you have a secure or private Web site that is not behind a firewall, you use this to keep anyone out. This is useful if you have employees who need to access your Web site so that they can do work at home. In this case, you choose All Will Be Denied Access and put in the IP addresses of users to whom you need to allow access. If you have a public Web site but find that a certain user is trying to break into your site, you choose All Will Be Allowed Access Except and put this user's IP address in Deny Access.

You use Limit Network Use if you find that a certain machine is taking up all your bandwidth. You can simply limit the amount of bandwidth going to or from that machine.

Other Features of IIS

This chapter has already mentioned your WWW/HTTP server. Next is Gopher, which you probably will not use often, if at all. Gopher is a piece of the puzzle that you will not be using for Commerce Server. (It just doesn't fit in.)

The last component that comes with IIS is the FTP (File Transfer Protocol) server. FTP is a good way to allow your clients to distribute software on the Internet. It is also a good way for you to allow your clients to upload their Web pages. Using FTP allows customers to completely maintain their Web sites without you as the ISP having to maintain their pages. Configuring FTP is basically exactly the same as configuring WWW. The only differences are that FTP uses port 21 and the default maximum number of connections is 1,000 instead of 100,000. FTP allows fewer connections because it uses a lot more bandwidth than WWW. When you are transferring files with FTP, you could be transferring several hundred kilobyte files or even several megabyte files. A well-written Web page is usually less than 50K.

The other difference is the way that authentication is handled. The default is to allow only anonymous connections. FTP sends user names and passwords in clear text over the Internet. At this time, you have no secure way to transmit user names, passwords, or files through FTP.

You do have the choice of giving users access with a user name and password. This is useful if you are going to allow your users to update their own Web pages or if you are giving customers write access to an anonymous FTP site. You should, of course, warn your users that they will be sending user names and passwords clear-text over the Internet and therefore, if someone is using a packet sniffer, they may be able to obtain the user name and password. If you need to transfer files by using a secure method, the best way to accomplish this is to either encrypt the file before allowing the file to be downloaded or to use HTTPS to transfer the file. Of course, HTTPS works only with a Web browser; it will not work with FTP at this time.

If you decide to allow non-anonymous access to your FTP server, IIS gives you a warning message, telling you that this type of authentication is insecure. For a user name and password, IIS simply uses the information that is in User Manager for Domains to authenticate users going through FTP. Users have the same read and write permissions that they would have if they were logged in over the network or logged in locally, so be careful what types of permissions you give your users and to which directories you allow access.

Part

V

Ch

21

Networking for the Internet and Intranet

After you configure IIS and any of its components, you want to apply IIS to your Internet, intranet, or both. This puzzle has a few pieces; one is a TCP/IP router. TCP/IP is the only protocol that works with IIS, because it is the only protocol that is accepted over the entire Internet.

A router is necessary if you want your machines to connect outside your network. A *router* takes packets destined for machines outside your local network and forwards them to the next "hop" over the Internet. In other words, if you have a T1 connection to BBNPlanet, and one of your users opens Internet Explorer and types **http://www.microsoft.com/**, the machine immediately notices that this IP address is not part of your local network and forwards the request to your router. Your router forwards that request over the T1 line to the router that it is connected to. The router forwards that packet to another router that is closest to that site, and so on, until it actually finds that site. Then that site sends a message back (most likely, the Web page that you are trying to view) and follows the same route in reverse. This process takes only a few seconds.

With your abilities to approach diverse networks within your own, these are what we call intranets. From those intranets, you can populate other Internet sites, and vice versa. Suppose that XYZ Company has an Internet site and 500 employees. All these employees could have their own personal home pages, which would give descriptions of them, what they like, and other little pieces of information about themselves. At the same time, the company could have its own internal home page, which could be http://*companyhomepage*, which is actually referring to a specific IP address for creating a newsletter, daily events, or a monthly calendar for referral by company personnel. Within this intranet, you could add more Internet sites (WWW), depending on the security setup of the specific LAN and its internal needs.

Name Resolution

Next, you need to provide name resolution for your machines. If you are using a firewall, you can have two sets of machine names: internal machines and external machines. If you are interested in securing your machines, you do not want to announce the names of your secure internal machines to the outside. For information about setting up a DNS server with Microsoft Windows NT 4.0 DNS Server, see Chapter 20, "Understanding DNS."

DHCP is a way to automatically configure all the machines on your local network. DHCP automatically configures TCP/IP in your machines, including IP address, default gateway, WINS server, and DNS servers. (See Chapter 19, "Understanding Microsoft Windows NT Server 4.0," for detailed instructions on setting up a DHCP server.) The benefit of using DHCP is that you do not need to configure all your machines; it also helps conserve IP addresses. With such a shortage of IP addresses left on the Internet, DHCP is a great way to do your part to "Save the Net."

If you are going to use DHCP, you also want to use a WINS server. WINS dynamically maps IP addresses to machine names. Because DHCP changes your IP address every time someone logs in, you need a way to keep up with these changes. WINS allows you to keep up with these changes on your local intranet. WINS does not broadcast these names outside to the Internet, as DNS does; it keeps them private in your intranet. If you are going to allow your users Internet access, you will, of course, need to set up a DNS server for name resolution on the Internet. You will not be including any internal host names in your DNS server because they constantly change and also because not announcing these IP addresses is more secure. If you do not announce these computer's IP addresses with DNS, it makes it that much more difficult for a hacker to break into your workstations.

Key Management

SSL (Secure Socket Layer) is a protocol developed for securing data transmission in commercial transactions on the Internet. By using public-key cryptography, SSL provides server authentication, data encryption, and data integrity for client/server communications. SSL is like a barrier or a protective layer allowing for some privacy. There are different strengths of encrypting when it comes to SSL. If you are in the United States or Canada as a Web provider, you will want to provide the strongest encrypting possible. At this time, the strongest encryption is 128-bit, which is almost impossible to break. 128-bit encryption means that there are 2^{128} possibilities for the encryption key. To date, the strongest key that has been broken is a 56-bit (2^{56}) key, and breaking that key took several computer users several months to break. Of course, if you were the government and had several hundred millions of dollars to spend, you could probably break 56-bit keys in a significantly less amount of time.

If you are a merchant in the United States or Canada and are sending information to customers outside the United States or Canada, the strongest encryption that you are allowed to use is 40 bit (2^{40}). This is very weak encryption and should under no circumstances be trusted to send sensitive information. A company that is willing to invest some time and money could intercept your transmission and break a 40-bit key without much effort if the information that they are breaking is worth it.

Recently, the US has eased up on export restrictions. If a user needs to use strong (128-bit) encryption for protecting a financial transaction with a bank, investment firm or other type of firm, the US government has decided that these type of transactions will be allowed. Several companies are trying to convince the US government that they should ease up on encryption restrictions. If you would like to find out more information on the ongoing controversy, you can visit **http://www.bsa.org/policy/encryption/encryption.html**.

SSL

To enable SSL, you have to obtain a key from an authority (VeriSign). You will find this exercise to be painless simply by following the prompts that are given to you when you go to Key Manager in IIS:

1. Choose Create a New Key from the Key menu. The Create New Key and Certificate Request dialog box appears (see Figure 21.4).
2. In the Key Name text box, choose a name for your key.

Part
V

Ch
21

A good name to choose is the customer's name that the key is going to be used for. Remember that this site is for a Web site. Key Manager asks you for your key name—a password for the key name that should be unique only to you. Remember that your security is only as good as your passwords. In the United States, you are allowed to have a 512-, 768-, or 1,024-bit key. The higher the number, the more secure your data is. Outside the United States, you can apply for only a 512-bit key, because of the U.S. State Department's regulations on exporting encryption schemes.

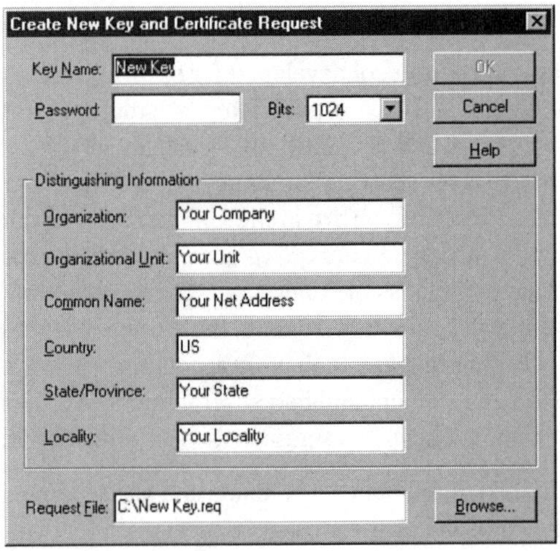

FIG. 21.4

The Create New Key and Certificate Request dialog box is where you type in all the information so that you can request your key from an authority such as VeriSign.

3. Fill out the Distinguishing Information for this key:

- *Organization.* Type the full legal company name in this text box.
- *Organizational Unit.* Type the company division, such as MIS, in this text box.
- *Common Name.* This would be the URL of the page. If you are going to be using http://www.c-systems.com for this key, you would need to type **www.c-systems. com** in this text box. Be very careful when you fill this in. If you type any information in this text box that is not in your URL—for example, if you type **www.c-systems.com** when the URL you are going to be using is actually secure.c-systems.com—your users are going to get a warning message saying that the site certificate is not valid for the URL that you are using. This can cost you sales, and you will be getting unnecessary questions in the form of phone calls and e-mail that can be avoided if you make sure that your information is accurate.
- *Country.* Type the country in which your business or site resides.
- *State/Province.* Type the state or province in this text box. You must type the full name of the state or province; do not use the state or province abbreviation, or your application will be rejected.
- *Locality.* This is the town or city in which your business or site resides.

4. The last text box is for the location of the key. Once you finish filling out the request, Key Manager will generate a key request file, which you must paste into a mail message and mail to VeriSign. From now on, we will use VeriSign because this is the key authority that Microsoft recommends for IIS. You, of course, can choose another company, if you desire.

5. When you have checked to be sure that all the information is filled in and accurate, click OK. You will see a dialog box asking you to verify the password.

6. Now you see a dialog box telling you that your key is being created. After your key is created, another dialog box asks for Administrator Information.

7. In the Administrator Information dialog box, you are asked for your e-mail address and phone number.

8. When you have entered your administrator information, a dialog box tells you that the key has been created and what you need to do to activate the key. Read these instructions carefully and click OK when you are finished.

9. Mail the request file to VeriSign. Open the key request file that was just created with a text editor, copy the whole file, and paste this file into an e-mail message. This text file will look like a bunch of "gibberish." Do not modify this file in any way. Address this e-mail message to **microsoft-request-id@verisign.com**. Do not simply attach this text file to an e-mail message. If you simply attach the file to an e-mail message, the auto-responder at VeriSign will not be able to decode the message and your request will be rejected.

   When you send your e-mail, an autoresponder will acknowledge your e-mail and you will receive a reference number and a time frame when you can expect to hear back with your certificate.

In a few days, you will receive your key, as long as all the information that you provided checks out and no other problems exist. You will receive your certificate as text in an e-mail. Copy the text between the –Cut here-sections and save this to a file. It does not matter what you save this file as or what the extension is as long as you know **where** you save the file.

When you have saved the file, go into Key Manager and go to your key. Right-click the key to bring up the shortcut menu and choose Install Key Certificate… You will see a dialog box asking you to select the key certificate. Browse to the directory that you saved the key certificate file and click open. You will be prompted for your password.

When you type in the proper password, your key will be activated. Now that your key has been activated, the first thing that you will want to create is a backup set. To create a backup set, follow these steps:

1. Click the key that you want to back up.

2. From the Key menu choose Export and then Backup. You will see a warning message telling you that you could possibly be compromising security by keeping a backup set on your computer.

3. Click OK. A dialog box will ask you what you want to name the key and where you would like to put the key.

Part

V

Ch

21

4. When you have named the key and placed it in a directory, click Save.

5. Now you have a backup key in case your computer ever crashes. You should move this key off your Web server or whatever computer this key resides on. You can either keep this key on a secure machine or save the file to a floppy disk and lock it in a safe somewhere.

ISAPI (Internet Server Application Programming Interface)

ISAPI is a subordinate with Windows NT and a replacement for CGI. ISAPI filters are powerful and can be used to facilitate several applications, including custom authentication schemes, compression, encryption, and logging. Depending on the options you chose, the filter application can act on several server operations, including reading raw data from the client, processing headers, and enabling communications over a secure port.

This is not to say that you can no longer use CGI scripts, but as Microsoft points out, CGI takes two processes. You have to call the CGI process, which then invokes the operation, which is called from a command given it from the browser. (An example is a mailto program in which you have a form. The information is parsed and then sent to the party that it is coded to in your form from a browser.) With ISAPI, the same process is streamlined. You invoke a thread because com is already invoked through DLLs that are already present in the operating system. Thus, you have a single process that increases the threads but does not call a second process. In turn, you have increased efficiency of your server by at least 50 percent. You have more speed (which is good) and less overhead taxing and slowing your system.

For more information on ISAPI filters, you can go to the help file in IIS or **www.microsoft.com**.

From Here...

This chapter went over the benefits of using IIS on your Windows NT server, how to set up IIS, and how to request and install an authority key for using SSL. You learned about virtual roots so that you can give multiple customers home directories, logging to either a text file or an SQL database. You learned how to restrict access so that if you have a private site, you can allow only authorized users to access the site or if you have a problem user, you can keep that user out.

The following chapters provide further information to help you go on with development of your commerce stores.

■ Chapter 3, "Setting Up Your Store," describes installing and configuring Microsoft Commerce Server. When you have IIS working, you want to set up Commerce Server as soon as possible so that you can start developing your store.

■ Chapter 7, "Using the Microsoft Site Analyst," describes how to use Microsoft Site Analyst. When you design and maintain your Web site, you need to make sure that all of your links are valid and that none of your pages are getting too large. Site Analyst will go through your entire Web site, inform you of broken links, tell you how large your pages are and provide you with a wealth of useful information.

■ Chapter 8, "Using the Microsoft Usage Analyst," describes how to use Microsoft Usage Analyst. When you are running a Web site, you will want to get detailed information about all your customers to use as marketing information.

Building the Order Processing Pipeline

This chapter discusses each step of the Order Processing Pipeline (OPP), showing you how you can change the OPP and how to ensure that your custom components follow the OPP rules. At the end of the chapter, you create your own custom OPP. ■

Order Processing Pipeline stages

The Order Processing Pipeline is composed of a set of stages which define the finalizing of an order.

Order Processing Pipeline modes

You can call the Order Processing Pipeline in different modes which allow you to manage order information more easily.

Order Processing Pipeline components

Components created for the Order Processing Pipeline must follow a defined set of rules.

Creating an Order Processing Pipeline

This is where we actually create an Order Processing Pipeline, discussing the standards to consider.

The POM is best described as the what COM stands for (COM)object of COM objects. When you think of a component, you think of a COM object that can be inserted into any ActiveX supporting application. While it is true that the OPP is a component, the OPP has a defined role that differentiates it from other components.

The OPP is a component that administrates a defined set of components. To fully understand the OPP, think of a soccer game. A soccer game consists of one or two officials, two soccer teams, and one or more coaches per team. Each of the players on the team has a distinct purpose, but all players must work together, sharing data such as where other players are and who is open for a pass. The coaches instruct the players with some form of strategy, and the official(s) make sure that the players and coaches are following a certain set of rules.

The OPP works much the same way. Think of the OPP as being both the coach and the officials, instructing each component with some strategy to complete an order, but also making sure that the components are following a certain set of rules. Other components are the team players on the field, each having a distinct purpose, but working together and sharing data to finalize the order.

Now that you have a good picture of what the OPP is and how it works, here's the official definition: The Order Processing Pipeline (OPP) is a Commerce Server 2.0 component that serves to administrate a defined set of other Commerce Server 2.0 components in the finalizing of an order. The OPP ensures that each component is called at the correct time and makes sure that the component follows a defined set of rules.

Order Processing Pipeline Stages

When the OPP component is called, the component is passed information via an OrderForm component for finalizing an order. The OPP passes this order form through a hard-coded set of components, called *stages*, that perform certain tasks that use, set, and correct the name-value pairs in that order form.

Table 22.1 lists the name-value pairs that are initialized when the OPP is instantiated.

Table 22.1   Initialized Name-Value Pairs

Name	Description
order.order_id	Contains the shopper's order ID for the current order. This string value is set by Commerce Server 2.0 and should not be changed.
order.shopper_id	Contains the shopper's ID. This string value is set by Commerce Server 2.0 and should not be changed.
order._messages	Contains the language to use for error messages. This string value is set by Commerce Server 2.0 and should not be changed.

Name	Description
order._error_shopper_change	An HTML list-delimited string containing all changes made in the current order due to errors. These errors are logged by the Purchasing component. This value is set to ("") if no errors occur.
order._error_shopper_error	An HTML list-delimited string containing all errors that prevented an order from finalizing. This value is set to ("") if no errors occur.
order._error_process_level	Used internally by the Order Form component passed in; initially set to 0.
order._locale_messages	Initialized to the locale ID for all messages.

When these values have been initialized, the Order Form component is passed through the stages of the OPP, so the stages can set, correct, or modify the existing name-value pairs of the Order Form.

Table 22.2 lists the stages supported by the Order Processing Pipeline component under Commerce Server 2.0.

Table 22.2   Order Processing Pipeline Stages

Stage	Description
Accept	Finalizes an order.
Handling	Checks for any handling costs and stores this information for later use.
Inventory	Checks the current inventory against the quantity of each item in the basket, making sure that all items purchased are in stock.
Item Price Adjust	Checks the price of each item in the basket and stores any deductions or promos that apply at the time when this stage is called. This stage does not change any information.
Merchant Information	Pulls the order's merchant information from a database and writes the information to the order form component passed into the OPP.
Order Check	Verifies that the order contains all the correct information needed to finalize the order.
Order Initialization	Creates a new OrderForm component for the OPP by copying information already stored by the Order Form component, passed into the OPP, as well as setting other fields.

continues

Table 22.2   Continued

Stage	Description
Order Price Adjust	Changes the price of each item in the basket, using information from the Item Price Adjust stage as well as the order itself.
Order Total	Writes to the order form the sum of the subtotal, shipping, handling, and tax values that were stored; then subtracts any further discounts.
Payment	Handles the payment of the order. This stage is where credit-card verification takes place.
Product Information	Pulls the order's product information from the Order Form component passed into the OPP.
Shipping	Checks for any shipping costs and stores this information for later use.
Shopper Information	Pulls the shopper's information from the Shopper object and writes the information to the Order Form component passed into the OPP.
Tax	Checks for any tax costs and stores this information for later use.

As explained earlier in this chapter, the OPP expects each component to follow certain rules. In other words, each stage must meet a set of requirements for the stage to exit successfully, and if these requirements are not met, the OPP resolves an error with that stage based on the condition not met.

The following sections briefly describe the OPP requirements for each stage.

Accept Stage

The Accept stage administrates the physical changes necessary for the finalizing of an order. These duties include, but are not limited to, the following:

- Reducing local inventory
- Writing purchase orders
- Saving receipt information to a database/file

Handling Stage

The Handling stage requires that the name-value pair order.order_handling_total be set. If this value is not set, the stage generates an error.

Any component attached to the Handling stage must first make sure that the_shipping_method name-value pair is set. If this value is not set, the component should *not* execute.

The Handling stage is essentially the same as the Shipping stage; therefore you can package both the shipping and handling requirements into the Shipping stage, but be aware that some tax software systems require that these requirements be met separately.

You should keep the functions separate for two reasons: The management of handling charges is easier, and if you ever change tax systems to one that requires the shipping and handling requirements to be met separately, you will not have to recode your pipeline.

Inventory Stage

The Inventory stage verifies that each item currently selected for purchase is in the local inventory. If one or more items fails to be found in the local inventory, the stage generates an error.

Item Price Adjust Stage

The Item Price Adjust stage calculates the regular and current prices of each item currently selected for purchase, setting the name-value pairs _iadjust_regularprice and _iadjust_currentprice, respectively.

If the name-value pair _iadjust_regularprice is not set, the _iadjust_regularprice defaults to _product_list_price. In relation, if the name-value pair _iadjust_currentprice is not set, _iadjust_currentprice defaults to _iadjust_regularprice.

You must understand two concepts of the Item Price Adjust stage:

- If your product database table does not have a column named _list_price, the name-value pair _product_list_price must be set to the name of the column containing the price information. If no column named _list_price exists, and the name-value pair _product_list_price is not set to a column containing this data, the OPP errors out the Item Price Adjust stage.

- When a shopper places an item in the basket, the name-value pair _price is set for that item. When the Item Price Adjust stage is run, the stage compares each item in the basket's _price value with the _iadjust_currentprice for that item. If the _price value does not match the _iadjust_currentprice for that item, the stage sets the _price value correctly, and the OPP sets a basket error to warn the user of the price change.

Merchant Information Stage

The Merchant Information stage retrieves any merchant information to write to the Order Form component passed into the OPP.

Order Check Stage

The Order Check stage serves two purposes. The first purpose is to ensure that the user selected at least one item for purchase. If not, the stage adds the purchase error pur_noitems to the Message Manager component.

The second purpose is to run the order through any merchant requirements that you specify. You can use this stage to require certain rules for your shoppers, which is a very useful tool.

Order Initialization Stage

The Order Initialization stage sets or registers any values that are needed for the finalizing of an order.

For integrity, the stage sets the following values to NULL:

```
_total_total
_oadjust_subtotal
_shipping_total
_tax_total
_handling_total
_tax_included
_payment_auth_code
```

Order Price Adjust Stage

The Order Price Adjust stage completes the following tasks:

- Sets the name-value pair _oadjust_adjustedprice
- Sets the name-value pair _oadjust_subtotal to the sum of _oadjust_adjustedprice for each item in the basket
- Sets the name-value pair _iadjust_currentprice for any items in the basket that is not already adjusted by the Item Price Adjust stage

Order Total Stage

The Order Total stage sets the name-value pair order._total_total to the sum of all charges and taxes, minus any handling or promotions.

Payment Stage

The Payment stage handles the credit-card authorization and sets the name-value pair order._payment_auth_code when the credit card is approved. If order._payment_auth_code is not set at the end of this stage, Commerce Server 2.0 generates a Bad Payment error.

When Creating a Component for the Payment Stage, Your Component Should Consider the Following Rules

When you create a component for this stage, it should conform to the following rules:

1. The name-value pair _payment_method must be set to the correct value; otherwise, your component should return S_FALSE.

2. If a previous component is called S_FALSE, your component should return S_FALSE.

3. If a credit card fails to charge the _total_total value, the component should return S_FALSE.

4. If a credit-card transaction times out, your component should return S_OK but do not set the name-value pair _payment_auth_code.

5. If _payment_auth_code is already set, your component should return S_OK.

Product Information Stage

The Product Information stage sets the name-value pairs _product_* for each item in the basket and removes any fields with the delete field set to 1.

N O T E The only valid value for the delete field is 1; all other values are undefined. ▪

Shipping Stage

The Shipping stage sets the name-value pair _shipping_total to the total shipping charges of the current order. If _shipping_total is not set, Commerce Server 2.0 generates an error.

N O T E Any custom Shipping stage components should first make sure the name-value pair _shipping_method is set. If this value is not set, the component should not execute. ▪

Shopper Information Stage

The Shopper Information stage sets the name-value pairs _shopper_* for each item in the basket.

Tax Stage

The Tax stage sets the name-value pairs item._tax_total, order._tax_total, and order._tax_included. order._tax_total, and order._tax_included must be set to some value; otherwise, Commerce Server 2.0 generates an error.

N O T E If a customer enters your store from a country that does not have a Tax stage component associated with it, the stage should not set order._tax_total, and order._tax_included to any value. ▪

The tax components shipped with Commerce Server are provided only for evaluation and testing purposes. As such, these components are not meant for a production environment.

You can purchase a tax component suitable for production use from independent tax providers such as TaxWare Inc. of Salem, Massachusetts.

Order Processing Pipeline Modes

The OPP can be called in any of three modes: Product, Plan, and Purchase. The mode in which the OPP is called determines what stages are called and how the stages are implemented.

The following examples illustrate how the OPP works in each mode. The mode the OPP is called in, essentially defines the set of stages the OPP is to run through, as shown in Figure 22.1.

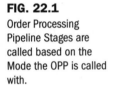

FIG. 22.1

Order Processing Pipeline Stages are called based on the Mode the OPP is called with.

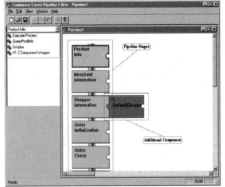

Order Processing Pipeline Components

OPP Components are COM objects that are designed to attach to the stages of the OPP. In other words, each stage of the OPP supports the direct attachment of any COM object designed for the OPP.

Following is an example of what this object-stage relationship looks like.

As you see in Figure 22.2, the QueryProdInfo component attaches to the Product Information stage. This probably is as cool as Commerce Server 2.0 can get, because you have the power to customize your store in absolutely any way that you want.

Before you get into the implementation of these cool components, first look at what components are installed by Commerce Server 2.0 and what each component does.

Table 22.3 lists the components that are available to each stage.

FIG. 22.2
Order Processing
Pipeline (OPP)
components attatch to
OPP Stages.

Table 22.3   Order Processing Pipeline (OPP) Components Listed by the Stages They are Available to

Stage	Supported Components
[ALL]	Scriptor Execute Process V1 C Component Wrapper
Product Information	[ALL] QueryProdInfo
Merchant Information	[ALL]
Shopper Information	[ALL] DefaultShopperInfo
Order Initialization	[ALL]
Order Check	[ALL] ValidateCCNumber
Item Price Adjust	[ALL] SaleAdjust ItemPromo
Order Price Adjust	[ALL] DbOrderPromo
Shipping	[ALL] FixedShipping LinearShipping TableShipping DefaultShipping
Handling	[ALL] DefaultHandling FixedHandling LinearHandling TableHandling

continues

Table 22.3 Continued

Stage	Supported Components
Tax	[ALL] DefaultTax SimpleUSTax SimpleJapanTax SimpleCanadaTax SimpleVATTax
Order Total	[ALL] DefaultTotal
Inventory	[ALL] FlagInventory LocalInventory
Payment DefaultPayment	[ALL]
Accept	[ALL] ReduceLocalInventory MakePO SaveReceipt SQLItem SQLOrder POtoFile ValidateCCNumber

Each component installed with Commerce Server 2.0, as well as any components that you add, has a distinct purpose associated with the finalizing of an order.

This section briefly discusses what each component installed with Commerce Server 2.0 does and provides some information that is useful in the implementation of that component. Later in this chapter, you see how to use these components and any new components that you add.

You should not try to read straight through the following section, which is long, but understanding the concept is important, so you should at least skim it. Besides, you can always come back to this section for reference.

If you want to get into the fun stuff, you can skip to "Creating an Order Processing Pipeline" later in this chapter. If you do skip ahead, remember to come back to this section for reference.

[ALL] Stage Components

The components discussed in this section are components that can be used in all OPP stages. When we create a component in Chapter 23, "Constructing Your Own Server Components" you will learn how components are linked with stages.

Scriptor

The Scriptor component runs a script written in an ActiveX scripting language (JavaScript or Visual Basic Scripting Edition). The component can be written internally (entered as one of the arguments) or externally (entered in a specified text file).

ExecuteProcess

The ExecuteProcess component runs a process with a specified set of parameters. In other words, you can have a program or batch file that can be called with this component. This component is typically run during the Accept stage but can be run in any stage.

Properties   Path Name of the Executable Complete path to the executable file that is to be run.

Command Line For the Executable

Command-line parameters (if any) to the executable process. This parameter may be %1, which is replaced by substitutionField, much the same way that you would use parameters in a batch file.

Field Name of Substitutable Parameter

Optional parameter containing the name of the field in the order form to be substituted.

The name-value pair po_text is set to the result of the execution unless manually overridden by the input_field name-value pair.

Version 1.0 Component Wrapper

The Version 1.0 Component Wrapper component encapsulates an existing component written in C for Merchant Server version 1.0 (using the 1.0 API set) in the new pipeline COM framework.

Product Information Stage Components

The Product Information stage components are used to set the name-value pairs _product_* for each item in the basket and remove any fields with the delete field set to 1.

QueryProdInfo

The QueryProdInfo component runs a database query and puts the returned data in the item value in the order form. For each item in the database, QueryProdInfo executes the query named by the Query parameter for the item's SKU. If no data is found for the item, it sets the item for deletion and continues. If data is found, the component sets the _product_attribute value. Thus, the data in the column called col is set in the name-value pair _product_col. QueryProdInfo has one parameter, which is described in the following section.

Query   The database query.

Order Check Stage Components

The Order Check stage components are used to verify that the order contains all the correct information needed to finalize the order.

ValidateCCNumber

The ValidateCCNumber component, which can also be run in the Payment stage, performs a standard checksum test on the credit-card number. If the ValidateCCNumber component fails, Commerce Server 2.0 generates an error, sending the error to the Message Object, and then returns S_FALSE.

> **N O T E** The ValidateCCNumber component tests only for well-formed credit-card numbers. The component works only on cards that use the standard credit-card numerical format (such as Visa, MasterCard, and American Express). ■

Item Price Adjust Stage Components

The Item Price Adjust stage components are used to check the price of each item in the basket and store any deductions or promos that apply at the time when the component is called. This stage should not change any information, but rather store the information.

SaleAdjust

The SaleAdjust component sets _iadjust_currentprice based on order._product_sale_* values. For each item currently stored in the basket, the component sets _iadjust_currentprice to _product_sale_price if the current date is between the values stored in the name-value pairs _product_sale_start and _product_sale_end.

> **N O T E** Commerce Server 2.0 generates an error if the name-value pairs sale_* are not set before the SaleAdjust component is called, because the component does not have the information needed to set the name-value pair _iadjust_currentprice. ■

ItemPromo Component

The ItemPromo component adjusts the current price of an item in the basket based on a promotional value. The following sections describe the component's seven parameters.

Condition Order Key   The name of the item attribute against which the promotion condition is checked. This field is set to the name of the column that stores the product description (_product_type, for example).

Condition Operator   This parameter is a comparison operator that compares parameter Condition Order Key with parameter Condition Value by using the equality operators =, <, and >.

Condition Value   An integer or string value indicating the product being promoted.

Discount Type   The type of discount that `Discount Value` is to be evaluated with—either % or $.

Discount Value   An integer value indicating the amount of the discount.

N O T E   Floating-point values are not valid. ■

Start Date   Optional parameter set to the date when the promotion begins.

N O T E   If this value is not set, the promotion is evaluated every day. ■

End Date   Optional parameter set to the date when the promotion ends.

N O T E   If this value is not set, the promotion is evaluated every day. ■

Order Price Adjust Stage Components

The `Order Price Adjust` stage components are used to change the price of each item in the basket, using information from the `Item Price Adjust` stage as well as the order itself.

DBOrderPromo

The `DBOrderPromo` component queries the database to determine a promotion amount. The following section describes the component's parameter.

Query   The name of a *stored procedure* specified in the `global.asa` file. Following is an example from the Sample Store Adventure Works:

```
Call MSCSContent.AddQuery("price-promo-system", "select promo_name, date_start,
➥date_end, shopper_all, shopper_column, shopper_op, shopper_value, cond_all,
➥cond_column, cond_op, cond_value, cond_basis, cond_min, award_all, award_column,
➥award_op, award_value, award_max, disc_type, disc_value from AW_promo_price
➥where active <> 0 order by promo_rank")
```

The database query to be performed must return at least one of the following columns:

> `cond_column`
>
> The name of the name-value pair against which the promotion condition is checked.
>
> `cond_op`
>
> One of the comparison operators (=, <, or >) that compares `cond_column` with `cond_value`.
>
> `cond_value`

An integer or string value set to the item being promoted.

cond_all

If cond_all is set to 1 (True), any product in the set of products to be purchased triggers this promotion. Otherwise, this promotion is triggered only by products that meet the criteria defined in cond_column, cond_op, and cond_value (the condition set).

award_column

Value indicating the award criterion.

award_op

One of the comparison operators (=, <, or >) that compares award_column with award_value.

award_value

Value set to the item being awarded.

award_all

If award_all is set to 1 (True), the award can be applied to any product. Otherwise, this award is applied only to products that meet the criteria defined in award_column, award_op, and award_value (the award set).

shopper_column

Value indicating the shopper-specific information. This can be @ (a wild card value), indicating that all shoppers are eligible for the promotion.

shopper_op

Should be set to = if a shopper is specified; otherwise, shopper_op is set to @.

shopper_value

Value indicating the type of shopper which can be @ (a wild card value), indicating any shopper.

shopper_all

Indicates whether this promotion is available to all shoppers. If this value is 0 (False), the promotion is available only to shoppers who meet the criteria defined in shopper_column, shopper_op, and shopper_value; otherwise, all shoppers are available for the promotion.

cond_min

A value set to the minimum purchase necessary to be eligible for the promotion. The interpretation of `cond_min` depends on `cond_basis`.

`cond_basis`

Determines whether the value stored in `cond_min` is measured in price (P) or quantity (Q).

`award_max`

The maximum number of awards to give.

`disc_value`

Value set to the amount of the discount based on the valued stored in `disc_type`.

`disc_type`

Value set to the type of discount (either % or $), which is used to evaluate the value stored in `disc_value`.

`date_start`

Value set to the date when the promotion begins.

`date_end`

Value set to the date when the promotion ends.

N O T E   An order promotion has three criteria: the shopper, condition, and award. If the shopper doesn't match the shopper criterion, the promotion is not applied. If the shopper does match the shopper criterion, the other two criteria are applied to all the items in the order, producing two sets: the condition set (those matching the condition criterion) and the award set (those matching the award criterion). ▓

Shipping Stage Components

The `Shipping` stage components are used to check for any shipping costs then store the cost information.

FixedShipping

The `FixedShipping` component charges a fixed amount to ship an order, based on the `Control` parameter. The following sections describe the component's three parameters.

Control   If `Control` is set to `"Always"`, the `Cost` parameter is always applied to the order. If set to `"Apply if shipping_method equals Method"`, the value of `Cost` is applied only if `shipping_method` equals `Method`. If set to `"Shipping method set in blackboard"`, `Method` should be left blank, and `Cost` is applied when `shipping_method` is set in the order form.

Method   The method is either a string or an empty string ("). If the method is a string other than the empty string, the price is applied only if `shipping_method` equals that string. If `Method` is an empty string, the `Cost` parameter is unconditionally used as the shipping charge for the order.

Cost   Value set to the price in cents (or whatever the currency unit is).

N O T E   If you connect multiple components to this component, the Method parameter must be set to `"fixed"` for this component; otherwise, the component runs but the action does not. ■

LinearShipping

The `LinearShipping` component charges a multiple of some aggregate value to ship an order based on the value of the `Control` parameter. The following sections describe the component's four parameters.

Control   If `Control` is set to `"Always"`, the `Cost` parameter is always applied to the order. If set to "Apply if `shipping_method` equals Method", the value of `Cost` is applied only if `shipping_method` equals `Method`. If set to `"Shipping method set in blackboard"`, `Method` should be left blank, and `Cost` is applied when `shipping_method` is set in the order form.

Method   The method is either a string or an empty string (""). If the method is a string other than the empty string, the price is applied only if `shipping_method` equals that string. If `Method` is an empty string, the `Cost` parameter is unconditionally used as the shipping charge for the order.

Basis Item Key   Value set to the name of the attribute of each item that is used to compute the shipping cost. The cost is computed based on the sum of all item `basis` fields. For `basis`, you can use quantity, `_iadjust_currentprice`, `_oadjust_adjustedprice`, or some other merchant-supplied value, such as weight. In the following descriptive examples, the weight (`_product_weight`) is used for the `basis`.

If the order has two items, one item weighing 2 pounds and the other item weighing 3 pounds, the `basis` sum is 5 pounds. If the order has two items, one item weighing 2 pounds with a quantity of 3 and the other item weighing 4 pounds with a quantity of 1, the `basis` sum is 10 pounds.

Rate   Value set to the number to multiply by the `basis` value to obtain the price. If you buy two units of one item and four of another, the `basis` is set to quantity, and the `rate` is 20.5, you pay $1.23 for shipping (20.5 * (2 + 4)).

N O T E   If you connect multiple components with this component, the Method parameter must be set to `"linear"` for this component; otherwise, the component runs, but the action may not be what you expect. ■

TableShipping

The `TableShipping` component looks up shipping costs in the database. The following sections describe the component's five parameters.

Control If `Control` is set to `"Always"`, the `Cost` parameter is always applied to the order. If set to `"Apply if shipping_method equals Method"`, the value of `Cost` is applied only if `shipping_method` equals `Method`. If set to `"Shipping method set in blackboard"`, `Method` should be left blank, and `Cost` is applied when `shipping_method` is set in the order form.

Method The method is either a string or an empty string (""). If the method is a string other than the empty string, the price is applied only if `shipping_method` equals that string. If `Method` is an empty string, the `Cost` parameter is unconditionally used as the shipping charge for the order.

Basis Item Key Value set to the name of the attribute of each item that is used to compute the shipping cost. The cost is computed based on the sum of all item `basis` fields. For `basis`, you can use quantity, `_iadjust_currentprice`, `_oadjust_adjustedprice`, or some other merchant-supplied value, such as weight. In the following descriptive examples, the weight (`_product_weight`) is used for the `basis`.

Query The name of the database query to be performed.

Order Key Value set to the name of a value in the order that is used for shipping calculation. This parameter is optional; if none is specified, it defaults to `ship_to_zip`.

Item Key Value set to the shipping-cost column name returned by the query. This parameter is optional; if none is specified, it defaults to cost.

N O T E The method name, the aggregated basis, and the value of the location are given as arguments to the query, which must return a single number as a result. With some databases, the query must refer to all three variables, even if it doesn't need them.

For example:

select cost, :2, :3 from shipping_costs

min_weight <= :1 and max_weight > :1.

:2 and :3 refer to the location and method, respectively. These references are the database column number references. The component ignores the return fields after the first, but some databases issue an error if you do not refer to them at all. :1 refers to the product weight. ▪

Handling Stage Components

The `Handling` stage components check for any handling costs and stores these handling costs.

FixedHandling

The `FixedHandling` component charges a fixed amount to handle any order. The following sections describe the component's three parameters.

Control   If Control is set to "Always", the Cost parameter is always applied to the order. If set to "Apply if handling_method equals Method", the value of Cost is applied only if handling_method equals Method. If set to "Handling method set in blackboard", Method should be left blank, and Cost is applied when handling_method is set in the order form.

Method   The method is either a string or an empty string ("). If the method is a string other than the empty string, the price is applied only if handling_method equals that string. If Method is an empty string, the Cost parameter is unconditionally used as the handling charge for the order.

Cost   Value set to the price in cents (or whatever the currency unit is).

LinearHandling

The LinearHandling component charges a multiple of some aggregate value to handle an order. The following sections describe the component's four parameters.

Control   If Control is set to "Always", the Cost parameter is always applied to the order. If set to "Apply if handling_method equals Method", the value of Cost is applied only if handling_method equals Method. If set to "Handling method set in blackboard", Method should be left blank, and Cost is applied when handling_method is set in the order form.

Method   This parameter has the same meaning as in FixedHandling.

Basis Item Key   Value set to the name of the attribute of each item that is used to compute the handling cost. The cost is computed based on the sum of all item basis fields. For basis, you can use quantity, _iadjust_currentprice, _oadjust_adjustedprice, or some other merchant-supplied value, such as weight. In the following descriptive examples, the weight (_product_weight) is used for the basis.

If the order has two items, one item weighing 2 pounds and the other item weighing 3 pounds, the basis sum is 5 pounds. If the order has two items, one item weighing 2 pounds with a quantity of 3 and the other item weighing 4 pounds with a quantity of 1, the basis sum is 10 pounds.

Rate   Value set to the number to multiply by the basis value to obtain the price. If you buy one unit of one item and three of another, the basis is set to "quantity", and the rate is 25, you pay $1.00 for handling (25 * (1 + 3)).

TableHandling

The TableHandling component looks up handling costs in the database. The following sections describe the component's five parameters.

Control   If Control is set to "Always", the Cost parameter is always applied to the order. If set to "Apply if handling_method equals Method", the value of Cost is applied only if handling_method equals Method. If set to "Handling method set in blackboard", Method should be left blank, and Cost is applied when handling_method is set in the order form.

Method   This parameter has the same meaning as in FixedHandling.

Basis Item Key   Value set to the name of the attribute of each item that is used to compute the handling cost. The cost is computed based on the sum of all item `basis` fields. For `basis`, you can use `quantity`, `_iadjust_currentprice`, `_oadjust_adjustedprice`, or some other merchant-supplied value, such as weight. In the following descriptive examples, the weight (`_product_weight`) is used for the `basis`.

Query   Value set to the name of the database query.

Order Key   Value set to the name of a value in the order that is used for handling calculation. This parameter is optional; if none is specified, it defaults to `ship_to_zip`.

Item Key   Value set to the handling cost column name returned by the query. This parameter is optional; if none is specified, it defaults to `cost`.

N O T E   The method name, the aggregated basis, and the value of the location are given as arguments to the query, which must return a single number as a result. With some database query languages, the query must refer to all three variables, even if it doesn't need them.

For example:

Select cost, :2, :3 from handling_costs

min_weight <= :1 and max_weight > :1.

:2 and :3 refer to the location and method, respectively. These references are the database column number references. The component ignores the return fields after the first, but some databases issue an error if you do not refer to them at all. :1 refers to the product weight. ■

Tax Stage Components

SimpleUSTax

The `SimpleUSTax` component applies a given rate to any order sent to a specified state. `SimpleUSTax` always sets the `_tax_included` name-value pairs to 0 (for both the item and the order). The component does not handle fractions of cents (or whatever currency unit is being calculated); all calculations are rounded to the nearest whole unit. The following sections describe the component's three parameters.

Control   If `Control` is set to `"Always"`, the rate is always applied to the order, even if `Country` is not set. If set to `"Apply if ship_to_country equals Country"`, the tax rate is applied only if `ship_to_country equals Country`. If set to `"Apply if ship_to_country is set in blackboard"`, the rate is applied if `ship_to_country` is set in the order form.

Country   Value set to the country for which to compute tax. This parameter can be a text string or @ (the wild card character). If the parameter is @, this tax model is used for any country.

State Rate List   Value set to the name of the state to which the order is to be shipped and the tax rate for that state, expressed as `State:Rate` pairs. This parameter can be @ (the wild card character), or any postal abbreviation. If the parameter is @, the rate applies for any other state not specified, but @ does not overwrite any previously specified state tax rates. Optionally, multiple State:Rate pairs can be specified.

SimpleJapanTax

The SimpleJapanTax component computes a tax rate for the Japanese tax model and can be used for any country that uses a similar model. The component does not handle fractions of currency units; all calculations are rounded to the nearest whole unit. The following sections describe the component's four parameters.

Control   If Control is set to "Always", the rate is always applied to the order, even if Country is not set. If set to "Apply if ship_to_country equals Country", the tax rate is applied only if ship_to_country equals Country. If set to "Apply if ship_to_country is set in blackboard", the rate is applied if ship_to_country is set in the order form.

Country   Value set to the country for which to compute tax. This parameter can be a text string or @ (the wild card character). If the parameter is @, this tax model is used for any country.

Include Item Key   A Boolean value that indicates whether the tax rate is to be added to the line item (in which case the item._tax_total value is set to the tax amount and item._tax_included is set to 0) or whether the tax rate is included in the price (in which case the item._tax_included value is set to the tax amount and item._tax_total is set to 0). In Japan, almost everything is taxed, but the tax may not be included in the price of the product. If this value comes from the product query run by the Product Information stage, this name is the database column name with _product_ prefixed to it. If the column is called jpn_prod_tax_included, the field becomes _product_jpn_prod_tax_included.

Rate Item Key   Value set to the name of the field in the item that contains the tax rate charged for the item. This tax rate is in addition to the tax rate specified by the Include Item Key parameter. If this value comes from the product query run by the Product Information stage, this name is the database column name with _product_ prefixed to it. If the column is called jpn_prod_tax_rate, the field becomes _product_jpn_prod_tax_rate.

SimpleCanadaTax

The SimpleCanadaTax component computes a tax rate for Canada, including goods and services tax (GST) and provincial sales tax (PST). SimpleCanadaTax always sets the _tax_included name-value pairs to 0 (for both the item and the order). The component does not handle fractions of cents (or whatever currency unit is being calculated); all calculations are rounded to the nearest whole unit.

GST is common throughout Canada, and almost all goods and services have a GST. If a product is taxed, the GST rate is the same throughout Canada. Some products are not taxed, however, and some service merchants (making less than a given amount) may elect to not charge GST. Each province has its own PST—typically, a fixed rate for all products—but PST still depends on the product (although a province may elect to tax an item not taxed by another province).

When shipping from one province to another, you do not pay any PST tax. Although the situation is not common, a product may have PST but not GST (and vice versa). The following sections describe the component's five parameters.

Control If `Control` is set to `"Always"`, the rate is always applied to the order, even if `Country` is not set. If set to `"Apply if ship_to_country equals Country"`, the tax rate is applied only if `ship_to_country equals Country`. If set to `"Apply if ship_to_country is set in blackboard"`, the rate is applied if `ship_to_country` is set in the order form.

Country Value set to the country for which to compute tax. This parameter can be a text string or @ (the wild card character). If the parameter is @, this tax model is used for any country.

GST Item Key Value set to the item's field name that contains the GST rate. If this value comes from the product query run by the `Product Information` stage, this name is the database column name with `_product_` prefixed to it. If the column is called `can_prod_gst_tax_rate`, the field becomes `_product_can_prod_gst_tax_rate`.

PST Item Key Prefix Value set to the item's field name that contains the PST rate for a province. If this value comes from the product query run by the `Product Information` stage, this name is the database column name with `_product_` prefixed to it and the province name removed from it. If the column is called `can_prod_pst_tax_rate_alb`, the field becomes `_product_can_prod_pst_tax_rate_`.

Province List Value set to the province or list of provinces (separated by spaces) for which to compute the tax. This parameter is used to look up the tax rate in the database table column. The parameter can be @ (the wild card character); if so, this tax model is used for any province. Optionally, multiple provinces can be specified.

SimpleVATTax

The `SimpleVATTax` computes a value-added tax (VAT) for the items. `SimpleVATTax` always sets the `_tax_total` name-value pairs to 0 (for both the item and the order). The component does not handle fractions of currency units; all calculations are rounded to the nearest whole unit. The following sections describe the component's three parameters.

Control If `Control` is set to `"Always"`, the rate is always applied to the order, even if `Country` is not set. If set to `"Apply if ship_to_country equals Country"`, the tax rate is applied only if `ship_to_country equals Country`. If set to `"Apply if ship_to_country is set in blackboard"`, the rate is applied if `ship_to_country` is set in the order form.

Country Value set to the country for which to compute tax. This parameter can be a text string or @ (the wild card character). If the parameter is @, this tax model is used for any country. Any country abbreviation can be used, as long as the merchant's shopping page is aware of its meaning.

Rate Item Key Value set to the name of the field in the item that contains the VAT rate included in the item price. If this value comes from the product query run by the Product Information stage, this name is the database column name with _product_ prefixed to it. If the column is called ger_vat_tax_rate, the field becomes _product_ger_vat_tax_rate.

Inventory Stage Components

The Inventory stage components are used to verify that every item ordered is in stock.

FlagInventory

The FlagInventory component verifies that none of the order items has the _product_in_stock value, which corresponds to the in_stock column in the items database table, set to 0. If any item does have this field set to 0, FlagInventory sets the _inventory_backorder parameter to the quantity ordered (indicating the shortage). If such a shortage occurs and the disallow_backorder parameter is set to 1, FlagInventory generates an error, which prevents the purchase from occurring. This component interacts with a manual inventory control process; the product database must be updated to reflect the actual stock on hand. The following section describes the component's parameter.

Disallow Backorder This parameter is optional; enabling it indicates that the _inventory_backorder value should be disallowed. In this case, FlagInventory generates an "out of stock" error as soon as _inventory_backorder is set (is greater than 0). If this parameter is 0 (the default) or is omitted, _inventory_backorder can be set, and no error is generated.

LocalInventory

The LocalInventory component checks to ensure that the order does not need more units of an item than are available. To provide the inventory control in your store, you should use the ReduceLocalInventory component in the Accept stage along with LocalInventory for the inventory stage.

The LocalInventory component sums the number of items of each SKU in the order and makes sure that the value of _product_local_inventory is at least that number. If not, the component sets the _inventory_backorder value to the difference. The following section describes the component's parameter.

Disallow Backorder This parameter is optional; enabling it indicates that the _inventory_backorder value should be disallowed. In this case, LocalInventory generates an "out of stock" error as soon as _inventory_backorder is set (is greater than 0). If this parameter is 0 (the default) or is omitted, _inventory_backorder can be set, and no error is generated.

Accept Stage Components

The `Accept` stage components handle the completed order and allow the order to be fulfilled.

ReduceLocalInventory

The `ReduceLocalInventory` component invokes a named database query with the appropriate parameters. The following section describes the component's parameter.

Query   Value set to the named database query to invoke.

MakePO

The `MakePO` component, formerly named `POGen`, generates a purchase order (PO) from an Active Server Pages template file and information on the order form. Database interaction is specified by the template file. The following sections describe the component's three parameters.

Template File Name   Value set to the complete path name for the template file. For example:

```
"C:\stores\common\potemplate.txt"
```

ProgID   Value set to the scripting language (for example, VBScript, which is the default) to be used.

Output Data Property Name   Optional parameter which indicates the name of the order form key to which the PO is output. The default is `po_text`.

SaveReceipt

The `SaveReceipt` component replaces `SaveOrderToDb` from version 1.0. The component saves an order to a database table. The following section describes the component's parameter.

Prefix   Value set to the name of the attribute's prefix.

SQLItem

The `SQLItem` component runs the specified SQL command for each item in the order, with the given fields from the order and item as arguments.

The first argument is the string containing the SQL command, which is executed once for each item. All subsequent arguments are parameters to the query. The following sections describe the component's two parameters.

Query   Value set to a string containing the SQL command, which is executed once for each item.

Example:

```
"insert into running_item_price values (:1,:2)"
```

Parameter List   Value set to the parameter to the query. If the parameter is the word `"count"`, it is interpreted as the number of line items in the order. If the parameter is the word `"index"`, it is interpreted as the (zero-based) index of this line item. If the parameter is of the form `order.`*`fieldname`*, that field from the order form is used. If the parameter is of the form `item.`*`fieldname`*, that field from the current line item is used.

Example:

```
order.order_id item._oadjust_adjustedprice
```

SQLOrder

The `SQLOrder` component runs the specified SQL command for each item in the order, with the given fields from the order as arguments.

The first argument is the string containing the SQL command. All subsequent arguments are parameters to the query. The following sections describe the component's two parameters.

Query   The string containing the SQL command, which is executed once for each item.

Example:

```
"insert into running_total values (:1, :2)"
```

Parameter List   Value set to the parameter to the query. If the parameter is the word `"count"`, it is interpreted as the number of line items in the order. If the parameter is of the form `order.`*`fieldname`*, that field from the order form is used.

Example:

```
order.order_id order.order_total
```

POToFile

The `POToFile` component sends a purchase order (typically, the result of `MakePO`) to a file. The following sections describe its five parameters.

Name of Field   The name of the field in the order form containing the text to be saved (`po_text` by default).

File Name   Value set to the name of the file in which to save the PO text data.

Example:

```
C:\log\polog.txt
```

File Named in Field   Value set to the name of the order form field that contains the name of the file in which to save the `POText` data.

Example:

```
save_filename.
```

Temporary File Value set to the name of the order form field that contains the name of the temporary file in which the `POText` data is stored.

Example:

`saved_filename.`

Append to File If this option is enabled, the `POText` is appended to the file; if unchecked, the component overwrites the file.

Creating an Order Processing Pipeline

Now that you have a good understanding of what the Order Processing Pipeline (OPP) is and what it consists of, you are ready to create your own. You are actually going to get to use all the information that you just read.

Microsoft provides two editors with Commerce Server 2.0 that enable you to create and manage your OPP. You can create and manage the OPPs by using either the Win32 Pipeline Editor or the HTML Based Editor. No difference exists between the editors in their implementation of the OPP, but they are slightly different in their use. As a result, this chapter shows both editors in use. First, you create your own custom OPP by using the Win32 Pipeline Editor; then you use the HTML Based Editor to modify the custom OPP.

Using the Win32 Pipeline Editor

The Win32 Pipeline Editor is a Windows 32-bit application that runs on Windows NT 4.0 or later versions. The executable is installed to the following path when you install Commerce Server 2.0 to `C:\Microsoft Commerce Server`:

```
C:\Microsoft Commerce Server\Server\Administration\Pipeline
➥Configuration\pipeedit.exe
Installation should also create a Start-menu icon for the Pipeline Editor in the
➥Commerce Server 2.0 program group.
```

N O T E If you do not install your Commerce Server 2.0 folder in the default location, substitute the custom location that you specified during the installation for `Commerce Server 2.0`. ■

To create a custom OPP, do the following:

1. Start the Win32 Pipeline Editor, which will start with a new configuration, shown in Figure 22.3.

The Pipeline Editor has four major sections:

■ Stage Selection

■ Pipeline Stages

■ Components Available for Stage Selected

■ Additional Component(s)

Stage Selection is where you select the stage for the components that you want to appear in the Components Available for Stage Selected window.

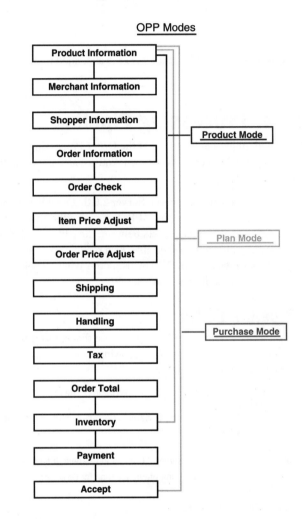

FIG. 22.3

The Win32 Order Processing Pipeline Editor.

OPP Modes

- Product Information
- Merchant Information
- Shopper Information
- Order Information
- Order Check
- Item Price Adjust
- Order Price Adjust
- Shipping
- Handling
- Tax
- Order Total
- Inventory
- Payment
- Accept

Product Mode

Plan Mode

Purchase Mode

The Pipeline Stages are the stages discussed earlier in this chapter, but in a graphical representation. The Additional Component(s) windows is where you add additional custom components to the Pipeline Stages.

The application supports active drag-and-drop technology—in other words, you can click a component in the Components Available for Stage Selection window and drag it to the Additional Component(s) window, where you drop the component onto the stage where you want it to be attached.

When you drop the component, it attaches itself to the puzzle-like groove of the Pipeline Stage that you dropped it on.

Exactly what does dropping the component into a stage do? This is the interesting part. When you drop components onto stages, the component is called with the specified parameters (if any) when the stage is run. One important concept to understand is that when a component is said to be associated with a stage, this is virtual.

Technically, you can drag and drop any component onto any stage, but the problem is that some components are looking for certain information to be set before they can be run.

Suppose that you drop the SimpleUSTax component onto the ProductInfo stage. The component inserts itself into the stage, but when the component is called, the _tax_* values are not set, and the component does not run correctly.

For the rest of this book, any reference to components associated with stages implies that the component does not have the correct information to run without or before that stage.

After you start the Pipeline Editor and have your basic pipeline, you should take a couple of steps every time you create a new Order Processing Pipeline (OPP).

Product Info *Stage* Drop the QueryProdInfo component into the ProductInfo stage. Then right-click the component and choose Properties from the drop-down menu. For the Query parameter, type a name that you can use to specify a query in the global.asa file.

The sample store Microsoft Press Bookstore, which is installed with Commerce Server 2.0, specifies this Query variable as the default value "product".

You need to edit the global.asa file for the store that you are creating this OPP for. After you open your global.asa file, insert the following code at the top of the file:

```
Call MSCSContent.AddQuery ("product", "select * from STORENAME_product where sku
= convert(varchar, :1)")
```

N O T E Substitute the name of your store for STORENAME. For the sample store Microsoft Press Bookstore, in this example you would substitute STORENAME with MSPress_product. ■

The query we just added to the global.asa file selects all the attributes for each of the items in the basket. This way, you can use this information during the rest of the stages.

You can leave the Merchant Information stage without any components, and you can also leave the Shopper Information stage with the DefaultShopper component. Now look at the Order Initialization stage.

Order Initialization *Stage* To understand the role of the Order Initialization stage, click the Scriptor component in the Components Available for Selected Stage window and drag it to the Order Initialization stage. When the component is attached to the stage, right-click the component and choose Properties from the drop-down menu.

When the Properties dialog box appears, select the programming language that you want to write in, then select Internal. If you select External, the File parameter will highlight, and you will be prompted to select a file to read the function from. For the purposes of this example, write the script as internal.

After you select the language to program and specify where you want the script to be stored, you should write a set of code that performs tasks similar to Listing 22.1 (taken from the sample store Microsoft Press Bookstore).

Listing 22.1

```
function MSCSExecute(config, orderform, context, flags)
  set df = context.datafunctions
  REM -- copy shopper info to bill-to address
  If IsNull(orderform.bill_to_name) then
   orderform.bill_to_name = df.CleanString(orderform.[_shopper_name])
  End If
  If IsNull(orderform.bill_to_street) then
                  orderform.bill_to_street =
➥df.CleanString(orderform.[_shopper_street])
  End If
  If IsNull(orderform.bill_to_city) then
   orderform.bill_to_city  = df.CleanString(orderform.[_shopper_city])
  End If
  If IsNull(orderform.bill_to_state) then
                  orderform.bill_to_state = df.CleanString(orderform.[_shopper_state])
  End If
  If IsNull(orderform.bill_to_zip) then
   orderform.bill_to_zip   = df.CleanString(orderform.[_shopper_zip])
  End If
  If IsNull(orderform.bill_to_country) then
   orderform.bill_to_country=df.CleanString(orderform.[_shopper_country])
  End If
  If IsNull(orderform.bill_to_phone) then
                  orderform.bill_to_phone   =
➥df.CleanString(orderform.[_shopper_phone])
                  End If
  REM -- copy shopper info to ship-to address
  If IsNull(orderform.ship_to_name) then
    orderform.ship_to_name    = df.CleanString(orderform.[_shopper_name])
  End If
  if IsNull(orderform.ship_to_street) then
    orderform.ship_to_street  = df.CleanString(orderform.[_shopper_street])
  End If
  If IsNull(orderform.ship_to_city) then
    orderform.ship_to_city    = df.CleanString(orderform.[_shopper_city])
  End If
  If IsNull(orderform.ship_to_state) then
    orderform.ship_to_state   = df.CleanString(orderform.[_shopper_state])
  End If
  If IsNull(orderform.ship_to_zip) then
    orderform.ship_to_zip     = df.CleanString(orderform.[_shopper_zip])
  End If
  If IsNull(orderform.ship_to_country) then
    orderform.ship_to_country = df.CleanString(orderform.[_shopper_country])
  End If
  If IsNull(orderform.ship_to_phone) then
    orderform.ship_to_phone   = df.CleanString(orderform.[_shopper_phone])
  End If
```

```
      REM -- Return Success
      MSCSExecute = 1
   End Function
```

Order Check Stage   Because this stage is used to check the order, before you continue to the stages that do most of the real work, you should add a Scriptor component, as you did for the Order Initialization stage.

After you add the Scriptor component, you should write a function that makes sure that the information added thus far is legal. Listing 22.2 is a clip from the Scriptor component attached to the Order Check stage of the sample store Microsoft Press Bookstore.

Listing 22.2

```
function MSCSExecute(config, orderform, context, flags)
   set errors = orderform.[_Purchase_Errors]
   set datafunctions = context.datafunctions
   result = 1
   REM -- validate shopper ship-to address
   If IsNull(datafunctions.CleanString(orderform.ship_to_name, 1, 100)) then
      errors.Add("ship to name must be a string between 1 and 100 characters")
      orderform.ship_to_name = ""
      result = 2
   End If
   If IsNull(datafunctions.CleanString(orderform.ship_to_street, 1, 100)) then
      errors.Add("ship to street must be a string between 1 and 100 characters")
      orderform.ship_to_street = ""
      result = 2
   End If
   If IsNull(datafunctions.CleanString(orderform.ship_to_city, 1, 100)) then
      errors.Add("ship to city must be a string between 1 and 100 characters")
      orderform.ship_to_city = ""
      result = 2
   End If
   If IsNull(datafunctions.CleanString(orderform.ship_to_state, 2, 2)) then
      errors.Add("ship to state must be a two character state code")
      orderform.ship_to_state = ""
      result = 2
   End If
   If IsNull(datafunctions.CleanString(orderform.ship_to_zip, 5, 10)) then
      errors.Add("ship to zip must be a string between 5 and 10 characters")
      orderform.ship_to_zip = ""
      result = 2
   End If
   If IsNull(datafunctions.CleanString(orderform.ship_to_country, 1, 100)) then
      errors.Add("ship to country must be a string between 1 and 100 characters")
      orderform.ship_to_country = ""
      result = 2
   End If
   If IsNull(datafunctions.CleanString(orderform.ship_to_phone, 8, 20)) then
      errors.Add("ship to phone must be a string between 8 and 20 characters")
      orderform.ship_to_phone = ""
      result = 2
```

continues

Listing 22.2   Continued

```
   End If
   MSCSExecute = result
End Function
```

You can leave the Item Price and Order Price Adjust stages without any components, and you can also leave the Shipping and Handling stages with their Default* components.

If you do not have a third-party shipping component, check out TanData Inc. on the Web at **http://www.tandata.com**, or by phone at (918) 499-2800.

Tax *Stage*   This section does not discuss this stage in detail. If you have a custom component from a third-party vendor, such as TaxWare Inc., you should insert the component and modify the component to the vendor's specifications.

If you do not have a third-party tax component, check out TaxWare Inc. on the Web at **http://www.taxware.com**, or by phone at (508) 741-0101.

For this example, leave the DefaultTax component attached to the Tax stage.

You can leave the Order Total stage with the DefaultTotal component attached, and you can also leave the Inventory stage without any components.

Payment *Stage*   For the Payment stage, leave the DefaultPayment component attached to the stage and add the ValidateCCNumber component. To add the ValidateCCNumber component, you need to select All Stage in the Select Stage drop-down list. Click the ValidateCCNumber component and drag it to the Payment stage on the Order Processing Pipeline.

You have no properties to configure for either of these components.

Accept *Stage*   The Accept stage is the last stage to discuss. Add two components. First, drag the SaveReceipt component to the Accept stage. You can leave the default value in the component's properties.

The second component to drop in is the SQLItem component. After you drag in the SQLItem component, right-click the component and choose Properties from the drop-down menu.

You have two parameters to configure. The first parameter, Query, should be set to the name of a stored procedure added in your store's global.asa file by using the AddQuery method.

The second parameter, Parameter List, should be a space-delimited list of variables to be used by the stored procedure. Following is an example from the sample store Microsoft Press Bookstore:

```
Query: insert-receipt-item
Parameter List: item._product_sku order.order_id index item.quantity
➥item._oadjust_adjustedprice
global.asa: Call MSCSContent.AddQuery("insert-receipt-item", "insert into
➥MSPress_receipt_item values
(:1,:2,convert(int, :3),convert(int, :4),convert(int, :5))")
```

To complete the custom Order Processing Pipeline, choose Save As from the File menu and save the file to your store's `Config` directory, using the file name `pipeline.pcf`.

Using the HTML-Based Editor

You have created a custom Order Processing Pipeline (OPP) with the Win32 Pipeline Editor. Now try using the HTML Based Editor.

In this section, you add a new component to the `Order Check` stage by using the HTML Based Editor. To open the editor, open Microsoft Internet Explorer 3.01 or later and go to your store's admin page.

When you get the admin page, click the Configure Order Pipeline button. You see the page that shows you the Pipeline stages as well as the components attached to the stages.

Scroll down to the `Order Check` stage and click the Add Component button. You see a page that allows you to select a component to add. Add the `Scriptor` component.

When you click the `Scriptor` component, you go back to the page that shows the Pipeline stages. The difference is that you now have the opportunity to edit this component's properties.

You just click to edit the properties for the components. Edit the component and add the code in Listing 22.3, which is taken from the sample store Adventure Works.

Listing 22.3

```
Language: VBScript
Internal
Script:
function MSCSExecute(config, orderform, context, flags)
  set errors = orderform.[_Purchase_Errors]
  set datafunctions = context.datafunctions
  result = 1
  REM -- validate shipping method
  If IsNull(datafunctions.CleanString(orderform.ship_to_name, 1, 50))
          or (orderform.shipping_method <> "fixed"
          and orderform.shipping_method <> "linear") then
errors.Add("shipping method must be 'fixed' or 'linear'")
orderform.ship_to_name = ""
result = 2
  End If
  MSCSExecute = result
End Function
```

After you add this code, click the Save button, and the pipeline configuration is saved.

From Here...

This chapter thoroughly discussed the Order Processing Pipeline (OPP) and showed you how to use the OPP with components, as well as how to create your own custom OPP configuration using the Win32 Pipeline Editor. This is the center of all data transfer for Commerce Server 2.0, and fully understanding its use is imperative. If you do not understand the OPP, read this chapter again. By reviewing this chapter, you pick up a great deal that you may not have understood the first time.

- Chapter 23, "Constructing Your Own Server Components," leads you step-by-step through the creation of your own custom component for the OPP, using Visual C++ 5.0.
- Chapter 27, "Using the Microsoft Buy Now and Wallet Components," introduces you to two new and very useful components for the OPP.
- Part VI, "Case Studies," will show you three different implementations of the OPP, which will reinforce your understanding of how components interact with the OPP.

CHAPTER 23

Constructing Your Own Server Components

Throughout this book, you have been teased, being told all about the advantages of the Commerce Server 2.0 order-processing pipeline (OPP), informed about its integrated COM features, and told how much time and effort it is going to save you. In the meantime, you have been secretly held back from this mystery, right?

You have been prepared, and you should now have a good understanding of the OPP and its internal representation. The purpose of this chapter is to lead you step-by-step through the creation of a component designed for the Commerce Server 2.0 OPP, but some topics must be discussed before you tackle this adventure.

Despite the fact that the focus of this chapter is to use the COM technology to create a component that is compatible with the OPP, each of these topics is intricate enough to have a book written about it. This chapter was written under the assumption that you read Chapters 13 through 19 which discuss Active Server Pages (ASP), as well as Chapter 22, "Building the Order Processing Pipeline," and that you have a good understanding of the development and implementation of Visual C++ in-proc COM objects.

Even though you can run through this chapter and accomplish the tasks in it without this knowledge, you can get much more from the chapter if you have this knowledge.

Review of previously discussed material

Reviewing previously discussed topics is a good idea, so this section reviews ASP, components, and the order-processing pipeline.

Introducing Commerce Server 2.0 SDK

Along with Commerce Server 2.0 comes an SDK that helps you develop components.

Creating your component

This section is where the fun stuff is; you create your component.

Adding your component to the OPP editor

A component isn't worth much unless you can add it to the OPP. In this section, you do just that.

If you are a daring go-getter who just jumps into things, jump right in, but you will find it to your benefit to read up before jumping in. ■

N O T E   At the time this book was written, the current version of Commerce Server 2.0 had problems with threading when custom components for the OPP were created in Visual Basic 5.0. Therefore, this chapter discusses creating a custom component with Visual C++ 5.0. A basic understanding of Visual C++ 5.0 is expected. This chapter walks you through the process of creating a component but does not discuss the advanced debugging features that are available with the MSDev Integrated Development Environment (IDE or Editor). ■

Reviewing Some Important Material

Up to now, the book has discussed material that may be new to you, so this section looks back at what the book has discussed so far and tells you where this material is used in this chapter and later.

Component Object Model (COM)

As you design objects for Commerce Server 2.0 (or any other application, for that matter), you face the task of conquering a technology that in the past few years has become popular for developing application tools. Developers have been intrigued by the capabilities of this technology, but Microsoft continues to amaze everyone by implementing the intricate features of COM into every project.

You may have a good understanding of what COM is and how it works, but if you have not had the pleasure, this section describes the methods and concepts behind the COM object. Component Object Model is a protocol by which a developer can create an application with the capability to talk with other applications.

Suppose that you open Microsoft Outlook to send your boss e-mail detailing last month's profits (at least, you hope that last month was profitable). The first thing that you do is click the New Mail button, and up comes an editor. You can use Microsoft Word as your editor, because Microsoft Outlook and Microsoft Word were both created with the COM technology, which allows them to talk with each other.

The purpose of this book and this chapter is not to explain how all this works, but you should at least understand this concept of communication between applications.

How is this example related to creating a component? When you create a component, you use this COM technology so that your components can talk with Commerce Server 2.0 as a whole, but also with other components and ASP pages.

Active Server Pages

To get your feet wet with ASP, refer to Chapter 13, "Introducing Active Server Pages;" Chapter 14, "Introduction to ASP Scripting;" Chapter 15, "Working with Active Server Web Pages;" Chapter 16, "Integrating VBScript into ASP;" and Chapter 17, "Practical ASP Programming."

The HTML Pipeline editor encapsulates your component's Property Page in .ASP format, so you must understand the logistics of ASP programming if you are going to use the HTML Pipeline Editor.

The .ASP aspects of this chapter are discussed in the section, "Create Active Server Pages For Your Component," later in this chapter. In that section, you create two ASP files that allow you to configure your component by using the HTML Pipeline Editor.

Commerce Server 2.0 Components

Understanding the Commerce Server 2.0 components before you continue in this chapter is crucial. If you are not educated in the design of these components, picturing how your component works with the OPP is difficult.

The purpose of this chapter is to teach you how to create a component that can be used in the Commerce Server 2.0 OPP. You must fully understand the components that are shipped with Commerce Server 2.0 before you can create a component to work with Commerce Server 2.0.

In addition to reading up on the components, you should start up the HTML or Win32 Pipeline Editor and play with the components. Move the components around, change their properties, and check out some of their limitations. This kind of hands-on experience helps prepare you for the sections ahead.

Order Processing Pipeline

The order processing pipeline is the backbone of the Commerce Server 2.0 store, and when you are done with this chapter, you will be able to quickly create components that help strengthen this backbone.

If you are not sure what the order-processing pipeline is, please refer to Chapter 22, "Building the Order Processing Pipeline." When you are familiar with the order-processing pipeline, you will understand the need for custom components.

Merchant Server 1.0 had many limitations in store functionality because the order-processing pipeline was hidden from the store developers. Commerce Server 2.0 solves the problem by making the order-processing pipeline a component supporting the insertion of custom components that store developers have easy access to. This functionality is by far the best improvement made in the Merchant Server 1.0 architecture.

Commerce Server 2.0 SDK

Along with Microsoft Commerce Server 2.0 comes an SDK that includes documentation, header files, libraries, and samples that assist developers in creating Commerce Server 2.0 components. Understanding the features that Microsoft provides with Commerce Server 2.0 is important.

Documentation

Microsoft provides some technical documentation that you can use to understand how to use the SDK. Due to the technical nature of the documentation, you may not want to read it straight through, but skimming it is a good idea.

Following is a list of the chapters in the Microsoft Commerce Server `\sdk\documentation` subdirectory:

```
Address Selector Ifaces.doc

Buy Now Overview.doc

CPCsmple.doc

MinMaxShip.doc

OCsmple.doc

OPP Interfaces.doc

Order Processing.doc

Payment Builder.doc

Payment Selector Ifaces.doc

Scripting API.doc

SDK Intro.doc

Wallet Controls.doc

WebKitOview.doc

Writing Components.doc
```

As you see, most of what is discussed in these chapters is discussed in this book. If you want to read about one of these subjects, look for it in this book first. This book is easier to understand, and after you master the concepts, you may later want to refer to some of this Microsoft documentation which is more technically oriented for the advanced user.

Header Files

Later in this chapter, you use header files to create your component, so look through them so that you have a good working knowledge of what each file does. The following list briefly describes the files:

`Commerce.h` contains the common Commerce Server 2.0 definitions, as well as the interface definitions.

`Commerce.idl` is the `.idl` definition file for the MIDL compiler, which defines the interfaces defined in the `commerce.h` file.

`Computil.cpp` implements some commonly used functions based on the `commerce.h` and `commerce.idl` definitions.

The functions implemented include:

```
HRESULT GetDictFromDispatch(IDispatch* pdisp, IDictionary** ppdict);
HRESULT GetSimpleListFromDispatch(IDispatch* pdisp, ISimpleList** pplist);
HRESULT GetNumValueOfVariant(VARIANT* pvar, int* pvalue);
HRESULT GetStringValueOfVariant(VARIANT* pvar, BSTR* pvalue);
HRESULT PutDictValue(IDictionary* pdict, LPCWSTR name, VARIANT& var);
HRESULT PutDictValue(IDictionary* pdict, LPCWSTR name, int value);
HRESULT PutDictValue(IDictionary* pdict, LPCWSTR name, LPCWSTR value);
HRESULT GetDictValue(IDictionary* pdict, LPCWSTR name, VARIANT* pvar);
HRESULT GetDictValue(IDictionary* pdict, LPCWSTR name, int* pvalue);
HRESULT GetDictValue(IDictionary* pdict, LPCWSTR name, BSTR* pvalue);
HRESULT GetListItems(IDispatch* pdictOrder, ISimpleList** pplistItems);
HRESULT GetNumItems(ISimpleList* pListItems, long* pcItems);
HRESULT GetNthItem(ISimpleList* pListItems, long iItem, IDictionary**
ppdictItem);
HRESULT GetListFromDict(IDictionary* pdictOrder, LPCWSTR wszName, ISimpleList**
pplist);
inline HRESULT GetListItems(IDictionary* pdictOrder, ISimpleList** pplistItems);
inline HRESULT DeleteNthItem(ISimpleList* plist, int iItem);
HRESULT AddErrToList(IDictionary* pdictOrder,LPCWSTR wszErrListName,IDispatch*
pdispContent,
LPCWSTR wszErrMsgName);
HRESULT GenUniqueID(unsigned short* buf, BOOL fAddRandom);
HRESULT InitKeyEnumInDict(IDictionary* pdict, IEnumVARIANT** ppenum);
HRESULT GetNextKeyInDict(IEnumVARIANT* penum, BSTR* pbstrKey);
inline HRESULT DeInitKeyEnumInDict(IEnumVARIANT** ppenum);
HRESULT RegisterCATID(const CLSID& clsid, IID newCATID);
HRESULT RegisterName(const CLSID& clsid, LPCWSTR wszName);
HRESULT RegisterThreadingModel(const CLSID& clsid, LPCWSTR wszThreadingModel);
```

N O T E Computil.cpp is not directly included in the Commerce OPP SDK include directory. Computil.cpp is taken from the MFCSample MinMaxShip project. ■

Computil.h simply defines the functions implemented in computil.cpp.

Merchext.h serves to define commonly used values for any custom components, as well as to define the basic functions that must be supported (such as exec). Merchext.h contains a definition of the order of the OPP stages, defined as follows:

```
/*
Stage index — uses as the third argument in
the call to Exec
 */
#define PRODUCT_INFO_INDEX          00
#define MERCHANT_INFO_INDEX     10
#define SHOPPER_INFO_INDEX      20
#define ORDER_INIT_INDEX        30
#define ORDER_CHECK_INDEX       40
#define IADJUST_INDEX               50
#define OADJUST_INDEX               60
#define SHIPPING_INDEX              70
#define HANDLING_INDEX              80
#define TAX_INDEX               90
#define TOTAL_INDEX                 100
#define INVENTORY_INDEX              110
#define PAYMENT_INDEX               120
#define ACCEPT_INDEX                130
```

N O T E These definitions are useful for any stage-components that you create, so that you know what stage is calling your component. Remember that these stages are numbered starting with 00, which is the first component. Forgetting this fact can throw your logic off. ■

Mscsadmin.h contains the definitions for the Administration interfaces.

Mspu_guids.h contains the GUID definitions for all the Commerce Server 2.0 interfaces, as well as the components shipped with Commerce Server 2.0.

Pipecomp.h contains the actual definition for the IPipelineComponent interface, as well as the core Pipeline component definitions.

Pipecomp.idl is the .idl definition file for the MIDL compiler, which defines the interfaces defined in the pipecomp.h file.

Pipeline.h contains the actual definition for the IPipeline interface, as well as the IPipelineAdmin interface.

Pipeline.h also defines the following important flags:

Mode

```
typedef enum tagOPPMODE_TYPE {
    OPPMODE_PRODUCT    = 1,
    OPPMODE_PLAN       = 2,
    OPPMODE_PURCHASE   = 4
} OPPMODE_TYPE;
```

Type

```
typedef enum tagOPPFLAGS_TYPE {
OPPFLAGS_DEBUG_COMPONENTS    = 1,
    OPPFLAGS_TRACE_PIPELINE     = 2
} OPPFLAGS_TYPE;
```

Error Level

```
typedef enum tagOPP_ERRORLEV {
    OPPERRORLEV_SUCCESS   = 1,
    OPPERRORLEV_WARN     = 2,
    OPPERRORLEV_FAIL     = 3,
    OPPERRORLEV_FATAL    = 4
} OPP_ERRORLEV;
```

Pipeline.idl is the .idl definition file for the MIDL compiler, which defines the interfaces defined in the pipeline.h file.

Pipeprx1.h contains only the definitions of the IPipeline interface defined in pipeline.h.

Pipeprx1.idl is the .idl definition file for the MIDL compiler, which defines the interfaces defined in the pipeprx1.h file.

Pipeprx1.h contains only the definitions of the IPipelineAdmin interface defined in pipeline.h.

`Pipeprx2.idl` is the `.idl` definition file for the MIDL compiler, which defines the interfaces defined in the `pipeprx2.h` file.

`Pipe_stages.h` contains the definitions for the CATIDs for each stage of the order-processing pipeline. These CATIDs are used in the Registry to tell the Pipeline Editor which stage(s) your component is allowed to be attached to.

`Pipe_stages.h` defines the following CATIDs:

```
CATID_MSCSPIPELINE_COMPONENT
{cf7536d0-43c5-11d0-b85d-00c04fd7a0fa}
CATID_MSCSPIPELINE_ANYSTAGE
{d2acd8e0-43c5-11d0-b85d-00c04fd7a0fa}
CATID_MSCSPIPELINE_ACCEPT
{d82c3490-43c5-11d0-b85d-00c04fd7a0fa}
CATID_MSCSPIPELINE_HANDLING
{d82c3491-43c5-11d0-b85d-00c04fd7a0fa}
CATID_MSCSPIPELINE_IADJUST
{d82c3492-43c5-11d0-b85d-00c04fd7a0fa}
CATID_MSCSPIPELINE_INVENTORY
{d82c3493-43c5-11d0-b85d-00c04fd7a0fa}
CATID_MSCSPIPELINE_MERCHANT_INFO
{d82c3494-43c5-11d0-b85d-00c04fd7a0fa}
CATID_MSCSPIPELINE_OADJUST
{d82c3495-43c5-11d0-b85d-00c04fd7a0fa}
CATID_MSCSPIPELINE_ORDER_CHECK
{d82c3496-43c5-11d0-b85d-00c04fd7a0fa}
CATID_MSCSPIPELINE_ORDER_INIT
{d82c3497-43c5-11d0-b85d-00c04fd7a0fa}
CATID_MSCSPIPELINE_PAYMENT
{d82c3498-43c5-11d0-b85d-00c04fd7a0fa}
CATID_MSCSPIPELINE_PRODUCT_INFO
{d82c3499-43c5-11d0-b85d-00c04fd7a0fa}
CATID_MSCSPIPELINE_SHIPPING
{d82c349a-43c5-11d0-b85d-00c04fd7a0fa}
CATID_MSCSPIPELINE_SHOPPER_INFO
{d82c349b-43c5-11d0-b85d-00c04fd7a0fa}
CATID_MSCSPIPELINE_TAX
{d82c349c-43c5-11d0-b85d-00c04fd7a0fa}
CATID_MSCSPIPELINE_TOTAL
{d82c349d-43c5-11d0-b85d-00c04fd7a0fa}
CATID_MSCSPIPELINE_REQUIREDCOMPONENT
{EA226CA1-8F48-11d0-BE9A-00A0C90DC855}
```

This section does not fully cover what each file entails, but it highlights the key points that you learn later in the chapter when you create your component. With these files come libraries that you can use in programming custom components.

Libraries

Microsoft has compiled some libraries that you can use. Following is a list of the libraries that are included with Microsoft Commerce Server 2.0 (for a description of their uses, refer to the preceding section of this chapter):

```
commerce.lib
merchext.lib
pipecompps.lib
pipeline.lib
pipeprx1.lib
pipeprx2.lib
```

Much as the header files are included in the `include` directory, the `.lib` files are located in the `lib\PROCESSOR_ARCHITECTURE` (I386) directory.

Samples

Microsoft provides some sample components that you can use as templates for your components. I actually used the `MinMaxShipping` sample component to template my first OPP component. Without the sample component one can easily get lost.

You have six examples for the OPP, but this chapter discusses only the `MinMaxShipping` sample because it was written with Visual C++ and MFC. Following is a list of the components that are shipped with Commerce Server 2.0:

`DumpOrder`	(Visual Basic)
`JavaMaxShip`	(Java)
`MaxShipV1`	(C++)
`AtlSample`	(Visual C++ 4.0 – ATL)
`MinMaxShipping`	(Visual C++ 4.0)
`TestScaffold`	(Visual C++ 4.0)

Order-Processing Pipeline Interfaces

This section describes the COM interfaces and methods for the Commerce Server 2.0 order-processing pipeline. You can use these interfaces to write a custom order-processing component.

Following is a list of interfaces discussed in this chapter:

```
IOrderPipeline Interface
IPipelineComponent Interface
IPipelineComponentAdmin Interface
IDictionary Interface
IPersistStreamInit Interface
ISpecifyPropertyPages Interface
```

IOrderPipeline Interface

The IOrderPipeline interface is derived from IDispatch Interface and acts as the execution interface for the Pipeline object. Remember that the role of the order-processing pipeline is to present the OrderForm to the components so they can read and write data to and from the OrderForm.

A component can then capture information from the OrderForm and do what it wants to with the information. The nice feature of this structure is that the OrderForm information is still encapsulated by the component. The IOrderPipeline methods can be called from an Active Server Page because the IOrderPipeline Interface is derived from the IDispatch Interface.

The following sections list the syntax for each IOrderPipeline interface method.

IOrderPipeline::OrderExecute The OrderExecute method runs the order-processing pipeline through the set of components attached to the stages included in the lMode parameter.

Syntax

```
HRESULT IOrderPipeline::OrderExecute(
long            lMode             // in
IDispatch *        pDispOrder           // in
IDispatch *        pDispContext    // in
long            lFlags            // in
long *          plErrorLevel    // out, return value
); // OrderExecute
```

Parameters

lMode

Informs the Pipeline what set of stages to run through. Valid values are as follows:

```
OPPMODE_PRODUCT = 1
OPPMODE_PLAN = 2
OPPMODE_PURCHASE = 4
```

pDispOrder

A pointer to the OrderForm object.

pDispContext

A pointer to the Context object, which is a Dictionary object containing pointers to the MessageManager, Shopper, and Content objects, as well as the store's language information.

lFlags

Should be 0.

plErrorLevel

Used as a flag that determines the status of the errors to be reported to the user. Valid values are as follows:

Value	Description
0	No errors; the pipeline exited successfully.
1	Basket or purchase errors occurred during the execution of the pipeline.
2	Serious errors occurred during the execution of the pipeline.

This error level is meant to supplement the HRESULT information returned by a function. The pipeline maps errors returned from components (E_xxxx errors) to an error level of 2.

Return Values

S_OK

(function ran successfully)

S_FALSE

(function ran into errors)

IOrderPipeline::EnableDesign   The EnableDesign method prepares the pipeline for execution by using either design mode or execution mode. Execution mode (the default) is analogous to the production mode and is also the default mode in which a pipeline starts.

The pipeline passes the design mode to the individual components (see IPipelineComponent::EnableDesign).

N O T E   Only administrative tools should call this method, because no reason should exist to call EnableDesign while the pipeline is executing. ▪

Syntax

```
HRESULT EnableDesign(
    BOOL     fEnable    // in
);
```

Parameters

fEnable

Informs the pipeline whether it should be run in execution mode (FALSE) or design mode (TRUE).

Return Values

S_OK

(function ran successfully)

S_FALSE

(function ran into errors)

Example

```
pPipe->EnableDesign(TRUE);
```

IOrderPipeline::LoadPipe   The LoadPipe method is an automation function used in environments in which IPersistFile::Load is unavailable. The function is used to bind to the Commerce Server 2.0 pipeline's configuration file (.pcf).

Syntax

```
HRESULT LoadPipe (
BSTR      pszFileName    // in
);
```

Parameters

pszFileName

The full path to the pipeline configuration file to be loaded.

Return Values

S_OK

(function ran successfully)

S_FALSE

(function ran into errors)

IOrderPipeline::SetLogFile   The SetLogFile method informs the order-processing pipeline to log debug information to the specified file.

Syntax

```
HRESULT SetLogFile (
BSTR      pszFileName    // in
);
```

Parameters

pszFileName

The full path to the log file to which the order-processing pipeline is to log debug information.

N O T E If *pszFileName* specifies a file that the current process does not have write access to, the log file is not written to without failure. To turn logging off, set *pszFileName* to NULL. ■

Return Values

S_OK

(function ran successfully)

S_FALSE

(function ran into errors)

Example

```
IOrderPipeline *pPipeline=NULL;
HRESULT hr=pPipeline->SetLogFile("c:\pipe.log");
```

IPipelineComponent Interface

All order-processing pipeline components must implement the `IPipelineComponent` interface, passing an `OrderForm` interface pointer to be passed between each component. If a component returns an error, the pipeline terminates and returns an error to the caller.

`IPipelineComponent::Execute`   The `Execute` method is the entry point of execution for a component.

Syntax

```
HRESULT Execute(
IDispatch *    pDispOrder     // in
IDispatch *    pDispContext   // in
long      lFlags      // in
long *     plErrorLevel   // out, return value
);
```

Parameters

`pDispOrder`

A pointer to the OrderForm object.

`pDispContext`

A pointer to the Context object, which is a Dictionary object containing pointers to the MessageManager, Shopper, and Content objects, as well as the store's language information.

`lFlags`

Should be 0.

`plErrorLevel`

Used as a flag that determines the status of the errors to be reported to the user. Valid values are as follows:

Value	Description
0	No errors; the pipeline exited successfully.
1	Basket or purchase errors occurred during the execution of the pipeline.
2	Serious errors occurred during the execution of the pipeline.

This error level is meant to supplement the HRESULT information returned by a function. The pipeline maps errors returned from components (E_xxxx errors) to an error level of 2.

Return Values

S_OK

(function ran successfully)

S_FALSE

(function ran into errors)

IPipelineComponent::EnableDesign   The EnableDesign method prepares the pipeline for execution by using either design mode or execution mode. Execution mode (the default) is analogous to the production mode and is also the default mode in which a pipeline starts.

Syntax

```
HRESULT EnableDesign(
BOOL     fEnable   // in
);
```

Parameters

fEnable

Informs the pipeline whether it should be run in execution mode (FALSE) or design mode (TRUE).

Return Values

S_OK

(function ran successfully)

S_FALSE

(function ran into errors)

Example

```
STDMETHODIMP CMyComponent::XPipelineComponent::
 EnableDesign (BOOL fEnable) {
return S_OK;
}
```

IPipelineComponentAdmin Interface

The IPipelineComponentAdmin is an optional interface provided to be used as an interface between a component and its user interface (UI). To support third-party components in the system, components must provide a UI code.

IPipelineComponentAdmin::GetConfigData   The GetConfigData method returns an IDictionary pointer with which the UI can read the configuration data for a component.

Syntax

```
HRESULT GetConfigData(
IDispatch **      ppDict        // out
);
```

Parameters

ppDict

An IDictionary pointer to an object containing the configuration data for a component that the UI can read.

Return Values

S_OK

(function ran successfully)

S_FALSE

(function ran into errors)

IPipelineComponentAdmin::SetConfigData   The SetConfigData method takes a pointer to an IDictionary object containing the configuration information for the component.

Syntax

```
HRESULT SetConfigData(
IDispatch *     pDict        // in
);
```

Parameters

pDict

An IDictionary interface pointer to the object containing the configuration information for the component.

Return Values

S_OK

(function ran successfully)

S_FALSE

(function ran into errors)

IDictionary Interface

The OrderForm object implements the IDictionary interface, which is used as the internal name–value representation of the order's data. The pipeline and the pipeline components use the IDictionary interface to access name–value pairs from the order.

The computil.cpp file installed with the Commerce Server 2.0 MinMaxShipping component implements the following methods by using the IDictionary interface:

```
HRESULT GetDictFromDispatch(IDispatch* pdisp, IDictionary** ppdict);
HRESULT GetSimpleListFromDispatch(IDispatch* pdisp, ISimpleList** pplist);
HRESULT GetNumValueOfVariant(VARIANT* pvar, int* pvalue);
HRESULT GetStringValueOfVariant(VARIANT* pvar, BSTR* pvalue);
HRESULT PutDictValue(IDictionary* pdict, LPCWSTR name, VARIANT& var);
HRESULT PutDictValue(IDictionary* pdict, LPCWSTR name, int value);
```

```
HRESULT PutDictValue(IDictionary* pdict, LPCWSTR name, LPCWSTR value);
HRESULT GetDictValue(IDictionary* pdict, LPCWSTR name, VARIANT* pvar);
HRESULT GetDictValue(IDictionary* pdict, LPCWSTR name, int* pvalue);
HRESULT GetDictValue(IDictionary* pdict, LPCWSTR name, BSTR* pvalue);
HRESULT GetListItems(IDictionary* pdictOrder, ISimpleList** pplistItems);
HRESULT GetNumItems(ISimpleList* pListItems, long* pcItems);
HRESULT GetNthItem(ISimpleList* pListItems, long iItem, IDictionary** ppdi
➥ctItem);
HRESULT GetListFromDict(IDictionary* pdictOrder, LPCWSTR wszName, ISimpleL
➥ist** pplist);
inline HRESULT GetListItems(IDictionary* pdictOrder, ISimpleList** pplistI
➥tems);
inline HRESULT DeleteNthItem(ISimpleList* plist, int iItem);
HRESULT AddErrToList(IDictionary* pdictOrder,LPCWSTR wszErrListName,IDispa
➥tch* pdispContent,
LPCWSTR wszErrMsgName);
HRESULT GenUniqueID(unsigned short* buf, BOOL fAddRandom);
HRESULT InitKeyEnumInDict(IDictionary* pdict, IEnumVARIANT** ppenum);
HRESULT GetNextKeyInDict(IEnumVARIANT* penum, BSTR* pbstrKey);
inline HRESULT DeInitKeyEnumInDict(IEnumVARIANT** ppenum);
HRESULT RegisterCATID(const CLSID& clsid, IID newCATID);
HRESULT RegisterName(const CLSID& clsid, LPCWSTR wszName);
HRESULT RegisterThreadingModel(const CLSID& clsid, LPCWSTR wszThreadingMod
➥el);
```

You should look over this file, because you will use it to create your custom component, and you can use this information later to create more of your own methods with the IDictionary interface.

IPersistStreamInit Interface

The IPersistStreamInit interface is a standard Win32 OLE interface that typically is implemented on any object that needs to support an initialized stream-based persistence, regardless of the object's task. In the context of the order-processing pipeline, the interface is used to load/save the component configuration in the pipeline configuration file (the order-processing pipeline calls on this interface as appropriate).

IPersistStreamInit::IsDirty   The IsDirty method checks to see whether a component has changed since it was last saved, to prevent you from losing information from components that have not yet been saved. The dirty flag for a component is conditionally cleared in the Save method.

Syntax

HRESULT IsDirty(void);

Parameters

None

Return Values

S_OK

(function ran successfully)

S_FALSE

(function ran into errors)

`IPersistStreamInit::Load`   The `Load` method loads a component's information from its associated stream. The seek pointer is set as it was in the most recent `IPersistStreamInit::Save` method, and the pointer must be positioned in the same position as it was passed in (the position immediately following the end of the component's data). This method can seek and read from the stream but does not have the right to write to it.

Syntax

```
HRESULT Load(
IStream *       pStm        // in
);
```

Parameters

pStm

A pointer to the IStream interface that the component should use to load its information.

Return Values

S_OK

(function ran successfully)

S_FALSE

(function ran into errors)

`IPersistStreamInit::Save`

The `Save` method saves a component into the specified stream and should reset its dirty flag. The component must call the `IStream::Write` method to write its data.

When the function is called, the seek pointer is positioned at the location in the stream at which the object should begin writing its data. Upon function exit, the seek pointer must be positioned immediately following the component's data written. The position of the seek pointer is undefined if an error returns.

Syntax

```
HRESULT Save(
IStream *   pStm       // in
   BOOL     fClearDirty   // in
);
```

Parameters

pStm

A pointer to the IStream interface that the component uses to save its data.

fClearDirty

Indicates whether to clear the dirty flag after the save is complete. If `fClearDirty` evaluates to TRUE, the flag should be cleared; otherwise, the flag should be left unchanged.

Return Values

`S_OK`

(function ran successfully)

`STG_E_CANTSAVE`

(function could not save the component's data to the stream)

This error could indicate, for example, that the object contains another object that is not serializable to a stream or that an `Istream::Write` call returned `STG_E_CANTSAVE`.

`STG_E_MEDIUMFULL`

(function could not save the component's data because the storage device is at capacity)

`IPersistStreamInit::GetSizeMax`

The `GetSizeMax` method returns the size (in bytes) that a component needs to save its data. You can call this method to determine the size of a component before calling the `IPersistStreamInit::Save` method on the component.

Syntax

```
HRESULT GetSizeMax(
ULARGE_INTEGER *   pcbSize        // out
);
```

Parameters

`pcbSize`

A pointer to a 64-bit unsigned integer value, indicating the size (in bytes) of the data to be saved for this component.

Return Values

`S_OK`

(function ran successfully)

`S_FALSE`

(function ran into errors)

`IPersistStreamInit::InitNew`   The `InitNew` method initializes a component to a default state and is called instead of `IPersistStreamInit::Load`. This is much like a constructor for a class.

Syntax

```
HRESULT InitNew(void);
```

Parameters

None

Return Values

S_OK

(function ran successfully)

E_NOTIMPL

(function may return this value for two reasons: orthogonality or in anticipation of a future need for this method)

ISpecifyPropertyPages Interface

The ISpecifyPropertyPages interface is a standard Win32 OLE interface used to allow the pipeline administration tool to invoke the component's Property Page UI.

ISpecifyPropertyPages::GetPages   The GetPages method is used to fill a counted array of UUID values. Each UUID specifies the CLSID of a particular property page that can be displayed in the property sheet for this object.

The CAUUID structure is caller-allocated but is not initialized by the caller. The ISpecifyPropertyPages::GetPages method fills the *cElements* field in the CAUUID structure. This method also allocates memory for the array pointed to by the *pElems* field in CAUUID by means of CoTaskMemAlloc; then it fills the newly allocated array. When this method returns successfully, the structure contains a counted array of UUIDs, each UUID specifying a property page CLSID.

Syntax

```
HRESULT GetPages(
CAUUID *    pPages     // out
);
```

Parameters

pPages

A pointer to a CAUUID structure that must be initialized and filled before returning.

The CAUUID structure is defined as follows:

```
typedef struct tagCAUUID{
ULONG       cElems;       // Size of pElems array.      GUID FAR*       pElems;
// Pointer to arr
➥ay of
// UUID values. The
// Callee is expected to
// manage array
// allocation (using
// CoTaskMemAlloc)
// and freeing (using
```

```
//CoTaskMemFree)
} CAUUID;
```

Return Values

S_OK

(function ran successfully)

E_POINTER

(the address stored in *pPages* is invalid)

Creating Your Component

You should now have a good understanding of how the Commerce Server 2.0 components encompass the COM technology and how the order-processing pipeline uses these components to manipulate order information. You can now move on to actually creating your first component, which leads you to the hardest task of all: figuring out what component to create? A useful tool would be a debugging tool which allows you to see the values of the OrderForm for each item in the basket, each time the OPP is called.

In this chapter you are going to create a component for debugging the order-processing pipeline information. Suppose that you write a component to figure special shipping prices, and when you test the component, your prices do not come out correctly. How would you figure out what the problem is? You could write down all the values and figure them out, but where would you get those values? The OPP does not show you all the values that are currently stored in the OrderForm. Wouldn't it be great to have a component that you could place on any stage, that would tell you all the values currently stored in the OrderForm? This component is what you create in this chapter.

As stated earlier in the chapter, Commerce Server 2.0 has threading problems in components created with Visual Basic 5.0, so you use Visual C++ 5.0 to create this component. You also use the Win32 Based Pipeline Editor to use and test the control.

Preparation

Now that you have a clear picture of what you are going to create, you need to plan the project to accomplish this task. First, draw what your component will accomplish.

As discussed in Chapter 22, "Building the Order Processing Pipeline," the primary goal of the order-processing pipeline is to give the store designer access to the values stored in the OrderForm so that those values can be read and written during a user's session. This availability to the OrderForm values implies that OPP components also have access to the OrderForm values, which means that you can write a component to output these values.

Following are the steps that you need to take to create this component:

1. Implement a basic OLE Inproc server component.
2. Prepare the component to implement Commerce interfaces.

3. Implement the `IPersistStreamInit` interface (or `IPersistPropertyBag`) if the component has any configuration data that needs to be persisted.

4. Implement `ISpecifyPropertyPages` and OLE Property Pages.

5. Implement the `IPipelineComponent` interface.

6. Register the component with the appropriate CATIDs that specify which stage(s) of the pipeline the component is intended for.

7. Design a dialog box to be used as the user interface for the component.

8. Register the DLL for the Win32 Pipeline Editor.

9. Implement Active Server Pages(ASP) for configuring the component from the HTML-based Pipeline Editor.

After you read the discussions of these steps in this chapter, you will have a solid foundation in the development of Commerce Server 2.0 components. When you master these techniques, you will be not only an accomplished developer, but also a great asset to your customers.

Implement a Basic OLE Inproc Server Component You create your component in the Visual Studio 97 Editor, using the Visual C++ 5.0 configurations. Open Visual C++ 5.0. You should see your main desktop (see Figure 23.1).

FIG. 23.1

The Microsoft Visual C++ 5.0 main desktop.

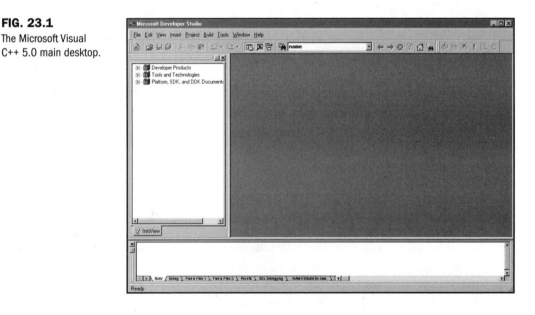

For this example, call the component `OPP_Debug` (for order-processing pipeline debug). Create the `OPP_Debug.DLL` project by following these steps:

1. Choose New from the File menu of Visual C++ 5.0.

   Visual C++ responds by displaying the New dialog box, shown in Figure 23.2.

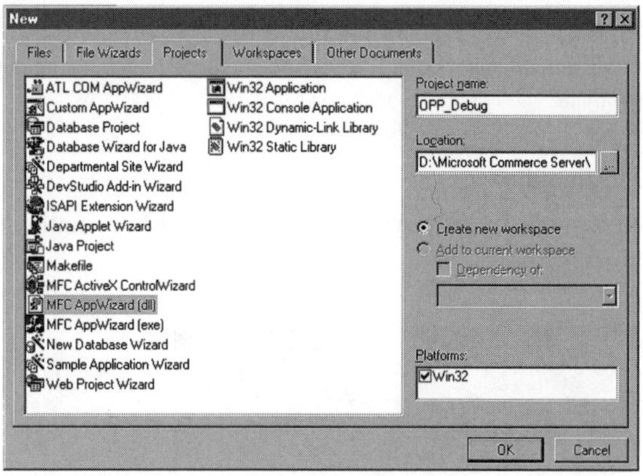

FIG. 23.2

The Visual C++ 5.0 New dialog box.

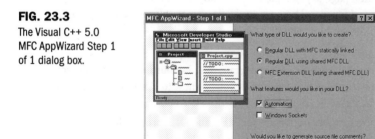

2. Choose the Projects tab and select MFC AppWizard (dll).

3. Enter **OPP_Debug** (the project name) in the Project Name box.

4. Set the Location box to point to your Commerce Server 2.0 SDK\OPP\OPP_Debug directory.

5. Make sure that the Win32 check box is selected in the Platforms section.

6. Click the OK button.

   Visual C++ responds by displaying the MFC AppWizard Step 1 of 1 dialog box, shown in Figure 23.3.

FIG. 23.3

The Visual C++ 5.0 MFC AppWizard Step 1 of 1 dialog box.

7. Choose the Regular DLL with MFC statically linked and Automation options.

   The Automation option allows you to attach variables to your component's Property dialog box and to map them to your component's internal coding.

8. Practicing the good programming habits that we all have, select "Yes, please" for comments.

N O T E   Selecting "Yes, please" is not necessary for this project, but if you don't, it might cause
serious programmers mind cramp later when someone tries to figure out what is happening
with your code, just kidding. ▦

9. Click the Finish button.

Visual C++ responds by displaying the New Project Information dialog box, shown in
Figure 23.4.

FIG. 23.4

The Visual C++ 5.0 New
Project Information
dialog box.

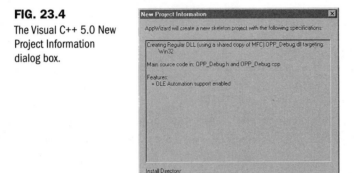

The New Project Information page is just a page description summarizing what the magical
Visual C++ editor just created for you. The page basically says that Visual C++ created the
following files with the following information:

ReadMe.txt is a generic file generated with every project, detailing some useful information for understanding Microsoft's MFC programming in your new project, as well as a
description of most of the files like this one. If you are new to Visual C++, check out this
file.

StdAfx.h contains the headers necessary for MFC and OLE programming.

StdAfx.cpp includes StdAfx.h so that the headers are in the project.

OPP_Debug.h contains the main class definition for your project. This class implements
the basic MFC and OLE features that are necessary for your COM object.

OPP_Debug.cpp creates the only global OPP_Debug object. This file also includes the entry
points for your DLL to register and unregister with Windows.

Resource.h stores the IDs that are used for the next Resource, Command, or Control
added to your project.

OPP_Debug.rc stores the main Resource information for your project.

OPP_Debug.clw contains information for the MFC ClassWizard such as Version,
ClassCount, and ResourceCount (among others).

OPP_Debug.def contains the Library, Description, and Exports definitions for your project. Other definitions may be added as you build your project.

OPP_Debug.dsp is your project definition file (previously .mdp in Visual C++ version 4.x). The file basically tells the Visual C++ editor what files to open and includes any previous debug information that you added when opening your project.

OPP_Debug.dsw is your project workspace definition file. This file is much like the .dsp file, except it contains only the information necessary for adding your project to the workspace. You use this file to reopen your project.

OPP_Debug.odl contains the Object Description Language code that you use to compile the type library for your project.

RES\OPP_Debug.rc2 is where you should store any resource information that the Visual C++ editor cannot display.

You now have a working COM object which, although it can't do anything productive, you can be built. If you want to build your component now (and at any other time in this chapter), you can choose the Build OPP_Debug.dll option from the Build menu of Visual C++.

Prepare Component to Implement Commerce Interfaces   Now that you have a working COM object, you can prepare it to implement the Commerce Server 2.0 order-processing pipeline interfaces. Follow these steps:

1. Choose Class Wizard from the View menu of Visual C++

   Visual C++ responds by displaying the Class Wizard dialog box, shown in Figure 23.5.

FIG. 23.5
The Visual C++ Class Wizard dialog box's Message Maps tab.

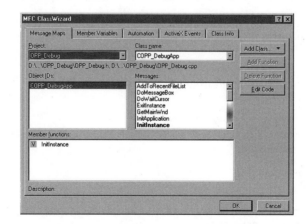

2. Make sure that the Message Maps tab is selected and that OPP_Debug Project is selected in the drop-down list, as shown in Figure 23.5.

3. Choose New from the Add Class button.

   Visual C++ responds by displaying the New Class dialog box, shown in Figure 23.6.

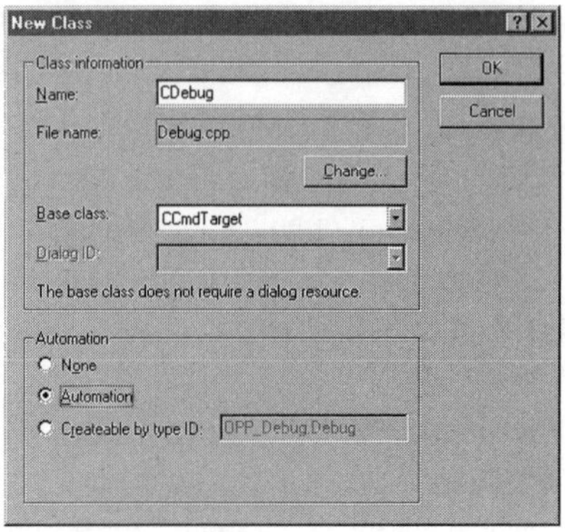

FIG.23.6

The Visual C++ New Class dialog box.

4. Type **CDebug** in the Name box.

5. Choose CCmdTarget from the Base Class drop-down list.

6. Choose Automation in the Automation section.

7. Click the OK button.

> Visual C++ responds by adding the following files:
>
> Debug.h contains the class definition of your new CDebug class.
>
> Debug.cpp contains the implementation of your new CDebug class. This file is where the bulk of your work is done.
>
> OPP_Debug.aps is used by the Visual C++ 5.0 editor to keep track of new project information.

Updating the following project files:

OPP_Debug.clw

Visual C++ changed ClassCount from 1 to 2 and LastClass from COPP_DebugApp to CDebug, and added the following lines:

```
Class2=CDebug
 LastTemplate=CCmdTarget

[CLS:COPP_DebugApp]
LastObject=COPP_DebugApp
 [CLS:CDebug]
Type=0
HeaderFile=Debug.h
ImplementationFile=Debug.cpp
BaseClass=CCmdTarget
Filter=N
LastObject=Cdebug
```

OPP_Debug.dsp

Visual C++ added the following lines:

```
SOURCE=.\Debug.cpp
# End Source File
# Begin Source File
SOURCE=.\Debug.h
# End Source File
# Begin Source File

OPP_Debug.odl
```

Visual C++ added the following lines:

```
//  Primary dispatch interface for CDebug

        [ uuid(77A2BD41-FAE7-11D0-A8D3-00403332871D) ]
        dispinterface IDebug
        {
                properties:
                        // NOTE - ClassWizard will maintain property information
here.
                        //    Use extreme caution when editing this section.
                        //{{AFX_ODL_PROP(CDebug)
                        //}}AFX_ODL_PROP

                methods:
                        // NOTE - ClassWizard will maintain method information here.
                        //    Use extreme caution when editing this section.
                        //{{AFX_ODL_METHOD(CDebug)
                        //}}AFX_ODL_METHOD
        };
        //  Class information for CDebug
        [ uuid(77A2BD43-FAE7-11D0-A8D3-00403332871D) ]
        coclass Debug
        {
                [default] dispinterface IDebug;
        };
```

Now click the ClassWizard dialog box OK button to close the ClassWizard.

You have done a great deal so far, but you just told the Visual C++ editor what to do; it took care of the rest. Now you take over.

8. Using the Project Workspace, edit the StdAfx.h file and search for _AFX_NO_OLE_SUPPORT.

9. Add the following lines (in bold) so that your project can support the common OLE controls:

```
#ifndef _AFX_NO_OLE_SUPPORT
#include <afxctl.h>    // MFC OLE controls
#include <afxole.h>    // MFC OLE classes
#include <afxodlgs.h>  // MFC OLE dialog classes
#include <afxdisp.h>   // MFC OLE automation classes
#endif // _AFX_NO_OLE_SUPPORT
```

10. Copy guids.cpp, computil.cpp, computil.h from the SDK\OPP\SAMPLES\MFCSample directory to the SDK\OPP\INCLUDE directory.

You use these files to include headers and some common functions needed to support order-processing pipeline components. Next, you add these files to your project.

11. Choose Files from the Add to Project submenu of the Project menu in Visual C++.

    Visual C++ responds by displaying the Insert Files into Project dialog box, shown in Figure 23.7.

FIG. 23.7

The Visual C++ Insert Files into Project dialog box.

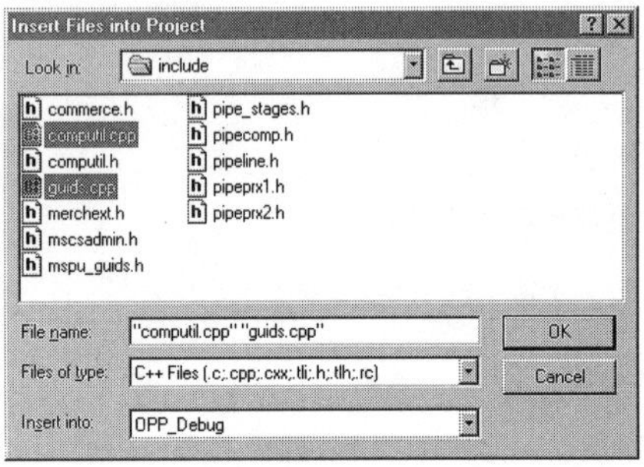

12. Choose the SDK\OPP\INCLUDE directory from the Directory drop-down list.

13. Select both guids.cpp and computil.cpp, as shown in Figure 23.8.

14. Click OK.

    Visual C++ responds by adding guids.cpp and computil.cpp to your project workspace.

N O T E Visual C++ does not copy these files to your project directory by default. If you do not want to modify the files contained in the INCLUDE directory, you need to first copy these two files to your project directory and then insert them into your project. ▨

The last thing that you need to do is add the SDK\OPP\INCLUDE directory to your project's include directories for compiling. Doing this allows you to include any files in that directory in your project by using the preprocessor directive #include without copying the files to your project's directory.

15. Choose Options from the Tools menu in Visual C++.

    Visual C++ responds by displaying the Options dialog box, shown in Figure 23.8.

FIG. 23.8

The Visual C++ Options dialog box's Directories tab.

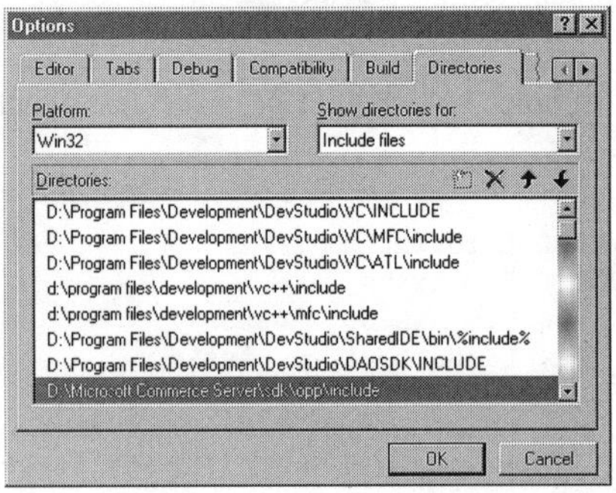

16. Select the Directories tab.

17. Choose Included Files from the Show Directories For drop-down list.

18. To add a directory, scroll to the bottom of the Directories list box and double-click the last (empty) entry; when you are prompted, select your SDK\OPP\INCLUDE directory.

19. Click OK.

Visual C++ responds by adding the directory to the list of directories that the preprocessor searches when processing the #include directive.

Part
V

Ch
23

You can now build your component again to ensure that you are not missing anything. When you have built your component successfully, you are ready to begin programming your project to support the order-processing pipeline (OPP) interfaces.

Everything that this chapter has discussed up to now, excluding the addition of the m_bActive property, can be used as a template for creating any COM object. The following section discusses what you can do to turn this COM object into an OPP-supporting COM object.

Adding Skeleton Order-Processing Pipeline Interfaces

You have designed a solid COM object; now you need to prepare it to be useful. First, you must get the class to support the order-processing pipeline (OPP) interfaces, so add the following to the Debug.h file (additions in bold):

> **N O T E** The entire file is not included (to save space), only what is necessary for you to know where to add the bold type. ■

```
#include <pipecomp.h>
/////////////////////////////////////////////////////////////////////////////
➡///
// CDebug command target
class CDebug : public CCmdTarget
{
// Attributes
public:
    BOOL m_fDirty;
// Implementation
protected:
    virtual ~CDebug();
    // Generated message map functions
    //{{AFX_MSG(CDebug)
        // NOTE - the ClassWizard will add and remove member functions here.
    //}}AFX_MSG
    DECLARE_MESSAGE_MAP()
    DECLARE_OLECREATE(CDebug)
    BEGIN_INTERFACE_PART(PipelineComponent, IPipelineComponent)
      STDMETHOD (Execute) (IDispatch* pdispOrder, IDispatch* pdispContext,
➡LONG lFlags, LONG* plErrorLevel);
      STDMETHOD (EnableDesign) (BOOL fEnable);
    END_INTERFACE_PART(PipelineComponent)
    BEGIN_INTERFACE_PART(PersistStreamInit, IPersistStreamInit)
```

```
        STDMETHOD (GetClassID) (CLSID *pClassID);
        STDMETHOD (IsDirty) (void);
        STDMETHOD (Load) (IStream *pStm);
        STDMETHOD (Save) (IStream *pStm, BOOL fClearDirty);
        STDMETHOD (GetSizeMax) (ULARGE_INTEGER *pcbSize);
        STDMETHOD (InitNew) ();
    END_INTERFACE_PART(PersistStreamInit)
BEGIN_INTERFACE_PART(SpecifyPropertyPages, ISpecifyPropertyPages)
    STDMETHOD(GetPages) (CAUUID * pPages);
    END_INTERFACE_PART(SpecifyPropertyPages)
    // Generated OLE dispatch map functions
    //{{AFX_DISPATCH(CDebug)
    BOOL m_bActive;
    afx_msg void OnBActiveChanged();
    //}}AFX_DISPATCH
    DECLARE_DISPATCH_MAP()
    DECLARE_INTERFACE_MAP()
};
```

To implement these definitions, add the following code to Debug.cpp (only the bold lines):

```
#include <computil.h>
#include <pipe_stages.h>
#include <pipeline.h>
BEGIN_INTERFACE_MAP(CDebug, CCmdTarget)
    INTERFACE_PART(CDebug, IID_IDebug, Dispatch)
    INTERFACE_PART(CDebug, IID_IPersistStreamInit, PersistStreamInit)
    INTERFACE_PART(CDebug, IID_IPipelineComponent, PipelineComponent)
    INTERFACE_PART(CDebug, IID_ISpecifyPropertyPages, SpecifyPropertyPages)
END_INTERFACE_MAP()
*** Paste the rest of this at the end of the file ***
/////////////////////////////////////////////////////////////////
// IPersistStreamInit
ULONG CDebug::XPersistStreamInit::AddRef()
{
METHOD_PROLOGUE(CDebug, PersistStreamInit)
return pThis->ExternalAddRef();
}
ULONG CDebug::XPersistStreamInit::Release()
{
METHOD_PROLOGUE(CDebug, PersistStreamInit)
return pThis->ExternalRelease();
}
STDMETHODIMP CDebug::XPersistStreamInit::QueryInterface(
 REFIID iid, void FAR* FAR* ppvObj)
{
METHOD_PROLOGUE(CDebug, PersistStreamInit)
return (HRESULT)pThis->ExternalQueryInterface(&iid, ppvObj);
}
STDMETHODIMP CDebug::XPersistStreamInit::GetClassID( CLSID* pCID )
{
return E_NOTIMPL;
}
STDMETHODIMP CDebug::XPersistStreamInit::IsDirty()
{
```

```
return E_NOTIMPL;
}
STDMETHODIMP CDebug::XPersistStreamInit::Load(IStream* pStm)
{
return E_NOTIMPL;
}
STDMETHODIMP CDebug::XPersistStreamInit::Save(IStream* pStm, BOOL fClearDi
➥rty)
{
return E_NOTIMPL;
}
STDMETHODIMP CDebug::XPersistStreamInit::GetSizeMax
(ULARGE_INTEGER* pcbSize)
{
return E_NOTIMPL;
}
STDMETHODIMP CDebug::XPersistStreamInit::InitNew()
{
return E_NOTIMPL;
}
////////////////////////////////////////////////////////////////
// ISpecifyPropertyPages
ULONG CDebug::XSpecifyPropertyPages::AddRef()
{
METHOD_PROLOGUE(CDebug, SpecifyPropertyPages)
return pThis->ExternalAddRef();
}
ULONG CDebug::XSpecifyPropertyPages::Release()
{
METHOD_PROLOGUE(CDebug, SpecifyPropertyPages)
return pThis->ExternalRelease();
}
STDMETHODIMP CDebug::XSpecifyPropertyPages::QueryInterface(
REFIID iid, void FAR* FAR* ppvObj)
{
METHOD_PROLOGUE(CDebug, SpecifyPropertyPages)
return (HRESULT)pThis->ExternalQueryInterface(&iid, ppvObj);
}
STDMETHODIMP CDebug::XSpecifyPropertyPages::GetPages(CAUUID *
pPages)
{
return E_NOTIMPL;
}
////////////////////////////////////////////////////////////////
// IPipelineComponent
ULONG CDebug::XPipelineComponent::AddRef()
{
METHOD_PROLOGUE(CDebug, PipelineComponent)
return pThis->ExternalAddRef();
}
ULONG CDebug::XPipelineComponent::Release()
{
METHOD_PROLOGUE(CDebug, PipelineComponent)
return pThis->ExternalRelease();
}
```

```
STDMETHODIMP CDebug::XPipelineComponent::QueryInterface(
 REFIID iid, void FAR* FAR* ppvObj)
{
METHOD_PROLOGUE(CDebug, PipelineComponent)
return (HRESULT)pThis->ExternalQueryInterface(&iid, ppvObj);
}
STDMETHODIMP CDebug::XPipelineComponent::Execute(IDispatch*
pdispOrder, IDispatch* pdispContext, LONG lFlags, LONG* plErrorLevel)
{
return E_NOTIMPL;
}
STDMETHODIMP CDebug::XPipelineComponent::EnableDesign(BOOL
fEnable)
{
return S_OK;
}
```

You have just added the basic OPP interface functionality for your component, and you can rebuild your project. You can use everything that you have done so far as a basic template for creating a component for the OPP.

Next, you customize the template for your own needs. In the next few sections, you customize these interfaces with code that takes care of the tasks that you set out to accomplish.

Implement the *IspecifyPropertyPages* Interface   The ISpecifyPropertyPages interface supports the addition of a property page for your component in the order-processing pipeline (OPP). You must take a couple of steps to implement this interface:

- Add a string table
- Add the CDebugPpg class
- Adding CLSIDs to the project
- Implement the ISpecifyPropertyPages interface

Add a String Table   When you call your property page by using the standard OLE calls, you need to pass the methods to a string ID containing the title of the property page, so create a string table with an ID that you can pass to these methods later. Follow these steps:

1. Select the ResourceView tab in the Project Workspace.
2. Right-click the OPP_Debug_resources folder and then choose Insert.

   Visual C++ responds by displaying the Insert Resource dialog box (see Figure 24.9).
3. Double-click String Table.

   Visual C++ responds by creating a string table to your resources and starts you editing the string table.
4. Double-click the empty string cell.

   Visual C++ responds by displaying the String Properties dialog box, shown in Figure 23.9.
5. Change the entry in the ID drop-down list to **IDS_CDEBUG_PPG**.

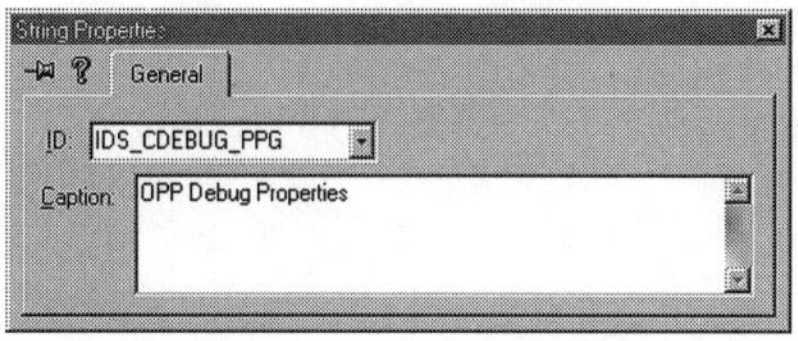

FIG. 23.9

The Visual C++ String
Properties dialog box,
General tab.

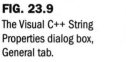

6. Type **OPP Debug Properties** in the Caption box.

   This caption is used as the dialog-box title for your property page. This is discussed
   more later in this chapter.

7. Close the dialog box by clicking the X in the top-right corner.

When you finish adding this string, you can close the string table. Take a step back and review
what has changed in your project. Since you last checked, the following has changed:

OPP_Debug.rc now contains a string table.

Resource.h defined the String IDS control, and adjusted the definitions for the next
available ID.

Other files were added, but they are all related to the Visual C++ project information and are
hidden, so this section does not mention them.

Adding the CDebugPpg Class   You are ready to add a class for your new property page dialog
box. Unfortunately, Microsoft does not support the addition of new classes derived from the
COlePropertyPage class, so you need to add this class manually by doing the following things:

- Creating the CDebugPpg class definition
- Creating the CDebugPpg methods
- Adding the CDebugPpg class to the ClassWizard

Creating the CDebugPpg Class Definition.   The first step is creating a basic MFC class
derived from the COlePropertyPage class. For this project, add your class definition and
methods to the existing Debug.h and Debug.cpp files.

To create a basic MFC class derived from the COlePropertyPage class, paste the following
right after the CDebug class definition in the Debug.h file:

```
/////////////////////////////////////////////////////////////
// CDebugPpg dialog
class CDebugPpg : public COlePropertyPage
{
    DECLARE_DYNCREATE(CDebugPpg)
public:
    CDebugPpg();
    //{{AFX_DATA(CDebugPpg)
      // NOTE - the ClassWizard will add and remove data here
    //}}AFX_DATA
    //{{AFX_VIRTUAL(CDebugPpg)
    protected:
    virtual void DoDataExchange(CDataExchange* pDX);
    //}}AFX_VIRTUAL
```

```
protected:
   //{{AFX_MSG(CDebugPpg)
      // NOTE: the ClassWizard will add member functions here
   //}}AFX_MSG
   DECLARE_MESSAGE_MAP()
};
```

Creating the CDebugPpg Methods   You need to implement the basic CdebugPpg MFC class methods so that the ClassWizard can add methods and variables, and map data to and from other classes.

Paste the following into the Debug.cpp file, right after the message handlers:

```
/////////////////////////////////////////////////////////////////////////////
// CDebugPpg property page
IMPLEMENT_DYNCREATE(CDebugPpg, COlePropertyPage)
BEGIN_MESSAGE_MAP(CDebugPpg, COlePropertyPage)
   //{{AFX_MSG_MAP(CDebugPpg)
      // NOTE: the ClassWizard will add message map macros here
   //}}AFX_MSG_MAP
END_MESSAGE_MAP()
CDebugPpg::CDebugPpg() : COlePropertyPage(NULL,
IDS_CDEBUG_PPG)
{
   //{{AFX_DATA_INIT(CDebugPpg)
      // NOTE: the ClassWizard will add member initialization here
   //}}AFX_DATA_INIT
}
void CDebugPpg::DoDataExchange(CDataExchange* pDX)
{
   //{{AFX_DATA_MAP(CDebugPpg)
      // NOTE: the ClassWizard will add class data mapping here
   //}}AFX_DATA_MAP
}
BOOL CDebugPpg::CDebugPpgFactory::UpdateRegistry(BOOL bRegister)
{
   return TRUE;
}
```

Adding the CDebugPpg Class to the ClassWizard   Because the ClassWizard does not support the addition of classes derived from the COlePropertyPage class, you need to change the ClassWizard's internal representation of classes so that the ClassWizard allows you to use your new class. To add the class to the ClassWizard, you need to modify OPP_Debug.clw (ClassWizard).

To assist you in these modifications, any old lines are typed here in *italics* and I will type any lines that you need to type in bold. Make the following changes in the OPP_Debug.clw file.

Change these lines:

```
[General Info]
ClassCount=2
ClassCount=3
LastTemplate=CCmdTarget
LastTemplate=COlePropertyPage
```

Add these lines:

```
[General Info]
Class3=ColePropertyPage

[CLS:CDebugPpg]
Type=0
HeaderFile=Debug.h
ImplementationFile=Debug.cpp
BaseClass=COlePropertyPage
Filter=D
LastObject=CdebugPpg

VirtualFilter=idWC
```

Now the ClassWizard recognizes your new class.

Adding CLSIDs to the Project You have already generated CLSIDs for both the OPP_Debug component and the property page, but if you need to generate your own CLSIDs later for other components that you create, you can choose Create GUID from the Tools menu in Visual C++.

For this project, add the following lines to the CDebugPpg class in the Debug.h file (additions in bold):

```
DECLARE_DYNCREATE(CDebugPpg)
DECLARE_OLECREATE_EX(CDebugPpg)
```

Add the following lines to the Debug.cpp file (additions in bold):

```
// {BB4F0FE0-FAEB-11d0-A8D3-00403332871D}
static const GUID CLSID_CDebugPpg =
{ 0xBB4F0FE0, 0xFAEB, 0x11d0, { 0xA8, 0xD3, 0x0, 0x40, 0x33, 0x32, 0x87, 0
➥x1D } };
// {BB4F0FE0-FAEB-11d0-A8D3-00403332871D}
IMPLEMENT_OLECREATE_EX( CDebugPpg, "OPP.DebugPpg.1", 0xBB4F0FE0, 0xFAEB, 0
➥x11d0, 0xA8, 0xD3, 0x0, 0x40, 0x33, 0x32, 0x87, 0x1D )

// {BB4F0FE1-FAEB-11d0-A8D3-00403332871D}
static const CLSID CLSID_CDebug =
{ 0xBB4F0FE1, 0xFAEB, 0x11d0, { 0xa8, 0xD3, 0x0, 0x40, 0x33, 0x32, 0x87, 0
➥x1D } };
// {BB4F0FE1-FAEB-11d0-A8D3-00403332871D}
IMPLEMENT_OLECREATE(CDebug, "OPP.Debug.1", 0xBB4F0FE1, 0xFAEB, 0x11d0, 0xa
➥8, 0xD3, 0x0, 0x40, 0x33, 0x32, 0x87, 0x1D )
```

Registering the Object with the Order-Processing Pipeline To register your object with the order-processing pipeline (OPP), you must first register your component as an OPP component and then register what stage you want your component to be added to. You can find a list of valid stages in the pipe_stages.h file in the SDK\OPP\INCLUDE directory.

The OPP_Debug component can be included in any stage, so modify the following function to register the following:

```
BOOL CDebugPpg::CDebugPpgFactory::UpdateRegistry(BOOL bRegister)
{
    if (bRegister)
```

```
    {
      RegisterCATID(CLSID_CDebug,
CATID_MSCSPIPELINE_COMPONENT);
      RegisterCATID(CLSID_CDebug,
CATID_MSCSPIPELINE_ANYSTAGE);
      RegisterName(CLSID_CDebug, L"OPP Debug");
      RegisterThreadingModel(CLSID_CDebug, L"both");
      // Notice this is where we use our String ID
// IDS_CDEBUG_PPG
      return
AfxOleRegisterPropertyPageClass(AfxGetInstanceHandle(),
        m_clsid, IDS_CDEBUG_PPG);
    }
   else
     return AfxOleUnregisterClass(m_clsid, NULL);
}

STDMETHODIMP CDebug::XSpecifyPropertyPages::GetPages(CAUUID * pPages)
{
 return S_OK;
}
```

Implement the *IPersistStreamInit* Interface   The IPersistStreamInit interface is used to store your property page variables, so the values are kept between sessions. The use is straightforward; you have an InitNew for new components and Load, Save, and GetMax (which returns the size of all your property variables) methods that administrate the storage of your properties.

Update the following methods in the Debug.cpp file:

```
///////////////////////////////////////////////////////////////
// IPersistStreamInit
STDMETHODIMP CDebug::XPersistStreamInit::GetClassID( CLSID* pCID )
{
    METHOD_PROLOGUE(CDebug, PersistStreamInit)

    if (!pCID)
      return E_INVALIDARG;
    *pCID = pThis->guid;
    return S_OK;
}
STDMETHODIMP CDebug::XPersistStreamInit::IsDirty()
{
    METHOD_PROLOGUE(CDebug, PersistStreamInit)

    return pThis->m_fDirty;
}
STDMETHODIMP CDebug::XPersistStreamInit::Load(IStream* pStm)
{
    METHOD_PROLOGUE(CDebug, PersistStreamInit)

    if (!pStm)
      return E_INVALIDARG;
    return S_OK;
}
```

```
STDMETHODIMP CDebug::XPersistStreamInit::Save(IStream* pStm, BOOL fClearDi
➥rty)
{
   METHOD_PROLOGUE(CDebug, PersistStreamInit)
   if (!pStm)
     return E_INVALIDARG;
   return S_OK;
}
STDMETHODIMP CDebug::XPersistStreamInit::GetSizeMax(ULARGE_INTEGER* pcbSiz
➥e)
{
   METHOD_PROLOGUE(CDebug, PersistStreamInit)

   if (!pcbSize)
     return E_INVALIDARG;
 return S_OK;
}
STDMETHODIMP CDebug::XPersistStreamInit::InitNew()
{
 METHOD_PROLOGUE(CDebug, PersistStreamInit)
   return S_OK;
}
```

Implement the *IPipelineComponent* Interface   The last and most important interface to
implement is the IPipelineComponent interface. The IPipelineComponent interface is to your
component what main() is to a C program.

You will need to add the following two helper functions before the Execute method:

```
// Forward Declaration
STDMETHODIMP EnumValues(IDispatch*, FILE**);

STDMETHODIMP EnumList(IDispatch* pdispList, FILE** fp)
{

        HRESULT                 hr                      = S_OK;
        ISimpleList           pList             = NULL;
        IDictionary           pDict             = NULL;
        long                  ListCount      = 0;

        hr = CoInitialize(NULL);
    if ( FAILED(hr) ) {
            fwprintf (*fp, L"EnumList: Unable to CoInitialize\n"), fflus
➥h(*fp);

        } else {
            hr = pdispList->QueryInterface(IID_ISimpleList,(void**) &pLi
➥st);
                if (SUCCEEDED(hr)) {
                    GetNumItems(pList, &ListCount);

                    for (int x = 0; x < ListCount; ++x) {
                        GetNthItem (pList, x, &pDict);
                        EnumValues (pDict, fp);
                        fwprintf (*fp, L"\n");
```

```
                              }
                    } else
                        fwprintf (*fp, L"EnumList: Unable to Query SimpleList Int
➥erface\n"), fflush(*fp);

            }
            if (pDict)
                    pDict->Release();
            if (pList)
                    pList->Release();
            CoUninitialize();

            return hr;
}
STDMETHODIMP EnumValues(IDispatch* pdispOrder, FILE** fp)
{
            HRESULT         hr        = S_OK;
        IDictionary*    pdict      = NULL;
            IDictionary     pDict2          = NULL;
            ISimpleList     pisl            = NULL;
            IUnknown        pUnk          = NULL;
            IEnumVARIANT*   penum         = NULL;
            static int              TimesCalled = -1;
            VARIANT         retvar;
            VARIANT               vvalue;
            BSTR                  pvalue;
            BSTR                  DictKey;
            int                          ivalue;

            VariantInit (&vvalue);
            VariantInit(&retvar);
            ++TimesCalled;
            hr = CoInitialize(NULL);
        if ( FAILED(hr) ) {
                    fwprintf (*fp, L"EnumValues: Unable to CoInitialize\n"),
fflush(*fp);
             return hr;
            }
            hr = pdispOrder->QueryInterface(IID_IDictionary,(void**) &pdict);
            if (SUCCEEDED(hr)) {

                    hr = pdict->get__NewEnum(&pUnk);
                    if (SUCCEEDED(hr)) {

                            //Note that IID_IEnumVARAINT and Next are standard CO
➥M stuff
                            hr = pUnk->QueryInterface(IID_IEnumVARIANT,(void**) &
➥penum);
                            if (SUCCEEDED(hr)) {

                                    while ((hr = penum->Next(1,&retvar,NULL))==S_O
➥K) {

                                            if (SUCCEEDED(hr = GetStringValueOfVariant(&re
➥tvar, &DictKey))) {
```

```
                              for (int i = 0; i<TimesCalled; ++i)
                                  fwprintf (*fp, L"  "), fflush(*fp);

                          // retvar
                          if (SUCCEEDED(hr = GetDictValue (pdict,
➥DictKey, &pvalue))) {
                                  if (wcscmp(DictKey, L"SKU") &&
➥TimesCalled > 0)
                                      fwprintf(*fp, L"\t");
                                  fwprintf (*fp, L"%s: %s\n", DictKey,
➥pvalue), fflush(*fp);
                              } else if (SUCCEEDED(hr =
➥GetDictValue (pdict, DictKey, &ivalue))) {
                                      fwprintf (*fp, L"%s : %i\n",
➥DictKey, ivalue), fflush(*fp);
                              } else if (SUCCEEDED (hr =
➥GetListFromDict(pdict, DictKey, &pisl))) {
                                          EnumList(pisl, fp);
                              } else if (SUCCEEDED (hr = Get
➥DictFromDispatch(pdict, &pDict2))) {
                                          fwprintf(*fp,
➥L"\nFound Dictionary: %s\n", DictKey), fflush(*fp);
                              } else
                                  fwprintf (*fp,
➥L"GetDictValue() FAILED! [%s]\n", DictKey), fflush(*fp);
                              } else
                                  fwprintf (*fp, L"Unable to
➥get DictKey\n"), fflush(*fp);
                          }

              } else
                          fwprintf (*fp, L"Shopper_ID:
➥GetDictValue() FAILED!\n"), fflush(*fp);
              } else
                      fwprintf (*fp, L"Shopper_ID: GetDictValue() FAILED!
➥\n"), fflush(*fp);
      }
      if (pdict)
              pdict->Release();
      if (penum)
              penum->Release();
      if (pDict2)
              pDict2->Release();
      CoUninitialize();
      -TimesCalled;
      return hr;
}
```

Now you can add the following Execute method to your Debug.cpp file.

```
STDMETHODIMP CDebug::XPipelineComponent::Execute(IDispatch*
pdispOrder, IDispatch* pdispContext, LONG lFlags, LONG* plErrorLevel)
{

      METHOD_PROLOGUE(CDebug, PipelineComponent)
      IDictionary* pdictOrder = NULL;
```

```
        if (pdispOrder == NULL)
                return E_INVALIDARG;
        if (SUCCEEDED(pdispOrder->QueryInterface(IID_IDictionary, (void**)&
➥pdictOrder)))
    {
            FILE* fp;
            if ((fp = fopen("C:\\OPP_Debug.out", "a")) == NULL) {
                    if ((fp = fopen("C:\\OPP_Debug.out", "w")) == NULL)
➥{

                            return E_FAIL;
                    }
            }
             BSTR OrderID;
              GetDictValue (pdictOrder, L"shopper_id", &OrderID);
              fwprintf (fp, L"********************** Order: %s *********
➥*************\n\n", OrderID), fflush(fp);
            EnumValues (pdispOrder, &fp);

              fwprintf (fp, L"\n********************** Order: %s ******
➥****************\n", OrderID), fflush(fp);
            fclose(fp);
            if (pdictOrder)
                    pdictOrder->Release();
        } else
                return E_INVALIDARG;
        return S_OK;
}
```

To ensure that your component locks and unlocks itself, add the following, in bold, to your Cdebug constructor and destructor.

```
CDebug::CDebug()
{
      EnableAutomation();
      // To keep the application running as long as an OLE automation
      //      object is active, the constructor calls AfxOleLockApp.
      AfxOleLockApp();
}
CDebug::~CDebug()
{
      // To terminate the application when all objects created with
      //      with OLE automation, the destructor calls AfxOleUnlockApp.
      AfxOleUnlockApp();

}
```

You have created your first Commerce Server 2.0 component. You can use this knowledge to create tons of your own components for your stores.

Now that you have created the component, you want to register it and then test it by using the Win32 Pipeline Editor.

Register the Component

After you build your component, you have to register the component before you can use it in the Pipeline Editor. This tells Windows and the Pipeline Editor what interfaces you support, as well as what stages your component can be used in.

To register your component, follow these steps:

1. Open a command prompt.
2. Change to the directory that contains your new component's .DLL.
3. Run REGSVR32.EXE OPP_Debug.DLL.

N O T E REGSVR32.EXE is stored in your computer's system32 directory. You need to run the program by using the entire path or ensure that system32 is in your current PATH system variable. You can add system32 to your PATH system variable by typing the following at the command prompt:

set PATH=%PATH%;%SystemRoot%\SYSTEM32 ▪

Create Active Server Pages for Your Component

To configure your order-processing pipeline by using the HTML editor, you must add two Active Server Pages to the Server\Administration\order-processing pipeline directory. The first file must be named after the ProgID for the component. The component that you just created has the ProgID "OPP.Debug.1". You registered this with the following lines in the Debug.cpp file:

```
// {C21F1C71-D9BF-11d0-A873-00403332871D}
IMPLEMENT_OLECREATE(CDebug, "OPP.Debug.1", 0xC21F1C71, 0xD9BF, 0x11d0, 0xA
➥8, 0x73, 0x0, 0x40, 0x33, 0x32, 0x87, 0x1D )
```

You must name your first file OPP_Debug_1.asp; call the second file OPP_Debug_1_post.asp. Open a new file, Server\Administration\Pipeline Configuration\OPP_Debug_1.asp, and paste the following into the file:

```
<!—#INCLUDE FILE="pe_global.asp" —>
<% REM ###############################################################
➥###### %>
<% REM
➥        %>
<% REM    OPP_Debug_1.ASP                                          %>
<% REM    Microsoft Commerce Server v2.00                          %>
➥        %>
<% REM
➥        %>
<% REM ###############################################################
➥###### %>
<!—#INCLUDE FILE="pe_cannotedit.asp" —>
```

Because the OPP_Debug component does not have any properties, you will not need to create an OPP_Debug_1_post.asp file for the component. You write a component with properties you will need to create this file by using one of the existing components COMPONENT_post.asp file as a template. The format is straight-forward and you can just modify the file to meet the needs of your component's properties.

Now you can edit and configure the new component by using the HTML Pipeline Editor.

From Here...

You should now be able to see just how powerful components are to the Commerce Server 2.0 order-processing pipeline. You designed a simple debugging tool for any store as well as any stage, but imagine expanding this component. Trying to do so helps you learn some of the intricate features that Microsoft provided with Commerce Server 2.0, and provides you a handy tool for debugging the advanced stores that you will be creating.

- Chapter 27, "Using the Microsoft Buy Now and Wallet Components," will take you through the usage of two components that are already created for you. You can learn much about the design of components by studying these two components.

- Chapter 28, "Building a New Site: Eddie Bauer," will help you understand the concepts behind building a new site as well as help you see component usage from the perspective of building a store from the ground up.

- Chapter 29, "Converting an Existing Site: Childs Hope," will help you understand the concepts behind converting an existing site as well as help you see component usage from the perspective of converting a store rather than building a new store.

Working with the Progistics Shipping Solution

- An overview of the Progistics architecture

- Detailed instructions for the setup of the Progistics shipping-and-handling electronic-commerce solution

- Configuring Commerce Server to work with the Progistics components

- Testing the Progistics environment

- Creating store accounts to use with Progistics

This chapter covers the installation and configuration of the TanData Progistics shipping-and-handling components to work with Microsoft Commerce Server 2.0. Configuring Commerce Server to handle the additional functionality that the Progistics components provide is also discussed in detail. Reading this chapter will provide you with a pretty good idea as to how the Progistics components work and what they can do for you and your Commerce Server site. ■

Shipping Basics

Microsoft Commerce Server 2.0 provides three basic methods of calculating the shipping charges for an order. These methods are fixed shipping, linear shipping, and table shipping. Each of these methods has its advantages and disadvantages, but none of the methods are able to provide the actual carrier shipping charges for an order as it is being placed.

Most electronic-commerce merchants assign conservatively high values to the shipping charges so that they don't end up paying for these costs themselves. Unfortunately, this conservative method of estimating often means that the customer is being overcharged for the cost of shipping. Although overcharging the customer for shipping may not be an issue in a noncompetitive market, most merchants are looking for any competitive advantage they can find.

TanData Corporation's Progistics.*Merchant* product allows Commerce Server to provide accurate shipping charges for an order on a per-carrier basis. Progistics.*Merchant* also allows for best-way carrier selection, tracking-number generation, and the implementation of a merchant's logistics business rules.

Logistics business rules are the internal rules that a merchant follows in shipping their product to their customers. For instance, a merchant may provide a discount on shipping charges when shipping to particular customers or particular areas. These merchants may agree to ship their product overnight to some of their larger customers but only charge these customers for the cost associated with second day shipping. Other merchants may define that United Parcel Service be used for all overnight shipments but that Federal Express be used for all two-day shipments. Any rules that define *how* a product is shipped from the warehouse to the customer is a logistics business rule.

Since Progistics.*Merchant* is based on Microsoft's Component Object Model (COM), any development tool capable of accessing COM objects can be used with Progistics.*Merchant* to implement the merchant's logistics business rules. Such development tools would include Internet Explorer's VBScript and JavaScript ActiveX scripting engines, Visual Basic, Visual J++, Visual C++, Delphi, Powerbuilder, and a host of others.

Progistics.*Merchant* also provides the merchant more flexible controls for the calculation and application of handling charges. Handling charges can be calculated as a percentage of the order subtotal, a percentage of the order shipping charges, or as a fixed amount. The computed handling charges can then be added directly to the shipping charges or itemized out as a separate item in the total cost of the order.

Progistics.*Merchant* Architecture

Progistics.*Merchant* implements the scalable architecture known as the TanData Merchant Interface (see Figure 24.1). This interface allows for the minimal implementation of a stand-alone commerce site, as well as for an enterprise-commerce site that is completely integrated with inventory-management, warehouse-management, shipping, and customer-service systems.

FIG. 24.1

The TanData Merchant Interface.

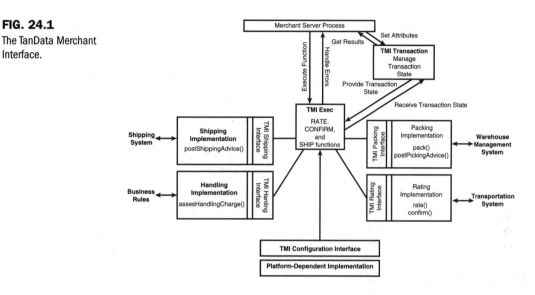

Such integration is possible because the Progistics.*Merchant* system is based on the client/server distributed-object model of TanData's Progistics architecture. The Progistics architecture is a full-blown, 32-bit, multithreaded, client/server-based, distributed logistics application.

Progistics.*Merchant* runs as a component in the Progistics CS (Component Solution) environment. Progistics CS is the base architecture that the various Progistics components use. Other components based on the Progistics CS architecture are Progistics.*Connect* (rating and routing across the internet) and Progistics.*Shipper* (browser based shipping and manifesting). Information on these components, as well as other component products, is available on the TanData Web site (**http://www.tandata.com**).

The Progistics environment is composed of a group of one or more machines running Progistics components, all of which are capable of interacting. Progistics.*Merchant* is the Progistics component that is responsible for processing shipments in an order-pipeline.

The order-pipeline process is different from the normal shipping process because the product being ordered has not yet been packed into boxes. As a result, the exact number of boxes and the respective box weights may not be known. To provide rates for a shipment, the carriers require the number of boxes and their individual box weights.

Progistics.*Merchant* uses a packing algorithm to simulate the packing process. This packing algorithm is implemented in Java and exposed as a COM object. The default algorithm supplied by TanData is based on weight. The store administrator assigns a maximum box weight that the packing algorithm uses to create virtual boxes.

Product is placed in a virtual box until the maximum box weight is reached. The system then creates another virtual box and continues packing the order. This process is repeated until all the items in the order are assigned to individual virtual boxes. These boxes are then

Part
V

Ch
24

individually rated by the system. Progistics.*Merchant* returns the sum of these rates to the order-pipeline.

In addition to setting a maximum box weight, each product can be associated with a no pack flag. This flag tells the system that a particular product cannot be packed with any other products. The no pack flag is useful when shipping large items, such as monitors and computer systems.

This default algorithm is a somewhat simplistic view of the packing process. But because the functionality is implemented as a plug-in object, a more realistic algorithm can easily be created and substituted with the default algorithm to better meet the individual needs of a particular merchant.

Although explaining the entire Progistics architecture is beyond the scope of this current chapter, the following sections describe the components that comprise the Progistics.*Merchant* and Progistics CS software suite.

Progistics Controller

The Progistics Controller component acts as the coordinator for a Progistics system, providing basic network-management functions for other Progistics components. The Progistics Controller enables each component on the network to locate other components, regardless of the size of the network or the network protocol that is used.

The Progistics Controller also manages the business entities that the store administrator establishes. These business entities are referred to as *shippers*. A Progistics environment can have more than one shipper. Each shipper has its own account with each carrier that a shipper uses. This feature is useful for an Internet Service Provider that is hosting an electronic mall for multiple merchants.

Only one Progistics Controller can run in a Progistics environment at a time.

Progistics Machine Manager

The Progistics Machine Manager component is a server program that runs locally on each computer that a Progistics base component is running on. The Progistics Machine Manager is responsible for all Progistics activity on that local system. All Progistics Machine Managers are in direct communication with the Progistics Controller.

RateServers

A RateServer is the component that provides individual carrier functionality. The RateServer implements all the rules that a given carrier mandates in its service guide for rating, routing, time-in-transit computation, and tracking-number generation. Any special services (such as

Saturday delivery, collect-on-delivery, and declared value) that a particular carrier supports are also implemented in the carrier-specific RateServer.

The standard rating, routing, and time-in-transit information (normally termed *book* information because it is published by the carriers) that the RateServers use is maintained by TanData. Carriers normally update book information yearly. TanData updates their RateServers as new book information is made available by the carriers. The updates are then either sent out by TanData to their user base or made available on TanData's Web site. TanData charges a nominal annual fee for updating their RateServers. Custom rate information (rates negotiated between the merchant and the carrier) is typically supplied directly by the carrier on diskette (known as a rate disk). The RateServer administration pages provide a method of loading the carrier rate disk into the appropriate RateServer.

The basic Progistics CS package includes RateServers for United Parcel Service, Roadway Package Service, DHL Worldwide Express, and the United States Postal Service. Airborne Express, Burlington Air Express, Emery, Federal Express, less-than-truckload (LTL) and smaller regional carriers are also available from TanData but are not provided as part of the Progistics CS base system at this time.

RateMan

RateMan supplies the uniform interface to each carrier RateServer. A client program uses RateMan to talk to a RateServer. RateMan also allows for configuration of best-way groups. A *best-way group* is a set of services that the store administrator defines. RateMan can select one of the services from this group or return a list of all the services and their respective rates for the group.

RateMan can be configured to automatically select a service from the best-way group, according to one or more selection algorithms. These algorithms allow for selection of the carrier by cost, delivery commitment, or a combination of cost and delivery commitment.

You could create a group called Best-Way Overnight, for example, containing the UPS Next Day Air Saver and Federal Express Standard Overnight services. You could present this best-way group to the shopper as a shipping option. RateMan automatically determines which service is the least costly to use in shipping the order to the destination.

RateMan can also be configured to return all the qualifying services, along with their rates and delivery commitments, from the group. A qualifying service is a service that can actually be used to ship to the destination within the commitment timeframe. Most carriers advertise priority (morning delivery) overnight shipping, but most carriers do not support this level of service for all destinations served. Progistics.*Merchant* will only return services that meet the criteria of selection. For instance, if the best-way group contains a list of priority overnight services, only those priority overnight services that can ship the shopper's order to the shopper's destination will be returned. The shopper could then choose the service that best fits his or her needs from the list of returned services.

Progistics Security Server

The Progistics Security Server provides a single point of entry into the Progistics environment from an outside source. This component is responsible for ensuring that only valid Progistics messages from known sources are passed into the Progistics system. This component is also responsible for mapping Java byte-code binaries to local machine binaries and for logging all transactions by account name.

Administrative Clients

Individual client interfaces comprise the portion of Progistics that a store administrator uses to configure the Progistics components. Each component of the Progistics system has its own special set of parameters that must be configured.

RateServer administrative clients allow the store administrator to configure the various account numbers for the carriers that a merchant uses. Tracking-number ranges, special services (such as UPS Delivery Track II and UPS Hundredweight), the origin point (the ZIP code from which the merchant is shipping orders), and any incentive programs that a carrier may have with the merchant can also be configured through this interface component.

The RateServer administrative clients also provide methods of updating any custom rate, route, and delivery-commitment information the merchant may have negotiated with the carriers.

The RateMan administrative client specifies which carrier RateServers are available to the rest of the Progistics system. Best-way groups are also maintained through this interface.

Functions are provided in the RateMan administrative client to dynamically list the available services and best-way groups. These functions would allow you to write client applications that do not need to specifically know which carriers and services are available. A store administrator could then modify the shipping methods that are available to the merchant's customers without having to rewrite any of the store functionality.

You can maintain the various Progistics components without having to shut down and restart the system. TanData implements these administrative clients as COM objects and presents them on Active Server Pages.

Progistics.*Merchant* Commerce Server Interface

Progsitics.*Merchant* is the Progistics component that implements the TanData Merchant Interface (TMI). This interface (shown in Figure 24.1) is a specification for the implementation of the shipping-and-handling component of a typical order-processing pipeline. (Refer to the TanData Web site at **http://www.tandata.com** for more information regarding this specification.)

The Progistics.*Merchant* component is responsible for validating and parsing TMI messages from the client application and sending them to the Progistics system as transactions. This component also receives the results from these transactions and formats them into TMI response messages for return to the client application.

The Commerce Server interface for Progistics.*Merchant* provides the store administrator with the interface that he or she needs to configure and use the Progistics functions that are directly related to the Commerce Server order-processing pipeline. Functions are provided to enumerate the available services, set the rating configuration, rate and confirm shipments, and so on.

The Progistics.*Merchant* Commerce Server interface exposes its functionality through COM and can be used through JavaScript or VBScript in HTML pages or Active Server Pages. The administrative clients provided by TanData use Progistics.*Merchant*'s functionality through JavaScript in Active Server Pages.

The Commerce Server interface for Progistics.*Merchant* is one of many interfaces that TanData currently supports. Interfaces for electronic-commerce products from iCat, INTERSHOP, and Oracle are also currently available.

Setting Up the Progistics Environment

Setup of the Progistics environment is a two-step process: installation and configuration. Installation of the Progistics components is a straightforward and simple process. Configuration consists of configuring the shipper and the individual RateServers for use.

Installing the Progistics Components

Follow these steps for a successful installation:

1. Double-click setup.exe on the installation CD-ROM to run the Progistics installation program. Once the Setup Wizard finishes loading, the Welcome dialog box will appear (see Figure 24.2).

2. Click Next in the Welcome dialog box. The Choose Destination Location dialog box will appear (see Figure 24.3).

3. Select the directory in which Progistics.*Merchant* should be24. installed. By default, the installation program will create a Progistics directory off your Web server's document root directory. If this directory is satisfactory, click Next. Otherwise click Browse and select the directory in which the Progistics directory should be created and then click Next.

   The system will update the registry entries and then a dialog box prompting for your Web server name will appear (see Figure 24.4).

FIG. 24.2

The Progistics Welcome dialog box.

FIG. 24.3

The Choose Destination Location dialog box.

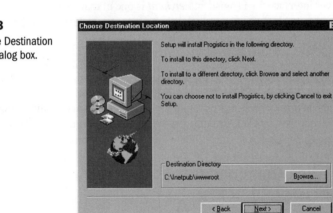

4. The Web Server Name dialog box will have the name of the system from which you are running the installation program listed as the name of your Web server by default. If this is not the name of the Web server you want Progistics to use, type in the correct name.

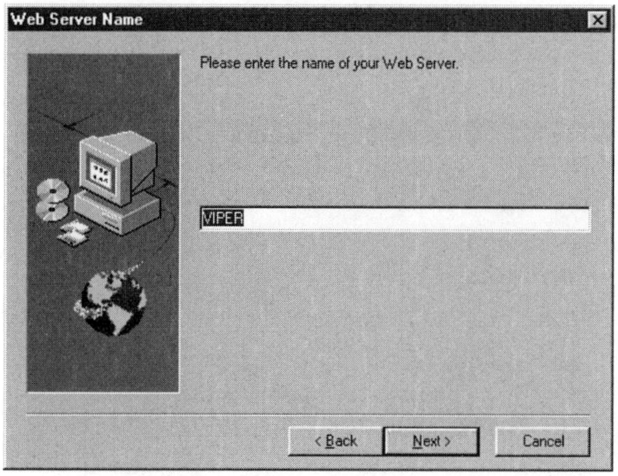

FIG. 24.4

The Web Server Name dialog box.

5. Once you have the name of the Web server that you want Progistics to use entered into the Web Server Name dialog box, click Next. The installation program will then proceed to copy files into the location you specified in step 3.

6. After all the Progistics files have been copied you will receive a dialog box stating that information has been successfully entered into the registry. Click OK to acknowledge this message. The Select RateServer Options dialog box will then appear (see Figure 24.5).

7. Select the RateServers you will be using to generate rates and/or tracking numbers. Currently only the UPS, RPS, DHL, and USPS RateServers are part of the Progistics CS base package. Other RateServers are available from TanData. You should email TanData (**info@tandata.com**) or check their Web site (**http://www.tandata.com**) for information regarding additional RateServers.

N O T E Any time after completing the installation, you can go back and add or remove carriers from the Progistics system. To do so, click the Start button in the taskbar to display the Start menu; choose Programs; choose TanData Progistics; and finally, click RateServer Setup.

The Select RateServer Options dialog box described in Step 6 of Installing the Progistics Components will then appear. You can then follow the instructions outlined in Step 7 of Installing the Progistics Components to modify your RateServer selections. ■

8. Once you have selected the carriers you wish to use with Progistics, click Next. The installation will finish and you will receive a message stating that setup has been

completed. Click OK to acknowledge this message. You will be prompted with a
question asking whether or not you want to view the readme file.

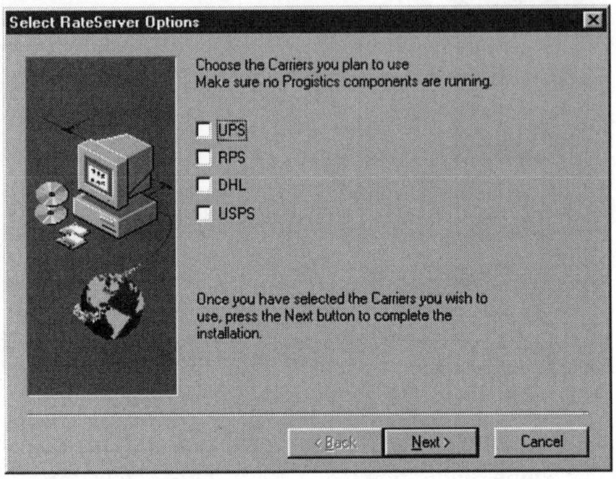

FIG. 24.5

The Select RateServer
Options dialog box.

9. You should click Yes to review the readme file. After clicking Yes, the installation
    program will open the readme file and display it using the Windows Notepad program.
    The readme file will contain any late breaking information on Progistics. After reviewing
    the file, close Notepad.

10. After closing Notepad the Progistics installation program will advise you to shut down
    and restart your system. Click OK to acknowledge this message. You will then receive a
    dialog box asking if you want to shut down and restart your system now or if you want to
    do it later. If you have any programs currently running, select the No option button and
    then click OK; otherwise simply click OK and your system will shutdown and restart
    automatically.

11. If you chose not to have the system automatically shut down and restarted for you, you
    should save any files you have open and close down all of your running programs. Once
    you have saved all of your open files and closed all of your running programs you should
    shut down and restart your system.

    Once your system is restarted, you will be ready to proceed and configure the Progistics
    software.

Configuring Progistics CS

You should now have the Progistics CS and Progistics.*Merchant* components successfully installed. You must configure Progistics CS before you can configure Progistics.*Merchant*. Configuration of Progistics CS consists of setting up the RateServers to work with the merchant's company. You will want to collect the carrier account numbers and tracking number ranges for any carriers that you plan to use with this system.

If you don't have the merchant's carrier account information, or just want to evaluate the Progistics software, the test configuration outlined below can be used. This test configuration can be modified later with the actual carrier account information once received from the merchant.

> **N O T E** Because the administration pages for Progistics.*Merchant* are Active Server Pages, make sure that you're using the latest version of Internet Explorer. If you experience problems running the Active Server Pages (such as JavaScript source code displayed in your browser when accessing the Progistics pages), you may need to tell the World Wide Web Server you're using that the `Progistics` directory is an executable directory. If you are using Internet Information Server 3.0, follow these steps to configure the `Progistics` directory as an executable directory: Start the Internet Service Manager. To do so, click the Start button in the taskbar to display the Start menu; choose Programs; choose Microsoft Internet Server; and finally, click Internet Service Manager. The Internet Service Manager window will open. Open the Properties dialog for the WWW service. To do so, double-click the computer name associated with your WWW service listed in the Internet Service Manager window. The WWW Service Properties dialog box will open (see Figure 24.6). Select the Directories tab in the WWW Service Properties dialog box and scroll down the list of directory entries until you locate the directory in which you installed Progistics. If you accepted the default installation path, you should find the entry `C:\InetPub\wwwroot\Progistics`. If you are able to locate the Progistics entry, double-click it; the Directory Properties dialog box will open. If you cannot locate the Progistics entry, you'll need to add it. To do so, click the Add button; the Directory Properties dialog box will open. In the Directory text box of the Directory Properties dialog box, if the name of the directory in which Progistics was installed is not already present, enter it now. If there is not an alias present in the Alias text box, type the `Progistics` into this field. Ensure that the Execute checkbox is checked and then click OK to close and save the property settings. You can now close the Internet Service Manager window and access the Progistics Active Server Pages. ▓

Follow these steps to successfully configure Progistics CS:

1. Click the Start button in the taskbar to display the Start menu; choose Programs; choose TanData Progistics; and finally, click Configure.

   The TanData Progistics Web page opens in your browser (see Figure 24.7).

FIG. 24.6

The Directory Properties dialog box with the Progistics directory configured properly.

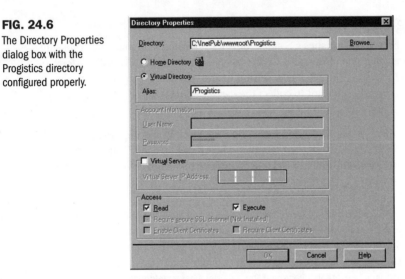

FIG. 24.7

The TanData Progistics Web page.

2. Click the Progistics box to the left of Before You Begin.

   The Before You Begin Web page will open. Read and follow the instructions on this page carefully; it contains any last minute information you may need in order to start the Progistics CS components.

3. To start the Progistics CS components click the Start button in the taskbar to display the Start menu; choose Programs; choose TanData Progistics; and finally, click Start Progistics.

   The Progistics Controller, the Progistics Machine Manager, the Progistics Security Server, the Progistics Merchant Server, and any RateServers that you chose to install will now be started.

N O T E You can stop all the Progistics CS components at any time by clicking the Start button in the taskbar to display the Start menu; choose Programs; choose TanData Progistics; and finally, click Stop Progistics.

Using the Stop Progistics program to close all of the Progistics components is the easiest way of shutting down the Progistics environment. If you want to close these components manually you must close them in a particular order: close RateMan; close all RateServers; close the Security Server; close the Machine Manager; and finally, close the Controller. ▨

4. When all the components start, click the Move On Now link at the bottom of the current page.

   This link takes you to a page similar to the one displayed in Figure 24.8. You should see the Progistics Machine Manager and Progistics Security Server listed below the heading Active Servers. Any RateServers that you chose to install should be listed below the heading Active RateServers. If these components are not listed, wait several seconds and then click the Click Here to Refresh the Program List link.

   When the servers are running and listed under the Active Servers and Active RateServers headings, you will be ready to continue.

5. Click the Progistics Machine Manager link.

   The Configuring the Progistics Server page will appear in your browser (see Figure 24.9).

6. Click the Add a New Shipper link.

   This link creates an undefined shipper and displays the page shown in Figure 24.10. The Invalid Country error displayed in red toward the top of the page is normal for a new shipper that has not yet been configured.

FIG. 24.8

The Configuring the Progistics Servers Configurations page.

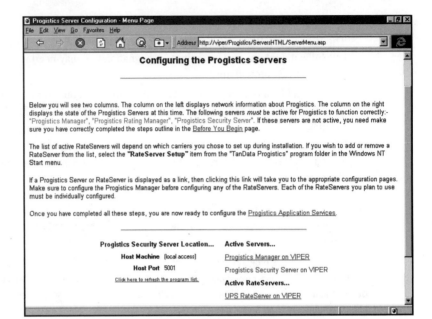

FIG. 24.9

The Configuring the Progistics Server page.

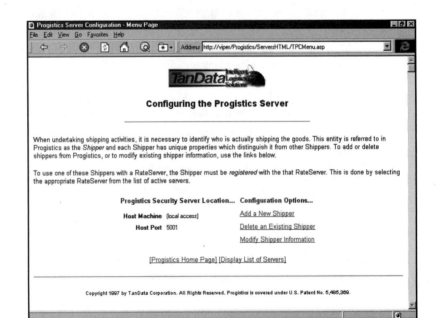

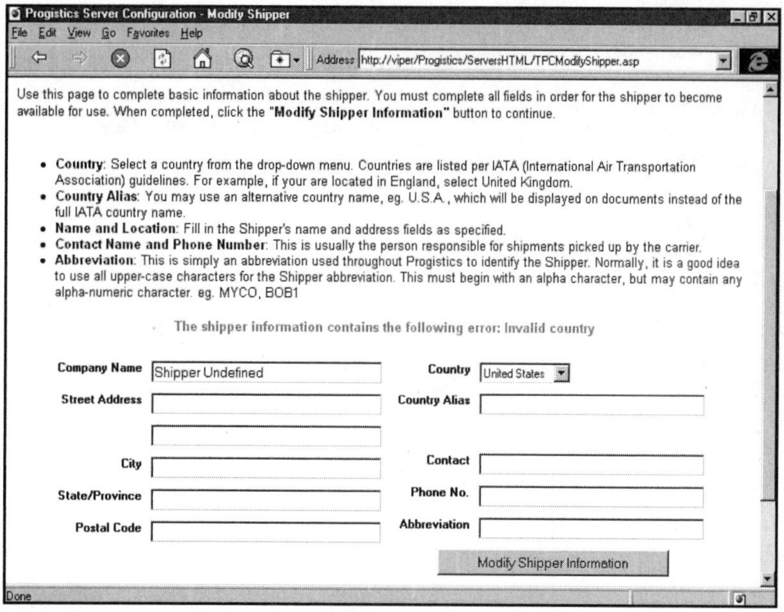

FIG. 24.10

The Modifying Shipper Information for the Progistics Server page.

7. Fill in the address information for the merchant whose store you are configuring.

   You can use the Country Alias field as a way of referring to a country by a name other than its International Air Transport Association (IATA) country code. If you want to refer to the United Kingdom as England, for example, you type **England** in this field. Country Alias is not a required field.

8. Next, enter an abbreviation for this shipper into the Abbreviation field. For example, if I were configuring a shipper for Microsoft, I might enter **MICROSOFT** into this field. You will want to make note of what you enter as the abbreviation. You will use the abbreviation to refer to the shipper entity you are currently creating when you configure the RateServers and shipping methods in later sections of the Progistics configuration.

9. When you finish typing the shipper information, click the Modify Shipper Information button.

   Provided that no problem occurs with the information that you entered (such as an invalid phone number or ZIP code), you return to the Configuring the Progistics Server page.

10. Click the Display List of Servers link.

    This link takes you back to the Configuring the Progistics Servers page.

N O T E The next step is to configure the RateServers that you selected to install on the system.
Although the UPS RateServer is used in the following steps as an example, all the carrier
RateServer configuration functions are the same, except the Modify Shipper Account Information
function. You need to consult the individual pages for the particular RateServer that you are installing
for instructions on how to configure that section. ■

11. Click the UPS RateServer link.

    This link displays the page shown in Figure 24.11.

FIG. 24.11

The Configuring the UPS
RateServer page.

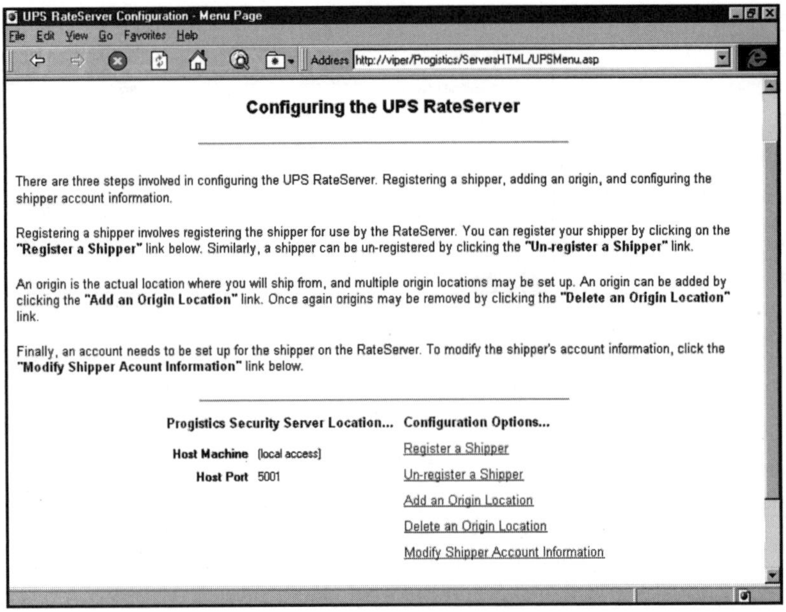

12. Click the Register a Shipper link.

    This link displays the page shown in Figure 24.12. You should see the company name
    that you entered earlier, when you created the shipper, displayed in the listbox.

13. Select the shipper and then click the Register Shipper button.

    You will be brought back to the Configuring the UPS RateServer page shown in
    Figure 24.11.

14. Click the Modify Shipper Account Information link.

    You will see a page entitled Selecting a Shipper to Modify that looks very similar to the
    Registering a Shipper with the UPS RateServer page discussed in Step 11.

15. Select the shipper and then click the Select Shipper button.

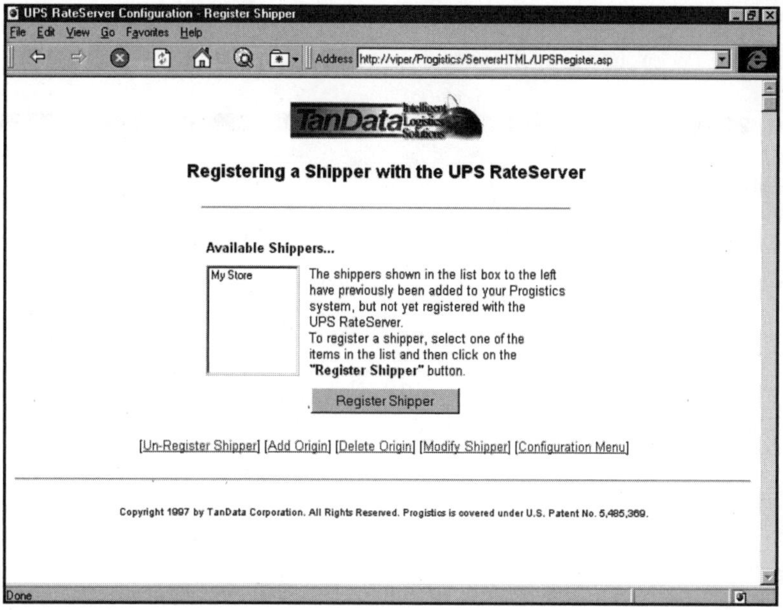

FIG. 24.12

The Registering a Shipper with the UPS RateServer page.

You should see a page similar to the one shown in Figure 24.13. This page contains carrier-specific information. (Not all carriers require the same information.) The first step in configuring a RateServer is adding an origin point. An *origin point* is the ZIP code that the merchant ships orders from.

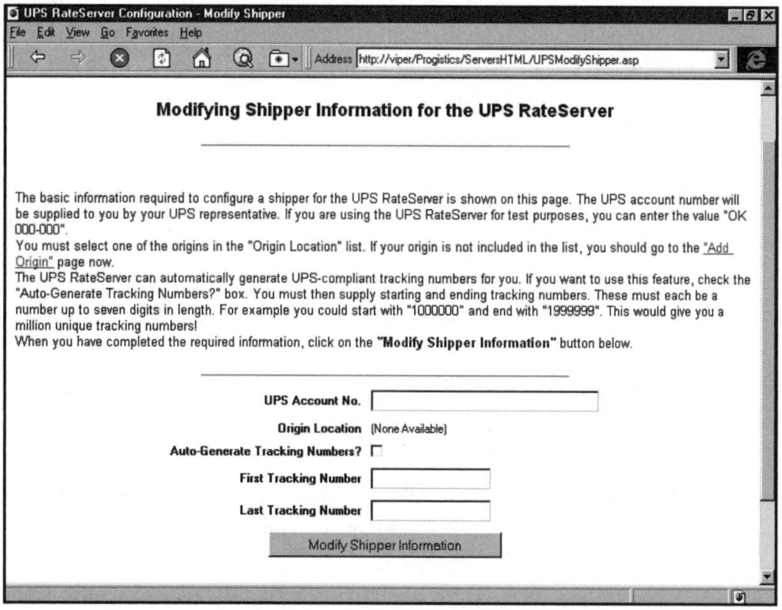

FIG. 24.13

The Modifying Shipper Information for the UPS RateServer page.

16. Click the Add Origin link toward the top of the page.

You will see the page displayed in Figure 24.14.

FIG. 24.14

The Adding an Origin to
the UPS RateServer
page.

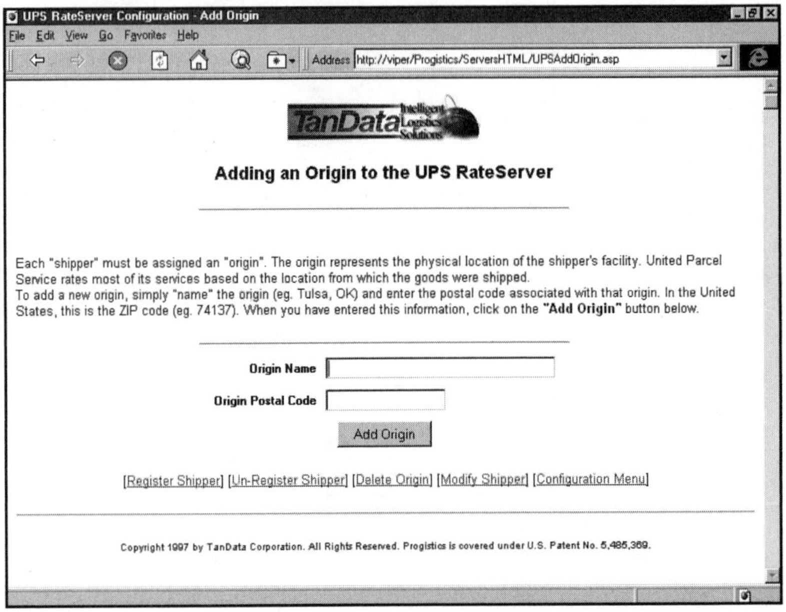

You must assign a name to the origin that you are adding. You can name the origin anything that suits your needs. Usually, the city name works well.

17. Type the origin name in the Origin Name field and enter the ZIP code that the merchant for which you are configuring the program ships from into the Origin Postal Code field.

18. Click the Add Origin button.

You return to the Modifying Shipper Information for the UPS RateServer page. You should see the origin that you just entered displayed in a drop-down list.

Make sure that you have your merchant's carrier-account information handy at this point (unless you're configuring this shipper for test purposes).

The next step of the configuration process is to enter the shipper's account number for the carrier. For the UPS RateServer, enter the shipper account number into the UPS Shipper No. field. A sample UPS account number is OK 123-456. The first two digits usually represent the shipper's state abbreviation; the next six digits comprise the actual UPS account number.

19. Ensure that the origin you added is selected in the Origin Location drop-down listbox.

20. If you want to make tracking numbers available to the shopper, check the Auto-Generate Tracking Numbers? checkbox and supply a starting number (usually, 1) and an ending number (usually, 9999999).

21. Click the Modify Shipper Information button.

   You should return to the Configuring the UPS RateServer page. If you receive an error, double-check that you entered the proper information into the fields. Figure 24.15 shows an example of valid data in the UPS Shipper Information page that you can use if you are unable to get your own data accepted by the system.

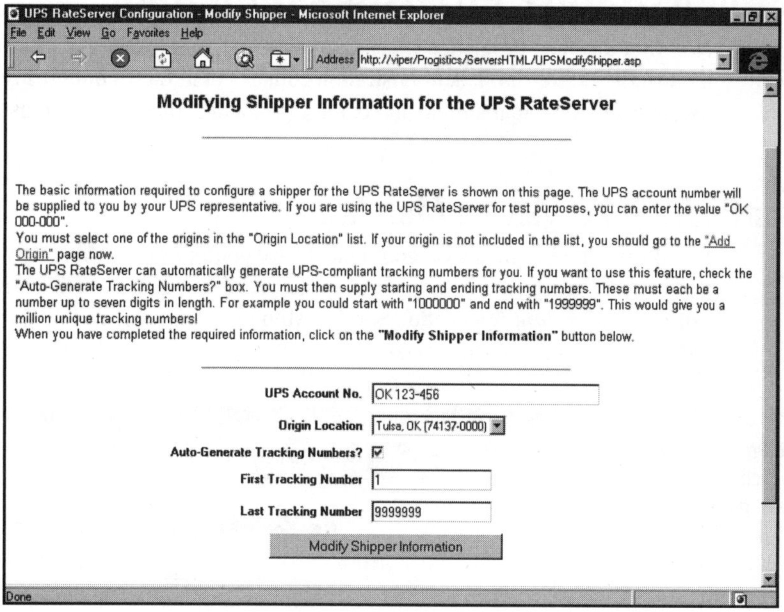

FIG. 24.15

An example of the UPS RateServer Shipper Information page filled-in with valid data.

22. Click the Display List of Shippers link to return to the Configuring Progistics Servers page.

   You can now configure any additional RateServers that you chose to install.

23. When you finish configuring the RateServers, click the Progistics Home Page link to return to the TanData Progistics home page.

If you run into any problems during the configuration process, the TanData Progistics home page contains a link called Resources. Clicking the Resources link will take you to the Resources Web page. This Web page contains links to the carrier Web sites and the TanData Web site.

The carrier Web sites should be consulted if you have any carrier-specific questions (such as questions about a carrier's service levels, establishing new carrier accounts, standard book rates, and so on). You should consult the TanData Web site for technical support information and technical documentation on Progistics CS and Progistics.*Merchant*.

The Resources Web page also contains instructions for accessing the TanData news server. The TanData news server is an excellent source for answers to technical questions regarding all of TanData's products. Although the TanData news server was primarily created to allow independent systems integrators and store administrators to converse with each other, TanData's technical support group, technical services group, and software development group can also be found participating in the discussions.

Administrating Progistics.*Merchant*

Now that the base Progistics CS components are configured, you're ready to start administrating Progistics.*Merchant*. Administration consists of initially configuring Progistics.*Merchant* for use, learning how to maintain and extend Progistics.*Merchant*, and testing the Progistics environment.

Configuring Progistics.*Merchant*

When the base Progistics CS components are configured, you're ready to look at the various ways of configuring Progistics.*Merchant* to better fit the merchant's business model. The Progistics.*Merchant* Application Service Menu page (as shown in Figure 24.16) contains methods of managing store accounts.

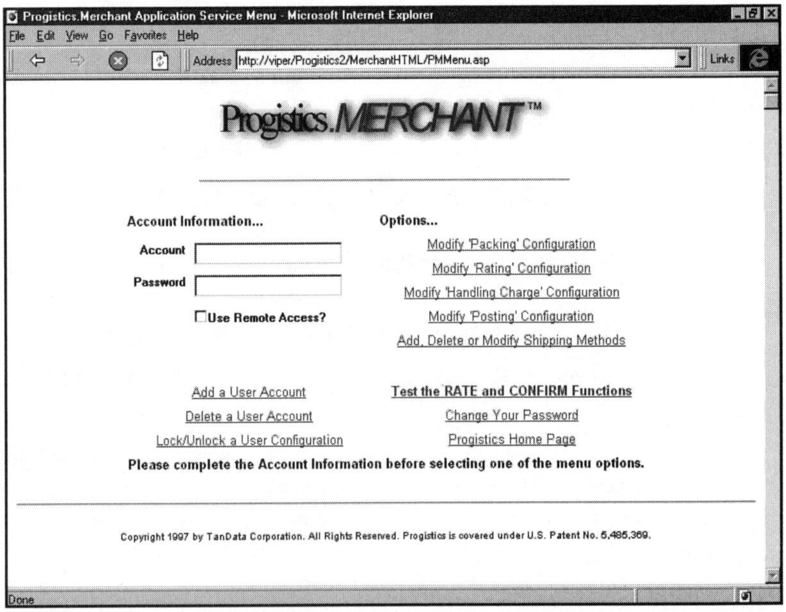

FIG. 24.16

The Progistics.*Merchant* Application Service Menu page.

Before selecting the Test the RATE and CONFIRM Functions link, ensure that the following Progistics components are running:

Progistics.*Merchant* is shipped with two basic accounts: TEST and ADMIN. Both accounts have blank as the default password. Links for administering accounts are provided on this page.

You want to create a separate account for every store that uses the Progistics system. Information regarding the packing, rating, handling, and shipping methods are associated with each account. Each account can contain custom settings for every store or shipper that uses Progistics to rate packages.

The Lock/Unlock link is provided to keep unauthorized users from modifying account settings after the store administrator sets them up. When the store administrator locks an account, that account cannot be modified until the store administrator unlocks it.

The Remote Access check box controls which mode Progistics.*Merchant* operates in. When you check Remote Access, you will be configuring Progistics.*Merchant* for client/server mode and two new fields will be displayed on the current page. The two new fields are Service Host and Service Port. These two fields tell the Progistics.*Merchant* client component where it can find the associated Progistics.*Merchant* server component. Normally, these components run as one component on the local machine, but for larger installations, the Progistics.*Merchant* interface component can be offloaded to a separate server machine.

You may want to run Progistics.*Merchant* in client/server mode if you have multiple Store Accounts, each on a separate machine, working with one instance of Commerce Server. In such a case, you would have multiple Progistics.*Merchant* client components connected to one Progistics.*Merchant* server component that is connected to Commerce Server. This makes the entire site easier to maintain from the shipping perspective. In such a case, you need to supply the name of the machine that is hosting the Progistics.*Merchant* server component. The port setting normally should remain 5004.

For testing purposes, the Remote Access check box should not be checked. The unchecked state indicates to the Progistics.*Merchant* component that the Progistics CS components are running on the local machine, which is the default configuration.

The Modify Packing Configuration link allows the store administrator to modify the maximum box weight for each virtual box that was created during the packing process (described earlier in this chapter under the Progistics.*Merchant* architecture section). The Modify Packing Configuration page can also be used to modify the weight format (kilograms or pounds).

The Modify Rating Configuration link is a little more complicated. Selecting this link takes you to a page similar to the one shown in Figure 24.17.

The Progistics Host Machine and associated Progistics Host Port fields contained on the Rating Configuration page tell the Progistics.*Merchant* component where to find the Progistics Security Server (and thereby the rest of the Progistics CS components). Normally, these components run on the local machine, but for larger installations, the Progistics CS components can be offloaded to a separate server machine. In such a case, you need to supply the name of the machine that is hosting the Progistics CS environment. The port setting normally should remain 5004.

This feature is also useful for creating a fault-tolerant system. If a problem occurs with one of the systems hosting the Progistics CS environment, you can simply change the Service Host name to point to a backup system that has the Progistics CS components installed on it. Progistics works equally well whether the backup system is located on a LAN or across the country on the Internet. In fact, TanData provides the ability of hosting backup RateServers, through their Progistics.*Connect* software, at their location for a nominal fee. The Progistics Security Server ensures that only valid users have access to the rate information.

FIG. 24.17
The Rating Configuration page.

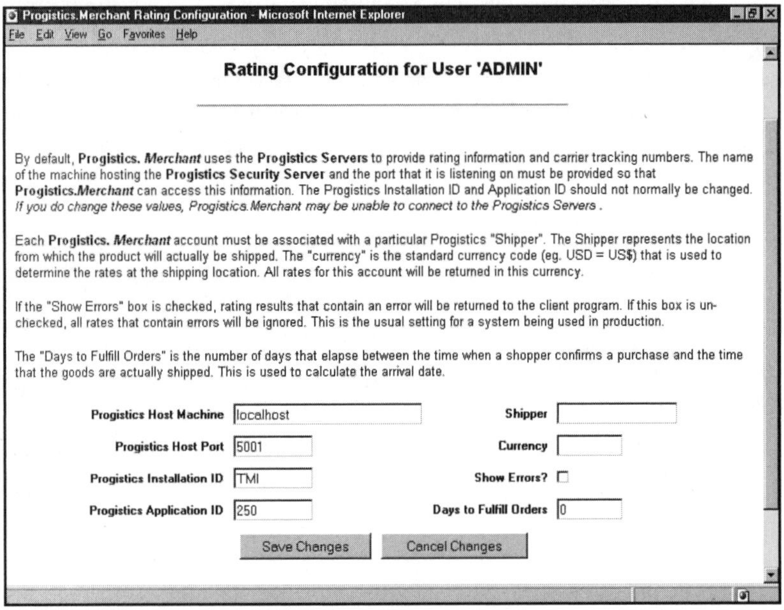

The Progistics Installation ID and Progistics Application ID fields are used internally by the Progistics.*Merchant* system. You do not need to modify these settings unless you are creating new application objects that must talk directly to the Progistics Security Server component. If you want more information on creating these types of objects, contact TanData.

You must enter the shipper abbreviation into the Shipper field. The shipper abbreviation was set up in Step 8 of the Configuring Progistics CS section of this chapter.

The Currency field contains the type of currency that you're dealing with at this particular store. All currency amounts are returned in the specified format. USD, the default currency type, stands for *United States dollar*. You should consult the TanData documentation for additional payment types supported by the system. Ensure that a supported currency type is entered into the Currency field.

The Show Errors? check box indicates whether errors should be returned to the client application when Progistics is unable to rate a shipment. You normally leave the Show Errors? check box unchecked for production systems. If Show Errors? is checked, even best-way groups containing a service that does not serve a particular destination return an error. Normally, you do not want the system to return an error under such conditions, but to simply return a service that does ship to the given location.

The Days to Fulfill the Order field shows the number of days that normally elapse between the time when the order is placed and the time when the order is shipped. Progistics uses this field in conjunction with the type of service that is used to calculate the anticipated arrival date for the shipment. This date is an added benefit to the customer who places the order.

Add, Delete, or Modify Shipping Methods is the link to the RateMan client-administration interface discussed in the Progistics.*Merchant* architecture section earlier in this chapter. You use this link to maintain the various shipping methods that are available to the shopper. After selecting this link, you will see a page similar to the one shown in Figure 24.18. Notice that there are currently no shipping methods setup in the system.

FIG. 24.18

The Shipping Method Configuration page.

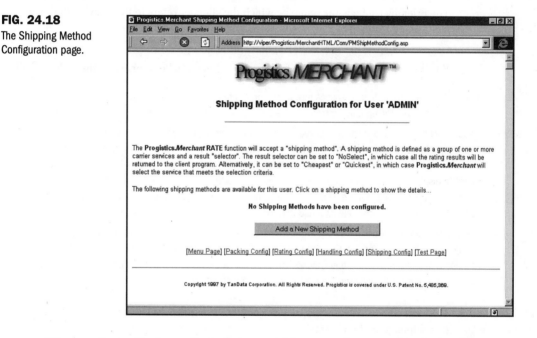

Part

V

Ch

24

There are three shipping methods that are useful as general purpose shipping methods for Progistics.*Merchant*: Least-Costly Overnight, Least-Costly Ground, and Customer's Choice. Least-Costly Overnight and Least-Costly Ground are best-way groups that contain several services from different carriers. When the shopper selects one of these groups, the system selects the least costly method of shipping the order to the delivery destination. Customer's Choice contains a list of services that the shopper can choose among when he or she selects the delivery method.

Follow these instructions to add the Least-Costly Overnight shipping method to the Progistics.*Merchant* system:

N O T E In order to setup the shipping method examples described in this section, you must have installed the UPS, RPS, DHL, and USPS RateServers. See the earlier section entitled Installing the Progistics Components if you need to install one or more of these RateServers. ▨

1. Click the Add a New Shipping Method button on the Shipping Method Configuration page.

   The Add a Shipping Method page is displayed (shown in Figure 24.19).

2. Enter NEXTDAY into the Symbolic Name field.

   The symbolic name is the name you would use in referring to this shipping method programmatically (using VBScript or JavaScript, for example).

3. Enter Least-Costly Overnight into the Friendly Name field.

   The Friendly Name is the name by which the shopper refers to this service (for example, when using a drop-down listbox to select a shipping method).

4. Choose Cheapest in the Selector option button group.

   When Cheapest is selected, the least-costly service will be returned to the order-pipeline.

N O T E The Selector tells Progistics how to respond to rating requests for the given shipping method. The options for this field are None, Cheapest, and Quickest.

If you select None, all the services that you selected in the Service listbox are returned to the client application. In this scenario, you need to accommodate the additional services. Commerce Server expects only one service and one rate to be returned to the order-pipeline. You could create additional pages to display all the available services that met the selection criteria, as well as the associated rates. The shopper could then be allowed to select the service that best fits his or her needs. The service and rate the shopper selects would then be returned to the Commerce Server order-pipeline.

If you want to use Progistics.*Merchant* with Commerce Server without creating additional Web pages to handle this type of shipping functionality, make sure that your shipping methods resolve to one service and one rate. To do so, select either Quickest or Cheapest as the selector that Progistics.*Merchant* uses in choosing the service from the best-way shipping method. ▨

5. The next step is to select the services you want to make available to shoppers who chose this shipping method.

   Ctrl+click UPS Next Day Air, DHL Overnight Delivery, and USPS Express Mail.

N O T E Choosing proper services is important to how well your best-way shipping method work.

You want to only include those services which offer the same or a similar level of service. For instance, it would not make sense to include UPS 2nd Day Air as an option in an Overnight Delivery shipping method. Aside from being misleading to the shopper, UPS 2nd Day Air would always be returned from this group because it would always be cheaper than an overnight service such as UPS Next Day Air.

Many carriers offer several delivery options for overnight delivery. For instance, UPS offers UPS Next Day Air Early A.M., UPS Next Day Air, and UPS Next Day Air Saver. The difference between such services is usually that one delivers next day very early in the morning, the next later in the morning, and the last in the afternoon. Federal Express offers comparable services. It is again important to select similar service levels between carriers.

For instance, choosing UPS Next Day Air Early A.M. (typically a $40+ delivery cost for the first pound) and DHL Overnight Delivery (typically a $20+ delivery cost for the first pound) will always return the DHL service as the less expensive service. The UPS Early A.M. service and the DHL Overnight Service are not fair comparisons. The first guarantees very early morning delivery (typically by 8:30 A.M.) while the latter guarantees an early afternoon delivery (typically by noon). UPS Next Day Air and DHL Overnight Delivery are fair services to compare since their delivery commitments are in close proximity with each other (10:30 A.M. and noon respectively).

One of the most useful best-way shipping method comparisons is between UPS Ground and USPS First-Class mail. Both services offer similar delivery timeframes, but both have different pricing structures. The USPS First-Class service is typically less expensive than the UPS Ground service for packages that weigh 2 pounds and less. The UPS Ground service, on the other hand, is significantly less expensive than the USPS First-Class service for packages weighing over two-pounds. Other services have less obvious pricing differences for similar services. One of the most powerful features of the Progistics system is its ability to quickly and automatically determine which service is the least costly method of delivery for any given package. ▪

6. Click the Add Now button to add the shipping method you just created to the Progistics system.

   The Shipping Method Configuration page will again be displayed in your browser. The shipping method you just added will be displayed on this page directly above the Add a New Shipper button. Your Overnight Delivery shipping method is now ready to use.

Follow these instructions to add a Least-Costly Ground shipping method to the Progistics.*Merchant* system:

1. Click the Add a New Shipping Method button on the Shipping Method Configuration page.

   The Add a Shipping Method page is displayed (shown in Figure 24.19).

2. Enter GROUND into the Symbolic Name field.

   The symbolic name is the name you would use in referring to this shipping method programmatically.

3. Enter Least-Costly Ground into the Friendly Name field.

   The Friendly Name is the name by which the shopper refers to this service.

4. Choose Cheapest in the Selector option button group.

   When Cheapest is selected, the least-costly service will be returned to the order-pipeline.

5. The next step is to select the services you want to make available to shoppers who chose this shipping method.

   Ctrl+click UPS Ground, USPS First-Class mail, and RPS Ground.

6. Click the Add Now button to add the shipping method you just created to the Progistics system.

   The Shipping Method Configuration page will again be displayed in your browser. The shipping method you just added will be displayed on this page directly above the Add a New Shipper button. Your Least-Costly Ground shipping method is now ready to use.

Follow these instructions to add the Customer's Choice shipping method to the Progistics.*Merchant* system:

1. Click the Add a New Shipping Method button on the Shipping Method Configuration page.

2. The Add a Shipping Method page is displayed (shown in Figure 24.19).

3. Enter CHOICE into the Symbolic Name field.

   The symbolic name is the name you would use in referring to this shipping method programmatically.

4. Enter Customer's Choice into the Friendly Name field.

   The Friendly Name is the name by which the shopper refers to this service.

5. Choose None in the Selector option button group.

   When None is selected, all services assigned to this shipping method will return rates. You must supply the Active Server or HTML pages necessary to allow the shopper to choose which service best fits his or her needs so that only one rate and service are returned to the Commerce Server order pipeline.

6. The next step is to select the services you want to make available to shoppers who chose this shipping method.

7. Ctrl+click all of the services listed in the Services listbox (or alternately, only choose the ones you feel are appropriate to the store you are implementing).

8. Click the Add Now button to add the shipping method you just created to the Progistics system.

   The Shipping Method Configuration page will again be displayed in your browser. The shipping method you just added will be displayed on this page directly above the Add a New Shipper button. Your Customer's Choice shipping method is now ready to use.

Testing the *RATE* and *CONFIRM* Functions

When both Progistics CS and Progistics.*Merchant* have been installed and configured, you should test the Progistics environment. The Test the RATE and CONFIRM Functions link on the Progistics.*Merchant* Application Service Menu page (see Figure 24.16) will allow you to test your Progistics environment.

- Progistics Controller
- Progistics Machine Manager
- Progistics Security Server
- At least one configured RateServer (such as the UPS RateServer)

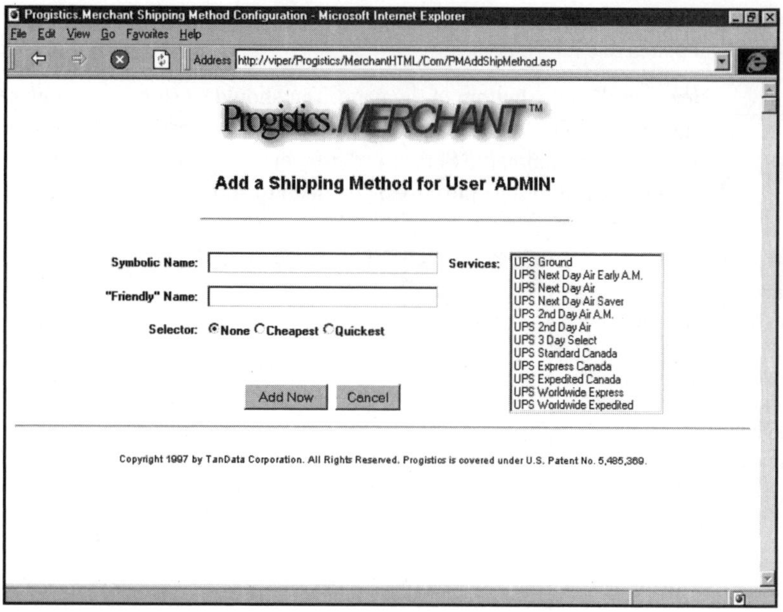

FIG. 24.19
The Add a Shipping
Method page.

Enter **ADMIN** into the Account text box in the Progistics.*Merchant* Application Services page. Leave the Password text box blank.

You can now click the Test the RATE and CONFIRM Functions link. You should see a screen similar to the one shown in Figure 24.20.

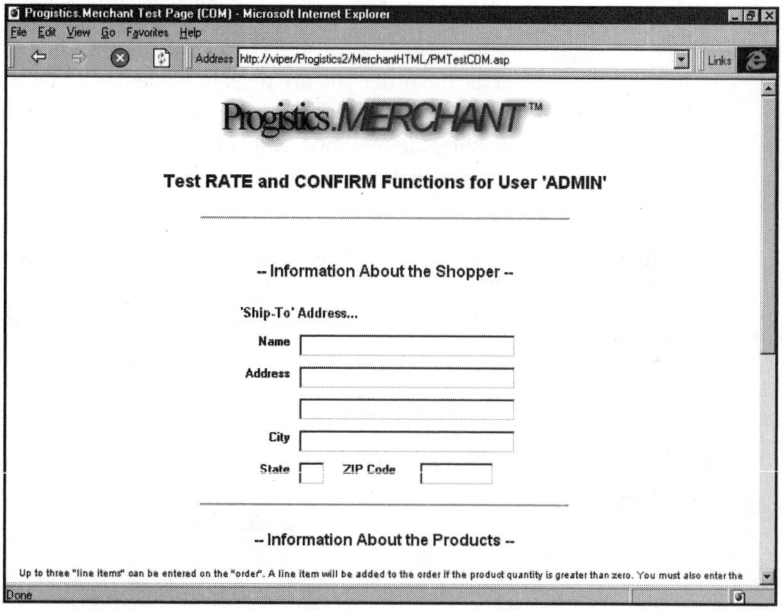

FIG. 24.20
The Progistics.Merchant
Test Page for the
Commerce Server
interface.

Part
V

Ch
24

Fill in the Ship-To name and address fields. The Commerce Server order-pipeline normally supplies this information.

Next, scroll to the bottom of the page. You should see a screen similar to the one shown in Figure 24.21. This screen is where you supply information about the products that are being ordered. The Commerce Server order-pipeline supplies this data to Progistics.*Merchant* behind the scenes. But for test purposes, you need to supply the information manually.

FIG. 24.21

The lower half of the Progistics.Merchant Test Page for the Commerce Server interface which contains the Information About the Products entry fields.

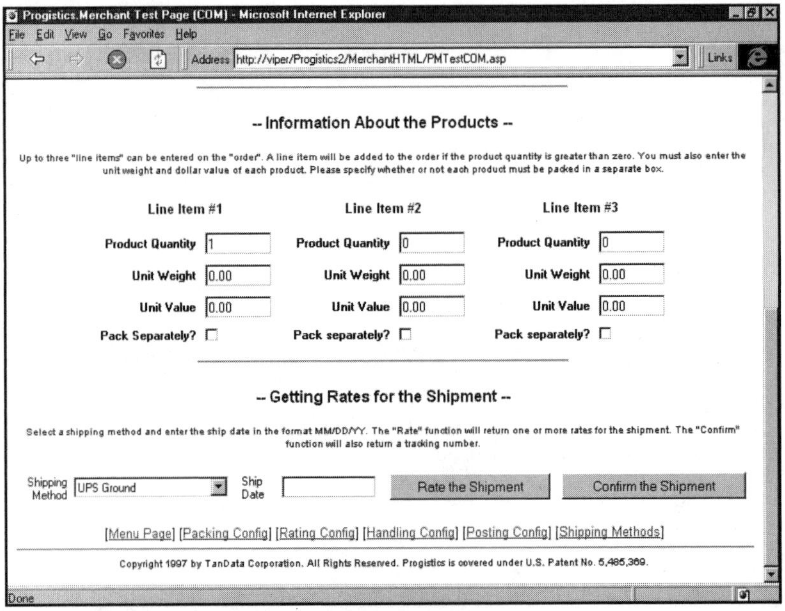

Fill in the information for the order you are testing. If you don't have a test order, enter some dummy data in the fields. If you open the Shipping Method drop-down listbox, you see a list of the currently available shipping methods. Select the shipping method that you want to use for this test. Type the date on which you are shipping the order, and click the Rate Shipment button.

Provided that everything was configured properly, you should see a new page similar to the one shown in Figure 24.22. The symbols with which you identify particular services are displayed in parentheses. The currency type is also displayed in the parentheses next to the dollar amounts.

If you click the browser's Back button and then click the Confirm the Shipment button, you see a page similar to the one shown in Figure 24.23. If you selected a service that provides a tracking number (such as UPS Next Day Air Saver), you see the tracking number displayed in this new page.

FIG. 24.22
The Results Returned
from the RATE Function
page.

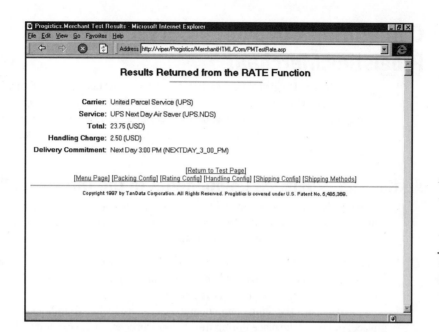

FIG. 24.23
The Results Returned
from the CONFIRM
Function page.

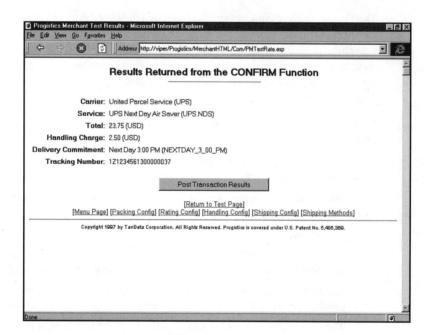

Now that you have tested the Progistics environment and it is functioning properly, you can
continue on to configure Commerce Server to make use of the new functionality that
Progistics.*Merchant* provides.

Configuring Commerce Server to Utilize Progistics.*Merchant*

When you have Progistics CS and Progistics.*Merchant* installed, configured, and tested you need to set up Commerce Server to use the new shipping-and-handling functionality. This configuration is a multi-step process: configuring the Commerce Server order-pipeline, adding shipping-related product attributes to the product database, and mapping the Progistics fields to Commerce Server fields.

Adding the Progistics Components to the Order-Pipeline

The Progistics.*Merchant* interface for Commerce Server 2.0 consists of two components that plug into the Commerce Server order-pipeline: the Progistics Shipping & Handling component and the Progistics Confirmation component.

The Progistics Shipping & Handling component is used by Commerce Server to select a carrier, compute a freight cost, and compute a handling charge. Because the handling charge can optionally be added into the freight cost, the Progistics Shipping & Handling component cannot be used as a Handling component in the order-pipeline. Handling calculations can still take place, but they take place during the shipping process of the order-pipeline.

The Progistics Shipping Confirmation component is used during the Accept stage in the Commerce Server order-pipeline to confirm the shipment, generate tracking numbers, and compute the arrival date of an order. The Progistics Shipping Confirmation component can also be used to perform external functions such as posting shipment data to an external data source for use with a shipping system (such as Progistics.*Shipper*) when the order is actually shipped from the warehouse.

Follow these steps to successfully configure the Commerce Server order-pipeline for use with Progistics.*Merchant*:

1. Click the Start button in the taskbar to display the Start menu; choose Programs; choose Commerce Server 2.0; and finally, click Pipeline Editor.

   You should see a screen similar to the one displayed in Figure 24.24.

2. Scroll down the right-hand side of the screen until you see the Order Price Adjust component.

   Just below the Order Price Adjust component is the Shipping component, which probably is currently assigned to Default Shipping (see Figure 24.25).

3. Right-click the component that is attached to the Shipping component in the order-pipeline (probably Default Shipping) and choose Delete from the pop-up menu.

   The component that was assigned to the Shipping component is now removed.

   Notice that the left listbox is now filled with the various shipping components that are available to Commerce Server. One of the available selections is Progistics Shipping & Handling.

FIG. 24.24
Commerce Server's
Pipeline Editor.

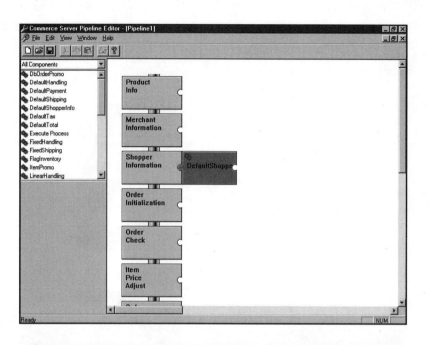

FIG. 24.25
The Pipeline Editor
positioned at the
Shipping component.

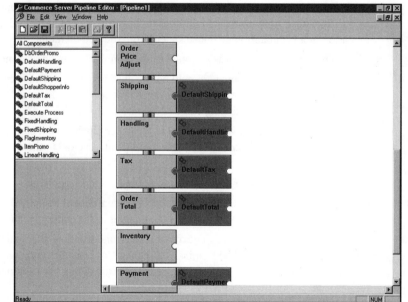

Part

V

Ch

24

4. Select the Progistics Shipping & Handling component from the listbox of available
   Shipping components and drag it to the Shipping component in the order-pipeline.

   The Progistics Shipping & Handling component should now be attached to the Shipping
   component in the order-pipeline (see Figure 24.26).

FIG. 24.26

The Progistics Shipping & Handling component when attached to the order-pipeline.

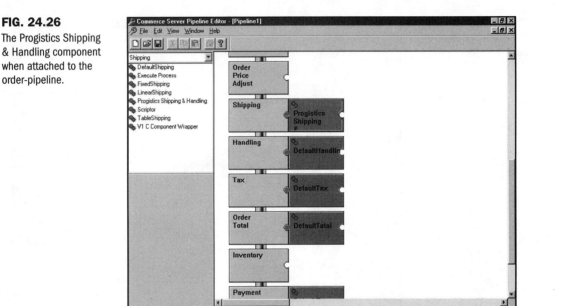

5. Directly beneath the Shipping component is the Handling component. Right-click the component that is attached to the Handling component in the order-pipeline (probably Default Handling) and choose Delete from the pop-up menu.

   The component that was assigned to the Handling component is now removed.

   The Handling component should not be used when using the Progistics Shipping & Handling component. Handling charges that need to be assessed to the order will be added during the shipping stage of the order-pipeline.

6. Scroll all the way down to the end of the order-pipeline and click the Accept component. Commerce Server does not have a component attached to the Accept component in the order-pipeline by default.

   The left listbox will show a list of available Accept components.

7. Drag the Progistics Shipping Confirmation component from the listbox of available Accept components to the Accept component in the order-pipeline.

   The Progistics Shipping Confirmation component is now attached to the order-pipeline (see Figure 24.27). The Progistics Shipping Confirmation component is responsible for generating tracking numbers, as well as for calculating final shipping-rate totals for the order.

The Commerce Server order-pipeline is now configured to use the Progistics.*Merchant* interface. Commerce Server will automatically invoke the necessary Progistics component at the appropriate point in the order process. To test this, you can start one of the Starter Stores, order a product, and receive shipping costs on your order total. The shipping costs generated will not be accurate for the product ordered until the store product data has been modified to include weight and other shipping-related information. The necessary modifications to the product data needed to generate accurate shipping rates for your products are discussed in the next section.

FIG. 24.27
The Progistics Shipping Confirmation component when attached to the order-pipeline.

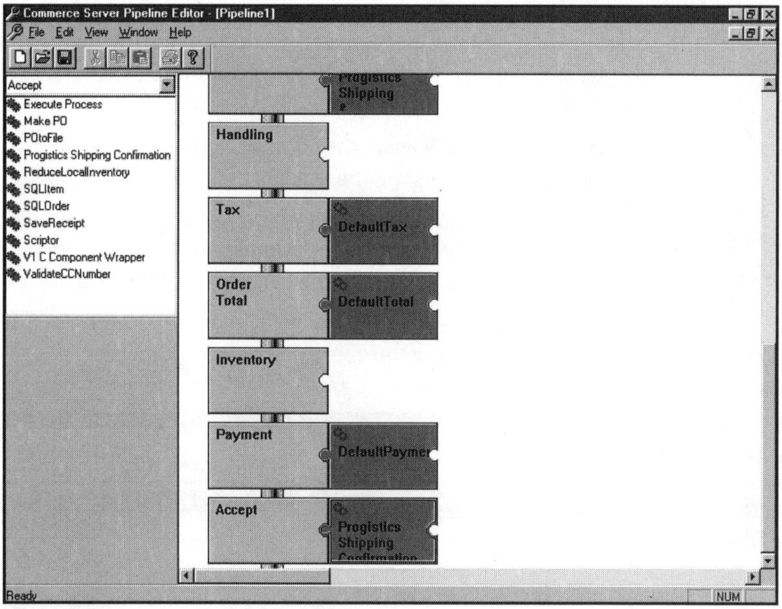

Modifying Store Product Tables to Work with Progistics.*Merchant*

In the previous section you configured the order-pipeline to use the Progistics.*Merchant* Commerce Server interface components. Although adding these interface components to the order-pipeline enabled you to generate shipping costs at the point-of-sale, the shipping costs generated were in accurate for the order. Progistics generated these inaccurate rates because, by default, a weight of 10 pounds is defaulted into the system. Accurate product weights must be provided to the Progistics system in order for the Progistics system to provide accurate shipping costs.

The product database must be altered to support the additional shipping-related fields that Progistics requires to rate orders. There are currently two shipping-related fields that need to be appended to the product database: weight and no_pack. The weight field will contain the weight of the product and the no_pack field contains a flag indicating whether or not the product can be packed with other products (for example, computer monitors would probably not be packed with other products while software packages may very well be packed with other products).

There are two areas that need to be modified when making changes to the product data structure: the product database table and the Product Maintenance Active Server Pages for the store. The Microsoft Press Starter Store will be used as an example demonstrating how to make the required changes. Changes to your own store, or other Starter Stores are very similar. The following steps assume that your Starter Store is using Microsoft SQL Server 6.5.

Follow these to successfully add the shipping-related fields to the Microsoft Press Starter Store product database:

1. Start the SQL Enterprise Manager. To do so, click the Start Button in the taskbar to display the Start menu; choose Programs; choose Microsoft SQL Server 6.5; and finally, select SQL Enterprise Manager.

   The SQL Enterprise Manager window will open and contain a Server Manager window with a directory tree listing the available SQL Server systems.

2. Expand the server system branch which hosts the Microsoft Press Starter Store; expand the Databases branch; expand the database branch of the database which your Microsoft Press Starter Store uses; expand the Objects branch; and finally, expand the Tables branch.

   Figure 24.28 shows an example of what your SQL Enterprise Manager window should look like after following the above steps.

FIG. 24.28

The SQL Enterprise Manager window with its branches expanded to the Tables entry.

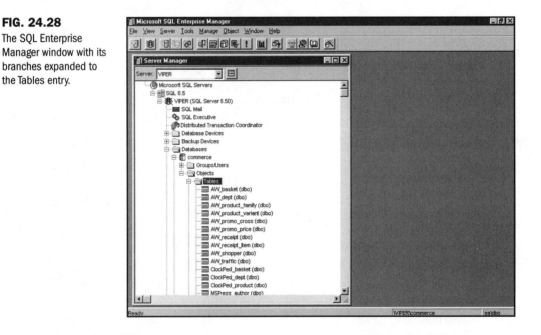

3. Double-click the MSPress_product table.

   The Manage Tables window opens with the list of column names and attributes associated with the MSPress_product table.

4. Scroll down the Manage Tables window until you reach the last column name entry. The last entry is date_changed. Click the blank column name entry directly under the date_changed column name entry.

   The cursor will start blinking in the blank field.

5. Enter the word **weight** into the blank field; tab to the Datatype column; select decimal from the datatype drop-down listbox; tab to the Size column and enter **5,2.**

6. Click the blank column name entry directly under the `weight` column name entry.

   The cursor will start blinking in the blank field.

7. Enter the word **no_pack** into the blank field; tab to the Datatype column; select varchar from the datatype drop-down listbox; tab to the Size column and enter **10**.

8. Close the Manage Tables window; the system will ask if you want to apply the changes, click Yes.

   The Manage Tables window will close and the changes will be applied to the database table.

9. Close the SQL Enterprise Manager window.

   The Microsoft Press Starter Store is now setup to hold shipping-related information. The next step is to provide a method of entering and maintaining the shipping-related information.

Modifying the Store Administration Pages

The `weight` and `no_pack` fields should now be present in the Microsoft Press Starter Store product database table. The Active Server Pages used to manage this Starter Store must now be modified to account for these two additional fields.

Once the Starter Store Manager pages are modified, you will be able to enter and maintain the `weight` and `no pack` flag for each product contained in the Starter Store. Progistics will be able to access this shipping-related information when computing shipping totals for orders.

Follow these steps to successfully configure the Manager Active Server Pages for the Microsoft Press Starter Store:

1. Using the Windows Notepad program, open the file `_add.asp` located in the `Stores\MSPress\Manager` directory off the Microsoft Commerce Server directory.

   If you chose to have Commerce Server installed in its default location, the complete path to the `_add.asp` file is: `C:\Microsoft Commerce Server\Stores\MSPress\Manager\ _add.asp`

2. Place the following code fragment under the `Case "product"` select statement directly under the `list_price end if` statement but before the `Case "author"` select statement (as shown in Figure 24.29):

```
weight = mscsPage.RequestString("weight", null, 0, 5000)
if IsNull(weight) then
errorFields("weight") = "weight must be a number between 0 and 5000"
end if
no_pack = mscsPage.RequestString("no_pack", null, 1, 10)
if no_pack = "on" then
   no_pack = "TRUE"
else
```

```
no_pack = "FALSE"
end if
if IsNull(no_pack) then
errorFields("no_pack") = "no_pack must be either TRUE or FALSE"
cx
```

FIG. 24.29

The _add.asp file with the appropriate modifications to the Case statement to handle the weight and no_pack variables.

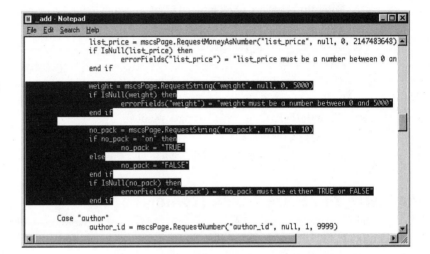

3. Scroll down the _add.asp file until you come to the Case "product" statement that contains a set of recordSet functions. Add the following code fragment directly after the recordSet("date_changed") function inside the Case "product" statement (as shown in Figure 24.30):

```
recordSet("weight").Value = weight
recordSet("no_pack").Value = no_pack
```

This code fragment will update the weight and no_pack fields in the product database table with the corresponding information passed in from the product_new.asp page discussed later in this section.

4. Save the changes to the _add.asp file.

5. Using the Windows Notepad program, open the file _update.asp located in the Stores\MSPress\Manager directory off the Microsoft Commerce Server directory.

If you chose to have Commerce Server installed in its default location, the complete path to the _update.asp file is: C:\Microsoft Commerce Server\Stores\MSPress\Manager\ _update.asp

6. Place the following code fragment under the Case "product" select statement directly under the date_changed end if statement but before the Case "author" select statement (as shown in Figure 24.31):

```
weight = mscsPage.RequestString("weight", null, 0, 5000)
if IsNull(weight) then
    errorFields("weight") = "weight must be a number between 0 and 5000"
end if
```

```
no_pack = mscsPage.RequestString("no_pack", null, 1, 10)
if no_pack = "on" then
    no_pack = "TRUE"
else
    no_pack = "FALSE"
end if
if IsNull(no_pack) then
    errorFields("no_pack") = "no_pack must be either TRUE or FALSE"
end if
```

FIG. 24.30

The _add.asp file
with the appropriate
additions to the
recordSet state-
ments handling the
weight and no_pack
variables.

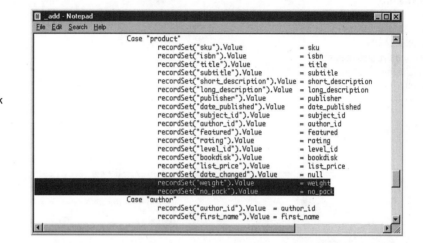

Part

V

Ch

24

FIG. 24.31

The _update.asp file
with the appropriate
modifications to the
Case statement to
handle the weight and
no_pack variables.

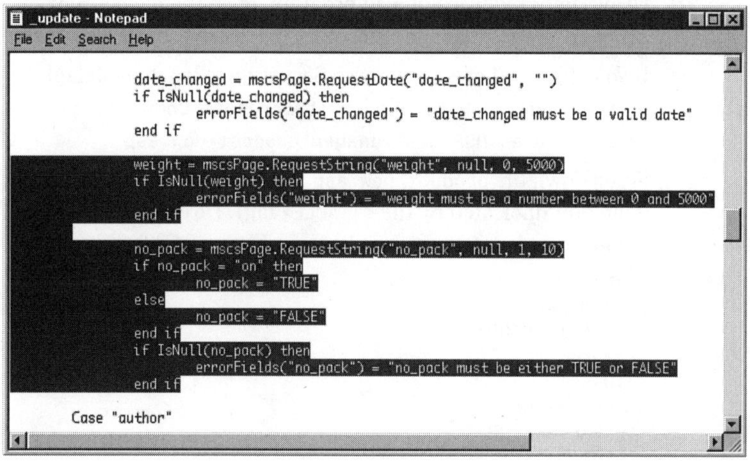

7. Scroll down the _update.asp file until you come to the Case "product" statement that contains a set of recordSet functions. Add the following code fragment directly after the recordSet("date_changed") function inside the Case "product" statement (as shown in Figure 24.32):

```
recordSet("weight").Value = weight
recordSet("no_pack").Value = no_pack
```

This code fragment updates the weight and no_pack fields in the product database table with the corresponding information passed in from the product_edit.asp page discussed later in this section.

8. Save the changes to the _update.asp file.

FIG. 24.32

The _update.asp file with the appropriate additions to the recordSet statements handling the weight and no_pack variables.

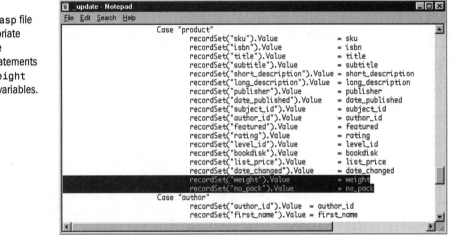

9. Using the Windows Notepad program, open the file product_new.asp located in the Stores\MSPress\Manager directory off the Microsoft Commerce Server directory.

If you chose to have Commerce Server installed in its default location, the complete path to the product_new.asp file is: C:\Microsoft Commerce Server\Stores\MSPress\Manager\product_new.asp

10. Scroll down the product_new.asp page until you come to the end of the HTML table definition (indicated by the </TABLE> tag). Directly before the </TABLE> tag, add the following code fragment (as shown in Figure 24.33):

```
<TR>
<% REM label:  %>
<TD VALIGN=TOP>
Weight:
</TD>
<% REM value:  %>
<TD VALIGN=TOP>
<INPUT
TYPE="text"
SIZE=32
NAME="weight">
</TD>
</TR>
<TR>
```

```
<% REM label:  %>
<TD VALIGN=TOP>
No Pack:
</TD>
<% REM value:  %>
<TD VALIGN=TOP>
<INPUT
TYPE="checkbox"
NAME="no_pack">
</TD>
</TR>
```

The product_new.asp page is the page that is displayed when you select the Add a New Product link on the Starter Store Product Management page. The product_new.asp page will now pass the user entered weight and no_pack data (along with the rest of the product data) through to the _add.asp page which will in turn add the product to the product database table.

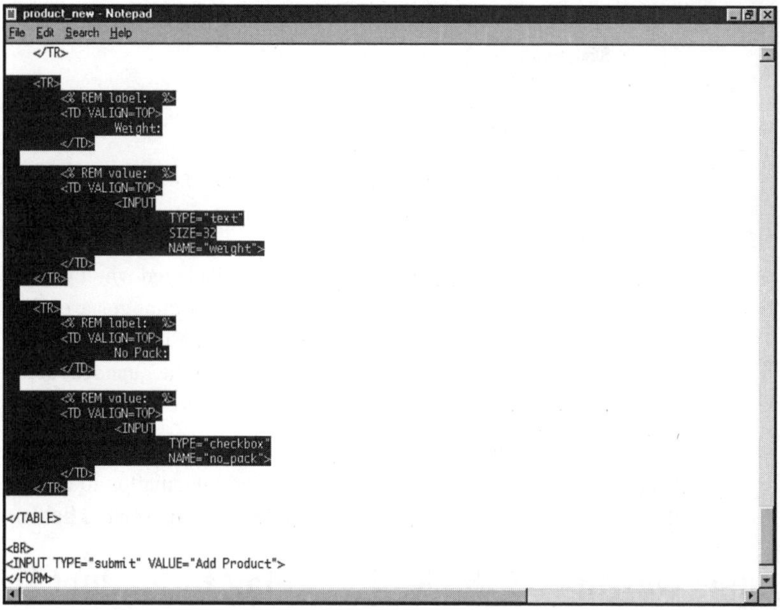

FIG. 24.33

The product_new.
asp file with the new
HTML statements to
handle the weight
and no_pack fields.

11. Using the Windows Notepad program, open the file product_add.asp located in the Stores\MSPress\Manager directory off the Microsoft Commerce Server directory.

    If you chose to have Commerce Server installed in its default location, the complete path to the product_add.asp file is: C:\Microsoft Commerce Server\Stores\MSPress\Manager\product_new.asp

12. Scroll down the product_new.asp page until you come to the end of the HTML table definition (indicated by the </TABLE> tag). Directly before the </TABLE> tag, add the following code fragment (as shown in Figure 24.34):

```
<TR>
<% REM label:  %>
<TD VALIGN=TOP>
Weight:
</TD>

<% REM value:  %>
<TD VALIGN=TOP>
<INPUT
TYPE="text"
SIZE=32
NAME="weight"
VALUE = "<% = product("weight") %>">
</TD>
</TR>
<TR>
<% REM label:  %>
<TD VALIGN=TOP>
No Pack:
</TD>

<% REM value:  %>
<TD VALIGN=TOP>
<INPUT
TYPE="checkbox"
NAME="no_pack"
<% if product("no_pack") = "TRUE" then Response.Write("CHECKED") %>>
</TD>
</TR>
```

The product_edit.asp page is the page that is displayed when you select the SKU link on the Starter Store Product Management List page. When changes are submitted through the product_edit.asp page the system will now pass the user modified weight and no_pack data (along with the rest of the product data) through to the _update.asp page which will in turn update the product data in the product database table.

The necessary framework is now in place in the Microsoft Press Starter Store to allow for adding the weight and no_pack shipping-related information to the product data. The next section describes how to make use of the new shipping-related fields.

Adding Weight and the No Pack Flag to Product Data

The last section walked you through changes to the Microsoft Press Starter Store that allowed for the addition of two shipping-related fields to the product data: weight and the no_pack flag. As mentioned earlier in the chapter under the Configuring Progistics.*Merchant* section, weight and the no_pack flag are used to determine how to pack boxes for shipment rating purposes.

The weight field contains the weight of a product. The no_pack flag indicates whether or not the particular product can be packed with any other products. When the no_pack is set true, the product will be rated as one box. When the no_pack flag is set false, the system will attempt to pack the product with other products in the order before determining freight costs.

FIG. 24.34

The product_edit. asp file with the new HTML statements to handle the weight and no_pack fields.

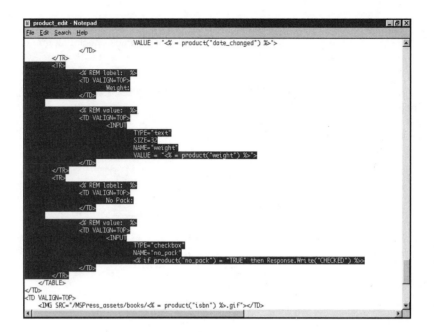

```
product_edit - Notepad
File  Edit  Search  Help
                                    VALUE = "<% = product("date_changed") %>">
                        </TD>
            </TR>
            <TR>
                <% REM label:  %>
                <TD VALIGN=TOP>
                        Weight:
                </TD>

                <% REM value:  %>
                <TD VALIGN=TOP>
                        <INPUT
                                TYPE="text"
                                SIZE=32
                                NAME="weight"
                                VALUE = "<% = product("weight") %>">
                </TD>
            </TR>
            <TR>
                <% REM label:  %>
                <TD VALIGN=TOP>
                        No Pack:
                </TD>

                <% REM value:  %>
                <TD VALIGN=TOP>
                        <INPUT
                                TYPE="checkbox"
                                NAME="no_pack"
                                <% if product("no_pack") = "TRUE" then Response.Write("CHECKED") %>>
                </TD>
            </TR>
        </TABLE>
</TD>
<TD VALIGN=TOP>
        <IMG SRC="/MSPress_assets/books/<% = product("isbn") %>.gif"></TD>
```

Follow these steps to populate the weight and no_pack fields for the Microsoft Press Starter Store product data:

1. Start the Commerce Server Host Administrator. To do so, click the Start button in the taskbar to display the Start menu; choose Programs; choose Commerce Server 2.0; and finally, select Host Administrator.

    The Commerce Server Host Administrator page will be opened in your browser.

2. Click the Manage link to the right of Microsoft Press under the Store heading.

    The MS Press Store Manager page will be displayed in your browser.

3. Click the Products link to the right of Merchandising.

    The Product List page will open.

4. Click an SKU number, preferably the first one.

    The Edit Product page will open.

5. Scroll down to the bottom of the page.

    You will see a page similar to the one shown in Figure 24.35.

6. You can now enter a weight for this product. Enter 3.50 into the Weight field. We will leave the No Pack check box unchecked for the current product.

    You must enter a date into Date Changed field before clicking the Update Now button. Otherwise an error will be generated asking you to go back and enter a valid date.

7. Click the Update Now button.

    The Product List page will be redisplayed in your browser.

Part

V

Ch

24

8. You can now continue entering weights for the various products contained in this Starter Store. You may also want to check the No Pack check box for some of the products as well.

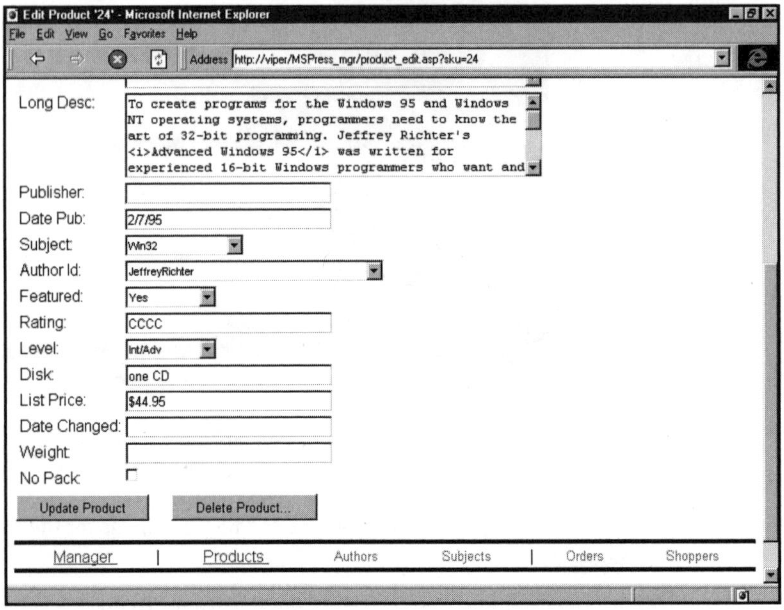

FIG. 24.35

The lower half of the Edit Product page displaying the weight and no_pack fields.

N O T E You will need to enter weights for any products that you may want to try purchasing during the testing phase later in this chapter. It is a good idea to fill in a weight for all products. Since the product database was modified to include the weight field (as opposed to being created from the onset with a weight field), any products that you do not enter a weight for will contain *null* as the weight. Orders which contain a product that has a *null* weight will not generate shipping costs. ■

The back-end of your Microsoft Press Starter Store is now configured to work with Progistics.*Merchant*. You're almost ready to begin receiving accurate shipping rates on your orders. The next, and last required, step is to remove the default values setup in the Progistics.*Merchant* Commerce Server interface during the installation process and map the Progistics shipping fields to the Commerce Server shipping fields.

Mapping the Progistics Fields to the Commerce Server Fields

Progistics uses its own internal set of fields to keep track of shipping-related information. Because Progistics was designed as a complete and robust shipping solution, it contains a large number of fields to keep track of data that are not required at the client-side of the interface.

Due to the highly specific nature of the Progistics field names, they must be mapped to the more simple order-pipeline field names. The steps outlined below describe how map the Progistics field names to the Commerce Server field names as well as how to set or remove the default settings for the Progistics.*Merchant* Commerce Server interface.

1. Open the Progistics.*Merchant* Commerce Server 2.0 Interface Documentation page in your browser. To do so, click the Start button in the taskbar to display the Start menu; choose Programs; choose TanData Progistics; choose Application Services; and finally, select Configure MSCS Interface.

   The Progistics.*Merchant* Commerce Server 2.0 Interface Documentation page opens in your browser (see Figure 24.36). There are a number of links on this page; not all of them are necessary for what needs to be configured in this section.

2. Click the Selecting a Shipping Method link under Configuring the Progistics Shipping & Handling Component.

   The Modifying Shipping Method Attribute Mapping (RATE function) is displayed in your browser.

FIG. 24.36

The Progistics.Merchant Commerce Server 2.0 Interface Documentation page.

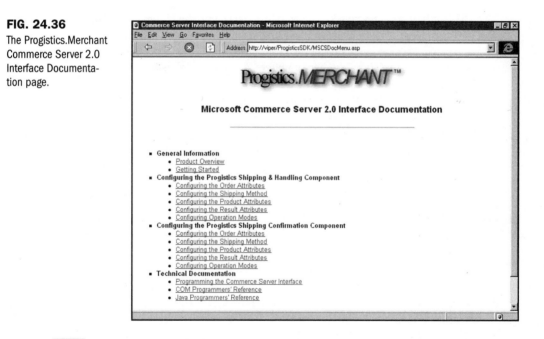

NOTE   You will notice there are two Selecting a Shipping Method links: one listed under the Configuring the Progistics Shipping & Handling Component link and the other under the Progistics Confirmation Component link; each of these components serve a very different role. The Progistics Shipping & Handling component is executed when the Shipping stage of the order-pipeline is reached. The Progistics Confirmation component executes when the Accept stage of the order-pipeline is reached.

continues

continued

The shipping method associated with the Shipping & Handling component is the shipping method that allows the possibility of more than one service being returned from Progistics; as when using a shipping method such as Customer's Choice (described earlier in the section entitled Configuring Progistics.*Merchant*). The store administrator must ensure that when the Shipping & Handling component completes only one service is returned to the order-pipeline. This one service is then used by the Progistics Confirmation component to actually ship the order and generate tracking numbers. The Progistics Confirmation component cannot ship one order by two different services; and this is why it must be passed only one service.

When the Progistics Shipping & Handling component is configured to return multiple results, the store administrator needs to have a Web page ready to display these results so the shopper can pick which service best fits his or her needs. This chosen service would then be returned to the order-pipeline for the Progistics Confirmation component to use.

Information on creating Web pages that interact with the Progistics Shipping & Handling component can be found in the Progistics.*Merchant* SDK available with the Progistics.*Merchant* software. ▪

3. A shipping method *symbol* needs to be entered into the Shipping Method Attribute field. The shipping method entered will be the shipping method used by Progistics.*Merchant* to rate packages with during the order-pipeline process. Shipping method symbols were discussed earlier in this chapter under Configuring Progistics.*Merchant*. You created two shipping methods during the configuration of Progistics.*Merchant*: Least-Costly Ground and Least-Costly Overnight (a third, Customer's Choice, was also created and the note on shipping methods should be consulted for information on how to use the Customer's Choice shipping method with Commerce Server).

   Enter NEXTDAY in the Shipping Method Attribute field. NEXTDAY was the symbol used during the creation of the Least-Costly Overnight shipping method created earlier in this chapter. If NEXTDAY is not the symbol you used when creating the Least-Costly Overnight shipping method, or you want to use a different shipping method, enter the shipping method symbol you want to use now.

4. Click the Save Changes button to save the modifications to the shipping method attribute.

   The Progistics.*Merchant* Commerce Server 2.0 Interface Documentation page is again displayed in your browser.

5. Click the Product Attributes link under Configuring the Progistics Shipping & Handling Component.

   The Modifying Product Attributes Mappings (RATE function) page is opened (see Figure 24.37).

6. Progistics is installed with the default product attributes shown on the Modifying Product Attributes Mappings page. The value shown in the Weight field under the MS Commerce Server 2.0 heading is ^10.00; which translates to 10 pounds. The Weight field should be modified to utilize the product weight information that we made available in earlier sections. To do so, click the Modify button to the right of the Weight field.

The Modifying Product Attribute for 'WEIGHT' (RATE function) is displayed in your browser (see Figure 24.38).

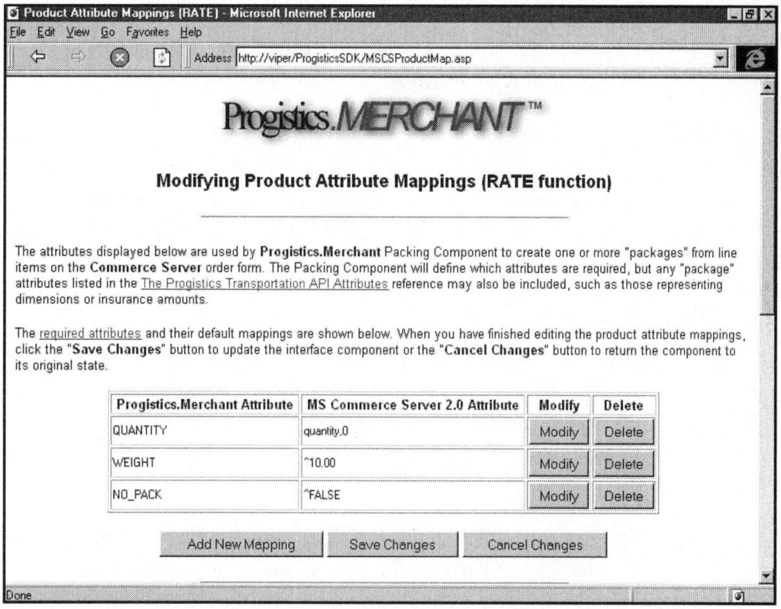

FIG. 24.37
The Modifying Product Attributes Mappings (RATE function) page.

FIG. 24.38
The Modifying Product Attributes Mappings for 'WEIGHT' (RATE function) page.

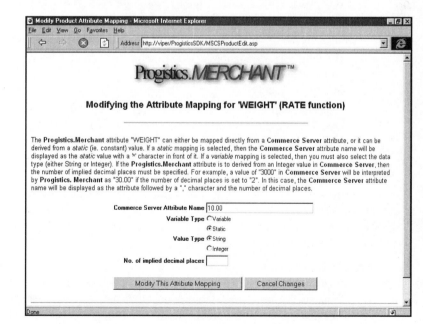

7. Enter **product_weight** into the Commerce Server Attribute Name field; select Variable as the Variable Type; select Integer as the Value Type; and finally, enter **2** into the Number of Implied Decimal Places field. Click the Modify This Attribute Mapping button to save the changes.

   Your changes will be saved and the Modifying Product Attribute Mappings page is again displayed in your browser.

> **N O T E**   As defined in the Commerce Server SDK, the Commerce Server Attribute Names for product information follow the convention of product_column name. This is why product_weight is used in the Weight field and product_no_pack is used in the NO_PACK field. weight and no_pack are the column name's of their respective fields in the MSPress_product table. ▦

8. By default, the no_pack flag is set to false; as indicated by the ^FALSE entry under the MS Commerce Server 2.0 heading. The NO_PACK field should be modified to utilize the product no_pack information that we made available in earlier sections. To do so, click the Modify button to the right of the NO_PACK field.

   The Modifying Product Attribute for 'NO_PACK' (RATE function) is displayed in your browser.

9. Enter **product_no_pack** into the Commerce Server Attribute Name field; select Variable as the Variable Type; and finally, select String as the Value Type. Click the Modify This Attribute Mapping button to save the changes.

   Your changes will be saved and the Modifying Product Attribute Mappings page is again displayed in your browser.

10. Click the Save Changes button on the Modifying Product Attribute Mappings page.

    The Progistics.*Merchant* Microsoft Commerce Server 2.0 Interface Documentation page is displayed in your browser.

11. Click the Configuring the Product Attributes link under the Configuring the Progistics Shipping Confirmation Component and repeat steps 6-10. You will be configuring the Progistics Shipping Confirmation component to use the shipping-related product information this time (the last time we configured the Progistics Shipping & Handling components; since they occur at separate stages in the order-pipeline, they are configured separately).

Progistics CS, Progistics.*Merchant*, the Progistics.*Merchant* Commerce Server interface, Commerce Server, and the Microsoft Press Starter Store are now all configured to and ready to use. You can start the Microsoft Press Starter Store, order product, and receive accurate shipping charges for the order placed.

This chapter has only touched-on some of the capabilities of the TanData Progistics.*Merchant* system. The capability to provide accurate rating and tracking number information at the point-of-sale is one of the most popular uses of the Progistics.*Merchant* system, but it is by no means the most important one. Integrating Progistics.*Merchant* with the merchant's warehouse management system provides the beginning of an accurate shipment planning and fulfillment solution.

Other Progistics components, such as the Progistics.*Shipper* component, can bring even higher levels of customer satisfaction. For instance, Progistics.*Shipper* could be configured to use the customer's email address recorded during the order-pipeline process to generate and send an email to the customer as the order is actually shipped from the warehouse, in real-time. Utilizing the capabilities of both Progistics.*Merchant* and Progistics.*Shipper* together can provide merchants with a closed-loop order fulfillment solution.

Consult the TanData Web site (**http://www.tandata.com**) for the latest developer's information for all the Progistics products. ●

CHAPTER 25

Internet Payment Authentication

The Internet is an exciting place to sell goods and services. By electronically linking millions of consumers and thousands of merchants around the world, the Internet has become a global marketplace. By the turn of the century, Internet users are expected to be buying hundreds of billions of dollars' worth of goods and services.

To date, however, few merchants accept payment over the Internet, because they are faced with confusing choices about software, standards, business processes, and security. VeriFone recognized the need for an easy-to-use, reliable, secure Internet commerce system and developed a suite of Internet software products to allow consumers to safely use their credit cards to pay for goods and services, merchants to accept online payment while performing the operational and administrative tasks necessary to run their businesses, and financial institutions to process credit-card transactions received over the Internet.

Combining proven Internet security technology, leading industry standards, and VeriFone's payment expertise developed the VeriFone Internet commerce solution. The company's Internet products fulfill the critical need to move payment transactions securely over the Internet from consumer to merchant to financial processor.

This chapter describes the key elements of the VeriFone Internet commerce solution. The discussion begins with an overview of VeriFone's experience in the development of payment systems. The company's products for consumers, merchants, and financial institutions are then detailed. Finally, the business process for distributing and setting up VeriFone's Internet payment solution is described. ■

VeriFone's Internet Commerce Products

VeriFone brings a wealth of payment knowledge and expertise to the Internet. The company has spent more than a decade solving secure payment problems and currently develops a variety of payment solutions, payment terminals, network systems, printers, and payment security products. These systems are used to deliver electronic payment services to financial institutions, retail merchants, and consumers, as well as to government agencies, health-care providers, and benefit recipients.

The Internet was the next logical step for VeriFone in the business of electronic payments. In 1995, VeriFone's Internet Commerce Division was formed, with the objective of accelerating the development of Internet commerce through the introduction of easy-to-use, highly secure payment products for consumers, merchants, and financial institutions.

Internet Payment

The current physical-world payment process for conventional credit-card transactions involves three separate parties: consumers, merchants, and financial institutions. After selecting goods or services, the consumer uses a credit card to pay for the products. The merchant uses point-of-sale software and hardware to capture the transaction and communicate with the financial institution, usually via a telephone line. The financial institution's host system then communicates through existing financial networks to get authorization for the purchase and sends this information back to the merchant to complete the transaction. When the merchant receives the authorization, the payment process is complete, and the consumer receives a credit-card receipt.

On the Internet, the credit-card-payment process with VeriFone's Internet commerce solution is similar. A consumer browses, shops, and selects goods or services to purchase. When ready, the consumer submits the order to the merchant, using secure Internet protocols. The vPOS software on the merchant's Web server captures the transaction in the same manner as the point-of-sale terminal at a physical store. The vPOS software then forwards an authorization request over the Internet to the merchant's acquiring bank/processor. The acquirer receives the authorization request from the merchant and uses its existing financial infrastructure to determine whether the authorization is approved or denied. Again using the Internet, the acquirer sends the authorization response to the merchant. The merchant then sends a digital receipt to the consumer and posts the transaction.

An End-to-End Payment Solution

The VeriFone Internet commerce solution allows transactions to move securely from the consumer to the merchant and from the merchant to the acquirer. The product suite is comprised of vPOS (point-of-sale) software and the vGATE Internet gateway.

■ vPOS software is a flexible point-of-sale application that can easily handle payments and provide payment-management functions for Internet merchants. vPOS is easy to use and install, and provides a browser interface for store operation. vPOS resides on the merchant's Web server, connects with the financial institutions Internet gateway, and provides merchants with a comprehensive set of tools for secure Internet payments. vPOS communicates directly with the financial institution and supports existing merchant business processes, including merchant-originated transactions, returns, and end-of-the-day reconciliation. vPOS merchant point-of-sale software interacts with a secure HTML payment form and in the future will interact with a consumer wallet.

■ vGATE Internet gateway software allows the financial institution to accept and process transactions from Internet merchants without altering their current host system. vGATE's principal purpose is to serve as a bridge between proprietary authorization and settlement hosts (and financial networks) and the open highly accessible Internet environment. VeriFone's vGATE Internet gateway and vPOS implement SET from the merchant to the acquirer/processor to safely complete the Internet transactions. VeriFone's Internet merchant and gateway payment products deploy the first implementation of the MasterCard/Visa SET protocol.

VeriFone's Internet payment products implement secure end-to-end payment transactions by allowing consumers to use widely available Secure Sockets Layer (SSL) -enabled browsers to purchase products from Internet merchants. They can then use SET from the merchant to the acquirer/processor to authorize and complete the transaction.

SET, the Secure Electronic Transaction protocol developed by MasterCard and Visa, focuses on the communication and interaction among partners in a payment transaction. If a consumer wants to buy a product on the Internet, he or she decides what to purchase and enters credit-card information in a secure SSL-based payment window. The merchant vPOS then sends the order and transaction information to the acquirer/processor for authorization, using SET. The acquirer/processor replies with the authorization to the merchant, also using SET. The merchant vPOS, upon receiving approval, sends a receipt to the consumer, using SSL, to complete the transaction.

The SET protocol specifies both the encryption (encryption scrambles the information so that no one can intercept the information and read it without having the proper tools to unscramble this information) and the authentication (authentication is a way to verify the identity of the parties involved in the transaction) methodologies, ensuring a secure transaction.

VeriFone's Internet payment products will migrate to a full SET implementation (consumer, merchant, and acquirer/processor) as the consumer infrastructure supporting SET becomes available. Full SET compliance requires the broad availability and adoption of consumer digital credentials (certificates and key pairs) and SET-compliant consumer software.

The vPOS in Microsoft Commerce Server 2.0

Microsoft and VeriFone have jointly integrated and bundled VeriFone's vPOS payment software with Microsoft's Commerce Server 2.0. The combination of Microsoft Commerce Server 2.0 and VeriFone vPOS software represents the first deployment of a bundled Internet retailing and payment solution. The combined product is designed to provide companies the most complete and easy-to-use solution for selling on the Internet.

The vPOS software, which is included with every copy of Microsoft Commerce Server 2.0, provides online merchants with an integrated payment solution designed to facilitate credit-card transactions and to test Internet payment functionality. By exercising payment functionality through a test gateway, the merchant can fully integrate Internet payment transactions before opening an online store.

The vPOS software consists of three main components: the vPOS engine, the payment component, and the software interface.

- The vPOS engine runs as an NT service and provides back-end payment protocol, configuration, and logging support to the other two components. This component provides the security protocols and functionality between the bank and the merchant.

- The payment component installs in the Microsoft Commerce Server 2.0 configuration and provides an interface between the merchant ordering process and the vPOS engine. The payment component executes the payment step of the ordering process through a dynamic link library (DLL) loaded in the Store Processes of the Microsoft Commerce Server 2.0. The Store Processes initialize the vPOS once and call the payment component for every transaction, posting the information to the Merchant System "blackboard." vPOS takes the information from the blackboard to construct and execute the payment transaction. When the transaction is executed, the system database stores the information that the merchant later uses to administer the store. After a complete transaction, vPOS places the receipt information on the blackboard, which is used to construct a digital receipt for the consumer.

- The vPOS software interface provides an HTML forms-based user interface for operator-initiated payment transactions, payment administration, and vPOS software configuration.

For consumer credit-card purchases, vPOS automatically processes the transaction and returns authorization results without merchant involvement. For additional payment functionality, a merchant can enter vPOS as either an operator or an administrator. As an operator, vPOS allows the merchant to manually enter payment transactions and review transactions from the vPOS terminal. Functions provided are:

- **Authorization.** Authorization verifies that the purchase amount is within the cardholder's limit and sets the transaction amount aside from the cardholder's available-credit amount. The amount then is available when the merchant captures the transaction.

- **Capture.** The merchant needs to capture a transaction to confirm to the acquirer that the authorized transaction has been completed (that the product has been shipped). The acquirer then deposits the transaction value in the merchant's account. If the merchant is selling products that a consumer receives online, the transaction is captured immediately.

- **Transaction review.** vPOS software allows the merchant to review the credit-card transactions based on search criteria entered by the merchant. The merchant can request a display of all transactions on a particular date or of a specific type (only transactions that have been authorized, for example). The Review Transactions function retrieves detailed transaction information from each entry in the vPOS terminal database. The merchant then can perform all applicable follow-on transactions, including capture, credit, retry capture, retry credit, and retry authorization.

As an administrator, the merchant can view transactions stored on the vPOS terminal and transactions stored at the acquiring bank. vPOS provides two different Administrator reports:

- **Terminal Totals Report.** This report displays the summary and total of transactions, grouped by payment instrument, stored in the current database in the vPOS terminal.

- **Host Totals Report.** This report displays the summary and total of transactions captured by the host for settlement, grouped by payment instrument, that are stored in the current database.

The vPOS software included with Microsoft Commerce Server 2.0 is used for setup and testing of the merchant's storefront payment functionality. A test gateway simulator and certificates are installed with the vPOS software. The test gateway simulates the actual acquirer/processor vGATE response and processes test transactions.

When the merchant is ready for deployment of live online transactions, a relationship with a bank must be established. The merchant's bank provides the final step by providing a merchant ID, certificates, and bank-specific vPOS software to complete the connection to the bank's Internet gateway and financial host system. The bank-specific vPOS provides the additional functionality to change the vPOS from exercising payment functionality through a test payment gateway to fully conducting secure online payment transactions over the Internet. When the bank-specific vPOS is installed, the merchant can process and administer payments in the online retailing environment equivalent to the functions available in the physical-retailing environment.

The evaluation version of the vPOS software included with Microsoft Commerce Server 2.0 does not provide the full functionality of the bank-specific vPOS product that the merchant obtains from a financial institution. The evaluation vPOS provides the following functionality:

- **Authorizations.** The evaluation vPOS has the capability to send authorization requests to a test gateway and receive authorization responses.

- **Capture.** A demonstration of the capture function is included. Capture is what actually charges the customers' credit card. When the customer enters their credit card number, vPOS authorizes the transaction, but it does not charge the customers' credit card.

Part

V

Ch

25

- **Review Transactions.** Review Transactions is fully functional even on the evaluation version of vPOS. Review Transactions allows you to review the transactions of any given day.

- **Terminal Totals Report.** Terminal Totals Report is fully functional even on the evaluation version of vPOS. Terminal Totals Report gives you the totals of each of your vPOS Terminals.

- **Host Totals Report.** An example screen is provided.

Configuring VeriFone 1.0 to work with Commerce 2.0   Although VeriFone was not written to work with Microsoft Commerce Server 2.0, there is a way to get it to work. In order to make VeriFone work with Commerce Server 2.0, you must add the vPOS service using the V1 C Component Wrapper to the Payment stage using the Commerce Server Pipeline Editor after you have installed the vPOS software. Before you edit the pipeline however, you should backup the PIPELINE.PCF file in case there is a problem. This file can be found in *X*:\Microsoft Commerce Server\Stores*storename*\config where *X* is the drive where Microsoft Commerce Server resides and *storename* is the name of your store).

1. To get to the Commerce Server Pipeline Editor, go to the Start menu, Programs, Commerce Server 2.0, Pipeline Editor. A default pipeline will come up automatically. Close this window and go to the file menu and choose Open. In the open dialog box, go to the path of the store that you would like to configure (usually *X*:\Microsoft Commerce Server\Stores*storename*\config where *X* is the drive where Microsoft Commerce Server resides and *storename* is the name of your store). Open the file named pipeline.pcf.

2. When you open the Pipeline Editor and open the pipeline to your store, you should have a screen that looks similar to this figure. Note that you can minimize or maximize the window and you can have multiple pipelines open as well.

3. Now you need to go to the Payment stage. Scroll down the pipeline until you see the Payment box on the left of the pipeline window. You should see several components next to Payment. These components look like red puzzle pieces. Delete *ALL* of these red pieces (you should see a ValidateCCNumber component, and 2 – 3 Scriptor components).

4. After you have deleted all of the components in the Payment stage, it is time to add the V1 C Component Wrapper. There is a window on the left of the Pipeline Editor with a drop-down menu. When you clicked the payment component, this window should have been changed to Payment. If you do not see Payment in the window on the left of the Pipeline Editor, choose Payment from the drop-down menu. You should see several components that you can choose from. Click the V1 C Component Wrapper and drag it on top of the Payment box. You should see the Grey payment box and a red box called V1 C Component Wrapper.

5. Double-click the V1 C Component Wrapper box to bring up the Component Properties dialog box.

6. Fill in all of the information. Note that most of these fields are case-sensitive so be very careful when you input this information.

   - Component Name: vpos
   - DLL Path. The full path to vpos.dll. This path should be in the bin directory in the directory that you installed the VeriFone program.
   - Config String: vpos.vpos @ *storename* 0
   - Store Name: *The name of your store*
   - Pipeline Stage: Payment
   - Leave the thread save box unchecked.

7. Click OK when you are finished.

8. Close the Pipeline Editor. You are prompted to save your changes to pipeline.pcf. Click Yes in the dialog box.

The next thing that you need to do is to give the Internet Server account (usually called IUSR_*machinename*) full access to the VeriFone registry key and all of the subkeys.

1. To change the permissions on this key, open regedt32 by going to the Start menu and choosing Run. Type regedt32 in the run dialog box and click OK. You cannot use regedit because regedit does not have a security menu, and therefore, you cannot change permissions using regedit.

2. Maximize the HKEY_LOCAL_MACHINE window and go to the key HKEY_LOCAL_MACHINE\SOFTWARE\VeriFone.

3. Go to the Security menu and choose Permissions to bring up the Registry Key Permissions dialog box.

4. Click the Add button to bring up the Add Users and Groups dialog box. Click the Show Users button to show a list of all users. Find the IUSR_*machinename* account and double click this account. This account should appear in the Add Names text box. Click the Type of Access pull-down menu and choose Full Control. Click OK to close the Add Users and Groups dialog box.

5. Check the Replace Permission on Existing Subkeys check box and click OK. A dialog box will appear asking if you are sure that you want to replace permissions on the whole subkey. Click Yes.

N O T E When you have finished these steps, there is one thing that vPOS will not do in Commerce 2.0 that it would do under Merchant Server 1.0. vPOS will not insert a" ink to the VeriFone vPOS Administration. If you would like to create a link on your manager page, you would simply create a link to http://*your commerce server*/vpos/cgi-bin/termint.exe/@storename@/ ▩

After you complete all of the above steps, the last thing that you need to do is to restart all of the IIS services and the vPOS service. The easiest way to restart the IIS services is to open the

Part

V

Ch

25

Internet Service Manager and stop all of the services that appear and then restart them. After you have stopped and restarted these services, go to Control Panel, Services and stop and start the vPOS Engine Service. Now when you visit, go to your Commerce Server page and make a purchase, Commerce Server should authorize the transaction for you.

Hosting Multiple Stores using one copy of VeriFone   If you have a need to host more than one store per server, VeriFone will support this. The requirements for hosting multiple stores per server are simply that you must have the same encryption key on each store. As long as each store has the same encryption key, you can use one copy of VeriFone for as many stores as you can use one copy of Commerce Server. Also, you only need to load the Gateway certificate and the two certificates from the vPOS CD once. For each additional store, you only need to load the two certificates that your acquiring bank issues you (the merchant certificates). For additional instructions on how to set up the vPOS software, you need to refer to the manual that comes with your vPOS software because setup is different for each acquiring bank.

The Role of Financial Institutions

VeriFone's vPOS software provides online merchants a payment solution designed to facilitate credit-card transactions and to enable Internet payment. Before a merchant can accept live online transactions, the merchant needs to establish a merchant account with an acquiring bank/processor, so that the acquiring bank can process transactions for the merchant and settle the payment between the consumer and the merchant. The merchant's bank/processor also supplies the merchant the means to connect to the financial institution's Internet gateway and host system.

More specifically, the merchant needs to contact an acquiring bank/processor that supports VeriFone's vPOS solution to apply for a merchant account. When the account is approved, the financial institution supplies the merchant a merchant ID and bank-specific vPOS software. The merchant installs the bank-specific vPOS software on the Web server and configures it to meet his business requirements (if the merchant accepts only certain credit cards, for example). Using the graphical user interface provided by the bank-specific vPOS software, the merchant applies for and obtains a digital certificate (using the merchant ID as one of the inputs) from a certification authority specified by the financial institution. The merchant then installs the certificate in vPOS point-of-sale software. At this point, the merchant is ready to conduct live Internet-based credit-card transactions.

N O T E   Certificates are a required element of the process, because they verify the merchant's identity to the acquirer and help prevent fraudulent merchants from conducting business under the name of the legitimate merchant. This certification is needed before merchants can send or receive secure transactions. ▪

CyberSource's Internet Commerce Services

CyberSource offers Internet Commerce Services, (ICS), a suite of turnkey, backoffice commerce applications that are critical to a merchants successful electronic commerce initiative.

ICS is a suite of services, not a product, which allows companies to outsource the complexities of electronic commerce to CyberSource. This helps companies focus their resources on marketing their Website to attract visitors and gives them an incentive to buy, rather than how to configure all the transaction processing requirements. CyberSource has developed a plug-in module that is included with Microsoft Commerce Server 2.0 that enables simple drag and drop setup of the service in the order processing pipeline, enabling merchants to quickly setup access to the CyberSource services. See the CyberSource Internet Commerce Service COM document for detailed information on merchant services setup.

Why use an Internet Commerce Service Provider (ICSP)?

Web merchants today have a very tough job differentiating themselves—no longer are physical locations and overnight delivery a competitive advantage. One-to-one marketing, relationship building, value-added services, and so on. are the things that will make web stores successful. With all these tasks to worry about, why would a merchant want to do the transaction processing piece too? There's no competitive advantage or cost savings of building and maintaining it in-house—only risks from upset customers if you don't get it right!

The Suite of Services

CyberSource commerce services include real-time credit card processing, IVS fraud screen (patent pending), export control, sales tax calculation, electronic fulfillment, customer support interfaces, and EDI. In addition CyberSource offers the CyberSource ClearingHouse™ which provides a trusted third-party rights registry for digital goods such as software, music, video clips, and so on.

- Real-time credit card transaction processing. This includes all steps in the credit card purchasing process: address verification service (AVS), pre-authorization, and completion of billing (settlement).

- IVSTM fraud protection. With the relative ease of false identification over the Internet, AVS alone is not sufficient protection. Internet transactions belong to the MOTO (mail order/telephone order) category, for which merchants are 100 percent liable—even when the transaction has been authorized by the bank! That's why CyberSource developed its unique IVS fraud screen. In addition to real-time bank validation, every CyberSource transaction is checked, analyzed, and cross-checked by Internet address, browser type, and over 100 other validation factors to uncover potential fraud. Based on artificial intelligence software we developed and a transaction history database of over 2 million transactions, the IVS fraud screen is an important safeguard you only get with CyberSource.

- Export control. The federal government prohibits sales to restricted countries and individual parties, according to detailed lists that change almost weekly (Denied Persons, Specially Designated Nationals, Restricted Countries, and more). Failure to comply can trigger six-figure U.S. State Department and Treasury Department penalties! So you'll need to have someone closely monitor these lists, analyze transactions against them, and keep the lists current. Or, you can simply avoid the hassle and expense by handing this function over to CyberSource. We'll mitigate the exposure by ensuring that your transactions conform to these government rules.

■ In addition, many publishers of intellectual property restrict the sale of their products by country or region, to comply with exclusive distribution agreements or for other marketing reasons. CyberSource technology ensures compliance with these contractual or marketing restrictions as well.

■ Sales tax services. The proper application of sales tax in electronic transactions is another potential nightmare for on-line merchants. Accordingly, CyberSource maintains up-to-date sales tax tables for all states, cities, and counties, covering virtually every jurisdiction in the United States and Canada.

■ Fulfillment. Once a customer has completed a purchase transaction, we can deliver digital products immediately via ESD, or arrange for physical product delivery via surface or air transport, using an EDI connection to a distributor or fulfillment house. CyberSource uses the approved ESD industry standards we helped develop with Microsoft, other publishers, and the Software Publishers Association, for encryption, secure delivery, returns, and clearinghouse functions. To ensure safe delivery, your digital product is encrypted and encased in a secure electronic container. The purchase is also electronically "branded" to discourage unauthorized duplication or distribution of the product. An Electronic License Certificate (ELC) is then sent separately to the customer to unlock the electronic container.

■ Electronic Data Interchange (EDI). CyberSource maintains immediate EDI connections to large distributors and fulfillment houses for easy, cost-effective, physical delivery of your products. By leveraging these established EDI links from CyberSource, merchants can avoid the effort and expense of setting up their own EDI connections.

Commerce Server 2.0 and CyberSource ICS Communications Protocol

CyberSource developed Simple Commerce Messaging Protocol (SCMP) for safe and secure transactions that pass through firewalls and proxy servers. SCMP uses public key cryptography to provide security and message authentication. In addition, encrypted messages are converted to ASCII format ("armored") for transmission over a HyperText Transfer Protocol (HTTP) connection. This encryption and armoring is done with RSA Public Key CryptoSystem from RSAData Security, Inc. SCMP messages consist of an encrypted series of fields in name=value pairs, separated by newline characters (ASCII \012).

Order Processing Component System

The Commerce Server order processing component system consists of a series of distinct stages called the order processing pipeline. After the shopper places an order, the order is passed through the pipeline, each stage of which consists of some number of components.

Each stage of the pipeline contains a set of order processing components that you specify and configure. Some of these components are optional; you can use whichever fit your needs.

Commerce Server includes a tool called Pipeline Editor. This editor provides a User interface for selecting the components run at specific stages of the order processing pipeline.

Using CyberSource Internet Commerce Services COM

When you start the Pipeline Editor, a new pipeline is immediately displayed. If you want to create a new pipeline, click New on the File menu. To Load and configure an existing pipeline, click Open on the File menu. Locate the .pcf file for the pipeline you wish to configure and load it.

To add the CyberSource Component to a stage, drag the component from the left-hand drop down list and drop it on the stage in which it is to be run. To configure the component, double-click the puzzle piece and the following Property sheet is displayed.

Enter the merchant name and select the Services you want to seek for that stage.

You can also use the right mouse button to delete or enter parameters for the component.

When you are finished configuring the pipeline, click Save on the File menu. Give the pipeline configuration file a name then click OK. For the newly configured pipeline to take effect, you must reload the store.

DataBase Field Requirements

Commerce Server supports all ODBC-compliant, ANSI-standard, SQL-based, database management systems. CyberSource Internet Commerce Service COM requires the following fields for the shopper information in the shopper table.

first_name, last_name, email, phone, address1, city, state, zip, country, ccnum, expmo, expyr

Also in the product table name, sku, type, price, and quantity are expected.

When the merchant executes the Pipeline object CyberSource Internet Commerce COM will be executed. The COM will read all the values about the shopper from the Order form and make the ics message structure. (Note: The commerce server automatically creates the name/value pair as found in the DataBase.)

It also will read the information about the products in the shopping basket and make an offer for each product in the basket. Then the services, which are selected for this COM object, will be executed from the online CyberSource Commerce Server. The result will be put in a database field called result. The COM will also process the results and any error that occurred during the process will be appended to the error object. The merchant can write an ASP program to display the errors.

From Here...

This chapter went over two of the different options that you as the merchant have when it comes to choosing your credit card authentication software. Of course, this is also dependent on the bank that you are using to do your credit card verification as well. VeriFone does not, as of the writing of this book, have a Commerce 2.0 solution. However, you learned how to integrate VeriFone 1.0 into your Commerce 2.0 server using the V1 C Component Wrapper. You also learned how to make the vPOS software work with multiple stores on the same machine. At this time, CyberSource does have a Commerce 2.0 solution and they also have several features that you as a merchant could find very useful such as export control. If you accidentally sell merchandise to a restricted country, you could find yourself in a whole lot of trouble.

The following chapters provide further information to help you continue with the development of your commerce stores.

- Chapter 3,"Setting Up Your Store." This chapter describes installing and configuring Microsoft Commerce Server. You may already have VeriFone of CyberSource working, and now you will want to setup Microsoft Commerce Server as soon as possible so that you can get started in developing your store.

- Part IV: "Creating Stores with Active Server Pages." Since Microsoft Commerce Server 2.0 uses ASP and not HTML anymore, you will want to familiarize yourself with ASP. These chapters go over setting up Commerce Server 2.0 stores with ASP.

- Part VI: "Case Studies." The case studies section goes over real-world stores including how to configure your store using credit card authentication software such as VeriFone and CyberSource.

CHAPTER 26

Enhancing Security with the PIX Firewall

When you are setting up your network, security is one of the things that you need to consider. As you know, the more popular your Web site is, the more tempting it will be for people to try to hack into it. Although you should not be paranoid about security, you should take steps to ensure that your site cannot be easily hacked. The best way to protect against break-ins is to make an investment in a firewall. By using a firewall, you are protected from almost any incoming traffic except what you decide to allow in.

For the C-Systems network, it was decided to go with the Cisco PIX Firewall. The reason that this particular firewall was chosen is because it is a hardware solution. Most of the firewalls out there are software-based and they run on either a Windows NT Server or a UNIX-based machine. Having a software-based firewall solution has a lot of disadvantages. The main disadvantages to using a software-based firewall are that 1) software-based firewalls are only as secure as the operating system that they are running on. If you subscribe to any type of security mailing list such as CERT, you will see that someone comes up with a new way to hack into the UNIX server as root (root is the account that can do absolutely anything on the machine regardless of file security) almost every week.
2) Having a software-based firewall could slow down incoming and outgoing traffic and not give the level of

An overview of the Cisco PIX Firewall

Understand what the Cisco PIX Firewall can do in maintaining the security and privacy of your network and your servers.

Booting the Cisco PIX Firewall for the first time

The first time that you boot the Cisco PIX Firewall, you will need to make sure that you have the correct number of licenses and are running the lastest version of the PIX Firewall operating system. You may also need to clear the configuration if there is an existing configuration.

Configuring the Cisco PIX Firewall

You can configure the Cisco PIX Firewall either using a command-line interface or an easy HTTP interface.

flexibility, protection, and speed that one would look for in a site that would be experiencing very heavy traffic. ■

Introducing the Cisco PIX Firewall

The Cisco PIX Firewall is guaranteed to work with speeds as high as two T3 lines without any loss in performance due to traffic being redirected through a firewall. The Cisco PIX Firewall also comes with 10/100 Base-T network cards. There are two versions of the Cisco PIX Firewall. The 133MHz version of the PIX will handle up to 45Mbps or a full T3 and the 200MHz version of the PIX (the Cisco PIX Firewall 1000) will handle up to 90Mbps or two T3's. This firewall is so fast because of the way that it handles incoming and outgoing traffic.

The way that a firewall works is that all traffic inside of the firewall is given a nonroutable IP address. Every computer on the Internet needs to have an IP address that is unique; no other computer can have the same address. An *IP address* is an address in the form xxx.xxx.xxx.xxx. By using these numbers, computers can find other computers on the Internet, and these computers can communicate with one another. In the interest of security, you do not want all these computers to be able to communicate with one another, so you need to make a way to protect these computers.

You set up your network so that all your computers have an IP address that does not belong to them. When computers within the network communicate, they have no problem communicating because they are all using the same block of IP addresses, so the routers know where all this traffic goes. Also, when a computer on the Internet tries to communicate with one of these machines, it is unsuccessful because it cannot locate this computer by the IP address assigned to it.

Using nonroutable IP addresses presents a problem, however, because if a computer is not using an IP address assigned by an Internet Service Provider, it cannot get to the Internet in the same way that computers on the Internet cannot get to it.

This is where the firewall comes in. The firewall is assigned at least two IP addresses: an IP address on the internal network that only internal computers can recognize and an IP address that was assigned by the Internet Service Provider so that the firewall can get to the Internet. When a computer tries to go to the Internet, it goes to the firewall and requests access to the Internet.

At this point, a traditional firewall does one of several things. The first thing is ask the user to authenticate with a user name and password. Many companies restrict access to the Internet by authorized personnel so that their employees are not wasting the company's bandwidth by surfing the Web. When the user is authenticated, the firewall checks to see whether that user has access to that particular site. If the user does have access, the firewall takes the traffic from the computer and resends it, using its own IP address. When traffic is returned through the firewall, the firewall must send it to the machine where the traffic originated.

Imagine a network of 1,000 computers that all have access to the Internet. Your network has sufficient bandwidth to handle all the requests, so you should not be slowing down at all, but your users notice that things are getting slow during peak times. You check your utilization logs, and you find that even during the busiest times, you are only at 60 percent utilization. As you continue to investigate, you find that the load on the firewall is much more than the machine should have to handle.

The reason that the machine is having this much trouble with all this traffic is that it is trying to account for up to 1,000 simultaneous connections going through the same IP address. Every time a user sends out a request, this computer needs to know where these requests came from and to send them back to the proper computer. With this much traffic, the computer is getting backlogged, and this is accounting for significant slowdowns out to the Internet.

Taking Advantage of the Cisco PIX Firewall

Cisco has come up with a solution to this problem. The Cisco PIX Firewall has one IP address for the internal network and one IP address for the Internet. The difference is that the Cisco PIX Firewall also keeps a pool of IP addresses available. When a user tries to get to the Internet, the firewall tries to authenticate the user, if it is configured to do so. When the user is authenticated and cleared to get to the site, the Cisco PIX Firewall assigns to that computer a unique IP address. Now, whenever that computer tries to get out, it goes through the same IP address, and all traffic going through that IP address is coming from and going to only that one computer.

This does a great deal to lighten the load from the firewall. Instead of the firewall having to account for all traffic going through the firewall, it has to keep track of only IP addresses. The one drawback to this solution is that with the other firewalls, you need only one IP address to handle a great amount of machine. With the Cisco PIX Firewall, you need one IP address per simultaneous connection. If you have 1,000 desktops that need to access the Internet at the same time, you are going to need at least 1,000 IP addresses.

If you do not have 1,000 IP addresses but you need 1,000 computers or even 10,000 computers to access the Internet at the same time, the Cisco PIX Firewall also supports this. The PIX has a feature called Port Address Translation. Port Address Translation allows a System Administrator to assign a single routable IP address to any number of internal IP addresses.

According to the Cisco documentation, if you have purchased enough licenses, you can assign one routable IP address to up to 64,000 internal IP addresses. You can use up to 16,384 simultaneous connections through the firewall.

Greater Response Time

By assigning a separate IP address to each computer, the firewall only needs to account for where all traffic to that one IP address should be routed. The firewall does not have to keep track of where each packet should be routed.

Greater Flexibility

Most firewalls need to know what the traffic is before they allow it out. Some firewalls allow only World Wide Web and FTP traffic to go out through a Web browser. You cannot Telnet to remote hosts, you cannot use real audio or real video, some ActiveX controls do not work, ping does not work (ping is a utility that allows you to see whether a remote host is available). You cannot connect to Microsoft Windows 95 or Windows NT machines by using Windows NT tools (if you have access to port 139 and have an administrative account, you can administer any Windows NT Server or Workstation over the Internet). You cannot connect to another machine's news or NNTP server (port 119).

As you can see, other firewalls do not allow you to do easily what the Cisco PIX Firewall allows you to do. Most of these firewalls can be configured to allow for most of this type of access, but configuration requires a great deal of work by the system administrator, if the firewall supports it at all. Also, most firewalls do not allow streaming audio or video because they do not use a specific port. With most firewalls, you cannot configure access if you do not know a predetermined port. With the Cisco PIX Firewall, you can restrict access to these types of applications, but by default, the firewall allows your users to use anything on the Internet.

Security

The Cisco PIX Firewall is secure because even though it loans all computers their own IP address for a period of time, if a computer tries to get to one of those IP addresses, it is not allowed access. That IP address can only send traffic out to the Internet; it cannot receive traffic from the Internet.

Conduits

The Cisco PIX Firewall allows you to make conduits. You can allow passage of specific traffic through these conduits. If you have a public Web server on your network, you need to allow access to this Web server through the firewall. First, you assign a static IP address to this machine. This IP address is an internal IP address; therefore, you cannot use this IP address to get to the Internet because it was not assigned by your ISP. Next, you assign an IP address in the firewall to correspond to that computer's internal IP address. In other words, if you are using 120.0.0.5 as the internal IP address of your server, because this address is not a valid IP address, you cannot get to the Internet by using this IP address. You decide to use 205.181.30.5, an IP address that was assigned by your ISP, as the IP address for this machine.

Now, whenever you go out to the Internet through this machine, all traffic uses the IP address 205.181.30.5. Even though all traffic going out uses this specific IP address, the firewall has not been told to allow any traffic in yet.

The next step is creating an access list of traffic that is allowed in. You have several options at this point. You can allow all traffic to a specific port, all traffic to the entire machine, all traffic from a specific IP address or block of IP addresses to the machine, and so on. You learn how to do this later in this chapter in the section "Configuring the Cisco PIX Firewall."

Easy Configuration

With the Cisco PIX Firewall, you need to type only about six commands and then you can configure it, using a user-friendly HTTP interface. Using this interface, you can configure everything that you would be able to do by using the command line. If you are familiar with the Cisco IOS operating system, you can do everything through the command line, if you want.

Full Compatibility with Authentication Methods

If you need to have strict access control for users to get out through the firewall, the Cisco PIX Firewall supports both Terminal Access Controller Access Control System+ (TACACS+) and Remote Authentication Dial-In User Service (RADIUS). The databases reside on a Windows NT Server or a UNIX server, and the Cisco PIX Firewall authenticates all outgoing traffic through these databases. If you have a dial-up server, you can use the same databases for the Cisco PIX Firewall that you use for dial-in authentication.

Full Redundancy

With the Cisco PIX Firewall, you can have complete fault tolerance. You can have two Cisco PIX Firewalls connected to each other via special cable, and if one should ever go down for any reason or need to be rebooted, the other one takes over without any noticeable downtime for your users.

Java Applet Filter

Some Java applets can do harm to users' computers. Because the user is running the program, most firewalls cannot protect against this type of application. Some firewalls block Java and ActiveX applications. The Cisco PIX Firewall has a Java applet filter, so you can allow certain types of applets to be run or none at all.

Mail Guard

As any junior system administrator knows, sendmail has been used for countless attacks and is still being used to hack into systems. For this reason, you most likely do not want to expose your mail server to the Internet. You may not even want to make a mail conduit, because you could be putting your systems at risk.

Cisco has built a secure mail-transfer program into the Cisco PIX Firewall. Mail Guard allows connections through the mail server, but it logs all transactions and allows only the minimum commands to send mail. Commands such as `vrfy` and `expn` are not allowed, because users can use these commands to find user names and hack into your system. Also, things like trying to flood the mail port to cause a buffer overflow and crash the system are not allowed.

Configuring the Cisco PIX Firewall

When you first get your Cisco PIX Firewall, you need to clear the configuration, reload it, and then configure it via the command line. After you do the initial configuration, you can configure the Cisco PIX Firewall by using HTTP. Make sure that you follow all these steps *before* turning on the Cisco PIX Firewall. You are going to want to look at some important information while the Cisco PIX Firewall is booting, so you need to connect it to your computer first.

To connect the Cisco PIX Firewall to your computer, you need just a regular serial cable. Unlike other Cisco products, the firewall does not require any special cables or a null-modem adapter. Connect the serial cable to the Cisco PIX Firewall and then to your computer. If you plan to configure the Cisco PIX Firewall via HTTP, you also need to connect the internal interface of the Cisco PIX Firewall to your network. Make sure that you plug the network cable into the internal port, because you cannot easily connect directly to the Cisco PIX Firewall through the outside interface.

Now open your terminal program. If you are using Windows 95 or Windows NT Server or Workstation, you can simply use HyperTerminal. Do not connect to a modem; connect directly to the serial port, into which you plugged the Cisco PIX Firewall. Turn on the Cisco PIX Firewall and watch it boot. Figure 26.1 shows the bootup screen.

FIG. 26.1

The PIX Firewall bootup screen also gives use restrictions.

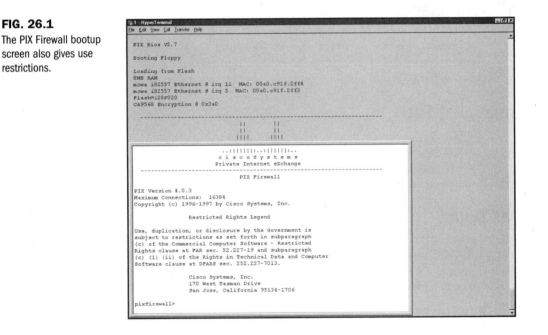

Booting the Cisco Pix Firewall

The first things that you are looking for is the amount of flash RAM. All the new Cisco PIX Firewalls should have at least 8M of RAM. If you recently purchased a Cisco PIX Firewall, and it has less than 8M of RAM, it could be an earlier model. Unless you agreed on purchasing a lesser model, check with your reseller to find out why you have a lesser amount of memory. If you have only 2M or 4M of RAM, you cannot upgrade your Cisco PIX Firewall to version 4 of the IOS software.

If you have an older Cisco PIX Firewall and need to upgrade to version 4 of the IOS software, you should be able to get in touch with your reseller and purchase an 8M upgrade card. If you are unsure whether you need to upgrade, or if you want to find out why it may be to your advantage to upgrade, you should check out http://www.cisco.com/pix for the latest information on version 4.0 of the IOS software. If you are going to be purchasing a new Cisco PIX Firewall, the easiest solution is to ask your reseller to make sure that you are getting an 8M RAM flash card with the latest 4.0 released revision of the software.

As you can see from the example, the Cisco PIX Firewall tries to boot from the 3.5-inch floppy drive first. If no disk is in the drive, it loads from flash, which is how you normally boot. Next, you see the Ethernet cards that you have installed in your Cisco PIX Firewall, the IRQs that the cards are on, and the hardware addresses of the cards. If you look down a little more, you see the version of the software.

At the time this book was published, the latest released version is 4.0.5. If you are running a version that is earlier than 4.0.5, you can upgrade, but unless you find that you are running beta software, that you have a bug in your version, or that you do not have some functionality, you do not necessarily need to upgrade.

The maximum number of simultaneous connections that the Cisco PIX Firewall supports is 16,384. When you purchased the Cisco PIX Firewall, you purchased the software for a specific number of simultaneous connections. You should see this number of connections under Maximum Connections when you first boot. If the number is incorrect, you need to contact your reseller for the correct version of the software. Fortunately, increasing the number of simultaneous connections involves only inserting a floppy disk and rebooting the Cisco PIX Firewall. When the Cisco PIX Firewall finishes booting from the floppy disk, you reboot it without the floppy disk, and you should be all set. You do not have to go through any type of hardware upgrade or hardware swap.

Part
V

Ch
26

Saving Your Configuration

If you find that you need to do an upgrade after you configure your firewall, you need to save your configuration to floppy disk. When you upgrade your flash card, your configuration is lost, so be sure to save your work before upgrading. To save your work, you simply need go into enable mode and type **save –f**. To restore your configuration, you simply type (in enable mode) **restore –f**.

Going into Enable Mode

Now you see a prompt that says pixfirewall>. With any Cisco product, you can tell which type of access you have by the prompt. As you notice, the prompt is >. This prompt means that you are not in privileged mode, so you can view only certain configuration options, and you cannot make any changes in the Cisco PIX Firewall. To make changes, you need to go to enable mode by typing **en**. You are prompted for a password. If you are in the Cisco PIX Firewall for the first time, simply press Enter. If you still see the password prompt, try typing **cisco** for the password. Now you should see pixfirewall#. Notice the pound sign (#). If you are ever logged into any Cisco product and see a prompt followed by a pound sign, you are in enable mode, and you can view or change any configuration.

Clearing an Existing Configuration

Now you need to find out whether your Cisco PIX Firewall has been configured. Type **show config**. When Cisco ships a firewall, the firewall will either have a configuration that does not suit the needs of your network or the configuration will be totally clear. If you see that the firewall has a configuration that is not correct to work on your network, you want to erase the configuration. If you see No Configuration, you do not need to perform the following steps.

To erase the configuration, type **write erase** and press Enter to confirm. Now you must reboot the Cisco PIX Firewall for it to completely clear the configuration. Type **reload** and press Enter to confirm that you want to reboot the Cisco PIX Firewall. The Cisco PIX Firewall should reboot in 30 seconds or less.

Performing the Initial Configuration

Now you are ready to actually start configuring the Cisco PIX Firewall. You can find the available commands by typing **?** at any time. Also, if you want to find out what a command does, type a command followed by a question mark (?).

You can abbreviate commands. The abbreviated command for **write memory** is **wr mem**. The abbreviated command for **config term** is **co t**.

To begin configuring the Cisco PIX Firewall, go to enable mode and type **config term**. You should see the config prompt (pixfirewall(config)#). Type the following commands:

```
pixfirewall(config)# interface ethernet inside auto
pixfirewall(config)# interface ethernet outside auto
```

These lines configure the network interface cards to autodetect the speed of the network. You need to be using Intel 10/00 auto-sensing network interface cards to be able to use this command. If you are using 3 Com cards, you need to replace **auto** with **10BaseT**. If you are using Token Ring cards, you need to replace **ethernet** with **token** and **auto** with **4mbps** or **16mbps**, depending on the speed of your network.

The following lines assign an IP address to the inside and outside interfaces of the Cisco PIX Firewall:

```
pixfirewall(config)# ip address inside ip_address netmask
pixfirewall(config)# ip address outside ip_address netmask
```

The inside should be a block of IP addresses that only your internal computers recognize. Certain blocks of IP addresses have been reserved for firewalls and other such purposes. You should use either 10.x.x.x or 120.x.x.x. You will have more than enough IP addresses by using either of these two blocks. You have a class-A of addresses—255^3 of IP addresses or more than 16 million IP addresses. If you decide to use 10, you most likely set your inside IP address to 10.0.0.1 and the netmask to 255.0.0.0. The outside IP address needs to be an IP address that has been assigned by your ISP, and the netmask corresponds to that IP address.

For the C-Systems network, the IP address of 205.181.30.254 with a netmask of 255.255.255.0 will be used.

Configuring the Cisco PIX Firewall using an existing IP address

When you first configure the firewall, you may need to set the IP address of the Cisco PIX Firewall to an IP address of your local network to configure it. Doing so is not a problem. When you go into production, you simply need to change the IP address of the inside interface to the IP address that you reserved for it.

When you first begin to configure the Cisco PIX Firewall, there are some commands that you must type in using a terminal program such as Hyperterimal.

```
pixfirewall(config)# passwd <password>
```

This command sets the password telnet password:

```
pixfirewall(config)# enable pass <password>
```

This command sets the enable password:

```
pixfirewall(config)# http 10.0.0.0 255.0.0.0
```

This command allows HTTP connections to come from any IP address beginning with 10:

```
pixfirewall(config)# write memory
```

Now you can write your configuration to memory and continue configuring the Cisco PIX Firewall by using a Web browser such as Microsoft Internet Explorer.

Configuring the Cisco PIX Firewall via HTTP

Go to your Web browser and type the internal interface of the browser. If you did everything correctly, you get a prompt to type a user name and password. Always use admin for the user name; the password is the enable password that you typed in the preceding section. When you enter the correct user name and password, you see the PIX Firewall Configuration home page (see Figure 26.2). Click PIX Firewall Configuration to continue configuring the Cisco PIX Firewall.

As you see in the illustration, you can configure many things to customize your Cisco PIX Firewall. You also see what you have already configured and saved up to this point.

Configuring the IP Addresses of the PIX Firewall Interfaces

The Interfaces box shows the IP addresses of each network interface card and the link type of either the Ethernet or Token Ring (see Figure 26.3). As you can see, the Cisco PIX Firewall has not been configured to use the IP address of what will be the internal network. Before the Cisco PIX Firewall is brought into production, the internal IP address of the PIX will need to be changed to 120.0.0.1.

Part

V

Ch

26

FIG. 26.2

The PIX Firewall
Configuration Home.

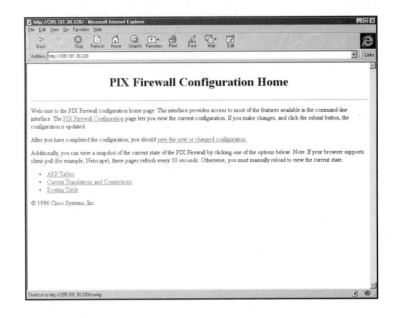

Make sure that you save your work before you reboot the PIX Firewall

When you make any changes, you need to submit your changes when you are done. You do not need to submit every change; you can make all your changes and submit only once. The reason that you see a `submit` button in every section is because the configuration page is so long. Cisco decided that it would be easier for users if they could submit their changes at any point in the configuration process rather than having to scroll to the top or bottom of the page to submit any changes. This also makes it much faster if you need to change only one item.

By submitting a change, however, you are not saving it to flash. When you submit your changes, you need to go back to the PIX Firewall Configuration home page and choose to save all your changes. Clicking the `save the new or changed configuration` link writes all of your changes to flash. If you do not save your changes to flash, the changes will be effective until you reboot your Cisco PIX Firewall; then it goes back to the old configuration.

If you are unsure about what you are doing or, are going to be doing a long configuration list, you will want to submit and save your changes often. Submitting your changes often also helps, because if you make a mistake and try to submit your changes, your changes are not submitted. If you submit your work after only a couple of sections, you will find your errors quickly.

CAUTION

Be careful when deciding what IP addresses you are going to use for your internal network. If you need to dial into another network, make sure that the network that you are dialing into is not using the same IP addresses that you have chosen for your internal network. For example, if you have a customer that is using a Cisco PIX Firewall and assigned 10.0.0 to their internal network, you should not use 10.0.0 for your internal network. When you go to dial in to your customers network, your workstations will be confused and the result is not going to be what you are trying to accomplish.

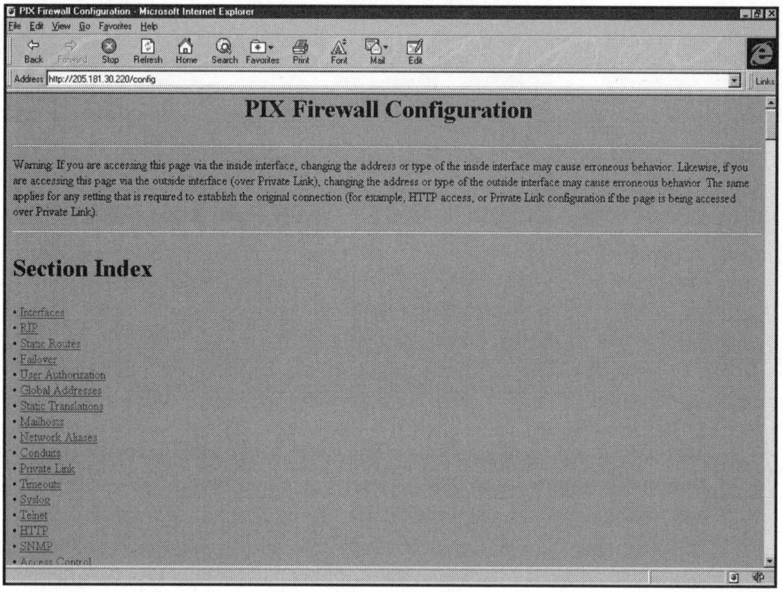

FIG. 26.3

Here, you configure the inside and outside IP addresses of each network card and you also need to configure what type of network link you are using.

Subnetting IP addresses in your local network

Instead of using a netmask of 255.0.0.0, which makes all traffic going to 10.x.x.x appear to be on the same local network, you can use a netmask of 255.255.255.0, which divides your addresses into 2,097,152 class-Cs. In other words, if you are using 10.0.0.1 with a netmask of 255.255.255.0, all traffic coming from any address in 10.0.0.x goes directly to the target machine. Any traffic coming from 10.0.0.1 and going to 10.0.x.x needs to go through the router and then be directed to the proper machine. Alternatively, if you need to have more than 254 machines connected to the same network, you can split your block into 65,534 class-B addresses by using the netmask 255.255.0.0. This means that you have about 65,000 IP addresses in each block, and 65,534 of these blocks are available. If you have a large network, you probably will split these addresses so that you can plan for traffic and loads going through each point.

Configuring RIP and Static Routes

The next two sections are RIP and Static Routes (see Figure 26.4). If you need to use RIP on your network to broadcast IP addresses and routes, you can enable Broadcast or Passive on your inside and outside network interfaces. If you do not use RIP, leave all of the RIP options disabled.

Part

V

Ch

26

FIG. 26.4

This figure shows where you configure RIP and Static Routes.

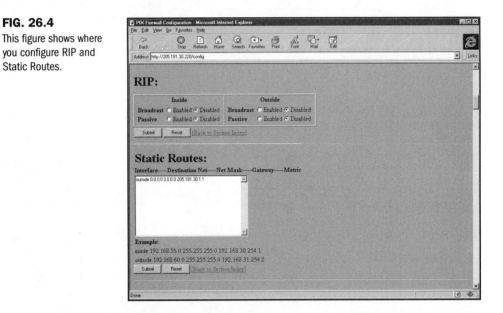

You need to set up at least one static route so that the Cisco PIX Firewall knows where to send traffic going out to the Internet. The command `route outside 0.0.0.0 0.0.0.0 205.181.30.1 1` sends all traffic that is not internal through the router that has an IP address `205.181.30.1`. The first `0.0.0.0` is the IP address, and it represents the entire Internet. The second IP address `0.0.0.0` is the netmask, and it also represents the entire Internet. `205.181.30.1` is the IP address of the router. `1` is the number of hops that the router needs to travel to get to the router. Most of the time, your router is only one hop away. If you have other routers on your internal network, you also need to add static routes to these routers. If you have multiple offices and are connected via frame relay, you connect through a frame relay router—a Cisco 2511 that is inside the firewall, for example.

In this case, you have a few choices of what to do. If you have only one router on your network, the easiest thing to do is have all traffic from your internal workstations and servers go through that router. If that router does not know where to send the traffic, it sends the traffic through the firewall. This method requires you to use only one static route.

The first thing that you have to do is to have the internal router use the firewall as its default gateway. This is nothing different from the way that you would normally set up any other machine. Next, you set up a static route in your firewall so that all internal traffic is routed through the router. If your router has the IP address `10.0.0.100`, you set your route to look like this: `route inside 0.0.0.0 0.0.0.0 10.0.0.100 1`. If you have more than one router on your network, you need to set up static routes for all your routers. Thus, if you have a network of `172.188.3` going through a router with the IP address `10.0.0.100`, you need to use the following command: `route inside 172.188.3.0 255.255.255.0 10.0.0.100 1`. This command tells the firewall to redirect any traffic going to `172.188.3.x` to `10.0.0.100`, which is one hop away.

Configuring Failover and Radius Server List

The next sections are Failover and Radius Server (see Figure 26.5). The Cisco PIX Firewall has the capability to run full redundancy. If you have two Cisco PIX Firewalls on your network, one acts as an active primary and the other as a secondary on standby. If the primary Cisco PIX Firewall should fail for any reason, get rebooted, or just become unavailable for 15 seconds or more, the secondary turns itself into the primary and takes over the role that the primary Cisco PIX Firewall was handling. This feature is on by default. If you are not using a backup Cisco PIX Firewall, you should disable Failover.

FIG. 26.5
You can either enable or disable Failover. You can also specify a Radius Server List for any Radius Servers on your network.

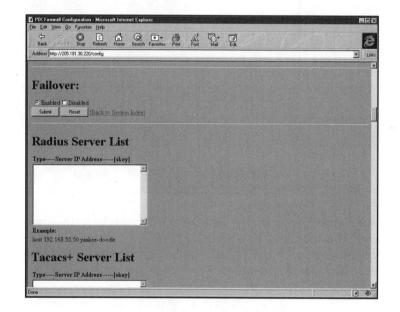

If you are using a Radius Server to authenticate your users before they can get through the Cisco PIX Firewall, you need to provide the IP address of your radius server and the secret key. If you are not using a Radius Server, you can leave the Radius Server List section blank. The syntax is host `<ip address> <secret key>`.

Configuring the Tacacs+ Server List

Use the Tacacs+ Server List if you are using a Tacacs server. The command syntax is the same as if you are using a Radius Server (see Figure 26.6).

Configuring Authentication and Authorization

The next two sections are Authentication and Authorization (see Figure 26.7). For authentication, users need to authenticate through a specific service before they are allowed through the firewall. The best way for your users to authenticate is through a Web browser. When your user has been authenticated, he or she can get out to the Internet. In other words, if a user wants to connect to a remote e-mail server, he first needs to go out, using a Web browser, and

Part
V

Ch
26

log in with his user name and password. After the user successfully logs in, he can go out with his mail program if he has sufficient access to get through the firewall.

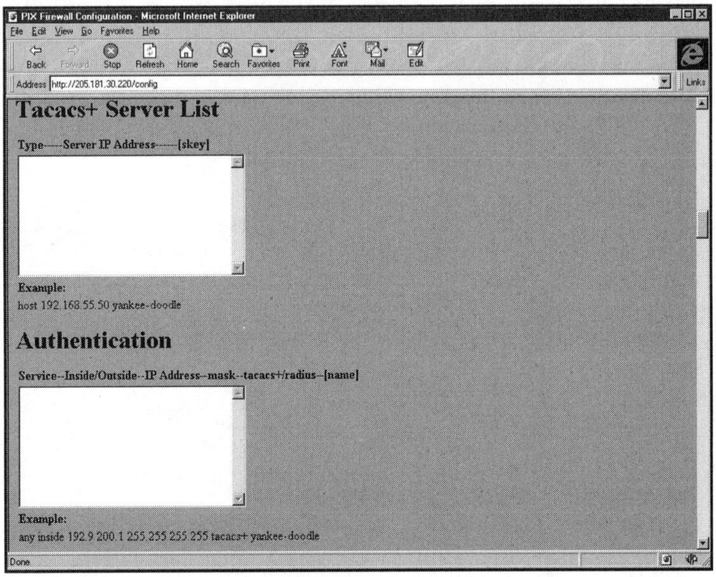

FIG. 26.6

If you are using a Tacacs+ Server for authentication, you can type in the IP addresses of your servers in this text box.

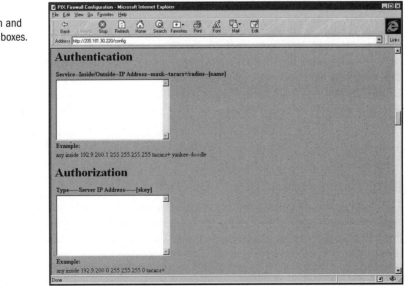

When a user is authenticated, the Cisco PIX Firewall checks the authorization to verify that the user can access the requested service. For a more in-depth description of how these two services work, visit `http://www.cisco.com/univercd/data/doc/netbu/hardware/pix/pixcncmd.htm#HDR7`.

FIG. 26.7

The Authentication and Authorization text boxes.

Configuring a Pool of Global IP Addresses

Global is for setting up your pool of global IP address (see Figure 26.8). These IP addresses enable your users to get to the Internet, so you must enter IP addresses assigned to you by your ISP. The command is `global 1 205.181.31.1-205.181.31.254`. Global is used only if you are using the command line. `1` is the global ID. You can have up to 256 global IP address pools. `205.181.31.1-205.181.31.254` is the range of IP addresses in the global IP address pool. When a user needs to go to the Internet, the Cisco PIX Firewall finds an available IP address from one of the global pools and assigns it to that machine.

FIG. 26.8

The Global Addresses text box is where you set up your pool of global IP addresses.

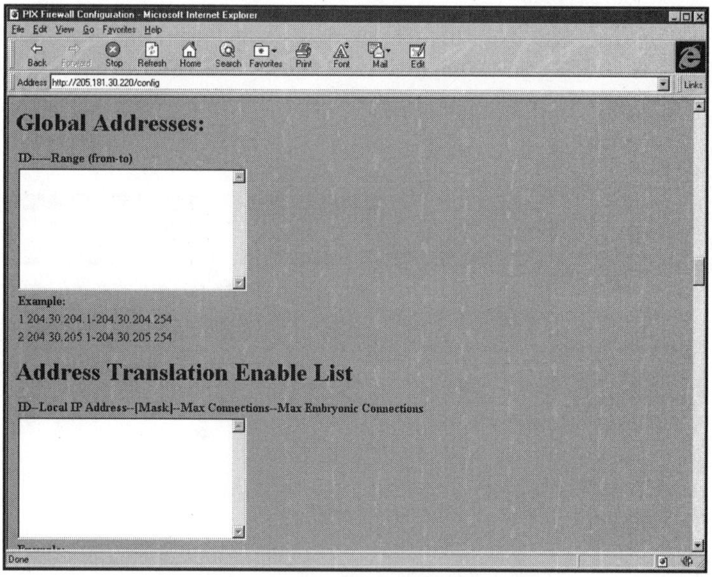

Configuring the Address Translation Enable List

Address Translation Enable List (`nat`) associates a network with a pool of global IP addresses (see Figure 26.9). The command is `nat 1 10.0.0.0 255.0.0.0 50 40`. nat is used if you are configuring via the command line. `1` is the global ID that you specified with the global command. `10.0.0.0` and `255.0.0.0` are the IP address and netmask that are allowed to use IP addresses in this global address pool. If you want to restrict access to the Internet by IP address, you can do so in the Address Translation Enable List text box. If you want to allow Internet access only by IP addresses in the range of `10.0.0.129` to `10.0.0.254`, you would type **10.0.0.129** and **255.255.255.128** for your IP address and netmask. `50` is the maximum simultaneous connections allowed through the firewall. `40` is the maximum number of embryonic connections allowed through the firewall. An *embryonic connection* is a connection that someone attempted but has not completed and has not yet seen data from. Every connection is embryonic until it sets up. The default is `0`, which means unlimited connections. The maximum is `65535`, and the minimum is `1`. If you have only 32 licenses, of course, you can get only 32 connections through the firewall.

Part

V

Ch

26

Another option (although it is not recommended) is to use IP addresses on your inside network that were assigned to you by your ISP. In this case, you do not need to use any type of network translation. Even though you are using routable IP addresses, you are still protected by the firewall, because it does not allow any traffic to pass through it unless it is specifically instructed to.

Some examples are:

nat 1 0. If you have only one network and want to allow all computers access to the Internet, you use this command. This command gives all computers access to global IP address pool 1.

nat 1 10.0.0.0 255.255.255.0. This command specifies that only computers coming from 10.0.0.x are allowed to use global address pool 1.

nat 1 10.0.0.0 255.255.255.126. This command specifies that only computers coming from 10.0.0.1 to 10.0.0.128 are allowed to use IP addresses in global pool 1.

FIG. 26.9

The Address Translation Enable List (nat).

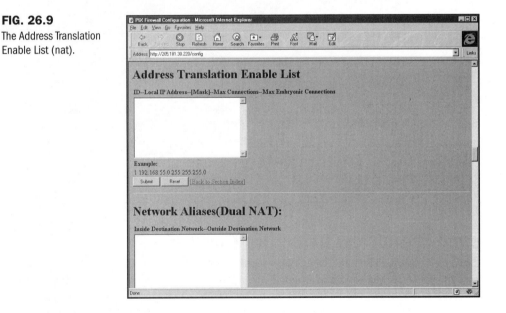

Using Network Aliases

Network Aliases are used if you are going to use IP addresses for your internal network that have been assigned to another network by an ISP (see Figure 26.10). Network Aliasing is something that you should never need to use, because more than enough reserved IP addresses are available, and you should never have an IP address conflict.

FIG. 26.10

The Network Aliases (Dual NAT) text box.

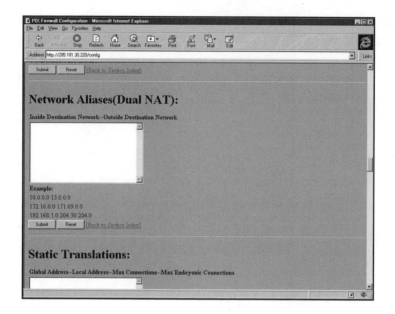

Configuring Static Translations

If you are going to allow traffic to come in through the firewall, you need to set up static address translations (see Figure 26.11). Static address translations configure the firewall so that all traffic originating from a specific machine always use the same IP address. Just because you configure a static IP address does not mean that traffic is allowed in through the firewall; you still need to configure conduits to allow access in. (Conduits are covered in the Setting up Conduits section.) If you are going to set up a static IP address to receive mail, you do not use the static command; you use the mailhost command instead. This command allows access to sendmail but restricts the commands that can be issued. The mailhost command prevents someone from trying to hack into your system by trying to use vulnerability in sendmail.

This command is issued as follows: static 205.181.30.20 10.0.0.20 100 75. Static is used only if you are using the command line. 205.181.30.20 is an IP address that was issued to you by your ISP; it can be part of your global_ip address pool (not recommended, however). 10.0.0.20 is an address on your local network. 100 is the maximum number of connections that are allowed to this static IP address, and 75 is the maximum number of embryonic connections that are allowed. max_connections and em_limit are, as always, optional.

You can also use net static. This command is used for blocks of IP addresses that need to have static IP address mapping. The syntax of this command is static 205.181.30.0 10.0.0.0 1000 750. Notice that ending the IP addresses with 0 means to use the entire block of addresses. 10.0.0.1 corresponds to 205.181.30.1, 10.0.0.15 corresponds to 205.181.30.15, and so on. Again, assigning static IP addresses to computers does not mean that computers are allowed into your network, it simply means that when computers go out through your network, they use the same IP address each time they go to the Internet.

Part
V

Ch
26

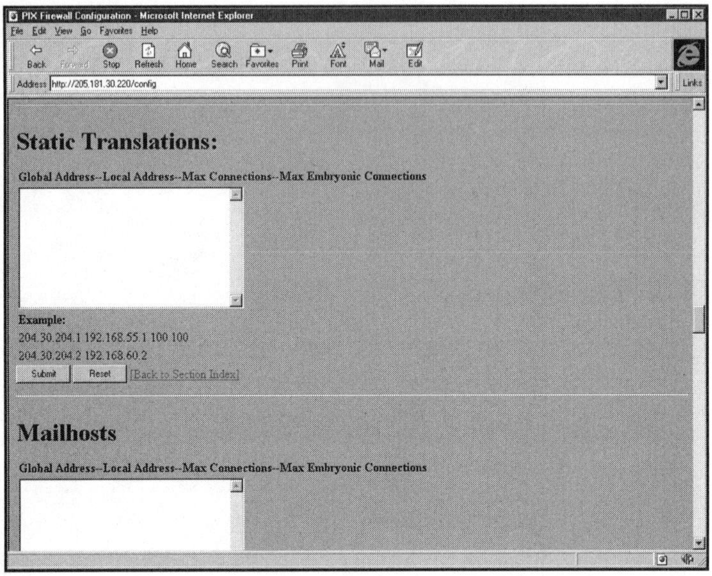

FIG. 26.11

The Static Translations text box.

Configuring Mailhosts

The mailhosts command works the same way as static does, except that it is used only for a mail server. This command cannot be used with static. If you specify a mailhost for a specific IP address, the mailhost command sets up a static mapping to that IP address and configures a conduit to allow access to port 25 (the SMTP port). You can then specify other conduits if you need to allow access to other services on that machine (see Figure 26.12).

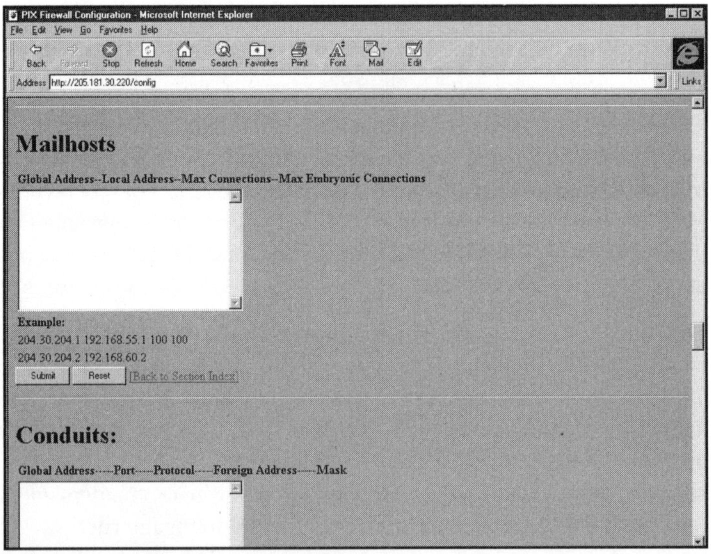

FIG. 26.12

The Mailhosts text box.

Setting up Condiuts

When you specify your mailhosts and static IP address mappings, you need to setup conduits (see Figure 26.13). A conduit provides a way to send traffic from the Internet to a specific machine on your network. You have a great deal of flexibility with conduits. You can allow access to the entire machine from anywhere on the Internet. You can allow access to the entire machine from only specific IP addresses. You can allow access from the Internet to only a specific service on the machine or any combination. You can allow access to any TCP or UDP port. The only type of traffic that you cannot get through the Cisco PIX Firewall is ICMP traffic—ping and traceroute, for example. You usually do not need to allow this type of traffic into your network, which is why no firewall supports this type of traffic at this time.

FIG. 26.13
The Conduits text box.

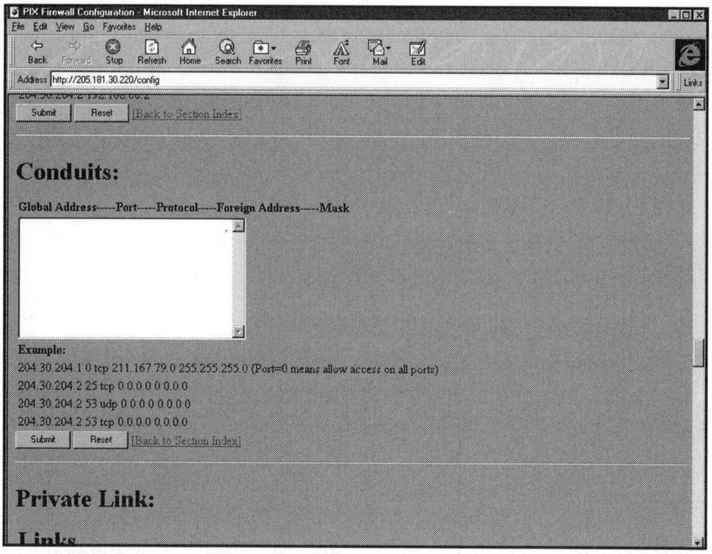

Part
V

Ch
26

Examples of conduit statements are:

conduit 205.181.30.181 0 tcp 205.232.68.0 255.255.255.0. You need to type **conduit** only if you are using the command line. 205.181.30.181 is an IP address that has been assigned by an ISP. You must already have a static IP address mapping for this IP address by using either the static command or the mailhost command. tcp means that traffic is allowed in through a TCP port. Your other choice is to allow access through a UDP port. 0 means to allow access to any TCP port. 205.232.68.0 255.255.255.0 means that any traffic coming from an IP address that begins with 205.232.68.x is allowed to access the machine on any TCP port.

conduit 205.181.30.21 ftp tcp 0.0.0.0 0.0.0.0. This statement allows any machine on the Internet to access the FTP service on host 205.181.30.21.

conduit 205.181.30.21 1000-2000 tcp 0. This statement allows any machine on the Internet to access ports 1000 to 2000. Notice that you simply type one 0 instead of 0.0.0.0 0.0.0.0. A single 0 is an abbreviation for the entire Internet.

conduit 205.181.30.21 http tcp 0. This statement allows access to the HTTP port, port 80, from the entire Internet. If you are running an e-commerce site, you need to use secure HTTP or HTTPS when a user purchases an item from your store. The following statement does not allow access to a secure Web server. If you are using an encryption certificate or HTTPS on your Web server, you need to issue the following command for users to send their information to you via a secure method.

conduit 205.181.30.21 443 tcp 0. Port 443 is the secure HTTP or HTTPS port.

With the Cisco PIX Firewall, you have the capability to create a private encrypted link between two or more networks that are behind a Cisco PIX Firewall. If you have an office in Boston and another office in Los Angeles, it will cost you several times more money to run a private high-speed link between the two offices than to use the Internet to connect the two offices.

The problem is that the Internet is insecure. If you are sending private e-mail and files, a good chance exists that a good hacker with a packet sniffer in the right place could gain access to these files while they are in transit. For this reason, Cisco has a card available for the Cisco PIX Firewall that allows you to send information between your two networks; it encrypts all of the information while it is in transit. This way, if someone is using a packet sniffer, he cannot do anything with the information that he acquires.

To use this feature, when you have the cards installed on both Cisco PIX Firewalls, you need to configure them to use the same encryption keys. The command syntax is:

link 205.232.68.21 1 1234567890abcd md5

link is used only if you are using the command line to configure. 205.232.68.21 is the IP address of the remote Cisco PIX Firewall running Private Link. 1 is the key ID. You can use up to seven keys to encrypt your data. You specify the age of a specific key, and when that time runs out, the Cisco PIX Firewall switches to another key. The firewall continually rotates among these seven keys to keep your data private. 1234567890abcd is the actual hexadecimal key that you use to encrypt your data. Your key is a 56-bit key and can be up to 14 hexadecimal digits long. If you select MD5 encryption, this option puts a digital signature in the AH/ESP header of each packet before being transmitted to the remote Private Link firewall.

You need to keep one thing in mind: The 56-bit encryption key has been proved to be break-able with the correct equipment. If a business has $300,000 to put into a system, any 56-bit key could be broken in a reasonable amount of time. If your data is important enough or worth enough money to someone, spending $300,000 is not a high price for a sophisticated computer system.

If you are transmitting sensitive data or any type of top-secret data, you should not use 56-bit encryption as a means of transmitting your data. If your data is of a private, top-secret nature, you should be using a key that is at least 90 bits. Even Web browsers that are used to send data that is nothing more than a person's credit-card number are now being encrypted with a 128-bit encryption key. If you want more information on encryption and the strength that is needed to keep your private information private, you should check out http://www.bsa.org/policy/encryption/cryptographers.html and http://www.bsa.org/policy/encryption/encryption.html.

After you set up your link and your encryption keys, you need to set up a link path (see Figure 26.14). The `linkpath` command specifies IP address information for the remote Private Link Cisco PIX Firewall. The command is `linkpath 10.0.0.0 255.255.255.0 205.181.32.154`. `10.0.0.0 255.255.255.0` is the network on the inside of the remote Cisco PIX Firewall. `205.181.32.254` is the IP address of the outside interface of the remote Cisco PIX Firewall.

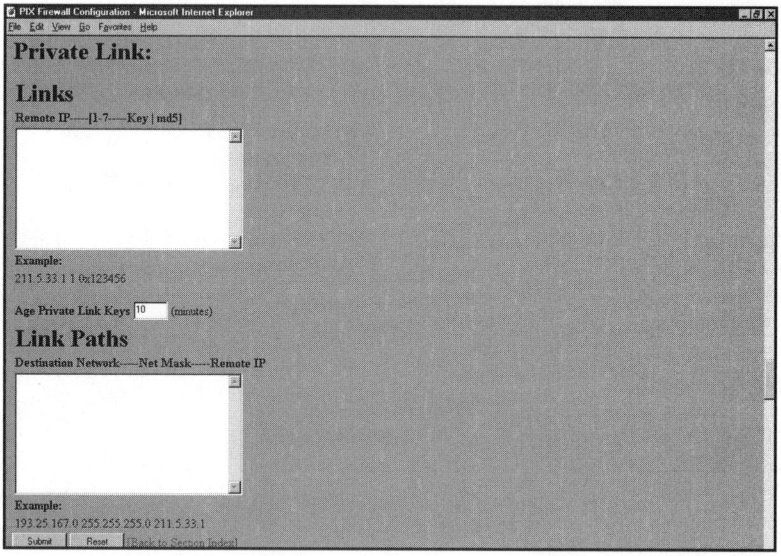

FIG. 26.14

In the Links text box, you will type the Remote IP address, the encryption key, and optionally you can choose MD5. The Link Paths text box allows you to configure the IP address and netmask of the destination network and the IP address of the remote machine.

Configuring Inactivity Timeouts, Syslog Options, and a Syslog Loghost

The Inactivity Timeouts disconnect users from certain services if they are connected and have been idle for a certain amount of time. You should set these timeouts accordingly.

You can use the syslog feature to log activity through the firewall. You need to choose a syslog facility. The default is 20. Eight facilities are available, LOCAL0(16) through LOCAL7(23); the default is LOCAL4(20). Hosts file the messages based on the facility number in the message. You also need to choose a syslog level. The levels are as follows:

0: System unusable

1: Take immediate action

2: Critical condition

3: Error message

4: Warning message

5: Normal but significant condition

6: Informational

7: Debug message

Now you need to choose a loghost (see Figure 26.15). If you do not have a machine running syslog available on your network, you can output syslog information to the console. Because this command works only when you are in command-line mode, you do not see this command on the HTTP configuration page. The commands to use are:

`syslog 20.4.20` is the syslog facility, and 4 is the syslog level

`syslog console`. This command turns on logging to the console.

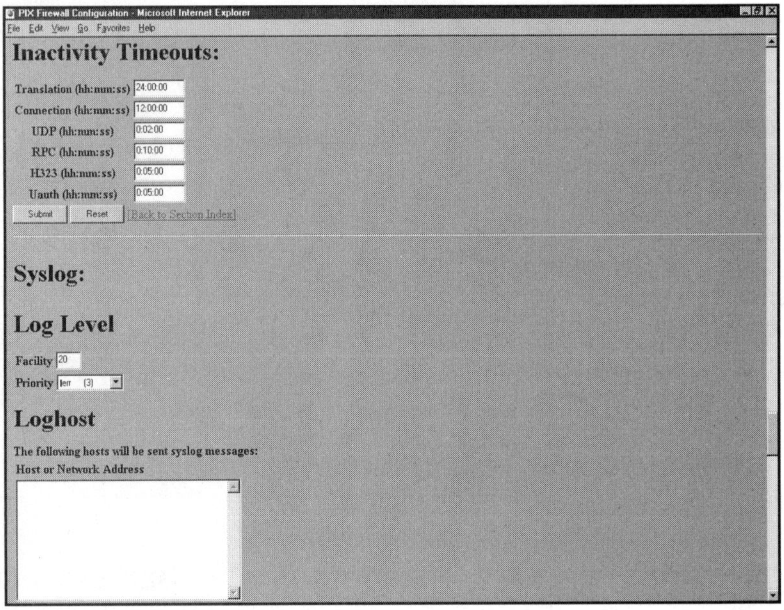

FIG. 26.15

In Inactivity Timeouts, you can choose how long a connection can remain idle before the Cisco PIX Firewall will close the session. Syslog allows you to log certain activities to a syslog loghost (usually a UNIX host but not always).

Configuring Access to the Cisco PIX Firewall via Telnet and HTTP

One of the things that needed to be done when initially configuring the Cisco PIX Firewall via the console port was to specify which hosts could access the Cisco PIX Firewall directly through HTTP and through Telnet. You can also reconfigure these hosts in the HTTP interface (see Figure 26.16). You have the option of specifying one host or specifying several hosts by entering a single IP address or a host address and netmask.

Configuring SNMP Traps

The Cisco PIX Firewall supports SNMP (Simple Network Management Protocol) traps (see Figure 26.17). You simply specify the hosts to receive SNMP traps (up to five hosts), the name of the system administrator, and the location of the Cisco PIX Firewall.

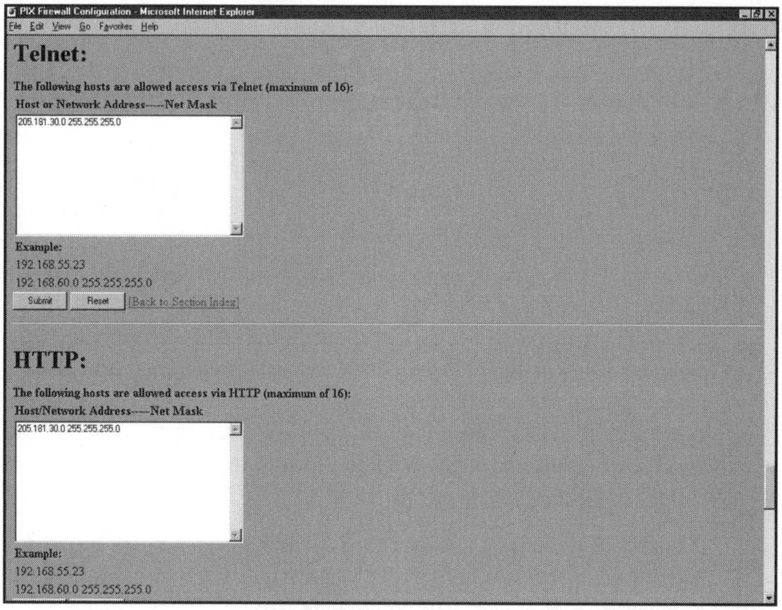

FIG. 26.16
In the Telnet and HTTP text boxes, you need to specify what IP addresses or blocks of IP addresses are allowed to access the Cisco PIX Firewall directly in order to configure it.

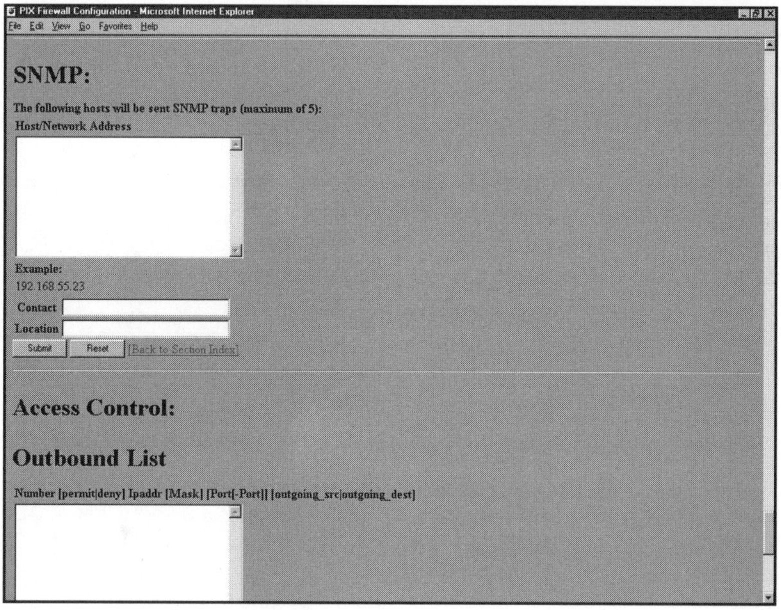

FIG. 26.17
The SNMP configuration text box.

Configuring Access Control Lists

The last thing that you can configure via HTTP is Access Control Lists (ACL) (see Figure 26.18). Using Access Control Lists, you can permit or deny access through the firewall to specific hosts and specific services on those hosts.

If you find that during football season, some of your employees are spending a great deal of time on http://espnet.sportszone.com, you can deny access to this site; the command is outbound 1 deny 204.201.32.0 255.255.255.0 0. outbound is needed only if you are configuring via the command line. 1 is the access number. You need to give each outbound list a number, because you later need to apply that outbound list by number. deny means that you are denying access to that host. If you deny all traffic to the Internet, you need to replace deny with permit to allow outbound traffic to reach permitted hosts. 204.201.32.0 255.255.255.0 means that no access is allowed to any traffic on the 204.201.32 network. 0 is the port number. If you specify 0, all access to this block of addresses is denied. You can also choose to block only a port or specific ports. After you have your access lists, you need to apply these lists. The command is apply 1 outgoing_dest.

If a particular user or a few users are spending far too much time surfing the Web, but those users need to access other services on the Internet, you could block that user or those users from accessing the Web. The commands are:

```
outbound 2 deny 10.0.0.158 255.255.255.255 80
apply 2 outgoing_src
```

Notice that this statement uses outgoing_src. This means that this access is to be used on traffic going from the internal network through the firewall. outgoing_dest means that you apply this ACL to a site that is on the Internet.

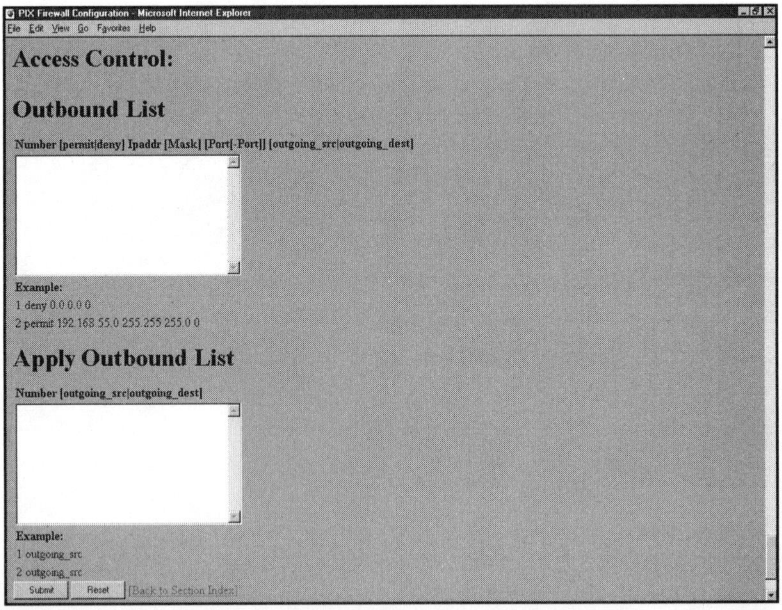

FIG. 26.18

The Access Control section.

Now that you have finished configuring the firewall, you want to submit the information. You have been submitting the information on a regular basis, of course, and now you are saving the last of what you have changed.

Implementing the Cisco PIX Firewall

You are ready to implement the Cisco PIX Firewall in a test environment. You should test the Cisco PIX Firewall in a small-scale lab for a few days or even a few weeks to make sure that you have it configured the way that you want and that it is going to work the way you expect.

You also have to prepare your network to implement the Cisco PIX Firewall. If all your workstations and servers are directly connected to the Internet, you need to renumber all your machines unless you decide to use routable IP addresses in your internal network. If you are using DHCP, this procedure is easy; you simply change the IP address pool in your DHCP server to use the new IP addresses that the Cisco PIX Firewall is going to route, and you also change the default gateway.

You may need to change some other information, so make sure that you test the configuration thoroughly in your testing lab. You need to change the IP addresses of any machines that are using static IP addresses, and you need to change the default gateway, the wins server, and (possibly but not necessarily) the DNS servers.

If you do decide not to change the IP addresses of your machines, you still may need to change the IP address of the default gateway. If your machines were pointing to the Internet router as their gateway, they no longer point to this router. You either have to change the IP address of the Internet router, which could cause many problems, or change the default gateway in all your machines to point to the Cisco PIX Firewall. For this reason, using DHCP for workstations is a good idea. This way, when you make a large-scale change, you need to change only one database. The worst thing that happens when you make these changes is that all your users need to reboot their machines when they come in the next morning.

When you get your Cisco PIX Firewall connected and all your servers and workstations configured, rebooting all your routers that are on that network segment is a good idea.

N O T E When you implement the Cisco PIX Firewall on your network, if you should re-number all of the IP addresses on all of your computers, make sure that you reboot not only all of the computers but also all of the routers on your network. If you do not reboot all of the computers and routers, you may run into a problem where the ARP tables still remember the old IP addresses. If this happens, traffic from that machine will not be able to reach any machines on the network until the ARP tables clear out. If this happens on a router then machines may not be able to get either in or out. ▪

Part
V

Ch
26

From Here...

This chapter covered the benefits of using the Cisco PIX Firewall and what it can do for your network. It also went over how to configure the Cisco PIX Firewall. At this time, the Cisco PIX Firewall is one of the more secure firewalls available because it is a hardware based firewall which means that you do not have to worry about any security holes in the operating systems like you would with a UNIX solution. Having a hardware-based firewall is also a much faster solution. We also covered how easy the Cisco PIX Firewall is to configure using the HTTP interface.

CHAPTER 27

Using the Microsoft Buy Now and Wallet Components

Microsoft has provided with Commerce Server 2.0 two controls (or components) that assist you in presenting the purchasing of your store's merchandise. The Wallet control helps your shoppers store their address and credit-card information, and the Buy Now control assists the site developer in the cross-store marketing necessary to be competitive in today's marketplace.

Probably the biggest topic today on the Web, and probably in the world, is transaction security in electronic commerce (better known as e-commerce). Commerce Server 2.0 has made a formidable effort to solve this problem for your shoppers. If you are going to expect your shoppers to come back time after time, your customers are going to expect you to keep their information protected.

This chapter discusses some of the features that the Wallet control provides for protecting your shoppers' information, as well as the benefits of using the Buy Now control to cross-market your store's merchandise. ■

Using the Buy Now Control

One of the most commonly used marketing techniques is partnering with another company and sharing advertisements—by far the most inexpensive form of advertising (most of the time, anyway). Companies have been making the same partnerships on the Web, too. This form of advertising calls for programming the HTML with the company's advertisement and making updates in the company logo and messages.

Wouldn't it be great if something could do all this marketing for you? Someone came up with the great idea to create a component that scrolls company advertisements on a Web page. This component not only scrolls company advertisements, but also allows you to purchase an item that you see and end up at the URL you were at before purchasing the item. You can see a sample of the Buy Now control on the left side of Figure 27.1.

FIG. 27.1

Web site hosting a Buy Now advertisement for the sample store Adventure Works, installed with Commerce Server 2.0.

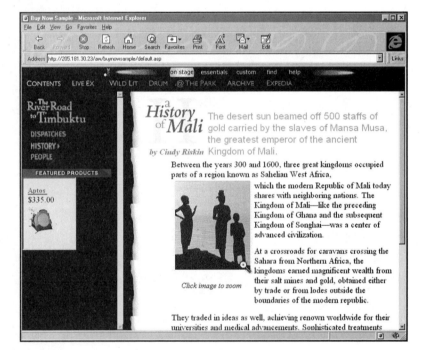

This component is great, isn't it? The component definitely provides a convenient service for your customers. Customers can shop anywhere while you can show them specials or products, and who knows—maybe they will see something that they have been looking for (which is the whole purpose, right?).

Preparing for the Buy Now Component

Understanding what the Buy Now component is and how it works is important. Most documentation calls this component the Buy Now control, but I like to call it the Buy Now component, because it really is just a component.

To use the Buy Now component, a site developer must be aware that several requirements must be met.

Customer Requirements

- Microsoft Internet Explorer or Netscape Navigator version(s) 3.x or later
- Installation of the Buy Now control when prompted

Merchant Requirements

- Microsoft Windows 95 or Microsoft Windows NT, version 4.0 or later
- Microsoft Internet Explorer version(s) 3.2 or later, or Netscape Navigator 3.x or later
- Web server (Microsoft Internet Information Server version 2.0 recommended)
- Commerce Server SDK
- Installation package for delivery to Internet sites

Hosting-Site Requirements

- Web server (Microsoft Internet Information Server version 2.0 recommended)
- Merchant's Buy Now installation package

Understanding the Buy Now Component

The Buy Now component displays merchandise advertising in an HTML page and, when the user clicks the item that he wants, opens a dialog box allowing the shopper to purchase the item.

When a shopper clicks the merchandise, the component redirects the shopper to a site contained in a wizard configuration file (.wcf), displaying this site in a dialog box without changing the user's URL in his current browser (see Figure 27.2). The shopper can purchase the item at his leisure (see Figure 27.3).

The dialog box that is redirected to the purchasing site is configured with the .wcf file and is a subset of the actual purchasing site. The cool thing about this dialog box is that the component actually picks up the information to create a page similar to what the user would see if he were actually at that site.

Using Buy Now Methods

You can use three documented methods to administrate the use of the Buy Now control. This section discusses the following three methods:

```
MSBuyNowCheckLoaded
MSBuyNowDisplay
MSBuyNowIECodebase
```

You can find the definitions of these methods in the BuyNow.asp file, which you can find in your Microsoft Commerce Server\Server\Administration\Host Administrator\Copy Blueprints\ aw\shop\include directory. You need to include this file in any project that uses the Buy Now control.

FIG. 27.2

Web site hosting Buy Now component, showing Buy Now Wizard dialog box after shopper clicks the merchandise.

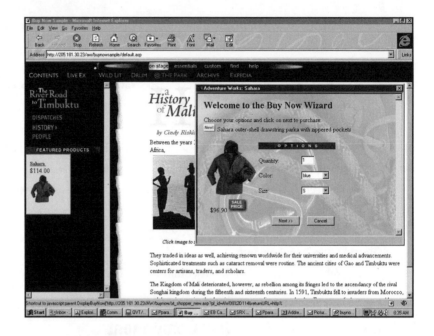

FIG. 27.3

Buy Now Wizard dialog box.

MSBuyNowCheckLoaded   The `MSBuyNowCheckLoaded` method ensures that the control has completely downloaded before the user attempts any other actions.

Syntax

MSBuyNowCheckLoaded(*buyNowObject*)

Parameters

buyNowObject

Buy Now control object.

Return Values

TRUE

Buy Now control has successfully downloaded.

FALSE

Buy Now control has not finished downloading.

Example

```
function MSBuyNowCheckLoaded(buyNowObject)
{
   if (!fMSBuyNowLoaded)
   {
     if (!(!buyNowObject))
        fMSBuyNowLoaded = true
     else
        alert("The Buy Now Control has not finished downloading, please wait.")
   }
   return fMSBuyNowLoaded
}
```

MSBuyNowDisplay   The `MSBuyNowDisplay` function displays the Buy Now control, starting at *startURL*.

Syntax

`MSBuyNowDisplay(buyNowObject, startURL)`

Parameters

buyNowObject

Buy Now control object.

startURL

The starting URL for the Buy Now control (`Xt_shopper_new.asp`, for example).

Return Values

None

Example

```
function MSBuyNowDisplay(buyNowObject, strStartURL)
{
   if (!MSBuyNowCheckLoaded(buyNowObject))
     return
   buyNowObject.URL = strStartURL
   buyNowObject.Display()
}
```

MSBuyNowIECodebase   The `MSBuyNowIECodebase` function is a server-side (ASP) VBScript routine that specifies the download location for the Buy Now control files. This function call should always be used for the CODEBASE value in the <OBJECT> tag. By default, this location is defined as TBD. In some situations, you want to override this default location and have the Wallet files downloaded from another location (if the shopper is not connected to the Internet, for example).

To use this function, set the strMSBuyNowDwnldLoc variable to the desired URL before including Selector.asp. The MSBuyNowIECodebase function uses this variable to determine the download location.

Syntax

MSBuyNowIECodebase ()

Parameters

None.

Return Values

strMSBuyNowDwnldLoc

Value set to the location of the the IE Codebase.

Using the Microsoft Wallet Control

The Microsoft Wallet control provides a secure way for your users to store credit-card and address information (see Figure 27.4). Users can make purchases by selecting this information by means of a nickname key, rather than having to type the information every time.

FIG. 27.4
The Microsoft Wallet Manager.

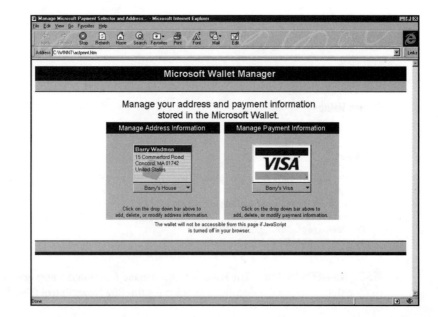

The Wallet control currently supports two interfaces: the Address Selector and the Payment Selector. The following sections describe these interfaces.

Using the Address Selector

The Address Selector, shown in Figure 27.5, stores a shopper's personal and business addresses securely locally on his computer. To add an address, a shopper fills in a dialog box with business or personal address information that is keyed based on a friendly name, or nickname. Shoppers can then select addresses from the Address Selector component by their nickname, instead of filling in the information every time. The great thing about this component is that the information is never transferred to the merchant asking for the information unless the shopper specifically tells the component to send the information.

FIG. 27.5

The Microsoft Wallet Address Selector.

Another appealing feature of the Address Selector is the fact that the component fully integrates the Windows Address Book (WAB). In other words, if the WAB is installed on the shopper's computer, the shopper can select addresses that have been entered externally in the WAB.

Using the Payment Selector

The Payment Selector component, shown in Figure 27.6, is much like the Address Selector component, in that it stores a shopper's credit-card information keyed with a nickname. The user can select a credit card to use by selecting the nickname instead of typing the information every time.

Part

V

Ch

27

The Payment Selector currently supports Visa, MasterCard, JCB (only in Japan), American Express, and Discover (only in North America) payment types. Although this list is limited, because the Payment Selector control is a component, the Payment Selector supports interfaces that allow third-party vendors to add other credit-card vendors to this list. Currently, third-party vendors are writing add-ins that allow users to select cards such as debit cards and branded credit cards.

FIG. 27.6

The Microsoft Wallet Payment Selector.

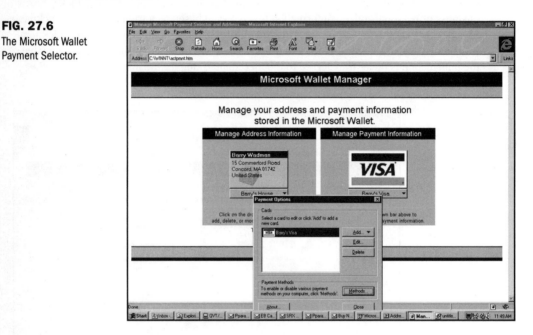

When a shopper adds a new Payment selection, the Payment Selector Setup Wizard allows the shopper to assign a password to the credit card and then stores the credit-card information in a Wallet Encrypted Storage format locally on the shopper's machine.

After the shopper installs the Wallet control on her machine, she can use this information on any site that uses the Wallet control. Because the shopper's credit-card information is stored on her machine, she can access all the information that she has written, no matter what store she added the information from.

N O T E   Because each credit card is protected by a password assigned by the cardholder, a single Payment Selector can store credit cards owned by different people without presenting any security issues.

Using the Microsoft Wallet Control Files

You can use the Wallet controls in your store by using the SDK provided with Commerce Server 2.0. You can find some files that help you use the Wallet control in the \SDK\Wallet\Samples\Webmaster subdirectory.

The following table lists the files that you should use when you use the Wallet control in a store.

File	Description
Payaddr.asp	Payaddr.asp simply sets the download location storing this information in the global variable strMSWltIEDwnldLoc (for Internet Explorer) and strMSWltNavDwnldLoc (for Netscape Navigator) for the Wallet control.
Pa.asp	Pa.asp includes Selector.asp and contains the code to download and display the Wallet control.
Selector.asp	Selector.asp defines the Wallet control's API. You should use this definition for any pages that you design that use the Wallet control.

Preparing Your Store for the Wallet API Calls

Now that you know what the Wallet control can do, you need to script your store to use the Wallet control's API calls. Following is a list of the API calls that you can use for your store's Wallet control:

MSWltCheckLoaded

MSWltLoadDone

MSWltLastChanceText

MSWltIECodebase

MSWltNavDwnldURL

MSWltPrepareForm

MSWltIEPaySelectorClassid

MSWltIEAddrSelectorClassid

The following sections discuss each of these functions in more detail.

MSWltCheckLoaded   The MSWltCheckLoaded() function, defined in Selector.asp, ensures that the control has completely downloaded before the user attempts any other actions.

Syntax

MSWltCheckLoaded()

Parameters

None.

Example

```
if (!MSWltCheckLoaded())
return FALSE
```

Return Values

TRUE

The Wallet control has finished downloading.

FALSE

The Wallet control is still downloading.

MSWltLoadDone   The MSWltLoadDone method determines whether the shopper has installed the Microsoft Wallet. If the Wallet is not installed, the method asks the shopper to install it. The MSWltLoadDone() method also handles installation and removal of the Wallet control in Netscape Navigator by comparing the version resource of the DLL and the version number of the <EMBED> tag, and offering to upgrade older versions of the control.

> **N O T E**   If the shopper refuses installation or upgrade of the Wallet control, the MSWltLoadDone() method loads a page containing the appropriate HTML-based form. ▨

Syntax

```
MSWltLoadDone(strDownlevelURL)
```

Parameters

strDownlevelURL

URL to go to if the shopper does not have a browser that supports the Payment and Address Selector.

Example   The following OnLoad event uses the MSWltLoadDone() method to finish initializing the Payment and Address Selector components when both components are installed:

```
<BODY>
<% If fMSWltUplevelBrowser Then %>
  ONLOAD="<% = MSWltLoadDone(strDownlevelURL) %>"
<% End If %>
```

MSWltLastChanceText   The MSWltLastChanceText() method allows the shopper to enter payment and address information in an HTML form if any difficulties occur in accessing the Payment and Address Selector components.

Microsoft suggests that you use the current page as the down-level page and then post the information back to the current page.

Syntax

```
MSWltLastChanceText (strDownlevelURL)
```

Parameters

strDownlevelURL

URL to the destination form.

Example

```
<!--#include file="selector.asp"-->
<P ALIGN=RIGHT>
<FONT SIZE=2>
  <% = MSWltLastChanceText(Request.ServerVariables("SCRIPT_NAME")) %>
</FONT>
```

MSWltIECodebase   The `MSWltIECodebase()` method specifies the download location for the Microsoft Wallet files for Microsoft Internet Explorer. This method should be used for the `CODEBASE` value in the `<OBJECT>` tag. This location is defined, by default, as `http://activex.microsoft.com/controls/mswallet/mswallet.cab`. To use a different location, set the `strMSWltIEDwnldLoc` variable to the desired URL before including `Selector.asp`.

Syntax

`MSWltIECodebase ()`

Parameters

None.

Example

```
<%
  ' Override default download location
  strMSWltIEDwnldLoc = "http://myserver/Retail/MSWallet.cab"
%>
<!--#include file="selector.asp"-->
<OBJECT ID="paySelector"
    CLASSID="clsid:87D3CB63-BA2E-11cf-B9D6-00A0C9083362"
    CODEBASE="<% = MSWltIECodebase() %>" HEIGHT="123" WIDTH="154" HSPACE="20" >
</OBJECT>
```

MSWltNavDwnldURL   The `MSWltNavDwnldURL()` method specifies a file name that contains download instructions for the Microsoft Wallet files for users of Netscape Navigator. Set the `strMSWltNavDwnldLoc` variable to the desired URL before including `Selector.asp`.

Syntax

`MSWltNavDwnldURL (strFileName)`

Parameters

`strFileName`

File to download.

Example

```
<%
  ' Override default download location
  strMSWltNavDwnldLoc = "http://MyURL"
%>
<!--#include file="selector.asp"-->
<EMBED NAME="paySelector" SRC="<% = strMSWltNavDwnldLoc & "empty.wlt" %>"
    PLUGINSPAGE="<% = MSWltNavDwnldURL("plginst.htm") %>"
```

Part
V

Ch
27

```
VERSION="<% = strMSWltDwnldVer %>"
ACCEPTEDTYPES="<% = strMSWltAcceptedTypes %>"
TOTAL="<% = strMSWltTotal %>" HEIGHT="123" WIDTH="154" HSPACE="20" >
```

MSWltPrepareForm   If the Payment and Address Selector components are present, the MSWltPrepareForm() method updates form values by using the current payment and address selections in the Payment and Address Selector.

Syntax

```
MSWltPrepareForm(form, cParams, [xlationArray])
```

Parameters

form

Name of the form that posts data retrieved from the Payment Selector and Address Selector to the server.

cParams

Number of incoming parameters. If no optional xlationArray parameters are specified, this number is always 2.

xlationArray
([form_field_name, selector_field_name,...])

You can use these optional parameters to map field names between the form field name and the Payment and Address Selector field names.

Example

```
<!--#include file="selector.asp"--><FORM NAME="payform" METHOD="POST"
ACTION="http://MyURL/Mirror.asp"
<%  If fMSWltUplevelBrowser Then %>
    ONSUBMIT="return MSWltPrepareForm(payform, 2)"
<% End If %>
<% If fMSWltUplevelBrowser = 1 Then %>
<% REM ... %>
<INPUT TYPE=SUBMIT VALUE="Pay Now">
```

MSWltIEPaySelectorClassid   The MSWltIEPaySelectorClassid() method specifies the CLSID for the Payment Selector control, depending on whether the user is downloading the Intel or Alpha version of the control. Be sure to include the file Selector.asp.

Syntax

```
MSWltIEPaySelectorClassid()
```

Parameters

None.

Example

```
<OBJECT ID="paySelector"
  CLASSID="<% = MSWltIEPaySelectorClassid() %>"
  CODEBASE="<% = MSWltIECodebase() %>" HEIGHT="123" WIDTH="154" HSPACE="20" >
```

```
     <PARAM NAME="AcceptedTypes" VALUE="<% = strMSWltAcceptedTypes %>" >
     <PARAM NAME="Total" VALUE="<% = strMSWltTotal %>" >
</OBJECT>
```

MSWltIEAddrSelectorClassid   The `MSWltIEAddrSelectorClassid()` method specifies the `CLSID` for the Address Selector control, depending on whether the user is downloading the Intel or Alpha version of the control. Be sure to include the `Selector.asp` file.

Syntax

```
MSWltIEPaySelectorClassid()
```

Parameters

None.

Example

```
<OBJECT ID="addrSelector"
   CLASSID="<% = MSWltIEAddrSelectorClassid() %>"
   CODEBASE="<% = MSWltIECodebase() %>" HEIGHT="123" WIDTH="154" HSPACE="20" >
</OBJECT>
```

For more examples of using the Wallet control, look at the Adventure Works sample store included with the Commerce Server 2.0 installation. The Microsoft Web site also has some useful information for using the Wallet control.

From Here...

In this chapter, we have discussed in detail the BuyNow and Wallet controls, and how they can benefit your store(s) or mall(s).

By using the Buy Now and Wallet controls, you can present a professional and secure method for your shoppers to purchase merchandise while protecting their personal information. As you probably know, this type of confidence brings shoppers back on the Web.

Part
V

Ch
27

P A R T VI

Case Studies

Building a New Site:
Eddie Bauer

This case study is an overview of the problems surrounding
developing a new Commerce Server site based on an
existing Internet commerce site. The issues discussed
here deal largely with porting functionality and data to
Commerce Server from an existing third-party system.

Site Owner and Manager, Eddie Bauer (www.ebauer.com)

Eddie Bauer is a worldwide retail chain based in Seattle, Washington. Established as a small sporting-goods shop in downtown Seattle in 1920, the Eddie Bauer company has grown to more than 460 stores on three continents, and the company's annual sales are now more than $1.6 billion.

Eddie Bauer's retail lines span a diverse set of products from clothing to housewares. Their retail outlets are broken into four distinct lines of merchandise:

- **Eddie Bauer Sportswear**: men's and women's clothing, shoes, and accessories
- **Eddie Bauer Home**: bedding and housewares
- **Sport Shop**: swimsuits and activewear
- **AKA Eddie Bauer**: a new line of "business casual" clothing

Each type of merchandise typically sports its own storefront.

In addition to physical retail locations, Eddie Bauer supports a strong catalog sales division. Regular catalog mailings are sent to millions of homes thoughout the U.S. and Canada. Catalog orders can be made though the mail or by phone. All the lines of merchandise that are carried in the stores are also available through the catalog sales outlet.

In 1996, Eddie Bauer launched its first storefront on the World Wide Web (**www.ebauer.com**). This established a third channel of distribution to complement the retail and catalog divisions. Starting with a small budget, the Internet commerce effort is now starting to attract attention thoughout the organization.

The original Web site was a custom-designed commerce package written in Perl on the Microsoft NT Server Platform. The application used extended Perl libraries to retrieve data from a Microsoft SQL Server database system. The Web server chosen for the system was Microsoft IIS 2.0.

Site Developer Fry Multimedia (www.frymulti.com)

Founded in 1993, Fry is an early adopter of the Microsoft Commerce Server technology. In the fall of 1996, the 1-800-FLOWERS site was ported from a proprietary UNIX-based system to Merchant Server.

Justifying Microsoft Commerce Server

Many key factors were involved in the decision to port the Eddie Bauer site to Commerce Server. The main reason for the port, however, focused on the scalability issues inherent in Commerce Server's multiple-CPU and multiple-server architecture. With the rapid growth in Internet use and the increasing acceptance of electronic commerce, Eddie Bauer's internal

Web team had doubts about whether the site's initial software package would be able to handle the expected future loads. With Commerce Server, however, a Web site can be designed with a scalable software architecture. In the future, when the load exceeds the current hardware, additional servers can be added without modifying the basic structure of the site.

In addition to providing scalability, Commerce Server facilitates remote maintenance and administration. The site can be designed with forms that allow direct interaction with the database. This way, changes in the products and their availability can be changed in real time as stock levels change.

Commerce Server also includes integrated shipping, taxation, and credit verification modules. These utilities did not exist in the old site and would have to have been written, tested, and debugged. Writing these functions would have been time-consuming and would have delayed implementation of the site. With Commerce Server, these functions are available from Microsoft or third-party software companies, no new code needs to be written. All you have to do is define a few parameters and the order pipeline takes care of adding in the correct charges to the order and presents the total to the shopper.

One of the goals of the redesign of the Web site was to increase the average revenue per sale. Two methods commonly used to effect this ratio are upselling and cross-selling. These techniques are used to offer additional products to the customer during the course of a sale. In upselling, a higher grade product is offered to the customer to replace a similar, but, cheaper product that has been selected and placed in the shopping cart. In cross-selling, add-on products are offered that somehow enhance a product that the user has selected.

Upselling and cross-selling were functions that the Eddie Bauer Web team wanted to have integrated into the commerce system. With their existing site, the Perl scripts and database would have to be rewritten to accommodate the new functionality. However, Commerce Server makes offering both of these sales methods a snap, by facilitating these actions as part of its base functionality.

An additional factor that led to the use of Commerce Server was its capability to work with Microsoft SQL Server databases. Because the previous Web site was based on SQL Server, a good deal of leveraging on existing knowledge and experience was available. In fact, much of the existing database schema was reused, which made porting the data from the old site to the new much easier.

Choosing a Starter Store

The starter stores that come with Commerce Server serve two important functions. First, they really are meant as a quick-start to build new stores on so that a site developer can get up and going with very little effort, as long as looking like one of the starter stores is no problem (only another Commerce Server developer would know for sure). Secondly, the starter stores serve as "live" documentation for the Commerce Server product. Since the product is so complex, it is very difficult to begin from scratch. It is much better to start off with a known good foundation and build up from there. If the foundation is weak, the store will be very buggy.

Part
VI

Ch
28

However, when implementing an existing design in Commerce Server, using one of the complex starter stores can make things very difficult. Not only do you have to understand the design for the store you are building, you will have to understand the whole design of the starter store. You have to understand what the base store is doing so that it can be appropriately adapted for your application's use. Since Eddie Bauer already had an established look and feel, and a complex design, none of the stores that come with Commerce Server really were appropriate.

However, after a bit of experimentation, the Clock Peddler store was chosen as the starter store due to its minimal framework. The other starter stores had many good concepts built in, but they more narrowly defined the shopping model. In essence, Clock Peddler's minimal setup would be less obtusive when the developers began to tweak it.

Starting with a simple store such as Clock Peddler, however, did not prevent the developers from taking pieces of the more advanced stores, such as Adventure Works, and adding them in. In fact, several pieces from the more complex stores were adapted for use with Eddie Bauer. These included some of the shopping cart and shopper management mechanisms from the Adventure Works store.

Converting Perl to ASP

A decision had to be made about much of the original store's code base. The original store was written in Perl, with extensions to allow interactions with SQL Server. These Perl scripts ran as traditional CGIs and dynamically created nearly every page of the site based on data contained in the database.

The portion of the store that ran the catalog and shopping area of course needed to be entirely rewritten to work with Commerce Server. However, other parts of the site, which served up articles and company information, porting the Perl code was optional. A decision needed to be made whether to leave that portion alone or move all the code to ASP.

Based on upkeep and maintenance analysis, it was decided to move all the code from Perl to ASP. Even though this meant rewriting and debugging working code, the developers could be assured that the store's code would be native to the IIS and Commerce Server environment. Any problems that arose would therefore not be due to any oddities in the interaction of Perl, IIS/ASP, and Commerce Server.

Recoding Perl into VBScript went very quickly. Since the functions that were being ported were outside of the complex shopping system, they were mostly standalone items. Most brought up an item from the database for display using a template. The existing Perl functions were therefore used as a baseline development spec. Then the VBScript functions were written to reproduce the functionality. When development was finished, the original Perl scripts served as the baseline for testing.

Updating Database Schema and Data

Because the old site was based on a SQL Server database, modifying the database schema for Commerce Server went smoothly. The basket, shopper, and receipt tables were added in. A few other changes were made based on the new site's requirements, but on the whole, 90 percent of the database schema was reused. This made porting the old data and tools a straightforward process.

The biggest problem porting the existing data to a Commerce Server application revolved around Commerce Server's requirement for a unique SKU for every product in the database. Eddie Bauer's existing inventory model calls for an SKU to identify the product, but not its size or color. To make Commerce Server work with Eddie Bauer's data, the data had to be denormalized to combine color and size information in the product data. An identity field was added to the table to create a unique key for every row. This technique is the way that Microsoft solved the problem in its Adventure Works starter store. The identity field's value, rather than the product's real SKU, was used to identify a unique product in the table.

This compromise between Eddie Bauer's merchandising model and Commerce Server's model means that managing the products in the database is now more time-consuming than in the previous version. Full product information must be maintained and edited for all combination of sizes and colors (S, M, L, XL, and XXL, and Red, Green, Blue, Black, White, and so on). This denormalization of the data greatly increased the size of the product table, increasing the time that product-search queries took.

Porting the Look and Feel

The original Eddie Bauer Web site design was developed by using HTML framesets to aid in the consistency of navigation and location of content. The design for the updated version in Commerce Server also used framesets to retain the look and feel from the original site.

Developing a framed site in Commerce Server posed very few design and engineering problems. ASP pages can be referenced just like standard HTML pages. In fact, using ASP actually made handling state information in the Web site much easier. Data and state information could be passed though the frameset to the content pages by using Request variables, something that can't be done with standard HTML.

However, framesets did cause some problems that held up development for some time. Even though caching was explicitly turned off by using the Response.Expires = 0 line of VBScript code. To overcome this problem, certain pages were developed to have two versions. The application then alternated between the two versions working around the cache problem. To avoid such headaches, you should probably avoid using framesets in the Commerce Server/ ASP environment.

Final Analysis

At this writing, the final version of the Eddie Bauer Web site is just beginning testing. There is no information yet comparing the previous version of the Web site to the current; however, simple experimentation shows the site to be much faster and handle high user loads with ease.

Both the Web design teams at Fry Multimedia and Eddie Bauer are looking forward to taking this application live and seeing how it operates in a real-world environment. ●

CHAPTER 29

Converting an Existing Site: Child's Hope

Site Developer: Child's Hope **http://www. childshope.org,** (see Figure 29.1) was developed and created by C-Systems Inc. **(http://www.c-systems. com)**, a leader in electronic commerce solutions for the Internet.

Child's Hope is the result of corporate partnerships and sponsorships. The companies that helped bring this site to the Internet are Microsoft **(http://www.microsoft.com)**, Hewlett Packard **(http://www.hp.com)**, C-Systems **(http://www.c-systems.com)**, Wells Fargo **(http:// www.wellsfargo.com)**, Verifone **(http://www.vfi.com)**, and Seidler's Jewelers of Boston **(www.seidlers.com)**. This simple idea helps the children and families of Boston's Children's Hospital through online donations (see Figure 29.2).

The development department of Boston's Children's Hospital wanted to broaden its capability to reach the public. Merchant Server 1.0 and now Commerce Server 2.0 offered both new flair and extension to an even newer population.

We looked at many models and found that the simplicity of the Clock Peddler sample store gave us just what we needed.

With the framework set, the Child's Hope site took its place on the World Wide Web, thus pioneering a new concept in the fund-raising community.

FIG. 29.1

The front page of **http://www.childshope.org**.

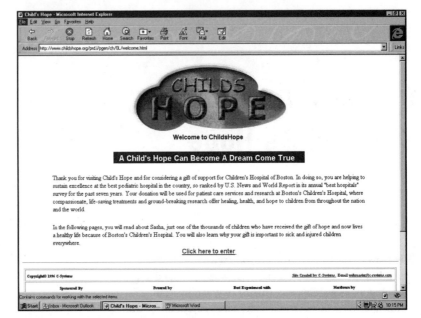

FIG. 29.2

The Donation section of the Child's Hope homepage includes an area for the selection of specific donation amounts.

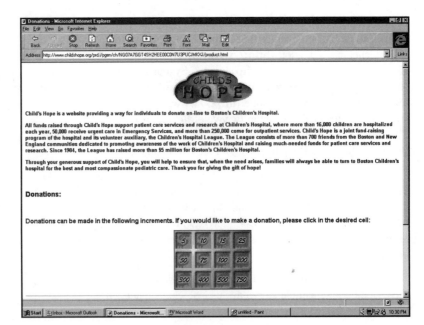

The original software was Merchant Server 1.0 running on Hewlett Packard's LX and LH Pro. We will continue to run the site on a Hewlett Packard hardware platform while we advance the software to Microsoft's Commerce 2.0. ■

An Overview of the Conversion Utilities

Converting a store from Merchant Server 1.0 to Commerce Server 2.0 is far from an exact science; it is more a matter of trial and error.

You can convert a store from Merchant 1.0 to Commerce Server 2.0 in several ways. The conversion utility provided with Commerce Server 2.0 is a useful tool for converting your stores. Although the utility does not convert the entire store and make it work with Commerce 2.0, the conversion utility usually is the best place to get started.

The conversion utility has come a long way since the early betas of Commerce Server. Microsoft has experimented with several ways of running the conversion utility, including trying to make the conversion utility completely convert the whole store over to Commerce 2.0 and Active Server Pages format. Unfortunately, because of the complexity and vast differences between all of the different Merchant Server 1.0 stores that exist, there was no way to create such a utility.

At a development lab that was held when an early beta version of Commerce Server 2.0 was released, Microsoft had several different programmers try to convert their Merchant Server 1.0 stores by using the conversion utility. After almost a week, there were some stores that were not even close to being finished. Child's Hope, as simple as it was, took almost the entire week to convert because of all the trouble with the first version of the conversion utility.

Because of the problems in trying to make a conversion utility that would completely convert a whole store, Microsoft decided to make a conversion utility that would convert only the templates, not the entire site. Finishing the conversion of the site was up to the programmers. Converting the Child's Hope site with the new conversion utility took about two hours—quite an improvement from the early beta.

Based on the first experience with the conversion utility, the approach of conversion was a two-step process. Because this site is simple, some shortcuts from what would be used in a complicated site can be taken.

The first thing to do is to create a store foundation. Child's Hope was created based on the Clockped (Clock Peddler) store, but it was decided that creating a new foundation would be easier than trying to use Clockped again. All the options that pertain to the store were chosen. No tax was chosen because donations are not taxable; no shipping charges were chosen, because the site has nothing to ship; and no receipts were chosen, because the site provides an electronic receipt. No items or fields to any products were chosen since there are only donations and it simply depends how much of a donation you would like to give. Also when going through the "Create a New Store Foundation" utility, search engines and shopper registration were not chosen as options.

When the site was finished, the tables in the existing database were overwritten, because the database would not convert with the receipt conversion utility. Backup copies of the existing database were created so that it will always be avaliable for reference, should anything come up. Most of the database tables remained intact but some of them were overwritten. The product table was overwritten, so the donations actually had to be added back in, which was no big deal because only 12 products needed to be added back in.

Now that the conversion on the templates has been completed, the store foundation has been created and the product tables have been added to the existing database, it is time to add the converted templates into the new store foundation. This is where you need to decide how to proceed. There will be converted templates that you are going to want to use and just change a couple of minor things. There are also going to be templates that you are not going to want to use at all. On some of the templates, you will find that there will be too many actions that you will need to convert, it will just take too long. You will instead want to use the templates that were built with the store foundation and customize them, cutting and pasting code from your old store's converted templates.

Customizing Your Templates

The first template that will be looked at is welcome.html, which was converted to default.asp. The following template is the finished product after conversion and modification:

```
<%
 REM Converted by the Microsoft Commerce Server 2.0 Template Conversion Utility
 REM Time: Mon Jun 02 10:43:39 1997

 Response.Buffer = TRUE

%>
<!--#INCLUDE FILE = "i_shop.asp" -->
```

Make sure that the file that gets included in the #INCLUDE statement is the correct file. i_shop.asp is the page that sets your variables for the database. It creates shopper IDs, and you can include any other actions that need to be handled on each page. When the templates were converted, the #INCLUDE statement pointed to include/shop.asp, which did not exist in the original store that was created with the Store Creator Wizard.

```
<HTML>

<HEAD>
<META HTTP-EQUIV CHARSET=ISO-IR-100>
<TITLE>Child's Hope</TITLE>
</HEAD>
<BODY BGCOLOR="#FFFFFF">
<CENTER>
        <TABLE WIDTH="85%">
                <TR>
                        <TD ALIGN="CENTER">
                                <IMG SRC="/ch_assets/images/choplogo.jpg" ALIG
```

```
                            N="absmiddle" BORDER="0" WIDTH="410" HEIGHT="177">
                </TD>
        </TR>
        <TR>
```

In this store, most of the images are in the assets directory. When the store was converted, the conversion utility changed where the images to point to the /MM_IMAGES directory, all the images needed to be in each page and changed to point to the correct directory, which is simply /ch_assets/images.

```
                <TD ALIGN="CENTER">
                        <FONT FACE="Arial"><STRONG>Welcome to ChildsHo
                        pe</STRONG></FONT>
                </TD>
        </TR>
        <TR>
                <TD ALIGN="CENTER">
                         
                </TD>
        <TR>
                <TD ALIGN="CENTER">
                        <APPLET CODE="RTLScroll.class"
                                CODEBASE="/ch_assets"
                                ALIGN="absmiddle"
                                WIDTH="500"
                                HEIGHT="30">
                        <PARAM NAME="bgcolor" VALUE=" 4194368">
                        <PARAM NAME="font" VALUE="times">
                        <PARAM NAME="jump" VALUE="1">
                        <PARAM NAME="message" VALUE="A Child's
                        Hope Can Become A Dream Come True">
                        <PARAM NAME="Notice" VALUE="Copyright
                        (c) 1997 OpenCube Technologies">
                        <PARAM NAME="size" VALUE="20">
                        <PARAM NAME="speed" VALUE="10">
                        <PARAM NAME="textcolor" VALUE="16777215
                        ">
                        </APPLET>
                </TD>
        </TR>
```

In Merchant Server 1.0, the assets directory always points to simply /ch instead of /ch_assets. In Commerce Server 2.0, /ch is the directory name of the store, so the codebase needed to be changed from looking in /ch to /ch_assets so that the Java applet will work.

The next section in default.asp that you see is the actual text of the first page.

```
        <TR>
                <TD>
                         
                </TD>
        </TR>
        <TR>
                <TD>
                        <P>
```

```
                                   Thank you for visiting Child's Hope and
                                   for considering a gift of support for
                                   Children's Hospital of Boston. In doing
                                   so, you are helping to sustain excellence at
                                   the best pediatric hospital in the country,
                                   so ranked by U.S. News and World Report in its
                                   annual "best hospitals" survey for the
                                   past seven years. Your donation will be used
                                   for patient care services and research at
                                   Boston's Children's Hospital, where
                                   compassionate, life-saving treatments and
                                   ground-breaking research offer healing,
                                   health, and hope to children from
                                   throughout the nation and the world.
                              </P>
                    </TD>
          </TR>
          <TR>
                    <TD>
                          
                    </TD>
          </TR>
          <TR>
                    <TD>
                              <P>
                                   In the following pages, you will read a
                                   bout Sasha, just one of the
                                   thousands of children who have received
                                   the gift of hope and now lives a healthy life
                                   because of Boston's Children's Hospital.
                                   You will also learn why your gift is important
                                   to sick and injured children everywhere.
                              </P>
                    </TD>
          </TR>
          <TR>
                    <TD ALIGN="CENTER">
                              <%
%>
<A HREF="<% = mscsPage.URL("when.asp") %>"><FONT FACE="Arial"><STRONG>
Click here to enter</STRONG></FONT></A>
                              </TD>
                    </TR>

          </TABLE>
</CENTER>
```

To enter the store in a Merchant Server 1.0 store, you need to register or enter as shopper.guest, which is a Merchant 1.0 action. The way the store is working now, users are given a cookie instead of having the shopper ID appear in the URL. Now whenever shoppers go to default.asp, first-time shoppers are automatically registered. For this reason, going to the next page does not require any type of action except simply going to the page. For this reason, instead of having to call any Commerce 2.0 scripts or actions, the user is simply taken to the next page, when.asp.

```
<!-- BEGIN COPYRIGHT INFORMATION -->
<!--#INCLUDE FILE = "include/copyright.asp" -->
```

The last line calls the copyright page. In the templates that come with Commerce Server, this file usually is called `footer.asp`, but `copyright.asp` is a more descriptive name for the file.

Now that you have seen what has been done with this file, go through the rest of your site and make similar changes. With Child's Hope, only one other template needed to be changed before the shopping page, and that template was `when.htm`. I followed the same steps as I did when I took the converted page and changed whatever references were incorrect for my new site.

The next page is the product page, `product.htm`. The convert page is now `product.asp`. Several more changes needed to be made in this page, because this page has several actions in it.

```
<%
REM Converted by the Microsoft Commerce Server 2.0 Template Conversion Utility
REM Time: Mon Jun 02 10:43:50 1997

Response.Buffer = TRUE
%><!--#INCLUDE FILE = "i_shop.asp" --><!DOCTYPE HTML PUBLIC "-//IETF//DTD HTML//
EN">
```

Again, you need to change the `include` file to be the correct `include` file.

This next section is the donation page. This page is the converted `product.html` template. When this page was converted, the conversion utility did not replace all of the Merchant Server 1.0 actions, it simply left notes to the programmer saying that these actions needed to be replaced.

```
<HTML>

<HEAD>
<META HTTP-EQUIV="Content-Type"
CONTENT="text/html; charset=iso-8859-1">
<TITLE>Donations</TITLE>
</HEAD>

<BODY BGCOLOR="#FFFFFF">

        <CENTER>
                <IMG SRC="/ch_assets/images/choplogosm.jpg" WIDTH="212" HEIG
                HT="92">
        </CENTER>

<P><FONT COLOR="#000000" SIZE="2" FACE="Arial"><STRONG>
Child's Hope is a website providing a way for individuals to donate
on-line to Boston's Children's Hospital.
</STRONG></FONT></P>


<P><FONT COLOR="#000000" SIZE="2" FACE="Arial"><STRONG>
```

All funds raised through Child's Hope support patient care services and research at Children's Hospital, where more than 16,000 children are hospitalized each year, 50,000 receive urgent care in emergency services, and more than 250,000 come for outpatient services. Child's Hope is a joint fund-raising program of the hospital and its volunteer auxiliary, the Children's Hospital League. The League consists of more than 700 friends from the Boston and New England communities dedicated to promoting awareness of the work of Children's Hospital and raising much-needed funds for patient care services and research. Since 1984, the League has raised more than $5 million for Boston's Children's Hospital.

```
</STRONG></FONT></P>
```

```
<P><FONT COLOR="#000000" SIZE="2" FACE="Arial"><STRONG>
Through your generous support of Child's Hope, you will help to ensure
that, when the need arises, families will always be able to turn to Boston
Children's
hospital for the best and most compassionate pediatric care. Thank you for giving
the gift of hope!
</STRONG></FONT></P>
```

```
<P> </P>
```

```
<H3><FONT FACE="Arial"><STRONG>Donations:</STRONG></FONT></H3>
```

```
<P> </P>
```

This is where it gets fun. This page has several lines of old actions. Following is an example of what this action looks like right after the page is converted using the conversion utility:

```
      <AREA SHAPE="rect" HREF="<%
 REM ### this use of a 1.0 action needs to be updated
 %><% = mscsPage.URL("actions/xt_order_additem.asp", "sku", 200) %>"
 COORDS="156,56 198,97">
```

As you can see, remarks are inserted at every action, so that you know that you need to change. Changing these actions to Commerce 2.0 code was simple. The only thing that needed to change was that every time `"actions/xt_order_additem.asp"` was called, it simply needed to be changed to `"xt_orderform_additem.asp"`. The `"xt_orderform_additem.asp"` file was supplied by the Store Creator Wizard as well, nothing needed to be changed in this file to get the donations to work. To make this change, a simple find-and-replace operation needed to be done in the text editor of choice.

The following text shows what the code is doing for the actual donations. As you can see, all of the code is very similar, the only differences are the sku's representing the dollar amount of the donation:

```
<P><FONT FACE="Arial"><STRONG>Donations can be made in the
following increments. If you would like to make a donation, please click
In the desired cell:</STRONG></FONT></P>
<MAP NAME="MONEY">
      <AREA SHAPE="rect" HREF="<%
```

```
%><% = mscsPage.URL("xt_orderform_additem.asp", "sku", 5)
%>" COORDS="5,6 46,46">
        <AREA SHAPE="rect" HREF="<%
%><% = mscsPage.URL("xt_orderform_additem.asp", "sku", 10)
%>" COORDS="57,6 96,46">
        <AREA SHAPE="rect" HREF="<%
%><% = mscsPage.URL("xt_orderform_additem.asp", "sku", 15)
%>" COORDS="10 8,6 146,47">
        <AREA SHAPE="rect" HREF="<%
%><% = mscsPage.URL("xt_orderform_additem.asp", "sku", 25)
%>" COORDS="15 6,5 196,47">
        <AREA SHAPE="rect" HREF="<%
%><% = mscsPage.URL("xt_orderform_additem.asp", "sku", 50)
%>" COORDS="5, 56 46,97">
        <AREA SHAPE="rect" HREF="<%
%><% = mscsPage.URL("xt_orderform_additem.asp", "sku", 75)
%>" COORDS="56,56 97,96">
        <AREA SHAPE="rect" HREF="<%
%><% = mscsPage.URL("xt_orderform_additem.asp", "sku", 100)
%>" COORDS="106,55 147,97">
        <AREA SHAPE="rect" HREF="<%
%><% = mscsPage.URL("xt_orderform_additem.asp", "sku", 200)
%>" COORDS="156,56 198,97">
        <AREA SHAPE="rect" HREF="<%
%><% = mscsPage.URL("xt_orderform_additem.asp", "sku", 300)
%>" COORDS="6,106 45,147">
        <AREA SHAPE="rect" HREF="<%
%><% = mscsPage.URL("xt_orderform_additem.asp", "sku", 400)
%>" COORDS="56,105 97,148">
        <AREA SHAPE="rect" HREF="<%
%><% = mscsPage.URL("xt_orderform_additem.asp", "sku", 500)
%>" COORDS="106,105 147,147">
        <AREA SHAPE="rect" HREF="<%
%><% = mscsPage.URL("xt_orderform_additem.asp", "sku", 750)
%>" COORDS="157,105 197,147">
</MAP>

<CENTER>
        <IMG SRC="/ch_assets/images/donations.jpg" WIDTH=202 HEIGHT=152
        BORDER=0 USEMAP="#MONEY">
</CENTER>

<!--
<TABLE BORDER="4" CELLPADDING="2" BORDERCOLOR="#008000"
BORDERCOLORDARK="#008000" BORDERCOLORLIGHT="#FF0000">
  <TR>
    <TD ALIGN="center"><FONT SIZE="5" FACE="Arial"><STRONG><%
%><A HREF="<% = mscsPage.URL("xt_orderform_additem.asp", "sku", 5) %>">$5
</A></STRONG></FONT></TD>
    <TD ALIGN="center"><FONT SIZE="5" FACE="Arial"><STRONG><%
%><A HREF="<% = mscsPage.URL("xt_orderform_additem.asp", "sku", 10) %>">$
10</A></STRONG></FONT></TD>
    <TD ALIGN="center"><FONT SIZE="5" FACE="Arial"><STRONG><%
%><A HREF="<% = mscsPage.URL("xt_orderform_additem.asp", "sku", 15) %>">$
15</A></STRONG></FONT></TD>
```

```
    <TD ALIGN="center"><FONT SIZE="5" FACE="Arial"><STRONG><%
%><A HREF="<% = mscsPage.URL("xt_orderform_additem.asp", "sku", 25) %>">$
25</A></STRONG></FONT></TD>
  </TR>
  <TR>
    <TD ALIGN="center"><FONT SIZE="5" FACE="Arial"><STRONG><%
%><A HREF="<% = mscsPage.URL("xt_orderform_additem.asp", "sku", 50) %>">$
50</A></STRONG></FONT></TD>
    <TD ALIGN="center"><FONT SIZE="5" FACE="Arial"><STRONG><%
%><A HREF="<% = mscsPage.URL("xt_orderform_additem.asp", "sku", 75) %>">$
75</A>
    </STRONG></FONT></TD>
    <TD ALIGN="center"><FONT SIZE="5" FACE="Arial"><STRONG><%
%><A HREF="<% = mscsPage.URL("xt_orderform_additem.asp", "sku", 100) %>">
$100</A></STRONG></FONT></TD>
    <TD ALIGN="center"><FONT SIZE="5" FACE="Arial"><STRONG><%
%><A HREF="<% = mscsPage.URL("xt_orderform_additem.asp", "sku", 200) %>">
$200</A></STRONG></FONT></TD>
  </TR>
  <TR>
    <TD ALIGN="center"><FONT SIZE="5" FACE="Arial"><STRONG><%
%><A HREF="<% = mscsPage.URL("xt_orderform_additem.asp", "sku", 300) %>">
$300</A></STRONG></FONT></TD>
    <TD ALIGN="center"><FONT SIZE="5" FACE="Arial"><STRONG><%
%><A HREF="<% = mscsPage.URL("xt_orderform_additem.asp", "sku", 400) %>">
$400</A></STRONG></FONT></TD>
      <TD ALIGN="center"><FONT SIZE="5" FACE="Arial"><STRONG><%
%><A HREF="<% = mscsPage.URL("xt_orderform_additem.asp", "sku", 500) %>">
$500</A></STRONG></FONT></TD>
      <TD ALIGN="center"><FONT SIZE="5" FACE="Arial"><STRONG><%
%><A HREF="<% = mscsPage.URL("xt_orderform_additem.asp", "sku", 750) %>">
$750</A></STRONG></FONT></TD>
  </TR>
</TABLE>
-->

<!--#INCLUDE FILE="include/copyright.asp" -->
</BODY>
</HTML>
```

From here, the templates that were provided by the Store Creator Wizard were found to be much easier to use than the pages of the converted templates. The reason is that using the templates that are provided, and changing some of the code and inserting any pictures or images is much simpler than changing the converted code. Also, the pages that are provided use the Microsoft Wallet with code that is more updated and more efficient than the code that is used for the Merchant 1.0 store.

When you change the payment, billing, and receipt page, and thoroughly test your store, you are ready for prime time. Converting all your stores is not as simple as **http:// www.childshope.org**, but this is the foundation of a successful conversion. To familiarize yourself with the conversion utility, you should try converting a simple store like Child's Hope so that you know what you are getting yourself into. When you familiarize yourself with conversion, you can convert much more complicated stores.

From Here...

This chapter discussed converting a very simple store, **http://www.childshope.org** or Child's Hope. In this chapter, you saw that conversion of even the simplest stores is a multi-step process. In this case of Child's Hope, the best way to convert the store was to first run the Store Creator Wizard to create a new store and store foundation and then to run the Template Conversion Utility. With the converted Merchant Server 1.0 templates and the new store templates, converting Child's Hope was a very simple and quick process.

The following chapters provide further information to help you go on with conversion of your Merchant Server 1.0 stores:

- Part VI: Case Studies. The chapters in this section all cover converting Merchant 1.0 stores from the simplest store, Child's Hope, to a much more complicated store, Seidler's Jewelers. This section also shows new store creation with the example of Eddie Bauer.

Reapplying a New Technology: Programmer's Paradise

Programmer's Paradise (PP) offers a valuable resource to programmers: an online source for purchasing software. The initial site, built with Merchant Server, also offered us an ideal opportunity to test the conversion path to Commerce Server 2.0.

The original base shell was taken from Volcano Coffee, and the enterprise hardware platform was Hewlett Packard. The site uses three Lx Pros to form a powerful foundation to absorb the huge number of users who use this popular site. ■

Converting to Commerce Server 2.0

We began our conversion by running the conversion wizard on the existing MMS site. The template conversion utility updates current Merchant Server 1.0 store templates to use Active Server Pages, including VBScript scripts and methods on Commerce Server components. The template conversion utility is automatically installed if you choose a complete setup during Commerce installation. If you choose a custom setup, you must choose the option to install the conversion utility. If you have already installed Commerce Server and did not install the template conversion utility, rerun the setup and choose the option to install the utility.

Upon launching the template conversion utility, the program detects existing MMS stores in the Registry and presents a dialog box, asking the user to specify the store to be converted, the path for the output of the converted store, and the path for the conversion log file.

We installed Commerce Server 2.0 on a machine that was not running MMS 1.0, so when I initially launched the conversion utility, no stores were in the registry. I was pleased to find, however, that if I dumped the key `HKEY_LOCAL_MACHINE\SOFTWARE\Microsoft\MerchantServer` from our production machine and imported it into the conversion machine, the next launch of the template conversion utility found the store's directory. Therefore, I was able to proceed with the conversion without installing MMS 1.0 first. I found out later, that to proceed with the conversion without dumping an MMS 1.0 Registry value, you can simply click the button next to the directory input box and choose a directory on a local, or a mapped drive. If you want to convert one template, simply create a directory, store your template in that directory, and point the template conversion utility to that directory.

Initially, I allowed the conversion utility to create the converted files to a subdirectory of `<drive>:\Commerce\Stores\paradise`, which is the default directory chosen by the utility. Later, however, I found that I should have approached the conversion differently. Therefore, I scrapped this directory and allowed the conversion utility to create the files in a directory separate from the `Commerce` directory.

After selecting the store, the path for converted files, and the path for the log file, the utility read through each template, converted it to an `.asp` file, and saved it in the path indicated. (Actions, directives, and value references are converted to VBScript and Commerce Server component methods, where possible.) The conversion utility left intact all the HTML defining the page layout.

Testing the Conversion of Templates

To determine whether my templates were successfully converted, I opened the conversion log file residing in the directory that I specified when running the utility. Following is an example of this log file:

```
==========================================================================
Log started at: Mon Apr 21 13:27:18 1997
---------------
Microsoft Commerce Server 2.0 Conversion Tool
==========================================================================
```

```
Beginning template conversion.
Source directory: E:\paradise1.0
Target directory: E:\commerce\Stores\paradise
===========================================================================
Checking directory: E:\paradise1.0
Skipping: .\welcome.bak
---------------
Converting: .\welcome.closed.html
---------------
Converting: .\welcome.html
===========================================================================
Checking directory: E:\paradise1.0\admin
(created: E:\commerce\Stores\paradise\admin)
---------------
Converting: admin\add.producttosubsection.html
 Found: action usage that needs to be updated
---------------
Converting: admin\admin.html
 Found: store_config.attr --- no longer supported
 Found: [simg] --- virtual root needs to be updated
 Found: [simg] --- virtual root needs to be updated
 Found: [simg] --- virtual root needs to be updated
 Found: [simg] --- virtual root needs to be updated
 Found: [simg] --- virtual root needs to be updated
```

The log file provides a detailed log for every step of the conversion. You should be aware of the following issues before proceeding with the conversion process:

- The conversion utility does not convert any file that does not maintain the `.html` or `.htm` extension.

  Skipping: `assets\products\smfhtml.jpg`

- All converted files include the file `shop.asp`, no matter in which directory they are located.

- Response buffering is set to true whether or not the template contains the `[nocache]` directive. The `Buffer` property of the `Response` object indicates whether to buffer page output. If page output is buffered, the server does not send a response to the client until all the server scripts on the current page have been processed or until the `Flush` or `End` method has been called.

- Files that require further editing are flagged to indicate that actions or functions are unsupported or operate differently in version 2.0. In addition, the templates that are flagged contain remarks about the required modifications. Templates containing the following items need to be modified to conform with the 2.0 architecture:

  - `actions`

    Converting: `admin\add.producttosubsection.html`

    Found: action use that needs to be updated

  - `dateinfo`

    Converting: `elements\date.args2var.html`

    Found: `dateinfo()`; no longer supported

- `[decode]`
- `(dynamic)`
- `[include]` with a variable file

    Found: `[include]` with variable file; no longer supported
- `[map]`
- `now`

    Found: `now`; result type has changed
- `[return]`

    Found: `[return]`; no longer supported
- `store_config.attr`

    Found: `store_config.attr`; no longer supported

Additional Modification Concerns

Other custom functionality that you developed in your 1.0 store may not convert properly, either, so the preceding list does not include all the modifications that you may encounter.

■ Virtual directories for images are handled differently in Commerce Server 2.0. When the conversion utility encounters the `[img]` or `[simg]` tag, it sets a flag notifying you to update these virtual directories. Due to the large amount of images in Programmer's Paradise, these remarks account for a majority of the log file.

Found: `[img]`; virtual root needs to be updated

■ Any files that include a file without the `.html` or `.htm` extension cause a remark informing you that you must upgrade these files manually. If you want, you can simply rename the files with the `.htm` or `.html` extension and run the conversion utility on them in a separate directory.

■ The conversion utility remarks on any subdirectories that it has to create to conform to the old store's directory structure.

Created: `E:\commerce\Stores\paradise\elements`

If you run the conversion utility twice with the same parameters, you find that the utility names the files with a `.backup.n` extension, so as to not overwrite any existing files.

Creating a Store Foundation

After what appeared to be a successful conversion, our next step was to avoid making required modifications to our templates for now and move on to creating a store foundation. We did this with the Store Foundation Wizard. The path to upgrading your store includes the following tasks:

■ Upgrading store directories
■ Upgrading the store database

- Upgrading the store configuration
- Upgrading the management access

Upgrading the Store Directories

You can create store directories manually, or you can use the Store Foundation Wizard. We chose the latter method, which proved to be a less arduous and completely reliable solution. Store directories in Commerce Server 2.0 maintain a different structure from an MMS 1.0 directory structure. The following changes exist:

- The shop folder contains all the files for new and guest shoppers, thus eliminating the use of a login folder for guest shoppers. The shop directory can contain `include` files, extensions, assets, and subdirectories.

- The administrative pages for the store now reside in the `manager` directory.

- The `elements` directory has been eliminated and is replaced by the `store name/include` directory.

- The `images` directory in the `store` directory no longer exists; instead, images are stored in the `assets` directory of individual stores.

- A new directory called `config` is created for each store and contains the order pipeline configuration file.

Upgrading Store Configuration

The Store Foundation Wizard is launched from the Commerce Server Host Administrator page, which, in a default installation, has the following location:

```
http://<machine name>/MSCS_HostAdmin/default.asp
```

CHAPTER 31

A New Look for Seidlers

Seidlers Jewelers is a well-known jewelry store in the Boston area. In order to expand its business, Seidlers was interested in developing a way to reach a broader customer base. The perfect solution? A Microsoft Merchant Internet site. In this chapter, we will take a look at how we converted the Seidlers site from Microsoft Merchant Server 1.0 to Microsoft Commerce Server 2.0. By the way, Seidlers is one of the original Microsoft banner sites—the first retail sites that were developed with Merchant Server—that was chosen to go live on the day that Microsoft released Merchant Server to the public (October 30, 1996).

Daniel Seidler & Sons Inc. has been a fixture in the Boston area for more than 60 years. In the early 1900s, the Seidler family owned a pawn shop named Provident Loan in the old Scollay Square section of Boston. In 1930, Daniel Seidler moved the shop to its present location in the Jewelers Exchange Building at 333 Washington Street in downtown Boston. At this time, he and his three sons also opened a jewelry store that was incorporated in 1936 and named Daniel Seidler and Sons, Inc. From its humble beginnings, this small pawn shop has grown into what Seidlers is today. Three exquisite jewelry stores now grace the Boston area and serve an international clientele, each store with its own personality.

Curiously, as much as Seidlers has grown, it still remains built on its original foundation focused on its original premise of personal service and attention to its customers. Still a family business, the Seidler name is known far and wide for its quality, service, and discount prices.

Seidlers's goal for its Commerce site was to establish a broader world presence on the Internet. The main goal for the site was to give customers a personalized touch and to make them feel as if they were shopping in person. In particular, Seidlers wanted its customers to know that the Seidler name represented quality and customer satisfaction in the world of jewelry. ■

Hardware/Software

We looked at many different configurations of hardware from many different manufacturers. We chose to serve our site from two HP NetServer LX Pro servers. We picked these machines because of their efficiency, ability to handle a high level of use, and speed.

In addition to Microsoft Commerce Server 2.0, we used Windows NT 4.0, SQL 6.5, and Internet Information Server 3. We kept our system in a Microsoft-approved configuration so that we would be able to get help from Microsoft more easily. This also prevented problems that might have occurred had we gone with nonstandard equipment.

Site Conversion: A Step Up and a Face Lift

When we decided to convert our next store, we decided to take the opportunity to give the site a face lift as well. Seidlers.com was built in 1.0 Merchant format and based on the "aw" store model. This model provides one of the most sophisticated user interfaces of the demo store templates. With frames and javascript driving much of the content of the frames, we decided that Seidlers did not need all that. After an evaluation of the changes that could be made, we decided that the site only needs to use frames for viewing products. For the rest of the site, the frames are too much. Therefore, we set out to redesign the site without frames, and use a frame set for the catalog only. The catalog demands a frame because we are trying to relay so much content to the user. We want to give the user a list of products, but we do not want to have to refresh that list every time the user views a single product (this was being done on the old Seidlers site). The user should be able to navigate all the departments easily while she is looking at a product. We wanted to give the user the ability to tab through the products one at a time like a catalog. And finally, we wanted the user to be able to navigate the rest of the site (search, basket, lobby, credits, and so on) easily. All of these demands put a damper on any attempt we made to build the catalog without a frame set.

Our model was now more in a form to agree with the 'vc' model. 'vc' provides us with the page flipping for the product catalog, and it does not use frames. However, the 'vc' model also does not allow guest shoppers. I have written an 'asp' page to simulate the 'shopper.guest' action of the 1.0 architecture and this template will work for this store as well.

When we are through, our site will be more navigatable, conform to basic design fundamentals, offer quicker downloads of pages, and implement an enhanced graphical front-end.

Seidlers store conversion notes follow: (note: I took the initial notes on some troubleshooting techniques I used during the conversion, and some errors I found as well. Towards the end of these notes, I outlined some of the design procedures)

```
Commerce.OrderPipeline error '80020009'
::OrderExecute() failed for component[0x8] hr: 0x80000008 PROGID:
Commerce.SaleAdjust.1 Cannot convert None to number
/sj/order_basket.asp, line 19
```

The sale adjust stage is causing the next problem. Here, is where we open the pipeline configuration editor and look into the stage that is causing the problem. The code: `PROGID:` `Commerce.SaleAdjust.1`from the error message above tells us that a SaleAdjust component failed. It is possible to have more than one component, but the number after the name of the component should also tell us that this is the first instance of this component.

In the pipeline editor, we find a saleadjust component in the `Item Price Adjust` stage. The Sale Adjust component sets the _iadjust_currentprice based on _product_sale_* values on the OrderForm.

For each item, it sets _iadjust_currentprice to _product_sale_price if the current date is between _product_sale_start and _product_sale_end.

This component relies on the data received from the Product Information Stage. Specifically the _product_sale_* name/value pairs set by QueryProdInfo.

This all comes down to a problem in the Query that is being executed in the Product Information Stage of the Order Pipeline. We are only querying the product_family table, because the query that is built with the default 'aw' foundation model fails to return any records. All of the sample stores that use variants are built so that if one product in your database does not have a variant, the store will not function. Therefore, you have to build a work around to it.

The query that is being executed is as follows:

```
select pf_id sku, * from sj_product_family where pf_id = :1
```

This executed properly and did return a sku, so it's back to the code in `xt_orderform_additem.asp` to see if we are not passing the sku properly.

It seems that my query needs to only fetch the sku. So, creating a new query :

```
select pf_id sku from sj_product_family where pf_id = :1
```

that only fetches the sku from the product table.

Then execute this query in the orderFormAddItem function of the `xt_orderform_additem.asp` template.

Looking at the page you will notice that the page that is calling `xt_orderform_additem.asp` (`feature.asp`) is sending the value `sku`, not `pf_id` . Thus, the query was receiving a null value. I fixed this, then I received the following error in the pipeline:

```
Commerce.OrderPipeline error '80020009'
::OrderExecute() failed for component[0x0] hr: 0x80000008
```

```
PROGID: Commerce.QueryProdInfo.1 Missing required attribute
item.sku in order process
/sj/order_basket.asp, line 19
```

It seems that the item name/value pairs are not being set. We then decided to set the order pipeline log file in the `'global.asa' : Call OrderPipeline.SetLogFile(Filename)` to see what was happening.

None of the products have variants. That is the issue.

`****************************`

error '80004005'

`/sj/xt_orderform_additem.asp, line 38`

Receiving this error on:

```
set item = orderForm.AddItem(productsku.sku, product_qty, 0)
```

Using sql trace to see what queries are being executed. The question arises as to whether we are passing null as the shopper id in one of my queries.

In SQL trace, we can see that the following call in the function `'orderformAddItem'` :

```
set productsku = DataSource.Execute("product-family",
Cstr(Request("pf_id")))
```

is being created:

SQL Trace:

```
create proc #odbc#sa4782322 @P1 char(1) as select pf_id sku, * from
sj_product_family where pf_id = @P1
```

When it is executed, it is being delivered a null value:

```
#odbc#sa4782322 NULL
```

The page that was calling this page was using a form with an action posted to `'xt_orderform_additem.asp'`. The field on the form was set to 'sku' when it should have been `'pf_id'`.

`*************************`

```
Commerce.Datasource.1 error '80040e07'
```

```
[Microsoft][ODBC SQL Server Driver][SQL Server]Disallowed implicit conversion
from datatype 'int' to datatype 'char' Table: 'seidler.dbo.sj_shopper', Column:
'shopper_id' Use the CONVERT function to run this query.
```

`/sj/product.asp, line 6`

The converted page `'product.asp'` was sending this message. This converted page was converted from an 'aw' model store template page called `'product.asp'`. Since I used the store wizard to build a store foundation modeled after the 2.0 'aw' store, I had a `'foundation'` page to refer to.

The error in the converted `'product.asp'` was generated by the following call:

```
ShopperID = Page.GetShopperId()
Set shopper = Application("MSCSShopperStorage").GetData(Page.Context, ShopperID)
```

The `'foundation'` page `'product.asp'` sets the shopper as follows:

```
if IsNull(mscsShopperID) then
        call Response.Redirect("welcome_body.asp")
end if
set shopper = MSCSShopperStorage.GetData(null, CStr(mscsShopperID))
```

Maybe if we swapped these two, then I would solve the problem. But prior to changing these, it was determined that the mistake was as simple as not passing the shopper id with the call. From the lobby, we called `'search.asp'` as:

```
<A HREF="search.asp"....>
```

It should be called with the page components URL method, which appends the shopper id onto the end of the url.:

```
<A HREF="<% = Page.URL("search.asp") %>"....>
```

The search page was not receiving the shopper id, therefore the results page was not receiving this and thus not passing it onto the product page.

Now we've deleted the store, and redesigned with Volcano Coffee. This uses variants as well, but in a much more universal matter. This means that the variants are simply named `attribute_1` through `attribute_4`. This is much more specific for the Seidlers environment, because each product line carries different variants.

I ran through the copy store wizard, using the vc templates. The tables were created and my old tables I had renamed to `*_data`. Now I can simply copy data from the sj data tables into the newly created vc model tables, which still contain vc data.

After a simple comparison, it was found that the old sj store tables had much in common with the vc modeled tables. After a few adjustments, I was able to bring my data over to the new tables. I now had all the functionality of the vc store and the aw store. This is because I added the sale information columns in the `product_family` table.

Next, I deleted all the files from the `'assets'` directory, and copied over the 'Seidlers' assets directory.

We now have a store built after the VC model, but named Seidlers Jewelry. The data in the tables is all Seidlers data, and the images are now Seidlers images. The next step is to bring up the Seidlers store to see if it works. Yes, it works. It is a complete model of Volcano Coffee, now we just have to adjust the templates to fit our store.

The first step in converting the vc templates into our Seidlers model is to open and configure `'default.asp'`. Prior to setting up the foundation for our Seidlers conversion, we ran the template conversion wizard on the old 1.0 Seidlers templates. We also went through these templates and adjusted all the errors. When we started this project, this was going to be a simple conversion based on the original 'aw' model. Therefore, we had built an 'aw' foundation, and inserted my converted Seidlers templates. Since the converted templates were based on the 'aw' model, we were able to begin troubleshooting the templates with minimal effort. I had finished the conversion of the templates (not the actions or directives) prior to moving our model over to the 'vc' foundation.

As we open the first page of the new site `'default.asp'` and open the first page of the converted template. We are taking this opportunity to not only convert the back-end of the site, but we are giving the site a face lift as well. Therefore, we need to structure my templates the way we want them to look in the new format. This is all done in a top-down format with the 'vc' model `'default.asp'` template. By using this template, I can push down all the html and asp that is currently in this template. By building my template into the 'default.asp' template, we are able to use the asp that was meant to be used with the 'vc' model.

The 'vc' model page `'default.asp'` consists of a couple of images, a welcoming paragraph of text, and options for the user to login or register. Our model needs to give the shopper the ability to browse without signing in. The asp page will simulate a `'shopper.guest'` action from the 1.0 merchant architecture. Essentially, this page will create a shopper_id and enter that id into the database. Before the shopper can purchase an item, he must register and provide the rest of his information to the database. We could develop a SQL stored procedure to clear out, at given intervals, any guest shoppers who did not sign in.

```
'XT_SHOPPER_GUEST.ASP' Template begin:
<%
        '-- XT_SHOPPER_GUEST.ASP
        '-- GIVES SHOP THE ABILITY TO ALLOW GUEST SHOPPERS
        '-- MATTHEW N. KLEIN 6/15/97
        '-- SET THE SHOPPER MANAGER , CONTEXT, PAGE AND SHOPPER STORAGE
        '--OBJECTS
        Set MSCSShopperManager = Application("MSCSShopperManager")
        Set MSCSShopperStorage = Application("MSCSShopperStorage")
        Set mscsPage = Server.CreateObject("Commerce.Page")
        Set Context = mscsPage.Context

        '-- CREATE A DICTIONARY OBJECT TO CONTAIN THE SHOPPER INFO
        Set mscsShopper = Server.CreateObject("Commerce.Dictionary")
        '-- GENERATE A SHOPPER ID
        mscsShopperID = MSCSShopperManager.CreateShopperID()
        '-- ADD THE SHOPPER ID TO THE SHOPPER DICTIONARY OBJECT
        mscsShopper.Shopper_id = mscsShopperID
        '-- ADD THE DATE CREATED TO THE SHOPPER DICTIONARY OBJECT
        mscsshopper.created      = CDate(Now)
        '-- INSERT THE DATA INTO THE SHOPPER DBSTORAGE OBJECT
        call mscsshopperStorage.InsertData(Context, mscsshopper)
        '-- PUT THE SHOPPER ID INTO THE URL
        call mscsPage.PutshopperId(mscsshopperID)
        '-- REDIRECT SHOPPER TO THE LOBBY
        Response.Redirect mscsPage.URL("main.asp")

%>
END 'XT_SHOPPER_GUEST.ASP'
```

To develop this page, we simply replace the html of the vc shop with the html that we want the Seidlers shop to use. Then, I use the links to the actions on my login button and register button. The browse button gets directed to `xt_shopper_guest.asp`.

With the `default.asp` file finished, we want to move on to configure the main 'lobby' page now. This page is entiteled 'main.asp'. Our version of the lobby uses a frame. The topmost frame is used as a navigation area, to navigate amongst the departments. The site navigation bar, which allows shoppers to navigate to various other activities on the site, is currently included on each page. I wanted to give this site more of a catalog feel. To do this I am going to swap the department navigation in the top frame with the site navigation that is included on each page. I also want to go away from frames. I don't feel that this site needs it and that is one reason why we chose the 'vc' model, which does not use frames.

The top of my page will consist of a header for the store, and a navigation header that allows the shopper to traverse all parts of the site. The department listing will now become the `catalog page`. The department listing will serve as the table of context for the catalog.

We chose to build the header as a seperate file called `head_navbar.asp`. This allows me to include it into all pages. I figure I may want to change the headings of the navbar to signify where a user currently is positioned within our site. This means that I may have to write a lot of code to manipulate the graphics, and I don't want to clutter up all my files with that code.

Again, building from the top down, we have modified the `main.asp` template to fit the Seidlers store. The department list is generated automatically from the code that the 'vc' template used. After some simple modifications, I now have a shopper registering as a guest and viewing the main page of our site.

One problem that we encountered was with the departments. In the old seidler model, we did not use departments and sub-departments. The vc model uses these departments to generate their pages. we were receiving a catastrophic error on the `product.asp` page, because we did not have a parent department for any of the other departments. We used the admin portion of the site to create a new department, then assign that department as the hierarchical superior to all the other departments. This cured the catastrophic error.

Now Seidler's is working with a new face lift and Microsoft Commerce 2.0. ●

CHAPTER 32

Building a New Site: MSN Store

This case study is an overview of the benefits for developing a new Internet electronic commerce site using Commerce Server. The issues discussed here deal with how Commerce Server facilitates the commerce experience, both for the shopper and the merchant. ∎

How to incorporate your viewing preferences into Excel's display settings

Windows 95 supports most five disk compression schemes, Double-Space, DriveSpace, Stacker, SuperStor, and AddStor.

Site Owner and Manager, The Microsoft Network (www.msn.com)

The idea behind the MSN Store was to sell MSN and other Microsoft brand name merchandise to consumers through the web. The idea of the Microsoft Network (MSN) was reworked in the fall of 1996 to an Internet only solution, www.msn.com. With the subsequent growth and expansion of that website, there has been a lot of consumer demand generated for branded MSN products.

The MSN electronic commerce manager, Deborah Levinger, came to MSN from E-Shop, where she was the manager of the E-Shop plaza. This has given her a strong background, not only in implementing electronic commerce, but in implementing Commerce Server's progenitor, the E-Shop commerce tool. Her experience made her well aware of the benefits of a merchant driven product like Commerce Server.

The MSN Store is planned to launch in the fall of 1997 and will have a wide assortment of products with the MSN logo, CarPoint, On Computing, Expedia, Investor, and others. The store will allow consumers to navigate quickly and easily either by type of product or brand. Consumer will also be able to get on-line help or e-mail questions.

A preview of the of the store's front page is shown in Figure 32.1. This page shows how the store will feature product navigation two ways; by type of product or by which of the MSN shows to which the product is related.

FIG. 32.1

The MSN Store's front page, shown here in development, features a "Hot" product selection and richly animated graphics for navigation.

Site Developer Fry Multimedia (www.frymulti.com)

Fry is an early adopter of the Microsoft Commerce Server technology. In the fall of 1996, the 1-800-FLOWERS site was ported from a proprietary UNIX-based system to Merchant Server. This site served as a Microsoft "Banner Site" for the launch of Merchant Server 1.0 and was one of the few actually accepting and fulfilling orders on the Merchant Server launch date.

On her decision to use Fry as the developer, MSN's electronic commerce manager, Deborah Levinger said, "We selected Fry Multimedia to do the development work because of their successful experience in building sites using Commerce Server such as 1-800-Flowers. I got several bids and determined that Fry not only had the best value, but I felt the most confidence in their ability to deliver a quality product on time. In addition, their ability to work with our merchandising source to make sure that the order pipeline is set up and working correctly."

Site Goals

Early in the development for the MSN store, Deborah, established some key concepts in how to implement the MSN shopping experience. These goals became the foundation for the store's design:

1. Know your audience—How is your audience different online, how will you target your audience?

2. Build it to work—Make it fast, don't put too many layers (these are road blocks to the consumer SHOPPING), close the sale—ask them to add the products to their basket and to check out, build a useful search tool if you have a large database, and finally make the ordering system safe and secure.

3. Merchandise—These are the keys to successful selling. Leverage tools already built into Commerce Server for cross-selling and up-selling, the Commerce Server and ASP's ability to incorporate seasonal themes, contests, and promotions, and so on.

4. Make it better—Give the consumer a reason to shop online versus another way. Give true added value and consider building added value features such as gift reminder, gift register, wish list, and more.

5. Continue to make it BETTER—Develop a plan and execute testing new ideas and see what works for your site. Keep your site fresh. It's better to start out with something simple, do it well, and then evolve it.

6. MAKE IT FUN!—Finally, don't forget to make it fun.

Ease of Merchandising

The first order of importance to the MSN store was to find a set of tools and technology that would deliver a robust electronic commerce application. With Commerce Server's evolution from E-shop to Merchant Server to its current form, the product has developed into an environment that fulfills these requirements.

Microsoft Commerce Server makes the creation of an interactive shopping area very easy. Using ASP templates and straight-forward database integration, developers can design pages that can react instantly to changes in the stores information. Product data, customer service information, sales, and promotions will all be stored in the database and pulled up on the stores pages from there. This way new information can be sent to one place and will populate the entire store.

Along with this active content, the design of the MSN store will take advantage of many of Commerce Server's advanced features.

- ability to do promotions to drive sales—dollar off, percent off, and so on
- ability to do cross-sells and up-sells at point of purchase
- ability to tag merchandise as out of stock
- rotating featured product—to drive traffic to best sellers

As with the active content, all of these abilities will be database driven. The store managers will be able to use simple HTML-based forms tools to manage their products, sales, and promotions. Meaning that managing the store is just that, managing the product, not the database or underlying software.

Ease of Order Processing

Another attractive feature of Commerce Server is its integrated order processing pipeline. This tool separates the order handling from the shopping model and makes order processing easily changeable. Using this tool, the MSN store can change its shipping model, or add in discounts without modifying the rest of the store.

In the order pipeline, the phases of calculating the order modular are separate, so each phase of processing the order—shipping, handling, and taxation can be distinct. The store management can change any phase without having to redevelop the others. This flexibility is a huge boon to a new store, like the MSN shop, which will be evolving over time.

Another big boost that the order pipeline gives to this store comes in its final phase where the purchase order is written. Because of the flexibility built into the pipeline architecture, the purchase order can be created in any format needed. This way, regardless of the changing needs of the fulfillment house for MSN, the orders can be generated and sent with only minor changes to the store.

Ease of Shopping

With electronic commerce being a very new venue for shopping, every effort has to be put into designing systems that are easy to use and present a highly reliable environment. Users of electronic commerce sites need to be comfortable with what is going on, or they will leave without buying and not come back. The "basket" shopping model in use by Commerce Server really helps build a comfort level while the user is shopping. Users can browse the store and place items in the basket until they are ready to check out. This is a very familiar paradigm, both from other electronic commerce site and from the real world.

That the basket is an integrated part of the Commerce Server system means there are fewer chances for problems to creep in. The quickest way to lose a sale is to have the shopping basket be broken or work incorrectly. Imagine if you went to the grocery store and the carts there were filthy and broken? What if in the middle of the store, suddenly the groceries you had selected disappeared from your cart and were replaced by those of another shopper? Scary stuff, unfortunately this kind of bug occurs quite often in some shopping systems.

Commerce Server is built around its shopping basket. Therefore this feature is directly integrated with the store application, the product data, and the order pipeline. This means that there is very little chance for problems to creep in as in the case where these functions were programmed separately.

Since an electronic store does not have a friendly clerk to help a customer find what they are looking for, another ability that the MSN store will be getting is a product search system. As with the shopping cart, a familiar tool needs to be provided to aid the customers and increase their comfort and confidence levels while shopping. As the number of products grows, the application will need to present the user with the ability to quickly locate products in the database.

Ease of Integration with Other Tools

Microsoft has developed several tools to be integrated with electronic commerce site. These tools help to make the on-line shopping experience be much less of a hassle for the customer.

The first of these tools to be integrated into the MSN site will be the "Buy Now" control. This gives the shopper the ability to quickly go through the purchase process. The "Buy Now" control allows site developers to implement a quick-buy scenario that takes the form of a Microsoft-style "Wizard."

Wherever a product is presented to the customer in the MSN shop, there will be two buttons, one labeled "See More" and one labeled "Buy Now." The "See More" button when clicked will go through the traditional route of presenting the user with the product's description and allowing them to place the product in their shopping basket. The "Buy Now" button, on the other hand, will activate the "Buy Now" control's wizard. In this case the user will be sent immediately to the checkout screen with the selected product placed in the basket. The user will then go through the billing, shipping, and credit card forms and the sale will be quickly completed.

The other tool that the site will make use of is the Microsoft Wallet control. This will make the check out process nearly painless for the customer. Using the Wallet, the customer's billing, shipping, and credit card information can be selected from information that they have already entered. No more reentering the same billing data time and time again for every sale. Since many of the complaints that on-line shoppers give have to do with the checkout process, integration with the Wallet will make the electronic shopping experience a more enjoyable time for all.

From Here...

The MSN shop will be an application in a constant state of evolution. Starting small, the venture plans to grow and change as quickly as the Web. Because of the wealth of growth options offered by the combination of Commerce Server and ActiveX technology, the MSN shop can easily take advantage of developing standards and technology as they become available. Oh, and one more thing, this combination is a great way to MAKE IT FUN!

PART VII

Appendix

Commerce 2.0 Components

The Commerce Server components are a group of Active Server Pages (ASP) server components that provide the runtime environment for the presentation of online stores. These components are registered on your system as Active Server components when you install Commerce Server. Like Internet Information Server (IIS) 3.0 components, Commerce Server components support methods and properties that you call and set from within the Visual Basic Scripting Edition (VBScript) server-side code that runs your Commerce Server store.

Commerce Server components, however, provide an extensive set of services that are unavailable in IIS 3.0—services that simplify and automate many of the tasks that you would have to perform manually to build a working store with IIS 3.0 components alone. Such tasks include the reliable maintenance of state data across multiple sessions, easy access to and modification of content stored in a database, the logging of store traffic for marketing and diagnostic purposes, and the automated processing of order data through the order-processing pipeline (OPP).

This chapter describes the Commerce Server components and includes definitions of the methods and properties that they support. For a tour of the online stores that use these components, see the chapters: Chapter 31, "Converting an Existing Site; Child's Hope," and Chapter 30, "Reapplying New Technology: Programmer's Paradise."

Commerce Server defines the server components listed in Table A.1.

Table A.1 Components installed with Commerce Server 2.0

Components	Description
Content	Provides a cache in which to store string variables that you associate with data-source names (DSNs) and SQL queries.
CookieStorage	Supports the simple creation, retrieval, and deletion of cookies from the shopper's system. These cookies are specifically designed to store purchase data.
DataFunctions	Supports a collection of functions that validate the format of data for database storage or for processing by the OPP.
Datasource	Executes queries that you specify. These queries can be SQL queries that you construct at runtime or that you associate with string variables and store in a Content component cache.
DBStorage	Supports flexible interaction with the database, primarily for the storage of receipt and order information.
Dictionary	Associates a value with a key.MessageManager Provides a cache to store shopper messages that the OPP uses to describe error conditions.
OrderForm	Supports the in-memory storage of shopper and purchase information for the current shopping session.
OrderPipeline	Loads the pipeline configuration file (.pcf) which contains the pipeline-configuration Information for your store.
Page	Simplifies the layout of HTML pages, as well as the interaction between these pages and the data sources that your store uses.
ShopperManager	Supports the creation, deletion, and retrieval of unique shopper identifiers.
SimpleList	Provides an array of VARIANT's which can be initialized as other components (usually Dictionary components).
TrafficLogFile	Supports logging store events to a text file.
TrafficTable	Supports logging store events to database tables.

Hexadecimal Codes for Countries

Many of the methods implemented in the Commerce Server components take locale variables as optional parameters. These variables are represented by unique hexadecimal codes, which are listed in Table A.4 at the end of this section.

Additionally, Commerce Server defines a group of optional application-level locale parameters, which you can initialize to the values listed in the table. For a list of these variables, refer to "Application-Level Commerce Server Components" earlier in this chapter.

The list of Locales and Languages IDs is in the National Language Support API (NLSAPI) Functional Specification, which you can find on the Microsoft Developer Network (MSDN) compact disc.

Appendix A of the specification lists locales and languages IDs; Table A.2 provides an extract of this information, listing only the locale IDs. This list is continually growing, and further locale support may be added to any future product.

Table A.2   Locales and Languages IDsPrimary

Language	Locale Name	ID
Albanian	Albania	(0x041c; SQI)
Arabic (16)	Saudi Arabia	(0x0401; ARA)
Arabic (16)	Iraq	(0x0801; ARI)
Arabic (16)	Egypt	(0x0C01; ARE)
Arabic (16)	Libya	(0x1001; ARL)
Arabic (16)	Algeria	(0x1401; ARG)
Arabic (16)	Morocco	(0x1801; ARM)
Arabic (16)	Tunisia	(0x1C01; ART)
Arabic (16)	Oman	(0x2001; ARO)
Arabic (16)	Yemen	(0x2401; ARY)
Arabic (16)	Syria	(0x2801; ARS)
Arabic (16)	Jordan	(0x2C01; ARJ)
Arabic (16)	Lebanon	(0x3001; ARB)
Arabic (16)	Kuwait	(0x3401; ARK)
Arabic (16)	United Arab Emirates	(0x3801; ARU)
Arabic (16)	Bahrain	(0x3C01; ARH)

continues

Table A.2   Continued

Language	Locale Name	ID
Arabic (16)	Qatar	(0x4001; ARQ)
Basque	Basque Provinces	(0x042D; EUQ)
Byelorussian	Byelorussia	(0x0423, BEL)
Bulgarian	Bulgaria	(0x0402, BGR)
Catalan	Catalan	(0x0403; CAT)
Chinese (4)	Taiwan	(0x0404; CHT)
Chinese (4)	People's Republic of China	(0x0804; CHS)
Chinese (4)	Hong Kong	(0x0C04; CHH)
Chinese (4)	Singapore	(0x1004; CHI)
Croatian	Croatia	(0x041a, SHL)
Czech	Czechoslovakia	(0x0405; CSY)
Danish	Denmark	(0x0406; DAN)
Dutch (2)	The Netherlands (Standard)	(0x0413; NLD)
Dutch (2)	Belgium (Flemish)	(0x0813; NLB)
English (6)	United States	(0x0409; ENU)
English (6)	United Kingdom	(0x0809; ENG)
English (6)	Australia	(0x0c09; ENA)
English (6)	Canada	(0x1009; ENC)
English (6)	New Zealand	(0x1409; ENZ)
English (6)	Ireland	(0x1809; ENI)
Estonian	Estonia	(0x0425, ETI)
Farsi	Farsi	(0x0429; FAR)
Finnish	Finland	(0x040b; FIN)
French	France (Standard)	(0x040c; FRA)
French	Belgium	(0x080c; FRB)
French	Canada	(0x0c0c; FRC)
French	Switzerland	(0x100c; FRS)
French	Luxembourg	(0x140c; FRL)
German	Germany (Standard)	(0x0407; DEU)

Language	Locale Name	ID
German	Switzerland	(0x0807; DES)
German	Austria	(0x0c07; DEA)
German	Luxembourg	(0x1007; DEL)
German	Liechtenstein	(0x1407; DEC)
Greek	Greece	(0x0408; ELL)
Hebrew	Israel	(0x040D; HEB)
Hungarian	Hungary	(0x040e; HUN)
Icelandic	Iceland	(0x040F; ISL)
Indonesian	Indonesia	(0x0421; BAH)
Italian (2)	Italy (Standard)	(0x0410; ITA)
Italian (2)	Switzerland	(0x0810; ITS)
Japanese	Japan	(0x0411; JPN)
Korean	Korea	(0x0412; KOR)
Latvian	Latvia	(0x0426, LVI)
Lithuanian	Lithuania	(0x0427, LTH)
Macedonian	Macedonia	(0x042f; MKD)
Norwegian (2)	Norway (Bokmal)	(0x0414; NOR)
Norwegian (2)	Norway (Nynorsk)	(0x0814; NON)
Polish	Poland	(0x0415; PLK)
Portuguese (2)	Portugal (Brazilian)	(0x0416; PTB)
Portuguese (2)	Portugal (Standard)	(0x0816; PTG)
Rhaeto-Romanic	Rhaeto-Romanic	(0x0417; RMS)
Romanian (2)	Romania	(0x0418, ROM)
Romanian (2)	Moldavia	(0x0818, ROV)
Russian	Russia	(0x0419; RUS)
Russian	Moldavia	(0x0819, RUM)
Serbian	Serbia	(0x081a; SHC)
Slovak	Slovakia	(0x041b; SKY)
Slovenian	Slovenia	(0x0424, SLV)
Sorbian	Germany	(0x042e, SBN)

continues

Table A.2 Continued		
Language	**Locale Name**	**ID**
Spanish (3)	Spain (Traditional Sort)	(0x040a; ESP)
Spanish (3)	Mexico	(0x080a; ESM)
Spanish (3)	Spain (Modern Sort)	(0x0c0a; ESN)
Swedish	Sweden	(0x041D; SVE)
Thai	Thailand	(0x041E; THA)
Turkish	Turkey	(0x041f; TRK)
Ukrainian	Ukraine	(0x0422; UKR)
Urdu	Urdu	(0x0420; URD)

Application-Level Commerce Server Components

Commerce Server components are per-application or per-page components, where a component has application/page scope based on the way the component is initialized.

`Application` component variables are declared, and should be initialized, in your store's `global.asa` file. An Application variable is initialized as an IIS 3.0 `Application` component variable, and as such is available to any page in your store. The `global.asa` file is an Active Server administration file which resides in each Commerce store's `shop` directory. This global configuration file defines the `Session_OnStart`, `Session_OnEnd`, `Application_OnStart` and `Application_OnEnd` event handlers, as well as the `Session` and `Application` variables. More on this later, for now we will concentrate on learning the components that make up a `global.asa` file.

Commerce Server stores generally avoid the use of `Session` variables and, thus, do not need to define `Session_OnStart` and `Session_OnEnd` event handlers. However, all Commerce stores use `Application` variables, to store references to component instances that need to be created and used on a per-application basis. Following is an example in which a store's `ShopperManager` component is created within the `global.asa` file, initialized to an `Application` variable:

```
Set ShopperManager = Server.CreateObject("Commerce.StandardSManager")

Set Application("MSCSShopperManager") = ShopperManager
```

In this example, because the "`MSCSShopperManager`" variable references a component instance, the `Set` keyword is required. When the `Application` variable "`MSCSShopperManager`" is set to the created `ShopperManager` component, you can use that `Application` variable to call `ShopperManager` methods, as follows.

```
ShopperID = Application("MSCSShopperManager").CreateShopperID()
```

Although the names that you assign to Application variables usually are arbitrary, the names that you assign to Application variables that reference Commerce Server components are hard-coded. This requirement arises from three facts:

- Commerce Server components occasionally need to retrieve information stored by other Commerce Server components.

- Commerce Server components must use the IIS 3.0 scripting context to retrieve the Application component that stores this information.

- The Application component requires that components querying its internally stored variables identify these variables specifically by their string variable names.

Thus, in the preceding example, the name that you assign to the ShopperManager component instance is arbitrary, but the Application component variable referencing this instance must be MSCSShopperManager.

Table A.3 lists the mandatory Application variable names that you use to store per-application component instances.

Table A.3   Mandatory per-application *Application* variables

Variable	Purpose
MSCSContent	Stores the instance of the Content component
MSCSDataFunctions	Stores the instance of the DataFunctions component
MSCSMessageManager	Stores the instance of the MessageManager component
MSCSOrderFormStorage	Stores the instance of the DBStorage or CookieStorage component that you use to store OrderForm data
MSCSOrderPipeline	Stores the application instance of the OrderPipeline component
MSCSReceiptStorage	Stores the instance of the DBStorage component that the OPP uses to store purchase data
MSCSShopperManager	Stores the instance of the ShopperManager component
MSCSShopperStorage	Stores the application instance of the DBStorage or CookieStorage component in which you store shopper data
MSCSTraffic	Stores the application instance of the TrafficTable or TrafficLogFile component that you use to log store traffic

The Application-level variables listed in Table A.4 are not required. However, for component methods requiring values that these variables reference, you must specify the values in the call to the component method or initialize these variables.

Table A.4   Optional *Application* Variables

Variable	Purpose
MSCSDefaultDatasource	Stores the default Datasource component instance for this store.
MSCSIDUrlKey	Indicates the name to be used in the name part of a name–value pair when the shopper's shopper ID is appended to a URL.
MSCSDisableHTTPS	A Boolean value that indicates whether secure HTTP is enabled.
MSCSInsecureHostName	The name of the insecure host. The URL method uses this name to generate a secure URL to a store page.
MSCSSecureHostName	The name of the secure host. The URL method uses this name to generate a secure URL to a store page.

The *SimpleList* Component

The SimpleList component is used throughout Commerce Server to pass data back and forth among Commerce Server components using the Dictionary component discussed in the next section, "The Dictionary Component." A SimpleList component is simply a list of VARIANTs. In the Commerce System, the SimpleList component is used to store the results of executed SELECT queries and to read and write data to and from storage through the DBStorage component.

The SimpleList component supports the methods listed in the following table:

Method	Description
AddItem	Adds the specified item to the list.
Delete	Deletes an item based on a specified index value.

The SimpleList component supports the properties listed in the following table:

Property	Description
Count	A read-only number that identifies the number of elements in the SimpleList.

To create a SimpleList component, use the Internet Information Server (IIS) 3.0 Server object's CreateObject method, specifying "Commerce.SimpleList" as the component's program identifier. After creating a SimpleList component, you can use the SimpleList's AddItem and Delete methods to add items to and remove items from the underlying list. To retrieve elements, you can index into the list just as though it were an array, and where a list consists of Dictionary components, you add a dot (.) operator between the SimpleList name and Dictionary key to reference the Dictionary.

To create a `SimpleList` component, use the IIS 3.0 `Server.CreateObject` method, specifying `"Commerce.SimpleList"` as the component's program identifier. The following is an example showing the creation of a Commerce.SimpleList component, followed by the addition of the item "Hello":

```
<%
    Set SimpleList = Server.CreateObject("Commerce.SimpleList")

    ' Add an item

    SimpleList.AddItem("Hello")
%>
```

The *Dictionary* Component

The `Dictionary` component consists of name-value pairs. The `Dictionary` component defines no methods, but supports the properties listed in the following table:

Property	Description
Count	A read-only number that identifies the number of elements in the `Dictionary`.
Value	A variable that identifies the value of a given `Dictionary` key.

To create a `Dictionary` component, specify the `"Commerce.Dictionary"` program identifier as follows:

```
<%

Set Dictionary = Server.CreateObject("Commerce.Dictionary")
Set SimpleList = Server.CreateObject("Commerce.SimpleList")

Dictionary.shopper_id = Page.GetShopperID

SimpleList.AddItem(Dictionary)

REM Later, to retrieve the added dictionary.

Set SrcDict = SimpleList(0)

%>
```

You can use Visual Basic Scripting Edition (VBScript) `For Each` statement to iterate through the elements of either a `SimpleList` or a `Dictionary`.

The following statement, sets the `Dictionary` component's key `shopper_id` value to the current shopper's shopper ID:

```
Dictionary.shopper_id = Page.GetShopperID(Page.Context)
```

The *Content* Component

The Content component provides a straightforward way for stores to create and maintain a cache of variables that identify the queries and data-source names (DSNs) needed to run a store. You can use Content component methods to associate string variables with configured system and file DSNs, to associate SQL query strings with application-wide variables, and to create the Datasource components through which these queries are executed.

The Content component supports the methods listed in Table A.5.

Table A.5   *Content* Component Methods

Methods	Description
AddDatasource	Associates a string variable with a configured system or file DSN and stores this variable in the Content component cache
AddQuery	Associates a string variable with an SQL statement and stores this variable in the Content component cache
Content	Returns the Datasource component for the specified DSN variable
Datasource	Functionally equivalent to the Content method, Datasource returns a Datasource component based on the variable name associated with a DSN variable

Overview

You can use the Content component to perform the following tasks:

- Add data-source name (DSN) variables to the Content component cache
- Add query variables to the Content component
- Retrieve Datasource components through which to execute queries

These operations are explained in more detail in the sections that follow.

N O T E   The Content and Datasource components, like the DBStorage component, simplify store interaction with the store content database. These components, however, typically are used to retrieve inventory data, whereas DBStorage manages store purchase and receipt data. For more information on DBStorage, see "The DBStorage Component" later in this chapter. ■

Creating a Content Component

To create a Content component, use the IIS 3.0 Server component's CreateObject method, identifying "Commerce.Content" as the component identifier, as follows:

```
Set Content = Server.CreateObject("Commerce.Content")
```

Although you can create a `Content` component anywhere in your store, you typically create this component in your store's `Application_OnStart` event, which you define in your `global.asa` file, and then set the `Application` component variable `MSCSContent`.

Adding DSN Variables

A data-source name (DSN) associates a name that you specify with a set of information about a data source, including the location of the data source and the user information necessary to connect to it. The data source can be a Microsoft Access database, an Excel spreadsheet, or any other application data for which an ODBC-compliant driver is installed on the system.

Before executing a query against an ODBC data source, you use the ODBC32 utility in the Windows NT Control Panel to configure a file or system DSN for that data source. The benefit of using a DSN is that applications querying the data source for which you configure a DSN do not need to know where the data is located; they need only know the name that you've assigned to the data source.

To create a DSN variable based on the configured DSN, call the `Content` component's `AddDatasource` method, as follows.

```
call Content.AddDatasource("clockped", "DSN=arnoldb1;
➥UID=sa;PWD=;DATABASE=eshop", 1, 0)

Set Datasource = Content.Datasource("clockped")
' or Set Datasource = Content("clockped")

' Execute the query
' Datasource.Execute(...)
```

The first part of `AddDatasource` is a string-variable name that you use in your store to refer to this DSN. The second part is a connection string that identifies security information and the location or (in the case of SQL Server) the name of the database.

You can add any number of data source variables to a store, and you can set the `Application`-level `MSCSDefaultDatasource` to the DSN that you want to be the store's default. After you add queries to the `Content` component to which you have added one or more data sources, you can use the `Datasource` or `Content` method to retrieve a `Datasource` component for any DSN variable in the `Content` component cache. For more information on the `Datasource` component, see "The Datasource Component" later in this chapter.

Adding Queries to the *Content* Component

Like DSNs, `Content` component queries can be identified within a store by the string-variable names that you associate with them.

Use the `AddQuery` method to add queries to a `Content` component. These queries should be added to your store in the `Application_OnStart` event, which is defined in the store's `global.asa` file discussed later at the end of this chapter.

The following example, from the AdventureWorks sample store, demonstrates how queries are added to the Content component:

```
REM Add all of the queries into Content component
Call MSCSContent.AddQuery("price-promo-system", "select promo_name, date_start,
▸date_end, shopper_all, shopper_column, shopper_op, shopper_value, cond_all,
▸cond_column, cond_op, cond_value, cond_basis, cond_min, award_all, award_column,
award_op, award_value, award_max, disc_type, disc_value from AW_promo_price where
active <> 0 order by promo_rank")

Call MSCSContent.AddQuery("receipts-for-shopper", "select shopper_id, order_id,
▸date_entered, total, status, marshalled_receipt from AW_receipt where shopper_id
▸= :1 order by date_entered")

' Rest of queries required for store operation...
```

The first part of AddQuery is a string resource identifier that you assign to the query, and the second part is the query's text.

Parameterized Queries

You can use the AddQuery method to add parameterized queries to the Content component cache. For more information on how to add and execute these queries, see "Using Parameterized Queries" later in this chapter.

The following sections describe Content component methods in more detail.

AddDatasource

The AddDatasource method associates a configured file or system data-source name (DSN) with a string alias.

Syntax

    Content.AddDatasource(Alias, ConnectionString, RowsetSize, MaximumRows)

Parameters

Alias

A string that identifies the name by which you reference the DSN in your store.

ConnectionString

A string that contains connection and login information.

RowsetSize

A number that specifies the number of rows to gather at one time. Specifying a default of 1 optimizes the server-side cursor by ensuring that the server never has to retrieve more than a single row in server memory at a time.

MaximumRows

The maximum number of rows to return.

Remarks

If you use multiple DSNs in a store, you should specify one of them as the default DSN for the store. To do so, set the Application object variable MSCSDefaultDatasource to reference that store.

Example

The following example, from the AdventureWorks sample store, creates a Content component, adds a DSN variable to the component, and makes that DSN the default DSN for the store:

```
REM Create a Content component for access to the database
Set  MSCSContent = Server.CreateObject("Commerce.Content")
Call MSCSContent.AddDataSource("AW", MSCSDSN, 1, 0)
Set  MSCSDatasource = MSCSContent.Datasource("AW")

' Later, in Application_OnStart
Application("MSCSDefaultDatasource") = MSCSDatasource
```

Applies To

Content

See Also

AddQuery

AddQuery

The AddQuery method adds a query variable to the Content component cache.

Syntax

Content.AddQuery *QueryName*, *QueryText*

Parameters

QueryName

A string variable that identifies the query.

QueryText

The SQL text of the query.

Example

Refer to "Adding Queries to the Content Component."

Applies To

Content

See Also

AddDatasource

Content

The Content method returns a Datasource component for the specified data-source-name (DSN) variable. *DSN* references a DSN variable added to the Content component cache through a previous call to AddDatasource.

Syntax

Content(*DSN*)

Parameters

DSN

A string that identifies the variable name associated with a DSN through a previous call to AddDatasource.

Remarks

This method is functionally equivalent to the Datasource method.

Example

The following example creates a Content component, adds a DSN variable to the component, and then uses the Content method to create a Datasource component for that DSN:

```
' In Application_OnStart event of Global.asa.
REM -- Create a content component and datasource for connection to the database
Set  MSCSContent = Server.CreateObject("Commerce.Content")
Call MSCSContent.AddDatasource("BikeShop", MSCSDSN, 1, 0)
Set  MSCSDatasource = MSCSContent.Content("BikeShop")
```

See Also

Datasource, AddDatasource

Datasource

The Datasource method returns a Datasource component for the specified data-source-name (DSN) variable. *DSN* references a DSN variable added to the Content component cache through a previous call to AddDatasource.

Syntax

Content.Datasource (*DSN*)

Parameters

DSN

A string that identifies the variable name associated with a DSN through a previous call to AddDatasource.

Remarks

This method is functionally equivalent to the Content method.

Example

The following example, from the Clock Peddler sample store, creates a Content component, adds a DSN variable to the component, and then uses the Datasource method to create a Datasource component instance for that DSN:

```
REM -- Create a content component and datasource for connection to the database
Set  MSCSContent = Server.CreateObject("Commerce.Content")
Call MSCSContent.AddDatasource("ClockPed", MSCSDSN, 1, 0)
Set  MSCSDatasource = MSCSContent.Datasource("ClockPed")
```

The *CookieStorage* Component

The CookieStorage component supports the creation, modification, lookup and deletion of cookies that are written temporarily to the shopper's system and that contain order information.

The syntax of CookieStorage methods corresponds to that of DBStorage methods, because you can use either type of method to store shopper data for a store. You should not, however, use CookieStorage to store purchase data for a shopping session; you should always use DBStorage to store purchase data.

The CookieStorage component supports the methods listed in Table A.6.

Table A.6 *CookieStorage* **Methods**

Methods	Description
CommitData	Updates the contents of a key
DeleteData	Deletes the contents of the specified key
DeleteDataKey	Deletes the key, including its contents
GetData	Returns the contents of a key in a Dictionary component
InitStorage	Initializes the CookieStorage component
InsertData	Inserts the contents of an OrderForm or Dictionary component into a cookie
LookupData	Returns a single record based on keys and values that you specify
LookupMultipleData	Retrieves multiple cookies from the client system and returns the cookies in a SimpleList of Dictionary components

Overview

The `CookieStorage` component gives Commerce Server stores an alternative to using the `DBStorage` component to store shopper information. Shopper-specific information typically is stored as a group of name–value pairs. The simplicity of this data format enables you to store shopper data in memory as a `Dictionary` component and to read and write this information to the client system as cookies.

The `CookieStorage` component supports methods that read cookie information into `Dictionary` components and that use initialized `Dictionary` components to retrieve cookies from the client system. For more information on the `Dictionary` component, refer to "The `SimpleList` and `Dictionary` Components" earlier in this chapter.

To use the `CookieStorage` component, you first use the Internet Information Server (IIS) 3.0 Server object's `CreateObject` method to create an instance of the component and then call `InitStorage` to initialize it, as follows:

```
Set CookieStorage = Server.CreateObject("Commerce.CookieStorage")

Call CookieStorage.InitStorage("clockped_shopper", "shopper_id",
➡"Commerce.Dictionary", "date_changed")
```

The parameters to `InitStorage` specify the following information:

- **Heading:** a prefix for cookies that you create to ensure their uniqueness on the client system.
- **Key name:** the `Dictionary` element that `CookieStorage` methods, such as `LookupData`, use to retrieve cookie information from the shopper's system.
- **Program identifier:** the component that you use to pass and retrieve data to and from `CookieStorage` methods. This component must be a `Dictionary` component (`"Commerce.Dictionary"`).
- **Date:** the date on which the cookie was written.

Attempting to call any other `CookieStorage` method before calling `InitStorage` results in an error.

DeleteData (CookieStorage)

The `DeleteData` method deletes a cookie containing the data that you specify.

Syntax

`CookieStorage.DeleteData(Context, Data)`

Parameters

Context

The `Page` component's `Context` property, a read-only property that is initialized by the `Page` component when the `Page` is created.

Data

A `Dictionary` component that describes the data to delete.

Remarks   To delete cookie data from the client system, initialize a `Dictionary` component to describe the item to delete. The following code sample demonstrates the addition and deletion of cookie data:

```
'Add Cookie Data
Set Dict = Server.CreateObject("Commerce.Dictionary")
Dict.key = "shopper_key"
Dict.shopper_id = Page.GetShopperID()
call CookieStorage.InsertData(Page.Context, Dict)

'Delete Cookie data
Dict.key = "shopper_key"
Dict.shopper_id = Page.GetShopperID()
call CookieStorage.DeleteData(Page.Context, Dict)
```

To remove a cookie based on a specified key, call `DeleteDataKey`.

Applies To

CookieStorage

See Also

DeleteDataKey (CookieStorage)

DeleteDataKey (*CookieStorage*)

The `DeleteDataKey` method deletes the data that corresponds to the value of the specified key.

Syntax

CookieStorage.DeleteDataKey(*Context*, *Key*)

Parameters

Context

The `Page` component's `Context` property, a read-only property that is initialized by the `Page` component when the `Page` is created.

Key

The key name for the cookie to delete, which is the key you specified in the previous call to `InitStorage`.

Remarks   The `DeleteDataKey` method differs from `DeleteData` in that the former requires only the key value to delete the key's data. This method requires the value stored in the `Dictionary` element that corresponds to the element identified as the `Key` in the initial call to `InitStorage`.

Thus, if you specify "shopper_id" as the Key for this cookie storage, you could delete a given shopper's information as follows:

```
Dict.shopper_id = Page.GetShopperID()
CookieStorage.DeleteData(Page.Context, Dict)
```

Applies To

CookieStorage

See Also

DeleteData (CookieStorage)

GetData (CookieStorage)

The GetData method retrieves the specified data from a CookieStorage, based on the provided key value, and returns the data in a Dictionary component.

Syntax

CookieStorage.GetData(*Context*, *Key*)

Parameters

Context

The Page component's Context property, a read-only property that is initialized by the Page component when the Page is created.

Key

The key value for the data you want to retrieve which is the value stored in the cookie element which you specified as the key through a previous call to InitStorage.

Remarks   Because the GetData method requires only the key as the basis of the data retrieval, you can retrieve the information for a given shopper as follows:

```
dictsrc.shopper_id = Page.GetShopperID()
dictdest = CookieStorage.GetData(Page.Context, dictsrc)
```

Applies To

CookieStorage

See Also

LookupData (CookieStorage)

InitStorage (CookieStorage)

The InitStorage method initializes a component. You must call this method before calling any other CookieStorage method.

Syntax

CookieStorage.InitStorage(*Heading*, *Key*, *ProgID*, *DateChanged*)

Parameters

Heading

A string to prepend to this cookie storage to ensure the uniqueness of the cookie on the client system.

Key

The name of the element to be used as a key to the cookie.

ProgID

The program identifier of the component to be used to store and retrieve data. This value must be `"Commerce.Dictionary"`.

DateChanged

The date on which the cookie was written or modified.

Applies To

CookieStorage

InsertData (*CookieStorage*)

The `InsertData` method creates a cookie on the client system and stores the information that you specify in the cookie.

Syntax

`CookieStorage.InsertData(Context, Data)`

Parameters

Context

The `Page` component's `Context` property, a read-only property that is initialized by the `Page` component when the `Page` is created.

Data

A `Dictionary` component initialized with the data to store on the client system.

Applies To

CookieStorage

LookupData (*CookieStorage*)

The `LookupData` method retrieves a single cookie containing the specified data from the client system and returns the cookie contents in a `Dictionary` component.

Syntax

`CookieStorage.LookupData(Context, Keys, Values)`

Parameters

Context

The Page component's Context property, a read-only property that is initialized by the Page component when the Page is created.

Keys

An array containing the key names to use as the basis for the lookup.

Values

An array containing the values that correspond to the key names to use as the basis for the lookup.

Remarks   The *Keys* and *Values* arrays that you pass to LookupData share an index-to-index relationship which means they must contain an identical number of members and that the value stored in *Value(N)* is searched for in the key specified by *Key(N)*.

Because the LookupData method returns only a single row of data, specifying column and value information that would result in the retrieval of more than one row results in an error. To retrieve multiple results, use the LookupMultipleData method.

Applies To

CookieStorage

See Also

LookupMultipleData (CookieStorage)

LookupMultipleData (CookieStorage)

The LookupMultipleData method retrieves multiple cookies from the client system and returns the cookies in a SimpleList of Dictionary components.

Syntax

CookieStorage.LookupMultipleData(*Context, Keys, Values*)

Parameters

Context

The Page component's Context property, a read-only property that is initialized by the Page component when the Page is created.

Keys

An array containing the key names to use as the basis for the lookup.

Values

An array containing the values that correspond to the key names to use as the basis for the lookup.

Remarks   As in the `LookupData` method, the *Keys* and *Values* parameters for `LookupMultipleData` are arrays that share an index-to-index relationship. Because `LookupMultipleData` is designed to retrieve multiple records, however, each element in the *Keys* array references keys in a distinct cookie, and each element of *Values* references the value to search for in the cookie key referenced by the corresponding *Key* element.

Applies To

`CookieStorage`

See Also

`LookupData (CookieStorage)`

The *DataFunctions* Component

The `DataFunctions` component supports a group of methods that convert string values to data types that can be properly inserted into a database or passed in an `OrderForm` to the order-processing pipeline (OPP).

The `DataFunctions` component supports the `Locale` property, which specifies the locale value to be used to format date, time, money and number values.

The `DataFunctions` component supports the methods listed in Table A.7.

Table A.7   *DataFunctions* component Methods

Methods	Description
`CleanString`	Processes a string, stripping out white spaces, modifying the case of the string, and validating that the length of the string falls within a given range
`ConvertDateString`	Returns a properly formatted date value based on a string representation of the date and on the specified locale
`ConvertTimeString`	Returns a properly formatted time value based on a string representation of the time and on the specified locale
`ConvertDateTimeString`	Returns a properly formatted date/time value based on a string representation of the date/time and on the specified locale
`ConvertFloatString`	Converts a string representation of a floating point number to a `Double Variant`.
`ConvertNumberString`	Returns a properly formatted number based on a string representation of that number and on the specified locale

continues

Table A.7   Continued

Methods	Description
ConvertMoneyStringToNumber	Returns a properly formatted monetary value based on a string representation of the money and on the specified locale
Date	Returns a string representation of the specified date, based on the specified locale
DateTime	Returns a string representation of the specified date/time value, based on the specified locale
Money	Returns a string representation of the specified monetary value, based on the specified locale
Time	Returns a string representation of the specified time value, based on the specified locale
ValidateDateTime	Checks the value of a date against a specified range
ValidateNumber	Checks the value of a number against a given range

Locale

The Locale property stores a number value that indicates the locale to be used by DataFunctions methods to format date, time, money and number information.

For a list of the numbers that you can store in this property, refer to "Hexadecimal Codes for Countries" earlier in this chapter.

The following code initializes the Locale property to the locale identifier for the United States:

```
DataFunctions.Locale = &H0409
```

Applies To

DataFunctions

CleanString

The CleanString method processes a string, stripping out white spaces, modifying the case of the string, and validating that the length of the string falls within a given range. If successful, CleanString returns the processed string.

Syntax

DataFunctions.CleanString(*String*, *MinLength*, *MaxLength*, *StripWhiteSpaces*, *StripReturn*, *Case*)

Parameters

String

The text of the string to process.

MinLength

An optional parameter that indicates the minimum length against which the length of *String* must be validated. The default value for this parameter is 0. If a value is specified and the string is shorter than the minimum length, CleanString returns FALSE.

MaxLength

An optional parameter that indicates the maximum number against which the length of *String* must be validated. The default value for this parameter is 65535. If a value is specified and the length of the string exceeds the specified maximum, CleanString returns FALSE.

StripWhiteSpaces

An optional Boolean value that indicates whether the white spaces should be stripped from the string. The default value is TRUE.

StripReturn

An optional Boolean value that indicates whether the carriage returns should be stripped from the string. The default value is TRUE.

Case

An optional value that indicates the case to which the string should be converted. The default value for this parameter is 0, which results in no modification to the case of the string. If *Case* is 1, the string is converted to uppercase. If *Case* is 2, the string is converted to lowercase.

Applies To

DataFunctions

ConvertDateString

The ConvertDateString method converts the specified string to a date, based on the specified locale, and returns the date.

Syntax

Page.ConvertDateString(*String, Locale*)

Parameters

String

A string representation of the date to convert.

Locale

An optional number representing the date locale. For a list of valid locale values, refer to "Hexadecimal Codes for Countries" earlier in this chapter.

If the *Locale* parameter is not specified, ConvertDateString uses the value stored in the DataFunctions component's Locale property.

Applies To

DataFunctions

See Also

ConvertTimeString, ConvertDateTimeString

ConvertDateTimeString

The ConvertDateTimeString method returns a date/time value from a string representation of that value, based on the specified locale.

Syntax

DataFunctions.ConvertDateTimeString(*DateTime, DateLocale, TimeLocale*)

Parameters

DateTime

A string that specifies the date/time value to format.

DateLocale

An optional parameter that specifies the locale to use to convert the date. For a list of valid locale values, refer to "Hexadecimal Codes for Countries" earlier in this chapter.

If the *Locale* parameter is not specified, the DataFunctions component's Locale property is used.

TimeLocale

An optional parameter that specifies the local to use to convert the time. For a list of valid locale values, refer to "Hexadecimal Codes for Countries" earlier in this chapter.

If the *Locale* parameter is not specified, ConvertDateTimeString uses the value of the Locale property.

Applies To

DataFunctions

See Also

ConvertDateString, ConvertTimeString

ConvertFloatString

The ConvertFloatString method converts a string expression of a floating-point number to a Double Variant, based on the specified locale. If successful, ConvertFloatString returns the Double Variant; otherwise, Null.

Syntax   *DataFunctions.**ConvertFloatString**(Float, Locale)*

Parameters

Float

A string expression of the number to convert.

Locale

Optional. This number specifies the locale to use to convert the string. For a list of valid locale values, see "Hexadecimal Codes for Countries." If this value is not specified, the value of the DataFunctions component's Locale parameter is used.

Applies To

DataFunctions

See Also

Float, ValidateFloat

ConvertMoneyStringToNumber

The ConvertMoneyStringToNumber converts the specified string as money, based on the specified locale, and returns the monetary value.

Syntax

DataFunctions.ConvertMoneyStringToNumber(*Money*, *Locale*)

Parameters

Money

A string representation of the money to convert.

Locale

An optional parameter that specifies the local to use to convert the money. For a list of valid locale values, refer to "Hexadecimal Codes for Countries" earlier in this chapter.

If the *Locale* parameter is not specified, ConvertMoneyStringToNumber uses the value of the Locale property.

Remarks   The ConvertMoneyStringToNumber method returns the monetary value time 100, based on the provided locale. Thus, given a value in dollars, ConvertMoneyStringToNumber returns the number of cents in the dollar value.

Applies To

DataFunctions

See Also

ConvertFloatString, ConvertNumberString

ConvertNumberString

The ConvertNumberString method returns an appropriately formatted number, based on a string representation of an integer and on the specified locale.

Syntax

DataFunctions.ConvertNumberString(*Number, Locale*)

Parameters

Number

A string representation of the number to convert.

Locale

An optional parameter that specifies the local to use to convert the number. For a list of valid locale values, refer to "Hexadecimal Codes for Countries" earlier in this chapter.

If the *Locale* parameter is not used, ConvertNumberString uses the value of the Locale property.

Remarks   The ConvertNumberString method is designed to accept only integers. Passing a floating-point number as the *Number* parameter results in an error. To convert floating-point numbers, use ConvertFloatString.

Example   The following example uses ConvertNumberString to convert 123,000 from a string to a number:

StrNum = "123,000"

NNum = DataFunctions.ConvertNumberString(StrNum)

In this example, the call to ConvertNumberString returns the following value:

123000

Applies To

DataFunctions

See Also

ConvertFloatString, ConvertMoneyStringToNumber

ConvertTimeString

The ConvertTimeString method returns a time value from a string representation of the time, based on the specified locale.

Syntax

DataFunctions.ConvertTimeString(*Time, Locale*)

Parameters

Time

A string that specifies the time to convert.

Locale

An optional parameter that specifies the local to use to convert the time. For a list of valid locale values, refer to "Hexadecimal Codes for Countries" earlier in this chapter.

If the *Locale* parameter is not specified, ConverTimeString uses the value of the DataFunction's Locale property.

Example   The following example converts the provided time value and outputs the value to the page:

```
<% Time = DataFunctions.ConvertTimeString("3:30PM") %>
<% =Hour(Time)%>
<%=Minute(Time)%>
<%=Second(Time)%>
```

Applies To

DataFunctions

See Also

ConvertDateString, ConvertDateTimeString

Date

The Date method returns the provided date value as a string, based on the specified locale.

Syntax

DataFunctions.Date(*Date*, *Locale*)

Parameters

Date

The date to format.

Locale

An optional number that specifies the locale to use to convert the date to a string. For a list of valid locale values, refer to "Hexadecimal Codes for Countries" earlier in this chapter.

If the *Locale* parameter is not specified, the Date method uses the value stored in the DataFunctions component's Locale property.

Applies To

DataFunctions

See Also

DateTime, ConvertDateString

DateTime

The `DateTime` method returns the provided date/time value as a string, based on the specified locale.

Syntax

`DataFunctions.DateTime(DateTime, Locale)`

Parameters

`DateTime`

The date/time value to format.

`Locale`

An optional hexadecimal number representing the date locale. For a list of valid locale values, refer to "Hexadecimal Codes for Countries" earlier in this chapter. If this value is unspecified, the `Date` method uses the `DataFunctions` component's `Locale` property.

Remarks

If the `Locale` parameter is not used, the `DateTime` method uses the values stored in the `DataFunctions` component's `Locale` property.

Applies To

`DataFunctions`

See Also

`Date, Time, ConvertDateTimeString`

Float

The `Float` method returns the specified floating-point number as a string, based on the specified locale.

Syntax

`DataFunctions.Float(Float, Locale)`

Parameters

`Float`

The floating-point number to convert.

`Locale`

An optional number identifying the locale to be used to perform the conversion. For a list of these values, refer to "Hexadecimal Codes for Countries" earlier in this chapter. If this value is unspecified, the `DataFunctions` component's `Locale` property is used as the basis for the conversion.

Applies To

DataFunctions

See Also

ConvertFloatString

Money

The Money method returns the specified money value as a string, based on the provided locale.

Syntax

DataFunctions.Money(*Money*, *Locale*)

Parameters

Money

The money value to convert to a string.

Locale

An optional hexadecimal number representing the locale to be used to convert the money. For a list of valid locale values, refer to "Hexadecimal Codes for Countries" earlier in this chapter.

If the *Locale* parameter is not used, the Money method uses the value stored in the DataFunctions component's Locale property.

Applies To

DataFunctions

See Also

ConvertMoneyStringToNumber

Time

The Time method returns the specified time value as a string, based on the specified locale.

Syntax

DataFunctions.Time(*Time*, *Locale*)

Parameters

Time

The time value to convert.

Locale

An optional number value representing the locale to use to convert the time. For a list of these values, refer to "Hexadecimal Codes for Countries" earlier in this chapter.

If the *Locale* parameter is not used, the Time method uses the value stored in the DataFunctions component's Locale property.

Applies To

DataFunctions

See Also

ConvertTimeString

ValidateDate

The ValidateDate method tests a date value against a specified range.

Syntax

DataFunctions.ValidateDate(*Date, LowDate, HighDate*)

Parameters

Date

The date to test against the provided range.

LowDate

An optional date parameter that specifies the low end of the date range.

HighDate

An optional date parameter that specifies the high end of the date range.

Remarks   If the specified value is within the provided date range, ValidateDate returns TRUE; otherwise, it returns FALSE. If no date range is specified, ValidateDate returns TRUE.

Applies To

DataFunctions

See Also

ValidateNumber

ValidateFloat

The ValidateFloat method tests a floating-point number against a specified numerical range.

Syntax

DataFunctions.ValidateFloat(*Value, MinimumValue, MaximumValue*)

Parameters

Value

The floating-point number to validate.

MinimumValue

The low end of the range.

MaximumValue

The high end of the range.

Remarks   The `ValidateFloat` method returns `FALSE` if the number is not in the given range; otherwise, it returns TRUE. If the *MinimumValue* and *MaximumValue* parameters are not used, `ValidateFloat` returns TRUE.

Applies To

DataFunctions

See Also

ValidateNumber

ValidateNumber

The `ValidateNumber` method tests the value of a number against a specified numerical range and returns a Boolean value that indicates the results of the test.

Syntax

DataFunctions.ValidateNumber(*Value, MinimumValue, MaximumValue*)

Parameters

Value

The value to compare with the low and high ends of the specified range.

MinimumValue

The low end of the range.

MaximumValue

The high end of the range.

Remarks   The `ValidateNumber` method returns `FALSE` if the number is not in the given range; otherwise, it returns TRUE. If the *MinimumValue* and *MaximumValue* parameters are not used, `ValidateNumber` returns TRUE.

Applies To

DataFunctions

See Also

ValidateDate

The *Datasource* Component

The `Datasource` component executes queries against a system or file DSN and, where appropriate, returns query results in a `SimpleList` of `Dictionary` components. The queries that you execute can be SQL statements declared as string variables in the page in which you execute the query or query variables cached in a Content component.

You do not use the IIS 3.0 Server object's CreateObject method to create a Datasource component. Instead, you use the Content component's Content or Datasource method, which creates the component based on the DSN variable that is cached by the Content component. When you create a Datasource component, the Datasource has access to the Content component's cache of queries.

For more information on the Content component, refer to "The Content Component" earlier in this chapter.

The Datasource component supports the Execute method, which executes the specified query against a data source and, where appropriate, returns the results in a SimpleList of Dictionary components.

Overview

Although you can use the Datasource component to perform any operation that you need to perform on your store database, Commerce Server stores generally use this component in two contexts:

- To execute queries that retrieve product information for display on a page
- To retrieve product information for storage in an OrderForm

Creating a *Datasource* Component

Use the Content component's Content or Datasource method to create a Datasource component, based on a DSN variable that you previously stored in the Content component's cache.

The following example, from the AdventureWorks sample store, illustrates the creation of both a Content and a Datasource component (this code appears in the AdventureWorks global.asa file, in the Shop directory):

```
REM Create a Content component for access to the database
Set  MSCSContent = Server.CreateObject("Commerce.Content")
Call MSCSContent.AddDataSource("AW", MSCSDSN, 1, 0)
Set  MSCSDatasource = MSCSContent.Datasource("AW")
```

Executing a Query

After using the Content component's Content or Datasource method to create a Datasource component, call the Datasource component's Execute method to execute a query. The query that you execute can be a query variable added to the Content component through its AddQuery method or the text of an SQL query.

The following sample code illustrates both methods:

```
<%

Set Content = Server.CreateObject("Commerce.Content")
```

```
 ' Add a single data source.

Content.AddDatasource("clockped", "DSN=arnoldb1;UID=sa;PWD=;DATABASE=eshop",
➥1, 0)

 ' Add a query.

Content.AddQuery("get_products", "SELECT * FROM Products")

Set Datasource = Content.Datasource("clockped")

' Call execute

Set RS = Datasource.Execute("get_products")

' Or
' Set RS = DataSource.Execute("SELECT * FROM Products")

%>
```

Using Parameterized Queries

In a *parameterized* query, the SQL query statement contains *parameter markers* that indicate search values that are supplied at runtime to the Datasource component's Execute method. For parameterized queries added to the Content component, a colon, followed by a number that designates the parameter's place in the parameter list, serves as the parameter marker. Optionally, you can use the question mark (?) as a parameter marker.

Where a parameterized query contains only one parameter marker, for example, this number is 1, as follows:

```
Call MSCSContent.AddQuery("receipts-for-shopper", "select shopper_id, order_id,
➥date_entered, total, status, marshalled_receipt from AW_receipt where shopper_id
➥= :1 order by date_entered")
```

In the following example, three parameter markers appear in the query, indicating that three values will be supplied at runtime and bound to the SQL statement:

```
Call MSCSContent.AddQuery("variant-sku", "select sku from AW_product_variant
➥where pf_id = :1 and (color_value = :2 or color_value is null or color_value='')
➥and (size_value = :3 or size_value is null or size_value='')")
```

The values to substitute for the parameter markers are supplied at runtime as an optional parameter list to the Datasource component's Execute method. The following call to Execute runs the preceding query and returns the first row in the query's results set:

```
Set productsku = DataSource.Execute("variant-sku", Cstr(Request("attr_1")),
➥Cstr(Request("attr_2")), Cstr(Request("attr_3")))(0)
```

If the number of parameter values supplied to Execute does not match the number of parameter markers in the SQL query, Execute generates an error.

Navigating the Results of a Query

When the Execute method is used to execute a SQL SELECT query against a data source, Execute returns the results of the query in a SimpleList of Dictionary components. You can navigate the results set by using the VBScript For Each statement to iterate through the SimpleList, or you can use an index to reference the Dictionary members of the SimpleList.

The following example, from the AdventureWorks store, illustrates the first method, using a For Each statement to read each member of the SimpleList into a Dictionary, and then using the Page component's Option method to display the sizes for an item:

```
<% set sizes = Datasource.Execute("sizes-for-family", Cstr(Request("pf_id"))) %>
<SELECT NAME="attr_3" size="1">
<% for each row_sizes in sizes %>
<% = Page.Option(row_sizes.size_value, "") %>
<% = Page.Encode(row_sizes.size_value) %>
<% next %>
</SELECT>
```

In the preceding group of statements, each iteration through the sizes SimpleList stores the current record in the row_sizes Dictionary. The value that appears to the right of the Dictionary's dot (.) operator references a column name in the queried table.

The following example performs the same operation as the preceding one but uses an index to iterate the SimpleList that contains the results set. In this example, the SimpleList acts as an array, and the SimpleList's Count property indicates the array's upper bound:

```
<% set sizes = Datasource.Execute("sizes-for-family", CStr(Request("pf_id")))%>
<SELECT NAME="attr_3" size="1">
<% for I = 0 to sizes.Count %>
<% = Page.Option(sizes(I).size_value, "")%>
<%=Page.Encode(sizes(I).size_value)%>
<% next %>
</SELECT>
```

If you are interested in retrieving only a single row in a result set, you can follow the call to Execute with a number value that indicates the SimpleList index that you want to retrieve, as follows:

```
<% set sizes = Datasource.Execute("sizes-for-family",
➥CStr(Request("pf_id")))(0)%>
```

For more information on SimpleList and Dictionary, refer to "The SimpleList and Dictionary Components" earlier in this chapter.

N O T E If the Dictionary element that stores a column value contains a Null value, that Dictionary entry is deleted. For this reason, a For Each iteration through a SimpleList of Dictionary components moves to the next non-Null value. When this situation occurs, the only way to retrieve the column name that contains the Null value is to index into the SimpleList and to reference the Dictionary key by name. ▪

Execute

The Execute method executes the specified query and returns the results of the query, if any, in a SimpleList of Dictionary components.

Syntax

```
Datasource.Execute(SQL, Parameters)
```

Parameters

SQL

The string resource identifier of a query added to a Content component through a previous call to AddQuery, or the SQL text of the query.

Parameters

One or more parameters to bind to the parameter markers in *SQL*.

Example   For an example of how to call the Execute method, see "Executing a Query." For examples of how to navigate the SimpleList of Dictionary components returned by the Execute method when a SQL SELECT statement is executed, see "Navigating the Results of a Query."

Applies To

Datasource

See Also

Datasource, AddQuery

The *DBStorage* Component

The DBStorage component provides for the easy management of routine store tasks, such as the retrieval, storage, and updating of order and shopper data.

Although the DBStorage component, like the Datasource component, interacts with the store's database-management system (DBMS), it fills a fundamentally different role within a store. The Datasource component typically is used for the general management of inventory data. In the Commerce Server sample stores, for example, product pages are populated by using the Datasource component to execute queries cached in the store's Content component. The Content component, as its name indicates, associates string variables with queries designed to manage store content.

The DBStorage component, on the other hand, generally is used to manage purchase and receipt data, reading such data out of OrderForm and Dictionary components that are initialized at runtime, and writing the data to the underlying database storage.

The DBStorage component supports the Mapping property, which maps a variable name to any entry in the OrderForm or Dictionary that DBStorage uses to insert and retrieve data.

The DBStorage component supports the methods listed in Table A.8.

Table A.8   *DBStorage* component Methods

Method	Description
CommitData	Updates a record in the data source to new values
DeleteData	Deletes specified data from the data source
DeleteDataKey	Deletes one or more elements based on the specified key value
GetData	Returns the data that you specify
InsertData	Inserts the data that you specify
InitStorage	Initializes the DBStorage component
LookupData	Returns a single record based on keys and values that you specify

Overview

The DBStorage and CookieStorage components support the management of shopper and receipt data for Commerce Server stores. Although the CookieStorage component can be used to store shopper data on the shopper's system, CookieStorage should never be used to store order or receipt information on the client system.

In the Commerce Server sample stores, which are included on the Commerce Server compact disc, the DBStorage component is used to store shopper, order, and receipt data. The following example, from the MS Press store, illustrates how DBStorage components are created and used in the routine operations of the store.

In the MS Press store's global.asa file, the store creates an applicationwide DBStorage component instance for its order, purchase, and shopper data. The DBStorage component that is created to temporarily store order data is the store's *orderform storage*. The component created for shopper data represents the store's *shopper storage*, and the receipt component represents the store's *receipt storage*.

Because these components are created on a per-application basis and are stored as IIS 3.0 Application object variables, they are created in the store's global.asa file, and the Application variables "MSCSOrderFormStorage", "MSCSShopperStorage", and "MSCSReceiptStorage" are set to reference these component instances, as follows:

```
REM  Create a Storage component for the shopper information
Set  MSCSShopperStorage = Server.CreateObject("Commerce.DBStorage")
Call MSCSShopperStorage.InitStorage(MSCSDatasource, "MSPress_shopper",
"shopper_id", "Commerce.Dictionary")

REM  Create a storage component for the order forms
Set  MSCSOrderFormStorage = Server.CreateObject("Commerce.DBStorage")
Call MSCSOrderFormStorage.InitStorage(MSCSDatasource, "MSPress_basket",
"shopper_id","Commerce.OrderForm","marshalled_order", "date_changed")
```

```
REM Create a storage component for receipts
Set MSCSReceiptStorage = Server.CreateObject("Commerce.DBStorage")
 call MSCSReceiptStorage.InitStorage(MSCSDatasource, "MSPress_receipt",
➥"order_id","Commerce.OrderForm", "marshalled_receipt", "date_entered")
MSCSReceiptStorage.Mapping.Value("_total_total") = "total"

' Later in global.asa
' Set up the Application intrinsic object
Application.Lock
        Set Application("MSCSOrderFormStorage") = MSCSOrderFormStorage
        Set Application("MSCSShopperStorage")   = MSCSShopperStorage
        Set Application("MSCSReceiptStorage")   = MSCSReceiptStorage
Application.Unlock
```

When a shopper visits the MS Press store, the store attempts to retrieve the shopper's shopper ID—a globally unique identifier that was assigned to this shopper during a previous visit to the store. If unable to retrieve this ID, the ShopperManager for MS Press creates an ID for the shopper, and that ID is ultimately committed to shopper storage.

If the shopper elects to add one or more of the books featured by MS Press to his or her shopping basket, the shopper's shopper ID, as well as purchased-item information, is added to an OrderForm, and the contents of that OrderForm are committed to the orderform storage. At any time during the session, should the shopper want to view the contents of the shopping basket, the contents of the shopper's orderform storage are read into an OrderForm, and the OrderForm contents are output to the page.

At the conclusion of a shopping session, if the shopper chooses to finalize the purchase of the selected items, the contents of the shopper's orderform storage are read into an OrderForm component, and this component is passed to the order-processing pipeline (OPP). After processing the purchase, the OPP writes the order information read from the OrderForm into the store's receipt storage, and the store deletes the information for this session from the orderform storage.

Creating and Initializing a *DBStorage* Component

Use the IIS 3.0 Server object's CreateObject method to create a DBStorage component, as follows:

```
Set Storage = Server.CreateObject("Commerce.DBStorage")
```

This function call returns an uninitialized instance of a DBStorage component. Use the InitStorage method to initialize the returned component instance, as follows:

```
Storage.InitStorage(MMDatasource, "mx_receipt1", "order_id",
➥"Commerce.Dictionary", "marshalled_receipt", "date_changed")
```

The parameters to InitStorage specify the following items of information:

- A Datasource component that you created with the Content component's AddDatasource method and that you retrieve by using the Content component's Datasource method.
- The name of the table in the referenced data source.

■ A key into that table, which is the column name that the DBStorage component uses to key into the table to perform routine tasks such as data insertion and retrieval. This variable should identify the primary key into the underlying table.

■ The program identifier of the component that you use to pass data to and retrieve data from DBStorage methods. This component must be an OrderForm or Dictionary component.

■ The name of a column for this DBStorage component instance to use for marshaling data. For more information on the marshaling column, see "InitStorage."

Attempting to call any other DBStorage method before calling InitStorage results in an error.

CommitData (DBStorage)

The CommitData method updates one or more records in the database storage.

Syntax

```
DBStorage.CommitData(Context, Data)
```

Parameters

Context

The Page component's Context property, a read-only property that is initialized by the Page component when the Page is created.

Data

A component initialized with the updated data. This component can be either an OrderForm or a Dictionary, but it must correspond to the component type specified as the program identifier in the initial call to InitStorage.

Example   The following example, from the AdventureWorks store, uses the Datasource component's Execute method to retrieve information from a database table, initializes an OrderForm to contain that information, and uses CommitData to write that OrderForm to storage:

```
REM -- add item to order form:
set productsku = DataSource.Execute("variant-sku", Cstr(Request("attr_1")),
➥Cstr(Request("attr_2")), Cstr(Request("attr_3")))(0)

sku = productsku.sku
set product = DataSource.Execute("product-purchase", CStr(sku))(0)

set item = orderForm.AddItem(sku, product_qty, product.list_price)
item.pf_name = product.pf_name
item.list_price = product.list_price
item.quantity = product_qty
item.color_value = product.color_value
item.size_value = product.size_value

REM -- commit order form back to storage:
call orderFormStorage.CommitData(ctx, orderForm)
```

Applies To

DBStorage

See Also

InitStorage (DBStorage), InsertData (DBStorage)

DeleteData (DBStorage)

The DeleteData method deletes data from a DBStorage component.

Syntax

DBStorage.DeleteData(*Context*, *Data)*

Parameters

Context

The Page component's Context property, a read-only property that is initialized by the Page component when the Page is created.

Data

A component initialized with the data to delete. This component can be either an OrderForm or a Dictionary, but it must correspond in type to the component type specified as the program identifier in the initial call to InitStorage.

Example   The following example, from the AdventureWorks store, appears in the OrderFormPurchase utility function in xt_orderform_purchase.asp. This user-defined routine, which is called after a purchase has been written by the OPP to receipt storage, uses DeleteData to delete the purchase data from orderform storage. The result is that should the user return to basket.asp, which reads from orderform storage to display the contents of the shopper's basket, the basket would be empty.

```
REM -- retrieve order form from storage:
on error resume next
set orderForm = orderFormStorage.GetData(ctx, shopperID)
on error goto 0
if IsEmpty(orderForm) then
    OrderFormPurchase = null
    exit function
end if

REM -- retrieve args from form:
success = OrderFormPurchaseArgs(orderForm)
if not success then
    OrderFormPurchase = null
    exit function
end if

REM -- commit:
call orderFormStorage.CommitData(ctx, orderForm)
```

```
REM -- purchase:
call page.RunPurchase(orderForm)

if orderForm.[_Basket_Errors].Count > 0 then
    REM show basket errors
    Response.redirect Page.URL("basket_errors.asp")
end if

if orderForm.[_Purchase_Errors].Count > 0 then
    for each item in orderForm.[_Purchase_Errors]
        errorStr = errorStr & "<LI>" & item
    next
Response.redirect page.URL("error.asp", "error", errorStr)
end if

order_id = orderForm.order_id

REM -- clear out basket:
call orderFormStorage.DeleteData(ctx, orderForm)
```

Applies To

DBStorage

See Also

InsertData (DBStorage)

DeleteDataKey (*DBStorage*)

The DeleteDataKey method deletes the data corresponding to the specified key.

Syntax

DBStorage.DeleteDataKey(*Context, Key*)

Parameters

Context

The Page component's Context property, a read-only property that is initialized by the Page component when the Page is created.

Key

The key value for the row to be deleted.

Remarks   The DeleteDataKey method differs from the DeleteData method in that the former requires only the value stored in the underlying table's key column. This column is specified as the key to the underlying table through a previous call to InitStorage.

Thus, if you specify an IDENTITY field in an SQL table as the key into the data source, you could delete all the columns for a specified row simply by providing the appropriate counter value. Alternatively, you could initialize a Dictionary component to the values stored in one or more columns and pass this initialized component to DeleteData.

Applies To

DBStorage

See Also

DeleteData (DBStorage)

GetData (*DBStorage*)

The GetData method retrieves the specified data from a DBStorage component and returns the data in an OrderForm or Dictionary component.

Syntax

DBStorage.GetData(*Context, Data*)

Parameters

Context

The Page component's Context property, a read-only property that is initialized by the Page component when the Page is created.

Data

A component initialized with the data to retrieve. This component can be either an OrderForm or a Dictionary, but it must correspond in type to the component type specified as the program identifier in the initial call to InitStorage.

Applies To

DBStorage

See Also

InitStorage (DBStorage), LookupData (DBStorage)

InitStorage (*DBStorage*)

The InitStorage method initializes a DBStorage component. You must call this method immediately after component creation and before calling any other DBStorage component methods.

Syntax

DBStorage.InitStorage(*Datasource, Table, Key, ProgID, MarshalColumn, DateChanged*)

Parameters

Datasource

A data source added to a Content component through a previous call to the Content component's AddDatasource method.

Table

The table within the data source.

Key

The column name that the DBStorage object uses as a key into the database table.

ProgID

The component in which data passed to or retrieved by DBStorage methods is stored. This parameter can be Commerce.Dictionary or Commerce.OrderForm.

MarshalColumn

A column that stores data for which no appropriate column exists in the data-source table. For more information on the MarshalColumn parameter, see the following "Remarks" section.

DateChanged

The date on which the change was made.

Applies To

DBStorage

Remarks   The InitStorage method initializes a data source for use by a Commerce Server component. The data source that you specify in InitStorage's *Datasource* parameter must be one that you added to a Content component by using AddDatasource and that you retrieved using the Content component's Datasource method.

The *ProgID* parameter references the component that is used to store the data that you pass to the DBStorage component's GetData, InsertData, and CommitData methods.

The *Keyname* parameter references a column in the table referenced by *Table* that the DBStorage component uses to key into the data source table. You should configure this column at table creation to store only unique values.

The *MarshalColumn* parameter is used to store data that does not appropriately belong in any other column in the data-source table. Should you specify "my_column" as the column in which you want to store data, and no such column exists, the value that you specify for that column is stored in the column that you specify as your marshaling column.

Example   The following example illustrates how to create and initialize a DBStorage component:

```
REM Create a Content component for access to the database

Set MSCSContent = Server.CreateObject("Commerce.Content")
Call MSCSContent.AddDataSource("AW", MSCSDSN)

REM Use the Datasource method to retrieve the Datasource component.

Set MSCSDatasource = MSCSContent.Datasource("AW")

REM Create a Storage component for the order form information

Set MSCSOrderFormStorage = Server.CreateObject("Commerce.DBStorage")
```

```
Call MSCSOrderFormStorage InitStorage(MSCSDatasource, "AW_basket", "shopper_id",
➥"Commerce.OrderForm", "marshalled_order", "date_changed")
```

See Also

Content, Datasource

InsertData (*DBStorage*)

The InsertData method inserts data into the database storage.

Syntax

DBStorage.InsertData(*Context*, *Data*)

Parameters

Context

The Page component's Context property.

Data

A component that contains the data to insert. The type of this component corresponds to the component type specified as the program identifier in the initial call to InitStorage.

Applies To

DBStorage

Example   The following example creates and initializes a Dictionary component to a set of values and then inserts the component's data into a database table:

```
<% Set Dictionary = Server.CreateObject("Commerce.Dictionary")
Dictionary.order_id = shopperID
Dictionary.shopper_id = shopperID
Dictionary.status = 5
call MSCSReceiptStorage.InsertData(Page.Context, Dictionary)
%>
```

See Also

InitStorage (DBStorage), CommitData (DBStorage)

LookupData (*DBStorage*)

The LookupData method retrieves a single row from the data source based on column names and values that you specify, and returns the results of the operation in a Dictionary component.

Syntax

DBStorage.LookupData(*Context*, *Column*, *Value*)

Parameters

Context

The Page component's Context property.

Column

An array containing the column names that you want to query.

Value

An array containing the values that you want to query.

Remarks   The *Column* and *Value* arrays that you pass to LookupData share an index-to-index relationship which means they must contain an identical number of members and that the value stored in *Value(N)* is searched for in the column specified by *Column(N)*.

Because the LookupData method returns only a single row of data, specifying column and value information that would result in the retrieval of more than one row results in an error.

Example   The following example uses two arrays to store column names and values, and passes these arrays to LookupData:

```
Column(0) = "shopper_id"
Value(0) = "23234"

Set Obj = Storage.LookupData(Page.Context, Column, Value)
```

Applies To

DBStorage.LookupMultipleData (DBStorage)

The LookupMultipleData method retrieves multiple results from the database table and returns these results in a SimpleList of Dictionary components.

Syntax

DBStorage.LookupMultipleData(*Context*, *Column*, *Values*)

Parameters

Context

The Page component's Context property, a read-only property that references the Internet Information Server (IIS) 3.0 scripting context and is initialized by the Page component during Page creation.

Column

An array containing the columns to query for the specified values.

Values

An array containing the values that correspond to the column names to use as the basis for the lookup.

Remarks   The *Column* and *Value* arrays that you pass to LookupMultipleData share an index-to-index relationship which means they must contain an identical number of members and that the value stored in *Value(N)* is searched for in the column specified by *Column(N)*. If the number of elements in *Column* does not equate to the number of values in *Value*, LookupMultipleData returns Null.

Applies To

DBStorage

See Also

LookupData (DBStorage)

The *MessageManager* Component

The MessageManager component provides for the storage and retrieval of language-specific messages that are used by the order-processing pipeline (OPP) to return errors generated during OrderForm processing.

The MessageManager component supports the DefaultLanguage property, which specifies the default language for the MessageManager.

The MessageManager component supports the methods listed in Table A.9.

Table A.9 *MessageManager* **component Methods**

Method	Description
AddLanguage	Adds a new language to the MessageManager
AddMessage	Adds a new message to the MessageManager
GetLocale	Returns the locale for the specified language
GetMessage	Returns the message associated with the specified string identifier

Overview

The MessageManager component is a cache that stores the messages that notify shoppers and store builders of error conditions that occur in order-processing-pipeline (OPP) components. Typically, the MessageManager component for a store is created in a store's global.asa file. A reference to the MessageManager for your store must be stored in the application-level "MSCSMessageManager" variable.

After you create a MessageManager component, you add languages to that component and then add messages that you associate with those languages. The addition of a language simply associates a string identifier with a hexadecimal code that identifies the language's locale. For a list of these codes, refer to "Hexadecimal Codes for Countries" earlier in this chapter.

Each message that you add to the MessageManager is associated with a language and identified by a string identifier. The name that identifies a message is hard-coded and depends on the message names that a given order-processing-pipeline (OPP) component expects to find in your MessageManager. For a list of the messages that you define for the default implementation of the OPP, see "The MessageManager and the Order-Processing Pipeline (OPP)" later in this chapter.

The string value that you associate with these hard-coded variable names can depend on a host of factors, including the store's locale and the cultural context that the store represents. Thus, a store that sells custom-tailored suits might initialize MessageManager variables to strings that represent standard American English usage, whereas a surfing-equipment shop might incorporate the slang usage typically associated with the surfer community.

N O T E   If you create a custom OPP component, you can define any message that the component is
programmed to retrieve from the MessageManager. You can add a message called
"wipeout" to your MessageManager, for example, provided that your OPP component knows that a
message called "wipeout" exists.

The *MessageManager* and the Order-Processing Pipeline (OPP)

The MessageManager's interaction with the OPP begins when a Page component method, such as RunPlan or RunPurchase, invokes the OPP on an OrderForm. As the OrderForm passes through each stage of the OPP, the OPP may encounter errors in the OrderForm. For example, when the price for an item listed in the OrderForm differs from the actual price for the referenced item, the OPP updates the price, and any other dependent OrderForm fields, such as the subtotal.

The OPP component in which the discrepancy was encountered typically is designed to associate a specific MessageManager message variable with this error condition. In such a case, the OPP uses the pipeline context to identify the MessageManager component instance associated with the "MSCSMessageManager" Application object variable and uses that MessageManager component to retrieve the message value associated with the appropriate message variable. Finally, the OPP writes the text of the error to the OrderForm's _Basket_Errors_ or _Purchase_Errors_ member.

Table A.10 lists the MessageManager messages that are used by the default implementation of the OPP and identifies the components that use these messages.

Table A.10 *MessageManager* Default Messages

Message...	Used by Component...	Under This Condition
pur_badplacedprice	RequiredItemAdjust	The price of an item does not correspond to the price contained in the OrderForm
pur_badhandling	RequiredHandling	The handling cost for an order cannot be computed
pur_badpayment	RequiredPayment	Credit-card information cannot be authorized
pur_badshopper	DefaultShopperInfo	The OrderForm does not identify a shopper

Message...	Used by Component...	Under This Condition
pur_badshipping	RequiredHandling	The shipping for an order cannot be computed
pur_badsku	RequiredProdInfo	An SKU in the OrderForm references an item that is not contained in the store's inventory
pur_badtax	RequiredTax	The tax on a purchase cannot be computed
pur_badverify	RequiredTotal	The data in an OrderForm has changed, requiring review by the shopper
pur_noitems	RequiredOrderCheck	The OPP has passed an empty OrderForm
pur_out_of_stock	FlagInventory, LocalInventory	An item referenced in the OrderForm is out of stock

AddLanguage

The AddLanguage method adds a new language/message set to the MessageManager.

Syntax

MessageManager.AddLanguage(*Language*, *Locale*)

Parameters

Language

A string identifier for the language/message set to add to the MessageManager.

Locale

A number that uniquely identifies the locale to associate with the added language. For a list of possible values for this parameter, refer to "Hexadecimal Codes for Countries" earlier in this chapter.

Remarks   The AddLanguage method adds a user-identified language to the MessageManager and associates that language with a system-defined locale. In subsequent calls to MessageManager component methods, the caller needs to identify the language but does not need to identify the locale.

Because the language name that you pass to AddLanguage is a string identifier that you choose, any number of languages can be associated with a single locale.

Example   The following example, from the AdventureWorks store, adds a language called "USA" to the MessageManager and uses the MessageManager's DefaultLanguage property to make the added language the default language for the store:

```
Call MSCSMessageManager.AddLanguage("usa", &H0409)
MessageManager.defaultLanguage = "usa"
```

Applies To

MessageManager

See Also

AddMessage, DefaultLanguage, GetMessage

AddMessage

The AddMessage method adds a message to the MessageManager.

Syntax

MessageManager.AddMessage (*Name*, *Value*, *Language*)

Parameters

Name

A string that identifies the message to add. This name must be known to the order-processing-pipeline (OPP) component that uses the message to identify an error condition.

Value

The text of the message to add.

Language

An optional parameter that designates the string resource identifier of the language with which to associate the message. This value, if specified, should designate a language added through a previous call to AddLanguage. If this value is not supplied, the language specified in the MessageManager's DefaultLanguage property is used.

Remarks   The *Language* part of the AddMessage method identifies a language identifier added to this MessageManager through a previous call to AddLanguage.

Example   The following example, from the AdventureWorks sample store, adds the pur_badpayment message to the MessageManager. The message associated with pur_badpayment is inserted into the _Purchase_Errors_ collection in the OrderForm if a customer provides invalid credit-card information:

```
Call MSCSMessageManager.AddMessage("pur_badpayment", "There was a problem
authorizing your credit.  Please verify your payment information or use a
different card.", "usa")
```

Applies To

MessageManager

See Also

GetMessage

GetLocale

The GetLocale method returns a hexadecimal number that identifies the locale for the specified language.

Syntax

MessageManager.GetLocale(*Language*)

Parameter

Language

The string identifier of the language for which you want to retrieve the locale. This identifier references a language that you added to the MessageManager through a previous call to AddLanguage.

The *Language* parameter is optional. If the language is not specified, GetLocale returns the locale for the default language for the message set.

Remarks   Like GetMessage, GetLocale typically is not called from within a store. Instead, GetLocale is used by the order-processing pipeline (OPP) to retrieve the locale for a message describing an error that the OPP encountered during a purchase.

Applies To

MessageManager

See Also

AddLanguage, DefaultLanguage, GetMessage

GetMessage

The GetMessage method returns the value of the specified message.

Syntax

MessageManager.GetMessage(*Name*, *Language*)

Parameters

Name

The name of the message to return which is the name associated with this message when it was added to the MessageManager through a call to AddMessage.

Language

The string name of the language with which the message is associated. This string specifies a language that was added to the MessageManager through a previous call to AddLanguage.

Remarks   The GetMessage method is seldom called from within a store. Instead, this method is used by order-processing-pipeline (OPP) components to retrieve messages describing errors that occur during the purchase process.

Applies To

MessageManager

See Also

GetLocale

DefaultLanguage

Use the DefaultLanguage property to specify the default language for the MessageManager. When you use AddMessage to add messages to the MessageManager and do not specify a language for those messages, they are associated with the language specified in this property.

The DefaultLanguage property is initialized in the global.asa file as follows, where "usa" references a language that has been added to the MessageManager by means of the AddLanguage method:

```
MessageManager.DefaultLanguage = "usa"
```

The *OrderForm* Component

The OrderForm component provides for the in-memory storage of shopper and purchase information. Commerce Server stores use the OrderForm component to store the items that a shopper chooses to purchase and to store receipt information that reflects a given shopper's purchase history.

The OrderForm component supports the methods listed in Table A.11.

Table A.11   *OrderForm* **Component Methods**

Method	Description
AddItem	Adds an item to the OrderForm
ClearOrderForm	Empties the OrderForm
ClearItems	Clears the *Items* collection from the OrderForm

Overview

The OrderForm component is defined internally as a structured group of SimpleList and Dictionary components, and includes the methods required to add items, clear items, and clear the entire OrderForm itself.

The base of the OrderForm component is a Dictionary component that contains information describing the entire order. This information includes shopper information (such as the shopper's shopper ID, name, and address), as well as order cost information (such as purchase subtotal, tax, shipping and total).

Several elements of the OrderForm's base Dictionary component include underscore characters. The appearance of an underscore character in an element name indicates that these items are not saved to the store's orderform storage. These elements are saved instead to the store's receipt storage when the purchase is finalized.

The *OrderForm* and *DBStorage*

Typically, an OrderForm component is created on a per-page basis and reflects the contents of the *orderform storage* which is a DBStorage component that you create in a store's global.asa file and assign to the Application-level MSCSOrderFormStorage variable. As shoppers add items to or remove items from their shopping baskets, these items are written to the orderform storage. When a shopper wants to view basket items, these items are read from the orderform storage into an OrderForm component and from the OrderForm component to a page that displays basket contents to the shopper.

The Clock Peddler store illustrates the OrderForm/storage interaction outlined in the preceding paragraph. When a Clock Peddler customer places an item in the shopping basket, the Clock Peddler calls OrderFormAddItem, a utility function defined by the Clock Peddler in xt_orderform_additem.asp. This routine retrieves from storage all items associated with the current shopper's shopper ID and loads these items into an OrderForm component. These items include all the items that the shopper has added to his or her basket during the current shopping session or a previous session, but not items that the shopper has actually purchased. The additional items that the shopper wants to purchase are also added to the OrderForm component, and this component is committed to the orderform storage.

The shopper is then redirected to basket.asp, which reads the orderform-storage information for this shopper into an OrderForm component and then reads the contents of that OrderForm to the page to display the current contents of the shopper's basket.

The *OrderForm* and the Order-Processing Pipeline

Throughout the course of a shopping session, the OrderForm component is presented by the Page component to the order-processing pipeline for preliminary processing. When a shopper finalizes a purchase, the Page component's RunPurchase method is used to finalize the purchase. The RunPurchase method invokes the order-processing pipeline on the OrderForm. The order-processing pipeline writes the purchased items to receipt storage, after which you can delete them from orderform storage.

The Clock Peddler store illustrates this process. In the Clock Peddler, each time a shopper adds items to the shopping basket, the additions are written to orderform storage. The shopper is then redirected to the basket.asp file, which loads the current shopper's basket from orderform storage into an OrderForm component and passes the initialized component to the Page component's RunPlan method.

The RunPlan method runs the OrderForm through the first 12 stages of the OPP and amends the OrderForm to contain the purchase subtotal, total, shipping cost, and tax. Additionally, where a discrepancy exists between the OrderForm's price for an item and the actual price of an item, the OrderForm is adjusted to reflect the actual price, and an error string is written to the _Basket_Errors_ list, which is included in the OrderForm component. The text of that error depends on the string that you associated with a given variable in the MessageManager for this store. For more information on the relationship between the order processing pipeline and the MessageManager, see "The MessageManager component" section.

At the conclusion of a shopping session, if the shopper opts to finalize the purchase, a store loads the orderform storage data into an OrderForm component a second time and uses the Page component's RunPurchase method on the OrderForm. Then the OPP writes the contents of the OrderForm to *receipt storage*. Receipt storage designates a DBStorage or CookieStorage component that is created for the storage of store receipts and that is assigned to the application-level MSCSReceiptStorage variable.

When a purchase has been successfully run through the OPP, the store can delete the order from orderform storage.

For more information on the relationship between the OrderForm and Page components, see "The Page Component."

AddItem

The AddItem method adds an item to the *items* element of an OrderForm component. For a list of the elements included as an *items* member, see "Overview" in the OrderForm section.

Syntax

OrderForm.AddItem (*SKU, Quantity, Price*)

Parameters

SKU

The SKU of the item to add.

Quantity

A number indicating the quantity of the items to add.

Price

The price of the item.

Remarks   Typically, at least one of the values that you pass to AddItems represents information that you retrieve from inventory by using the Datasource component's Execute method to run a query cached in the Content component for the store.

The Clock Peddler store, for example, defines an OrderFormAddItem utility function that uses the IIS 3.0 Request component to retrieve the SKU and the quantity from the calling page; then it uses the Datasource component to execute a query against the search on the product SKU to locate the product's list price.

Applies To

OrderForm

See Also

ClearOrderForm, ClearItems

ClearItems

Empties the items collection on the OrderForm.

Syntax

OrderForm.ClearItems()

Remarks   A store uses the ClearItems method to respond to a shopper's having opted to cancel a purchase. This method affects only the information in the items collection. Other OrderForm information, such as _oadjust_subtotal and _total_total, are modified only if you run the order-processing pipeline on this OrderForm by calling the Page component's RunPlan or RunPurchase method.

To empty the entire contents of the OrderForm, call the ClearOrderForm method.

Applies To

OrderForm

See Also

ClearOrderForm

ClearOrderForm

The ClearOrderForm method empties the entire OrderForm component.

Syntax

OrderForm.ClearOrderForm()

Applies To

OrderForm

See Also

ClearItems

The *OrderPipeline* Component

The OrderPipleline component is a file-based component that you use to identify the configuration of the Order Processing Pipeline (OPP) for your store, and to identify the file to which the OPP should log errors that occur during the purchase process.

The OrderPipeline component supports the methods listed in Table A.12.

Table A.12 *OrderPipeline* **Component Methods**

Method	Description
LoadPipe	Loads the OPP configuration settings for your store from a pipeline configuration(.pcf) which is located in your store's Config sub-directory.
SetLogFile	Specifies a file which the OPP will use to log OPP errors as they occur.

LoadPipe

The LoadPipe method loads the order processing pipeline (OPP) configuration settings for your store from a pipeline configuration file located in your store's \Config directory.

Syntax

OrderPipeline.LoadPipe(*Filename*)

Parameters

Filename

The path to the configuration file.

Applies To

OrderPipeline

See Also

SetLogFile

SetLogFile

The SetLogFile method identifies the file to which the order processing pipleline (OPP) logs errors that occur when the OPP is run on an OrderForm.

Syntax

OrderPipeline.SetLogFile(*Filename*)

Parameters

Filename

The name of the file to which to log transactions

Applies To

OrderPipeline

See Also

LoadPipe

The *Page* Component

The Page component supports methods that simplify the creation and layout of Active Server Pages (ASP) HTML pages.

Page component methods fall into the following categories.

- **The** Formatting **methods.** These methods include Justify, Option, and Check, and enable you to easily format HTML page items and, where applicable, to determine HTML item values based upon a runtime evaluation of other variables used in your page.

- **The** Validation **methods.** These methods include the Request* (ie. RequestFloat, RequestNumber, RequestString, ...) methods, which retrieve values from the QUERY_STRING server variable or posted form fields and convert the values to given data types, based on a locale value.

The Page component supports the properties listed in Table A.12.

Table A.12 *Page* **Component Properties**

Property	Description
Context	A read-only value that contains the IIS 3.0 scripting context
Messages	A number that identifies the language to use to return basket and purchase errors

The Page component supports the methods listed in Table A.13.

Table A.13 *Page* **Component Methods**

Method	Description
Check	Generates the word CHECKED based on a supplied value.
Encode	Encodes an argument in HTML.
Decode	Decodes an HTML argument.
GetOrderForm	Returns an existing OrderForm.
GetShopperID	Returns the unique shopper ID for the current shopper.
IncrShopperPerfCtrs	Increments the value of the Total New Shoppers Performance Monitor counter.
Option	Generates an option button on a page.
ProcessVerifyWith	Reads the contents of hidden fields created using the VerifyWith method into an OrderForm's _verify_with dictionary

continues

Table A.13   Continued

Method	Description
RequestDate	Retrieves the value of a date variable in the query string, checks that value against a specified range, and performs locale-based validation on the value.
RequestDateTime	Retrieves the date/time value of a variable in the query string, checks the value against a specified range, and performs locale-based validation on the value.
RequestDefault	Retrieves a specified URL argument, and returns a specified value if the retrieved argument has no value.
RequestFloat	Retrieves a floating-point value from the query string; checks the value against a specified range; and then validates the value, based on the specified locale.
RequestMoneyAsNumber	Retrieves a monetary value from the query string; checks the value against a specified range; and then validates the value, based on the specified locale.
RequestNumber	Retrieves a number value from the query string; checks the value against a specified range; and then validates the value, based on the specified locale.
RequestString	Retrieves a string value from the query string and performs extensive processing on a string, based on the specified locale.
RequestTime	Retrieves a time value from the query string; checks the value against a specified range; and validates the value, based on the specified locale.
SURL	Generates a secure URL based on the local path to a file. This URL includes the shopper ID, where applicable.
URL	Generates a full URL based on the local path to a file. This URL includes the shopper ID, where applicable.
VerifyWith	Outputs to the page's hidden fields that contain verification values.

The *Page* Component's Request Methods

The Page component supports a group of methods, beginning with Request*, that are designed to perform data-type conversion, locale-based validation, and optional range checking on values retrieved from the HTTP QUERY_STRING variable or from a posted form field.

These methods convert the retrieved values to the data types and perform locale-based validation on these values, ensuring that they can be inserted without error into the database storage that underlies many Commerce Server components.

The following example illustrates how to use one of these methods—RequestDate—to perform data-type conversion and locale-based validation on a query string variable. This example assumes that the date value is entered via the following form:

```
<FORM METHOD ="POST" ACTION="PROCESS.ASP">
<INPUT TYPE="Text" NAME="Date">
<INPUT TYPE="SUBMIT" NAME="ACTION" VALUE="Send Info">
</FORM>
```

If the user enters the date in the text box in this form and clicks the Send Info button, the value of this form field can be retrieved by the RequestDate method as follows:

```
TheDate = RequestDate("Date", "2/28/97", "1/1/97", "12/31/97")
```

The first parameter of RequestDate specifies, in this case, the name of the form field from which the data was submitted. If this text box is empty, the second parameter of RequestDate—"2/28/97"—becomes the date that RequestDate processes. First, the string expression of the date is converted to a date value, based on a specified locale. In the preceding example, this locale is not specified, so RequestDate uses the value of the DataFunctions component's Locale property as the basis of the conversion. Finally, the RequestDate method checks the date to ensure that it is within the range specified by the third and fourth parameters.

Context

The Context property is a read-only property of the Page component that contains the Internet Information Server (IIS) 3.0 scripting context, which comprises the state of IIS server objects at the time when the Page is created.

A store builder never needs to retrieve the contents of the Context property and uses it only as a parameter of other Commerce Server methods that need access to the IIS 3.0 context.

Messages

The Messages property contains a number that specifies the language to use to return basket and purchase errors in the OrderForm. This value must identify one of the languages added to the MessageManager through a call to that component's AddLanguage method.

Check

The Check method generates the word CHECKED into a page if the value specified in the *Value* parameter is a nonzero value.

Syntax

Page.Check(*Value*)

Parameters

Value

An integer that is evaluated to determine whether the word CHECKED should be inserted at the place in a page where the call to Check appears.

Example   The following example, from the AdventureWorks management pages, checks the option button if the recordset column "award_all" evaluates to TRUE:

```
<INPUT NAME="award_all"  VALUE=0  TYPE="radio"
<% = Page.Check(Cbool(promo("award_all") = 0)) %>>
```

Applies To

Page

See Also

Option

Decode

The Decode method evaluates *Value* against 0 and, on the basis of this evaluation, returns the corresponding appropriate argument in the argument list. If *Value* evaluates to 0, for example, the first argument in the argument list is returned; if *Value* evaluates to 1, the second argument is returned; and so on.

Syntax

Page.Decode(*Value, Argument*)

Parameters

Value

A number to evaluate against zero.

Argument

One or more arguments to return, based on the result of a base-zero evaluation of the *Value* parameter.

Applies To

Page

Encode

The Encode method applies HTML encoding to the specified expression.

Syntax

Page.Encode(*Expression*)

Parameters

Expression

The expression to encode.

Example   The following script example will generate the text below it into a page.

```
<%=Page.Encode("The following products are on sale: <P>")%>
The following products are on sale: &lt;P&gt;
```

Applies To

Page

GetOrderForm

The GetOrderForm method returns an initialized OrderForm for the current shopper.

Syntax

Page.GetOrderForm()

Remarks

The GetOrderForm method returns an OrderForm initialized from orderform storage. If no orderform storage data exists for the current shopper (if the shopper has not placed any items in her shopping basket), the returned OrderForm is initialized with shopper information loaded from shopper storage, and the OrderForm's *Items* collection is empty. If the current shopper does not have a shopper ID, GetOrderForm returns a Null value.

Applies To

Page

See Also

OrderForm

GetShopperID (Page)

The GetShopperID method returns the unique shopper ID for the current shopper.

Syntax

Page.GetShopperID()

Remarks   If the current shopper does not have a shopper ID, GetShopperID returns an empty string.

See Also

PutShopperID (Page)

Option

The Option method generates a list option on a page, and assigns to it the value and selection state that you specify.

Syntax

Page.Option(*Value*, *State*)

Parameters

Value

A variable containing the option's value.

State

A number that indicates whether list option is the selected option. If this value is greater than zero, the HTML keyword SELECTED is inserted into the definition of the option list.

Applies To

Page

See Also

Check

ProcessVerifyWith

The `ProcessVerifyWith` method reads into an `OrderForm`'s `_verify_with` dictionary the contents of hidden fields created with the `VerifyWith` method. When the `RunPurchase` method runs the `OrderForm` through the order-processing pipeline, the contents of this dictionary are compared with the contents of the appropriate fields of the `OrderForm` to ensure that a page has not been altered between presentation and final purchase.

Syntax

Page.ProcessVerifyWith(*OrderForm*)

Parameters

OrderForm

An `OrderForm` component that contains the shopper storage for the current shopper.

See Also

VerifyWith

PutShopperID (Page)

The `PutShopperID` method writes the specified shopper ID to a cookie, or stores it in a URL or SURL, depending on the initialization mode of the `ShopperManager` for the store.

Syntax

Page.PutShopperID(*ShopperID*)

Parameters

ShopperID

An ID that uniquely identifies this shopper.

Remarks   Where the `PutShopperID` method stores the specified shopper ID depends on the `ShopperManager` initialization mode. In URL mode, this method writes the shopper ID to the request, so that the URL and SURL methods add the shopper ID to the URL from this page.

Applies To

Page

See Also

GetShopperID (Page), SURL, URL

RequestDate

The RequestDate method retrieves the value of the requested QUERY_STRING element or posted form field; converts it to a date; checks the date against a date range; and validates the date, based on the specified locale. If the requested value has no value in the query string, RequestDate uses the default value that you specify as the basis for conversion, range-checking, and validation.

If RequestDate succeeds, it returns the validated value; otherwise, it returns Null.

Syntax

Page.RequestDate(*Name, Default, LowDate, HighDate, Locale*)

Parameters

Name

The query-string variable or posted form field that contains the value to validate.

Default

A default value to assign to the query-string variable if it contains no value. This value can be either a string or a date.

LowDate

An optional date value that specifies the low end of the range against which to validate *Date*. The default value is 0.

HighDate

An optional date value that specifies the high end of the range against which to validate *Date*. The default value is 0.

Locale

A number that specifies the locale to use to convert the date. If this value is not specified, the DataFunctions component's Locale property is used to validate the date.

Example   See "The Page Component's Request Methods"

Applies To

Page

See Also

RequestDateTime, ConvertDateString, ValidateDate

RequestDateTime

The `RequestDateTime` method retrieves the value of the requested `QUERY_STRING` element or posted form field; converts the value to a date/time value; and validates the date/time value, based on the specified locale. If the query value that you specify does not exist or has no value, `RequestDateTime` uses the default value that you specify as the bases of the conversion, range-checking, and validation.

If `RequestDateTime` succeeds, it returns the converted, validated value; otherwise, it returns `Null`.

Syntax

`Page.RequestDateTime( Name, Default, LowDateTime, HighDateTime, Locale)`

Parameters

Name

The name of the query string or form field that contains the value to process.

Default

A string that contains the value to process if the requested query-string variable does not exist or contains no value.

LowDateTime

An optional value that specifies the low end of the range. The default value for this parameter is 0.

HighDateTime

An optional value that specifies the high end of the range. The default value for this parameter is 0.

Locale

A number that identifies the locale to be used to convert the date/time string. If this parameter is not specified, `RequestDateTime` uses the value of the `DataFunctions` component's `Locale` property.

Example   See "The `Page` Component's Request Methods"

Applies To

Page

See Also

`RequestDate, RequestTime`

RequestFloat

The `RequestFloat` method retrieves the value of the requested `QUERY_STRING` element or posted form field; converts it to a floating-point number; checks that number against the specified range; and validates the number, based on the specified locale. If the requested query string or form field name does not exist or does not contain a value, RequestFloat uses a specified default value as the basis for the conversion, range-checking, and validation.

If RequestFloat succeeds, it returns the converted, validated value; otherwise, it returns Null.

Syntax

Page.RequestFloat(*Name, Default, LowFloat, HighFloat, Locale*)

Parameters

Name

The name of the query-string variable or form field that contains the value to convert and validate.

Default

A string expression of the value on which to base validation if the specified query-string variable does not exist or contains no value.

LowFloat

An optional number that specifies the low end of the range of values against which to validate the converted value. The default value for this parameter is 0.

HighFloat

An optional number that specifies the high end of the range of values against which to validate the converted value. The default value for this parameter is 0.

Locale

An optional number that identifies the locale to use to convert the value. If this value is not specified, the value of the DataFunctions component's Locale property is used.

Example   See "The Page Component's Request Methods"

Applies To

Page

See Also

RequestNumber

RequestMoneyAsNumber

The RequestMoneyAsNumber method retrieves the value of the requested QUERY_STRING element or posted form; converts the string value to money; checks the converted value against a specified range; and validates the value, using the specified locale. If the requested query string or form field does not exist or does not contain a value, RequestMoneyAsNumber uses a specified default value as the basis for the conversion, range-checking, and validation.

If `RequestMoneyAsNumber` succeeds, it returns the converted, validated value; otherwise, it returns `Null`.

Syntax

`Page.RequestMoneyAsNumber(Name, Default, LowMoney, HighMoney, Locale)`

Parameters

Name

The name of the query-string or form-field variable to retrieve.

Default

A string expression of the value on which to base validation if the specified query-string variable does not exist or contains no value.

LowMoney

An optional monetary value that specifies the low end of the range against which to validate the converted value.

HighMoney

An optional monetary value that specifies the high end of the range against which to validate the converted value.

Locale

An optional number that specifies the locale to use to convert *Value*. If this parameter is not used, the `DataFunctions` component's `Locale` property is used to convert *String*.

Example

See "The `Page` Component's Request Methods"

Applies To

Page

See Also

`RequestFloat`, `RequestNumber`

RequestNumber

The `RequestNumber` method retrieves the value of the requested `QUERY_STRING` element or posted form field; converts the value to a number; checks the converted number against a range; and validates it, based on the specified locale. If the requested query string or form field does not exist or does not contain a value, `RequestNumber` uses a specified default value as the basis for the conversion, range-checking, and validation.

If `RequestNumber` succeeds, it returns the converted, validated value; otherwise, it returns `Null`.

Syntax

`Page.RequestNumber( Name, Default, LowNumber, HighNumber, Locale)`

Parameters

Name

The name of the query-string part of the form field from which to retrieve the value.

Default

A string expression of the value on which to base conversion and validation if the specified query-string variable does not exist or contains no value.

LowNumber

An optional number value that specifies the low end of the range against which to validate the converted value.

HighNumber

An optional number value that specifies the low end of the range against which to validate the converted value.

Locale

An optional number that specifies the locale to use to convert *Value*. If this parameter is not used, the `DataFunctions` component's `Locale` property is used to convert *String*.

Example   See "The `Page` Component's Request Methods"

Applies To

Page

See Also

`RequestFloat`

RequestString

The `RequestString` method retrieves the value of the requested `QUERY_STRING` element or posted form field and then processes the string. This processing may involve stripping out leading and trailing white spaces; stripping out carriage returns; checking the string's length against a specified range; and validating the string, based on the specified locale. If the requested query string does not exist or does not contain a value, `RequestString` bases processing on the default string that you specify.

If `RequestString` succeeds, it returns the processed string; otherwise, it returns `Null`.

Syntax

`Page.RequestString(Name, Default, MinStrLen, MaxStrLen, StripWhite, StripReturn, Case, Locale)`

Parameters

Name

The name of the query-string part of the form field associated with the queried value.

Default

The string on which to base conversion and validation if the specified query-string variable does not exist or contains no value.

MinStrLen

An optional parameter that indicates the minimum length against which the length of *String* must be validated. The default value for this parameter is 0. If a value is specified and the string is shorter than *MinStrLen*, RequestString returns Null.

MaxStrLen

An optional parameter that indicates the maximum length against which the length of *String* must be validated. The default value is 65,535. If a value is specified and the length of the string exceeds the specified maximum, RequestString returns Null.

StripWhiteSpaces

An optional Boolean value that indicates whether the leading and trailing white spaces should be stripped from the string. The default value for this parameter is FALSE.

StripReturn

An optional Boolean value that indicates whether the carriage returns should be stripped from the string. The default value for this parameter is FALSE.

Case

An optional value that indicates the case to which the string should be converted. The default value for this parameter is 0, which results in no modification of the case of the string. If *Case* is 1, the string is converted to uppercase; if *Case* is 2, the string is converted to lowercase.

Locale

An optional number that specifies the locale to be used as the basis of the conversion. If this value is not specified, RequestString uses the value of the DataFunctions component's Locale property.

Example   See "The Page Component's Request Methods"

Applies To

Page

RequestTime

The RequestTime method retrieves the value of the specified QUERY_STRING element or posted form field, converts the value to time based on the specified locale, and checks the time against a specified range. If the QUERY_STRING or form-field element does not exist or contains no value, the default value that you specify becomes the basis of the conversion and validation.

If RequestTime succeeds, it returns the converted, validated value; otherwise, it returns Null.

Syntax

Page.RequestTime(*Name, Default, LowTime, HighTime, Locale*)

Parameters

Name

The name of the variable in the HTTP query string to retrieve, or the name of the a form field.

Default

A string expression of the value on which to base the conversion if the element referenced by *Name* does not exist or contains no value.

LowTime

An optional value that specifies the low end of the range. The default value is 0.

HighDateTime

An optional value that specifies the high end of the range. The default value is 0.

Locale

A number that specifies the locale to use to convert the date/time value. If this value is not specified, the DataFunctions component's Locale property is used to convert the date/time value.

Remarks

If the specified time is within the provided range, RequestTime returns TRUE; otherwise, it returns FALSE. If no time range is specified, RequestTime returns TRUE.

Applies To

Page

See Also

RequestDate

RunPlan

The RunPlan method invokes the order processing pipeline (OPP) to perform preliminary processing on an OrderForm component that contains the contents of the current shopper's orderform storage. For more information on orderform storage, see the "Overview" section in the section on the DBStorage component.

Syntax

Page..RunPlan(*OrderForm*)

Parameters

OrderForm

An OrderForm component that contains the contents of the orderform storage for the current shopper.

Remarks

The RunPlan method does not result in the purchase of the items referenced in the specified OrderForm's Items collection. Instead, RunPlan runs the OrderForm through all but the last two stages (the Payment and Accept stages) of the order-processing pipeline.

Typically, RunPlan is used to set nonsensitive information (such as shipping, billing address data, and adjusted price information) in the OrderForm and then compute the total. If the order-processing pipeline encounters errors, it stores these errors in the OrderForm's _Basket_Errors_ collection.

When RunPlan has been run on an OrderForm and the shopper has confirmed the purchase, the store calls RunPurchase on the modified OrderForm to write the OrderForm's contents to receipt storage.

Applies To

Page

See Also

RunProduct, RunPurchase, RunProduct

RunPurchase

The RunPurchase method runs the order-processing pipeline on an OrderForm component that contains the contents of orderform storage for the current shopper.

Syntax

Page.RunPurchase(*OrderForm*)

Parameters

OrderForm

An OrderForm component that contains the contents of orderform storage for the current shopper.

Remarks   In contrast with the RunPlan method, which runs all except the last two stages (Payment and Acceptance) of the order-processing pipeline on the OrderForm, RunPurchase runs the entire order-processing pipeline on the OrderForm. If no errors are encountered in the OrderForm, the order-processing pipeline writes the OrderForm's contents to receipt storage.

For more information on receipt and orderform storage, see the "Overview" section for the `DBStorage` component.

Applies To

Page

SURL

The `SURL` method generates a properly formatted secure HTTP URL, based on the provided file name and an optional list of name–value pairs. This URL includes the server name, the virtual directory in which the file is stored, and the name of the file itself.

Additionally, if the `ShopperManager` for the application is initialized in `"url"` mode, the `SURL` method uses the value stored in the `MSCSIDUrlKey` `Application` object variable as the name in a name–value pair, the value of which is the current shopper's shopper ID.

For more information on how the `Page` component coordinates with the `ShopperManager` component, see `URL`.

Syntax

Page.SURL(*Filename, Arguments*)

Parameters

Filename

The name of the file for the SURL to reference.

Arguments

An optional list of arguments that identifies the name–value pairs to be appended to the SURL.

Applies To

Page

See Also

URL

URL

The `URL` method generates a URL based on the specified file name and an optional list of name–value arguments. This URL includes the server name, the virtual directory in which the file is stored, and the name of the file itself.

Additionally, if the `ShopperManager` for the application is initialized in `"url"` mode, the SURL method uses the value stored in the `MSCSIDUrlKey` `Application` object variable as the name in a name–value pair, the value of which is the current shopper's shopper ID.

Syntax

Page.URL(*Filename, Arguments*)

Parameters

Filename

The name of the file to reference in the URL.

Arguments

An optional list of name–value pairs.

Remarks　　The URL method serves several purposes within the context of a Commerce Server store.

```
First, URL is a useful HTML utility function that spares the store builder the
➥need to map a file to the HTTP path to that file, or to manually build name-
➥value pairs into the query string appended to the URL. The following example
➥calls to URL reliably resolves to the correct HTTP path to filename.asp, and
➥appends the "sku" name and sku value to that URL as shown below the example.<%=
➥Page.URL("shop/filename.asp", "sku", sku) %>
```

```
Http://servername/virtual_directory/filename.asp?sku=13428
```

More importantly, when the ShopperManager is initialized in url mode, a call to URL appends the value stored in the Application object's MSCSIDUrlKey variable, along with the current shopper's shopper ID, to the resulting HTTP path. So, using our earlier example, initializing the Application object's MSCSIDUrlKey variable and setting the ShopperManager to run in url mode, the example changes as follows.

```
'Set this in the global.asa
```

```
Application("MMSURLKey") = "current_shopper")
```

```
<%= Page.URL("shop/filename.asp", "sku", sku) %>
```

```
Http://servername/virtual_directory/filename.asp?sku=13428&current_shopper=12345
```

For more information on ShopperManager initialization modes, see the documentation on the InitManager in the section, "The ShopperManager Component."

Applies To

Page

See Also

InitManager, SURL

VerifyWith

The VerifyWith method outputs a group of hidden fields to identify the OrderForm fields that verify that an order has not been altered between presentation of the OrderForm and final purchase. When the form is submitted, the ProcessVerifyWith method on the target page stores these fields in a dictionary in the OrderForm and then passes that OrderForm to the order-processing pipeline. In the order-processing pipeline, the RequiredTotal component compares the values in these fields with the _verify_with dictionary on the order form and generates an error if a mismatch occurs.

Syntax

page.VerifyWith(*OrderForm*, *Arguments*)

Parameters

OrderForm

The OrderForm component that contains the values to verify.

Arguments

One or more arguments that identify the OrderForm fields to use for verification.

Example The following example generates hidden fields containing the values stored in the _total_total, ship_to_zip, and _tax_total fields of the supplied OrderForm component:

```
<% = Page.VerifyWith(order, "_total_total", "ship_to_zip", "_tax_total") %>
```

When the page containing this call is loaded in the client browser, the document source for the page contains the following HTML script (assuming a total of 1A.00, a ZIP code of 98029, and a tax of 8.75 percent):

```
<INPUT TYPE="HIDDEN" NAME="_VERIFY_WITH_" VALUE="1A.00">
<INPUT TYPE="HIDDEN" NAME="_VERIFY_WITH_" VALUE="98029">
<INPUT TYPE="HIDDEN" NAME="_VERIFY_WITH_" VALUE="8.75">
```

Applies To

Page

See Also

ProcessVerifyWith

The *ShopperManager* Component

The ShopperManager component supports methods that facilitate the run-time creation, deletion, and retrieval of shopper IDs.

The ShopperManager component supports the methods listed in Table A.14.

Table A.14 *ShopperManager* Component Methods

Method	Description
CreateShopperID	Creates and returns a unique shopper ID
DeleteShopperID	Deletes a shopper ID
GetShopperID	Retrieves the shopper ID from the cookie, if available; otherwise, returns an empty string
InitManager	Initializes the ShopperManager with information that determines how shopper IDs are stored and retrieved
PutShopperID	Stores the shopper ID in a cookie on the client system

Shopper Identifiers and IIS 3.0 Session Identifiers

The ShopperManager component, like the IIS 3.0 Session object, can issue per-user identifiers that facilitate the maintenance of state data across a session. Significant differences exist, however, in how the ShopperManager and the Session object function, both internally and within the context of a store. Because of these differences, you should never use IIS 3.0 session identifiers in a Commerce Server store to identify a store user.

First, the IIS 3.0 session ID is unique only across a single user session. When that session concludes, a server running IIS may assign that session ID to another user. Consequently, using an IIS-issued session ID as a unique key is not advisable.

Shopper IDs, on the other hand, are designed to be unique across multiple sessions on a single server, so you can use these identifiers as a reliable key into the database tables in which you maintain shopper information.

Additionally, in a multiple-server environment, the IIS 3.0 session ID carries no guarantee of uniqueness. Two IIS 3.0 server Session objects are likely to issue the same session ID to different users. Shopper IDs, on the other hand, are designed to be unique even across multiple servers, so that when the same store is running across multiple servers, the shopper ID remains a reliable means of tracking shopper information, both for state maintenance and for persistently stored purchase operations.

Creating a *ShopperManager* Component

Use the IIS 3.0 Server object's CreateObject method to create a ShopperManager component, specifying the "Commerce.StandardSManager" program identifier.

```
Set ShopperManager = Server.CreateObject("Commerce.StandardSManager")
```

The ShopperManager is created on a per-application bases and, in the store's global.asa file, should be assigned to the MSCSShopperManager Application variable.

CreateShopperID

The CreateShopperID method creates and returns a new shopper ID.

Syntax

```
ShopperManager.CreateShopperID()
```

Remarks The CreateShopperID method has no parameters and returns the newly created shopper ID. Because the process of shopper-ID creation does not depend on a particular ShopperManager mode, you can create a shopper ID before initializing the ShopperManager. You must call InitManager before calling methods such as PutShopperID and GetShopperID, however, because these methods function in accordance with a provided shopper mode.

For more information on ShopperManager modes, see the section InitManager.

Applies To

ShopperManager

See Also

InitManager

GetShopperID (*ShopperManager*)

The GetShopperID method returns the shopper ID from a cookie stored on the client system.

Syntax

ShopperManager.GetShopperID(*Context*)

Parameters

Context

The Page component's Context property, a read-only property that contains the IIS 3.0 scripting context and is initialized during the process of Page-component creation.

Remarks   If no cookie is stored on the client system, GetShopperID returns an empty string.

Applies To

ShopperManager

See Also

PutShopperID (ShopperManager)

InitManager

The InitManager method initializes the ShopperManager component to the specified store key and mode.

Syntax

ShopperManager.InitManager(*StoreKey, Mode*)

Parameters

StoreKey

The name of the store.

Mode

A string that indicates how shopper information is to be stored (see the following "Remarks" section).

Remarks   The mode that you specify indicates whether the ShopperManager runs in cookie or url mode. The mode in which the ShopperManager runs determines how shopper IDs are stored and retrieved. Table A.15 lists the possible values of this parameter.

Table A.15 Valid *ShopperManager Mode*'s

Mode	Description
cookie	Indicates that the ShopperManager should store the shopper ID in a cookie
url	Indicates that the ShopperManager should store the shopper ID in a URL
cookieurl	Indicates that the ShopperManager should first attempt to write the shopper ID to a cookie and then, if this attempt fails, to a URL
urlcookie	Indicates that the ShopperManager should first attempt to write the shopper ID to a URL and then, if this attempt fails, to a cookie

Applies To

ShopperManager

See Also

PutShopperID (ShopperManager)

PutShopperID (*ShopperManager*)

The PutShopperID method stores a shopper ID in the cookie or a URL/SURL, depending on the mode in which the ShopperManager is running.

Syntax

ShopperManager.PutShopperID(*Context, ShopperID*)

Parameters

Context

The Page component's Context property.

ShopperID

The shopper ID to store.

Remarks   If the shopper ID is put to a URL, you can retrieve it by passing the value you set for the application-level MSCSSIDURLKey to the IIS 3.0 Request object.

Applies To

ShopperManager

The *TrafficLogFile* Component

The TrafficLogFile component gives Commerce Server stores the capability to log user information and store events to a plain-text file.

The `TrafficLogFile` component supports the methods listed in Table A.16.

Table A.16 *TrafficLogFile* Component Methods

Method	Description
InitTraffic	Initializes the `Traffic` component with the data source or file name to which to log traffic and, where applicable, a store key
LogTraffic	Logs traffic data to a data source or file

The `TrafficLogFile` component supports the properties listed in Table A.17.

Table A.17 *TrafficLogFile* Component properties

Property	Description
BlankSubstitution	Specifies the character to substitute for blank spaces.
ColumnDelimiter	Specifies the character to use to delimit columns.
ColumnSubstitution	Specifies the character to be used as the column delimiter if the data itself contains the character previously specified as the `ColumnDelimiter`.
LocaleDate	Identifies the locale to be used to format the date on which logged store events occur. The default is American (0x0409).
LocaleTime	Identifies the locale to be used to format the time at which logged store events occur. The default is American (0x0409).
RowDelimiter	Specifies the character to use to delimit rows. The default is a carriage return followed by a line feed (Chr(10) & Chr(13)).
RowSubstitution	Specifies the character to be used as the row delimiter if the data itself contains the character previously specified as the `RowDelimiter`.

Overview

To create a `TrafficLogFile` component, use the `Server.CreateObject` method, specifying `"Commerce.TrafficLogFile"` as the component's program identifier.

```
Set Traffic = Server.CreateObject("Commerce.TrafficLogfile")
```

After creating the component and before calling its `LogTraffic` method, use the `InitManager` method to initialize the component, specifying the types of information that you want to log. Table A.18 lists the items of information that you can log.

Table A.18 Items Available to Log

Field	Description
store_name	Used to store the store name
event	Used to store the event description
shopper_id	The unique identifier of the current shopper
item_requested	The SKU of the requested item
event_time	The time at which the event was logged

If you create a TrafficLogFile component in your store's global.asa file, you should initialize the Application object variable MSCSTraffic to reference the component instance. When you do so, the Page component calls LogTraffic for you to log store events automatically.

InitTraffic (TrafficLogFile)

The InitTraffic method initializes the TrafficLogfile component by identifying the kinds of store events to log.

Syntax

TrafficLogfile.InitTraffic(*StoreName*, *FileName*, *Arguments*)

Parameters

StoreName

The name of the store. This value is written to the log file to identify the store that logged the event.

FileName

The local path to the file to which events and data are logged.

Arguments

A list of arguments that identifies the events that you want to log. These events include the events defined by Commerce Server, as well as events that you define. If the events that you identify are prefixed with "args_", the value that follows the underscore character is assumed to reference a form field or query-string variable, and the value of this variable is logged to *FileName* when a page is posted.

Applies To

TrafficLogfile

LogTraffic (TrafficLogFile)

The LogTraffic method logs event or shopper information to the logfile for this TrafficLogFile component.

Syntax

`TrafficLogFile.LogTraffic(ShopperID, Event, ItemRequested, Context)`

Parameters

ShopperID

The shopper ID of the shopper that loaded the page that triggered the event.

Event

A string that identifies the event to log. This value can identify any of the events that you identified through a previous call to `InitManager`.

ItemRequested

The SKU of the requested item.

Context

The `Page` component's `Context` property. This read-only property is initialized when the `Page` component is created and references the Internet Information Server (IIS) 3.0 scripting context.

Remarks If you initialized the `Application` object variable `MSCSTraffic`, this method is called for you automatically.

Applies To

`TrafficLogFile`

The *TrafficTable* Component

The `TrafficTable` component gives Commerce Server stores the capability to log user information and store events to a database table.

The `TrafficTable` component supports the methods listed in Table A.19.

Table A.19 *TrafficTable* **Component Methods**

Method	Description
InitTraffic	Initializes the `Traffic` component with the data source or file name to which to log traffic and, where applicable, a store key
LogTraffic	Logs traffic data to a data source or file

Overview

To create a `TrafficTable` component, use the `Server.CreateObject` method, specifying `"Commerce.TrafficTable"` as the component's program identifier.

```
Set Traffic = Server.CreateObject("Commerce.TrafficTable")
```

After creating the component and before calling its `LogTraffic` (`TrafficTable`) method, use the `InitManager` method to initialize the component, specifying the types of information that you want to log. Table A.20 lists the items of information that you can log.

Table A.20 Items Available to Log

Field	Description
store_name	Used to store the store name
event	Used to store the event description
shopper_id	The unique identifier of the current shopper
item_requested	The SKU of the requested item
event_time	The time at which the event was logged

If you create a `TrafficTable` component in your store's `global.asa` file, you should initialize the `Application` object variable `MSCSTraffic` to reference the component instance. When you do so, the `Page` component calls `LogTraffic` (`TrafficTable`) for you to log store events automatically.

InitManager (*TrafficTable*)

The `InitManager` method initializes the `TrafficTable` component with data such as the data source or file to which store events are logged; the store key; and, where applicable, the table name.

Syntax

Traffic.InitManager(*Datasource*, *StoreKey*, *TableName*)

Parameters

Datasource

A variable that identifies a DSN variable

Content

Component cache.

StoreKey

The name of the store. The value specified in this parameter is used by `TrafficTable` to identify the store that logged the event.

TableName

The name of the table in the referenced data source. This parameter is used only if you are logging to a database table.

App
A

Arguments

An argument list that specifies the columns for the log file.

Applies To

TrafficTable

See Also

LogTraffic (TrafficTable)

LogTraffic (TrafficTable)

The LogTraffic method logs event information to a database table.

Syntax

Traffic.LogTraffic(*ShopperID, Event, ItemRequested, Context*)

Parameters

ShopperID

The ID of the current shopper.

Event

The event to log.

ItemRequested

The SKU of the item requested.

Context

The Page component's Context property.

Applies To

TrafficTable

See Also

InitManager (TrafficTable): The global Files

If you have read this whole chapter through, big kudo's to you! If you have not, don't worry, this is a long chapter, and filled with much technical information and jargon. It is not important that you have read all the material, but that you have understood what is happening with the information that has been discussed.

Although this chapter has the appearance of a good reference, the chapter leads you down a much longer path, and this path leads to the architectural design of a store. Without the components discussed in this chapter, you cannot create a Commerce Server 2.0 Store.

Much like a human's blood is essential to the body, architectural design is crucial to a Commerce Server 2.0 store. In much the same manner a human's heart pumps the blood throughout the body, and a store's `global.asa` outlines the architectural design of a store, pumping information throughout the store.

This compulsory architectural design compels Commerce Server 2.0 store designer's to have a good understanding of the `global.asa` and its presence in the Commerce Server environment.

The following outlines the general concepts that every `global.asa` file will need:

```
<SCRIPT RUNAT=Server Language=VBScript>
Sub Application_OnStart
End Sub
Sub Session_OnStart
End Sub
</SCRIPT>
```

Commerce Server stores support the existence of the following two global files:

Global	Description
global.asa	File that contains the .asa definitions for a Commerce Store that is open for business.
global_closed.asa	File that contains the .asa definitions for a Commerce Store that is closed.

The following sections will discuss the features of each file, and their use in the Commerce Server 2.0 environment.

Introducing *global.asa*

To fully understand the `global.asa` and its pressence in the Commerce Server 2.0 environment, let's take a look at the MSPress `global.asa` file.

> **N O T E**   I have numbered the lines, these numbers are not included in a `global` adminstration file, and should not be use for anything but these discussion purposes. Also, I have not fully included the `global.asa` file due to it's length, any lines I have taken out, have been replaced with "...". ■

```
1.  <!-- REM include DSN and DB connect string info from setup -->
2.  <!--#INCLUDE FILE="include/dsn_include.asp" -->
3.  <SCRIPT LANGUAGE=VBScript RUNAT=Server>
4.  Sub Application_OnStart
5.      REM -- ADO command types
6.          adCmdText       = 1
7.          adCmdTable      = 2
8.          adCmdStoredProc = 4
9.          adCmdUnknown    = 8
10.     REM -- ADO cursor types
11.         adOpenForwardOnly = 0
12.         adOpenKeyset      = 1
```

```
13.    adOpenDynamic     = 2
14.    adOpenStatic      = 3
15.    REM  Create a content object and store named queries
16.     Set  MSCSContent = Server.CreateObject("Commerce.Content")
17.     Call MSCSContent.AddDatasource("MSPress", MSCSDSN, 1, 0)
A.     Set  MSCSDataSource = MSCSContent.Datasource("MSPress")
19.    REM Add queries to the content object for use in our pages
20.     Call MSCSContent.AddQuery("product","select sku, isbn, title, subtitle,
       ➥short_description, publisher, date_published, subject_id, author_id,
       ➥featured, rating, level_id, bookdisk, list_price, date_changed,
       ➥long_description from MSPress_product where sku = convert(varchar, :1)",
       ➥0, adCmdText, 0, adOpenForwardOnly, 0)
21.    ...
22.     Call MSCSContent.AddQuery("products_by_subject","select msp.sku, msp.isbn,
       ➥msp.title, msp.subtitle, msp.short_description, msp.publisher,
       ➥msp.date_published, msp.subject_id, msp.author_id, msp.featured,
       ➥msp.rating, msp.level_id, msp.bookdisk, msp.list_price, msp.date_changed,
       ➥upper(substring(mss.subject_name,1,1)) first_letter, mss.*,
       ➥msp.long_description from MSPress_product msp, MSPress_subject mss where
       ➥msp.subject_id = mss.subject_id order by mss.subject_name, msp.title", 0,
       ➥adCmdText, 0, adOpenForwardOnly, 0)
A.     ...
24.    REM  Create the Order Process Pipeline
25.     Set  MSCSOrderPipeline = Server.CreateObject("Commerce.OrderPipeline")
26.     pathPipeConfig = server.mappath("/MSPress") & "\..\config\pipeline.pcf"
27.     Call MSCSOrderPipeline.LoadPipe(pathPipeConfig)
28.    REM  Create a Shopper Manager to deal with shopper ids
29.     Set  MSCSShopperManager =
       ➥Server.CreateObject("Commerce.StandardSManager")
30.     Call MSCSShopperManager.InitManager("MSPress", "cookieURL")
31.    REM  Create a Storage object for the shopper information
32.     Set  MSCSShopperStorage = Server.CreateObject("Commerce.DBStorage")
33.     Call MSCSShopperStorage.InitStorage(MSCSDataSource, "MSPress_shopper",
       ➥"shopper_id", "Commerce.Dictionary")
34.    REM  Create a storage object for the order forms
35.     Set  MSCSOrderFormStorage = Server.CreateObject("Commerce.DBStorage")
36.     Call MSCSOrderFormStorage.InitStorage(MSCSDataSource, "MSPress_basket",
       ➥"shopper_id","Commerce.OrderForm","marshalled_order", "date_changed")
37.    REM Create a storage object for receipts
38.     Set MSCSReceiptStorage = Server.CreateObject("Commerce.DBStorage")
39     Call MSCSReceiptStorage.InitStorage(MSCSDataSource, "MSPress_receipt",
       ➥"order_id","Commerce.OrderForm", "marshalled_receipt", "date_entered")
40.     MSCSReceiptStorage.Mapping.Value("_total_total") = "total"
41.    REM  Create a message manager and initialize for rest of system
42.     Set  MSCSMessageManager = Server.CreateObject("Commerce.MessageManager")
43.     Call MSCSMessageManager.AddLanguage("usa", &H0409)
44.     MSCSMessageManager.defaultLanguage = "usa"
45.     Call MSCSMessageManager.AddMessage("pur_out_of_stock", "At least one item
       ➥is out of stock.")
46.    Call MSCSMessageManager.AddMessage("pur_badsku", "Products in your basket
       were deleted because they don't exist in this store.")
47.    ...
48.    REM — Create a data functions object for validation
49.     Set  MSCSDataFunctions = Server.CreateObject("Commerce.DataFunctions")
50.     MSCSDataFunctions.Locale     = &H0409
```

```
51.   REM Set up the Application instrinsic object
52.       Application.Lock
53.       Set Application("MSCSContent")          = MSCSContent
54.       Set Application("MSCSOrderPipeline")    = MSCSOrderPipeline
55.       Set Application("MSCSOrderFormStorage") = MSCSOrderFormStorage
56.       Set Application("MSCSShopperManager")   = MSCSShopperManager
57.       Set Application("MSCSShopperStorage")   = MSCSShopperStorage
58.       Set Application("MSCSMessageManager")   = MSCSMessageManager
59.       Set Application("MSCSReceiptStorage")   = MSCSReceiptStorage
60.       Set Application("MSCSDataFunctions")    = MSCSDataFunctions
61.       Application("MSCSDefaultDatasource") = "MSPress"
52.       Application("MSCSSIDURLKey")          = "mscssid"
53.       Application("MSCSDisableHTTPS")       = 1
54.       Application("MSCSInsecureHostName") = ""  ' use this host
55.       Application("MSCSSecureHostName")   = ""  ' use this host
56.       REM These are temporary but needed by the system
57.       Application("DBTableReceipt")        = ""
58.       Application("DBQueryOrderProduct") = "product"
59.       Application("db_table_traffic")      = ""
60.       Application("db_table_receipt")      = ""
61.       Application("db_table_sql")          = "MSPress_sql"
62.       REM -------------------------------------------
63.       REM CONSTANTS
64.       REM -------------------------------------------
65.       Application("StoreName") = "The MS Press Online Book Store"
66.       Application("OPPMODE_PRODUCT")   = 1
67.       Application("OPPMODE_PLAN")      = 2
68.       Application("OPPMODE_PURCHASE") = 4
69.       Application.Unlock
70.End Sub
71.</SCRIPT>
```

Although this global.asa file is not the only way to write one, it serves as a very good example of what a global.asa file should look like.

Lines 1-3 are basic ASP scripting, which include a file and set compiling to run at the server. Line 4 begins the Appliction_OnStart function, which is where all Commerce Server 2.0 processing will be declared. Commerce Server 2.0 stores generally avoid the use of Session_* functions for structural reasons, and I suggest that you follow this rule. If you don't you may run into detrimental problems later.

Lines 5-14 set variables that the sample store MSPress uses, I will not discuss their use in the script, but I would like to note the use of initialization at the top of the function. Initializing variables at the top of functions is generally a good rule to follow when coding.

Lines 15-18 initialize the Content and Datasource components, while lines 19-23 add queries to our Content component. If you have ever worked with SQL programming before, you will recognize the likeness of these queries to Stored Procedures. Actually, these queries, in their basic implementation, are set up as stored procedures.

Lines 24-27 create the OrderPipeline component that your store will use to complete orders. Line 25 creates the actual OrderPipeline component, while line 26 informs the component what file to read when the call to LoadPipe is made in line 27.

Lines 28-30 create and initialize the ShopperManager component, notice how the MSPress sample store initializes the component in the cookieURL mode.

Lines 31-40 all use the DBStorage component to create storage areas for the shopper, order form, and receipt information. Consider these storage areas very important, and ensure they are set aside.

Lines 41-47 creates the MessageManager component which is used to store messages that your store will use throughout the application runtime.

Lines 48-50 initializes a DataFunctions component which will allow you to test your difference data types for their validity.

Lines 51-69 are the most significant in this example. These lines are what initialize your Application-Level variables with the ASP Application.

Remember that your store's global.asa file is what will bring order to your store, and will help you understand how many of your Application's methods are related to the store. I suggest that you take a look at the other sample stores and understand each store's implementation of the global.asa file within the Application.

Understanding each of these global.asa files, will give you a good understanding of what your store will need. As you move on to the more advanced sample stores (such as Adventure Works) you will begin to see how the global.asa file can make the .asp programming your project needs, easier to write, understand, and maintain.

Introducing *global_closed.asa*

```
<SCRIPT RUNAT=Server Language=VBScript>
Sub Application_OnStart
   Application.Lock
     Application("StoreName") = "Microsoft Press"
   Application.Unlock
End Sub
Sub Session_OnStart
   startPage = "/MSPress/closed.asp"
   currentPage = Request.ServerVariables("SCRIPT_NAME")
   if strcomp(currentPage,startPage,1) then
     Response.Redirect(startPage)
   end if
End Sub
</SCRIPT>
```

There is not much to say about the global_closed.asa except to say that the file is a cool way to let your customers know that the store is closed. I would suggest that you note the way the sample store MSPress redirects the customers to a file "closed.asa," this is a classy way to let your customers know that the store is closed for business or construction, or whatever.

The global_closed.asa administration file is not necessary for your store, but is definitely a file you will want to consider implementing for your customers. I can assure you that your customers will want to know why your store is down, and when they can expect it to be running again. I know I would.

From Here...

We have spent much time explaining the components that are installed with Commerce Server 2.0, as well as how they fit into the a Commerce store, and integrate with each other. There has been much time concentrated in this chapter for several good reasons:

- Commerce Server 2.0 components are the key to data storage, data access, and store integrity.

- Commerce Server 2.0 stores cannot be created without the direct use of components. Components such as the DBStorage component make creating a Commerce store impossible without their interaction.

- Commerce Server 2.0's backbone is itself a component. The OrderPipeline component serves to finalize orders, and without understanding this component, you loose many features that will help you design a solid architecture for your store.

In this chapter we have learned what most of the components are, and how they are used in the Commerce Server 2.0 store. In the following chapters, we will further our discussion by showing you the advanced features of Commerce Server 2.0 and components.

- In Chapter 18, "Constructing a Server Component Using ASP," we discuss some of the Client/Server considerations to take when creating components.

- While in Chapter 22, "Building the Order Process Pipeline," we will show you how to actually create your own custom OPP. This chapter will help put together the integration of components within Commerce Server 2.0.

- Finally, in Chapter 23, "Constructing Your Own Server Components," we will create our own component using Visual C++ 5.0. Here you will be enlightened with the reason Commerce Server 2.0, "takes the cheese," with Internet related software in today's market.

Index

B

backing up
Registry, 365
Windows NT Server, 349

BackOffice Live Web site, 88

Backup, 365-366

Backup Domain Controller (BDC), Windows NT Server, 354-355

bandwidth, Internet connections, 11-12

bank relationships, electronic commerce, 13

BASIC, history of, 282-283

Basic Authentication (MPS authentication methods), 100

BIND DNS server, 381

blocks in scripting, 290-292

booting Cisco PIX Firewall, 568-569

Browser Capabilities component, Active Server, 247

bugs
Internet Information Server (IIS), 355-358
regedt32, 374

building
server components, 481-500
Web businesses
adding new content, 23
graphics and design tools, 18
hiring site developers, 18-19
maintaining development, 23
opening your site, 21-22
programming tools, 18
quality assurance tests, 19-21
updating current content, 23
vision, 16-17
Web-authoring tools, 18

business shipping and handling component, *see* **Progistics.Merchant**

Buy Now component, 590-594
customer requirements, 591
hosting-site requirements, 591
merchant requirements, 591
methods, 591-595

C

C-Systems Web site, 611

caching
tracking, Session object, 320-322
user information, Session object, 319-320

capture, vPOS Commerce Server software, 555

case studies
Eddie Bauer
choosing starter stores, 607-608
Commerce Server justification, 606-607
Perl to ASP conversion, 608
porting the look and feel, 609
site developer profiles, 606
site owner profiles, 606
updating database schema, 609
Programmer's Paradise, converting to Commerce Server 2.0, 624-626

categories, displaying in Commerce Server, 223-230

Categories page code, global.asa file, 224-225

Category-Products page, global.asa file, 226-227

CDebugPpg
class
adding to ClassWizard, 494
definition, 493
methods, 494-502

Certificate Request dialog box, 425

Change Your Customization Options page, MPS, 106

Check Disk, 368-369

Check method, Page component, 701-702

Child's Hope Web site, 38, 611

Choose Destination Location dialog box, 509

Cisco PIX Firewall, 564-565
Address Translation Enable List, 577-578
advantages, 565-567
authentication/authorization, 575-576

booting, 568-569
conduits, 566
configuring, 567-571
access, 584
erasing, 570
initial, 570-571
saving, 569
with HTTP, 571-587
enable mode, 569-570
Failover, 575
global IP address pool, 577
implementing, 587
interfaces, 571-573
Mail Guard, 567
Radius Server, 575
Remote Authentication Dial-In User Service, 567
RIP, 573-574
Static Routes, 573-574
Tacacs+ Server List, 567, 575

Class C addresses, DNS name service setup, 407-410

classes, 265-266
abstractions, 265-266
CDebugPpg, definition, 493
COM (Component Object Model), 270-273
design goals, 271-272
interfaces, 272-273
naming conventions, 273
servers, 274-277
creating components, 326-330
creating class objects, 327
destroying class objects, 327
error handling, 330
instantiating objects, 327-328
methods, 328
property procedures, 328-329
public procedures, 330
CTransact, Public Transact method, 339-342
developing applications, 269-270
encapsulation, 266
exposing OLE servers, 331
inheritance, 266-269
composition, 268
polymorphism, 267-268
reusing objects, 269
static versus dynamic binding, 268
transaction, 335-342
VBScript, 286

ClassWizard, adding CDebugPpg class, 494

CleanString method, Datafunctions component, 666-667